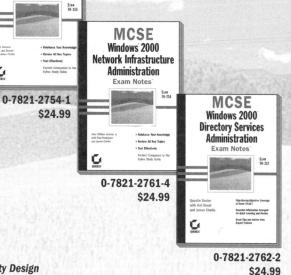

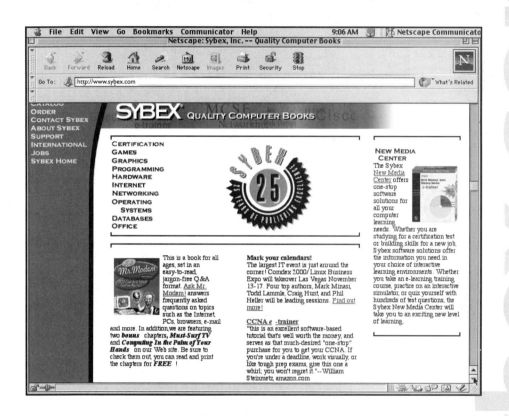

GET CISCO CERTIFIED WITH THE EXPERTS!

The Complete MCSE Solution

SYBEX®

Microsoft's® new exam track for the Windows 2000 MCSE requires four core and three elective exams. The core, design, and additional elective exams for the Windows 2000 MCSE are listed in the table below.

For more information, visit **www.microsoft.com/trainingandservices**.

Exam #	Exam Title	Product Title	ISBN
Required Core Exams			
70-210	Installing, Configuring, and Administering Microsoft Windows 2000 Professional	MCSE: Windows 2000 Professional Study Guide	ISBN: 0-7821-2751-7
		MCSE: Windows 2000 Professional Exam Notes	ISBN: 0-7821-2753-3
		MCSE: Windows 2000 Professional e-trainer	ISBN: 0-7821-5008-X
		MCSE: Windows 2000 Professional Virtual Test Center	ISBN: 0-7821-3000-3
70-215	Installing, Configuring, and Administering Microsoft Windows 2000 Server	MCSE: Windows 2000 Server Study Guide	ISBN: 0-7821-2752-5
		MCSE: Windows 2000 Server Exam Notes	ISBN: 0-7821-2754-1
		MCSE: Windows 2000 Server e-trainer	ISBN: 0-7821-5009-8
		MCSE: Windows 2000 Server Virtual Test Center	ISBN: 0-7821-3001-1
70-216	Implementing and Administering a Microsoft Windows 2000 Network Infrastructure	MCSE: Windows 2000 Network Infrastructure Administration Study Guide	ISBN: 0-7821-2755-X
		MCSE: Windows 2000 Network Infrastructure Administration Exam Notes	ISBN: 0-7821-2761-4
		MCSE: Windows 2000 Network Infrastructure Administration e-trainer	ISBN: 0-7821-5007-1
		MCSE: Windows 2000 Network Infrastructure Administration Virtual Test Center	ISBN: 0-7821-3002-X
70-217	Implementing and Administering a Microsoft Windows 2000 Directory Services Infrastructure	MCSE: Windows 2000 Directory Services Administration Study Guide	ISBN: 0-7821-2756-8
		MCSE: Windows 2000 Directory Services Administration Exam Notes	ISBN: 0-7821-2762-2
		MCSE: Windows 2000 Directory Services Administration e-trainer	ISBN: 0-7821-5010-1
		MCSE: Windows 2000 Directory Services Administration Virtual Test Center	ISBN: 0-7821-3003-8

(Already have your MCSE for NT 4 or taken the three core "NT" exams? If so, then you qualify to take the Accelerated Windows 2000 Exam in lieu of the four new core exams in the Windows 2000 MCSE track. The MCSE: Accelerated Windows 2000 Study Guide covers all objectives sets from the four core exams in a more consise manner on the assumption that you already have a pretty good sense of what the technology is about.)

Exam #	Exam Title	Product Title	ISBN
70-240	Microsoft Windows 2000 Accelerated Exam for MCPs Certified on Microsoft Windows NT 4.0.	MCSE: Accelerated Windows 2000 Study Guide	ISBN: 0-7821-2760-6
		MCSE: Accelerated Windows 2000 Exam Notes	ISBN: 0-7821-2770-3
Choose 1 More Core Exam			
70-219	Designing a Microsoft Windows 2000 Directory Services Infrastructure	MCSE: Windows 2000 Directory Services Design Study Guide	ISBN: 0-7821-2757-6
		MCSE: Windows 2000 Directory Services Design Exam Notes	ISBN: 0-7821-2765-7
or			
70-220	Designing Security for a Microsoft Windows 2000 Network	MCSE: Windows 2000 Network Security Design Study Guide	ISBN: 0-7821-2758-4
		MCSE: Windows 2000 Network Security Design Exam Notes	ISBN: 0-7821-2766-5
or			
70-221	Designing a Microsoft Windows 2000 Network Infrastructure	MCSE: Windows 2000 Network Infrastructure Design Study Guide	ISBN: 0-7821-2759-2
		MCSE: Windows 2000 Network Infrastructure Design Exam Notes	ISBN: 0-7821-2767-3
Choose 2 Electives			
70-222	Migrating from Microsoft Windows NT 4.0 to Microsoft Windows 2000	MCSE: Windows 2000 Migration Study Guide	ISBN: 0-7821-2768-1
		MCSE: Windows 2000 Migration Exam Notes	ISBN: 0-7821-2769-X
70-224	Installing, Configuring, and Administering Microsoft Exchange 2000 Server	MCSE: Exchange 2000 Server Administration Study Guide	ISBN: 0-7821-2898-X
		MCSE: Exchange 2000 Server Administration e-trainer	ISBN: 0-7821-5012-8
		MCSE: Exchange 2000 Server Aministration Virtual Test Center	ISBN: 0-7821-3017-8
70-225	Designing and Deploying a Messaging Infrastructure with Microsoft Exchange 2000 Server	MCSE: Exchange 2000 Design Study Guide	ISBN: 0-7821-2897-1
70-227	Installing, Configuring, and Administering Microsoft Internet Security and Acceleration (ISA) Server 2000	MCSE: ISA Server 2000 Administration Study Guide	ISBN: 0-7821-2933-1
70-228	Installing, Configuring, and Administering Microsoft SQL Server 2000 Enterprise Edition	MCSE: SQL Server 2000 Administration Study Guide	ISBN: 0-7821-2921-8
		MCSE: SQL Server 2000 Administration Virtual Test Center	ISBN: 0-7821-3016-X
70-229	Designing and Implementing Databases with Microsoft SQL Server™ 2000 Enterprise Edition	MCSE: SQL Server 2000 Design Study Guide	ISBN: 0-7821-2942-0

MCSE:
Exchange 2000 Server Administration
Study Guide

MCSE:
Exchange 2000 Server Administration
Study Guide

Walter Glenn

with James Chellis

San Francisco • Paris • Düsseldorf • Soest • London

Associate Publisher: Neil Edde
Contracts and Licensing Manager: Kristine O'Callaghan
Acquisitions and Developmental Editor: Heather O'Connor
Editors: Emily K. Wolman, Julie Sakaue
Production Editors: Shannon Murphy, Judith Hibbard
Technical Editors: James Kelly, Ed Crowley
Book Designer: Bill Gibson
Graphic Illustrator: Tony Jonick
Electronic Publishing Specialists: Jangshi Wang, Judy Fung
Proofreaders: Andrea Fox, Emily Hsuan, Nelson Kim, Laurie O'Connell, Yariv Rabinovitch, Nancy Riddiough
Indexer: Ted Laux
CD Coordinator: Erica Yee
CD Technician: Kevin Ly
Cover Designer: Archer Design
Cover Photographer: Tony Stone Images

SYBEX

To Our Valued Readers:

In recent years, Microsoft's MCSE program has established itself as the premier computer and networking industry certification. Nearly a quarter of a million IT professionals have attained MCSE status in the NT 4 track. Sybex is proud to have helped thousands of MCSE candidates prepare for their exams over these years, and we are excited about the opportunity to continue to provide people with the skills they'll need to succeed in the highly competitive IT industry.

For the Windows 2000 MCSE track, Microsoft has made it their mission to demand more of exam candidates. Exam developers have gone to great lengths to raise the bar in order to prevent a paper-certification syndrome, one in which individuals obtain a certification without a thorough understanding of the technology. Sybex welcomes this new philosophy as we have always advocated a comprehensive instructional approach to certification courseware. It has always been Sybex's mission to teach exam candidates how new technologies work in the real world, not to simply feed them answers to test questions. Sybex was founded on the premise of providing technical skills to IT professionals, and we have continued to build on that foundation, making significant improvements to our study guides based on feedback from readers, suggestions from instructors, and comments from industry leaders.

The depth and breadth of technical knowledge required to obtain Microsoft's new Windows 2000 MCSE is staggering. Sybex has assembled some of the most technically skilled instructors in the industry to write our study guides, and we're confident that our Windows 2000 MCSE study guides will meet and exceed the demanding standards both of Microsoft and you, the exam candidate.

Good luck in pursuit of your MCSE!

Neil Edde
Associate Publisher—Certification
Sybex, Inc.

SYBEX Inc. 1151 Marina Village Parkway, Alameda, CA 94501
Tel: 510/523-8233   Fax: 510/523-2373   HTTP://www.sybex.com

Acknowledgments

This book has been a great project to work on. I'd like to thank the people at Sybex who helped put this book together: Julie Sakaue and Emily Wolman for their wonderful editorial work, Shannon Murphy for cracking the scheduling whip and helping keep us all organized, Judy Fung and Jangshi Wang for making sure all the pages fit, and Heather O'Connor and Neil Edde for their guidance throughout.

Another big thanks to James Kelly and Ed Crowley for a relentless technical review. They put in a lot of work, and it shows.

I'd also like to thank James Chellis and Matt Sheltz for giving me the chance to work on the book and for helping to put the CD content together.

And, as always, many thanks to the staff at Studio B for their help in putting the project together.

Contents at a Glance

Contents

Table of Exercises

Each chapter teaches you how to perform important tasks, including the following:

- Installing and upgrading to Exchange 2000 Server

- Creating and managing recipients and public folders

- Configuring storage, routing, and administration in an Exchange organization

- Configuring client applications and Internet protocols

- Using Exchange 2000 Server's advanced security components

Throughout the book, you will be guided through hands-on exercises, which give you practical experience for each exam objective. At the end of each chapter, you'll find a summary of the topics covered in the chapter, which also includes a list of the key terms used in that chapter. The key terms represent not only the terminology that you should recognize, but also the underlying concepts that you should understand to pass the exam. All of the key terms are defined in the glossary at the back of the study guide.

Finally, each chapter concludes with 20 review questions that test your knowledge of the information covered and provide thorough explanations of the answers. In Appendix A, you'll find an entire practice exam, with 50 additional questions. Many more questions, as well as multimedia demonstrations of the hands-on exercises, are included on the CD that accompanies this book, as explained in the "What's on the CD?" section at the end of this Introduction.

The topics covered in this book map directly to Microsoft's official exam objectives. Each exam objective is covered completely.

How Do You Become an MCSE?

Attaining MCSE certification has always been a challenge. However, in the past, individuals could acquire detailed exam information—even most of the exam questions—from online "brain dumps" and third-party "cram" books or software products. For the new MCSE exams, this simply will not be the case.

To avoid the "paper-MCSE syndrome" (a devaluation of the MCSE certification because unqualified individuals manage to pass the exams), Microsoft has taken strong steps to protect the security and integrity of the new MCSE track. Prospective MCSEs will need to complete a course of study that provides not only detailed knowledge of a wide range of topics, but true skills derived from working with Windows 2000 and related software products.

In the new MCSE program, Microsoft is heavily emphasizing hands-on skills. Microsoft has stated that "Nearly half of the core required exams' content demands that the candidate have troubleshooting skills acquired through hands-on experience and working knowledge."

Fortunately, if you are willing to dedicate time and effort with Windows 2000, you can prepare for the exams by using the proper tools. If you work through this book and the other books in this series, you should meet the exam requirements successfully.

This book is a part of a complete series of MCSE Study Guides, published by Sybex, that covers the five core Windows 2000 requirements as well as the new Design exams and electives you need to complete your MCSE track. Titles include the following:

- *MCSE: Windows 2000 Professional Study Guide*

- *MCSE: Windows 2000 Server Study Guide*

- *MCSE: Windows 2000 Network Infrastructure Administration Study Guide*

- *MCSE: Windows 2000 Directory Services Administration Study Guide*

- *MCSE: Windows 2000 Network Security Design Study Guide*

- *MCSE: Windows 2000 Network Infrastructure Design Study Guide*

- *MCSE: Windows 2000 Directory Services Design Study Guide*

- *MCSE: Exchange 2000 Server Administration Study Guide*

Exam Requirements

Successful candidates must pass a minimum set of exams that measure technical proficiency and expertise:

- Candidates for MCSE certification must pass seven exams, including four core operating system exams, one design exam, and two electives.

- Candidates who have already passed three Windows NT 4 exams (70-067, 70-068, and 70-073) may opt to take an "accelerated" exam plus one core design exam and two electives.

NOTE If you do not pass the accelerated exam after one attempt, you must pass the five core requirements and two electives.

The following table shows the exams that a new certification candidate must pass.

All of these exams are required:

Exam #	Topic	Requirement Met
70-216	Implementing and Administering a Microsoft Windows 2000 Network Infrastrucuture	Core (Operating System)
70-210	Installing, Configuring, and Administering Microsoft Windows 2000 Professional	Core (Operating System)
70-215	Installing, Configuring, and Administering Microsoft Windows 2000 Server	Core (Operating System)
70-217	Implementing and Administering a Microsoft Windows 2000 Directory Services Infrastructure	Core (Operating System)

One of these exams is required:

Exam #	Topic	Requirement Met
70-219	Designing a Microsoft Windows 2000 Directory Services Infrastructure	Core (Design)
70-220	Designing Security for a Microsoft Windows 2000 Network	Core (Design)
70-221	Designing a Microsoft Windows 2000 Network Infrastructure	Core (Design)

Two of these exams are required:

Exam #	Topic	Requirement Met
70-219	Designing a Microsoft Windows 2000 Directory Services Infrastructure	Elective
70-220	Designing Security for a Microsoft Windows 2000 Network	Elective
70-221	Designing a Microsoft Windows 2000 Network Infrastructure	Elective
Any current MCSE elective	Exams cover topics such as Exchange 2000 Server, SQL Server, Systems Management Server, Internet Explorer Administrator's Kit, and Proxy Server (new exams are added regularly)	Elective

For a more detailed description of the Microsoft certification programs, including a list of current MCSE electives, check Microsoft's Training and Certification Web site at www.microsoft.com/trainingandservices.

The Exchange 2000 Server Exam

The Exchange 2000 Server exam covers concepts and skills required for administering Exchange 2000 Server, emphasizing the following areas:

- Standards and terminology
- Planning
- Implementation
- Troubleshooting

This exam can be quite specific regarding Exchange 2000 Server, and it can be particular about how administrative tasks are performed. It also focuses on fundamental concepts relating to Exchange 2000 Server's operation as an enterprise messaging system. Careful study of this book, along with hands-on experience, will help you prepare for this exam.

Microsoft provides exam objectives to give you a very general overview of possible areas of coverage of the Microsoft exams. For your convenience, we have added in-text objectives listings at the points in the text where specific Microsoft exam objectives are covered. However, exam objectives are subject to change at any time without prior notice and at Microsoft's sole discretion. Please visit Microsoft's Training and Certification Web site (www.microsoft .com/trainingandservices) for the most current exam objectives listing.

Types of Exam Questions

In the previous tracks, the formats of the MCSE exams were fairly straight-forward, consisting almost entirely of multiple-choice questions appearing in a few different sets. Prior to taking an exam, you knew how many questions you would see and what type of questions would appear. If you had purchased the right third-party exam preparation products, you could even be quite familiar with the pool of questions you might be asked. As mentioned earlier, all of this is changing.

In an effort to both refine the testing process and protect the quality of its certifications, Microsoft has introduced adaptive testing, as well as some new exam elements. You will not know in advance which type of format you will see on your exam. These innovations make the exams more challenging, and they make it much more difficult for someone to pass an exam after simply "cramming" for it.

Microsoft will be accomplishing its goal of protecting the exams by regularly adding and removing exam questions, limiting the number of questions that any individual sees in a beta exam, limiting the number of questions delivered to an individual by using adaptive testing, and adding new exam elements.

Exam questions are in multiple-choice format, and many are more lengthy scenario-type questions. You may also find yourself taking an adaptive format exam. Let's take a look at the exam question types and adaptive testing, so you can be prepared for all of the possibilities.

Multiple-Choice Questions

Multiple-choice questions include two main types of questions. One is a straightforward type that presents a question, followed by several possible answers, of which one or more is correct.

The other kind of multiple-choice question is more complex. This type presents a set of desired results along with a proposed solution. You must then decide which results the proposed solution would achieve.

The questions throughout this study guide and on the accompanying CD are presented in the same multiple-choice format that you will see on the exam.

Adaptive Exam Format

Microsoft presents many of its exams in an *adaptive* format. This format is radically different from the conventional format previously used for Microsoft certification exams. Conventional tests are static, containing a fixed number of questions. Adaptive tests change, or "adapt," depending on your answers to the questions presented.

The number of questions presented in your adaptive test will depend on how long it takes the exam to ascertain your level of ability (according to the statistical measurements on which the exam questions are ranked). To determine a test-taker's level of ability, the exam presents questions in increasing or decreasing order of difficulty.

Unlike the previous test format, the adaptive format will *not* allow you to go back to see a question again. The exam only goes forward. Once you enter your answer, that's it—you cannot change it. Be very careful before entering your answer. There is no time limit for each individual question (only for the exam as a whole). Your exam may be shortened by correct answers (and lengthened by incorrect answers), so there is no advantage to rushing through questions.

How Adaptive Exams Determine Ability Levels

As an example of how adaptive testing works, suppose that you know three people who are taking the exam: Herman, Sally, and Rashad. Herman doesn't know much about the subject, Sally is moderately informed, and Rashad is an expert.

Herman answers his first question incorrectly, so the exam presents him with a second, easier question. He misses that, so the exam gives him a few more easy questions, all of which he misses. Shortly thereafter, the exam ends, and he receives his failure report.

Sally answers her first question correctly, so the exam gives her a more difficult question, which she answers correctly. She then receives an even more difficult question, which she answers incorrectly. Next, the exam gives her a somewhat easier question, as it tries to gauge her level of understanding. After numerous questions of varying levels of difficulty, Sally's exam ends, perhaps with a passing score, perhaps not. Her exam included far more questions than were in Herman's exam, because her level of understanding needed to be more carefully tested to determine whether or not it was at a passing level.

When Rashad takes his exam, he answers his first question correctly, so he is given a more difficult question, which he also answers correctly. Next, the exam presents an even more difficult question, which he also answers correctly. He then is given a few more very difficult questions, all of which he answers correctly. Shortly thereafter, his exam ends. He passes. His exam was short, about as long as Herman's test.

Benefits of Adaptive Testing

Microsoft has begun moving to adaptive testing for several reasons:

- It saves time by focusing only on the questions needed to determine a test-taker's abilities. An exam that might take an hour and a half in the conventional format could be completed in less than half that time when presented in adaptive format. The number of questions in an adaptive exam may be far fewer than the number required by a conventional exam.

- It protects the integrity of the exams. By exposing a fewer number of questions at any one time, it makes it more difficult for individuals to collect the questions in the exam pools with the intent of facilitating exam "cramming."

- It saves Microsoft and/or the test-delivery company money by reducing the amount of time it takes to deliver a test.

We recommend that you try the EdgeTest Adaptive Exam, which is included on the CD that accompanies this study guide.

Exam Question Development

Microsoft follows an exam-development process consisting of eight mandatory phases. The process takes an average of seven months and involves more than 150 specific steps. The MCP exam development consists of the following phases:

Phase 1: Job Analysis   Phase 1 is an analysis of all of the tasks that make up a specific job function, based on tasks performed by people who are currently performing that job function. This phase also identifies the knowledge, skills, and abilities that relate specifically to the performance area to be certified.

Phase 2: Objective Domain Definition   The results of the job analysis provide the framework used to develop objectives. The development of objectives involves translating the job-function tasks into a comprehensive set of more specific and measurable knowledge, skills, and abilities. The resulting list of objectives—the *objective domain*—is the basis for the development of both the certification exams and the training materials.

Phase 3: Blueprint Survey   The final objective domain is transformed into a blueprint survey in which contributors are asked to rate each objective. These contributors may be past MCP candidates, appropriately skilled exam development volunteers, or Microsoft employees. Based on the contributors' input, the objectives are prioritized and weighted. The actual exam items are written according to the prioritized objectives. Contributors are queried about how they spend their time on the job. If a contributor doesn't spend an adequate amount of time actually performing the specified job function, his or her data is eliminated from the analysis. The blueprint survey phase helps determine which objectives to measure, as well as the appropriate number and types of items to include on the exam.

Phase 4: Item Development   A pool of items is developed to measure the blueprinted objective domain. The number and types of items to be written are based on the results of the blueprint survey.

Phase 5: Alpha Review and Item Revision During this phase, a panel of technical and job-function experts reviews each item for technical accuracy, then answers each item, reaching a consensus on all technical issues. Once the items have been verified as technically accurate, they are edited to ensure that they are expressed in the clearest language possible.

Phase 6: Beta Exam The reviewed and edited items are collected into beta exams. Based on the responses of all beta participants, Microsoft performs a statistical analysis to verify the validity of the exam items and to determine which items will be used in the certification exam. Once the analysis has been completed, the items are distributed into multiple parallel forms, or *versions*, of the final certification exam.

Phase 7: Item Selection and Cut-Score Setting The results of the beta exams are analyzed to determine which items should be included in the certification exam based on many factors, including item difficulty and relevance. During this phase, a panel of job-function experts determines the *cut score* (minimum passing score) for the exams. The cut score differs from exam to exam because it is based on an item-by-item determination of the percentage of candidates who answered the item correctly and who would be expected to answer the item correctly.

Phase 8: Live Exam As the final phase, the exams are given to candidates. MCP exams are administered by Sylvan Prometric and Virtual University Enterprises (VUE).

 Microsoft will regularly add and remove questions from the exams. This is called item *seeding*. It is part of the effort to make it more difficult for individuals to merely memorize exam questions passed along by previous test-takers.

Tips for Taking the Exchange 2000 Server Exam

Here are some general tips for taking the exam successfully:

- Arrive early at the exam center so you can relax and review your study materials. During your final review, you can look over tables and lists of exam-related information.

- Read the questions carefully. Don't be tempted to jump to an early conclusion. Make sure you know *exactly* what the question is asking.

- Answer all questions. Remember that the adaptive format will *not* allow you to return to a question. Be very careful before entering your answer. Because your exam may be shortened by correct answers (and lengthened by incorrect answers), there is no advantage to rushing through questions.

- Use a process of elimination to get rid of the obviously incorrect answers first on questions that you're not sure about. This method will improve your odds of selecting the correct answer if you need to make an educated guess.

Exam Registration

You may take the exams at any of more than 1,000 Authorized Prometric Testing Centers (APTCs) and VUE Testing Centers around the world. For the location of a testing center near you, call Sylvan Prometric at 800-755-EXAM (755-3926), or call VUE at 888-837-8616. Outside the United States and Canada, contact your local Sylvan Prometric or VUE registration center.

You should determine the number of the exam you want to take, and then register with the Sylvan Prometric or VUE registration center nearest to you. At this point, you will be asked for advance payment for the exam. The exams are $100 each. Exams must be taken within one year of payment. You can schedule exams up to six weeks in advance or as late as one working day prior to the date of the exam. You can cancel or reschedule your exam if you contact the center at least two working days prior to the exam. Same-day registration is available in some locations, subject to space availability. Where same-day registration is available, you must register a minimum of two hours before test time.

You may also register for your exams online at www.sylvanprometric.com or www.vue.com.

When you schedule the exam, you will be provided with instructions regarding appointment and cancellation procedures, ID requirements, and information about the testing center location. In addition, you will receive a registration and payment confirmation letter from Sylvan Prometric or VUE.

Microsoft requires certification candidates to accept the terms of a Non-Disclosure Agreement before taking certification exams.

What's on the CD?

With this new book in our best-selling MCSE Study Guide series, we are including quite an array of training resources. On the CD are numerous simulations, practice exams, and flashcards to help you study for the exam. Also included are the entire contents of the book. These resources are described in the following sections.

The Sybex E-Book for Exchange 2000 Server

Many people like the convenience of being able to carry their whole study guide on a CD. They also like being able to search the text to find specific information quickly and easily. For these reasons, we have included the entire contents of this study guide on a CD, in PDF format. We've also included Adobe Acrobat Reader, which provides the interface for the contents, as well as the search capabilities.

Sybex WinSim 2000

We developed WinSim 2000 to allow you to get some hands-on practice with the skills you need to know to pass the exam. The WinSim 2000 product provides both audio/video files and hands-on experience with key features of Exchange 2000 Server. Built around the exercises in this study guide, WinSim 2000 can give you the knowledge and hands-on skills that are invaluable for understanding Exchange 2000 Server (and passing the exam). A sample screen from WinSim 2000 is shown below.

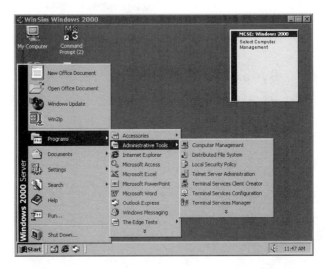

The Sybex MCSE EdgeTests

The EdgeTests are a collection of multiple-choice questions that can help you prepare for your exam. There are three sets of questions:

- Bonus questions specially prepared for this edition of the study guide, including 50 questions that appear only on the CD

- An adaptive test simulator that will give the feel for how adaptive testing works

- All of the questions from the study guide presented in a test engine for your review

A sample screen from the Sybex MCSE EdgeTest is shown below.

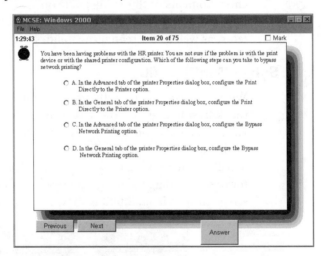

Sybex MCSE Flashcards for PCs and Palm Devices

The "flashcard" style of exam question offers an effective way to quickly and efficiently test your understanding of the fundamental concepts covered in the Exchange 2000 Server exam. The Sybex MCSE Flashcards set consists of 100–150 questions presented in a special engine developed specifically for this Study Guide series. The Sybex MCSE Flashcards interface is shown below.

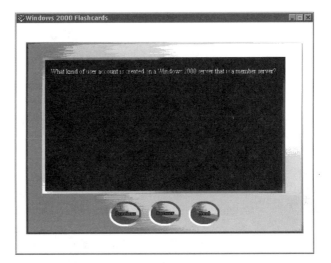

Because of the high demand for a product that will run on Palm devices, we have also developed, in conjunction with Land-J Technologies, a version of the flashcard questions that you can take with you on your Palm OS PDA (including the PalmPilot and Handspring's Visor).

How Do You Use This Book?

This book can provide a solid foundation for the serious effort of preparing for the Exchange 2000 Server exam. To best benefit from this book, you may wish to use the following study method:

1. Study each chapter carefully. Do your best to fully understand the information.

2. Complete all hands-on exercises in the chapter, referring back to the text as necessary so that you understand each step you take. If you do not have access to a lab environment in which you can complete the exercises, install and work with the exercises available in the WinSim 2000 software included with this study guide.

3. Answer the review questions at the end of each chapter. If you would prefer to answer the questions in a timed and graded format, install the

EdgeTests from the CD that accompanies this book and answer the chapter questions there instead of in the book.

4. Note the questions you did not understand, and study the corresponding sections of the book again.

5. Make sure you complete the entire book.

6. Before taking the exam, go through the training resources included on the CD that accompanies this book. Try the adaptive version that is included with the Sybex MCSE EdgeTest. Review and sharpen your knowledge with the MCSE Flashcards.

In order to complete the exercises in this book, you'll need to have access to at least one machine running Windows 2000 Advanced Server and preferable two such machines networked together. You will also need access to Exchange 2000 Server Enterprise edition, of which you can order a trial version through Microsoft. Some exercises may require you to have administrative access, or to be part of an Active Directory domain. If possible, we strongly recommend that you do not install Exchange on a network that is actually connected to your production network, as the interaction with other Exchange servers on the network and with Active Directory could produce unwanted results.

To learn all of the material covered in this book, you will need to study regularly and with discipline. Try to set aside the same time every day to study and select a comfortable and quiet place in which to do it. If you work hard, you will be surprised at how quickly you learn this material. Good luck!

Contacts and Resources

To find out more about Microsoft Education and Certification materials and programs, to register with Sylvan Prometric or VUE, or to get other useful information, check the following resources.

Microsoft Certification Development Team

www.microsoft.com/trainingandservices/mcp/exam info/certsd.htm

Contact the Microsoft Certification Development Team through their Web site to volunteer for one or more exam development phases or to report a problem with an exam. Address written correspondence to:

> Certification Development Team
> Microsoft Education and Certification
> One Microsoft Way
> Redmond, WA 98052

Microsoft TechNet Technical Information Network

www.microsoft.com/technet/subscription/about.htm

(800) 344-2121

Use this Web site or number to contact support professionals and system administrators. Outside the United States and Canada, contact your local Microsoft subsidiary for information.

Microsoft Training and Certification Home Page

www.microsoft.com/trainingandservices

This Web site provides information about the MCP program and exams. You can also order the latest Microsoft Roadmap to Education and Certification.

PalmPilot Training Product Development: Land-J

www.land-j.com

(407) 359-2217

Land-J Technologies is a consulting and programming business currently specializing in application development for the 3Com PalmPilot Personal Digital Assistant. Land-J developed the Palm version of the EdgeTests, which is included on the CD that accompanies this study guide.

Prometric

www.prometric.com

(800) 755-EXAM

Contact Sylvan Prometric to register to take an MCP exam at any of more than 800 Prometric Testing Centers around the world.

Virtual University Enterprises (VUE)
www.vue.com

(888) 837-8616

Contact the VUE registration center to register to take an MCP exam at one of the VUE Testing Centers.

Assessment Test

1. You are testing Exchange 2000 Server to determine whether it is worth upgrading to. You have just finished installing an Exchange server and are exploring the directories in which the files were created when you come across two files named PUB.EDB and PUB.STM. You recognize from earlier versions of Exchange Server that the PUB.EDB file is the database for your public folders. What is the PUB.STM file used for?

    A. Allowing Web access to the public folders

    B. Storing information about the folders that are compatible with earlier versions of Exchange server

    C. Storing certain types of media files in their native format

    D. Providing a backup of the PUB.EDB file

2. You have installed multiple public folder trees in your organization. Which of the following clients will be able to access the default public folder tree and all of the additional trees? (Choose all that apply.)

    A. Outlook

    B. A Web browser

    C. An Office 2000 application

    D. A generic POP3 client

3. You are the administrator of a large Exchange organization and have been given the task of creating a connector between two routing groups. You have the following requirements:

    ▪ Use the simplest connector possible in terms of configuration and maintenance.

    ▪ Configure multiple bridgehead servers.

    ▪ Assign a low cost to this connector so that is it more likely to be used than other connectors between the same routing groups.

    ▪ Have servers issue authentication before sending any mail.

You implement the following solution:

Install a Routing Group Connector between the two routing groups.

Which of the requirements does the proposed solution meet? (Choose all that apply.)

- A. Use the simplest connector possible in terms of configuration and maintenance.

- B. Configure multiple bridgehead servers.

- C. Assign a low cost to this connector so that is it more likely to be used than other connectors between the same routing groups.

- D. Have servers issue authentication before sending any mail.

4. You are the Exchange administrator for a large network and are about to install the first Exchange server in the organization. Before you do that, however, you must run the ForestPrep utility to prepare your forest. To which of the following groups must you belong in order to run the ForestPrep utility? (Choose all that apply.)

- A. Server Admins

- B. Domain Admins

- C. Schema Admins

- D. Enterprise Admins

5. You have five computers on which you are considering installing Exchange 2000 Server as a testing environment. Which of the following systems meet the requirements for installing Exchange 2000 Server? (Choose all that apply.)

- A. Pentium 90, 64MB RAM, 500MB disk space

- B. Pentium 133, 64MB RAM, 2500MB disk space

- C. Pentium 166, 256MB RAM, 1000MB disk space

- D. Pentium II 400, 128MB RAM, 250MB disk space

- E. Pentium III 500, 128MB RAM, 2000MB disk space

× **6.** What does the Delete Mailbox Storage right allow a person to do?

    A. Delete items from a mailbox.

    ‒ **B.** Delete a mailbox from a Private Information Store.

    C. Delete a Private Information Store from a storage group.

    D. Delete a storage group from a server.

✓ **7.** Which of the following MAPI components is a replaceable component that communicates with the server-side of the messaging system?

    A. Client Application Layer

    B. MAPI subsystem

    C. Common Mail Call

    ‒ **D.** MAPI service provider

✓ **8.** Your company has hired an outside agency to provide accounting services. Many of your employees need to e-mail messages to people in this agency using the Internet. You want to set it up so that the people in the agency appear in the Exchange Global Address List. What type of recipient object do you need configure for each person in the outside agency?

    A. Mailbox

    B. Mail-enabled user

    ‒ **C.** Contact

    D. A mailbox with a foreign owner

✓ **9.** Your organization has three routing groups: RG1, RG2, and RG3. Each group consists of three Exchange servers configured with about 500 users each. RG1 and RG2 are connected with a 256KB wide area network (WAN). RG2 and RG3 are connected with a switched 56K connection. RG1 is not directly connected to RG3. You have created a public folder that contains 600MB of data. Users in RG1 and RG3 need access to the folder throughout the day. Users in RG2 need only occasional access. The folder data is updated on a daily basis. On what servers should replicas be placed?

   A. On every server

   B. On one server in each routing group

   C. On every server in RG1 and RG3

   D. Only on the server where the public folder was originally created

   E. Only on domain controllers

✓ **10.** You are the administrator of a large network running Microsoft Mail for PC Networks. As part of a plan for moving to Exchange 2000 Server, you have just installed the first Exchange 2000 server and created a new Exchange organization. You would like to gradually migrate users from the MS Mail system and allow users of both systems to exchange messages during the migration. In order to do this, first you must set up a way for the two systems to communicate. What component of Exchange 2000 would you use?

   A. Migration kit

   B. Connector

   C. Import/Export tool

   D. None of the above

✓**11.** You are the administrator of a large Exchange organization that is running Key Management Server to provide security keys to your users. The computer on which KMS is installed fails. You repair the computer and reinstall the same version of Windows that was on the computer before. What should your next step be?

   A. Run Exchange Server in Disaster Recovery Mode.

   — **B.** Restore the System State data from backup.

   C. Restore the Exchange Server databases from backup.

   D. Reinstall the KMS Service.

✗ **12.** Lou has a notebook computer for doing work away from the office and a desktop computer at the office. Microsoft Outlook is installed on his computer at the office, and he uses Outlook Express on his notebook, which does not have a continuous connection to the office server. Lou has the following requirements:

   ▪ Retrieve all messages from all private folders while using either computer.

   ▪ Read and compose messages while using the notebook offline.

   ▪ Access public folders while using the notebook online.

   You propose the following solution:

   Configure Outlook Express to act as an IMAP4 client for accessing the Exchange server.

   Which of the requirements does the proposed solution meet? (Choose all that apply.)

   — **A.** Retrieve all messages from all private folders while using the notebook.

   — **B.** Read and compose messages while using the notebook offline.

   — **C.** Access public folders while using the notebook online.

   D. The proposed solution meets none of the requirements.

13. You are running a mixed-mode organization that contains a number of Exchange 2000 and Exchange 5.5 servers in several different sites. How do Exchange 5.*x* servers in different sites exchange directory information?

   A. Using e-mail messages

   B. Using MAPI

   C. Using RPCs

   D. Using LDAP

14. Which of the following objects can an administrative group hold? (Choose all that apply.)

   A. Servers

   B. Routing groups

   C. Recipients container

   D. System policy containers

   E. Tools container

15. Which of the following MS Mail directory synchronization events does a requestor use to rebuild its Global Address List?

   A. T1

   B. T2

   C. T3

   D. T4

X **16.** You are planning your company's Exchange 2000 deployment and are deciding how to group servers into routing groups. Which of the following criteria must servers meet to be in the same routing group? (Choose all that apply.)

   A. All servers must be in the same forest.

   B. All servers must be in the same domain tree.

   C. All servers must be in the same domain.

   D. All servers must be capable of supporting SMTP connectivity.

   E. All servers must be in the same administrative group.

   F. All servers must be capable of supporting high-speed connectivity.

✓ **17.** You have configured four storage groups on your Exchange server. One group holds five mailbox stores and no public stores. The other two groups are configured with two public stores each and no mailbox stores. The final group has one mailbox store and one public store. How many sets of transaction logs are maintained on the server?

   A. One

   B. Four

   C. Six

   D. Seven

   E. Nine

X **18.** You have just configured your Exchange server for IMAP4 client access. IMAP4 clients can be authenticated with either Basic or Basic with SSL authentication. The administrator of your firewall informs you that the firewall will allow traffic from SMTP (port 25), IMAP4 (port 143), and HTTP (port 80). What additional traffic must the firewall be configured to allow for your Exchange server POP3 configuration to be used?

   A. 993

   B. 995

   C. 137

   D. 135

19. You are the administrator of a large Exchange organization. Recently, you have become aware that users on the Internet have been using an SMTP server that you configured outside your firewall to relay messages not bound for your organization. How can you stop this?

    A. Use the Relay setting on the SMTP virtual server object's Access property page.

    B. Use the Inbound Security settings on the SMTP virtual server object's Advanced property page.

    C. Use the Authentication setting on the SMTP virtual server object's Access property page.

    D. Configure the Relay settings for the SMTP Connector object.

20. You suspect that one of your Exchange 2000 servers is too heavily utilized after noticing that response times are slow and that the hard disk is constantly active. You use the Windows 2000 Performance tool and collect the following statistics:

%Processor time = 95

%Disk free space = 72

Pages/sec = 3

Avg. Disk sec/Transfer = 0.02

What should you do to improve server response time?

    A. Install more RAM.

    B. Install a faster CPU.

    C. Create additional swap files.

    D. Install an additional hard disk.

    E. Replace the hard disk with a faster hard disk.

21. Management would like for you to configure the Exchange 2000 organization at your company so that users can access their mailboxes and other Exchange-based folders over the Internet. You have decided that the easiest way to do this would be for the users to be able to connect with a Web browser. Which of the following components work together to allow Web browsers to access an Exchange server? (Choose all that apply.)

    A. Internet Information Server

    B. Outlook Browser Access

    C. Outlook Web Access

    D. Exchange Web Server

22. Which of the following types of Windows authentication are used in a native-mode Windows 2000 network? (Choose all that apply.)

    A. Kerberos V3

    B. Kerberos V5

    C. NTLM

    D. Basic

    E. Basic over SSL

23. Which of the following permissions would you assign to an object if you wanted an administrator to be able to view the contents of a container in System Manager, but not access the object's properties?

    A. Read

    B. Write

    C. Read Properties

    D. List Contents

    E. Read Contents

$\times$ **24.** You have just received a message encrypted using a public-key encryption system. What key will be used to decrypt the message?

    A. The sender's public encryption key

    B. The sender's private encryption key

    C. Your public encryption key

    D. Your private encryption key

25. A user named Mary is the owner of a public folder. Mary leaves your company, and the former administrator deletes her user account. As the current administrator, you now need to modify the permissions on the public folder. What will you have to do?

    A. Create a new account with the same user information as the deleted account.

    B. Restore a backup tape of the server that was created before the user was deleted.

    C. Designate your account as the owner of the folder.

    D. Create a new public folder and move the contents of the old folder to it.

26. Which of the following tools provides a way to log the operation statistics of a computer's resources over time?

    A. Performance snap-in

    B. Computer Management

    C. Monitoring and Status

    D. Task Manager

✓ **27.** You are planning a deployment of Instant Messaging for your company network. You estimate that 22,000 users will use Instant Messaging. These users are divided into three e-mail domains: sales.widgets.com, eng.widgets.com, and hr.widgets.com. 12,000 users are in the sales.widgets.com domain, 6,000 users are in the eng.widgets.com domain, and 4,000 users are in the hr.widgets.com domain. You do not want to provide Internet access to Instant Messaging users. How many home servers and routing servers will you need?

A. Three home servers and no routers

B. Three home servers and one router

C. Four home servers and no routers

D. Four home servers and one router

E. Four home servers and two routers

F. Four home servers and three routers

G. Four home servers and four routers

✗ **28.** You are taking a long-overdue vacation and want system notifications regarding public folders to be sent to one of your assistants while you are away. What permission would you assign the assistant on each of the folders?

A. Folder Owner

B. Folder Manager

C. Folder Contact

D. Folder Notification

✗ **29.** Your Windows 2000 forest consists of a two domain trees. The first tree consists of a single root-level domain and four child domains of that root domain. The second tree consists only of a single root domain. You plan to install Exchange 2000 servers in both root domains and in one child domain of the first root domain. How many times would you need to run the DomainPrep utility?

 A. 1

 B. 2

 C. 3

 D. 6

✓ **30.** Which of the following installation modes would allow Outlook 2000 to act as an Exchange Server client? (Choose all that apply.)

 A. Internet Mail Only

 B. Corporate or Workgroup

 C. Shared-Messaging

 D. Client/Server

✓ **31.** What would you need to configure in order for clients to reach an IM server using an SMTP address such as user@im.widgets.com?

 A. An MX record in DNS

 B. An "A" record in DNS

 C. An IM record in DNS

 D. An SRV record in DNS

✕ **32.** You are the Exchange administrator for an organization that is currently running Exchange Server 5.5. You are going to upgrade to Exchange 2000 Server, but plan to do so in stages. During this time, your organization must operate in mixed mode. Which of the following are limitations of working in a mixed-mode organization? (Choose all that apply.)

 A. Administrative groups and Exchange 5.5 sites must be mapped on a one-to-one basis.

 B. Routing groups and Exchange 5.5 sites must be mapped on a one-to-one basis.

 C. You can only create one administrative group for your Exchange 2000 organization, and all Exchange 5.5 sites must be contained in that group.

 D. You can only create one routing group for your Exchange 2000 organization, and all Exchange 5.5 sites must be contained in that group.

✕ **33.** For security reasons, you have decided to configure your mailbox storage group to zero out deleted databases. When does this process occur?

 A. During routing information store maintenance

 B. Every four hours by default, but you can change this setting

 C. Once per day by default, but you can change this setting

 D. After an online backup is performed

✕ **34.** Which of the following constructs is used to track the set of root Certificate Authorities whose certificates can be trusted in a domain?

 A. Certificate Revocation List

 B. Certificate Trust List

 C. Certificate Authority List

 D. Root CA List

X **35.** You have an Exchange server that contains four storage groups. The first storage group contains a single mailbox store that consumes 20GB of disk space. The second storage group contains two mailbox stores that consume 10GB of disk space each. The third storage group holds a single public store that consumes 10GB of disk space. The fourth storage group holds a mailbox store that consumes 5GB of disk space. You want to enable full-text indexing on all of these stores. How much total disk space should the stores consume after indexing is complete?

A. 55GB

B. 60.5GB

C. 66GB

D. 71.5GB

E. 82.5GB

36. You are the Exchange administrator for a large mixed-mode organization that is gradually upgrading to Exchange 2000 Server. You are about to decommission one of your Exchange 5.5 servers and need to move all of the mailboxes on that server to a single mailbox store on one of your Exchange 2000 servers. You connect to the Exchange 5.5 server using Exchange Administrator and try to move the mailboxes, but during the process you get an error, and the operation fails. What is the likely problem?

A. You cannot use Exchange Administrator to move mailboxes from Exchange 5.5 to Exchange 2000.

B. You must first configure a temporary one-way connection agreement between the Exchange 5.5 server and the Exchange 2000 server.

C. The mailbox store must be dismounted before this operation can take place.

D. The mailbox store is not empty.

✕ **37.** Which of the following backup types would cause the archive bit for a file that is backed up to be set to the on position?
(Choose all that apply.)

   A. Normal

   B. Copy

   C. Incremental

   D. Differential

   – **E.** None of these

✓ **38.** You are configuring a connector between two routing groups that are in different buildings. You have a dedicated, high-speed link between the buildings, but have decided to create a routing group for each building anyway. You would like to use a connector that is fairly easy to set up and configure, but you also need the connector to support TLS encryption. What type of connector would you choose?

   A. Routing Group Connector

   B. Site Connector

   C. X.400 Connector

   – **D.** SMTP Connector

✓ **39.** You have configured directory synchronization between your Exchange organization and a legacy MS Mail system. You want all of the users in the Exchange organization to be replicated to the MS Mail system, but do not want contacts to be replicated. What is the best way to prevent the contacts from being replicated?

   A. Mark the contacts as hidden in the Global Address List.

   B. Create a new organizational unit for the contacts, and move the contacts to this container.

   C. Create a dirsync distribution list, and add the contacts to this list.

   – **D.** Configure the trust levels for the contacts to be higher than that of the MS Mail Connector.

40. You have just configured your Exchange server for HTTP client access. Your company has a front-end server running outside the company firewall that can accept the HTTP client requests. This server authenticates HTTP clients with either Basic (Clear-Text) or Basic over SSL. The firewall currently allows traffic via SMTP (port 25) and POP3 (port 110). What additional ports must be opened on the firewall to allow clients to connect using HTTP? (Choose all that apply.)

- **A.** 80

- **B.** 135

- **C.** 443

- **D.** 2890

- **E.** 3268

Answers to Assessment Test

1. C. An Exchange 2000 database represents two physical database files, a rich-text (.EDB) file and a streaming media (.STM) file. The rich-text file holds messages and works much like the database files in previous versions of Exchange Server. The streaming media file has been added to provide native support for many types of streaming media, including voice, audio, and video. See Chapter 2 for more information.

2. B, C. MAPI clients, such as Outlook, can only access the default public folder tree in an organization. Clients that can directly access the file system, such as Office applications, Web browsers, and Windows Explorer, can access multiple public folder trees. POP3 clients have no mechanism for accessing public folders at all. See Chapter 5 for more information.

3. A, B, C. The Routing Group Connector (RGC) is preferred for connecting routing groups, as it is robust and simple to configure and maintain. It allows the use of multiple bridgehead servers and cost assignment. Only the SMTP Connector can issue authentication before sending mail, specify TLS encryption, and remove mail from queues on remote servers. See Chapter 7 for more information.

4. C, D. In order to run the ForestPrep utility, a user must belong to both the Schema Admins and Enterprise Admins global groups. The user must also belong to the local Administrators group on the computer on which the utility is actually run. See Chapter 1 for more information.

5. C, E. Exchange 2000 Server requires a minimum of a Pentium 133, 128MB RAM, and 500MB disk space. See Chapter 3 for more information.

6. B. The Delete Mailbox Storage right allows a user to delete the actual mailbox from the Information Store. This right is given only to administrators by default. See Chapter 9 for more information.

7. D. MAPI service providers are replaceable components that communicate with the server-side of the messaging system. There are three types of service providers: address book providers, message store providers, and message transport providers. See Chapter 6 for more information.

8. C. A contact holds the address of a non-Exchange mail recipient. Contacts are made visible in the Global Address List. See Chapter 4 for more information.

9. B. There is really no need to have replicas configured on multiple servers in each routing group. However, because of the slow link speed between routing groups (especially RG2 and RG3), it is important that at least one server in each routing group have a replica. Since there is more available bandwidth at night, and since the public folder data is not time-critical, you could also schedule replication to occur only at night. See Chapter 7 for more information.

10. B. Connectors provide a way to connect Exchange servers in different routing groups and a way to connect Exchange organizations to external messaging systems. The MS Mail Connector is one of the connectors supplied with Exchange 2000. Once the connector is configured, you will be able to migrate users and messages to Exchange 2000 Server. See Chapter 1 for more information.

11. B. After a full system failure, you should reinstall the same version of Windows that was on the computer before the failure. However, you should not join a domain during the installation. Next, you should restore the System State data from backup. This rejoins the computer to whatever domain of which it was a member and restores the Windows Registry and IIS metabase data. Finally, you should run Exchange setup in Disaster Recovery Mode and then restore the Exchange databases. See Chapter 13 for more information.

12. A, B, C. IMAP4 allows access to multiple private folders and to public folders. In addition, IMAP4 allows users to retrieve messages while connected to the server and then process them while offline. See Chapter 6 for more information.

13. A. All Exchange 5.x servers in the same site automatically replicate directory information using RPCs. Replication of directory information between Exchange 5.x servers in different sites must be configured manually and occurs by sending e-mail messages over whatever connector is used to connect the sites. See Chapter 11 for more information.

14. A, B, D. Administrative groups can contain servers, routing groups, public folder trees, system policies, conferencing services, and chat communities. See Chapter 7 for more information.

15. C. Three primary events occur during synchronization: a requestor sends directory information to the server (T1), the server compiles the Global Address List and sends it to requestors (T2), and a requestor rebuilds its Global Address List (T3). See Chapter 12 for more information.

16. A, D. In order to be in the same routing group, all servers must have reliable, permanent, and direct network connectivity that supports SMTP. They must also belong to the same Active Directory forest and be able to connect to a routing group master. See Chapter 7 for more information.

17. B. Only one transaction log set is maintained for each storage group. See Chapter 8 for more information.

18. A. IMAP4 uses TCP port 110. If Secure Sockets Layer (SSL) is being used to create an encrypted authentication channel, port 993 is used instead. See Chapter 6 for more information.

19. A. By default, an SMTP virtual server will accept messages from any host, but will only relay messages sent from authorized clients. This allows clients in your domain using POP3 or IMAP4 clients to send SMTP messages using the SMTP virtual host. If you want to configure your SMTP virtual server to act as a smart host for relay messages coming in from other domains, you can configure the specific clients to relay messages by using this button. See Chapter 12 for more information.

20. B. The %Processor Time value indicates a high level of CPU usage. All other values indicate a normal range of activity, which suggests that the CPU is the bottleneck slowing the system down. See Chapter 9 for more information.

21. A, C. Internet Information Server is a Web server service built into Windows 2000 that provides the Internet protocol support for Exchange 2000 Server. Outlook Web Access is a component that allows IIS to access the Web Store and then present information to Web browsers in HTML format. See Chapter 2 for more information.

22. B, D, E. The Basic (Clear-Text) and Basic over SSL authentication methods may be used on any type of network. The third method available is Integrated Windows authentication. When running a mixed-mode Windows 2000 network, Integrated Windows authentication uses the NTLM protocol supported by Windows NT 4.0. When running in native mode, Integrated Windows authentication used Kerberos V5. See Chapter 14 for more information.

23. D. The List Contents permission lets a user view the contents of a container object but not access its properties. See Chapter 9 for more information.

24. D. The recipient's public key is used to encrypt a message, and the recipient's private key is used to decrypt the message. See Chapter 14 for more information.

25. C. An administrator has the permission to change the owner of a folder. Once the administrator takes ownership of the folder, they can then perform administrative tasks, such as adding rules and installing forms. See Chapter 5 for more information.

26. A. The Performance snap-in lets you create a log of the performance of certain resources over time and then use that log to chart results. Other tools on this list also provide some performance data, but none allow for logging. See Chapter 9 for more information.

27. F. Since the sales.widgets.com domain has 12,000 users and a single home server can support only 10,000 users, you know that you will need two home servers for that domain. You will also need a home server in the eng.widgets.com domain and in the hr.widgets.com domain, since there must be at least one home server per domain. Even though no Internet access is needed, you also need to have one router for every domain and for every two home servers if there is more than one in a domain. See Chapter 10 for more information.

28. C. A person with the Folder Contact permissions can receive e-mail notifications relating to a folder. Notifications include replication conflicts, folder design conflicts, and storage limit notifications. See Chapter 5 for more information.

29. C. DomainPrep is a tool used to prepare each domain in which Exchange will be installed. The tool is run using the /domainprep switch for the SETUP.EXE program. See Chapter 3 for more information.

30. B. The Corporate or Workgroup mode allows Outlook to connect to a local messaging system such as Exchange Server and to use using Internet protocols such as POP3 and IMAP4. The Internet Mail Only mode only allows connections using the Internet protocols. Outlook has no Shared-Messaging or Client/Server modes. See Chapter 6 for more information.

31. B. When users enter their IM address into the client logon screen, the address is translated into a URL that is used to access the IM server. Therefore, you must create DNS "A" records for any Instant Messaging servers. See Chapter 10 for more information.

32. A. Exchange 5.5 sites are mapped directly to Exchange 2000 administrative groups and vice versa. This gives you less flexibility in setting up administrative groups than when working in native mode. See Chapter 11 for more information.

33. D. The Zero Out Deleted Database Pages option is used to remove all 4k pages of data for items when they are deleted from a database by writing zeros to these pages within all stores of the storage group. This process occurs after an online backup is performed. This option can significantly reduce server performance, though, because of the additional overhead of writing to all the pages. See Chapter 8 for more information.

34. B. The Certificate Trust List (CTL) for a domain holds the set of root CAs whose certificates can be trusted. Trust in root CAs can be set by policy or by managing the CTL directly. See Chapter 14 for more information.

35. C. An indexed store requires about 20% more disk space than a non-indexed store. Before indexing, the combined space consumed by the stores was 55GB. Following indexing, this would increase by 20%, making the combined space consumed 66GB. See Chapter 8 for more information.

36. A. Moving mailboxes from Exchange 5.5 to Exchange 2000 with Exchange Administrator is not supported. You must use Active Directory Users and Computers. See Chapter 11 for more information.

37. E. No backup type sets the archive bit to on. When a file is created or modified, the archive bit is set to on. When some types of backups run, the archive bit is set to off, which indicates that the file has been backed up. The normal and incremental backup types set the archive bit to off so that the same files will not be backed up in subsequent backups unless the files change. See Chapter 13 for more information.

38. D. The Routing Group Connector is the fastest and simplest to set up. However, only the SMTP Connector offers the ability to use authentication and encryption of the connection. See Chapter 7 for more information.

39. D. The trust level is used to select objects for synchronization with a remote requestor. All Exchange objects with a trust level less than or equal to this value will be synchronized. See Chapter 12 for more information.

40. A, E. Since the front-end server is outside the firewall, it can already accept HTTP and HTTP over SSL connections. The front-end server must be able to look up information from the Global Catalog server using port 3268 and transfer information with the back-end server using port 80. Therefore those two ports must be opened on the firewall. See Chapter 14 for more information.

Chapter

1

Introduction to Microsoft Exchange

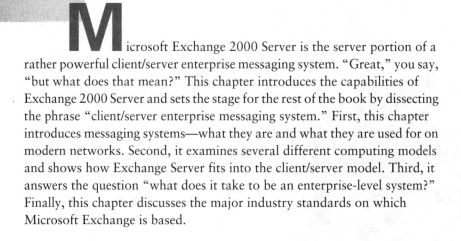

Microsoft Exchange 2000 Server is the server portion of a rather powerful client/server enterprise messaging system. "Great," you say, "but what does that mean?" This chapter introduces the capabilities of Exchange 2000 Server and sets the stage for the rest of the book by dissecting the phrase "client/server enterprise messaging system." First, this chapter introduces messaging systems—what they are and what they are used for on modern networks. Second, it examines several different computing models and shows how Exchange Server fits into the client/server model. Third, it answers the question "what does it take to be an enterprise-level system?" Finally, this chapter discusses the major industry standards on which Microsoft Exchange is based.

Messaging Systems

An enterprise needs information in order to get work done. For this reason, electronic messaging has become a mission-critical function in most organizations. While electronic mail (*e-mail*) is still the core ingredient of any messaging system, other applications are becoming more popular. Messaging can be divided into the following categories:

- E-mail
- Groupware
- Other messaging applications

Each of these categories, and how Exchange addresses them, are briefly discussed in the following text.

Due to the multiple functionality of some of the client programs, a single program could fit into more than one of the categories listed. For example, Microsoft Outlook includes e-mail functions and groupware functions like group scheduling.

E-Mail

An e-mail program allows a user to create, send, read, store, and manipulate electronic messages and attachments. E-mail is an example of *push-style* communication, meaning that the sender initiates the communication. Because of the importance of e-mail in the overall communication of organizations, e-mail client programs have evolved from merely creating and sending text messages into multifeatured programs.

Microsoft Exchange 2000 Server ships with the Outlook 2000 client application for Microsoft Windows 9x/NT/2000 and Outlook 98 client application for the Macintosh. Although older clients, such as Outlook 98 for Windows and Microsoft Exchange Client, will connect to an Exchange 2000 Server just fine, they are neither shipped with the product nor supported by Microsoft any longer.

Microsoft also has server components that enable standard Internet clients to be Exchange e-mail clients. Those Internet clients include those that follow:

- Web browsers through the Outlook Web Access component

- Internet e-mail programs with the Post Office Protocol, version 3 (POP3)

- Internet e-mail programs with Internet Message Access Protocol, version 4 (IMAP4) support

Figure 1.1 illustrates these e-mail client applications.

FIGURE 1.1   E-mail clients to Exchange Server

Microsoft Outlook 2000

Microsoft Outlook 2000 is an e-mail client that ships with Exchange 2000 Server and Microsoft Office 2000 as a stand-alone product. Outlook is referred to as a desktop information manager because it is more than just an e-mail client. It also performs such tasks as calendaring, scheduling, and task and contact management. Outlook is intended to be a central program for management of data of all types.

Microsoft Outlook includes a vast feature set, some of which are listed here:

Universal inbox (mailbox)   This central storage area can hold not only e-mail messages, but other data such as word processing documents, spreadsheet files, faxes, electronic forms, even voicemail files.

Two terms refer to a user's mailbox: mailbox and inbox. The most common usage in this book will be mailbox. This is our primary term for two reasons. One, Microsoft divides a mailbox into folders, one of which is labeled the inbox. Using the term inbox for only the folder helps prevent confusion. The other reason is that the server-based storage area for a user's messages is also called a mailbox.

Hierarchical data storage   Outlook organizes the client's *mailbox* into four default folders: Inbox, Outbox, Deleted Items, and Sent Items. Users can also create their own folders, thereby personalizing the organization of their data.

Customized views   Users have the ability to determine what and how data is presented to them on their screens. Messages can be ordered by sender, date, priority, subject, and other properties.

Search tool   Users can search and retrieve messages in their mailboxes using a variety of search criteria, such as sender, date, and subject.

Rich-text message content   Historically, most e-mail content was simple text. Outlook enables the creation of rich-text message content that can include multiple fonts, sizes, colors, alignments, and other formatting controls.

Microsoft Word as message editor   Even though Outlook includes a rich message editor, it can also be configured to use Microsoft Word as its message editor. This ability provides access to many of the standard Word features, such as tables, embedded pictures, and linked objects, right inside the e-mail message.

Compound messages and drag-and-drop editing   Outlook is *OLE 2 (Object Linking and Embedding)* compliant and, therefore, allows the creation of compound documents. For example, a user could drag and drop a group of cells from a spreadsheet into Outlook.

Secure messages   *Digital signatures* and message *encryption* are advanced security features built into Outlook.

Offline access   Because more and more employees spend part of their work day outside of the office, special features allow users to create folders on their local computers that synchronize with folders on an Exchange server when the local computer is connected to a network. When the computer is not connected, the folders that have been synchronized are available and users can create, work with, and send messages. Sent messages are placed in an outbox and are actually delivered the next time the offline folders are synchronized.

Delegate access   Some users need to allow other users to access their mailbox. For example, a manager might want a secretary to read meeting request messages in order to handle the manager's schedule. In many mail systems, this would be accomplished by having the secretary log on as the manager. This creates an obvious security problem. Microsoft solves this problem by allowing the manager to grant the secretary limited permission to access the manager's mailbox. This permission can be restricted to certain folders. The secretary can also be granted permission to send messages on behalf of the manager or even send messages as the manager, using the Send As feature.

Voting   Outlook supports the ability to add voting buttons in the header of a mail message and to collect the responses. This allows surveys to be conducted through e-mail.

AutoCreate   Outlook can automatically convert one Outlook item into another. For example, a mail message may contain an action item that the user can simply drag and drop into the Task folder. Outlook would automatically convert the mail message into a task.

Recover deleted items   Users of Outlook can recover deleted items in a mailbox or public folder for a certain amount of time determined by the Exchange administrator.

Expanded storage capacity   Users can store up to 64,000 items in their personal folder or an offline folder.

These are just some of the e-mail features of Microsoft Outlook. This client program and others are discussed further in Chapter 6.

Web Browsers

Exchange 2000 Server includes a component named *Outlook Web Access (OWA)* that runs in conjunction with Microsoft *Internet Information Server (IIS)*. OWA enables Web browsers to access Exchange resources such as mailboxes and public folders. Any standard Web browser can be used, such as Microsoft Internet Explorer or Netscape Navigator, though only Internet Explorer 5 or later supports some of the advanced features that OWA provides. This Exchange functionality permits users of other operating system platforms, such as Unix or IBM's OS/2, to also be Exchange clients. Chapter 6 covers the Exchange components required for Web browser clients.

Internet E-Mail Programs with POP3

Exchange has built-in support for the *Post Office Protocol, version 3 (POP3)*. POP enables mail clients to retrieve mail messages stored on a remote mail server. Exchange's support for this protocol allows Internet e-mail programs that support

POP3 to access their Exchange mailbox and download their messages. Chapter 6 covers POP3 in the Exchange environment.

Internet E-Mail Programs with IMAP4

Exchange also has built-in support for the *Internet Message Access Protocol, version 4 (IMAP4)*. IMAP is similar to POP in that it is a mail retrieval protocol. But IMAP has more features than POP, such as the ability to select the messages to download rather than having to download all new messages. Chapter 6 provides further details on IMAP4.

Groupware

A simple definition of *groupware* is any application (the ware in groupware) that allows groups to store and share information. That is a very broad definition, and one that includes applications like e-mail and electronic forms. And indeed, as you will see, these applications are important ingredients in groupware. However, the emphasis in groupware is collaboration—not merely sending an item, but enabling many people to cooperatively use that item. Microsoft Outlook incorporates many groupware functions, such as the ability to share a calendar, schedule, task list, and contact list.

Another example of groupware is folder-based applications. These applications utilize public folders. A *public folder* is a special storage area for group access. Various types of information can be contained in a public folder, such as documents, spreadsheets, graphics, e-mail messages, forms, and many other types of information. Along with storing information, a public folder can be assigned security, so that only selected users or groups can access the public folder. Other features like views and rules can also be assigned to a public folder. Using a simple folder-based application, a Sales department could place all of their sales letters in a specified public folder for the department. Only the employees in the Sales department would be given permission to access this public folder.

Folder-based applications can also utilize electronic forms. A specific electronic form or set of forms can be associated with a public folder. Users can fill out and post the form to the public folder. Other users can then access the public folder and view the posted information. An example of this type of application is a discussion-and-response application. A product manager could create a public folder for discussion about a product under development. That manager could also create customized electronic forms that people could use to enter their comments and that they could then send, through e-mail, to the public folder. The product manager and product developers could then access the public folder to read the comments. It is even possible to set up customized views of the content in the public folder in order to view only data on a specific topic. A marketing person, for example, might want to see only comments related to the possible market for the product.

Folder-based applications are examples of *pull-style* communication, because users go to the information and decide what is relevant to them. See Chapter 9 for more on the topic of public folders. Figure 1.2 illustrates folder-based applications.

FIGURE 1.2 Folder-based applications

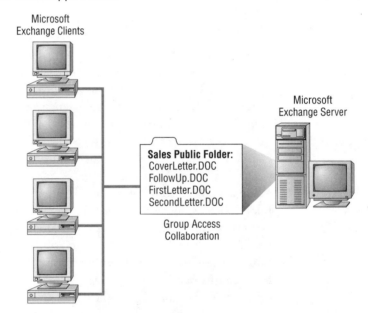

Other groupware elements of Exchange are the Microsoft Exchange *Chat Service* and *Instant Messaging Service*. The Chat Service enables users to conduct online meetings, discussions, or collaborate on documents or projects online and in real time. The Chat Service is based on the Internet protocol *Internet Relay Chat (IRC)*. The Instant Messaging Service allows users to communicate in real time using the Microsoft Instant Messenger. Chapter 11 discusses these services.

FIGURE 1.3 Host-based computing model

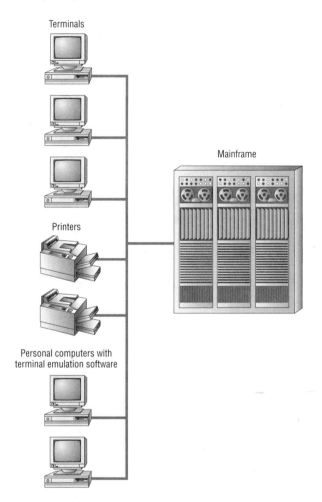

Using this model, a *shared-file messaging system* has active clients and passive servers. Each mail user is assigned a mailbox. A mailbox is actually a directory on the server where mail messages are placed. The server software is passive in that its main task is to store mail messages. The client software is said to be active because it performs almost all mail activities. Along with the normal mail activities of creating and reading mail, the client software is also responsible for depositing mail in the correct recipient mailboxes and checking its own mailbox for new mail (this is referred to as *polling)*.

This model could be compared to a postal system where people must take their outgoing mail to the post office and place it in the respective recipients' mail slots and also visit the post office to check their mail slots for any new mail. The primary duty of the post office is to store the mail. This is analogous to the shared-file messaging system in that the people (clients) are active and the post office (server) is passive.

The advantages of shared-file messaging systems include the following:

Minimal server requirements   Because the server has a passive role, it does not need to run on a high-end hardware platform.

Minimal server configuration in a single-server environment   Because the server is mainly a storage location, it does not need a lot of configuration.

The disadvantages of shared-file messaging systems include the following:

Limited security   Because the client software is responsible for sending mail to a recipient's mailbox, each client must have write permissions on each mail directory. Each client must also have read permissions on the entire mail directory structure in order to read forwarded or copied messages. From a security standpoint, this is considered an excessive level of permissions.

Increased network traffic   The periodic client polling of mailboxes for new mail increases network traffic.

Increased client load   The active clients do almost all of the processing work.

Limited scalability   These systems cannot accommodate large numbers of users due to the shared-file model. Users must access common files that can be opened by only one process at a time.

Figure 1.4 illustrates a shared-file messaging system.

FIGURE 1.4   Shared-file messaging system

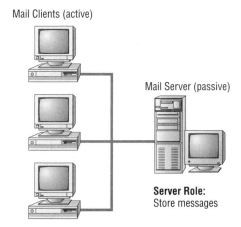

Mail Clients (active)

Mail Server (passive)

Server Role:
Store messages

Client Role:
– Poll mail directory for new mail
– Read mail (necessitates read
   permission over entire mail
   directory structure)
– Create mail
– Send mail (necessitates write
   permission over entire mail
   directory structure)

Client/Server Computing

In *client/server messaging*, a task is divided between the client processes and server processes. Each side works to accomplish specific parts of the task. The two processes are usually running on separate computers and are communicating over a network. The communication is in the form of requests and replies passed back and forth through messages.

The client side includes a user's personal computer or workstation and client software. The client software provides the interface for the user to employ when manipulating data and making requests to and receiving replies from the server. The processing power to carry out those tasks is provided by the client's computer.

The server side includes the server computer and server software. The server software receives and processes client requests, provides storage capabilities, implements security, provides for administrative functions, and performs many more duties. The server's processor, or processors, power these functions.

When this model is applied to a mail system, both the client side and the server side are active participants. Mail activities are divided between the two sides in a way that takes advantage of both parties. The client software enables users to initiate mail activities like creating, sending, reading, storing, and forwarding mail and attachments.

The server software also has an active role. Some of its tasks are implementing security, placing messages in mailboxes (as opposed to the client software doing it), notifying clients of new mail (which eliminates the need for clients to poll their mailboxes), and performing specified actions on mail, such as applying rules, rerouting messages, and many other tasks. Many of the mail activities that are initiated by the client software are actually implemented on the server. For example, when a client initiates the reading of a message, the client software sends a read request to the server where the message physically resides. The server software receives this request, processes it (for example, checks security to see if this user is permitted to read this message), and then sends the message to the client. The user can then use the client software and processor to manipulate the message (edit the message, for example). This illustrates how both sides are active.

In this model, the software running on the client machine is frequently referred to as the front-end program, while the software running on the server is referred to as the back-end program.

Exchange 2000 Server now supports front-end and back-end servers, a designation that allows an Exchange administrator to balance the various loads placed on Exchange servers among multiple computers. This concept is discussed in detail in Chapters 2 and 6. Do not confuse front- and back-end programs with front- and back-end servers.

The advantages of the client/server model include the following:

Distributed computer processing   The computer processing power of both the client and server machines are utilized. The client processor handles the end-user mail activities, such as creating, reading, and manipulating mail, while the server processor (or processors) handles the security, routing, and special handling of mail. This spreads the processing load over a multitude of client processors, while still utilizing the powerful processing of the server machine.

Tight security   The server software is responsible for the security of the mail system. The server software is the entity that actually places messages in mailboxes. The clients therefore do not need permissions to all mailboxes. This creates a much more secure mail system.

Reduced network traffic   Because the server software informs clients of new mail, the client software does not have to poll the server, thus reducing network traffic.

Scalable   The term *scalable* relates to the ability to grow easily. A client/server mail system can scale to any size organization.

The primary disadvantage of the client/server model is the following:

Increased server hardware requirements   Because the server has an active role in the messaging environment, there are greater requirements for the server hardware platform. This should not be seen as much of a disadvantage in light of the advantages of scalability, central administration, backup, and other advantages.

Figure 1.5 illustrates the client/server mail system.

Exchange is a client/server messaging system. The Exchange 2000 Server software runs as a series of services on a Windows 2000 server. It provides server-side messaging functions for the client applications. Exchange also ships with the Outlook client application noted earlier in this chapter. These programs, along with other client applications like Web browsers, provide client-side functions such as making requests to the server and creating and manipulating data.

So far, we have learned what features make up Exchange 2000 Server and how the system is implemented, namely the client/server model. Now we need to turn our attention to the context or scale in which Exchange can be implemented.

FIGURE 1.5 Client/server mail system

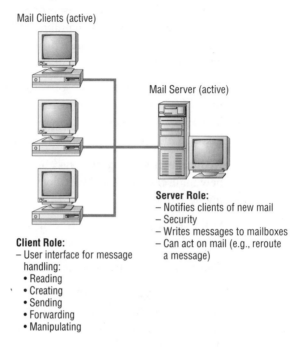

Mail Clients (active)

Mail Server (active)

Server Role:
– Notifies clients of new mail
– Security
– Writes messages to mailboxes
– Can act on mail (e.g., reroute a message)

Client Role:
– User interface for message handling:
  • Reading
  • Creating
  • Sending
  • Forwarding
  • Manipulating

Enterprise-Quality Features

Microsoft Exchange 2000 Server actually comes in two editions. The first is the Standard edition (or, simply, Microsoft Exchange 2000 Server), which is targeted for use by small- to medium-sized businesses. The other edition is Microsoft Exchange 2000 Enterprise Server. It is designed to be an enterprise messaging system, meaning one that is more scalable and includes features meant for larger organizations. In addition to the basic features supported by Exchange 2000 Server, Exchange 2000 Enterprise Server supports the following:

- No limit on the size of databases. The Standard edition limits the size of databases to 16GB.

- Multiple mailbox stores per server. The Standard edition supports only one database per server.

- Support for Active/Active clustering. This feature requires that Exchange 2000 Enterprise Server be installed on Windows 2000 Advanced Server.

- Support for distributed configuration (front-end and back-end servers).

For Exchange to be an enterprise messaging system, a large number of technologies had to be included or leveraged from other products (such as Microsoft Windows 2000 Server). This section briefly discusses the technologies that make Exchange a true enterprise messaging system. Those technologies fall into six categories:

- Enterprise-quality application platform

- Scalability

- Interoperability

- Performance

- Administration

- Reliability

Enterprise-Quality Application Platform

Before a determination can be made as to whether or not a product can scale to the size an organization needs, it must be determined that the product can do the things it needs to do. Exchange provides the necessary application platform to meet the requirements of almost any organization. The following are some of the elements of the Exchange application platform:

Supports a large number of messaging services   E-mail, electronic forms, groupware, and add-on products for faxing, paging, video conferencing, voicemailing, and many other services are supported.

Supports a large number of client platforms   There is client software that runs on MS-DOS, Windows 3.*x*, Windows 95, Windows 98, Windows NT, Windows 2000, Apple Macintosh, Unix, and IBM OS/2.

Integrates with other client applications   The Outlook client program that ships with Exchange tightly integrates with the most popular application suite on the market, Microsoft Office.

Provides open architecture/extensibility   Exchange is based on an open architecture, meaning that the specifications of many of its protocols are available in the public domain. Examples of published protocols include the *Messaging Application Programming Interface (MAPI)*, Internet protocols, and various Comit Consultatif International Telegraphique et Telephonique (CCITT) protocols. Developers can use this openness to create additional applications and programs that work with or extend Exchange. That is what is meant by extensible. One example of the way Microsoft encourages this is by including a single-user version of the Microsoft Visual InterDev product with Exchange Server. Developers can use Visual InterDev to create Web-based applications that enable Web clients to access Exchange resources. Chapter 6 briefly covers this topic.

Based on industry standards   The Exchange protocols, along with being open and extensible, are based on industry standards (protocols can be open and extensible but not based on industry standards). The MAPI protocol is considered an industry standard. Some of the industry standard Internet and CCITT protocols used in Exchange are as follows:

Internet mail   *Simple Mail Transfer Protocol (SMTP)*, Post Office Protocol, version 3 (POP3), and Internet Message Access Protocol, version 4 (IMAP4). See Chapter 6.

Internet chat   Internet Relay Chat (IRC). See Chapter 10.

Internet directory access   *Lightweight Directory Access Protocol (LDAP)*. See Chapter 6.

Internet news services   *Network News Transfer Protocol (NNTP)*. See Chapter 6.

Internet management   *Simple Network Management Protocol (SNMP)*. See Chapter 9.

Internet security   *Secure MIME (S/MIME)*, Secure Sockets Layer, version 3 (SSL), and Simple Authentication and Security Layer (SASL).

Internet Web protocols   *HyperText Transfer Protocol (HTTP)* and HyperText Markup Language (HTML). See Chapter 6.

CCITT message transfer   Comit Consultatif International Telegraphique et Telephonique (International Telegraph and

Telephone Consultative Committee): X.400. See the section "Industry Standards" later in this chapter.

CCITT directory   X.500. See the section "Industry Standards" later in this chapter.

Security features   Using the Internet security protocols listed above, along with other protocols, Exchange can provide advanced security features. For example, messages can be sent with a digital signature to confirm the identity of the sender, and message content can be encrypted to prevent unauthorized viewing. Chapter 14 discusses the protocols and administration of advanced security in Exchange. Further security features, and ones that are leveraged from Microsoft Windows 2000 Server, include:

Mandatory logon   A user must have a domain account and password to log on to a Windows 2000 Server domain.

Discretionary access control   An Exchange administrator can use Windows 2000 security to control access to Exchange resources. For example, one administrator could have permission to manage particular Exchange servers or features, but not others.

Auditing   Windows 2000 can be configured to monitor and record certain events. This can help diagnose security events. The audit information is written to the Windows 2000 Event Log.

Scalability

Once a product has been determined to accomplish the types of things you need to get done, then you must find out if it can do it on the scale you need. Exchange is extremely scalable due to the following features:

Software scalable   Exchange can be implemented with a single Exchange server, or dozens of servers, depending on the messaging requirements. Even with multiple Exchange servers, a single enterprise messaging system exists. This is due to the Exchange features that enable communication between servers. This functionality permits Exchange to scale from single server to multiple server implementations. Microsoft itself uses Exchange for its worldwide messaging system.

Hardware scalable   Scalability is also evidenced by the maximum hardware specifications that Exchange can utilize.

CPUs Scalable from one to eight processors, depending on the operating system.

RAM Maximum is 4GB.

Disk storage Storage is limited only by hardware capacity. The Standard edition of Microsoft Exchange 2000 Server has a 16GB storage limit on each of the Exchange databases. The Enterprise edition has no limit on either of those databases.

Interoperability

For a product to fit into an enterprise, it might need to work with an existing messaging system. This is called interoperability or *coexistence*. An organization might need to move all of its existing messaging data to a new messaging product. This is called a *migration*. Exchange addresses both of these issues.

To interoperate with various non-Exchange systems, referred to as foreign systems, Microsoft had to write special software programs called *connectors*. Connectors are similar to translators who understand both Exchange and the foreign system and translate between them. Third-party companies have also written similar programs. Microsoft refers to these programs as gateways. Some of the messaging systems that Exchange can interoperate with include the following:

- Internet mail

- X.400 mail systems

- Microsoft Mail

- Lotus cc:Mail

- Lotus Notes

- Digital Equipment Corporation (DEC) All-IN-1

- Verimation MEMO

The Standard edition of Exchange 2000 Server ships with connectors for Internet mail, Microsoft Mail, Lotus cc:Mail, Lotus Notes, X.400 mail systems, IBM OfficeVision/PROFS, and IBM SNADS–based systems. Connectivity to other systems, such as DEC ALL-IN-1 or Verimation MEMO, is provided through third-party gateway products.

For Exchange to interoperate with some of the previous systems, third-party software is required. Chapter 12 discusses interoperability in more detail.

Some of the messaging systems that Exchange can perform a migration from include the following:

- Microsoft Mail for PC Networks
- Lotus cc:Mail
- Lotus Notes
- Novell GroupWise 4.*x* and 5.*x*
- Netscape Collabra Share forums
- IBM PROFS and OfficeVision
- DEC All-IN-1
- Verimation MEMO
- LDAP-compliant directory information and IMAP4-based information from Internet e-mail systems

Performance

A messaging system requires adequate performance to be used on an enterprise scale. Exchange meets that requirement by being a 32-bit, multi-threaded program running on a high-performance operating system, Microsoft Windows 2000 Server. Many features are built into the Exchange System Manager to help optimize server performance.

Administration

An important element of any enterprise application is the ability to effectively and efficiently administer it. Exchange meets this need by including powerful administration programs, one of which is the *Exchange System Manager* snap-in for the Microsoft Management Console (MMC). This program provides a single point of administration for an entire Exchange organization. Exchange servers anywhere in the enterprise can be managed from this program, as well as such activities as configuring a server, managing connections to foreign systems, and monitoring services centrally.

Along with its own administrative utilities, Exchange can leverage the administrative capabilities of the Windows 2000 Server operating system. Exchange integrates with Windows 2000 Server utilities like Performance Monitor and Event Viewer. Another powerful administration feature in Exchange 2000 Server involves Active Directory. Exchange-related user features (such as mailbox properties) are now managed using the Active Directory Computers and Users utility—the same tool used by Windows 2000 administrators to manage users and groups.

Exchange 2000 Server also supports the Simple Network Management Protocol (SNMP). This enables third-party SNMP monitor programs to collect various management information about an Exchange server, such as the performance information gathered by Performance Monitor. The topic of Exchange Server administration is covered in Chapter 9.

Reliability

Because of the importance of a messaging system to an enterprise, it must be reliable. Exchange provides reliability through the following ways:

Transaction log files   Data that is to be written to an Exchange database is first written to these log files (which can be done very fast). The data is later written to the appropriate database, which takes longer because of the structured nature of a database. If, for whatever reason, a server has an unintended shutdown, data that has not been written to the database is not lost; it can be automatically reconstructed from the transaction log files. Chapters 2 and 13 discuss this topic further.

Windows 2000 Backup program   When Exchange is installed, it adds extensions to the Windows 2000 Backup program, allowing that program to back up Exchange information.

Replicas   Exchange can be configured to have multiple copies, called replicas, of a single public folder on different servers. This prevents a single point of failure in terms of data access and provides quicker access by putting folders on servers closer to the users in an organization.

Intelligent message routing   This feature allows multiple routes to a destination, thereby preventing a single point of failure for message delivery.

Windows 2000 Server fault tolerance   Exchange takes advantage of the many fault tolerant features of the Windows 2000 Server operating system, such as disk mirroring and disk striping with parity. Exchange 2000 Enterprise Server also supports Windows 2000 Server Active/Active clustering, which provides fault tolerance in the event of a server malfunction. If one server fails, another server can take its place, thereby providing uninterrupted service to users.

Industry Standards

Microsoft Exchange is based on industry standard technologies, ensuring an open architecture and, therefore, extensibility (i.e., the ability to easily add on to the product). An adequate understanding of the standards used in Exchange will help in utilizing it. This section presents a brief explanation of the following standards:

- Messaging Application Programming Interface (MAPI)
- The Remote Procedure Call (RPC) protocol
- X.400
- X.500

The Internet standards are also very important in Exchange, and they will be discussed in Chapters 2 and 6.

Messaging Application Programming Interface (MAPI)

To understand MAPI, you must first understand what an application programming interface is. At the code level, a program's functions are invoked through specific instructions. The collection of those instructions are referred to as an *application programming interface (API)*. That phrase is appropriate because the API allows a programmer to interface with the functions of a program. For example, if a program has the ability to read a message, there is a specific API instruction, also called a function call, that can invoke that ability. If two programs need to interact, they must do so with an API they both understand. For example, if program A sends the instruction Read_Message 4 to program B, but program B only understands the instruction Message_4_Read, then the instruction will not be understood. Humans can use slightly different grammar and still understand one another, but computers are not that forgiving.

In the past, many client/server messaging products had their own APIs for the client/server interaction. If someone wrote a client program, it would only work with the messaging system whose API it used. If a user needed to connect to multiple messaging systems, multiple client programs were needed. See Figure 1.6.

FIGURE 1.6 Multiple messaging APIs require multiple programs

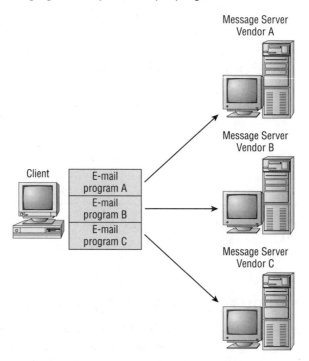

Microsoft decided to remedy that situation by creating a standard messaging architecture, referred to as the Messaging API (MAPI). MAPI accomplishes two broad goals. One, it provides a standard API for client/server messaging interaction. This role makes MAPI a type of middleware, meaning that it stands in the middle between clients and servers. Some authors refer to middleware as the slash (/) between the words client and server. MAPI makes it possible for a single client application to access different messaging servers. See Figure 1.7 for an illustration.

FIGURE 1.7 Accessing different messaging servers through MAPI

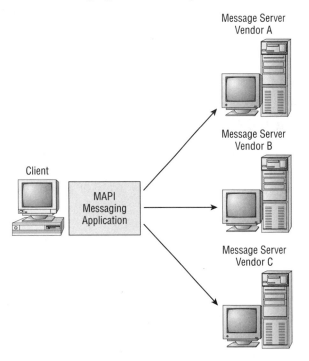

The second broad goal of MAPI is to provide a standard set of services to client messaging applications. These services include address books, message storage, and transport mechanisms. Even when using different types of MAPI applications, like e-mail, fax, and voicemail, a user can access a single address book (a universal address book) and store different data types in the same folder (a universal inbox). The transport mechanisms relate to a single client application that can connect to different messaging systems. A single MAPI e-mail application can access an Exchange server, a Microsoft Mail post office, an Internet mail server, and others.

Although MAPI includes individual API instructions, it most often communicates those instructions in an object-oriented manner. An object is a container; in this context, it functions as a container of API instructions. The Microsoft specification for object-oriented programming is called the

Component Object Model (COM). MAPI, OLE, ActiveX, and other technologies are part of the COM standard.

The original version of MAPI (called Simple MAPI) was developed by Microsoft. But in the subsequent version (MAPI 1), Microsoft worked with over 100 different vendors to develop an industry standard. Microsoft has also turned over the vast majority of the MAPI specification to standards organizations, while still taking a leadership role by including the core MAPI component with its Windows operating systems.

While MAPI deals with instructions, the next section discusses the protocols that enable those instructions to be passed between clients and servers.

Procedure Calls

We now know the instruction standard used by the Exchange client/server messaging applications, namely MAPI. But client/server applications are divided across physical machines. When a client issues a read instruction for a message, that message could be on the server. The server could understand that instruction and could send the message, but the instruction has to get to the server and the message has to get back to the client. MAPI does not handle those procedures. From MAPI's perspective, the physical distinction of the client and the server does not exist, it is transparent. Microsoft uses the Remote Procedure Call (RPC) protocol to pass instructions and data between machines. Before discussing the RPC protocol, we will first define what a procedure call is and then discuss the two types of procedure calls, local and remote.

In previous versions of Exchange Server, servers in the same Exchange site relied on RPCs to transfer messages and directory information between them. Exchange 2000 Server now uses SMTP to exchange this information between servers. You'll learn more about this in Chapter 2.

Procedure calls handle the transfer of instructions and data between a program and processor, or processors. When a program issues an instruction, that instruction is passed to the processor for execution, and the results of the execution are passed back to the program. Now, let's look at the two main types of procedure calls.

Local Procedure Calls

When a program issues an instruction that is executed on the same computer as the program executing the instruction, the procedure is referred to as a *local procedure call*. When Exchange Server components perform activities on that server, they issue instructions that are executed by that server's CPU or CPUs. That is an example of a local procedure call. Exchange uses a Microsoft protocol called the Local Procedure Call (LPC) to implement this mechanism.

Remote Procedure Calls

A *remote procedure call* is similar to a local procedure call in that it relates to the transfer of instructions and data between a program and processor. But unlike a local procedure call, a remote procedure call enables an instruction issued on one computer to be sent over the network to another computer for execution, with the results being sent back to the first computer. The computer making the instruction and the computer performing the execution are remote from each other. The transfer of instructions and data between the computers is totally transparent to the original program and to the user. To the program issuing the instruction, all of its instructions appear to be locally executed. Remote procedure calls are a key ingredient in distributed processing and client/server computing.

The RPC mechanism permits the optimization of performance by assigning different computers to do specific tasks. For example, some programs require lots of processor power, memory, or storage or all three. It would be impractical to give every computer running these applications the necessary levels of resources. But one specialized computer could be given, for example, four processors, 512MB of RAM, and 16GB of storage. Clients could use those resources through the RPC mechanism.

Because the request/reply aspect of RPC is intended to be transparent to the client program and user, the speed of network communication is a factor. The computers involved in an RPC session need to have a high-speed permanent link between them, such as a local area network (LAN) or a high-speed wide area network (WAN).

Exchange uses remote procedure calls in many of its communications. The protocol that Exchange uses to implement remote procedure calls is called the Remote Procedure Call (RPC) protocol. This protocol is discussed in the following section.

Remote Procedure Call (RPC) Protocol

As previously stated, the protocol that Exchange uses to implement remote procedure calls is called the Remote Procedure Call (RPC) protocol. It is based on a protocol created by the standards group Open Software Foundation (OSF) and is part of the OSF's Distributed Computing Environment (DCE) protocol suite. Microsoft includes the RPC protocol with their Windows 2000 operating system. In previous versions of Exchange, servers within an Exchange site transferred messages between themselves using RPCs. In Exchange 2000, this functionality has been largely taken over by SMTP. RPCs are still used to communicate with Exchange 5.5 servers, but SMTP is now used for all communications between Exchange 2000 servers inside and outside the boundaries of a routing group.

When a user chooses to read a message, the client program issues a MAPI instruction (MAPIReadMail). The RPC protocol on the client transfers this instruction to the Exchange server where the message physically resides. This is called a request. The RPC protocol on the server receives this request, has it executed, and sends the message back to the client's screen. This is called a reply. RPC clients make requests, and RPC servers make replies. RPC is sometimes referred to as a request/reply protocol. RPCs are also used in some Exchange server-to-server communications. Figure 1.8 illustrates the RPC mechanism.

FIGURE 1.8 The Remote Procedure Call protocol

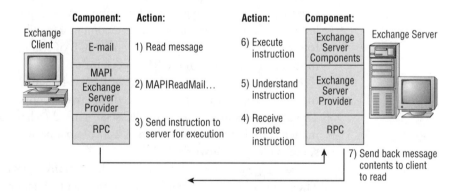

Note that being an RPC client or server doesn't really have anything to do with being a messaging client or server. In the example in Figure 1.8, the messaging client is also the RPC client, but an RPC client is really just the computer that issued the RPC. Exchange servers often communicate information between themselves using RPCs. The computer that initiates the connection request is the RPC client, and the computer that receives the request is the RPC server.

CCITT X.400

For most of the history of electronic messaging in the private sector, there were no widely accepted messaging standards. Different messaging products used vastly different messaging protocols. This made interoperability between different systems difficult and costly, sometimes impossible. To address this situation, different standards organizations began to develop what they hoped would become internationally recognized messaging standards. One of those standards organizations was the Comit Consultatif International Telegraphique et Telephonique (CCITT). This is translated in English as the International Telegraph and Telephone Consultative Committee. One of the standards they developed was the *X.400* Message Handling System (MHS) standard. Exchange uses some of the technologies of the X.400 standard.

The CCITT is now a subdelegation of the International Telegraph Union (ITU), which is an agency of the United Nations. The State Department is the voting member from the United States.

The different versions of the X.400 standard are referred to by the year they were officially published and by a specified color. Versions to date are as follows:

- 1984 "Red Book"
- 1988 "Blue Book"
- 1992 "White Book"

The Message Handling System (MHS) discussed in this section is not the same standard as the Novell-related Message Handling System (MHS).

X.400 is a set of standards that relates to the exchange of electronic messages (messages can be e-mail, fax, voicemail, telex, etc.). The goal of X.400 is to enable the creation of a global electronic messaging network. Just as you can make a telephone call from almost anywhere in the world to almost anywhere in the world, X.400 hopes to make that a reality for electronic messaging. X.400 only defines application-level protocols and relies on other standards for the physical transportation of data (e.g., X.25 and others).

X.400 Addressing: Originator/Recipient Address

Try to imagine what the American telephone system would be like if different parts of the country used different numbering schemes: different number lengths, different placement of the area code, etc. Obviously that would lead to a lot of complexity and problems, hence a standard numbering scheme exists. Electronic messaging also needs a standard addressing scheme to avoid the same sort of chaos.

One might think that you could simply list people's names in alphabetical order. But there are many problems with that scheme. The addressing scheme needs to be able to potentially scale to the entire world's population. An alphabetical list would be quite long. There is also the problem of what constitutes a last name; different countries have different methods (e.g., Anwar el-Sadat, Willem de Kooning). A truly global addressing scheme needs to be totally unambiguous.

The addressing scheme that X.400 uses is called the Originator/Recipient Address (O/R Address). It is similar to a postal address in that it uses a hierarchical format. While a postal address hierarchy is country, zip code, state, city, street, and recipient's name, the O/R Address hierarchy consists of countries, communication providers (like AT&T), companies or organizations, and other categories. Figure 1.9 and Table 1.1 present some of these categories, called fields.

FIGURE 1.9   X.400 Originator/Recipient Address example

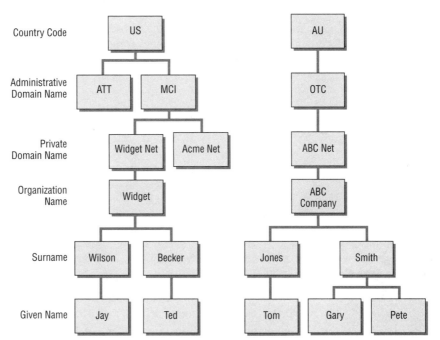

TABLE 1.1   X.400 Originator/Recipient Address Example

Field	Abbreviation/ Example	Description
Country code	c=US	Country
Administrative Management Domain (ADMD)	a=MCI	The third-party networking system used (e.g., AT&T, MCI, Sprint, etc.)
Private Management Domain (PRMD)	p=WidgetNet	Subscriber to the ADMD (company name)

TABLE 1.1 X.400 Originator/Recipient Address Example *(continued)*

Field	Abbreviation/ Example	Description
Organization	o=Widget	Name of company or organization
Surname	s=Wilson	Last name
Given name	g=Jay	First name

The O/R Address specifies an unambiguous path to where the recipient is located in the X.400 network (it does not specify a path the message might take, only the path to where the recipient is located).

In actual practice, this addressing scheme is not as standardized as Table 1.1 makes it seem, nor is it used in the standardized way. Although the address fields have always been specified, the order in which to write them was not specified until 1993. Consequently, you will see them written in different ways. Some X.400 implementations have modified the standard.

X.400 Message Format: Interpersonal Messaging (IPM)

X.400 also specifies the protocols for formatting messages. The most common one is called Interpersonal Messaging (IPM) and is used for e-mail messages. There are other protocols for other types of messaging, such as Electronic Data Interchange (EDI).

X.400 Message Routing: Message Transfer Agent (MTA)

Another very important X.400 protocol is Message Transfer Agent (MTA). MTA is the protocol that runs in the message routing machines (i.e., routers). MTA is like a local post office, in that it receives and routes messages to their ultimate destinations. And just like a postal system (a snail-mail system), electronic messages can go through several MTAs before they arrive at their ultimate destinations. This type of delivery method is called store and forward. An MTA machine receives a message, stores it so it can calculate its next route, and then forwards it either to another MTA machine or its ultimate destination. This method eliminates the need for the sender's application and the recipient's application to perform any simultaneous actions in order to exchange data. A sender's message is simply packaged with all the necessary addressing information and is sent to the next store-and-forward MTA machine (i.e., router). That MTA can route it to the next MTA, and so on, until it reaches it final destination.

Other X.400 Information

While the X.400 standard does not define the protocols for the physical transportation of messages, it does specify what other standards it can use. They include the following OSI (Open Systems Interconnection) protocols:

- TP0/X.25
- TP4 (CLNP)
- TP0/RPC 1006 to TCP/IP

 TP stands for Transport Protocol.

Third-party X.400 networks that can be subscribed to include: AT&T Mail, AT&T EasyLink, MCI Mail, Sprintmail, Atlas 400 (France), Envoy 100 (Canada), Telebox 400 (Germany), and Telecom Australia. Microsoft Exchange is an X.400 messaging product.

CCITT X.500

The CCITT X.500 standard defines the protocols for a global directory service. A directory service is a database of information on resources. Resources can be user accounts, user groups, mailboxes, printers, fax machines, and many other items. These resources are officially referred to as objects. The information about an object, such as a mailbox, can include the owner of the mailbox and the owner's title, phone number, fax number, as well as many other types of information. The information about an object is referred to as its properties or attributes. A directory enables objects and their properties to be made available to users and administrators.

The directory's importance cannot be overstated. To use a telephone analogy, imagine the current global telephone system without telephone directories. The technology to make a call would be in place, but you would have a hard time locating a person's number to call. The creation of a global electronic yellow pages could go a long way toward solving the "I know it's out there, I just can't find it" problem.

To create a directory service, X.500 addresses two main areas:

Directory structure   How resources should be organized.

Directory access   How one is able to read, query, and modify a directory.

X.500 Directory Structure

The X.500 directory structure is hierarchical, which facilitates a logical organization of information. Figure 1.10 illustrates the X.500 directory structure, and Table 1.2 explains it.

FIGURE 1.10   X.500 directory structure example

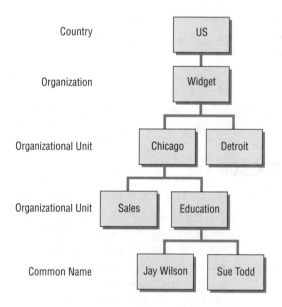

TABLE 1.2 Descriptions of X.500 Objects

X.500 Object	Abbreviation/Example	Description
Country	c=US	Country of the organization
Organization	o=Widget	Name of the organization
Organizational Unit	ou=Chicago	Subcategory of the organization
	ou=Detroit	
Organizational Unit	ou=Sales	Subcategories under the ou=Chicago
	ou=Education	
Common Name	cn=JayWilson	Name of a specific resource (username, fax name, printer name, etc.)

The X.500 terminology for the structure of a directory is the Directory Information Tree (DIT). The term for the information in the directory is Directory Information Base (DIB).

To communicate the location of an object in the directory hierarchy, list the path to that object, starting at the top and moving down. This is called a Distinguished Name (DN). The DN of the example in Figure 1.10 is as follows:

c=US; o=Widget; ou=Chicago; ou=Education; cn=JayWilson

The differences between an X.500 address, the Distinguished Name (DN), and an X.400 address are due to their different purposes. A DN is the location of an object in the directory, whereas the X.400 address is the location of an object in a messaging system. Getting back to the telephone analogy, a DN is the location of a person in the phone book, and an X.400 address is where they are in the physical telephone system. This is illustrated by the fact that an X.400 address can include information about third-party messaging networks that are used to physically deliver a message, some examples being AT&T, MCI, and Sprint.

The 1988 release of X.400 incorporated the use of a DN address instead of, or along with, an O/R Address. Some implementations of X.400 also incorporated some of the X.500 fields, like ou=x and cn=x.

A directory also puts a more natural interface on network resources. Many communication objects have long numeric identifiers that are hard to remember. A directory allows objects to be presented to users by a natural descriptive term. The directory then maps the descriptive term to the numeric identifier.

X.500 has a 1988 version and a 1993 version.

Directory Access

Having a directory is only half the equation. Users and administrators must also be able to access it to read, query, and write to it. A user might query the directory for a printer on the fourth floor in the Sales department, and the directory could respond with the needed information about the printer. Other issues that must be addressed are security (e.g., who can access an object and modify its properties) and directory replication (a true global directory would need to be on more than one machine). These issues are addressed by directory access protocols.

The standard access protocol in the X.500 recommendations is the Directory Access Protocol (DAP). DAP is considered more of a model than a real-world protocol. This is because DAP is very computer-resource intense (i.e., heavy) on client machines, and the few implementations of it are proprietary. But a newer access protocol that is getting a lot of attention today is the Lightweight Directory Access Protocol (LDAP). LDAP is an Internet protocol derived from the X.500 DAP. One of the reasons LDAP is called lightweight is because it requires fewer computer resources on the client. While LDAP is an Internet protocol, it is designed to enable access to an X.500-type directory. Almost every major software vendor has pledged support for LDAP.

Summary

T he Exchange product is a powerful client/server enterprise messaging product.

The types of applications in an Exchange environment are as follows:

- Electronic mail (e-mail)

- Groupware

- Other applications, such as fax, paging, video conferencing, and voicemail

The client application that is shipped with Exchange is as follows:

- Outlook

The network computing model that Exchange uses to implement its messaging system is the client/server model. This model utilizes the computing power of both client computers and server computers.

Exchange was designed for enterprise-wide implementations and, consequently, meets the following requirements:

- Enterprise-quality application services

- Scalability

- Interoperability

- Performance

- Administration

- Reliability

The following industry standards are used by Exchange:

- Messaging Application Programming Interface (MAPI)

- Internet protocols (e.g., SMTP, POP3, IMAP4, LDAP, SNMP, and others)

- Remote Procedure Call (RPC)

- X.400

- X.500

Key Terms

Before you take the exam, be certain you are familiar with the following terms:

application programming interface (API)	mailbox
Chat Service	Mainframe computing
client/server messaging	Messaging Application Programming Interface (MAPI)
coexistence	Microsoft Exchange 2000 Conferencing Server
connectors	migration
Digital signatures	Network News Transfer Protocol (NNTP)
e-mail	OLE 2 (Object Linking and Embedding)
encryption	Outlook Web Access (OWA)
Exchange System Manager	Post Office Protocol, version 3 (POP3)
groupware	public folder
HyperText Transfer Protocol (HTTP)	remote procedure call
Instant Messaging Service	scalable
Internet Information Server (IIS)	Secure MIME (S/MIME)
Internet Message Access Protocol, version 4 (IMAP4)	shared-file messaging system
Internet Relay Chat (IRC)	Simple Mail Transfer Protocol (SMTP)
Lightweight Directory Access Protocol (LDAP)	Simple Network Management Protocol (SNMP)
local procedure call	X.400

Review Questions

1. You are currently running Verimation MEMO on your network, but are considering deployment of Exchange 2000 Server. Once you install Exchange 2000 Server, Standard edition, which of the following options will be available to you? Choose all that apply.

   A. Install a connector to MEMO so that the two systems can coexist and interoperate.

   B. Use a migration tool to import data from MEMO to Exchange 2000 Server.

   C. Upgrade the MEMO servers to Exchange 2000 Server.

   D. You will not be able to use your legacy MEMO data.

2. You are evaluating client applications for use with Exchange 2000 Server. Many of your users need to be able to have offline access to all their mail folders and address books. Which of the following clients provide this? Choose all that apply.

   A. Outlook 2000

   B. POP3 clients

   C. IMAP4 clients

   D. Web browsers via Outlook Web Access

3. What is the name of the mechanism used when two Exchange components on the same machine pass instructions and data?

   A. Remote procedure call

   B. Remote instruction call

   C. Local instruction call

   D. Local procedure call

4. Which of the following operating systems can be used to run client applications that let users access Exchange 2000 Servers? Choose all that apply.

A. Windows 3.*x*

B. Windows 98

C. Windows 2000

D. Macintosh

E. UNIX

F. OS/2

5. You have just installed a new Exchange 2000 server and would like to migrate users and messages from a legacy Microsoft Mail system. In order to do this, you must first set up a way for the two systems to communicate. What component of Exchange 2000 would you use to do this?

A. Migration Kit

B. Connector

C. Import/Export tool

D. You cannot do this

6. You are preparing a report on the features of Exchange 2000 Server for your manager. Which of the following would you list as features that are available in Exchange 2000 Enterprise Server that are not available in the Standard edition? Choose all that apply.

A. Multiple databases per server

B. Instant Messaging support

C. Front-end and back-end server support

D. Active/Active clustering

E. Video conferencing

7. You are considering deploying Exchange 2000 on your network. You need to provide your users with basic messaging functionality and also advanced data conferencing. Which of the following editions of Exchange do you need?

   A. Exchange 2000 Server

   B. Exchange 2000 Enterprise Server

   C. Exchange 2000 Conferencing Server

   D. Exchange 2000 Collaboration Server

8. Which of the following protocols can be used to *retrieve* messages from Exchange 2000 Server? Choose all that apply.

   A. LDAP

   B. PNP

   C. PPP

   D. POP3

9. Which of the following services of Exchange 2000 Server would allow two or more users to collaborate on documents in real time?

   A. Chat Service

   B. Instant Messaging Service

   C. Public Folders

   D. Workflow Service

10. Which Outlook feature enables e-mail content to include multiple format types, such as fonts, sizes, and colors?

   A. WordPerfect

   B. This software cannot do this

   C. Richman message content

   D. Rich-text message content

11. Which of the following components work together to allow Web browsers to access an Exchange server? Choose two.

    A. Internet Information Server

    B. Outlook Browser Access

    C. Outlook Web Access

    D. Exchange Web Server

12. You are the manager of a large Exchange organization. Recently, you began to suspect that someone was attempting to log on to resources without permission. You enabled auditing on your servers to keep track of suspicious activity. Which utility would you use to view the audited information?

    A. Exchange System Manager

    B. Active Directory Users and Computers

    C. Computer Management

    D. Security Manager

    E. Windows 2000 Event Log

13. You are a consultant that has been hired by the Arbor Shoes Company. Some time ago, their network administrator set up a messaging system. The administrator has left the company, and the company now wants you to help them decide whether to keep the existing system or move to Exchange 2000 Server. In either case, you will need to train someone how to manage the system. A person at the company describes the messaging system to you in the following way. There is one server on their network that functions as the mail server. Whenever a new person needs a mailbox, the administrator creates a new folder and assigns it permissions. Then, the client application must be pointed to that folder. What type of messaging system do you suspect the company is running?

    A. Client/server messaging system

    B. Shared-file messaging system

    C. Mainframe messaging system

    D. Host-based messaging system

14. You have created a set of public folders on one of the six Exchange servers. Since their creation, the public folders have become an important resource in your organization, and you are concerned that having all of the folders on one server creates a single point of failure; should that server fail, no one will have access to the folders. What is the simplest way to remedy this situation?

    A. Back the public folders up hourly so that you may quickly restore them to another server if necessary.

    B. Configure two of the servers as a cluster.

    C. Configure replicas of the public folder on another Exchange server.

15. You are currently making recommendations for the purchase of Exchange 2000 software. You expect that the size of your databases on several servers will run around 25GB. Which edition of Exchange 2000 would you need for these servers?

    A. Exchange 2000 Server

    B. Exchange 2000 Advanced Server

    C. Exchange 2000 Enterprise Server

    D. Exchange 2000 Datacenter Server

16. In X.500, which of the following constructs describes the location of an object in a directory?

    A. Distinguished Name

    B. X.500 Address

    C. Organizational unit

    D. Common name

17. Your company is currently running Microsoft Mail, a shared-file messaging system. You have been trying to convince your manager to move to Exchange 2000 Server. In telling your manager about the features of client/server messaging systems, which of the following features would you NOT include?

    A. Distributed processing

    B. Tight security

    C. Passive client application

    D. Reduced network traffic

18. Which of the following is an Internet management protocol supported by Exchange 2000 Server?

    A. SNMP

    B. SMTP

    C. MMX

    D. MID

19. Which of the following protocols are used by Web browsers?

    A. HTTP

    B. HTML

    C. SNMP

    D. SMTP

20. Which of the following is the X.400 component whose primary responsibility is to receive and route messages to their ultimate destination?

    A. Message Routing Agent

    B. Message Transfer Agent

    C. Message Handling Agent

    D. Message Delivery Agent

Answers to Review Questions

1. B. Exchange 2000 Server comes with a migration tool for use with Verimation MEMO. Although coexistence with MEMO is supported, a third-party gateway connector is required. It does not come with Exchange 2000 Server. Also, Exchange 2000 Server does not support upgrades from foreign messaging systems.

2. A. Only Outlook 2000 and some previous versions of Outlook provide support for using folders and address books offline.

3. D. A local procedure call is an instruction passed between two components on the same computer. A remote procedure call is passed between two components on different computers that are linked via a permanent high-speed network.

4. A, B, C, D, E, F. Any operating system that can run a Web browser (and there is one available for every OS out there) or a POP3 or IMAP4 client can access Exchange 2000 Server as long as Exchange is configured correctly.

5. B. Connectors provide a way to connect Exchange servers in different routing groups and a way to connect Exchange organizations to external messaging systems. In migrating from existing messaging systems to Exchange, you must first set up a connector so that the two systems can communicate. Once the connector is configured, you will be able to migrate users and messages to Exchange 2000 Server.

6. A, C, D. Instant Messaging support is available in the Standard edition of Exchange 2000 Server. All of the other features listed require the Enterprise edition except for video conferencing, which requires Exchange 2000 Conferencing Server.

7. A, C. Microsoft Exchange 2000 Conferencing Server is a separate product from Exchange 2000 Server. It provides services that allow two or more people to communicate and collaborate as a group over the Internet or a private intranet in real time. Specifically, Exchange 2000 Conferencing Server provides data conferencing, audio and video conferencing, and advanced schedule management.

8. D. POP3 is a message retrieval protocol. LDAP is a directory access protocol. PPP is a remote access protocol.

9. A. The Chat Service enables users to conduct online meetings and discussions or collaborate on documents or projects online and in real time.

10. D. Outlook enables the creation of rich-text message content that can include multiple fonts, sizes, colors, alignments, and other formatting controls.

11. A, C. Internet Information Server is a Web server service built into Windows 2000 and provides the Internet protocol support for Exchange 2000 Server. Outlook Web Access is a component that allows IIS to access the Web Store and then present information to Web browsers in HTML format.

12. E. Windows 2000 can be configured to monitor and record certain events. This can help diagnose security events. The audit information is written to the Windows 2000 Event Log.

13. B. A shared-file messaging system is one in which a passive server is basically configured with a set of shared folders. Client applications are configured to regularly poll the shared folders to see if new mail has been deposited there.

14. C. Exchange 2000 allows you to configure replicas of public folders on multiple servers.

15. C. Exchange 2000 Server (the Standard edition) has a 16GB limit on the size that a database may reach. Exchange 2000 Enterprise Server does not have this limit. There is no such edition as Exchange 2000 Advanced Server or Datacenter Server.

16. A. In X.500, the Distinguished Name (DN) describes the location of an object in the X.500 directory.

17. C. In a shared-file messaging system, servers are relatively passive, and clients perform almost all active messaging functions. Even though the server in a client/server system plays a much more active role, the client is still by no means passive.

18. A. Simple Network Management Protocol (SNMP) is a TCP/IP-based management protocol supported by Exchange 2000 Server in the form of the MADMAN MIB, an information base of manageable Exchange components.

19. A, B. HTTP is the protocol used to define how messages are sent between a Web browser and Web server. HTML is the markup language that a Web browser uses to determine how a page should be displayed in the browser window.

20. B. The Message Transfer Agent (MTA) is the protocol that runs in the message routing machines (i.e., routers). An MTA machine receives a message, stores it so it can calculate its next route, and then forwards it to either another MTA machine or its ultimate destination.

Chapter

2

Microsoft Exchange Architecture

An *architecture* is the structure of something. When applied to a software product, an architecture is a description of the software components of the product, what they are, what they do, and how they relate to each other. In Exchange, examples of these components are the Information Store service that manages the databases of messages on a server or the System Attendant service that performs routine maintenance on a server. Part of what software components do is create and manage objects (i.e., resources) like servers, mailboxes, public folders, address books, etc. How those objects are structured or organized is also part of software architecture.

There are many practical benefits to understanding the architecture of Microsoft Exchange. It will aid a person in designing, installing, administering, and troubleshooting an Exchange system. For example, understanding component functionality will assist in deciding what optional components, if any, to choose during an installation. Troubleshooting can frequently benefit from a good understanding of architecture; just understanding some error messages requires such knowledge. This chapter provides you with a good conceptual background of the topics covered in the remainder of the book.

In this chapter, we will address the following issues:

- The Windows 2000 Active Directory and its integration with Exchange 2000 Server

- Information storage on an Exchange server

- Message flow in the Exchange environment

Active Directory

The *Active Directory* is one of the most important new concepts in Windows 2000 networking. Although a full discussion of Active Directory is outside the scope of this book, the nature of Exchange 2000 Server's tight integration with Active Directory warrants a brief discussion of the technology itself and an examination of how it affects the Exchange environment.

To learn more about Active Directory, start by checking out the Windows 2000 product documentation. It provides an overview of the technology and illustrates many of the benefits of using Active Directory. If you are interested in going past the basics, take a look at *MCSE: Windows 2000 Directory Services Administration Study Guide,* by Anil Desai and James Chellis (Sybex, 2000).

Active Directory in Windows 2000

To understand Active Directory, it is first necessary to understand what a *directory* is. Put simply, a directory is a hierarchy that stores information about objects in a system. A directory service is the service that manages the directory and makes it available to users on the network. Active Directory stores information about objects on a Windows 2000 network and makes this information easy for administrators and users to find and use. Active Directory uses a structured data store as the basis for a hierarchical organization of directory information.

You can use Active Directory to design a directory structure tailored to your organization's administrative needs. For example, you can scale Active Directory from a single computer to a single network or to many networks. Active Directory can include every object, server, and domain in a network.

What makes Active Directory so powerful, and so scalable, is that it separates the logical structure of the Windows 2000 domain hierarchy from the physical structure of the network itself.

Logical Components

In previous versions of Exchange, resources were organized separately in Windows and Exchange. Now, the organization you set up in Windows 2000 and

the organization you set up in Exchange 2000 are the same. In fact, the Active
Directory Users and Computers tool (whose use is covered in Chapter 4) is
now used to configure Windows 2000 users and Exchange 2000–related user
features, such as mailbox storage and protocol use. This requires a shift in
thinking from previous versions of Exchange, where the duties of Windows
and Exchange administrators were more clearly separated. Now, it is often
advantageous to have one user administrator manage all aspects of user configuration. In Active Directory, the domain hierarchy is organized using a
number of constructs to make administration simpler and more logical.
These logical constructs, which are described in the following subsections,
allow you to define and group resources so that they can be located and
administered by name rather than by physical location.

Objects

An *object* is the basic unit in Active Directory. It is a distinct named set of
attributes that represents something concrete, such as a user, printer, computer, or application. Attributes are the characteristics of the object; for
example, a computer is an object, and its attributes include its name and location, among other things. A user is also an object. In Exchange, a user's
attributes include the user's first name, last name, and e-mail address.
User attributes also include Exchange-related features, such as whether
the object can receive e-mail, the formatting of e-mail it receives, and the
location where it can receive e-mail.

Organizational Units

An *organizational unit* (OU) is a container in which you can place objects
such as user accounts, groups, computers, printers, applications, file shares,
and other organizational units. You can use organizational units to hold
groups of objects, such as users and printers, and you can assign specific permissions to them. An organizational unit cannot contain objects from other
domains and is the smallest unit you can assign or delegate administrative
authority to. Organizational units are provided strictly for administrative
purposes and convenience. They are transparent to the end user and have no
bearing on the user's ability to access network resources.

You can use organizational units to create containers within a domain
that represent the hierarchical, logical structures within your organization.
This enables you to manage how accounts and resources are configured
and used.

Organizational units can also be used to create departmental or geographical
boundaries. In addition, they can be used to delegate administrative authority
over particular tasks to particular users. For instance, you can create an OU for

all your printers and then assign full control over the printers to your printer administrator.

Domains

A *domain* is a group of computers and other resources that are part of a network and share a common directory database. A domain is organized in levels and is administered as a unit with common rules and procedures. You can think of a domain as the security boundary of a Windows 2000 network. Permissions granted in one domain do not apply in other domains. All objects and organizational units exist within a domain.

You create a domain by installing the first domain controller inside of it. A domain controller is simply a Windows 2000 server that has Active Directory enabled on it. Once a server has been installed, you can use the Active Directory Wizard to install Active Directory. In order to install Active Directory on the first server on a network, that server must have access to a server running DNS (Domain Name Service). If it does not, you'll be given the chance to install and configure DNS during Active Directory installation.

A domain can exist in either *mixed mode* or *native mode*, with mixed mode being the default installation. In mixed mode, a Windows 2000 domain controller acts like a Windows NT 4 domain controller. Active Directory domains in mixed mode endure the same limitations of the security accounts database as does a Windows NT 4 domain controller. For example, in mixed mode, there is a restriction on the size of the directory to 40,000 objects—the same limitation imposed by the Windows NT 4 model. The reason for this is that running in mixed mode assumes that legacy Windows NT 4 domain controllers exist on the network and that they need connectivity and synchronization with the Windows 2000 domain controllers.

Running Windows 2000 in native mode means that you no longer have any Windows NT 4 domain controllers on your network. The switch to native mode is a one-time, one-way switch and is irreversible. Native mode allows your Windows 2000 domain controllers to scale into the millions of objects per domain. In addition, running in native mode allows for the nesting of groups, something that is advantageous to Exchange 2000 if large distribution groups are anticipated.

Domain Trees

A *domain tree* is a hierarchical arrangement of one or more Windows 2000 domains that share a common namespace. *Domain Name Service (DNS)* domain names represent the tree structure. The first domain in a tree is called the *root domain*. For example, a company named Widgets (that has the Internet domain name widgets.com) might use the root domain widgets.com in its primary domain tree. Additional domains in the tree under the root domain are called *child domains*. For example, the domain hsv.widgets.com would be a child domain of the widget.com domain. Figure 2.1 shows an example of a domain tree.

FIGURE 2.1 A domain tree is a hierarchical grouping of one or more domains.

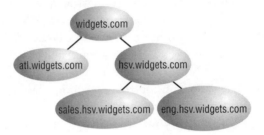

Domains establish trust relationships with one another that allow objects in a trusted domain to access resources in a trusting domain. Windows 2000 and Active Directory support transitive, two-way trusts between domains. When a child domain is created, a trust relationship is automatically configured between that child domain and the parent domain. This trust is two-way, meaning that resource access requests can flow from either domain to the other. The trust is also transitive, meaning that any domains trusted by one domain are automatically trusted by the other domain. For example, in Figure 2.1, consider the three domains named widgets.com, hsv.widgets.com, and sales.hsv.widgets.com. When hsv.widgets.com was created as a child domain of widgets.com, a two-way trust was formed between the two. When sales.hsv.widgets.com was created as a child of hsv.widgets.com, another trust was formed between those two domains. Though no explicit trust relationship was ever defined directly between the sales.hsv.widgets.com and widgets.com domains, the two domains trust each other anyway because of the transitive nature of trust relationships.

Domain Forests

A *domain forest* is a group of one or more domain trees that do not form a contiguous namespace, but may share a common schema and global catalog. There is always at least one forest on the network, and it is created when the first Active Directory–enabled computer (domain controller) on a network is installed. This first domain in a forest is called the *forest root domain* and is special because it is really the basis for naming the entire forest. It cannot be removed from the forest without removing the entire forest itself. Finally, no other domain can ever be created above the forest root domain in the forest domain hierarchy. Figure 2.2 shows an example of a domain forest with multiple domain trees.

FIGURE 2.2 A domain forest consists of one or more domain trees.

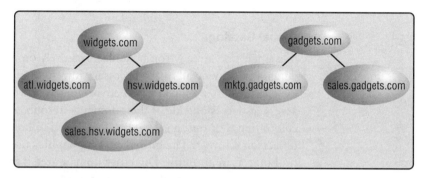

A forest is the outermost boundary of Active Directory; the directory cannot be larger than the forest. You can create multiple forests and then create trust relationships between specific domains in those forests; this would let you grant access to resources and accounts that are outside of a particular forest. However, an Exchange organization cannot span multiple forests.

Physical Components

The physical side of Active Directory is primarily represented by domain controllers and Windows 2000 sites. These enable organizations to optimize replication traffic across their networks and to assist client workstations in finding the closest domain controller to validate logon credentials.

Domain Controllers

Every domain must have at least one *domain controller*, a computer running Windows 2000 Server that validates user network access and manages Active Directory. To create a domain controller, all you have to do is install Active Directory on a Windows 2000 server. During this process, you have the option of creating a new domain or joining an existing domain. If you create a new domain, you also have the option of creating or joining an existing domain tree or forest. A domain controller stores a complete copy of all Active Directory information for that domain, manages changes to that information, and replicates those changes to other domain controllers in the same domain. Schema and infrastructure configuration information is replicated between all domain controllers in a forest.

In previous versions of Windows, a distinction was drawn between Primary and Backup Domain Controllers. In Windows 2000, all domain controllers are considered peers, and each holds a complete copy of Active Directory.

Global Catalog

In a single domain environment, users can rely on Active Directory for the domain to provide all of the necessary information about the resources on the network. In a multi-domain environment, however, users often need to access resources outside of their domain—resources that may be more difficult to find. For this, a *global catalog* is used to hold information about all objects in a forest. The global catalog enables users and applications to find objects in an Active Directory domain tree if the user or application knows one or more attributes of the target object.

Through the replication process, Active Directory automatically generates the contents of the global catalog from the domain controllers in the directory. The global catalog holds a partial replica of the Active Directory. Even though every object is listed in the global catalog, only a limited set of attributes for those objects are replicated in it. The attributes listed for each object in the global catalog are defined in the schema. A base set of attributes is replicated to the global catalog, but you can specify additional attributes to meet the needs of your organization.

By default, there is only one global catalog in the entire forest and that is the first domain controller installed in the first domain of the first tree. All others must be configured manually. We recommend adding a second global catalog for backup and load balancing.

Windows 2000 Sites

A *Windows 2000 site* is basically a group of computers that exist on one or more IP subnets. Computers within a site must be connected by a fast, reliable network connection. Using Windows 2000 sites helps maximize network efficiency and provide fault tolerance. Windows 2000 sites also help clients find the closest domain controller to validate logon credentials.

In previous versions of Exchange Server, the concept of a site was used to identify a group of Exchange servers that shared a permanent, high-bandwidth connection and also represented an administrative boundary in Exchange. The concept of Windows 2000 sites and sites in earlier versions of Exchange are unrelated. Exchange 2000 Server has replaced the concept of Exchange sites with routing groups and administrative groups. Routing groups are used to define groups of Exchange servers that share a reliable (but not necessarily high-bandwidth) connection. Administrative groups are used to define administrative boundaries within an Exchange environment.

 Exchange 2000 Server makes extensive use of Active Directory information on global catalog servers. For efficient communication, Exchange 2000 Server requires direct access to a global catalog server in your LAN.

Sites are created using the Windows 2000 Active Directory Sites and Services tool. No direct relationship exists between Windows 2000 domains and sites, so a single domain can span multiple sites and a single site can span multiple domains.

Schema

A *schema* represents the structure of a database system—the tables and fields in that database and how the tables and fields are related to one another. The Windows 2000 Active Directory information is also represented by a schema. All objects that can be stored in Active Directory are defined in the schema.

Installing Active Directory on the first domain controller in a network creates a schema that contains definitions of commonly used objects and attributes. The schema also defines objects and attributes that Active Directory uses internally. When Exchange 2000 Server is installed, Exchange setup extends the schema to support information that Exchange needs. Updates to the schema require replication of the schema across the forest and also to all domain controllers in the forest. For more information about how Exchange updates the schema, see Chapter 3.

Active Directory and Exchange 2000

In previous versions of Exchange Server, Exchange maintained a directory of its own through a service known as the Directory Service. On each Exchange server, the Directory Service maintained a copy of the directory in a database file on the Exchange server and took care of replicating changes in the directory to other Exchange servers. In Exchange 2000 Server, Directory Service has been removed altogether. Exchange is now totally reliant on Active Directory to provide its directory services.

This new reliance caused a shift in the way that the Exchange directory is maintained. This first section examines the effects that boundaries of a forest place on Exchange. It then looks at the interaction of DNS in an Exchange organization. Finally, it looks at the differences in directory replication now that Exchange itself no longer handles the directory information and the use of the Active Directory Connector to exchange data with previous versions of Exchange Server.

Forests

By default, the global catalog shows only objects within a single Windows 2000 forest, so an Exchange organization must be within the boundaries of a forest. This is different from earlier versions of Windows NT and Exchange. In previous versions, an Exchange organization could span domains that did not trust one another because Exchange 5.5 did not rely so much on the underlying security structure of Windows NT. With Active Directory and Exchange 2000 Server, the security structure is integrated, which means that a single Exchange organization cannot span forests but it can span domains.

Domain Name Service (DNS)

In previous versions of Windows NT, the *Windows Internet Naming System* (WINS) was the primary provider of name resolution within an organization because it provided dynamic publishing and full names to network address mapping. DNS was really only required for organizations that needed Internet connectivity, though it was usually recommended practice to use DNS with earlier versions of Exchange Server as well. Windows 2000 relies almost exclusively on DNS as it provides maximum interoperability with Internet technologies. In order for Exchange 2000 Server to function, a DNS service must be running in your organization. Outlook Web Access, SMTP connectivity, and Internet connectivity all rely on DNS.

Active Directory is often called a *namespace*, which is similar to the directory service in earlier versions of Exchange and means any bounded area in which a given name can be resolved. The DNS name creates a namespace for a tree or forest, such as widgets.com. All child domains of widgets.com, such as sales.widgets.com, share the root namespace. In Exchange 2000 Server, Active Directory forms a namespace in which the name of an object in the directory can be resolved to the object. All domains that have a common root domain form a *contiguous namespace*. This means that the domain name of a child domain is the child domain name appended to the name of the parent domain.

In Windows 2000 domains using DNS, a domain name such as hsv.widgets.com does not affect the e-mail addresses for Exchange users created in that domain. Although a user's logon name might be user@hsv.widgets.com, you control how e-mail addresses are generated using recipient policies in System Manager and Active Directory Users and Computers.

Directory Replication

In earlier versions of Exchange, the directory was a part of Exchange, and replication of that directory was handled by Exchange Server. When attributes of directory objects changed, the entire object was replicated throughout the organization.

Now, all directory functions have been passed to Active Directory, which replicates at the attribute level instead of the object level. This means that if a change is made to an attribute, only that attribute (and not the entire object) is replicated to other domain controllers in the domain, resulting in less network traffic and more efficient use of server resources.

Active Directory Connector (ADC)

Exchange 2000 supports coexistence with Exchange 5.5 through the Active Directory Connector. For organizations using earlier versions of Exchange, this is a critical component in upgrading to Exchange 2000 Server.

Because Exchange 2000 Server uses Active Directory as its directory service, directory information is managed in one location. The Active Directory Connector is a Windows 2000 service that synchronizes the Exchange 5.5 directory with Active Directory. This allows you to administer your directory from Active Directory or the Exchange 5.5 directory service. You can also use ADC to migrate objects from the Exchange directory service to Active Directory. For more information on configuring Exchange 2000 to work with Exchange 5.5, see Chapter 11.

Information Storage

In Exchange 2000 Server, a service named the *Information Store* is responsible for data storage and management. It supports access by MAPI clients and by numerous Internet protocols via Internet Information Server. It also supports access through application programming interfaces (APIs) such as Collaboration Data Objects (CDO), ActiveX Data Objects (ADO), and the Active Directory Services Interface (ADSI). What all of this means is that the Exchange Information Store has become much more than a place where messages and data are stored. It has become a single repository in which an entire network of users and applications can store and manage information of just about any type. Since it holds all types of data and provides such varied access methods, Microsoft describes the Information Store in Exchange 2000 as the *Web Store.*

With this new version of Exchange, the support and management of protocols have been passed from the Exchange software itself to Internet Information Server. Separating the protocols from the storage system and providing other features, such as an Installable File System, front-end/back-end servers, and Active/Active clustering support, have allowed Exchange 2000 Server to become much more robust and scalable than previous versions of Exchange.

Web Storage System

The Exchange 2000 Server Web Store combines features of the Web, the file system, and Exchange 2000 Server into a single, unified system for storing and accessing information. The Web Store serves as the sole repository for managing diverse types of information within a single infrastructure. In addition, almost every resource in the Web Store is now addressable through a solitary *Uniform Resource Locator (URL)* location.

Although much ado has been made of the "new" Web Store in Exchange 2000 Server, it is important to understand that the Web Store is not so much a specific entity or technology, as it is a new concept of how Exchange information is stored and used. Just like in previous versions of Exchange, information is still stored in databases and still managed by a service named the Information Store. Sometimes the storage system as a whole is called the Information Store, sometimes the Web Store. Both of these terms refer to the same system, but you may find them used in different situations based on context. For example, in the product documentation, Microsoft likes to call it the Web Store when they are pointing out new, Web-related features. New features such as supporting multiple databases per server that can be grouped into storage groups makes Exchange all the more powerful. The Web Store moniker is really just a way to get across the idea that the information databases of Exchange can be used for more than just storing e-mail messages. They can be used to store almost any kind of information or document, and they can be accessed by not only e-mail clients, but by Web browsers and custom applications as well.

Exchange Databases

An Exchange 2000 database is actually a logical entity that represents two physical database files, a *rich-text (EDB) file* and a *streaming media (STM) file*. For example, a single mailbox database might consist of the files `priv1.edb` and `priv1.stm`. Each database incorporates both files, and Exchange 2000 treats them as a single unit. Furthermore, the reported Information Store size will be the combination of both the rich-text store and the native content store along with the transaction logs. Both types of data are stored in an *Extensible Storage Engine (ESE)* database format.

The rich-text file holds messages and works much like the database files in previous versions of Exchange Server. The streaming media file has been added to provide native support for many types of streaming media, including voice, audio, video, and others. To do this, the streaming media file is designed to store files as *Multipurpose Internet Mail Extensions (MIME)* content, a specification for formatting non-ASCII messages so that they can be sent over the Internet. This means that multimedia content can be delivered to the Exchange server using non-MAPI protocols in the media's native format, stored, and then passed along to clients without ever having to be converted into a MAPI-acceptable format. This minimizes the time needed to deliver the files to the client and thereby helps to reduce network traffic and also eliminates the risk of introducing errors into the media during a conversion process.

Multiple Databases and Storage Groups

Exchange 2000 Server provides support for multiple databases and *storage groups* on a single server. Exchange allows up to five databases per storage group and up to four storage groups per server. Each database must exist inside a storage group.

Although each instance of a database runs under the same *Web Storage System* process, you can mount or dismount individual databases on the fly. This means that you can take one database down for maintenance while others continue to service client requests. Also, each database is checked for consistency when the Web Storage System process starts. Should one database be unable to mount, other databases remain unaffected and will mount normally.

Each storage group is represented by a single instance of the ESE and shares a single set of transaction log files. Whenever a transaction occurs on an Exchange server, the responsible service first records the transaction in a *transaction log*. Using transaction logs allows for faster completion of the transaction than if the service had to immediately commit the transaction to a database because the transaction log structure is much simpler than the database structure. Data is written to these log files sequentially as transactions occur. Regular database maintenance routines commit changes in the logs to the actual databases later, when system processes are idle. Consequently, the most current state of an Exchange service is the EDB database and STM database, plus the current log file.

The *checkpoint files* are used to keep track of transactions that are committed to the database from a transaction log. Using checkpoint files ensures that transactions cannot be committed to a database more than once. Checkpoint files are named edb.chk and reside in the same directories as their log files and databases.

The use of multiple databases and storage groups allows you to plan your organization's data storage by classifying various types of data or assigning separate databases to more important users. You can learn more about using multiple databases and storage groups in Chapter 8.

Public Folders

Public folders provide centralized storage of just about any type of data that is meant to be accessed by multiple users in an organization. The primary use of public folders is to serve as a sort of discussion forum, allowing users to post and reply to messages in a setting where conversations are threaded by subject. However, public folders can also be used for much more, including the storage of Microsoft Office documents, administrative messages generated by Exchange Server, and even as the basis for advanced workflow applications.

Like other databases in Exchange, a public folder is actually comprised of two database files—a rich-text file and a streaming content file. The addition of the streaming content file means that Web sites can actually be hosted from within a public folder. The HTML or Active Server Pages (ASP) files reside in the streaming file of the public folder store and are accessible from any Web browser using simple URLs. Also, because Exchange stores the Web sites, pages in the sites can make use of Exchange-specific functionality such as calendars and messaging.

Also like other databases, Exchange 2000 Server now supports the storage of multiple public folder stores on a single Exchange server. In addition, Exchange 2000 now supports multiple public folder trees in an organization.

In previous versions of Exchange, it was only possible to have one *public folder tree*, a hierarchy that forms the boundaries of the entire set of public folders available in the organization. Now, you can create multiple public folder trees and thus multiple sets of public folders. There is one caveat, however. When Exchange 2000 is installed, a default public folder tree, named All Public Folders, is created. This tree is accessible by all MAPI, IMAP4, NNTP (Network News Transfer Protocol), and Web clients. Additional public folder trees will only be available to NNTP, Web, and other clients that can use individual folders mapped as network drives. Additional trees are not accessible by any MAPI clients such as Outlook 2000. Additional trees such as these are intended for use as file repositories for groups or projects.

Learn more about the structure, creation, and management of public folders in Chapter 5.

Internet Information Server

One of the great strengths of Exchange 2000 Server lies in the way it supports standard Internet protocols for message transfer. In previous versions of Exchange, the Exchange Server software itself provided and managed the Internet protocols. Now, the responsibility of managing protocol support has been passed entirely to *Internet Information Server (IIS)*, a built-in component of Windows 2000 Server. All Exchange 2000 protocols are hosted within the IIS process. When Exchange 2000 Server is installed, it enhances the SMTP service built into IIS with a more robust version capable of handling the demanding Exchange routing environment.

Exchange 2000 subsystems, such as protocols and storage, can now be placed on separate servers to improve scalability. For this to work, a fast, reliable method of exchanging information between IIS and the Exchange storage system, the Web Store, is needed. This need is met by a component named the *Exchange Interprocess Communication Layer (ExIPC)*. ExIPC is basically a high-performance queue that allows IIS and the Web Store to exchange data. Figure 2.3 illustrates the basic Exchange architecture.

The Information Store (a process named `store.exe`) is the Exchange service that manages the Information Store on an Exchange server. One instance of `store.exe` runs for each storage group on a server. `Store.exe` manages processes such as store replication; maintains the ESE databases; and provides protocol stubs, interfaces that allow the ExIPC to transfer data between the IIS (a process named `inetinfo.exe`) and the Information Store. As you can see in Figure 2.3, a protocol stub exists for each protocol handled by IIS. The queuing process used by ExIPC is asynchronous, meaning that Exchange is able to allocate memory immediately after one portion of a process finishes.

FIGURE 2.3   Exchange 2000 architecture

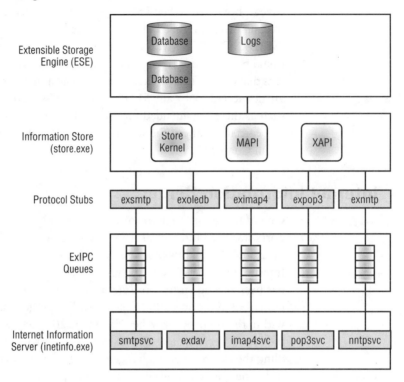

Installable File System

The *Installable File System (IFS)* permits normal network client redirectors, such as Exchange, to share folders and items. This is a means of exposing the Exchange Information Store to users and applications on the network. Because your local computer can assign, or map, a drive letter to these resources, standard applications like Windows Explorer and Office 2000 can access resources in the Exchange Store. A user could, for example, map a drive letter to their mailbox or open a public folder from within Microsoft Word.

The primary benefit of the IFS is that it allows clients to access Exchange data with no special software other than standard operating system components. During installation, an Exchange server creates an M: drive that serves as the portal into the Exchange Store for Windows applications. By default, the M: drive is shared using the share name BackOfficeStorage.

Front-End/Back-End Servers

Since Exchange 2000 Server now separates its databases from the client access protocols (now managed by IIS), there is now a distinction between store management and protocol management. Exchange now allows administrators to configure *front-end servers* that handle client access and *back-end servers* that handle the databases themselves. The front-end server becomes the point of contact for all client applications.

MAPI clients must connect directly to a back-end server and cannot use a front-end server, but other types of clients (POP3, IMAP4, etc.) can. Clients that can connect to a front-end server do so using the following process:

1. The client connects to the front-end server and makes a request using a particular protocol.

2. The front-end server relays the request to the back-end server using the same protocol used by the client.

3. The back-end server returns the requested data.

4. The front-end server returns the data to the client.

This arrangement provides load balancing for servers and also creates a unified namespace for clients.

Clustering

An Exchange 2000 *cluster* consists of between two and four connected computers referred to as *nodes*. These nodes share a common storage device, such as a RAID-5 array. Exchange 2000 Server can run on every node in the cluster. This provides a redundant hardware solution, since clients can connect to any node in the cluster rather than to just one computer. Clustering also provides fault tolerance. Should one node in the cluster fail, the Windows Clustering service restarts or moves the services on the failed node to a functional node in the cluster. During scheduled maintenance of a node, an administrator can also manually move services to other nodes, thus reducing or eliminating any client downtime.

Exchange 2000 Server uses a type of clustering known as Active/Active clustering, in which all members of the cluster are online at the same time and all are able to accept client requests. Previous versions of Exchange Server supported only Active/Passive clustering, in which only one member of the cluster at a time could provide services.

While Exchange 2000 Server will run on any version of Windows 2000 Server, only Windows 2000 Advanced Server and Windows 2000 Datacenter Server support clustering, and the same operating system must be used on all nodes that will participate in a cluster. Windows 2000 Advanced Server supports two nodes in a cluster. Windows 2000 Datacenter Server supports up to four nodes in a cluster.

Full-Text Indexing

The Information Store creates and manages indexes for common fields using the *Microsoft Search Service*. In previous versions of Exchange, searches were conducted on every item in every folder, resulting in long search times for larger databases. With *full-text indexing*, every word in all mailboxes and public folders is indexed, making searches much faster and more accurate. The service can index all messages, attachments, Microsoft Office documents, HTML files, text files, and even PDF files. Users can also search on document properties of many types of data, including properties such as author, file size, and modification dates.

All searches are passed through Exchange 2000 Server, which is responsible for handling security. If users do not have permissions to access particular objects, they are not allowed to bypass this using the Search Service.

An indexed database usually requires around 20 percent more available drive space than a non-indexed database, so you should allow for this when planning your Exchange server hardware. You should also be aware that indexing large databases can be quite time-consuming. Because indexes are created for each database, creating multiple databases can often make the indexing process easier.

You'll learn more about how to configure indexing in Chapter 8.

Message Flow

The flow of messages between components of an Exchange environment can be complicated. As an administrator, it would serve you well to learn how messages flow from one place (a sender) to another place (a recipient) in that environment. On a single Exchange server, component communication is relatively simple. As servers are added and grouped together into routing groups, this communication grows more complex. This section provides an introduction to the Exchange components involved in message flow and then examines the actual flow of messages in different situations.

Routing Architecture

Before we can look at the process of message flow in Exchange, it is first necessary to become familiar with some of the basic components that play a part in the routing of a message. Specifically, we will examine SMTP, the protocol used to transfer most messages in Exchange, routing groups that are used to define the routing topology of an organization, and connectors that are used to connect routing groups to one another and provide a way to transfer messages outside of an Exchange organization altogether.

SMTP

SMTP is now the native transport protocol in Exchange 2000 used to route messages within and between routing groups. In previous versions of Exchange Server, a component named the *Message Transfer Agent (MTA)* used a protocol named X.400 to provide most routing functions. The MTA and X.400 still exist in Exchange 2000, but are now used only to provide communications with earlier versions of Exchange Server and with foreign messaging systems using the X.400 protocol. SMTP has replaced X.400 over the past few years as the standard messaging protocol throughout the world, and so it has found acceptance in Exchange 2000 Server as the protocol of choice.

IIS handles SMTP and transfers information with Exchange via the ExIPC service that you learned about earlier in this chapter. The basic SMTP support in IIS is extended in a number of ways when Exchange 2000 is installed:

- A secondary store driver, `drviis.dll`, is added that provides message pickup and drop-off using the ExIPC.

- An enhanced routing engine is installed that adds link-state information—nearly instant information about the state of links to other servers.

- Additional command verbs are added that support the exchange of link-state information with other servers.

The adoption of SMTP provides a great advantage to Exchange 2000. In earlier versions of Exchange, servers were divided into Exchange sites that served as both routing and administrative boundaries. Within a site, communications between servers took place using *Remote Procedure Calls*

(RPCs), a method for invoking services on a remote computer. While RPCs are effective for message transport, they require full-time, relatively high-bandwidth connections between computers. This means that Exchange sites could really only span groups of computers that were connected by high-speed networking.

SMTP offers an advantage over RPCs: SMTP does not require a high-performance network connection. This and the elimination of Exchange sites in Exchange 2000 have led to much greater flexibility in the deployment of servers. Exchange 2000 now supports routing groups, which are groups of servers connected by a permanent connection, and administrative groups, which group servers and components according to administrative needs. The result of all this is that administrative needs can now be balanced with topology requirements in the deployment of Exchange servers.

Routing Groups

A *routing group* is a collection of servers with full-time, reliable connectivity. Topologically, a routing group is similar to the Exchange site used in previous versions of Exchange Server but, unlike the site, it imposes no administrative restrictions. Within a routing group, all messages are transferred directly between servers using SMTP. If you have a single Exchange server or if all your Exchange servers are connected over full-time, reliable connections, there will probably not be much reason for you to create more than one routing group. In fact, unless you create a second routing group, the fact that a routing group even exists is not evident in the Exchange System Manager (see Figure 2.4). When a second routing group is added, the Routing Groups container appears in System Manager, and servers are grouped according to the routing group they belong to.

FIGURE 2.4   The System Manager when only one routing group is used (left) and when multiple groups are used (right)

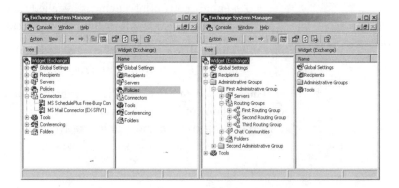

There are several reasons you may choose to set up multiple routing groups in your organization:

- Many Exchange servers do not have full-time, reliable, and direct SMTP connectivity to one another. This may be the case if your organization spans large geographic distances.

- You must control the path that messages travel between servers. You can create a routing group boundary to force computers in one group to use a single bridgehead server (BHS) to send messages to another group.

- You have a large number of servers and plan to divide them according to server function.

You can learn more about using routing groups in Chapter 7.

Connectors

Communications between servers in different routing groups and with foreign messaging systems outside the Exchange organization are established using *connectors*. You'll learn more about configuring and managing connectors in Chapter 7, but a brief introduction is useful here.

Three types of connectors may be used to connect routing groups to one another:

- Routing Group Connector

- SMTP Connector

- X.400 Connector

Routing Group Connector

The *Routing Group Connector* is the preferred method of connecting two routing groups in the same organization; it is fast, reliable, and the simplest to configure (since it has the fewest settings). SMTP is the native protocol used by the Routing Group Connector, and the connector consults Exchange 2000 Server's new link state table for routing information.

The Routing Group Connector is a unidirectional connection that goes from one server to another. Therefore, when you configure a Routing Group Connector, you'll need to create two connectors to form a logical bidirectional link between the two routing groups. However, to reduce administrative effort, you can autoconfigure the other side of a Routing Group Connector when installing the first end of the connector just like a Site Connector in Exchange Server 5.5.

A *bridgehead server* is a server that is designated to pass messages from one routing group to another, as shown in Figure 2.5. The Routing Group Connector offers a level of fault tolerance by allowing multiple source and destination bridgehead servers. Bridgehead servers can be used in one of three ways:

- No bridgehead server is designated, and all of the servers in the routing group function as bridgehead servers for message transmission.

- One bridgehead server is designated, and all mail destined for other routing groups flows through that one server. This gives the administrator great control over messaging configuration.

- Multiple bridgehead servers are used, and all mail flows through one of these designated servers. This configuration offers the advantages of load balancing and fault tolerance. Should one bridgehead server be unavailable for message transport, another will be available.

FIGURE 2.5 Bridgehead servers are responsible for transferring messages between routing groups.

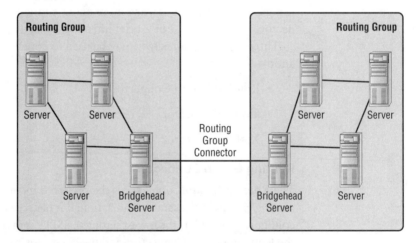

Routing Group Connectors offer administrators the ability to control connection schedules, message priority, and message size limits.

SMTP Connector

Although the Routing Group Connector uses SMTP as its native transport mechanism, Exchange 2000 Server also provides an *SMTP Connector* that can be used to link routing groups. There are three reasons that you might want to use an SMTP Connector instead of a Routing Group Connector:

- The SMTP Connector is more configurable than the Routing Group Connector and thereby offers the ability to more finely tune the connection. The SMTP Connector also offers the ability to issue authentication before sending mail, specifying TLS encryption and removing mail from queues on remote servers.

- The SMTP Connector always has to use SMTP. When you are connecting an Exchange 2000 server with an Exchange 5.5 server, the Routing Group Connector uses RPCs to communicate because it has no way of knowing whether the Exchange 5.5 server is configured to use SMTP, which was provided through the Internet Mail Service in previous versions of Exchange. There is no way to force the Routing Group Connector to use SMTP, so an SMTP Connector may be used instead.

- The SMTP Connector is also capable of connecting independent Exchange forests within an organization so that messages can be transferred.

Another advantage of the SMTP Connector is that it can be used to connect an Exchange organization to the Internet or to a foreign (non-Exchange) messaging system that uses SMTP.

When connected to the Internet, the SMTP Connector uses a smart host or mail exchange (MX) record in DNS for next-hop routing. When configured internally between two routing groups, this connector will relay link state information between routing groups but will still depend on the MX records in DNS for next-hop information.

X.400 Connector

The *X.400 Connector* can be used to link Exchange routing groups and also to link an Exchange organization to a foreign, X.400-based messaging system. X.400 Connectors are useful for linking routing groups when there is very little bandwidth (less than 16Kbps) available between servers or when X.400 is the only connectivity available. When linking routing groups with the X.400 Connector, a single server in each group must be designated as the bridgehead server. You must set up multiple X.400 Connectors between multiple servers in each routing group to gain a load-balancing feature. Note that you can also install a Routing Group Connector alongside an X.400 Connector.

Link State Algorithm

Whenever multiple routing groups are connected, the connections over which messages are transferred are referred to as links. Every *link* can exist in one of two states: up (available) or down (unavailable). In addition, every link is assigned a value that represents the cost of using that link relative to other available links. By default, the cost of any connector created is one, but cost can range from 1 to 100. You can configure the cost of connectors in your organization to create a bias for certain routes.

Exchange 2000 Server uses link state tables to provide all servers in the system with information that lets the servers determine whether any given link is functioning. The link state information also lets servers determine the best route to send a given message based on the total cost of all connectors a route will use. For example, a route that crossed two connectors whose individual costs were two (for a total cost of four) would be favored over a route that crossed two connectors with individual costs of three (for a total cost of six). Connectors that are in a down state are never considered. The information in these link state tables is based on a protocol named the *Link State Algorithm*.

Support for the Link State Algorithm is new to Exchange 2000, though it has been around for many years. In fact, it forms the foundation of the *Open Shortest Path First (OSPF)* protocol that is used extensively by routers today. Exchange 2000 still incorporates routes and costs, but relies heavily on link state information to route messages between routing groups.

The Link State Algorithm propagates the state of the messaging system in almost real time to all servers in the organization. There are several advantages to this:

- Each Exchange server can make the best routing decision before sending a message downstream where a link might be down.

- Message ping-pong is eliminated, because alternate route information is also propagated and considered in the routing calculations.

- Message looping is eliminated.

In each routing group, one server is designated as the *Routing Group Master* and will become the bridgehead server to the other routing group. By default, the first server added to a particular routing group becomes that group's master. When one bridgehead server connects to another bridgehead server in a different routing group and link state information is exchanged, this is done with SMTP. The Routing Group Master holds the information of who is up or down and propagates that information to each Routing Group Master in each routing group.

Message Transport

All good messaging systems rely on a strong transport and routing engine to deliver messages, and Exchange 2000 Server is no different. A solid understanding of how messages are transferred between Exchange Server components is essential to managing a reliable organization and to troubleshooting any failure in message transfer.

For the most part, messages are submitted to an Exchange server using the SMTP protocol. These messages may come from a client within the Exchange system or from an outside system such as the Internet. Though messages may also be submitted to the Exchange server via direct submission from a client using IFS or via the MTA from a foreign system, we will concern ourselves here with the SMTP process.

Here's the basic procedure that occurs when a client submits a message to the Exchange server (see Figure 2.6):

1. An SMTP client opens a connection on the SMTP Service.

2. The IIS process on the SMTP Service responds.

3. After negotiation, the SMTP process receives and processes the message.

4. The SMTP process hands the message to an advanced queuing engine, which places it into a Pre-Categorizer queue.

5. A *Categorizer* resolves the sender and recipient for the message, expanding any distribution lists as needed and resolving all recipients in the list. In previous versions of Exchange Server, this task was performed by the MTA.

6. Next, the advanced queuing engine passes the message to the routing engine, which parses the message against its Domain Mapping and Configuration table. The routing engine checks Active Directory and decides whether the message is destined for the local store or a remote server. If destined for a remote server, a *Destination Message queue* is created for the message as a temporary queue from which the SMTP service can read the message and pass it along.

FIGURE 2.6 A client submits a message to an Exchange server using SMTP.

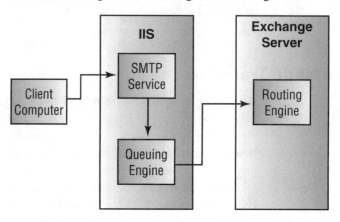

Once the message has been submitted, the routing engine decides where the message is supposed to go. In all, Exchange 2000 messages can get from a sender to a recipient in one of four contexts. A message can be sent as follows:

- From a sender to a recipient on the same server. This may be the case when two users have mailboxes on the same server and transfer messages between them, when a user posts a message to a public folder that exists on the same server, or when an Exchange Server component delivers a message to a local recipient.

- Between different servers in the same routing group.

- Between different routing groups.

- From a sender in the Exchange organization to a user on a foreign messaging system outside of the Exchange organization.

On the Same Server

If the message is destined for the local store, it is placed in the Local Delivery queue, and the `store.exe` process reads the message out of the queue and writes it to the local database. Thereafter, the message is associated with the destination mailbox, and the user is notified that new mail has arrived. This is the simplest of the message transport contexts.

Between Servers in the Same Routing Group

Messages routed between servers in the same routing group use SMTP as their transport. The steps involved in routing a message between two servers in the same group are slightly more complicated than on a single server:

1. Since the message is not intended for local delivery, the message is passed to the routing engine.

2. Once in the routing engine, the message is parsed against the Domain Mapping and Configuration table and then placed in the outgoing SMTP queue for the destination server.

3. The sending server looks up the recipient's home directory in Active Directory, conducts a DNS lookup for the MX record associated with the destination server on which the recipient's mailbox is stored, then creates a TCP connection to that server.

4. The message is transmitted to the destination server.

5. Once the destination server receives the message, it processes it in different ways depending on the destination of the message. If it determines that the message goes to a recipient in its local store, it follows the procedure discussed in the previous section. If it determines that the message goes to a different server or outside of the organization, the above process is repeated to route the message to the correct server.

Between Routing Groups

Messages routed between servers in multiple groups incur the use of a bridgehead server at each end of the connector. The steps involved in routing messages between servers in different routing groups are as follows (see Figure 2.7, where the solid line represents the flow of messages and the dashed line represents queries):

1. Since the message is not intended for local delivery, the message is passed to the routing engine.

2. The routing group information is gathered from the configuration naming context of Active Directory.

3. The link state information is consulted to determine the best routing path.

4. The message is passed to the bridgehead server.

5. The bridgehead server passes the message to the destination bridgehead server in the other routing group.

6. The receiving bridgehead server passes the message to the destination server in its group.

7. The message is brought into the destination server via the SMTP service and is placed in the Local Delivery queue.

8. The message is tⵊaken out of the queue by the `store.exe` process and associated with the recipient's inbox.

FIGURE 2.7 Routing messages between routing groups

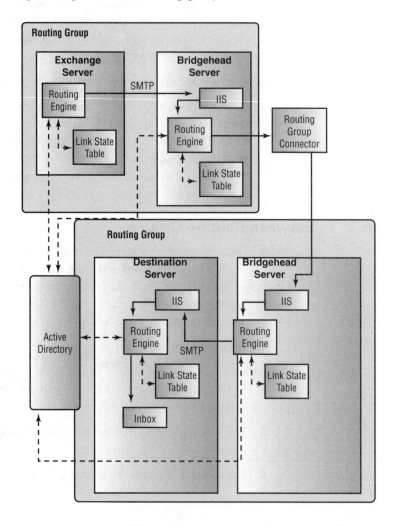

Outside the Exchange Organization

Message delivery outside of the Exchange organization is similar to delivery to another routing group in that a connector must be used to pass the message. Here are the steps involved in routing to another e-mail system:

1. Since the message is not intended for local delivery, the message is passed to the routing engine.

2. The routing group information is gathered from the configuration naming context of Active Directory.

3. The link state information is consulted to determine the best routing path. In this case, the path must end with the connector to the foreign system.

4. The routing server then either sends the message over the appropriate connector to the foreign system or, if the connector is in a different routing group, sends the message to that routing group.

5. The message is passed over the appropriate connector to the foreign system.

Summary

The better you understand how the system works, the better you'll be able to plan a viable network and troubleshoot that network when problems occur. This chapter examined three basic aspects of Exchange 2000 architecture: how Exchange is integrated with the Windows 2000 Active Directory, how information is stored on an Exchange server, and how messages flow within an Exchange organization.

At the top of the Active Directory hierarchy is the domain forest, which represents the outside boundary that any Exchange organization can reach. A domain tree is a hierarchical arrangement of domains that share a common namespace. The first domain in a tree is called the root domain. Domains added under this are called child domains. Within the domain tree, domains establish trust relationships with one another that allow objects in a trusted domain to access resources in a trusting domain. A domain is a group of computers and other resources that are part of a network and share a common directory database. Each domain contains at least one domain controller. Multiple domain controllers per domain can be used for load balancing and fault-tolerance.

When Exchange is installed, many objects, such as users, are enhanced with Exchange-related features. A global catalog is used to hold information about all of the objects in a forest. Objects can be grouped into containers called organizational units that allow administrators to effectively manage large groups of similar objects at the same time.

In Exchange 2000 Server, the Information Store is responsible for data storage and management. It supports access through numerous Internet and application programming protocols. This Information Store is also referred to as the Web Store, a nod to its support for Web-based protocols and access.

SMTP is now the native transport protocol in Exchange 2000, and it's used to route messages within and between routing groups. Internet Information Server (IIS) handles the SMTP protocol and transfers information with Exchange via the ExIPC service.

Multiple servers in an Exchange 2000 organization are grouped in routing groups. Servers within a routing group must share full-time reliable connectivity. Different routing groups are linked to one another using one of three types of connectors: the Routing Group Connector, which is the easiest to set up; the SMTP connector, which can be fine-tuned a bit more than the Routing Group Connector; and the X.400 Connector, which is used for very low-bandwidth connections.

Key Terms

Before you take the exam, be certain you are familiar with the following terms:

Active Directory	connectors
architecture	contiguous namespace
attributes	Destination Message queue
back-end servers	directory
bridgehead server	domain
Categorizer	domain controller
checkpoint files	domain forest
child domains	Domain Name Service (DNS)
cluster	domain tree

Exchange Interprocess Communication Layer (ExIPC)

Extensible Storage Engine (ESE)

forest root domain

front-end servers

full-text indexing

global catalog

Information Store

Installable File System (IFS)

Internet Information Server (IIS)

link

Link State Algorithm

Message Transfer Agent (MTA)

Microsoft Search Service

mixed mode

Multipurpose Internet Mail Extensions (MIME)

namespace

native mode

nodes

object

Open Shortest Path First (OSPF)

organizational unit

public folder tree

public folders

Remote Procedure Calls (RPCs)

rich-text (EDB) file

root domain

routing group

Routing Group Connector

Routing Group Master

schema

SMTP Connector

storage groups

streaming media (STM) file

transaction log

Uniform Resource Locator (URL)

Web Storage System

Web Store

Windows 2000 site

Windows Internet Naming System (WINS)

X.400 Connector

Review Questions

1. You are currently running Windows 2000 in mixed mode and are considering making the switch to native mode. Which of the following would be valid concerns to take into account before making the switch?

   A. The switch to native mode is irreversible.

   B. If you later decide to switch back to mixed mode, all object configuration is lost.

   C. Exchange Server 5.5 may not be run in a native mode environment.

2. Which of the following statements is true of domains in a single domain tree?

   A. Domains are not configured with trust relationships by default.

   B. Domains are automatically configured with one-way trust relationships flowing from parent domains to child domains.

   C. Domains are automatically configured with two-way non-transitive trusts.

   D. Domains are automatically configured with two-way transitive trusts.

3. What is the relationship between a Windows 2000 site and an Exchange site?

   A. The terms are used interchangeably.

   B. There must be a one-to-one mapping of Windows 2000 sites and Exchange sites.

   C. A Windows 2000 site can span multiple Exchange sites.

   D. An Exchange site can span multiple Windows 2000 sites.

   E. There is no relationship between Exchange sites and Windows 2000 sites.

4. A hierarchical arrangement of one or more Windows 2000 domains that share a common namespace is referred to as a:

    A. Windows 2000 site

    B. Domain site

    C. Domain tree

    D. Domain forest

5. You have just installed the first Windows 2000 server on your network and want to make it a domain controller. How would you do this?

    A. The first Windows 2000 server is automatically made a domain controller.

    B. Install Active Directory on the computer.

    C. Install DNS on the computer.

    D. Install the Schema on the computer.

6. Which of the following statements is true?

    A. An organizational unit cannot contain objects from other domains.

    B. An organizational unit can contain objects only from other trusted domains.

    C. An organizational unit can contain objects only from other domains in the same domain tree.

    D. An organizational unit can contain objects only from other domains in the same domain forest.

7. What service is the primary provider of name resolution on a Windows 2000 network?

    A. X.400

    B. DNS

    C. WINS

    D. SMTP

8. Which of the following tasks can the Active Directory Connector be used for? Choose all that apply.

A. Connecting the Active Directory information on a Windows 2000 server to the security database on a Windows NT 4 server

B. Connecting the Exchange-related Active Directory information on a Windows 2000 server to an Exchange 5.5 directory service

C. Migrating objects from an Exchange 5.5 directory service to Active Directory

D. Synchronizing the Active Directory between Windows 2000 domain controllers

9. You are backing up the database files created by Exchange and come across two files named `pub.edb` and `pub.stm`. You recognize that the `pub.edb` file is the database for your public folders. What is the `pub.stm` file used for?

A. Maintaining a log of transactions made to the `pub.edb` file

B. Storing information about the folders that are compatible with earlier versions of Exchange server

C. Storing certain types of media files in their native format

D. Providing a backup of the `pub.edb` file

10. What is the maximum number of databases that may exist on a single Exchange server?

A. 5

B. 6

C. 10

D. 20

11. You are performing a backup of an Exchange private Information Store that uses the default store name and need to make sure that you back up all of the necessary files for that store. Which of the following files compose the Exchange 2000 Server message database? Choose all that apply.

    A. `priv.edb`

    B. `priv.dat`

    C. `priv.stm`

    D. `edb.chk`

    E. `edb.log`

12. You have installed multiple public folder trees in your organization. Which of the following clients would only be able to access the default public folder tree and none of the additional trees?

    A. Outlook 2000

    B. A Web browser

    C. An Office 2000 application

    D. A generic POP3 client

13. Which of the following technologies permits normal network client redirectors, such as Exchange, to share folders and items?

    A. Installable File System

    B. SMTP

    C. Clustering

    D. Exchange Interprocess Communication Layer

14. You are configuring a Windows 2000 cluster to run your main Exchange mail servers and are planning to use Windows 2000 Advanced Server. How many nodes will you be able to configure in the cluster?

    A. 2

    B. 4

    C. 8

    D. 10

15. An HTTP client is attempting to access a mailbox on an Exchange 2000 server. Which of the following represents the correct sequence of components that are involved in the process?

    A. IIS, Information Store

    B. SMTP, ExIPC, Information Store

    C. W3svc, ExIPC, Information Store

    D. Information Store, ExIPC, IIS

16. You are configuring a connector between two routing groups and want to have servers issue authentication before sending any mail. Which connector allows this?

    A. Routing Group Connector

    B. SMTP Connector

    C. X.400 Connector

    D. Active Directory Connector

17. Which of the following connector types may use multiple bridgehead servers? Choose all that apply.

    A. Routing Group Connector

    B. SMTP Connector

    C. X.400 Connector

    D. TCP Connector

18. Your organization consists of two routing groups linked by a very slow link (you average around 8Kbps). Which type of connector is the best for supporting this type of link?

   A. Routing Group Connector

   B. SMTP Connector

   C. X.400 Connector

   D. TCP Connector

19. What primary advantage does SMTP offer over RPCs for connectivity between servers within a routing group?

   A. SMTP is faster.

   B. SMTP does not require full-time connectivity.

   C. SMTP does not require high-speed connectivity.

   D. SMTP does not require reliable connectivity.

20. What two constructs new to Exchange 2000 Server replace the Exchange site in previous versions of Exchange? Choose all that apply.

   A. Windows 2000 sites

   B. Routing groups

   C. Administrative groups

   D. Organizational units

Answers to Review Questions

1. A. The switch to native mode is a one-time, one-way switch and is irreversible. Native mode allows your Windows 2000 domain controllers to scale into the millions of objects per domain instead of the 40,000 accounts that Windows NT 4 can support.

2. D. Windows 2000 and Active Directory support transitive two-way trusts between domains. When a child domain is created, a trust relationship is automatically configured between that child domain and the parent domain. This trust is two-way, meaning that resource access requests can flow from either domain to the other.

3. E. Exchange sites are a construct from Exchange 5.5 that defined administrative and routing boundaries. Sites are no longer used in Exchange 2000. Windows 2000 sites are groups of computers on the same IP subnet.

4. C. A domain tree is a hierarchical arrangement of one or more Windows 2000 domains that share a common namespace. Domain Name Service (DNS) domain names represent the tree structure. The first domain in a tree is called the root domain.

5. B. To create a domain controller, all you have to do is install the Active Directory service on it. During this process, you have the option of creating a new domain or joining an existing domain. If you create a new domain, you also have the option of creating or joining an existing domain tree or forest.

6. A. An organizational unit is a container in which you can place objects such as user accounts, groups, computers, printers, applications, file shares, and other organizational units. An organizational unit cannot contain objects from other domains and is the smallest unit you can assign or delegate administrative authority to. Organizational units are provided strictly for administrative purposes and convenience.

7. B. DNS is now the primary provider of name resolution for Windows 2000–based networks. In fact, Windows 2000 domain structure is now based on DNS structure, and Active Directory requires that DNS be used.

8. B, C. The Active Directory Connector is a Windows 2000 service that synchronizes the Exchange 5.5 directory with Active Directory. This allows you to administer your directory from Active Directory or the Exchange 5.5 directory service. You can also use ADC to migrate objects from the Exchange directory service to Active Directory.

9. C. An Exchange 2000 database is actually a logical entity that represents two physical database files, a rich-text (EDB) file and a streaming media (STM) file. The rich-text file holds messages and works much like the database files in previous versions of Exchange Server. The streaming media file has been added to provide native support for many types of streaming media, including voice, audio, video, and others.

10. D. Exchange allows up to five databases per storage group and up to four storage groups per server. Each database must exist inside a storage group.

11. A, C, D, E. The most current state of any Exchange store is the EDB database, the STM database, the current log file, and the current checkpoint file.

12. A. MAPI clients, such as Outlook, can only access the default public folder tree in an organization. Clients that can directly access the file system, such as Office applications, Web browsers, and Windows Explorer, can access multiple public folder trees.

13. A. This is a means of exposing the Exchange Information Store to users and applications on the network. Because your local computer can assign, or map, a drive letter to these resources, standard applications like Windows Explorer and Office 2000 can access resources in the Exchange Store.

14. A. Windows 2000 Advanced Server supports two nodes in a single cluster. Windows 2000 Datacenter Server supports up to four nodes in a cluster.

15. C. First, the HTTP client (Web browser) sends out a request. That request is received by the W3svc service of Internet Information Server. W3svc passes the request through the ExIPC queues to the Information Store.

16. B. The SMTP Connector is more configurable than the Routing Group Connector, and thereby offers the ability to more finely tune the connection. The SMTP Connector offers the ability to issue authentication before sending mail, specifying TLS encryption and removing mail from queues on remote servers.

17. A, B. Both the Routing Group Connector and SMTP Connectors can be configured to use multiple source and destination bridgehead servers. The X.400 Connector can only support one bridgehead server. There is no such thing as a TCP connector.

18. C. X.400 Connectors are useful for linking routing groups when there is very little bandwidth (less than 16K) available between servers or when X.400 is the only connectivity available.

19. C. SMTP does not require a high-performance network connection. This and the elimination of Exchange sites in Exchange 2000 have led to much greater flexibility in the deployment of servers.

20. B, C. Exchange 2000 Server has replaced the concept of Exchange sites with routing groups and administrative groups. Routing groups are used to define groups of Exchange servers that share a reliable (but not necessarily high-bandwidth) connection. Administrative groups are used to define administrative boundaries.

Chapter

3

Installing Microsoft Exchange 2000 Server

MICROSOFT EXAM OBJECTIVES COVERED IN THIS CHAPTER:

- ✓ Install Exchange 2000 Server on a server computer.
- ✓ Diagnose and resolve failed installations.
- ✓ Upgrade or migrate to Exchange 2000 Server from Exchange Server 5.5.
- ✓ Diagnose and resolve problems involving the upgrade process.

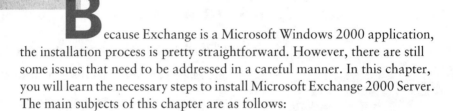

Because Exchange is a Microsoft Windows 2000 application, the installation process is pretty straightforward. However, there are still some issues that need to be addressed in a careful manner. In this chapter, you will learn the necessary steps to install Microsoft Exchange 2000 Server. The main subjects of this chapter are as follows:

- Standard edition vs. Enterprise edition of Microsoft Exchange 2000 Server
- Pre-installation considerations
- Installing Microsoft Exchange Server
- Upgrading Microsoft Exchange Server
- Installing Exchange Server on a cluster
- Post-installation considerations
- Troubleshooting a Microsoft Exchange installation

Exchange 2000 Server: Standard Edition vs. Enterprise Edition

Microsoft Exchange 2000 Server is available in two editions: a *Standard edition*, which is simply called Exchange 2000 Server, and an *Enterprise edition*. The main difference between them is the advanced features supported in the Enterprise edition.

Standard Edition Features

The Standard edition includes the following features:

- Basic messaging functionality

- Microsoft Exchange Web Storage System

- Instant messaging support

- Connectors for Microsoft Mail, Lotus cc:Mail, Lotus Notes, and X.400

- A full version of Exchange Server 5.5 with the Exchange Server 5.5 Service Pack 3

- Microsoft Outlook 2000 Service Release 1

- Microsoft Outlook for the Macintosh 8.2.2

- Microsoft Office 2000 Developer Tools

Additional Enterprise Edition Features

The Enterprise edition includes all of the features of the Standard edition and adds the following:

- No limit on database size (the Standard edition is limited to 16GB)

- Multiple mailbox stores per server (the Standard edition only supports one per server)

- Active/Active clustering support (requires Windows 2000 Advanced Server)

- Distributed (front-end/back-end) configuration of servers

- Chat services

Microsoft Exchange 2000 Conferencing Server is an add-on product for Exchange 2000 Server that adds groupware capabilities, such as data conferencing, application sharing, and multicast video teleconferencing, to Exchange. Conferencing Server was originally intended to be a part of Exchange 2000 Server, but is now offered separately.

Pre-Installation Considerations

You must address several important issues before installing Exchange Server. Having the correct information and making the right decisions about these issues will go a long way toward ensuring a successful installation. The following pre-installation issues are covered in this section:

- Minimum system requirements
- Windows 2000 user accounts related to the Exchange installation
- Licensing issues
- Preparing the Active Directory
- Other pre-installation steps

Microsoft ✓ **Exam Objective** | **Install Exchange 2000 Server on a server computer.**

Minimum System Requirements

This section lists the minimum requirements for the computer system upon which Exchange is to be installed. These minimums are valid when you install only the core components. Using additional Exchange components, and depending on your particular performance demands, could require more resources than the following minimum requirements.

Hardware Requirements

The minimum hardware requirements for installing Exchange are listed below:

Microprocessor	Intel Pentium 133MHz or higher (recommended: Pentium 166MHz or higher)
Random Access Memory	128MB (recommended: 256MB)
Hard disk space	500MB free disk space on the drive where Exchange is installed (recommended: 4GB free disk space); 200MB free disk space on the system partition

The Microsoft Exchange Server software comes on a CD. If the machine intended to be the Exchange server has no CD-ROM drive, the administrator may copy the necessary files from the CD to a shared hard disk or share a CD-ROM drive on another machine.

Software Requirements

The software requirements for an Exchange installation are listed below:

Operating system	Microsoft Windows 2000 Server, Advanced Server, or Datacenter Server with Windows 2000 Service Pack 1.
	The operating system needs to be configured for a page file size equal to 50MB of disk space plus the amount of RAM in the machine. (For example, if the machine has 48MB of RAM, the page file size should be 50 plus 48, equaling 98MB. The recommended size, however, is 100MB of disk space plus the amount of physical RAM.)
Active Directory	In a forest where Exchange 2000 servers are installed in more than one domain, at least one server in each domain must be configured as a global catalog server.
DNS	At least one Windows 2000 server in a domain where Exchange 2000 is to be installed must provide the Windows 2000 DNS service, configured to allow dynamic updates.
TCP/IP	Windows 2000 Transmission Control Protocol/Internet Protocol (TCP/IP) is required on all Exchange servers and on all clients that need to access Exchange Server using POP3/IMAP4/HTTP.
IIS	Internet Information Server, along with its NNTP and SMTP subcomponents, must be installed on any server on which Exchange 2000 Server will be installed.

Novell NetWare clients (optional)	Microsoft Gateway Services for NetWare (GSNW) is required on the Exchange server if NetWare clients will be accessing mail. If the NetWare clients are using IPX/SPX, then the Exchange server will also require Microsoft NWLink.
Advanced fault tolerance (optional)	As stated earlier, the Enterprise edition of Exchange 2000 Server can work with Windows 2000 clustering.

Remember that the minimum requirements may not provide the optimal operational performance, or take into account the requirements for any future growth of system demand. The actual system requirements of any installation will depend on the particulars of a specific environment. To determine your real-world requirements, refer to *Microsoft Exchange 2000 Server Planning and Installation*, the book that is included with Microsoft Exchange 2000 Server.

Windows 2000 User Accounts Related to the Exchange Installation

Because of Exchange 2000 Server's involvement with Active Directory, its installation involves a number of Windows 2000 user and group security accounts. Following are some of the more pertinent accounts:

Schema Admins	Members of this group have the rights and permissions necessary to modify the schema of the Windows 2000 Active Directory. To run the ForestPrep tool (described later in this chapter) that modifies the schema for Exchange 2000 Server, you must belong to the Schema Admins group, the Enterprise Admins group, and the local Administrators group on the computer on which you actually run the tool.

Enterprise Admins	Members of this group have the rights and permissions necessary to administer any domain in a forest. To run the ForestPrep tool, you must be a member of the Enterprise Admins group, the Schema Admins group, and the local Administrators group on the computer running the tool.
Domain Admins	Members of this group have the rights and permissions necessary to administer any computer or resource in a domain. You must be a member of this group in order to run the DomainPrep tool (also discussed later in this chapter) that prepares each domain for Exchange 2000 Server installation.
Administrators	Members of this local group are given the rights necessary to administer a local computer and install software on it. To install Exchange 2000 Server on a Windows 2000 server, you must be a member of this group. This level of privileges is needed because, during installation, services will be started, and files will be copied to the \<winnt_root>\SYSTEM32 directory.
Exchange Domain Servers	Along with the Exchange Enterprise Server local group, this global security group provides Exchange servers with the permissions necessary to access one another and perform necessary Exchange functions. All Exchange servers are placed into the Exchange Domain Servers group, and this group is placed into the Exchange Enterprise Servers local group on each Exchange computer.
Exchange Enterprise Servers	See the description of the Exchange Domain Servers group above.
Site Services Account	Exchange Server 5.5 services use this account to log on to the Windows system and carry out their functions.

Licensing Issues

Licensing issues relate to matters of legality (specifically, the number of servers Exchange can be installed on and the number of clients that can access a server). Three main licenses pertain to the various Microsoft Exchange product packages:

- Server License
- Client Access License (CAL)
- Client License

Server License

The basic *Server License* provides the legal right to install and operate Microsoft Exchange 2000 Server on a single-server machine. In addition, the Exchange System Manager Microsoft Management Console snap-in (the primary utility used to administer an Exchange organization) can be installed on additional machines without additional licenses.

Since many licensing policies can change over time, always check for the latest policy to ensure your compliance. You can find the licensing policies for Exchange 2000 Server at www.microsoft.com/exchange.

Client Access License (CAL)

A *Client Access License (CAL)* gives a user the legal right to access an Exchange server. An organization designates the number of CALs it needs when a Microsoft Exchange server is purchased. Each CAL provides one user the legal right to access the Exchange server. Any client software that has the ability to be a client to Microsoft Exchange Server is legally required to have a CAL purchased for it. Microsoft Exchange Client, Microsoft Outlook, and third-party client messaging programs require a CAL. Microsoft Exchange 2000 Server uses a per seat licensing mode.

Client Access Licenses are NOT included in any version of Microsoft Windows or Microsoft Office. For example, the version of Outlook 2000 that comes with Office 2000 requires by law that a separate CAL be purchased before accessing an Exchange server.

Client License

In addition to having a CAL, each piece of client software must also be licensed for use on the client computer. This means that each piece of client software needs its own license to be legally installed on the client computer plus a CAL to legally connect to an Exchange server.

Exchange 2000 Server comes with Outlook 2000 for Windows and Outlook 8.2.2 for Macintosh. For each CAL that you purchase with Exchange 2000 Server, you are licensed to distribute a version of Outlook to a client computer. For example, suppose you purchase Exchange 2000 Server with 25 CALs. You may then distribute Outlook 2000 (the version that comes with Exchange 2000 Server) to 25 client computers. If you then purchase additional copies of Outlook 2000 (say, along with Office 2000), you will need to purchase additional CALs to legally connect to Exchange 2000 Server.

Preparing the Active Directory

Before installing the first Exchange Server in an organization, you may need to prepare the forest and each domain into which Exchange will be installed. For these tasks, you will use two tools provided with the Exchange installation software: *ForestPrep* and *DomainPrep*. ForestPrep must be run once in a forest. It extends the Active Directory schema with the objects necessary to run Exchange 2000 Server. DomainPrep must be run in each domain to identify the domain's address list server and to create special domain accounts that Exchange needs to run properly.

Though this seems like a complicated installation routine, it does provide a significant advantage. Many networks separate administrative responsibilities of domain management, schema management, and Exchange management. For example, one group may be in charge of administering the schema and the primary domains of the forest, another may be in charge of managing resource domains, and still another group will manage Exchange.

These additional setup tools provide the ability for separate administrators to perform their necessary part of the Exchange installation and simplify the Exchange deployment. For example, the group in charge of managing the schema will have the permissions required to run the ForestPrep tool to extend the schema. Domain administrators will have the permissions required to use the DomainPrep tool that modifies domains. Once these tasks are done, Exchange administrators can install and manage Exchange without having to be given permissions for the other preparation tasks.

If a single administrator or group runs the network and has all the appropriate permissions (or if there is only one domain in your forest), the installation of Exchange is simplified. If the account with which you install the first Exchange server belongs to the Schema Admins, Enterprise Admins, and Administrators groups for the local computer, you do not need to run ForestPrep at all.

Preparing a Windows 2000 Forest

In order to run the ForestPrep tool, you must belong to the Schema Admins and Enterprise Admins security groups. In addition, you must belong to the local Administrators group on the server on which Exchange will be installed. If you are not a member of these groups, the appropriate administrator will have to run the ForestPrep tool before you can install Exchange 2000 Server.

When ForestPrep is run, it performs several tasks:

- It extends the Active Directory schema with Exchange-related information.

- It creates the organization object in Active Directory.

- If the forest contains no existing versions of Exchange Server, ForestPrep prompts you for an Exchange organization name and then creates the organization object in the Active Directory. If the forest contains a previous version of Exchange, ForestPrep creates the organization object in the Active Directory based on information in the Exchange 5.5 organization. The organization is at the top of the Exchange hierarchy. This case-sensitive field can be up to 64 characters in length. The organization name is associated with every object in the Exchange directory, such as mailboxes, public folders, and distribution lists. The organization name cannot be modified after installation.

- It assigns the Exchange Full Administrator role to the account that you specify. This account and the permissions associated with it are discussed later in the chapter.

Exercise 3.1 outlines the steps for running ForestPrep in a forest that does not have a previous version of Exchange running. Exercise 3.2 outlines the steps for running ForestPrep in a forest that is running Exchange Server 5.5.

EXERCISE 3.1

Running ForestPrep in a Forest with No Previous Versions of Exchange

1. Insert the Microsoft Exchange Server CD into the server's CD-ROM drive. If your CD-ROM drive is set to automatically run CDs, this will automatically open the Exchange 2000 Installation Wizard. If not, browse to the \setup\i386 directory. (Other options are to share the CD on another machine on the network and then connect to that share, or to copy the CD to the server's hard drive.)

2. Close the Wizard page by clicking the Cancel button.

3. On the Start menu, click Run.

4. In the Run dialog box, type **D:\setup\i386\setup /ForestPrep**, where D is the letter for your CD-ROM drive.

5. On the Welcome screen, click Next.

6. On the End User License Agreement screen, click I Agree, and then click Next.

7. On the Component Selection screen, click Next.

8. On the Installation Type screen, click Create An Exchange Organization, and then click Next.

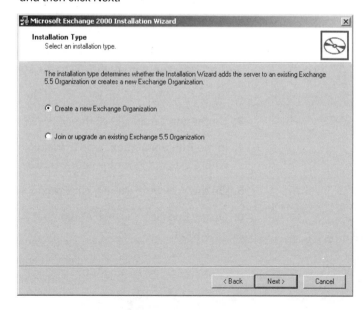

EXERCISE 3.1 *(continued)*

9. On the Organization Name screen, type the name for your organization, and click Next. Be careful, though: Once you click Next, you cannot go back and change the organization name.

10. On the Exchange 2000 Administrator Account screen, type the name of the user or group for administering Exchange, and click Next. This account is assigned the Exchange Full Administrator role and will have the permissions to install Exchange 2000 Server and to create other types of Exchange administrator accounts.

11. Next, ForestPrep begins to update the schema and may prompt you with a dialog to verify the update. If it does, click OK to go on.

12. Once the schema is updated (and this can take quite a long time, depending on the size of your forest), the Completion screen appears. Click Finish.

EXERCISE 3.2

Running ForestPrep in a Forest That Is Already Running Exchange Server 5.5

1. Insert the Microsoft Exchange Server CD into the server's CD-ROM drive. If your CD-ROM drive is set to automatically run CDs, this will automatically open the Exchange 2000 Installation Wizard. If not, browse to the \setup\i386 directory. (Other options are to share the CD on another machine on the network and then connect to that share, or to copy the CD to the server's hard drive.)

2. Close the Wizard page by clicking the Cancel button.

3. On the Start menu, click Run.

4. In the Run dialog box, type **D:\setup\i386\setup /ForestPrep**, where D is the letter for your CD-ROM drive.

5. On the Welcome screen, click Next.

6. On the End User License Agreement screen, click I Agree, and then click Next.

7. On the Component Selection screen, click Next.

8. On the Installation Type screen, click Join Or Upgrade An Existing Exchange 5.5 Organization, and then click Next.

9. On the Select A Server From An Exchange 5.5 Organization screen, type the name of a server in the Exchange 5.5 organization, and click Next. This server must be running Exchange Server 5.5 with Exchange Server 5.5 Service Pack 3 or higher.

10. On the Exchange 2000 Administrator Account screen, type the name of the user or group responsible for administering Exchange, and click Next. This account is assigned the Exchange Full Administrator role and will have the permissions to install Exchange 2000 Server and to create other types of Exchange administrator accounts.

11. On the Service Account page, type the name and password for the existing Exchange 5.5 site service account, and click Next.

12. Next, ForestPrep begins to update the schema and prompts you with a dialog to verify the update. Click OK to go on.

13. Once the schema is updated (and this can take quite a long time, depending on the size of your forest), the Completion screen appears. Click Finish.

Preparing a Windows 2000 Domain

Once the Windows 2000 forest is prepared using ForestPrep, each domain in the forest that will run Exchange 2000 Server must also be prepared using a tool named DomainPrep. To run DomainPrep, you must be a member of the Domain Admins group for that domain and the Administrators group on the local computer where you will be running DomainPrep. DomainPrep performs the following tasks:

- Determines the address list server for the domain, and grants it rights within the Active Directory
- Creates the Exchange Domain Servers global group
- Creates the Exchange Enterprise Servers local group

- Adds the Exchange Domain Servers group to the Exchange Enterprise Servers group
- Grants permissions for Exchange 2000 administrators and servers

Exercise 3.3 outlines the steps for running DomainPrep.

EXERCISE 3.3

Running DomainPrep

1. Insert the Microsoft Exchange Server CD into the server's CD-ROM drive. If your CD-ROM drive is set to automatically run CDs, this will automatically open the Exchange 2000 Installation Wizard. If not, browse to the \setup\i386 directory. (Other options are to share the CD on another machine on the network and then connect to that share, or to copy the CD to the server's hard drive.)

2. Close the Wizard page by clicking the Cancel button.

3. On the Start menu, click Run.

4. In the Run dialog box, type **D:\setup\i386\setup /DomainPrep**, where D is the letter for your CD-ROM drive.

5. On the Welcome screen, click Next.

6. On the End User License Agreement screen, click I Agree, and then click Next. Note that if you are running DomainPrep in the same domain where ForestPrep has already been run, you may not see this step or step 7.

7. On the Recipient Update Server screen, type the name of the computer that will be your Exchange Recipient Update server for the domain, and click Next. A computer account must exist in the domain for this computer, but Exchange 2000 Server should not yet be installed on it. The first instance of Exchange 2000 Server that you install in the domain must be installed on this computer.

8. On the Completion screen, click Finish.

Other Pre-Installation Steps

Prior to installing the Exchange Server software, you should consider these additional steps:

- Verify that the Windows 2000 Server domain controller is operational.

- Close any messaging-aware applications.

- Back up your existing Exchange installation if you will be performing an upgrade.

- Verify that Clustering Services is installed and properly configured if you will be installing Exchange in that environment.

Installing Exchange Server

This section explains several installation scenarios and component options and then walks you through an actual installation of the first server in an organization. So boot up your Windows 2000 server, grab your Exchange CD, and get ready.

Microsoft ✔ *Exam Objective*	**Install Exchange 2000 Server on a server computer.**

There are three basic contexts in which Exchange 2000 Server can be installed:

- As the first installation in an organization

- As a subsequent installation

- As an upgrade to a current installation of a previous version

In addition to these three contexts, this section also covers installing Exchange on a cluster.

Installing the First Exchange Server

Installing the first Exchange 2000 Server in an organization is a fairly important task. If you have already run (or had someone else run) the ForestPrep
and DomainPrep tools, then the Active Directory and Windows 2000
domain are all ready for the Exchange installation. You must also install the
software onto the same server as the one you specified as the Address List
Server when DomainPrep was run.

If you are a member of the Schema Admins, Enterprise Admins, and local
Administrators groups, you can forgo running the ForestPrep tool; it is possible to update the schema during the setup of the initial Exchange Server. In
addition, if you are installing into a single domain environment, you can forgo
running the DomainPrep tool. *Be warned, though: If you install Exchange
without running the ForestPrep tool into a forest where no version of
Exchange already exists, SETUP creates an organization based on the name
of the domain.*

When installing the first Exchange server, you will be prompted to enter
information on the following topics:

Name of the directory for installation   The default directory location
and name is C:\Program Files\Exchsrvr, but this can be modified by
the installer.

CD Key   The setup program will present you with a dialog box
requesting the CD Key or product ID (PID) number. The CD Key is
a unique 25-digit number found on the back of the Exchange Server
CD case.

Choosing Installation Components

Exchange Server setup can be initiated by simply inserting the Exchange
Server CD into the CD-ROM drive. This will automatically cause a Web-like
page to load that contains the option to set up Exchange 2000 Server.

Another way to initiate setup is to execute the file SETUP.EXE, which is found
on the Exchange Server CD (or on a shared network drive if the setup files have
been stored there). This file is found in the \Setup\I386\ directory.

When SETUP runs, it checks for a current installation of Exchange on that
machine. If it finds one, it goes into maintenance mode and lets you add or
remove components and reinstall or remove all components.

If SETUP does not find a current installation, it prompts you for the specific components to install, as shown in Figure 3.1.

FIGURE 3.1 A typical installation of Exchange

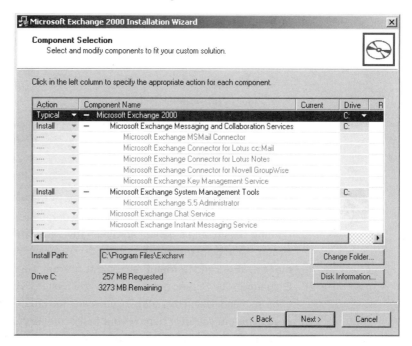

There are four main categories of components available under the main Microsoft Exchange 2000 entry:

- Messaging and Collaboration Services, which includes the basic Exchange routing engine and optional subcomponents for the various available messaging connectors and the Key Management Service.

- System Management Tools, which includes the System Manager snap-in for managing Exchange and a single optional subcomponent—the Exchange 5.5 Administrator tool for managing Exchange 5.5 servers.

- Chat Service, which is only available in the Enterprise edition of Exchange 2000 Server and provides tools for creating and administering chat communities. Users can connect to these communities with standard chat software.

- Instant Messaging Service, which provides support for Microsoft's Instant Messenger software.

In addition, there are three installation types that you can choose using the drop-down menu to the left of the Microsoft Exchange 2000 component at the top of the component list:

- *Typical*, which installs the Messaging and Collaboration Services and the System Management Tools components, but none of their sub-components. A Typical installation also does not include Chat Service and Instant Messaging Service.

- *Minimum*, which installs only the Messaging and Collaboration Services component itself.

- *Custom*, which you can use to select individually only the components you want.

When you install Exchange 2000 Server into a forest where no version of Exchange already exists, SETUP creates a default routing group, named First Routing Group, and a default administrative group, named First Administrative Group. If you want to create groups with more imaginative (or useful) names, run the ForestPrep and DomainPrep tools as normal. Then, perform an installation of Exchange 2000 Server, but select only the System Manager snap-in component to be installed. Using this snap-in, you can then create routing and administrative groups before you ever deploy your first actual Exchange server. If you are running in native mode, you can also rename the First Administrative Group after installing the first server. In either native or mixed mode, you can rename the First Routing Group after you install the first server.

Performing an Installation

Exercise 3.4 provides the actual steps to install Microsoft Exchange 2000 Server. This exercise assumes that both the ForestPrep and DomainPrep tools have already been applied and that you are installing the first Exchange server in an organization.

Please review the system requirements needed by your lab computer to perform these exercises. Those requirements are found in the introduction of this book in the section "How to Use This Book."

EXERCISE 3.4

Installing Microsoft Exchange 2000 Server

1. Insert the Microsoft Exchange Server CD into the server's CD-ROM drive. If your CD-ROM drive is set to automatically run CDs, this will automatically open the Exchange 2000 Installation Wizard. If not, browse to the \setup\i386 directory on the CD and run SETUP.EXE. (Other options are to share the CD on another machine on the network and then connect to that share, or to copy the CD to the server's hard drive.)

2. Click Next to go past the Welcome page.

3. The End User License Agreement page appears next. If you agree with the license, select I Agree, and click Next.

4. Enter the 25-digit CD-key that appears on the back of your Exchange 2000 Server setup disk cover.

5. The Component Selection page lists the installation options, as well as the option to choose the directory into which Exchange Server will be installed. This latter option is accessed through the Change Folder button. For this exercise, we will assume the installation directory is the default, C:\Program Files\Exchsrvr. The installation option we will use for this exercise is the Typical option, which includes most messaging components and management tools. If you would like to see the individual components that can be selected, choose the Custom option from the drop-down menu to the left of the first item in the list, Microsoft Exchange 2000. You can then choose whether or not to install each individual option using that option's drop-down menu. Once all of your decisions are made, click Next to go on.

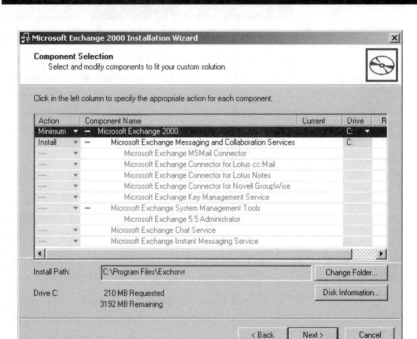

6. A Licensing screen appears explaining the need for you to pur-chase Client Access Licenses before clients can access this Exchange server. Exchange 2000 Server only supports the per seat licensing mode. Once you have read and agreed to this licensing, click the I Agree That check box, then click Next.

7. The Component Summary screen now appears, asking you to con-firm your installation choices. You can use the Back button to change any settings you have made. When you are satisfied with your choices, click Next to install Exchange 2000 Server.

8. The installation process can take some time. When it is done, a Congratulations screen appears informing you that the installation is complete. Click the Finish button.

After the initial setup, you can add and remove individual components by running the setup program again using the same procedure outlined above. You can also access the setup program using the Windows Add/Remove Programs Control Panel applet.

Installing Subsequent Exchange Servers

There are many reasons to add additional Exchange servers to an organization. The primary reasons are performance, capacity and scaling, and fault tolerance. Each is briefly discussed below.

Performance An organization could place certain Exchange services on additional Exchange servers, dedicating those servers to those functions. Examples are as follows:

Public and/or private information stores These databases could be located on an additional Exchange server dedicated to performing as a mailbox server or public folder server.

Connector software The same principle relates to running connector software on a dedicated Exchange server.

Capacity and scaling If the physical limits of a particular system are being approached, Exchange services and their related physical resources (e.g., disk space) can be spread out among multiple Exchange servers. This issue also relates to performance issues.

Fault tolerance through redundancy Many Exchange services and resources are replicated throughout an Exchange organization. This redundancy implements a built-in level of fault tolerance. For example, all the Exchange servers within a site share the same directory information through replication. If one particular Exchange server is taken offline, its directory information is automatically updated by another Exchange server through the replication mechanism when it comes back online.

The actual process of adding a subsequent Exchange server to an existing organization is nearly identical to installing the first server. The only difference is if you have defined more than one administrative or routing group in your organization (as detailed in Chapter 7). In this case, you will see two extra screens while using the installation Wizard. The first lets you choose the administrative group you want the new server to be a part of. The second screen, shown in Figure 3.2, lets you choose a routing group within the chosen administrative group that the server should be a part of. If you have not configured more than one administrative or routing group, you will see neither of these screens, and the installation will be identical to installing the first server.

FIGURE 3.2 Choosing a routing group for a subsequent installation

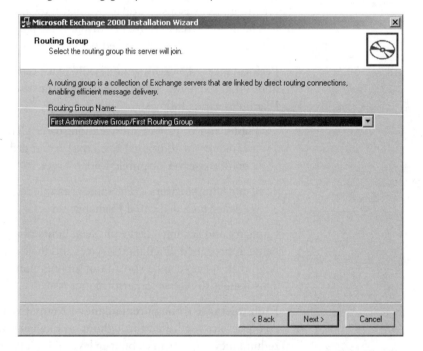

Upgrading an Existing Installation of a Previous Version

Exchange 2000 Server supports upgrades only for servers that are running Exchange Server 5.5 with the Exchange Service Pack 3 installed. If you are currently running a previous version of Exchange Server, you must first upgrade to version 5.5 and apply Service Pack 3 before you can upgrade to Exchange 2000 Server. In addition, the server computer needs to be running Windows 2000 Server, Advanced Server, or Datacenter Server with Windows 2000 Service Pack 1. Finally, you must run the ForestPrep and DomainPrep utilities described earlier in this chapter. Once all of these requirements are in place, upgrading to Exchange 2000 Server is not too difficult.

Microsoft ✔ *Exam Objective*

Upgrade or migrate to Exchange 2000 Server from Exchange Server 5.5.

WARNING

Before undertaking an upgrade, you should always perform a complete backup of your current installation. If something goes drastically wrong with the upgrade, you can then go back to your previous installation.

Microsoft defines three types of server upgrades for bringing an Exchange 5.5 organization up to Exchange 2000 Server:

- Upgrading in-place
- Upgrading by moving mailboxes
- Upgrading using the swing server method

Upgrading In-Place

An *in-place upgrade* is simply one where the server running Exchange Server 5.5 is taken offline and the Exchange 2000 Server software is installed on it. It is by far the simplest type of upgrade and is started in the same way as the initial setup: by executing SETUP.EXE. SETUP first checks for any existing Exchange Server components on that computer. If it finds any, it performs an upgrade. The same Installation Wizard is used as when you install an Exchange 2000 Server normally, and you can simply step through the pages of the Wizard in the same way as described previously. However, during an upgrade, you will not be allowed to add any additional components to those already installed on the server running Exchange Server 5.5. If you want to install additional components, you must run the setup program again after the upgrade is finished and add those components.

Upgrading by Moving Mailboxes

One potential disadvantage to the in-place upgrade is that your server must be taken offline during the time it takes to upgrade. If this kind of downtime is not acceptable, or if the computer running Exchange Server 5.5 is simply not powerful enough to support Exchange 2000 Server, you might consider *upgrading by moving mailboxes*.

In this method, you install Exchange 2000 Server on a new server running Windows 2000 Server. Once that is done, you join the new server to the existing Exchange site using the Active Directory Connector and the procedures discussed in Chapter 12. Next, you move any mailboxes and public folders from the old server to the new server. Finally, you take the old server offline.

This method offers the advantage of upgrading to a more powerful server while reducing the amount of downtime experienced by the user to only the period needed to move mailboxes. It also offers the advantage of having the Exchange 2000 installation occur on a new server that is not used by clients, reducing the risk of downtime due to installation problems.

Upgrading with the Swing Server Method

The *swing server method of upgrading* is really just a fancier version of the moving mailboxes method. There are essentially three steps in this method:

1. Install Windows 2000 and Exchange 2000 onto a new server, and join that server to an existing Exchange 5.5 site.

2. Move mailboxes from a server running Exchange Server 5.5 to a new one running Exchange 2000 Server.

3. Upgrade the server running Exchange Server 5.5 to Exchange 2000 Server and move mailboxes from another server running Exchange Server 5.5 to the newly upgraded server.

This method offers essentially the same advantages as the moving mailboxes method, but it also provides a way to preserve the use of existing hardware while minimizing downtime during the upgrade process. It is also a better choice than the moving mailboxes method when you have multiple servers to upgrade.

Installing Exchange 2000 Server on Clustered Servers

As stated earlier in this chapter, the Enterprise edition of Exchange 2000 Server is designed to work with the *Windows Clustering Service*. Clustering groups servers logically into an interdependent system, called a *cluster*, for the purpose of fault tolerance. This cluster appears as a single server to clients and applications. In the event of a failure on one system, the Clustering Service moves the affected services to a functioning node in the cluster. Where Exchange 5.5 supported only Active/Passive clustering, in which only one node of a cluster was active at a time, Exchange 2000 Server now supports Active/Active clustering, in which all nodes function simultaneously. Server clusters allow you to enable *resource groups* that are not bound to a specific computer and can fail over to another node. Exchange considers each resource group as a separate instance of Exchange, called a *virtual server*.

Each resource group in a cluster running Exchange must share the following resources:

- IP address

- Network name

- A physical disk or disk system, such as RAID5

- Exchange System Attendant service

Obviously, there is a lot more to clustering than a single chapter can go into. For more detailed information on Windows 2000 Clustering Service, consult your Windows 2000 documentation.

In order to run Exchange with Windows Clustering Service, you must be running Windows 2000 Advanced Server or Windows 2000 Datacenter Server. When installing Exchange 2000 Server into a cluster, it must be completely installed on one node before being installed on another node. In addition, you must install Exchange on each node using the same user account that you used to install Cluster Service. You must also install Exchange on the same drive letter and directory on all nodes. Finally, you must install the same Exchange components on all nodes.

Post-Installation Considerations

This section discusses some of the results of the Exchange installation. During the installation of Exchange, some of the activities of SETUP.EXE include creating an Exchange directory structure, copying files to that directory structure, creating share points to the directory structure, and adding keys and values to the Windows 2000 Registry. Knowing the results of these activities is helpful for the Exchange administrator, especially in troubleshooting situations (which will be discussed later in this chapter).

Default Directory and File Structure for Exchange

The default root directory for Exchange is \Program Files\Exchsrvr. SETUP creates subdirectories under that root directory and copies Exchange files to those subdirectories. Table 3.1 is a listing of the default Exchange subdirectories under the root and the type of files in those subdirectories.

TABLE 3.1 Default Exchange Directories and Their Contents

Folder	Contents
ADDRESS	This directory contains subdirectories with program files (DLLs) that can be used to generate foreign addresses for Exchange recipients. When an Exchange server uses a connector or gateway to create interoperability with a foreign system, the System Attendant component automatically generates a foreign address for each Exchange recipient. This foreign address, also referred to as a proxy address or simply an e-mail address, is what the users of the foreign mail system see and where they send mail. The program files in the subdirectories can generate these proxy addresses. The complete installation downloads files for the following foreign mail systems: Lotus cc:Mail, Microsoft Mail, Internet mail (SMTP), and X.400 mail.
BIN	This directory contains many of the files that are the components and services of Microsoft Exchange Server.
CCMCDATA	This directory is used for temporary storage by the Connector for cc:Mail.

TABLE 3.1 Default Exchange Directories and Their Contents *(continued)*

Folder	Contents
CONNECT	This directory contains subdirectories that hold the files that are the Microsoft connectors. The complete installation downloads files for the following connectors: the Microsoft Mail Connector, the Microsoft Schedule+ Free/Busy Connector, and the Microsoft Exchange Connector for Lotus cc:Mail. An additional subdirectory (Trn) contains files for translating messages into other languages.
DXADATA	This directory contains the file (XDIR.EDB) that is the Directory Synchronization database when Exchange 2000 Server is connected with an existing server that's running Exchange Server 5.5.
ExchangeServer _computername	This directory is named using the NetBIOS name of the computer and holds miscellaneous files for global Exchange support.
exchweb	This directory holds files for Outlook Web Access.
Computername .log	This directory holds log files for message tracking.
Mailroot	This directory holds working directories for message transfer.
kmsdata	This directory holds files supporting the optional Key Management Service.
MDBDATA	This directory is one of the most important on your server, as it contains the Information Store database. This database is composed of the following files: Private Information Stores (EDB and STM), which are the server-based storage of mailboxes; the Public Information Stores (EDB and STM), which are the server-based storage of public folder data; and the database transaction log files (LOG), which are the files to which data is initially written in order to provide for faster performance and fault tolerance.
MTADATA	This directory holds the files that make up and relate to the Message Transfer Agent (MTA).

TABLE 3.1 Default Exchange Directories and Their Contents *(continued)*

Folder	Contents
RES	This directory holds files that contain message strings used when Exchange logs events to the Windows 2000 Event Log.
SCHEMA	This directory holds the XML files that support the Exchange extension of the Windows 2000 Active Directory Schema.

Share Points and Permissions for Exchange Directories

Table 3.2 lists the Exchange directories that are shared on the network with the specified share names and permissions, assuming that Exchange was installed on the C: drive.

TABLE 3.2 Microsoft Exchange Share Points and Permissions

Folder	Shared As	Permissions
C:\EXCHSRVR\ADDRESS	Address	Administrators group: Full Control; Everyone group: Read
C:\EXCHSRVR\RES	Resources	Administrators group: Full Control; Everyone group: Read
C:\EXCHSRVR\TRACKIN G.LOG	tracking. log	Administrators group: Full Control; Everyone group: Read

Exchange Entries in the Windows 2000 Registry

During installation, SETUP creates entries in the Windows 2000 Registry. Some of these entries are mentioned here.

Registry information about the presence of the Exchange application on a machine, as well as the directory location of the installation, is found in the following Registry location:

```
HKEY_LOCAL_MACHINE
    \SOFTWARE
        \Microsoft
```

```
\Exchange
    \Setup
```

The following Registry location records the settings for the various Event Logs created by the different Exchange components:

```
HKEY_LOCAL_MACHINE
    \SYSTEM
        \CurrentControlSet
            \Services
                \EventLog
                    \Application
                        \<Exchange components>
```

The Exchange component settings are stored in the Registry at the following location:

```
\HKEY_LOCAL_MACHINE
    \SYSTEM
        \CurrentControlSet
            \Services
                \<Exchange component>
```

License settings for Exchange are stored in the following location:

```
\HKEY_LOCAL_MACHINE
    \SYSTEM
        \CurrentControlSet
            \Services
                \LicenseInfo
                    \MSExchangeIS
```

Exchange System Manager Snap-In

One powerful feature of Microsoft Exchange is the ability to centrally administer an entire Exchange organization. This is accomplished through a snap-in for the Microsoft Management Console named *Exchange System Manager* (see Figure 3.3). This snap-in can run on any Windows 2000 computer on the Exchange network. From this single point, an administrator can administer all the Exchange servers in an organization. This is sometimes referred to as single-seat administration.

FIGURE 3.3 The Exchange System Manager

The actual snap-in file for System Manager is Exchange System Manager.msc and is stored in the \EXCHSRVR\BIN directory. While the Exchange setup program can install the snap-in on the Exchange Server machine, the administrator will probably also want this program on their workstation. Installing this program also installs a new version of Windows 2000 Backup and extensions to the Active Directory Users and Computers and Performance Monitor programs. These changes enable those programs to work with Exchange 2000 Server.

Troubleshooting an Exchange Installation

If any problems arise during an Exchange installation, there are several areas you may want to investigate first.

Microsoft ✓ Exam Objective	Diagnose and resolve failed installations.
	Diagnose and resolve problems involving the upgrade process.

Should you run into installation problems, you should begin your troubleshooting efforts by checking that the following has been done:

Internet Information Server (IIS) and the necessary protocol support have been installed.   IIS is installed along with Windows 2000 Server during a default installation. However, this default installation does not include the NNTP service that, along with SMTP, is necessary in order to install Exchange 2000 Server. The NNTP service must be installed before Exchange 2000 Server is installed.

Windows 2000 Service Pack 1 has been installed.   Installing Exchange 2000 Server requires Windows 2000 Server, Advanced Server, or Datacenter Server, with Windows 2000 Service Pack 1 (SP1) applied. Without SP1 applied, the installation will fail.

You have the appropriate permissions to install the software.   In order to install Exchange 2000 Server, you must have local Administrator permission on the server on which you want to install. In order to run the ForestPrep tool, you must be a member of the Enterprise Admins and Schema Admins groups and the local Administrators group on the computer on which you run the utility. In order to run DomainPrep, you must be a member of the Domain Admins group and the local Administrators group on the computer on which you run the utility.

The forest and domain have been properly prepared.   In order to install Exchange 2000 Server in all but the simplest single domain situation, the ForestPrep tool may need to be run once in the forest, and the DomainPrep tool may need to be run in each domain in which Exchange 2000 Server will be installed.

Share point permissions are established.   Make sure the necessary Exchange directories are shared if other servers are having problems connecting to the Exchange server after installation.

Observe the Exchange Server boot process for alert messages and to ensure that all necessary services have been started.   If there are any problems with the Exchange boot process, alert messages can be sent to the console and/or written to the Windows 2000 Event Log. You may also want to check that all the necessary Exchange services have been started. This can be done by going to Administrative Tools/Services or to a command prompt and executing NET START. Some Exchange services are dependent on other Windows 2000 services being started. If the dependent service is not started, the Exchange service will not start.

Use the setup log to determine problems that the Exchange 2000 Server setup program may have logged.   While SETUP is running, it creates a log of what it is attempting. This log file, called `Exchange Server Setup Progress.txt`, is stored in the root directory of the drive on which Exchange is installed. If you run into problems during installation, the log file can help you find out what part of the installation failed or, at least, where in the installation process the failure occurred.

Summary

Although installing Microsoft Exchange Server is a straightforward process, there are still some important concepts for you to understand.

One of the most important phases of an installation is pre-installation. Before starting the actual installation, you must make sure the minimum requirements for Exchange are met. Licenses must be addressed to ensure compliance with legal issues. Because Exchange utilizes user accounts from Windows 2000 Server accounts databases, Exchange sites must interface with Windows 2000 domains. Finally, you must prepare the Windows 2000 forest by running ForestPrep (or by having someone with the appropriate permissions do so) and prepare each domain that will host Exchange 2000 Server by running DomainPrep.

Exchange installation happens in one of three contexts: as the first server in an organization, as a subsequent server, and as an upgrade. During the first or a subsequent installation, you will select the various components that make up an Exchange server. During an upgrade, you may not select any components that were not already installed on the original server running Exchange Server 5.5.

There are three types of installation options:

Typical   This option installs the Exchange Server software, the basic Messaging and Collaboration components, and the System Manager snap-in program. It does not include the additional connectors, the Chat Service, or the Instant Messaging Service.

Custom   This option lets you choose exactly which components should be installed.

Minimum   This option installs only the Exchange Server software and the basic Messaging and Collaboration components.

After an Exchange Server installation, you should know the directory structure that SETUP has created. The default directory name for the installation is `Program Files\Exchsrvr`. SETUP also makes share points and modifications to the Windows 2000 Registry.

Key Terms

Before you take the exam, be certain you are familiar with the following terms:

Client Access License (CAL)	resource groups
Custom installation	Server License
DomainPrep	Standard edition
Enterprise edition	swing server method of upgrading
Exchange System Manager	Typical installation
ForestPrep	upgrading by moving mailboxes
in-place upgrade	Windows Clustering Service
Minimum installation	

Review Questions

1. One of your company's locations contains an Exchange server with 25 users, each using Microsoft Outlook. You have purchased 25 Client Access Licenses. The company hires 10 new employees who will connect to the site remotely. Five of the new users will be using POP3 applications, and five will be using HTTP applications. How many additional Client Access Licenses must you purchase?

   A. 0

   B. 2

   C. 5

   D. 6

   E. 10

   F. 12

2. You are the Exchange administrator for a large network. You do not have the appropriate permissions to update the Active Directory Schema on your network, so you must get another administrator to do this before you can install Exchange 2000 Server. To which of the following groups must that person belong in order to run the ForestPrep utility? (Choose all that apply.)

   A. Server Admins

   B. Domain Admins

   C. Schema Admins

   D. Enterprise Admins

3. The messaging system at your company consists of a single Exchange Server 5.5 computer. You decide to install Exchange 2000 Server on a spare computer and add it to your existing Exchange Server 5.5 site. You think that this will allow you to avoid any downtime that an installation problem might cause if you simply upgraded the computer. What must you do before installing Exchange 2000 Server? (Choose all that apply.)

A. Install Windows 2000 with Service Pack 1 on the computer running Exchange Server 5.5.

B. Install Exchange Service Pack 3 on the computer running Exchange Server 5.5.

C. Install the Active Directory Connector on the computer running Exchange Server 5.5.

D. Run the DomainPrep tool on the computer running Exchange Server 5.5.

4. Your company is running a messaging system that consists of four Exchange sites, each with computers running Exchange Server 5. Which of the following steps must you take in order to upgrade all of your servers to Exchange 2000 Server? (Choose all that apply.)

A. Apply Exchange Server 5 Service Pack 1 to all servers.

B. Upgrade all servers to Exchange Server 5.5.

C. Apply Exchange Server 5.5 Service Pack 3 to all servers.

D. Install the Active Directory Connector on all servers.

E. Install Windows 2000 Server on all servers.

F. Apply Windows 2000 Service Pack 1 to all servers.

G. Install Exchange 2000 Server on all servers.

5. You have four computers on which you are considering installing Exchange 2000 Server as a testing environment. Which of the following systems would you have to upgrade before installing Exchange 2000 Server? (Choose all that apply.)

   A. Pentium 90, 64MB RAM, 500MB disk space

   B. Pentium 133, 64MB RAM, 2500MB disk space

   C. Pentium 166, 256MB RAM, 1000MB disk space

   D. Pentium II 400, 128MB RAM, 250MB disk space

6. You have just finished an installation of Exchange 2000 Server and have restarted the computer. When the computer restarts, you get a message saying that several services were unable to start. You verify this fact using the Event Viewer and then determine that none of the Exchange services are running. Which file would you use to see the details of the Exchange installation?

   A. Exchange Server Setup Progress.txt

   B. Exchange Server Setup Progress.log

   C. Exchange Server Setup Log.txt

   D. Exchange Server Error.log

7. You have recently set up your Exchange 2000 Server to communicate with a legacy cc:Mail server using the Connector for cc:Mail. You would like to set up auditing on all of the directories involved in the communication between the two systems. Which of the following default Exchange directories would you need be concerned with? (Choose all that apply.)

   A. \ADDRESS

   B. \CCMCDATA

   C. \CONNECT

   D. \KMSDATA

8. You are configuring a custom Microsoft Management Console snap-in for an assistant administrator who will be taking care of certain Exchange tasks for you. You would like to configure the System Manager snap-in so that the assistant can run it on their personal workstation instead of giving them access to the Exchange server. What file from the Exchange server would you need to install on the workstation?

   A. \EXCHSRVR\BIN\Exchange System Manager.msc

   B. \EXCHSRVR\BIN\System Manager.mmc

   C. \EXCHSRVR\Exchange System Manager.msc

   D. \EXCHSRVR\BIN\Exchadmin.msc

9. Your network is running Windows 2000 and Windows NT 4 in a single mixed-mode domain. You are using an Exchange Server 5.5–based messaging system that consists of multiple sites. One of the servers running Exchange Server 5.5 is configured with a connector to communicate with the company's legacy Microsoft Mail messaging system. You are planning to upgrade to Exchange 2000 Server.

   Required result:

   The new Exchange installation must still be able to connect to the legacy Microsoft Mail messaging system.

   Optional results:

   Your company would like to offer the Instant Messaging Service.

   Your company would like to offer the Chat Service.

   Proposed solution:

   Do not upgrade the server running Exchange Server 5.5 with the MS Mail Connector. Upgrade all other servers running Exchange Server 5.5 with Exchange 2000 Server. Configure an Active Directory Connector to allow the servers running Exchange Server 5.5 and Exchange 2000 Server to communicate.

Which result does the proposed solution produce?

A. The proposed solution produces the required result and both optional results.

B. The proposed solution produces the required result and one of the optional results.

C. The proposed solution produces the required result, but neither of the optional results.

D. The proposed solution does not produce the required result.

10. You are installing Exchange 2000 Server in an organization that must allow Novell NetWare clients to connect to the Exchange server. Which of the following is required?

A. The Microsoft Gateway Services for NetWare (GSNW) is required on the Exchange server.

B. The Microsoft Gateway Services for NetWare (GSNW) is required on at least one Windows 2000 server in the same domain as the Exchange server.

C. The Microsoft Gateway Services for NetWare (GSNW) is required on at least one domain controller in the same domain as the Exchange server.

D. The Microsoft Gateway Services for NetWare (GSNW) is required on all domain controllers in the same domain as the Exchange server.

11. Your Windows 2000 forest consists of a single domain tree. That tree consists of a single root level domain and four child domains of that root domain. You are about to prepare the root level domain for an Exchange 2000 installation. Which of the following commands would you use?

A. forestprep.exe

B. forestprep.exe /setup

C. setup.exe /domainprep

D. setup.exe /domain

12. Which of the following features are included in a Typical setup of Exchange 2000 Server?

    A. System Manager snap-in

    B. Chat Service

    C. Instant Messaging Service

    D. Key Management Service

13. You are preparing to install Exchange 2000 Server on a computer running Windows 2000 Server. During Windows 2000 setup, Internet Information Server was installed with the default components. Which of the following components of Internet Information Server should you make sure are installed prior to installing Exchange 2000 Server? (Choose all that apply.)

    A. SMTP

    B. SNMP

    C. FTP

    D. NNTP

14. You are planning to create a Windows 2000 cluster on which to install Exchange 2000 Server. Which of the following is a requirement for Exchange 2000 Server to work with Windows Clustering Service? (Choose all that apply.)

    A. The purchase of a 1000-user license

    B. Microsoft Windows 2000 Advanced Server

    C. The purchase of the optional Windows 2000 Clustering Server

    D. The Enterprise Edition of Exchange 2000 Server

15. You are about to install Exchange 2000 Server as the messaging system for your network. Your network is running a single native-mode Windows 2000 domain, and all servers are running Windows 2000 Advanced Server. Two servers are configured as domain controllers, and you have already prepared three servers to have Exchange 2000 Server installed on them.

Required result:

You want to create two different administrative groups, and you want to name them differently from the default names that Exchange setup provides.

Optional result:

You want to create a single routing group and name it differently from the default name that Exchange setup provides.

Proposed solution:

Install Exchange 2000 Enterprise Server on one of the servers. Next, run DomainPrep, and use the advanced options for that tool to rename the routing and administrative groups created during the Exchange installation. Install Exchange 2000 Enterprise Server on another server, and choose to create a new administrative group during the process. Finally, run DomainPrep to rename the new administrative groups.

Which of the results does the proposed solution produce?

A. The proposed solution produces the required result and the optional result.

B. The proposed solution produces the required result, but not the optional result.

C. The proposed solution produces the optional result, but not the required result.

D. The proposed solution produces neither the required result nor the optional result.

16. You are about to install Exchange 2000 Server as the messaging system for your network. Your network is running a single native-mode Windows 2000 domain, and all servers are running Windows 2000 Advanced Server. Two servers are configured as domain controllers, and you have already prepared three servers to have Exchange 2000 Server installed on them.

Required result:

You want to create two different administrative groups, and you want to name them differently from the default names that Exchange setup provides.

Optional result:

You want to create a single routing group and name it differently from the default name that Exchange setup provides.

Proposed solution:

Run the ForestPrep tool to prepare the Active Directory Schema. Next, use the Active Directory Users and Computers tool to modify the default routing and administrative groups created by the Forest-Prep tool. Finally, create a new administrative group object in the Schema, and provide it with the name you want.

Which of the results does the proposed solution produce?

A. The proposed solution produces the required result and the optional result.

B. The proposed solution produces the required result, but not the optional result.

C. The proposed solution produces the optional result, but not the required result.

D. The proposed solution produces neither the required result nor the optional result.

17. You are about to install Exchange 2000 Server as the messaging system for your network. Your network is running a single native-mode Windows 2000 domain, and all servers are running Windows 2000 Advanced Server. Two servers are configured as domain controllers, and you have already prepared three servers to have Exchange 2000 Server installed on them.

    Required result:

    You want to create two different administrative groups, and you want to name them differently from the default names that Exchange setup provides.

    Optional result:

    You want to create a single routing group and name it differently from the default name that Exchange setup provides.

    Proposed solution:

    Run the ForestPrep and DomainPrep tools as normal. Then, perform an installation of Exchange 2000 Server, but select only the System Manager snap-in component to be installed. Using this snap-in, you can then create routing and administrative groups before you ever deploy your first actual Exchange server.

    Which of the results does the proposed solution produce?

    A. The proposed solution produces the required result and the optional result.

    B. The proposed solution produces the required result, but not the optional result.

    C. The proposed solution produces the optional result, but not the required result.

    D. The proposed solution produces neither the required result nor the optional result.

18. Which of the following methods of upgrading an Exchange Server 5.5 organization results in the least perceived downtime for the client?

   A. Upgrading in-place

   B. Upgrading by moving mailboxes

   C. Upgrading by importing Windows NT 4 user information

   D. Upgrading online

19. Exchange 2000 Server supports which of the following types of clustering?

   A. Active/Active

   B. Active/Passive

   C. Passive/Passive

   D. Unified

20. With which of the following resources must each resource group in a cluster running Exchange 2000 Server be configured? (Choose all that apply.)

   A. IP address

   B. A physical disk drive

   C. Exchange System Attendant Service

   D. Exchange Message Transfer Agent Service

   E. System Manager snap-in

Answers to Review Questions

1. E. Every user who connects to the Exchange server will need a Client Access License, no matter what client software is used to connect.

2. C, D. In order to run the DomainPrep utility, a user must belong to both the Schema Admins and Enterprise Admins global groups. The user must also belong to the local Administrators group on the computer on which the utility is actually run.

3. B. If you are actually going to upgrade a server running Exchange Server 5.5 to Exchange 2000 Server, you must first install Windows 2000 Server with Service Pack 1 and the Exchange Service Pack 3 on the server running Exchange Server 5.5. Since you are installing Exchange 2000 Server on a different system, you need to make sure that Exchange Service Pack 3 is installed.

4. B, C, E, F, G. Exchange 2000 Server supports upgrading only servers that are running Exchange Server 5.5 with the Exchange Service Pack 3 installed. If you are currently running a previous version of Exchange Server, you must first upgrade to version 5.5 and apply Service Pack 3 before you can upgrade to Exchange 2000 Server. In addition, the server computer needs to be running Windows 2000 Server, Advanced Server, or Datacenter Server with Windows 2000 Service Pack 1. The Active Directory Connector is not necessary if you plan an in-place upgrade of all the servers. The Connector would only be necessary if you needed to keep some Exchange Server 5.5 servers online and allow them to communicate with new Exchange 2000 Server computers.

5. A, B, D. Exchange 2000 Server requires a minimum of a Pentium 133, 128MB RAM, and 500MB disk space.

6. A. While SETUP is running, it creates a log of what it is attempting. This log file, called `Exchange Server Setup Progress.txt`, is stored in the root directory of the drive on which Exchange is installed.

7. A, B, C. The ADDRESS directory contains subdirectories with program files (DLLs) that can be used to generate foreign addresses for Exchange recipients. When an Exchange server uses a connector or gateway to create interoperability with a foreign system, the System Attendant component automatically generates a foreign address for each Exchange recipient. The CCMCDATA directory is used for temporary storage by the Connector for cc:Mail. The CONNECT directory contains subdirectories that hold the files that are the Microsoft connectors.

8. A. The actual snap-in file for System Manager is Exchange System Manager.msc and is stored in the \EXCHSRVR\BIN directory.

9. B. The required result is met because the server running Exchange Server 5.5 will maintain communications with the Microsoft Mail system. However, upgrading the server to Exchange 2000 Server would also maintain the communication because the Microsoft Mail Connector is included with the Standard edition of Exchange 2000 Server. The first optional result, providing Instant Messaging Service, is met because this service is included with the Standard edition of Exchange 2000 Server. The second optional result, providing Chat Service, is not met because Chat Service is only included with Exchange 2000 Enterprise Server.

10. A. The Microsoft Gateway Services for NetWare (GSNW) is required on the Exchange server. If the NetWare clients are using IPX/SPX, then the Exchange server will also require Microsoft NWLink.

11. C. DomainPrep is used to prepare each domain in which Exchange will be installed. The tool is run using the /domainprep switch for the SETUP.EXE program.

12. A. A Typical setup of Exchange 2000 Server includes basic messaging functionality, support for connectors to foreign systems, and the System Manager snap-in. Key Management Service requires a Custom setup and Chat Service requires Exchange 2000 Enterprise Server.

13. A, D. Both SMTP and NNTP must be installed on the Windows 2000 server before Exchange can be installed. If these protocols are not installed, the Exchange setup program will terminate.

14. B, D. The Enterprise edition of Exchange 2000 Server is designed to work with the Windows Clustering Service that is built in to Windows 2000 Advanced Server and Windows 2000 Datacenter Server.

15. D. The DomainPrep tool cannot be used to create or modify administrative or routing groups. In order to create groups with more imaginative (or useful) names, run the ForestPrep and DomainPrep tools as normal. Then, perform an installation of Exchange 2000 Server, but select only the System Manager snap-in component to be installed. Using this snap-in, you can then create routing and administrative groups before you ever deploy your first actual Exchange server.

16. D. The ForestPrep tool does not create administrative or routing groups. The Active Directory Users and Computers utility cannot be used to modify administrative or routing groups. In order to create groups with more imaginative (or useful) names, run the ForestPrep and DomainPrep tools as normal. Then, perform an installation of Exchange 2000 Server, but select only the System Manager snap-in component to be installed. Using this snap-in, you can then create routing and administrative groups before you ever deploy your first actual Exchange server.

17. A. Only the System Manager snap-in can be used to create and modify administrative and routing groups.

18. B. With the upgrading by moving mailboxes method, you install Exchange 2000 Server on a new server running Windows 2000 Server. Once that is done, you join the new server to the existing Exchange site using the Active Directory Connector. Next, you move any mailboxes and public folders from the old server to the new server and then take the old server offline. This reduces the amount of downtime experienced by the user to only the period needed to move mailboxes.

19. A. Exchange 5.5 supported only Active/Passive clustering, in which only one node of a cluster was active at a time. Exchange 2000 Server now supports Active/Active clustering, in which all nodes function simultaneously.

20. A, B, C. Each resource group in a cluster running Exchange must contain an IP address, a network name, a physical disk drive, and the Exchange System Attendant Service.

Chapter

4

Creating and Managing Recipients

MICROSOFT EXAM OBJECTIVES COVERED IN THIS CHAPTER:

✓ **Configure a user object for messaging.**

- Configure a user object for e-mail.
- Configure a user object for Instant Messaging.
- Configure a user object for Chat.

✓ **Create and manage address lists.**

- Create security groups.
- Create distribution groups.

✓ **Diagnose and resolve Recipient Update Service problems.**

One of an administrator's most important tasks is to create and configure Exchange *recipients*. A recipient is an object in the Windows 2000 Active Directory that references a resource that can receive a message. The resource might be a mailbox in a private Information Store, such as in the case of a user, or a public folder in the public Information Store that is shared by many users. No matter where an actual resource exists, though, a recipient object is always created in the Active Directory.

In this chapter, we will discuss the types of Exchange recipients, their creation, and their properties. Exchange has four basic types of recipients:

Users   A *user* is an Active Directory object that typically represents a person who uses the network. Once Exchange is installed and updates the schema, each user in the Active Directory can be mailbox-enabled, mail-enabled, or neither. A *mailbox-enabled user* has an associated mailbox in a private Information Store on an Exchange server. Each user's *mailbox* is a private storage area that allows an individual user to send, receive, and store messages. A *mail-enabled user* is one who has an e-mail address but does not have a mailbox on an Exchange server.

Groups   A *group* in Active Directory is like a container to which you can assign certain permissions and rights. You can then place users (and other groups) into that group, and they automatically inherit the group's permissions and rights. Exchange uses the concept of mail-enabled groups to form distribution lists. Messages sent to a group are redirected and sent to each member of the group. These groups allow users to send messages to multiple recipients without having to address each recipient individually.

Contacts   A *contact* is a pointer object that refers to an e-mail address for a non-Exchange recipient. Contacts are most often used for connecting your organization to foreign messaging systems, such as Microsoft Mail, Lotus cc:Mail, or the Internet. As an administrator, you would create contacts so that frequently used e-mail addresses are available in the Global Address List (GAL) as real names. This makes it easier to send mail because users do not need to guess at cryptic e-mail addresses.

Public Folders   A *public folder* is like a public mailbox. It is a container for information to be shared among a group of people. Public folders can contain e-mail messages, forms, word-processing documents, spreadsheet files, and files of many other formats. Public folders can also be configured to send information to other recipients.

The rest of this chapter discusses the creation and configuration of these four recipient objects, as well as related management tasks.

Users

In previous versions of Exchange, both the tool used to create user accounts (User Manager for Domains) and the tool used to administer Exchange (Exchange Administrator) could be used to create and manage mailboxes. This has changed with Exchange 2000. Now, one tool, named Active Directory Users and Computers, is used to create and manage mail-related user properties. Although the concept of the mailbox as a physical area of storage on an Exchange server is still valid, the concept of a mailbox as a recipient object in the Exchange directory no longer is. Now, there are only user objects in the Active Directory. Property pages of the user object are now used to configure Exchange-related properties.

Microsoft
Exam
Objective

Configure a user object for messaging.

- Configure a user object for e-mail.

- Configure a user object for Instant Messaging.

- Configure a user object for Chat.

Create and manage address lists.

- Create security groups.

- Create distribution groups.

See Chapter 10, "Configuring Auxiliary Services," for coverage of the "Configure a user object for Instant Messaging" and "Configure a user object for Chat" subobjectives.

This tying together of user accounts and mailbox properties means that Exchange administrators and Windows 2000 administrators will now have to work more closely than ever before. Though many Exchange administrators may hate the idea of giving up control of mailbox administration, this is usually what happens. Since all of the user-related functions of mailbox management are now accessed through Active Directory Users and Computers, it makes sense to have one account administrator handle all of the user-management details.

Exchange 2000 Server supports two mail configurations for a user: mailbox-enabled and mail-enabled. The creation and management of each type is discussed in the following sections.

Mailbox-Enabled Users

Every user in an organization needs access to an Exchange-based mailbox in order to send and receive messages. One of the principal administrative tasks in Exchange is the creation and management of these mailboxes. In Exchange 2000, a user with an associated mailbox is called a mailbox-enabled user. Mailbox-enabled users are able to send and receive messages, as well as store messages on an Exchange server.

Creating a Mailbox-Enabled User

When the Active Directory forest is prepared for Exchange 2000, a number of important changes are made. One is that the Active Directory schema is updated with attributes for objects that relate to Exchange. Another important change is that the Active Directory Users and Computers snap-in is updated with extensions that allow the automatic creation of mailboxes whenever users are created. It is also easy to create mailboxes for existing users. Exercise 4.1 outlines the steps for creating a new user and an associated mailbox using Active Directory Users and Computers. Exercise 4.2 outlines the steps for creating a mailbox for an existing user. Both exercises assume that Exchange 2000 Server has been installed in the domain.

EXERCISE 4.1

Creating a New User and Mailbox

1. Click Start, point to Programs, point to Administrative Tools, and select Active Directory Users and Computers.

2. From the Action menu, point to New, and select User.

3. On the New Object-User screen, fill in the information for the new user. This includes the user's full name and logon name. When you are done, click Next.

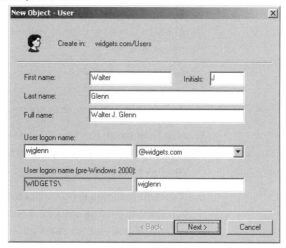

4. On the next screen, enter and verify the user's password, and set any password restrictions you want. When you are done, click Next.

5. Next, you are given the opportunity to create an Exchange mailbox for the user. To do so, first make sure the Create An Exchange Mailbox option is selected.

EXERCISE 4.1 *(continued)*

6. An *alias* is suggested based on the logon name that you chose for the user. The alias is an alternate means of addressing a user that is used by foreign messaging systems that may not be able to handle a full display name. You can change this if you have a specific policy in place for creating aliases, or you can leave it at the Windows default.

7. By default, the first Exchange server is selected as the server on which the mailbox should be created. Use the drop-down menu to change this if you want to create the mailbox on a different server.

8. Also by default, the first storage group on the selected server is chosen for you. Use the drop-down menu to alter that choice. Once you have made your selections, click Next to go on.

9. A summary screen is now displayed asking you to confirm choices. If you want to change any of the settings, you can use the Back button to do so. Once you are satisfied with your choices, click Finish to exit the Wizard, create the new user object in the Active Directory, and create the new mailbox on the selected Exchange server.

EXERCISE 4.2

Creating a Mailbox for an Existing User

1. Click Start, point to Programs, point to Administrative Tools, and select Active Directory Users and Computers.

2. In the Tree pane on the left, click the Users container.

3. In the Results pane on the right, find and select the user object for which you want to create a mailbox.

4. From the Action menu, select Exchange Tasks.

5. Click Next to bypass the Welcome screen of the Wizard.

6. On the Available Tasks screen, make sure that Create Mailbox is selected, and click Next.

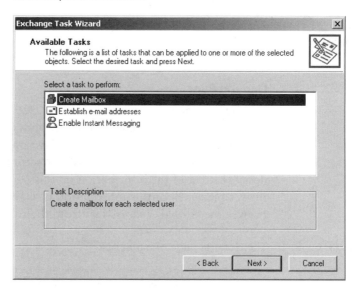

7. On the Create Mailbox screen, make sure that the alias, server, and storage group selections are all appropriate, and then click Next.

8. A summary screen is now displayed asking you to confirm your choices. If you want to change any of the settings, you can use the Back button to do so. Once you are satisfied with your choices, click Finish to exit the Wizard and create the new mailbox on the selected Exchange server.

Configuring Mailbox Properties

A user object, like all objects, has properties. Those properties are configured and viewed through property pages and the individual attributes on those property pages. Mailbox properties are configured using several Exchange-related property pages of the user object. The property pages of a user object are accessed in one of two ways. With the user highlighted, you can use the Properties command on the Action menu to access the property pages. A quicker way is simply to double-click the user object.

Many of the attributes that you can configure are straightforward and do not warrant much explanation (e.g., phone number). This section describes most of the property pages and the important individual attributes.

The terms "properties" and "attributes" are used interchangeably in this chapter.

General Page

The General page, shown in Figure 4.1, records general information about the user object. The first name, middle initial, and last name that you enter are used to generate a display name, which is the name of the recipient as it appears in the Active Directory Users and Computers window. The rest of the information on this page is used to further identify the recipient. All of this information is available to users when they browse the Global Address List from their e-mail client.

FIGURE 4.1 The General page of a mailbox

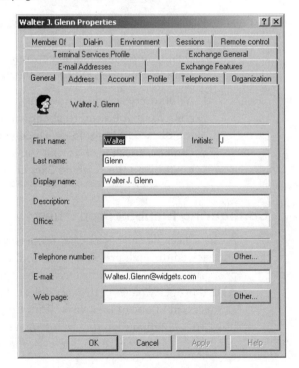

Organization Page

The Organization page contains fields for recording the organization information for the user, the name of the user's manager, and the people who report to the user. These people are referred to as *direct reports*. All of these fields are optional. All the information configured on this property page is also available in the Global Address List.

Address and Telephones Pages

The Address and Telephones pages contain information on addresses and phone numbers, as well as a place for free form notes about the user. All of this information is also available in the Global Address List.

Exchange General Page

The Exchange General page, shown in Figure 4.2, is used to configure general properties governing the Exchange mailbox associated with the user. The mailbox store that the user belongs to is displayed, but cannot be changed. The alias is an alternate means of addressing a user that is used by foreign messaging systems that may not be able to handle a full display name.

FIGURE 4.2   The Exchange General page of a mailbox

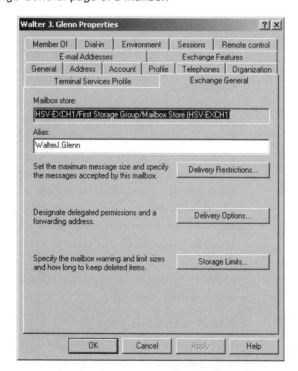

You will also find three buttons on this page that lead to more important settings: Delivery Restrictions, Delivery Options, and Storage Limits.

DELIVERY RESTRICTIONS

The Delivery Restrictions dialog box contains information regarding from whom this mailbox will accept or reject messages. The default is to accept messages from everyone (All), and to reject messages from nobody (None).

DELIVERY OPTIONS

The Delivery Options dialog box specifies a list of users who can send mail "on behalf of" this mailbox user. It also allows mail sent to this mailbox to be rerouted to another mailbox, referred to as an *alternate recipient*. The alternate recipient can be configured to receive mail instead of the original mailbox, or along with the original mailbox.

Send On Behalf Of permission can also be helpful in troubleshooting. If you assign this permission to yourself, as administrator, it allows you to test messages from any recipient in the organization. However, you should always use test mailboxes created for this purpose and not actual user mailboxes. Many users would consider having extended access into their e-mail an intrusion.

STORAGE LIMITS

The Storage Limits dialog box lets you set two parameters: *storage limits* and *deleted item retention time*. Storage limits refer to the limits placed on the size to which a mailbox can grow and what happens when that limit is crossed. By default, the Information Store (IS) settings will be used. However, this can be overridden. If it is overridden, you can set values (in kilobytes) for when warnings will be issued, when sending messages will be prohibited, and when sending and receiving messages will be prohibited.

The deleted item retention feature enables mailbox users to retrieve deleted items. But to prevent excessive build-up of deleted items, Exchange allows you to set a retention time for deleted items. That length of time can be configured through this setting or at the IS object. The IS default value will be used, but you can configure a mailbox to override that setting by specifying the number of days for deleted item retention. You can also configure a mailbox to keep deleted items (i.e., not permanently deleted) until the mailbox has been backed up.

E-Mail Addresses Page

Each time an Exchange mailbox is created, a number of non-Exchange mail addresses, also called *foreign mail addresses* or *proxy addresses*, are automatically generated for that Exchange mailbox. This allows Exchange mailboxes to be prepared to receive mail from foreign mail systems. The E-mail Addresses page lets you configure these addresses. Microsoft Exchange can automatically generate foreign addresses for the following systems:

- Lotus cc:Mail
- Microsoft Mail
- SMTP
- X.400

Exchange Features Page

The Exchange Features page, shown in Figure 4.3, lets you enable and disable advanced Exchange features for an individual mailbox. Such features include instant and voice messaging, along with other collaboration features of Exchange 2000 Server.

FIGURE 4.3 The Exchange Features page

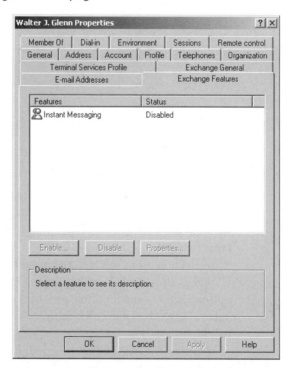

Exchange Advanced Page

The Exchange Advanced page, shown in Figure 4.4, lets you configure a number of miscellaneous features that the Exchange designers decided were advanced for one reason or another.

FIGURE 4.4 The Exchange Advanced page

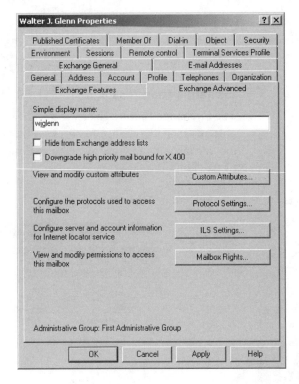

The *simple display name* is an alternate name for the mailbox. It appears when, for some reason, the full display name cannot. This situation often occurs when multiple language versions of System Manager are used on the same network.

By default, all recipients except public folders are visible to users via the Global Address List. You can use the Hide From Exchange Address Lists option to hide a mailbox from that list or other lists created in System Manager. The mailbox will still be able to receive mail; it just will not be included in address lists.

If the Downgrade High Priority Mail Bound For X.400 option is selected, the current mailbox cannot send high-priority messages to X.400 systems.

If a high-priority message is sent, it will automatically be downgraded to normal priority.

In addition to the attributes just mentioned, four buttons lead to separate dialogs with more configuration options: Custom Attributes, Protocol Settings, ILS Settings, and Mailbox Rights.

CUSTOM ATTRIBUTES

The Custom Attributes page lets you enter information about a mailbox in 15 custom fields. These fields can be used for any information that you need to include that isn't available on the other property pages. For example, if your company uses a special employee identification numbering system, you could create a custom field for that number. These fields are available to users in the Global Address List only if they are using a special template that displays them; or if they perform a specific LDAP query. By default, these fields are labeled extensionattribute1 through extensionattribute15, but they can be customized to suit your needs. Just select a field, and click Edit to enter a new value.

PROTOCOL SETTINGS

This page can specify various protocols and character sets that can be used with this mailbox. The protocols include HTTP, IMAP4, LDAP, NNTP, and POP3. By default, each of these is enabled, but this can be overridden at the mailbox or server level. The settings for each of these protocols can also be configured through this page. Encoding methods and character sets are examples of configurable settings.

ILS SETTINGS

Two fields on this page allow you to specify the server name of a Microsoft Internet Locator Service (ILS) and the account name (ILS account) for this mailbox. This is applicable if your network is using Microsoft NetMeeting for online meetings.

MAILBOX RIGHTS

This page allows you to view and configure the permissions that users and groups have for this mailbox. It should be noted that multiple users could be assigned as the owner of a mailbox. This is useful when you want to create a mailbox that will be used by a group of people, such as a Help Desk department. A single mailbox could be created, and all users of that department could be made an owner of that mailbox.

You can modify the particular rights of any user in the list by selecting the user and modifying the Allow and Deny check boxes beside the individual mailbox rights. Here are the rights that you can assign:

The Delete Mailbox Storage right   Allows a user to delete the actual mailbox from the Information Store. This right is only given to administrators by default.

The Read Permissions right   Lets the user read mail in the mailbox. You could use this right alone to allow a user to read another user's mail, but not send, change, or delete messages.

The Change Permissions right   Allows a user to delete or modify items in the primary user's mailbox.

The Take Ownership right   Allows a user to become the owner of a mailbox. By default, only administrators are given this permission.

The Mailbox Owner right   Allows a user to access a mailbox and read and delete messages. It also allows the user to send messages using the mailbox.

The Send As right   Another type of delegate access that can only be assigned by an administrator, this right lets a user send messages as though he/she were the owner of the mailbox. This differs from the Send On Behalf Of type of delegate access in that the sender's real identity is not sent along with the message.

The Primary Mailbox Owner right   Differs from the Mailbox Owner right in that only one user can be assigned as the primary mailbox owner.

Member Of Page

This page specifies the distribution groups of which this mailbox is a member. Not only can you manage a group from a user's properties, but you can manage a group from the group's properties. For more information on distribution lists, see the section "Groups" later in this chapter.

Mail-Enabled Users

A mail-enabled user is simply a user who has an e-mail address, but not a mailbox on an Exchange server. This means that the user can receive e-mail through their custom address, but cannot send mail using the Exchange system. You cannot enable mail for a user during user creation. The only way to create a mail-enabled user is first to create a new user that is not mailbox-enabled and then to enable mail for that user. Exercise 4.3 outlines the steps for mail-enabling a user.

EXERCISE 4.3

Creating a Mail-Enabled User

1. Click Start, point to Programs, point to Administrative Tools, and select Active Directory Users and Computers.

2. In the tree pane on the left, click the Users container.

3. In the results pane on the right, find and select the user object for which you want to enable mail.

4. From the Action menu, select Exchange Tasks.

5. Select the Establish E-Mail Addresses option from the list, and click Next.

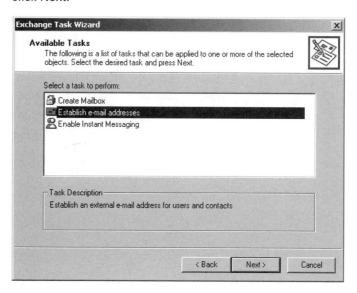

6. Make sure the alias and administrative group information is correct, and then click Modify.

7. The New E-mail Address dialog appears with a list of address types. From this list, select the type of e-mail address you want to create for the user, and click OK.

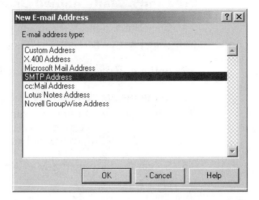

8. The Internet Address Properties dialog opens. On the General tab of the dialog, enter the e-mail address for the user.

9. Switch to the Advanced tab and override the Internet Mail Service default settings for the user by checking the Override Internet Mail Service Settings For This Recipient box and configuring your own message format settings. When you are done, click OK.

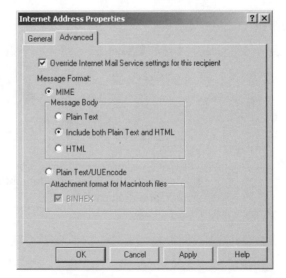

10. You are now returned to the Exchange Task Wizard, and the new e-mail address appears in the appropriate field. Click Next to go on.

11. A summary screen is now displayed asking you to confirm your choices . If you want to change any of the settings, you can use the Back button to do so. Once you are satisfied with your choices, click Finish to exit the Wizard.

Once you enable mail for a user following this procedure, you can configure the mail settings in the same way you would for a mailbox-enabled user.

Groups

In Windows 2000, a group is an Active Directory object that can hold users and other groups. Permissions can be assigned to a group and are inherited by all of the objects in that group. This makes the group a valuable Windows 2000 security construct. Exchange 2000 Server also uses the group for another purpose. A group can be made mail-enabled and then populated with other mail- or mailbox-enabled recipients to make a distribution list, a term you may be familiar with from earlier versions of Exchange Server. A group can contain users, contacts, public folders, and even other groups. When a message is sent to a mail-enabled group, the list of members is extracted, and the message is sent to each member of the list individually. Groups are visible in the Global Address List.

Windows 2000 supports two distinct types of groups. A security group can be assigned permissions and rights and be mail-enabled. A distribution group can only be mail-enabled.

Microsoft
Exam
Objective

Create and manage address lists.

- Create security groups.
- Create distribution groups.

Creating a Group

Creating and configuring a new group object is very simple. Exercise 4.4 outlines the steps involved.

EXERCISE 4.4

Creating a New Group in Active Directory

1. Click Start, point to Programs, point to Administrative Tools, and select Active Directory Users and Computers.

2. From the Action menu, point to New, and select Group.

3. In the Group Name field, type a name that represents the members of the group you are creating. Notice that Windows automatically fills in a pre–Windows 2000 compatible group name for you.

4. Next, you must choose a group scope. This determines at what level the group will be available in Active Directory—local, global, or universal. If you are going to create a simple distribution group (shown in the next step), it is usually best to make the group universal in scope so that it will be available throughout the organization. Otherwise, you may find that the group is limited by local or domain boundaries. Note that a domain must be running in native mode to support universal groups.

5. Next, you must define a group type. This determines whether the group is for security or distribution purposes. A *security group* can be made mail-enabled and used for distribution purposes. Security groups can also be assigned permissions and made part of Access Control Lists (ACLs) for resources. A *distribution group* is used for e-mail purposes only and cannot be used for security purposes.

6. Click Next to go on.

7. Select the Create An Exchange E-Mail Address option.

8. If you want, you can change the Alias name or the administrative group to which the new group belongs. When you are done, click Next to go on.

9. The final page summarizes the setup. Click Finish to create the new group.

Properties of a Distribution Group

Once you have created a new group, you will configure it the same way you configure other objects—with property pages. Three Exchange-related property pages connected with distribution groups need to be explained: Members, Managed By, and Exchange Advanced.

Members Page

The Members property page lists every member of the group. Use the Add button to access the Active Directory list, from which you can add new members to the group. Use the Remove button to remove selected members.

Managed By Page

The Managed By property page, shown in Figure 4.5, lets you assign an owner whose job it is to manage the group's membership. By default, the administrator who creates the group is the owner, but you can designate any user, group, or contact in the GAL as the owner. If you give ownership to another user, that user can use Outlook to modify the group's membership and does not need access to Active Directory Users and Computers. You can relieve yourself of a great deal of work by specifying the owners of a group. As groups grow larger, they can consume a considerable amount of management time.

FIGURE 4.5 Using the Managed By page to let other users manage a group

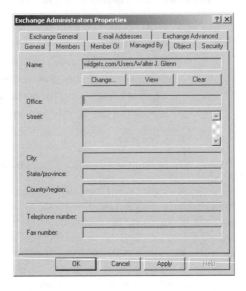

Exchange Advanced Page

The Exchange Advanced property page, shown in Figure 4.6, holds several configuration items that may be familiar to you, such as a simple display name and a button to assign custom attributes.

FIGURE 4.6 Setting advanced group properties with the Exchange Advanced page

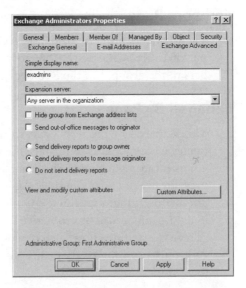

You can, however, also configure several options that are particular to distribution lists. They are as follows:

Expansion Server   Whenever a message is sent to a group, the group must be expanded so that the message can be sent to each member of the group. The Message Transfer Agent Service of a single Exchange server performs this expansion. The default choice is Any Server In The Organization. This choice means that the home server of the user sending the message always expands the group. You can also designate a specific server to handle the expansion of the group. The choice of a dedicated expansion server is a good one if you have a large group. In this case, expansion could consume a great amount of server resources, which can compromise performance for busy servers.

Hide Group From Exchange Address Lists   If you enable this option, the group is not visible in the GAL.

Send Out-of-Office Messages To Originator   Users of Exchange clients can configure rules that enable the clients to automatically reply to messages received while the users are away from their offices. When this option is enabled, users who send messages to groups can receive those automatic out-of-office messages from members of the list. For particularly large groups, it's best not to allow out-of-office messages to be delivered because of the excess network traffic they generate.

Send Delivery Reports to Group Owner   If you enable this option, notification is sent to the owner of the group whenever an error occurs during the delivery of a message to the group or to one of its members. Note that this option is unavailable if the group has not been assigned an owner.

Send Delivery Reports to Message Originator   If you enable this option, error notifications are also sent to the user who sent a message to the group.

Contacts

A contact is a pointer object that holds the address of a non-Exchange mail recipient. Contacts are made visible in the Global Address List and, therefore, permit Exchange clients to send messages to non-Exchange mail users. This functionality assumes that the necessary connector or gateway is in place between the Exchange system and the foreign system.

Creating a Contact

Like other objects, contacts are created using the Active Directory Users and Computers tool. When creating a contact, you must be prepared to select the type of e-mail address to create and to enter the foreign e-mail address. The standard options for the types of foreign addresses are as follows:

- cc:Mail address
- Microsoft Mail address
- MacMail address (this is Microsoft Mail for AppleTalk)
- Internet address
- X.400 address
- Other address

Exercise 4.5 walks you through the creation of this type of recipient.

EXERCISE 4.5

Creating a Contact

1. Click Start, point to Programs, point to Administrative Tools, and select Active Directory Users and Computers.

2. From the Action menu, point to New, and select Contact.

3. Enter the full name and display name of the user for whom you want to create a contact object, and then click Next.

4. Make sure the alias is correct, and then click Modify.

5. From the list of address types in the New E-Mail Address dialog that appears, select the type of e-mail address you want to create for the user, and click OK.

6. On the General page of the Internet Address Properties dialog that opens, enter the e-mail address for the user.

7. Switch to the Advanced page to override the Internet Mail Service default settings for the user and configure your own message format settings. When you are done, click OK.

8. You are now returned to the Exchange Task Wizard, and the new e-mail address appears in the appropriate field. Click Next to go on.

9. A summary screen is now displayed asking you to confirm your choices. If you want to change any of the settings, you can use the Back button to do so. Once you are satisfied with your choices, click Finish to exit the Wizard and create the new contact object.

Properties of a Contact

The properties of a contact are very similar to those of a standard Exchange mailbox. The main difference is that the attributes dealing directly with the capabilities or restrictions of a mailbox are not available. For example, you cannot set storage limits on a contact since there is no storage on the Exchange server to limit. Additionally, you cannot configure protocol settings for a contact.

Public Folder Recipients

A public folder is a sharable container of information. It is a recipient object because, in addition to being able to view information in it, users can send information to it.

Like mailboxes, public folders are created and stored on a specific home server. But because users on different servers and in different sites could need access to that public folder, public folders can be configured to be copied automatically to other Exchange servers. This is called *replication*, and each copy of the same public folder is called a *replica*.

While the other recipients are created from Active Directory Users and Computers, public folders are created and managed using either a Microsoft Exchange client application (like Outlook) or through the Exchange System Manager snap-in. All properties of a public folder are available for management within System Manager, and many are also available using an Exchange client. This allows users to take over much of the management of public folders.

The creation and configuration of public folders is covered in Chapter 5.

Basic Management of Recipient Objects

Even after they have been created, recipient objects still require care from administrators. Some of the basic management activities are as follows:

- Using templates for recipient creation
- Filtering a recipient
- Finding a recipient
- Moving a mailbox
- Using address lists

Each of these activities is covered briefly in the following discussions.

Using Templates for Recipient Creation

A *template* is a pattern that can be used to more efficiently create something—in this case, a recipient object. A template recipient, or multiple template recipients, can be created with the desired default values. These default values can then be used when creating actual recipient objects.

Any object can be used as a template. A simple method is to create an object, such as a user, that holds all of the default attribute settings you desire. Once the template is created, use it by highlighting it and then selecting the Copy command from the Action menu of the Active Directory Users and Computers tool. The New Object Wizard will open, just as when you create a new object, except that all of the default information configured in the template will already appear in the new object. The exception is that no matter what type of template object is used, the first name, last name, display name, alias name, directory name, and e-mail address are not copied to the new recipient objects created from the template.

When you create a recipient to use as a template, you probably will want to hide the recipient from the address book using the template's Exchange Advanced property page. This way, users won't be able to view it in the GAL. You will always be able to see it in Active Directory Users and Computers, though. You should also name your template in such a way that it is both easy to find and easy to distinguish from regular recipients. For example, you might name all of your templates with a dollar sign ($) or underscore (_) at the beginning so that they all appear at the top of the list.

Filtering a Recipient

By default, all types of recipients are shown when you select the Users container, including public folders. You can filter that view with the View menu so that only select types of recipients are shown. Filtering your recipient view can be useful if you are looking for a specific recipient and the list based on recipient type is not very long, or if you need to select all the recipients of a certain type.

In addition to using the View menu, you can also apply more advanced filters that let you view sets of objects according to selected attribute settings. To apply a filter, select the Users container in Active Directory Users and Computers, and choose Filter Options from the View menu. This opens the Filter Options dialog shown in Figure 4.7.

FIGURE 4.7   Filtering recipients

The default setting is to view recipients of all types. Click the Show Only The Following Types Of Objects option, and check the types of recipients you want to view. When you click OK, only the recipients of those types are displayed in the Users container. The Filter Options dialog also lets you specify how many recipients should be displayed per folder.

The filter options you set apply to the entire Active Directory hierarchy, not just the Users container. This means that if you set the filter to show only users and groups, for example, no computers will show up in your Computers folder until you reset the filter.

Finding a Recipient

Active Directory Users and Computers provides a recipient search tool with sophisticated search criteria. Open this tool by selecting the Find command in the Action menu. This command opens the Find Users, Contacts, And Groups window, shown in Figure 4.8.

FIGURE 4.8 Finding a recipient

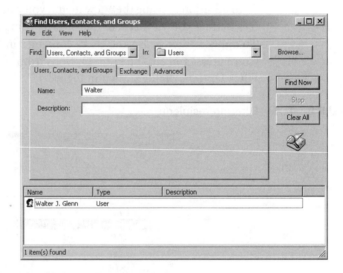

Use the Find field to specify what types of objects you want to find. The default is to find users, groups, and contacts. Use the In field to specify the container in which you want to perform the search. The default is to search in the Users container. Enter any part of a name or description, and click Find Now to begin the search. The Find window is expanded to display the results. You can manipulate objects in the Find window just as you would in the main Active Directory Users and Computers window by right-clicking them to access their shortcut menus.

There are also a few advanced options you can use to narrow down your search. The Exchange tab in the Find window lets you specify that you only want to view Exchange recipients in your search results and even lets you set the specific types of recipients you want displayed.

Moving a Mailbox

Physically, mailboxes and their contents reside on their home server. Mailboxes can be moved to other servers or to other mailbox stores on the same server.

This is done through Active Directory Users and Computers. Simply highlight the user whose mailbox you want to move, and select the Exchange Tasks command from the Action menu. On the first screen, select the Move Mailbox option. The Exchange Tasks Wizard will then step you through choosing a new server and storage group for the mailbox. When you finish the Wizard, the mailbox is moved.

When moving mailboxes, the size of the mailbox can increase. When a message is sent to multiple recipients in the same storage group, Exchange stores only one copy of the message on the server and gives all the recipients on that server a pointer to that single copy. This is called *single-instance storage*. But when a mailbox is moved outside of the storage group, the single-instance storage for that mailbox is lost in the new location because each message must be copied there. For example, suppose 10 mailboxes take up 55MB of disk space in the Private Information Store. Each mailbox has five messages of 1MB and a pointer to five single-instance messages of 1MB. If those 10 mailboxes were moved to another server, the single-instance storage would be lost, and each mailbox would have 10MB of storage. The Private Information Store on the new server would increase by 100MB.

Mailboxes might be moved for several reasons:

- To balance the load between servers

- To move mailboxes to a server that is on the same local area network as the mailbox owners

- To take a server down for maintenance reasons and still allow users access to their mailboxes

Because groups and contacts are primarily logical entities, they do not need to be moved and, therefore, cannot be moved.

Using Address Lists

Users on your network normally search for other users using the Global Address List (GAL), which contains all messaging recipients in an organization. If your network contains a large number of recipients, searching through the GAL for a specific recipient can become a daunting task. Fortunately, you can configure your own address lists that limit the scope of recipients included in the list.

Microsoft
✓ *Exam*
Objective

Create and manage address lists.

- Create security groups.
- Create distribution groups.

See the sections, "Users" and "Groups," that appear earlier in this chapter for coverage of the "Create security groups" and "Create distribution groups" subobjectives.

Default Address Lists

Exchange 2000 comes with several default address lists built in. When a user opens their address list in a client application, they can choose which address list to view. Table 4.1 shows the default address lists.

TABLE 4.1 Default Address Lists in Exchange 2000

Address List	Contains
All Contacts	All mail-enabled contacts in the organization.
All Groups	All mail-enabled groups in the organization. These include both security and distribution groups.
All Users	All mailbox-enabled and mail-enabled users in the organization.
Public Folders	All mail-enabled public folders in the organization that are not hidden from the address list.
Default Global Address List	All recipients in the organization.

Custom Address Lists

Exchange 2000 also lets you create your own custom address lists based on most of the fields available on recipient objects. For example, you could create an address list that showed only the users based in a certain city or in a certain department. Address lists are created in the Recipients container in System Manager, as shown in Figure 4.9.

FIGURE 4.9 Viewing address lists in System Manager

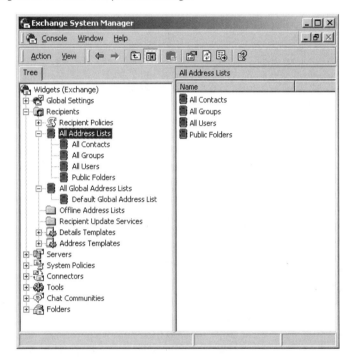

All address lists must be created inside other address lists. To create a top-level address list, create it inside the All Address Lists list. Since address lists can be nested, you can get pretty sophisticated in creating an address list structure. For example, suppose you wanted all of your users to be able to find one another easily by location. You might first create an address list called By Location. Within that, you could create a separate address list for each country in which your company is located. Within each of those country-based address lists, you could create a separate list for each city and, within those, for each building. Figure 4.10 shows a hierarchy like this example.

FIGURE 4.10 Creating nested address lists

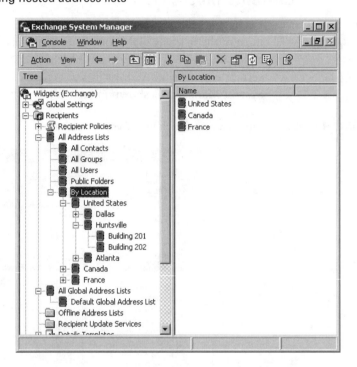

 Nesting address lists also provides a way to hide address lists from users. You can deny access to an address list by denying the user the Open Address List permission on the list's Security property page. However, this only prevents the user from viewing the contents of the list, not from viewing the list itself. The way around this is to create an empty address list and deny the Open Address List permission on that list. Name this list whatever you like. Then, create any address lists you want to be hidden from view inside this address list.

When you create a new address list, a dialog box opens that lets you name the list and set up filter rules that define the recipients contained in the list. You can set up the filter rules when you create the list or go back and do it later by opening the property pages for the list. If you are creating a nest of address lists, we often find it helpful to go ahead and create the structure by simply creating and naming the lists and then going back later to set up the filter rules.

You create filter rules using an interface much like the one used for finding recipients in Active Directory that we discussed earlier in the chapter (see Figure 4.11). Use the General tab of this dialog box to choose the types of recipients you want included on the list. Use the Storage tab to specify the server on which mailboxes or public folders are stored. Use the Advanced tab to restrict membership on the list by selecting criteria for specific fields for a recipient, such as their city, department, or any custom attribute.

FIGURE 4.11 Setting up filter rules for an address list

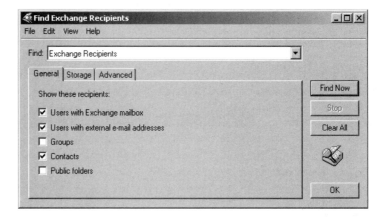

Offline Address Lists

Offline address lists are typically used by people who are not always connected to the Exchange network. Offline address lists are copies of online address lists that are stored on a user's local computer using an OAB extension. By default, the Default Global Address List is used to generate a Default Offline Address List. You can also create custom offline address lists by right-clicking the Offline Address Lists container in System Manager (refer to Figure 4.9) and choosing New Offline Address List. When creating the new offline address list, you will specify the list's name, a server that will store the new list, and any address lists (default or custom) that will be used to generate the new offline address list.

Recipient Update Service

The Recipient Update Service (RUS) is a component of the System Attendant service that is responsible for building and maintaining address lists. RUS polls Active Directory for updated recipient information on a predefined schedule (every one minute, by default) and updates address lists based on any new information. The RUS is also responsible for updating the e-mail addresses of any recipients that are attached to a recipient policy. Recipient policies are covered in Chapter 9.

The Recipient Update Services container in System Manager is shown in Figure 4.12.

FIGURE 4.12 Viewing RUS objects in System Manager

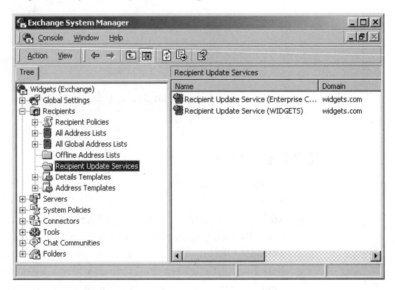

By default, two RUS objects are created:

- The Recipient Update Service (Enterprise Configuration) object updates the e-mail addresses of objects in the configuration partition of Active Directory. This includes objects such as the Information Store, MTA, and System Attendant.

- One Recipient Update Service (installation Active Directory domain) object exists for each Active Directory domain that contains an Exchange server. This RUS object updates the e-mail addresses for recipients found in the domain partition of Active Directory, including users, groups, public folders, and contacts. This RUS object also updates address lists based on changes to recipient objects in a domain.

Even though the RUS runs automatically, you can also update address lists manually using one of the following two commands available by right-clicking a specific address list:

- The Update Now command updates the address list with any new changes in recipient information.

- The Rebuild command rebuilds the entire membership of the address list.

In addition, you can modify the parameters of the RUS object itself by right-clicking it and choosing Properties. The following four properties are available:

- The domain serviced by the RUS. This is not directly modifiable.

- The server in the domain responsible for generating and updating address lists for the domain.

- The Windows 2000 domain controller that the server connects to for updated Active Directory information.

- The update interval at which the RUS will run. The Run Always option sets the RUS to run at its default—every one minute.

Summary

Recipients are Active Directory objects that are used to reference resources that can receive messages. The four main types of recipients are as follows:

- Users

- Groups

- Contacts

- Public folders

A user is an Active Directory object that usually represents a person with an Exchange mailbox. A mailbox-enabled user has an associated mailbox in a Private Information Store on an Exchange server. Each user mailbox is a private storage area that allows an individual user to send, receive, and store messages. A mail-enabled user is one who has an e-mail address and can receive, but not send, messages.

A group is a container into which you can place other recipients. Recipients in a group automatically inherit that group's permissions and rights. Exchange uses mail-enabled groups to form distribution lists. Messages sent to a group are redirected and sent to each member of the group. These groups allow users to send messages to multiple recipients without having to address each recipient individually.

A contact is a pointer to an e-mail address for a non-Exchange recipient. Contacts are most often used for connecting your organization to foreign messaging systems, such as Microsoft Mail, Lotus cc:Mail, or the Internet. As an administrator, you would create contacts so that frequently used e-mail addresses are available in the Global Address List as real names.

A public folder contains information that is shared among a group of people. Public folders can contain e-mail messages, forms, word-processing documents, spreadsheet files, and files of many other formats.

With the exception of public folders, all recipient objects are created and managed using the Active Directory Users and Computers utility. When you create a new user, you are automatically given the chance to create a mailbox for that user. You can also create mailboxes for existing users. Contacts and groups are usually made mail-enabled when they are created.

Recipient objects are mostly configured with property pages, which are groups of attributes that pertain to the object. Other Exchange-related tasks can be accessed through the Exchange Tasks command in the Action menu of Active Directory Users and Computers.

Public folders are created and managed using either an Exchange client or the System Manager snap-in for Exchange.

Key Terms

Before you take the exam, be certain you are familiar with the following terms:

alias	public folder
contact	recipients
deleted item retention time	security group
distribution group	simple display name
group	single-instance storage
mailbox	storage limits
mailbox-enabled user	template
mail-enabled user	user

Review Questions

1. A user named Aaron leaves your company. Management would like a user named Bobbi to assume Aaron's responsibilities. What could you do so that Bobbi can receive Aaron's e-mail messages? Select the best answer.

   A. Make Bobbi's mailbox an alternate recipient for Aaron's mailbox.

   B. Disable Aaron's user account, and give Bobbi profile permission to access Aaron's mailbox.

   C. Delete Aaron's mailbox, and forward all undeliverable messages to Bobbi.

   D. Create a rule in Aaron's mailbox so that all of Aaron's mail is forwarded to Bobbi.

2. You want to allow all of the personnel in the technical support group to send and receive messages from the same mailbox. What can you do to enable this?

   A. Create a distribution group, and designate the mailbox as the owner of the distribution group.

   B. Designate each technical support person as an owner of the mailbox.

   C. Allow each technical support person to send messages on behalf of the mailbox.

   D. Configure each technical support person's account as the primary Windows 2000 account for the mailbox.

3. You have become aware that a few of your users have signed up for a daily newsletter that often attaches large files to their messages. You would like to prevent this from happening with these users. What is the best way to do this?

    A. Configure delivery restrictions for the user that block messages from the message sender.

    B. Configure delivery restrictions for the user that only allow messages from within the Exchange system and from select originators outside the system.

    C. Configure a size limit on messages that may be sent to these users.

    D. Configure a storage limit on these users' mailboxes.

4. You configure a three-day deleted item retention for all deleted items in a particular user's mailbox. You perform a full backup on the server every Tuesday night. What can you do to allow the user to recover deleted e-mail messages after the retention period expires?

    A. Use the Delivery Options button on the Exchange General page for the user to configure items not to be deleted until the store has been backed up.

    B. Use the Storage Limits button on the Exchange General page for the user to configure items not to be deleted until the store has been backed up.

    C. Use the Storage Limits button on the Exchange Advanced page for the user to configure items not to be deleted until the store has been backed up.

    D. Use the Storage Options button on the Exchange Features page for the user to configure items not to be deleted until the store has been backed up.

5. What does the Delete Mailbox Storage right allow a person to do?

    A. Delete items from a mailbox.

    B. Delete a mailbox from a Private Information Store.

    C. Delete a Private Information Store from a storage group.

    D. Delete a storage group from a server.

6. You have a distribution group with a large number of members. Whenever messages are sent to that distribution group, the server experiences high CPU utilization. What could you do to minimize the performance loss on your server?

    A. Remove all unnecessary address spaces from all recipients.

    B. Move all members into their own recipients container.

    C. Specify another server as the expansion server.

    D. Move all recipients to another server.

7. On what user object property page would you find the command for configuring delivery restrictions?

    A. Exchange General

    B. Exchange Features

    C. Exchange Delivery

    D. Exchange Advanced

8. You need to move 10 mailboxes to another server. Each mailbox has five unique messages of 1MB each. Each mailbox also has five single-instance messages of 1MB each. After you move the mailboxes to the new server, how will the size of the Private Information Store on the new server change?

    A. The Private Information Store will increase by 55MB.

    B. The Private Information Store will increase by 100MB.

    C. The size will not increase.

    D. The size will decrease.

9. What is the default limit on the size of outgoing messages from a mailbox?

   A. 2MB

   B. 8MB

   C. 15MB

   D. It is the same as the limit set at the Information Store level.

   E. There is no default limit.

10. Which of the following foreign e-mail address types are automatically generated for a user object? (Choose all that apply.)

    A. X.400

    B. SMTP

    C. Lotus Notes

    D. OfficeVision

11. Which of the following protocols cannot be disabled at the individual mailbox level?

    A. POP3

    B. NNTP

    C. IMAP4

    D. LDAP

12. Which of the following statements is true?

    A. Protocols can be enabled or disabled for individual mailboxes.

    B. Protocols can be enabled or disabled for individual mailboxes if the default setting for the Information Store object is to enable the protocol.

    C. Protocols can be enabled or disabled for individual mailboxes if the default setting for the Information Store object is to disable the protocol.

    D. Protocols cannot be enabled or disabled for individual mailboxes.

13. Betty, a sales executive, is going away for vacation. Carl, her assistant, will be taking care of her office while she is away.

Required results:

Carl must be able to read and respond to Betty's e-mail.

Carl should not be required to log on to Betty's computer.

Optional result:

E-mail that Carl sends for Betty should make it clear that he is sending the mail for her.

Proposed solution:

Open the recipient object for Carl's mailbox in Active Directory Users and Computers. On the Exchange General property page, click the Delivery Options button. Add Betty's mailbox to the list of mailboxes for which Carl is an alternate recipient. Switch to the Exchange Advanced property page, and assign Carl the Send As permission for Betty's mailbox.

Which of the results does the proposed solution produce?

A. The proposed solution produces both the required results and the optional result.

B. The proposed solution produces both the required results, but does not produce the optional result.

C. The proposed solution does not produce the required results.

14. Betty, a sales executive, is going away for vacation. Carl, her assistant, will be taking care of her office while she is away.

Required results:

Carl must be able to read and respond to Betty's e-mail.

Carl should not be required to log on to Betty's computer.

Optional result:

E-mail that Carl sends for Betty should make it clear that he is sending the mail for her.

Proposed solution:

Open the recipient object for Betty's mailbox in Active Directory Users and Computers. On the Exchange General property page, click the Delivery Options button. Add Carl's mailbox to the list of users who can send mail on behalf of Betty. Also specify that Carl's mailbox should be an alternate recipient for Betty's mailbox.

Which of the results does the proposed solution produce?

A. The proposed solution produces both the required results and the optional result.

B. The proposed solution produces both the required results, but does not produce the optional result.

C. The proposed solution does not produce the required results.

15. Your company has hired an outside marketing agency to create marketing materials. Many of your employees often need to e-mail messages to people in this marketing agency. Since both the marketing agency and your network have Internet access, Internet e-mail seems the best method. However, you want to set it up so that the people in the marketing agency appear in the Exchange Global Address List. What type of recipient object would you configure to achieve this?

A. Mailbox

B. Mail-enabled user

C. Contact

D. A mailbox with a foreign owner

16. Which of the following permissions allows a user to read and send messages using a mailbox?

    A. Send As

    B. Full

    C. Mailbox Owner

    D. Change

17. In a native-mode organization, where can a mailbox be moved to?

    A. Only to other databases in the same storage group

    B. Only to other storage groups on the same server

    C. Only to other servers in the same routing group

    D. To any server in the organization

18. Which of the following statements is true regarding security and distribution groups?

    A. Only a security group can be mail-enabled.

    B. Only a distribution group can be mail-enabled.

    C. Both types of groups can be mail-enabled.

    D. Neither type of group can be mail-enabled.

19. Which of the following types of objects can a distribution group contain? (Choose all that apply.)

    A. User

    B. Group

    C. Contact

    D. Public Folder

20. Which of the following tools can you use to manage a public folder's properties? (Choose all that apply.)

A. Outlook 2000

B. Active Directory Users and Computers

C. Public Folder Manager

D. System Manager

Answers to Review Questions

1. A. Making Bobbi's mailbox an alternate recipient ensures that both mailboxes receive a copy of all messages sent to Aaron's mailbox. Creating a rule in Aaron's mailbox that forwarded mail to Bobbi would also work, but would require more configuration on your part.

2. B. Only a user with Mailbox Owner permissions can send messages from a mailbox.

3. A. The default delivery restrictions are to accept messages from everyone and reject messages from nobody. You can enter specific originators from whom you would like to block messages for individual users.

4. B. To prevent excessive build-up of deleted items, Exchange allows you to set a retention time for deleted items. That length of time can be configured on this page or at the Information Store (IS) object. The IS default value will be used, but you can configure a mailbox to override that setting by specifying the number of days for deleted item retention. You can also configure a mailbox to keep deleted items (i.e., not permanently deleted items) until the mailbox has been backed up. This is configured on the Exchange General page for a user via the Storage Limits button.

5. B. The Delete Mailbox Storage right allows a user to delete the actual mailbox from the Information Store. This right is only given to administrators by default.

6. C. Whenever a message is sent to a group, the group must be expanded so that the message can be sent to each member of the group. The Message Transfer Agent Service of a single Exchange server performs this expansion. The default choice is Any Server In Site. This choice means that the home server of the user sending the message always expands the group. You can also designate a specific server to handle the expansion of the group. The choice of a dedicated expansion server is a good one if you have a large group.

7. A. Delivery restrictions, delivery options, and storage limits for an object are all configured through the object's Exchange General property page.

8. B. Each mailbox has five messages of 1MB and a pointer to five single-instance messages of 1MB. If those 10 mailboxes were moved to another server, the single-instance storage would be lost, and each mailbox would have 10MB of storage. The Private Information Store on the new server would increase by 100MB.

9. D. By default, all storage limits set at the Information Store level are used for individual mailboxes.

10. A and B. Microsoft Exchange automatically generates foreign addresses for Lotus cc:Mail, Microsoft Mail, SMTP, and X.400.

11. D. LDAP is the only protocol that may not be disabled for individual mailboxes.

12. B. Protocols can be enabled or disabled for individual mailboxes, but only if the protocol is enabled at the Information Store level.

13. C. You cannot configure any properties for Betty's mailbox using the recipient object for Carl's mailbox. In addition, The Send As permission would let Carl send mail as if it were coming directly from Betty, which does not meet the required results.

14. A. Adding Carl to Betty's Send On Behalf Of list gives Carl the ability to send mail that looks like it comes from Betty, but also has Carl's name on it. This satisfies the optional result. Assigning Carl's mailbox as an alternate recipient for Betty's mailbox satisfies the required results, since Carl can use his own computer to receive and respond to Betty's mail.

15. C. A contact is a pointer object that holds the address of a non-Exchange mail recipient. Contacts are made visible in the Global Address List and, therefore, permit Exchange clients to send messages to non-Exchange mail users.

16. C. Only a user with Mailbox Owner permission can send messages using a mailbox.

17. D. Mailboxes and their contents reside physically on their home server. Mailboxes can be moved to other servers or to other mailbox stores on the same server. This is done through Active Directory Users and Computers.

18. C. Any type of group can be mail-enabled.

19. A, B, C, D. A distribution group can contain any other type of recipient object, including other distribution groups.

20. A, D. Both Outlook and System Manager can be used to create public folders. Each utility can also be used to manage certain properties of public folders.

Chapter

5

Using Public Folders

MICROSOFT EXAM OBJECTIVES COVERED IN THIS CHAPTER:

✓ **Create, configure, and manage a public folder solution.**

- Configure the Active Directory object attributes of a public folder.
- Configure the store attributes of a public folder.
- Configure multiple public folder trees.

✓ **Configure and manage system folders.**

✓ **Manage public folder connectivity.**

- Configure and monitor public folder replication.
- Diagnose and resolve public folder replication problems.

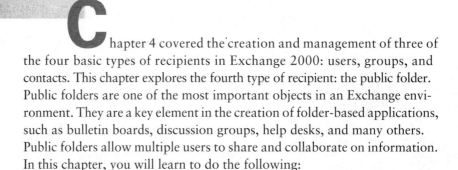

Chapter 4 covered the creation and management of three of the four basic types of recipients in Exchange 2000: users, groups, and contacts. This chapter explores the fourth type of recipient: the public folder. Public folders are one of the most important objects in an Exchange environment. They are a key element in the creation of folder-based applications, such as bulletin boards, discussion groups, help desks, and many others. Public folders allow multiple users to share and collaborate on information. In this chapter, you will learn to do the following:

- Create public folders.

- Configure public folders.

- Use public folders.

- Manage public folders.

An Overview of Public Folders

Public folders provide centralized storage for almost any type of information, including mail messages, electronic forms, documents from other applications, and even Web pages.

Thus, public folders can be used to provide a number of advantages to your users:

- A public folder can serve as a forum where users can participate in threaded discussion forums with other users, similar to Internet newsgroups. In fact, public folders can even be used to provide your organization with access to Internet newsgroups.

- Public folders can provide a centralized storage area for documents for different groups or projects in your organization.

- Public folders can store data for custom-designed workflow applications and, since public folders are exposed via Exchange's new Installable File System, they can store data for standard applications, as well.

- Public folders can store Web pages that are delivered to browsers via the Internet Information Server service.

Public Folder Configuration

The configuration of public folders in Exchange 2000 happens in two places. Public folders can be created using either the System Manager snap-in or a *MAPI client* such as Microsoft Outlook. System Manager and Outlook are used in the following respects to manage public folders:

- System Manager is used to configure the public folder store of an Exchange server and server-related aspects of individual public folders.

- Outlook is used to configure aspects of public folders such as permissions and electronic forms associated with the folders.

The reason why much of the public folder creation and management occurs in the Outlook client is that public folders are often used for workflow applications, and because most users work solely in the Outlook client, the administration of public folders was developed to reflect the application with which a user works.

Public Folder Storage

When you first install Exchange, a single *public folder tree* named *All Public Folders* is created. In previous versions of Exchange Server, an organization was stuck with only this default tree. In Exchange 2000 Server, you can create multiple public folder trees that appear alongside the All Public Folders tree. Each public folder tree uses a separate database on an Exchange server.

While having multiple public folder trees sounds great, there is a catch: MAPI clients like Outlook can only access the default public folder tree. The following types of clients can access the default public folder tree, but they are also the only ones that can access any additional trees that may have been created:

- Applications such as Microsoft Word and Excel

- Web browsers

- Windows Explorer

- NNTP clients

The actual procedures for creating and using new public folder trees is covered later in this chapter.

An Exchange organization can host multiple public folder trees. A public folder tree is organized hierarchically, like a directory structure (see Figure 5.1). The root, or highest level, of a tree is called the top level, and folders created here are called *top-level folders*. By default, all users may create folders at this level, but the System Manager snap-in can be used to modify the list of users who have permissions to create top-level folders. It is important to have this administrative control so that users don't clutter up the root of the tree and make it difficult to navigate.

FIGURE 5.1   Public folder hierarchy

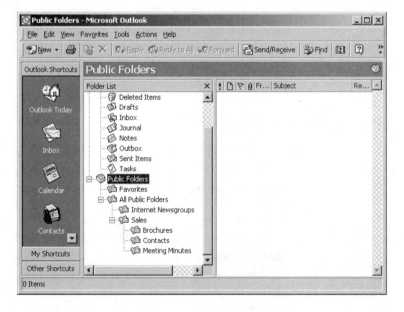

All public folders are created in the public folder store of a particular Exchange server. Any Exchange server that has a public folder store can host a public folder. In a typical organization, some folders exist on one server, others on another server, and so on.

When a user creates a top-level public folder, it is placed in the Public Information Store on that user's home server. When a user creates a lower-level public folder, it is placed in the Public Information Store of that new folder's parent folder. In addition, each individual public folder can be replicated to other servers in the organization. As you can see, this situation could get complicated. Public folders in the same tree may exist on different servers, and some public folders have instances on multiple servers.

A public folder is actually considered to have two parts. The first part is the public folder content—the actual messages inside the public folder. The second part is that folder's place in the *public folder hierarchy*. The contents of a public folder exist on a single server, unless you specifically configure the content to be replicated to other servers.

To ensure that information about public folders is distributed throughout the Exchange system, the Active Directory maintains a public folder hierarchy for each public folder tree, which is a single hierarchical structure that contains information about all the public folders in that tree. This hierarchy is automatically made available to every Exchange user in the organization.

Public Folder Web Access

Exchange dynamically creates a URL for each item in the Information Store. This means that users can access any piece of Exchange information, including mailboxes, messages, and public folders, from a standard Web browser. You can access the contents of any public folder using a simple address like `http://servername/public/foldername`.

Each public folder also has an HTML page associated with it. When you create a folder, Exchange automatically creates a default HTML page. You can replace the automatically generated Web page with a custom page, or you can change the URL to point to another Web site. You can gain access to all of the contents in a folder by accessing the folder container or by accessing a dynamically generated URL. This functionality is provided by Internet Information Server, whose integration with Exchange is discussed in detail in Chapter 2.

Public Folders and Active Directory

Every public folder in a public folder store can appear as a mail recipient in the Global Address List. You can mail-enable a public folder by right-clicking it in System Manager, pointing to All Tasks, and selecting Mail Enable from the shortcut menu.

After a public folder is mail-enabled, the Exchange System Attendant service connects to Active Directory and creates an object for the public folder in a container named Microsoft Exchange System Objects in Active Directory Users and Computers.

System Folders

System folders are special public folders that are hidden by default and are only accessible through the System Manager snap-in (see Figure 5.2). You can view them by right-clicking the Public Folders container and selecting View Hidden Folders from the shortcut menu.

Microsoft ✓ *Exam* *Objective*

Configure and manage system folders.

FIGURE 5.2   Viewing system folders

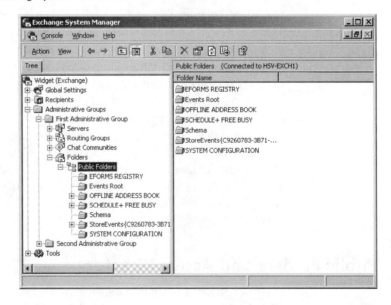

System folders contain items that facilitate the capabilities of many Exchange clients, such as collaborative scheduling in Outlook. For the most part, you will want to leave these folders alone. Much of their functionality is configured through other areas in the System Manager. Nonetheless, it may be helpful to know what a few of the folders are used for:

- EFORMS Registry contains the organization forms library created for an organization. This library is used when Outlook users create new electronic forms for messages and public folders.

- Events Root contains objects for the configuration of event information on Exchange servers.

- Offline Address Book contains a subset of the Global Address List that remote users can download and use for addressing mail when they are not connected to the Exchange server.

- Schedule+ Free/Busy contains objects that support the scheduling capabilities of Exchange clients.

- Schema contains objects related to the Windows 2000 Active Directory Schema.

- StoreEvents contains objects for the configuration of event information that specifically relates to the Information Store service.

- SYSTEM CONFIGURATION contains objects related to the configuration of the Exchange server.

Managing Public Folders with Outlook

Microsoft Outlook 2000 can be used to create public folders and perform a certain degree of public folder management. You can also use previous versions of Outlook, the Microsoft Exchange Client, and certain generic mail clients (specifically IMAP4 clients) to create public folders, but these applications may not provide the same level of management as Outlook 2000. Because the procedures for creation are fairly similar, this section focuses only on the use of Outlook 2000 in working with public folders.

Microsoft
✓ *Exam*
Objective

Create, configure, and manage a public folder solution.

- Configure the Active Directory object attributes of a public folder.
- Configure the store attributes of a public folder.
- Configure multiple public folder trees.

More detailed coverage of the topics associated with these subobjectives can be found throughout this chapter.

Creating Public Folders in Outlook

Creating folders in Outlook 2000 is simple. Just make sure that the All Public Folders object (or the folder in which you want to create a new folder) is highlighted, and select the New Folder command from the File menu. The process for creating a new folder is outlined in Exercise 5.1.

EXERCISE 5.1

Creating a Public Folder in Outlook

1. Start Outlook.

2. Make sure that the public folder tree is showing by selecting the List command from the View menu.

3. In the List view, expand the Public Folders item.

4. To create a top-level folder, select the All Public Folders object. You can also select another folder in which you want to create a subfolder.

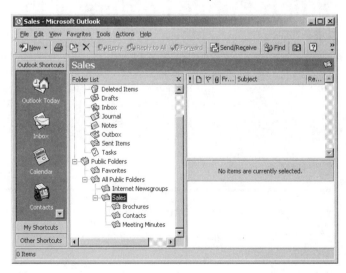

5. With a public folder selected, choose New Folder from Outlook's File menu. This opens the Create New Folder dialog box.

6. Enter the name of the public folder you want to create and the type of items the folder should contain, and select the folder in which the new folder should be created. The default folder is the one that was selected when you issued the New Folder command.

7. Once everything is set, click OK to create the new folder.

8. Assuming you have the appropriate permissions to create a folder in the chosen location (and, by default, all users can create folders wherever they want), the folder is created and may be accessed by other users immediately. Keep in mind, though, that it may take some time for the public folder hierarchy to replicate itself through-out Active Directory, so it may take some time before all users can see the folder in their lists.

Configuring Public Folders from Outlook

After a public folder is created, it is managed using both Outlook and System Manager. Because users can create public folders with Outlook, it is advantageous to allow them certain managerial responsibilities, which is why part of the management occurs in the client.

When a user creates a public folder, that user automatically becomes the folder's owner. The owner is responsible for the folder's basic design, which includes access permissions, rules, and the association of electronic forms. To perform these management tasks, the user can simply open the property sheets for a particular public folder in Outlook. Public folders can also be managed to a degree from within System Manager (discussed later), but the Outlook option means that the user has only a single application with which to be concerned.

The key configuration elements of public folders in Outlook are as follows:

- Permissions

- Forms

- Rules

- Views

These elements are managed through a set of property pages that are used for configuration. There are two ways to display these property pages. One way is to highlight the public folder, click the right mouse button, and choose Properties from the pop-up menu that appears. Another way is to highlight the public folder, and then choose Folders ➤ Properties for *<public folder name>* from the File menu.

Permissions

By assigning permissions, a public folder owner can choose which users have access to the folder and what actions those users may perform. There are eight individual permissions and nine groupings of permissions, called *roles*, that can be assigned. Table 5.1 describes these permissions, descending from the permission with the most capabilities to the permission with the fewest capabilities. The word "items," as used in this table, refers to the contents of the public folder, such as e-mail messages, forms, documents, and other files. Table 5.2 lists the predefined groupings of permissions according to role.

TABLE 5.1 Public Folder Permissions

Permission	Description
Folder Owner	Can change permissions in a folder and perform administrative tasks, such as adding rules and installing forms on a folder.
Create Items	Can create new items in a folder.
Create Subfolders	Can create subfolders within a folder.
Edit Items	Can edit (modify) items in a folder.
Delete Items	Can delete items in a folder.
Read Items	Can open and view items in a folder.
Folder Contact	Receives e-mail notifications relating to a folder. Notifications include replication conflicts, folder design conflicts, and storage limit notifications.
Folder Visible	Determines whether the folder is visible to the user in the public folder hierarchy.

Outlook 2000 uses a number of legacy permissions held over from Windows NT 4. If you configure public folder permissions using Outlook, Exchange 2000 automatically configures the corresponding Windows 2000 permissions for you.

TABLE 5.2 Predefined Roles and Their Permissions

Role	Folder Owner	Create Items	Create Subfolder	Edit Items	Delete Items	Read Items	Folder Contact	Folder Visible
Owner	✓	✓	✓	✓ (all)	✓ (all)	✓	✓	✓
Publishing Editor		✓	✓	✓ (all)	✓ (all)	✓		✓
Editor		✓		✓ (all)	✓ (all)	✓		✓

TABLE 5.2 Predefined Roles and Their Permissions *(continued)*

Role	Folder Owner	Create Items	Create Subfolder	Edit Items	Delete Items	Read Items	Folder Contact	Folder Visible
Publishing Author		✓	✓	✓ (own)	✓ (own)	✓		✓
Author		✓		✓ (own)	✓ (own)	✓		✓
Nonediting Author		✓			✓ (own)	✓		✓
Contributor		✓						✓
Reviewer						✓		✓
None								✓

Custom roles consisting of any combination of individual permissions may also be assigned.

When a public folder is created, the following three users are included on the permissions list by default (see Figure 5.3):

The user who created the public folder This user is automatically assigned the Owner role. In Figure 5.3, the owner of the folder is the Administrator account. The owner of a folder may also grant other users this role.

A special user named Default This user represents all users who have access to the public folder store but aren't explicitly listed in the permissions list. In top-level folders, the Default user is automatically granted the Author role (this can be modified). The Author role enables users to create subfolders under the top-level folder. Below the top-level folders, the Default user automatically inherits the permissions it has at its parent folder.

A special user named Anonymous The Anonymous user represents all users logged on with Anonymous access. For example, an Exchange server could contain public folders holding promotional information for public viewing. People without user accounts could use a Web browser or newsreader program and the Anonymous account to access the Exchange server and read the promotional information. Any permissions assigned to the Anonymous account are applied to these users.

FIGURE 5.3   The Permissions property page of a public folder

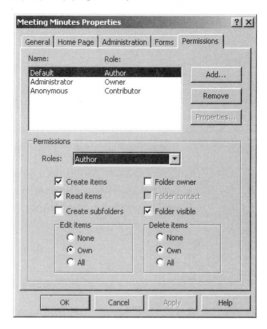

These three users cannot be removed from the permissions list of a public folder. However, the particular roles and permissions they have can be modified. All other users can be removed from a permissions list.

Exchange administrators can always designate themselves as the owners of public folders. This is especially important if the recipient who is the owner of a public folder (or all Windows 2000 accounts that are on the permissions list of that recipient) is deleted.

Exercise 5.2 outlines the steps to configure the permissions on a public folder.

EXERCISE 5.2

Configuring the Permissions on a Public Folder

1. In Outlook, highlight the public folder. Click the right mouse button, and choose Properties from the pop-up menu. The Properties dialog box for the folder appears.

2. Click the Permissions tab. Notice the permissions given to the Default user. The Default user is given the Author role by default for top-level folders and whatever permissions it has for the parent folder of all other folders. Notice also that the user who created this public folder has the Owner role.

3. Highlight the Default user, and then click the down-arrow in the Roles field. Choose the None role from the list.

4. Click Add, and highlight a new user from the list. Next, click Add, and then click OK. The user is added to the access list for the public folder with the role of None. This role was automatically assigned because the Default user's role is None.

5. Change the new user's role to Author. Notice that the new user now has the Create Items and Read Items permissions. This role also allows the user to edit and delete the user's own items.

6. Click OK to save the configuration.

Hiding Public Folders

Public folders can be hidden from the GAL and the public folder hierarchy. Hiding public folders can be part of your security plan.

Hiding a public folder from the GAL   By default, each public folder is hidden from the GAL. A public folder can be made visible by clearing the Hide From Exchange Address Lists check box found on its Exchange Advanced property page.

Hiding a public folder from the public folder hierarchy By default, all public folders and their contents are visible in the public folder hierarchy to all other recipients. To hide the contents of a particular public folder, you must revoke the Read Items permission for the recipient or recipients at that particular folder. If you wanted to hide not merely the contents of a public folder, but also its very listing in the hierarchy, you can revoke the Read Items permission for the parent folder of the folder you want hidden. Since a subfolder is considered part of the contents of its parent folder, revoking this permission at the parent folder can prevent the viewing of that sub-folder in the hierarchy.

Many times, an organization will create a top level called Hidden Folders that will contain all the folders they want hidden from the majority of their users. The Default user will be assigned the None role for Hidden Folders, which will prevent them from viewing all subfolders. Even the top-level folder Hidden Folders could be made invisible by revoking the Folder Visible permission from the Default user. To enable the users who do need to access the subfolders under this root, distribution lists would be created and assigned the relevant permissions at this root and any subfolders.

Forms

Forms can be associated with a public folder, allowing users to submit structured data into the folder. The list of forms associated with a public folder is found in the folder's property pages. Exercise 5.3 walks through the steps to associate a form with a public folder.

EXERCISE 5.3

Associating a Form with a New Public Folder

1. In Outlook, highlight the public folder in the hierarchy in the Folder List. Choose File ➢ Folders ➢ Properties to open the Properties dialog box for the folder.

EXERCISE 5.3 *(continued)*

2. Click the Forms tab. Notice that there are currently no forms associated with this public folder, but that the Allow These Forms In This Folder field is set to Any Form. You are going to associate a specific form with this folder and configure it as the only form to be used with this folder.

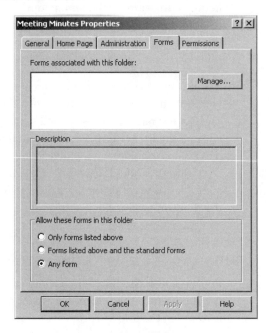

3. Click the Manage button. The Forms Manager appears, listing the forms published in the Organization Forms library.

4. Click a form, and then click Copy. If the form was already installed, all you have to do now is click Close. Otherwise, you'll be walked through some extra steps for installing the form. Notice that the form is now associated with this public folder.

5. Under the Allow These Forms In This Folder field, choose Only Forms Listed Above, then click OK. The form installation performed in this exercise will be tested in the upcoming section "Using Public Folders."

Rules

Rules consisting of conditions and actions can be configured on public folders. Rules allow a public folder to automate certain procedures. The following is a list of some of the conditions (or *criteria*) that can be used in a rule:

From   A message from specified recipients

Sent To   A message sent to specified recipients

Subject   Specified text in the Subject heading of a message

Message Body   Specified text or phrase in the body of a message

Size   A specified size of a message, "At least x size" or "At most x size"

Received   A specified date range that a message was received within

The following actions can be triggered if the preceding conditions are met:

Delete   Delete the message.

Reply With   Reply to the message's sender with a specified message template.

Forward To   Forward the message to specified recipients.

A rule could be used, for example, to keep postings separate from replies. If a company had a public folder named Company Events containing information on upcoming company events, users could be given permission to provide feedback on these events by sending replies to this folder. However, the number of replies in this folder could hinder users from finding the original events posting. To resolve this, the owner of this folder could create a subfolder called Discussions. The owner could then create a rule for Company Events that states that all replies to this folder should be forwarded to the Discussion folder. For this example to work, the preceding folders must be visible in the GAL.

Rules are added to public folders by clicking the Folder Assistant button on a folder's Administration property page. Clicking this button displays the Folder Assistant dialog box, which enables you to add, edit, delete, and order rules for a public folder. Exercise 5.4 outlines the steps involved in creating a rule on a public folder.

EXERCISE 5.4

Creating a Rule on a Public Folder

1. In Outlook, highlight the public folder. Click the right mouse button, and choose Properties from the pop-up menu. The Properties dialog box for the folder appears.

2. Click the Administration tab.

3. Click the Folder Assistant button. The Folder Assistant dialog box appears.

4. Click Add Rule. The Edit Rule dialog box appears. In the Subject field, type a word that should appear in the subject, and type the same word again in the Message Body field. This is the condition part of the rule and stipulates that any message that contains the chosen word in the subject or body of the message fits the criteria.

5. Now set the action part of the rule. Click the Forward check box, and then click To. The Choose Recipient dialog box appears. In the Show Names from The field, choose Global Address List.

6. Choose the user you want to automatically forward the message to, and then click the To button.

7. Click OK, and then click OK on the next three dialog boxes. The rule is now saved within the properties of the public folder.

Views

Outlook includes many powerful features to view items in a folder. Some of the features in Outlook are listed in Table 5.3.

TABLE 5.3   Outlook Features for Viewing Folder Items

Feature	Examples
Sort	Order items by sender, recipient, importance, subject text, sensitivity, or other properties.
Filter	Filter items by words or phrases contained in the subject text or message body, sender, recipient, what time they were sent, or other properties. Only items that pass through the filter are displayed in the Contents pane.

TABLE 5.3 Outlook Features for Viewing Folder Items *(continued)*

Feature	Examples
Group By	Group items by when they are due, sender, recipient, importance, subject text, sensitivity, or other properties.

Using Public Folders

This section and its exercises cover how to add content to a public folder. The three primary methods to add content to a public folder are as follows:

- Posting forms
- Sending e-mail messages
- Saving documents with an application

Posting

If a public folder is configured to accept postings, which is the default, users who have the necessary permissions can post data to the public folder. To post, a user must highlight the public folder and either click the Post tool on the toolbar or choose New Post In This Folder from the Compose menu. Posting is an easy and efficient method of adding content to a public folder, because the user does not have to address the message as they do when sending a mail message to a public folder. Exercise 5.5 outlines the steps for this procedure.

EXERCISE 5.5

Posting Information to a Public Folder

1. In Outlook, highlight the public folder.

2. Choose File ➢ New ➢ Choose Form. The New Form dialog box appears.

3. Highlight the appropriate form, and click OK. The form appears.

4. Enter a name in the Full Name field.

5. Enter a company name in the Company field, if you want to.

6. Enter some text in the body.

EXERCISE 5.5 *(continued)*

7. Click the More Info tab to view the page you designed. Enter some information.

8. When you are finished entering information, click the Save And Close toolbar button.

9. Notice the new entry in the public folder. If you double-click that entry, you will see the information you just entered.

Mail Messages

A mail message can be sent to a public folder. As you may recall, a public folder is a recipient and, therefore, can receive and send messages. Exercise 5.6 outlines the steps to send a mail message to a public folder.

In order for someone to send a mail message to a public folder using their client's address book, the public folder must be visible in the address book. By default, public folders are not visible in the address book. To perform this exercise, you must make the public folder visible.

EXERCISE 5.6

Sending a Mail Message to a Public Folder

1. In the System Manager snap-in, find and highlight the public folder in the All Public Folders container. Click File ≻ Properties. The folder's property pages appear. Click the Exchange Advanced tab. Notice the check box labeled Hide From Exchange Address Lists. It is checked by default. For this exercise, clear this check box. Click OK. This public folder is now visible in the address book.

2. In Outlook, choose Compose ≻ New Message. An untitled mail-message window appears.

3. Click To. In the Show Names From The field, choose Global Address List. Find the public folder in the Global Address List.

4. Select the public folder, click the To button, and then click OK.

5. Type an appropriate subject in the Subject field.

6. Type some information in the body of the message.

7. Click the Options tab. In the Importance field, choose High. For Tracking options, choose Tell Me When This Message Has Been Read.

8. Click the Send tool in the toolbar.

Saving from Applications

Another method of adding content to a public folder, made possible by the new Installable File System (IFS) in Exchange 2000, is simply to save a document from just about any application that can save to disk. Important pieces of the Exchange Web Store are exposed to the file system as the M: drive on each Exchange Server computer (the M: drive is used by default; see the upcoming sidebar "Changing the IFS Drive to Another Drive Letter"). You can use the Save dialog from most applications to browse to that drive and save documents in the public folders accessible there. You can also drag and drop a document directly into the folder using Windows Explorer.

Changing the IFS Drive to Another Drive Letter

By default, Exchange 2000 Server uses drive M: as the drive for the IFS. If you are willing to edit the Windows 2000 Registry, however, you can change the drive letter used. Be sure you follow the Registry Editor's instructions for backing up the Registry before you make any changes. Use the following procedure to change the drive letter used by IFS:

1. Start the Registry Editor by selecting Run from the Start menu and typing **regedt32.exe** in the Run field.

2. Select the following key in the Registry: HKEY_LOCAL_MACHINE\SYSTEM\CurrentControlSet\Services\EXIFS\Parameters.

3. On the Edit menu, select the Add Value command and add the following information for the new value:

   • Value Name: DriveLetter

- Data Type: REG_SZ

- Value: *<whatever drive letter you want to use>*

4. Exit the Registry Editor.

5. Restart the computer.

Managing Public Folders with System Manager

The System Manager snap-in provides a second way to create public folders and also provides many configuration options that are different than those available from within Outlook. In addition, Outlook cannot be used to create top-level folders in the hierarchy; only System Manager can be used for that.

Microsoft ✓ *Exam Objective*

Create, configure, and manage a public folder solution.

- Configure the Active Directory object attributes of a public folder.

- Configure the store attributes of a public folder.

- Configure multiple public folder trees.

Creating Public Folders in System Manager

In previous versions of Exchange Server, you could only create public folders using an Exchange client such as Outlook. Fortunately, Exchange 2000 Server has added that capability to the System Manager snap-in, offering Exchange administrators an easier way to create and manage public folders using only one tool. Exercise 5.7 outlines the steps for creating a public folder using System Manager.

EXERCISE 5.7

Creating a Public Folder in System Manager

1. Expand the public folder tree in which you want to create a new folder. If you have not created additional trees beyond the All Public Folders default tree, then expand that default tree.

2. If you want to make a top-level folder, select the tree object itself. Otherwise, navigate through the tree, and select the folder in which you want to create the new subfolder.

3. From Outlook's Action menu, select the New Public Folder command. This opens the property pages for the new public folder.

EXERCISE 5.7 *(continued)*

4. In the Name field, enter a name for the new public folder.

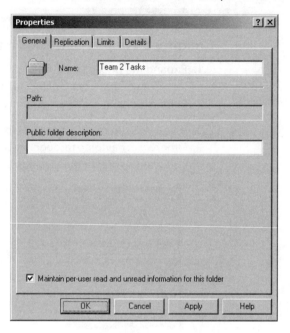

5. Optionally, type a description for the public folder that will appear in the Global Address List.

6. Click the OK button to create the new public folder. The folder will immediately be available to users.

Mail-Enabling a Public Folder

Once you have created a new public folder, you may still need to mail-enable the folder and configure mail-related settings if you want the public folder to be able to receive e-mail messages. If you choose not to do this, users will only be able to post messages using a MAPI client.

Microsoft ✓ Exam Objective

Create, configure, and manage a public folder solution.

- Configure the Active Directory object attributes of a public folder.

In *mixed-mode* Exchange organizations (those supporting both Exchange 2000 and Exchange 5.5), folders created in the default public folder tree are mail-enabled by default and cannot be disabled. By default, these folders are also hidden from the Global Address List. Folders created in any additional public folder trees (also referred to as *general-purpose trees*) are not mail-enabled by default. If they become mail-enabled, the default setting is to make them visible in the GAL. In *native-mode* Exchange organizations (those running only Exchange 2000), all folders in the default tree and any general-purpose trees are not mail-enabled by default. If any folder in any tree is made mail-enabled, it becomes visible in the GAL by default.

To mail-enable a folder, select the folder in System Manager and choose All Tasks ➤ Mail Enable from the Action menu. The command should take effect immediately, although you will get no feedback from System Manager after executing it. Once you have mail-enabled a folder, that folder's property sheet shows several extra mail-related property pages, including Exchange General, E-Mail Addresses, and Exchange Advanced. These property pages work the same as the similar property pages for other recipients and allow you to perform functions like setting delivery options and restrictions, changing the display name and alias, and setting custom attributes. Since Chapter 4 provides detailed coverage of performing these actions on other types of recipients, we refer you to that chapter for the specifics.

Latency Issues with Public Folder Hierarchy and Content

One Exchange 2000 Server service (the Public Folder Replication Agent) manages the replication of public folders while another service (the System Attendant) manages the listing of public folders in the Global Address List. Because of this segregated management, you may notice a number of latency issues, especially when working with large public folder trees. These issues include the following:

- You may sometimes notice that public folder trees appear differently when managed from two different servers. This is usually because changes to the public folder hierarchy have not yet been replicated to all servers.

- Users may see the public folder hierarchy in their MAPI client, but not be able to see the individual public folders in their address book until both services have replicated their information.

- Certain properties may appear incorrectly (or not at all) in System Manager because the replication of the hierarchy has taken place faster than the directory information.

Configuring Public Folders in System Manager

No matter how you create a public folder, it becomes accessible to users almost immediately, using the default configurations. As you saw earlier in the chapter, a good bit of public folder configuration is available from within the Outlook client so that users can take on some of the administrative burden of creating and maintaining public folders. However, there is also a good bit of configuration available for public folders that can only be accomplished using the System Manager snap-in.

Within System Manager, public folders are managed at two distinct levels. The first is at the level of the public folder store, where you will configure settings governing how the public folder store should handle public folders in general. The second is at the level of the public folder itself, where you will configure properties that control certain aspects of the folder and often override settings made at the store level.

Configuring Public Folder Store Properties

The public folder properties managed at the level of a public folder store govern the default settings for all public folders in that store. As with most other objects, the settings for the public folder store are managed through property pages. Each public folder store exists on a specific server. The Public Folder Store object is found inside the container for that server in System Manager (see Figure 5.4). To access the store's property pages, right-click the Public Folder Store object, and select Properties from the shortcut menu.

Microsoft ✓ *Exam* *Objective*

Create, configure, and manage a public folder solution.

- Configure the store attributes of a public folder.

FIGURE 5.4   Viewing the public folder store

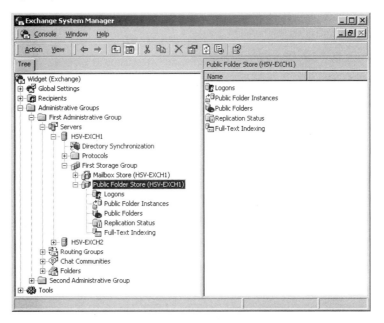

Most of the property pages for the public folder store are used to control the replication of public folders to other Exchange servers. These pages, and replication itself, are discussed later in the chapter. The one property page that is important now is named Limits, shown in Figure 5.5.

When a user deletes a message from a folder, that message is marked as hidden and is actually kept on the server for a certain number of days before being permanently deleted. Within that period, called the *deleted-item retention time*, the user can recover the item. To do so, however, the user must be using Microsoft Outlook 8.03 or a later version. (Outlook 2000, which is actually version 9, ships with Exchange 2000 Server.) Simply set the number of days that you want to keep deleted items on the server. The default setting is 0. In addition, you can specify that items not be permanently removed from the Information Store until at least one backup has occurred.

You can also use the Limits property page to set a default storage limit for public folders in a public folder store. This storage limit represents a size (in kilobytes) that the public folders can reach before a storage warning is issued to the folders' contacts. You can override this storage limit at the folder level for individual folders, as you see a bit later in the chapter.

FIGURE 5.5 The Limits property page for the public folder store

Public Folder Store (HSV-EXCH1) Properties

| Full-Text Indexing | Details | Policies | Security |
| General | Database | Replication | Limits |

Storage limits

☑ Issue warning at (KB):   10000

☑ Prohibit post at (KB):   15000

☐ Maximum item size (KB):

Warning message interval:

[Use custom schedule ▼]   [Customize...]

Deletion settings

Keep deleted items for (days):   7

☑ Do not permanently delete items until the store has been backed up

Age limits

☑ Age limit for all folders in this store (days):   6

[OK]   [Cancel]   [Apply]   [Help]

The final limit that you can set on the Limits property page is the default number of days for which items are kept in the public folders for the public folder store. The default is no *age limit* at all.

NOTE Public folder age limits work in combination with deleted-item retention time. Suppose that you set a 10-day age limit on your public folders and a 6-day deleted-item retention period. An item is deleted on day 9—one day before it would automatically expire. The deleted-item retention period starts at this point. If the item is recovered within the deleted-item retention period, the age limit for the newly recovered item is reset to add 10 more days.

Examining Public Folder Store Subcontainers

The Public Folder Store container in System Manager (refer to Figure 5.4) has a number of subcontainers that offer valuable information about your public store and the folders inside:

- The Logons container provides information about who is logged on and using public folders.

- The Public Folder Instances container lets you view the folders in a public store, configure properties of a folder (discussed in the next section), and configure replication of a folder (discussed later in the chapter).

- The Public Folders container provides details such as the path, size, and number of items inside the public folders in the store.

- The Replication Status container lists all folders and the number of servers that contain a replica of each folder. It also lists the current replication state and the time of the last replication. Replication of public folders is discussed later in the chapter.

- The Full-Text Indexing container shows the current state of the indexing of public folders in the store. This is covered in Chapter 8.

Configuring Public Folder Properties

Public folders are also managed at the individual folder level in the System Manager snap-in. This management is performed using the property pages of the folders themselves. As with the public folder store property pages, a number of the property pages for the folder deal with replication, which is discussed later. The two pages that are germane here are the General and Limits pages.

Microsoft ✓ *Exam* *Objective*

Create, configure, and manage a public folder solution.

- Configure the Active Directory object attributes of a public folder.

General Properties

The General property page, shown in Figure 5.6, lets you change the description of the folder that appears in the GAL. You'll also find an option named Maintain Per-User Read And Unread Information For This Folder. If you select this option, then the folder itself will keep track of and mark as read messages that each individual user of the folder has read. If a folder has been mail-enabled, as mentioned previously, another important setting is added to the General page. The Address List Name field governs whether you want the name that is visible in address books to be the same as the public folder name or a different name that you can enter.

FIGURE 5.6 Setting general properties for a public folder

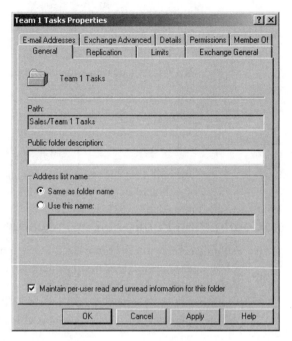

Limits Properties

The Limits property page, shown in Figure 5.7, defines messaging limits for the public folder. You can define the following limits on this property sheet:

- Storage limits indicate the amount of disk space, in kilobytes, a folder can take up before a warning is issued to the folder's owner. This setting works the same way that the setting at the public folder store level works, as discussed previously. Any settings made at the public folder level override settings made for the server.

- Deletion settings define the number of days that deleted messages are retained in the folder before being permanently removed. You can use the default defined for the public folder store level or override those settings for this particular folder.

- Age limits set the maximum amount of time in days that a message remains in this public folder before it expires, or you can use the defaults set at the public folder store level.

FIGURE 5.7   Setting messaging limits for a public folder

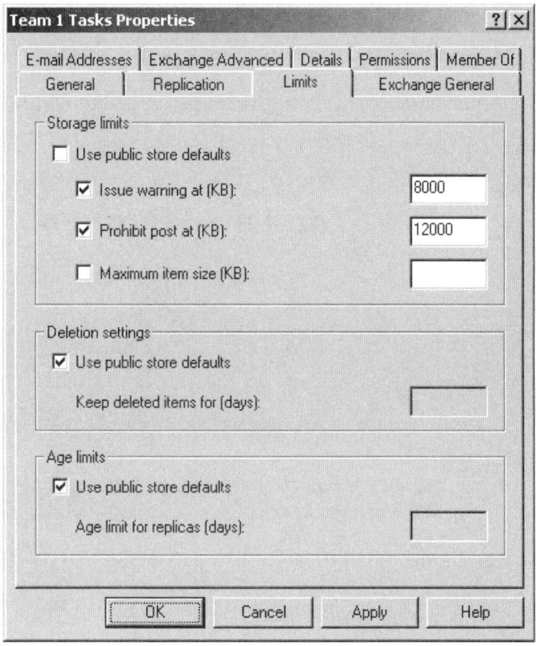

Creating New Public Folder Trees

Unlike previous versions of Exchange, Exchange 2000 Server allows the creation of more than one public folder tree structure. You could, for example, create separate public folder tree structures for different departments of the company. You could also create a public tree for a specific project. This helps you to better organize your public folders and more efficiently delegate authority over those folders. Keep in mind, though, that MAPI clients like Microsoft Outlook will only be able to view information in the default tree for the organization. For users to see other trees, they must use clients such as Web browsers or newsreaders.

Microsoft Exam Objective

Create, configure, and manage a public folder solution.

- Configure multiple public folder trees.

There are three steps to creating a new public folder tree. First, you will create a new top-level root folder that will house the new tree structure. Second, you will create a new public folder store on the server to hold the new tree structure. Finally, you will connect the new top-level folder to the new public folder store. This last step can be performed during the creation of the public folder store or later.

Creating a New Top-Level Root Folder

The first step in creating a new public folder tree is to create a new top-level root folder. Each top-level root folder exists on the same level as the public folder tree and uses its own database on each Exchange server that contains replicas of any of the folders in the tree's hierarchy. Exercise 5.8 outlines the steps for creating a new top-level root folder.

EXERCISE 5.8

Creating a New Top-Level Root Folder

1. First, open the System Manager snap-in, and highlight the Folders container for the administrative group in which you want to create the folder. If you only have one administrative group, or if you have System Manager set not to display administrative groups, the Folders container should appear directly under the root node. Otherwise, you will need to drill down into the appropriate administrative group.

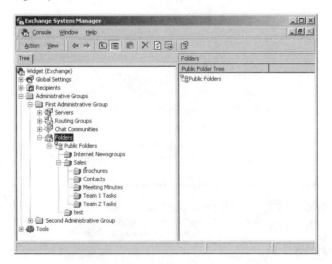

EXERCISE 5.8 *(continued)*

2. Next, choose New Public Folder Tree from the Action menu. This opens the Properties dialog box for the new folder.

3. Enter a name for the new tree in the Name field of the General property page.

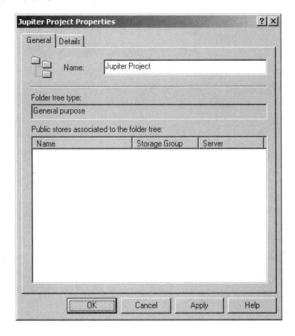

4. Once you are finished, click OK to close the property sheet and create the new public folder tree.

Creating a New Public Folder Store

Public folders reside in a Public Information Store. Each public folder tree uses its own database in the store. Once you create the new top-level root folder for a tree, you must then create a new public folder store to hold that tree. Exercise 5.9 outlines steps for creating a new public folder store.

EXERCISE 5.9

Creating a New Public Folder Store

1. In System Manager, locate and select the container for the storage group on the server on which you want to create the new tree. You will create the new public folder store in this storage group.

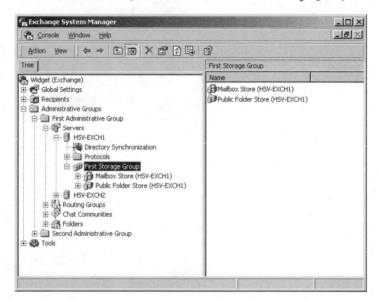

2. Once you have selected the storage group, choose New Public Store from the Action menu. This opens the Properties dialog box for the new store.

3. Enter a name for the new store in the Name field of the General property page.

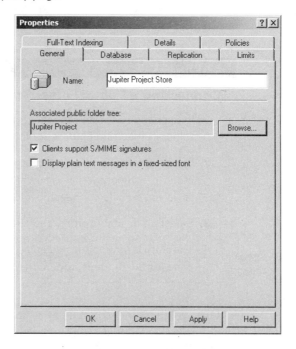

4. Click the Browse button to open a dialog that lets you associate the new store with a public folder tree. In the dialog, select the tree you created previously. If you choose not to do this now, you can connect the tree and the new store later following the procedure outlined in the next section.

5. Once you are finished, click OK to close the property sheet.

6. System Manager prompts you to mount the new store once it has been successfully created. Click Yes to mount the new store.

Connecting a New Top-Level Folder to a New Public Folder Store

If you created a new public folder store but did not associate it with the public folder tree during the process, you can do so later. Exercise 5.10 outlines the steps involved in this process.

EXERCISE 5.10

Connecting a Public Folder Tree to Its Store

1. In Exchange System Manager, find and select the top-level root folder in the main Folders container.

2. Once the folder is selected, choose Connect To from the Action menu. This opens a dialog in which you can select the public folder store you want to connect the folder to from a list of available stores.

3. Select an available store, and click OK.

4. The store is now connected and is listed on the Public Store property page for the top-level root folder.

Once you have created and connected a new public folder tree, another thing you may want to do is set permissions governing which users can make changes to the root level of that tree. To do that, just open the property sheet for the top-level folder, and switch to the Security property page. By default, only the Domain and Exchange Administrators groups have permissions to modify the root level. Click the Add button to select additional users to whom you want to grant permissions.

Creating Dedicated Public Folder Servers

A *dedicated public folder server* is an Exchange server that is used to store public folders and has no mailboxes. Dedicating a server for this purpose can increase client access to public folder data and can make for a more central backup strategy.

Implementing a dedicated public folder server involves the following steps:

1. Move public folders to the designated server. This can be done via replication, which is discussed later in the chapter.

2. If there are any mailboxes on the designated public folder server, they must be moved to another server or mail-disabled. Techniques for performing these actions are discussed in Chapter 4.

3. Remove any mailbox stores and unneeded storage groups from the server by right-clicking them and choosing Delete from the shortcut menu. For protection, you will not be allowed to delete any mailbox store that still has mail-enabled mailboxes in it.

Dedicated public folder servers can be an appropriate part of an Exchange environment when there are large amounts of public folder data and you need to offload processing and disperse the workload. Dedicated servers also provide for a more central backup strategy.

Public Folder Replication

Public folders can be copied to other Exchange servers. Each copy of a public folder is called a *replica*. Each replica contains the same information as the original public folder, but resides on a different Exchange server. Replicas can reside in the same routing group as the home server of the original public folder, and they can reside on servers in different routing groups.

Microsoft
✓ *Exam*
Objective

Manage public folder connectivity.

- Configure and monitor public folder replication.

- Diagnose and resolve public folder replication problems.

Reasons for using public folder replicas include the following:

Load balancing If a large number of users access a particular public folder, access times could be slow. A solution is to create public folder replicas and disperse user access to the various replicas.

Fault tolerance   Having a public folder replicated eliminates a single point of failure.

Easier access for remote users   If routing groups are geographically separated and users are accessing public folders in a remote group, it can make sense to distribute those public folders to the other routing groups through the use of replicas. This can be especially useful when users in one routing group are accessing public folders in another routing group over an unreliable network connection. Creating replicas in each remote group would allow users to access the public folders on their own local networks.

The following is a scenario that could warrant the use of public folder replicas. Suppose your organization has four routing groups, each group consisting of two Exchange servers and 500 users. The four routing groups are connected with a 256KB wide area network (WAN). The available bandwidth during the workday is less than 64KB, while at night the available bandwidth is 128KB or more. You have created a public folder that contains 600MB of data that is not time critical. Users access that folder approximately every fifteen minutes, and the folder data is only updated twice a week. A good strategy would be to create a replica of that public folder on an Exchange server in each of the four routing groups.

Public folder replication follows the *multimaster replication model*, in which every replica of a public folder is considered a master copy. When you decide which folders you want to replicate, you manually create and configure those replicas. Any change made to a public folder is automatically replicated to other replicas of that folder by the Exchange *Public Folder Replication Agent (PFRA)* service based on settings you configure. Replication is a mail-based process that uses SMTP as its transport mechanism.

Creating Public Folder Replicas

The method for configuring replication involves pushing replicas from one public folder store to other public folder stores using the property pages of the public folder that you want to replicate. Exercise 5.11 outlines the steps for creating a replica of a public folder

EXERCISE 5.11

Creating a Replica of a Public Folder

1. In System Manager, open the property page of the public folder for which you want to create replicas, and switch to the Replication property page.

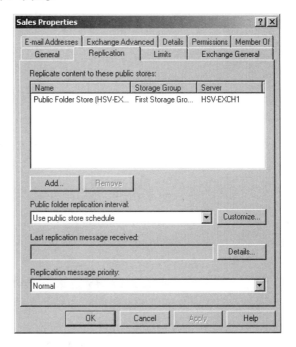

2. On this property page, you'll find a list of public stores that already contain a replica of the public folder. Click the Add button to open a dialog that contains a list of available public stores in your organization that do not already have replicas of the folder.

3. Select the store to which you want to replicate the folder, and click OK.

4. The public store is added to the list of stores that contain replicas. Below the list of public folder stores, you'll find a drop-down menu named Public Folder Replication Interval. Use this menu to schedule the replication of the public folder to the other public folder stores. You have several options here:

- The Never Run option turns off replication of the public folder, which is handy if you want to stop the replication temporarily to do something like troubleshoot a bad connector.

- The Always Run option essentially keeps replication going all of the time. As this would cause excessive traffic, it is generally a poor option to choose. However, there is one time when it is a useful option. When you first configure a new replica and you want the public folder content of that new replica to be transferred as soon as possible, you can turn on the Always Run option to ensure that the content will be replicated quickly. Be sure that you set the schedule to something more reasonable afterward, however.

- The Run Every 1, 2, Or 4 Hours options cause replication to occur at the defined intervals.

- The Use Custom Schedule option allows you to click the Customize button to bring up a dialog with a calendar of hours that you can use to set up the replication schedule.

- The Use Public Store Schedule option is the default setting and causes the folder to replicate according to the default replication schedule set for the public folder store to which the public folder belongs.

5. Click the Details button to bring up a dialog with information about the last replication message Exchange Server generated regarding the current public folder.

6. Use the Replication Message Priority drop-down list to set the priority that replication messages concerning this folder should take in your Exchange system.

Once you have created replicas of a public folder and configured how replication should behave at the folder level, you can also configure how replication should behave at the public store level. To do this, open the property page for the Public Folder Store object, and switch to the Replication property page, shown in Figure 5.8.

FIGURE 5.8   Configuring replication for a public folder store

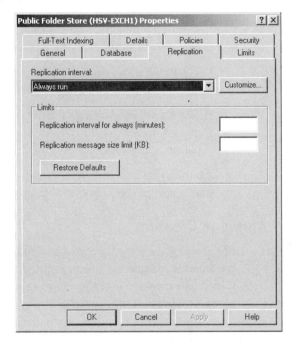

The first action you can perform on this page is to configure replication defaults that apply to all of the folders in that store. Do this using the same type of drop-down menu that you used to configure a schedule for the individual folder. If you do not specifically set a schedule for an individual folder (if you leave it at its default setting), the folder will use the schedule set for the public folder store to which the folder belongs. If you set a schedule for an individual folder, that schedule overrides the public folder store schedule.

The second action you can perform on the Replication property page is to define limits for replication. By default, no limits are defined, but you can specify the maximum time, in minutes, that replication is allowed to go on when replication occurs. You can also define the maximum size, in kilobytes, that a single replication message may be.

Synchronizing Replicas

The Public Information Store uses three primary constructs to keep track of replication throughout an organization and to determine whether a public folder is synchronized. These constructs include the following:

- A *change number* is made up of a globally unique identifier for the Information Store and a change counter that is specific to the server on which a public folder resides. When a user modifies (or creates) a message in a public folder, the PFRA for that Information Store assigns a new change number to the message.

- The PFRA also assigns a *time stamp* to messages as soon as they arrive in a public folder and a new time stamp whenever a message is modified.

- The *predecessor change list* for a message is a list of all of the Information Stores that have made changes to a message and the most recent change number assigned by each Information Store on the list.

Together, these constructs are referred to as *message state information* and play a role in message creation, deletion, and modification.

Message Creation

When a new message is created in a folder, the Information Store receiving the message assigns a change number to the message and deposits it in the folder. The message is replicated to other replicas of the folder during the normal replication schedule.

Message Deletion

When a message is deleted from a folder, the Information Store running the replica in which the message is deleted sends a replication message to all other Information Stores that host a replica of the folder. When each Information Store receives the replication message, it removes the deleted message from its own replica.

Message Expiration

When a message expires (reaches the configured age limit for messages in the folder), the Information Store deletes the message from the folder, but does not send a replication message to other Information Stores. Each Information Store removes expired messages from its own folders based on settings made for the store itself and for the folder. Thus, it is possible for different stores to expire a message at different times.

Message Modification

When a change is made to a message in one replica of a public folder, the PFRA for that Information Store updates the message state information for that message and sends a replication message to other Information Stores on which replicas of the folder exist. This replication message contains the modified messages and all of its attachments.

When another Information Store receives such a replication message, the modified message inside is used to replace the original message in that store if the message state information determines that the message is indeed newer than the original.

While the PFRA sends out replication messages, there is no mechanism in place for ensuring that replication messages reach their destination. The logic behind this is that generating an extra confirmation message for each replication message would unnecessarily double the amount of traffic involved in replication. Thus, it is possible for a message in different replicas of a public folder to become out of sync. A process known as *backfill* is used to remedy this situation. During regular maintenance, status messages are sent between servers, and change numbers for messages on different replicas are compared. If a server is found to be out of sync, it then generates a backfill request for any changes that have not yet been received.

Customizing Public Folders

Public folders can be turned into customized applications through the use of the *Microsoft Exchange Scripting Agent* and *Microsoft Exchange Event Service*. Each of these elements, plus the topics of security and Microsoft Outlook, are introduced in the following paragraphs.

Scripts

One of the properties that a public folder can have is a script written in Microsoft VBScript or Microsoft JScript. A script can contain the instructions for carrying out various actions. For example, a script could be created that would read the amount of a purchase request posted to a folder, compare that amount to a database containing the people with approval ability of various amounts, and then forward the posting to the appropriate person.

Microsoft Exchange Event Service and Event Sinks

The Microsoft Exchange Event Service is a component that monitors public folders containing scripts and provides backwards compatibility with Exchange Server 5.5. Exchange 2000 Server now uses *event sinks* both to watch for designated events to occur in folders and to serve as a trigger mechanism for scripts to be executed.

Microsoft Exchange Scripting Agent

The Scripting Agent is the component that reads and executes the script attached to the public folder. It can carry out instructions by accessing databases, spreadsheets, gateways, and many other programs and services.

Security

To create, edit, or save a script for a folder, the user must have the Author role set of permissions. This is done in the System Manager snap-in. In that program, under the System Folders object is an object called Events Root. The Events Root object contains a folder called EventConfig_<*server name*> that allows the administrator to assign the Author role to the users needing to create, edit, or save scripts. When a user has these permissions in the EventConfig folder, they will see the Agents tab when viewing the properties of a public folder through their client application.

Microsoft Outlook and Scripts

Microsoft Outlook enables users to create, edit, or save a script for a public folder. If a user has the necessary permissions, they can access the Agents property page of a folder. There they can create an agent or agents that define the events that will be the trigger mechanism for the script, and create or edit the script (Edit Scripts button). By default, Outlook will use Microsoft Notepad as the editor for the script. But if the user has Microsoft Visual InterDev installed, it also can be used as the editor.

For more information on these topics, see the Microsoft Platform Software Development Kit (SDK).

Summary

Public folders are an efficient and effective way to share data among several people. Permissions, forms, rules, and views can be configured on public folders to create folder-based applications. Users can easily create public folders and perform certain management functions using Outlook.

Permissions enable a folder owner to specify who can access a folder and what users can do in that folder. Associating a form with a public folder assists users in submitting structured information into the folder. Rules on public folders can perform automated actions when the appropriate conditions are met. Public folders can hold a large quantity and variety of information, so views can be leveraged to display the pertinent items in a desired way.

Adding content to public folders is very easy. It can be done by posting directly to a public folder, by sending the public folder regular e-mail messages, or by saving documents using a standard application.

Public folders can be created using the System Manager snap-in. In addition, System Manager offers many more management options than are available in Outlook. You can configure public folder–related settings at the level of the Public Information Store for a server and at the level of the individual server. Settings made at the folder level typically override settings made at the Public Information Store level.

Exchange 2000 now offers the ability to use multiple public folder trees. The default tree in an organization, named All Public Folders, is also referred to as a MAPI top-level hierarchy. This public folder tree can be accessed by any type of client, including MAPI, NNTP, and HTTP. Additional public folder trees are referred to as general-purpose trees and may not be accessed by MAPI clients such as Outlook. They can be accessed by other types of clients.

Each public folder is created on a single Exchange server, but replicas of that folder may be created on other servers. Once replicas are created, replication of folder content happens according to a predetermined schedule. Public folder replication follows the multimaster replication model, in which every replica of a public folder is considered a master copy.

Key Terms

Before you take the exam, be certain you are familiar with the following terms:

age limit	native mode
All Public Folders	predecessor change list
backfill	public folder hierarchy
change number	Public Folder Replication Agent (PFRA)
dedicated public folder server	public folder tree
deleted-item retention time	public folders
general-purpose trees	replica
MAPI client	roles
message state information	Rules
Microsoft Exchange Event Service	system folders
Microsoft Exchange Scripting Agent	time stamp
mixed mode	top-level folders
multimaster replication model	

Review Questions

1. A user named Perry is the owner of a public folder named Research. Perry leaves your company, and another administrator deletes Perry's user account. What would you as an administrator have to do to modify the permissions on the Research folder?

   A. Create a new account with the same user information as the deleted account.

   B. Restore a backup tape of the server that was created before Perry was deleted.

   C. Designate your account as the owner of the Research folder.

   D. Create a new public folder and move the contents of the Research folder to it.

2. You want to create a public folder hierarchy that has both visible and hidden folders. You have created a distribution group named HR that contains the users who do need to view the hidden folders. What would be an efficient way of providing the users who do need to view the hidden folder hierarchy with the ability to do that?

   A. Give the List permission to the HR distribution group at each hidden folder.

   B. Give the Folder contact permission to the HR distribution list at each hidden folder.

   C. Create a root folder that contains all the hidden folders. Revoke all permissions for the Default user. Give Folder Visible permission to the HR distribution group at the root of the hidden folder hierarchy. Ensure that the HR distribution group has the Read Items permission on each of the root's subfolders either explicitly or through the Default entry.

   D. Give the Create subfolders permission to the HR distribution group on each hidden folder.

3. You own a public folder named Company Events. Because of the large number of comments about the events sent as replies, users have a hard time distinguishing the original postings from the replies. You decide to create a subfolder named Discussions that you want to hold the replies to the Company Events postings. What is the most efficient way to ensure that all replies to Company Events go to the Discussions folder?

   A. Tell users to use the Discussions folder as a Cc recipient whenever they reply to Company Events.

   B. Configure a rule for Company Events that forwards everything to the Discussions folder except items from users who need to post company event items to the Company Events folder.

   C. Have all users add the Discussions folder to their Favorites folder.

   D. Configure Company Events to delete everything it receives.

4. Which of the following system folders contains Global Address List information downloaded by remote clients?

   A. Offline Address Book

   B. Schedule+ Free/Busy

   C. Address Lists

   D. System Configuration

5. Your organization has four routing groups, each group consisting of two Exchange servers and 500 users. The four groups are connected with a 256KB wide area network (WAN). The available bandwidth during the workday is less than 64KB. At night, the available bandwidth is 128KB or more. You have created a public folder that contains 600MB of data that is not time critical. Users access that folder only every fifteen minutes or so, and the folder data is updated only twice a week. On what servers should replicas be placed?

   A. On every server

   B. On one server in each group

   C. Only on the server where the public folder was originally created

   D. Only on domain controllers

6. Which of the following predefined public folder roles enables a user to delete items other than the items they created? (Choose all that apply.)

    A. Owner

    B. Reviewer

    C. Editor

    D. Publishing Author

7. You have replicas of a public folder configured on two servers in your organization. You configured the age limit of messages in the public folder store on the server hosting the original folder to be eight days before replicating the folder. One of the instances of the public folder seems to be expiring the messages right on schedule, but the other never does. You check the message logs on the server where the messages are being properly deleted, but find no replication messages regarding the expired messages. What could be the problem and solution?

    A. The Public Folder Replication Agent service is not running properly. Check the Services Control Panel applet to restart it.

    B. Your server is not set to log replication messages. Set it to log replication messages, and check the logs later.

    C. Expiration of messages is not replicated between replicas. You need to check the age limit configured on each replica individually.

    D. Expiration of messages is not supported in multiple replicas of a public folder.

8. You have a public folder that is used by your executive staff. Certain executive assistants are also given access to the public folder, but there are two subfolders in that public folder that the assistants should not be able to view at all. What must you do to hide the subfolders from particular recipients?

    A. Revoke the Read Items permission from those recipients at the parent folder.

    B. Revoke the Read Items permission from those recipients at the subfolders.

    C. Remove the Folder Visible permission from the subfolders for those recipients.

    D. Hide the subfolders from the Global Address List.

    E. A subfolder cannot be hidden, only its contents.

9. You are running an Exchange organization that consists of nine Exchange servers. Two of these servers are configured as dedicated mailbox servers and are running Exchange 2000 Server. Two servers are configured as dedicated public folder servers and are also running Exchange 2000 Server. One server is running Exchange Server 5.5 and is configured to operate connectors to several legacy gateway systems. You have just created a number of public folders in the default public folder tree for use by members of the sales staff. You do not want the folders to be mail-enabled, but System Manager does not allow you to disable them. What do you suspect is the reason for this?

    A. You can only change the mail-enabled status of a folder from Active Directory Users and Computers.

    B. You can only change the mail-enabled status of a folder from a MAPI client such as Outlook.

    C. Folders created in the default public folder tree in a mixed-mode organization may not be mail-disabled.

    D. You need to hide the folders from the Global Address List to mail-disable a folder.

10. The age limit on your public folders is set to 14 days. The deleted-item retention time is set to 7 days. A user deletes an item 12 days after it was created. That same user then recovers the deleted item 7 days later. How long will it be until the item expires?

   A. The item will expire immediately

   B. 2 days

   C. 5 days

   D. 14 days

11. In addition to a list of each of the Information Stores that have made changes to a message, which of the following items appear on a predecessor change list for a message? (Choose all that apply.)

   A. The last time stamp applied to the message by each Information Store on the list

   B. All of the time stamps applied to the message by each Information Store on the list

   C. The last change number applied to the message by each Information Store on the list

   D. All of the change numbers applied to the message by each Information Store on the list

12. Which of the following tools can you use to associate a form with a particular public folder? (Choose all that apply.)

   A. The property pages of the public folder in Outlook

   B. The property pages of the public folder in System Manager

   C. The property pages of the EFORMS System Folder in System Manager

   D. A separate utility called Electronic Forms Designer

13. What three users are included by default on the permissions list of a new public folder?

    A. The user who created the folder

    B. The local Administrator account

    C. A special user account named Default

    D. A special user account named Anonymous

    E. The Exchange Administrator account

14. One of your users has complained to you that he cannot create top-level folders using his Outlook client. Checking into it, you discover that he is using Outlook 98 on a computer running Windows NT 4 Workstation. Your Exchange organization is running both Exchange 2000 and Exchange Server 5.5. Which of the following may be the problem?

    A. Only Outlook 2000 supports the creation of top-level public folders.

    B. His computer needs to be upgraded to Windows 2000 Professional with Service Pack 1 in order for Outlook to support the creation of top-level folders.

    C. Top-level folders cannot be created from a client application when an Exchange organization is running in mixed mode.

    D. The user does not have the correct permissions to create top-level folders.

15. In a native-mode organization (one running only Exchange 2000), which of the following is true?

    A. All public folders created are mail-enabled by default.

    B. All public folders created are not mail-enabled by default.

    C. Only folders created in the default public folder tree are mail-enabled by default.

    D. Only folders created in the general-purpose public folder trees are mail-enabled by default.

16. You recently created a public folder that employees of your company can use to post personal announcements, such as marriages and births. You have now become aware that a number of people are also posting large attachments to messages in the form of photos or other documents. This is causing the public folder to swell considerably in size. People enjoy the Announcements folder, and you would like to keep it available. However, you want to keep users from posting large messages or attachments. What is your best option?

A. Set a limit on the size of messages that each user may send, using the property pages for that user.

B. Set a limit on the size of messages that can be posted in the public folder, using the folder's property pages.

C. Set a limit on the maximum size that a public folder can reach before new posts are prohibited, and then manually delete large posts.

D. Set a limit on the maximum size that a public folder can reach before new posts are prohibited, and then create a script that deletes large posts automatically.

17. Where in System Manager would you go to find out the current replication state of public folders on a server?

A. The property pages for that server

B. The property pages for the public folder

C. The property pages for the public folder store

D. The Replication Status subcontainer of the public folder store

E. The Public Folders subcontainer of the public folder store

18. Which of the following statements is true of public folder trees?

A. Each public folder store may have only one public folder tree.

B. Each public folder store may have only one default public folder tree, but up to five general-purpose trees.

C. Each public folder store may have only one default public folder tree, but any number of general-purpose trees.

D. Each public folder store may have any number of public folder trees.

19. When a public folder is mail-enabled, which Exchange service connects an object for the public folder to Active Directory?

    A. Microsoft Exchange Event Service

    B. Internet Information Server service

    C. System Attendant service

    D. Information Store service

    E. Public Folder Replication Agent (PFRA) service

20. You have just created a new public folder. Both the public folder and the public folder store use the default settings for age limits and deleted-item retention time. What would happen if a user deleted a message that was eight days old?

    A. The user would have four days to recover the message before it was removed from the server.

    B. The user would have seven days to recover the message before it was removed from the server.

    C. The user could not recover the message.

    D. The user could not delete the message because it would have already expired due to an age limit.

Answers to Review Questions

1. C. An administrator has the permission to change the owner of a folder. Once the administrator takes ownership of the folder, they can then perform administrative tasks, such as adding rules and installing forms.

2. C. The Folder Visible permission specifies whether the folder is visible to the user or group in the public folder hierarchy.

3. B. Rules consisting of conditions and actions can be configured on public folders. Rules allow a public folder to automate certain procedures.

4. A. The Offline Address Book folder contains a subset of the Global Address List that remote users can download and use for addressing mail when they are not connected to the Exchange server.

5. B. Since the folders are not accessed a great deal, there is really no need to have replicas configured on multiple servers in each routing group. However, because of the slow link speed during the day, it is important that at least one server in each routing group have a replica. Since there is more available bandwidth at night and since the public folder data is not time critical, you could also schedule replication to occur only at night.

6. A, C. Only the Owner, Editor, and Publishing Editor of a public folder can delete items other than their own. The Publishing Author, Author, and Nonediting Author can delete their own items only. All other roles cannot delete any items.

7. C. When a message expires (reaches the configured age limit for messages in the folder), the Information Store deletes the message from the folder, but does not send a replication message to other Information Stores. Each Information Store removes expired messages from its own folders based on settings made for the store itself and for the folder. You relied on the public folder store's age limit setting on the original instance of the folder, but the age limit might be set differently for the public folder store on the other server.

8. C. The only way to hide a folder from recipients altogether is to remove the Folder Visible permission from those recipients. Revoking the Read Items permission from the parent folder would render all items in the folder unreadable. For better security, it would also be a good idea to revoke the Read Items permission from the recipients. To simply hide the folder, however, this action is not necessary.

9. C. Folders created in the default public folder tree in a mixed-mode organization (one running Exchange 2000 and Exchange 5.5) are mail-enabled by default and may not be mail-disabled.

10. D. Since the item was recovered after the original expiration date, a new expiration date is set equal to the original expiration period. If the item had been recovered before the original expiration date, it would have then expired on the original expiration date.

11. C. A change number is made up of a globally unique identifier for the Information Store and a change counter that is specific to the server. When a message is modified, the Information Store updates the predecessor change list with the name of the Information Store and a change number. Only the last change number is listed in the predecessor change list.

12. A. You can only associate electronic forms with a public folder using Outlook. The EFORMS System Folder contains a library of forms that is used when associating a form in Outlook.

13. A, C, D. When a public folder is created, the user who created the folder is given the role of folder owner. The Default user represents all users who have access to the public folder store and aren't explicitly listed in the permissions list. The Anonymous user represents all users logged on with anonymous access.

14. D. Outlook can be used to create top-level folders in the default public folder tree, assuming the user has the correct permissions.

15. A. In a native-mode organization, all folders created in either the default public folder tree or any general-purpose trees are not mail-enabled by default. You can mail-enable any folder using System Manager.

16. B. The Limits property page for a public folder contains a number of settings that govern public folder limits. One setting allows you to specify the maximum size of messages that may be posted to the public folder. This is the best way to ensure that large posts are not made. Setting a limit on the size of the messages that users may send would also restrict the sending of regular e-mail messages. Deleting posts, whether done manually or automatically, may be considered intrusive and arbitrary by users.

17. D. The Replication Status container lists all folders and the number of servers that contain a replica of each folder. It also lists the current replication state and the time of the last replication.

18. A. Though a single server may host multiple public folder trees, a separate public folder store must be created for each tree.

19. C. The System Attendant is responsible for creating objects in the Active Directory for mail-enabled public folders.

20. C. No age limit or deleted-item retention time is set by default. This means that the age of the message in question would have no effect on deleting or recovering the item. Once the message was deleted, the user could not recover it because retention time is in effect.

Chapter

6

Configuring Client Access

MICROSOFT EXAM OBJECTIVES COVERED IN THIS CHAPTER:

✓ Perform client deployments. Clients include Microsoft Outlook 2000, Outlook Web Access, POP3, IMAP4, and IRC.

  ▪ Configure Outlook Web Access.

  ▪ Configure client access protocols.

✓ Configure and monitor client connectivity. Clients include Outlook 2000, Outlook Web Access, POP3, IMAP4, and IRC.

✓ Diagnose and resolve client connectivity problems. Problems include DNS structure, server publishing structure, DS Proxy/ DS Access, address resolution, Instant Messaging clients, various connection protocols, and non-Windows 2000 environments.

Outlook 2000, a MAPI client, includes many powerful features and is the primary Exchange client used in most organizations. In this chapter, you will learn about the installation and configuration of various Microsoft Exchange client programs. We discuss how to configure and take advantage of Outlook 2000, and we examine several important Internet protocols that can be used to access Exchange Server. Outlook Web Access provides a way for standard Web browsers to access Exchange information. We also cover the POP3 and IMAP4 message retrieval protocols.

Specifically, this chapter covers the following topics:

- Client platforms for Microsoft Exchange

- The MAPI architecture

- Microsoft Outlook

- Virtual servers

- Outlook Web Access

- POP3 clients

- IMAP4 clients

- NNTP clients

Client Platforms for Microsoft Exchange

The very first order of business is to define what is meant by *clients* for Microsoft Exchange. The best way to do that is to compare and contrast an Exchange client with an Exchange correspondent (this term is the authors').

An Exchange client application has the ability to access an Exchange mailbox as the owner of that mailbox, whereas an Exchange correspondent has only the ability to send and receive mail to and from an Exchange user. If an Exchange mailbox were a physical mailbox at the post office, a client would have the key for accessing their mailbox, while a correspondent would only be able to send mail to that mailbox or receive mail sent from it.

An example of a client application is Microsoft Outlook 2000. An example of a correspondent might be a user on the Internet. This latter functionality is enabled through Microsoft Exchange connectors or gateways. Applications that can only correspond with Exchange are also referred to as *foreign mail clients*. The users of foreign mail applications are defined as contacts within the Active Directory, as you learned in Chapter 4. This allows Exchange users to address mail to the foreign mail users (Exchange interoperability with foreign systems is covered in Chapter 12).

There are two main Exchange client application architectures:

MAPI (Messaging Application Programming Interface)   *MAPI* is the Microsoft API used for messaging functions. Microsoft Outlook 2000 for Windows and Outlook 98 for Macintosh are the only MAPI clients now shipping with Exchange 2000 Server.

Following are examples of MAPI client applications that can still be used with Microsoft Exchange Server, but are not necessarily supported:

- Microsoft Exchange Client (the version that shipped with previous versions of Exchange Server)

- Microsoft Schedule+ 7.5 (this product has been replaced by the Outlook Calendar function)

- Microsoft Outlook 97 version 8.03 (there are also versions of this product for Microsoft Windows 3.*x*, Windows 95, Windows NT, and Apple Macintosh)

Internet protocols   Some Internet protocols can also be used by clients to access Microsoft Exchange. Examples are as follows:

Post Office Protocol version 3 (POP3)   Retrieves mail from the Inbox folder of a mailbox on a remote server.

Internet Message Access Protocol version 4 (IMAP4)   Retrieves mail from a mailbox on a remote server. Access includes personal and public folders, as well as the Inbox folder.

HyperText Transfer Protocol (HTTP)   Handles data transfer between World Wide Web servers and browsers.

Lightweight Directory Access Protocol (LDAP)   Provides access to directory information. Clients and servers use LDAP to retrieve information from Active Directory. In previous versions of Exchange Server, clients used LDAP to access directories managed by Exchange.

Network News Transfer Protocol (NNTP)   Transfers data between newsgroup servers and between newsgroup servers and newsgroup reader programs.

Figure 6.1 illustrates foreign mail users communicating with Exchange, and Figure 6.2 illustrates various types of Exchange clients communicating with Exchange.

FIGURE 6.1   Foreign mail user communication with Exchange

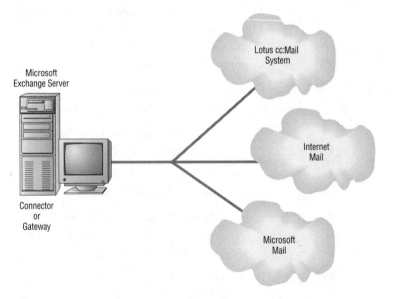

FIGURE 6.2 Exchange clients

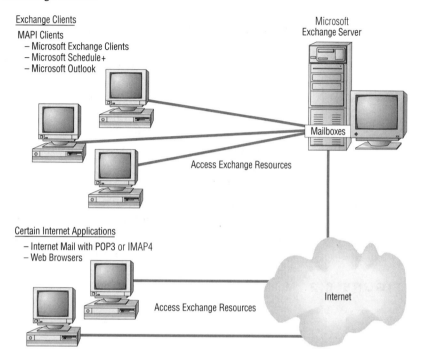

Exchange Clients

MAPI Clients
- Microsoft Exchange Clients
- Microsoft Schedule+
- Microsoft Outlook

Microsoft
Exchange Server

Mailboxes

Access Exchange Resources

Certain Internet Applications
- Internet Mail with POP3 or IMAP4
- Web Browsers

Access Exchange Resources

Internet

MAPI Architecture

Many messaging systems are divided into a client side and a server side. The client side provides an interface to users and permits them to read, save, create, and send mail. The server-side programs carry out the client requests. For example, if a client issues a read request for a certain message, the server responds by transmitting the message to the client. The client software is sometimes referred to as the *front end* to the server software, which can be referred to as the *back end*. The front-end programs can be thought of as consumers and the back-end programs as producers.

Do not confuse the front end and back end of a client/server system with the concept of front-end and back-end servers used in Exchange 2000. You can learn more about front-end and back-end servers in Chapters 8 and 14.

Historically, messaging systems have been implemented using "closed" application programming interfaces (APIs). An API is a collection of instructions, also called function calls. When a user wants to read a message stored on the server, the client program issues the relevant API function call, and the server responds accordingly.

The problem with the closed API model is that each model is proprietary, and thus each vendor has their own APIs. When someone wrote a client program to be used with one of these proprietary systems, it only worked with that system. With this architecture, multiple client programs were needed to connect to multiple messaging systems (see Figure 6.3).

FIGURE 6.3 Multiple client programs for multiple message systems

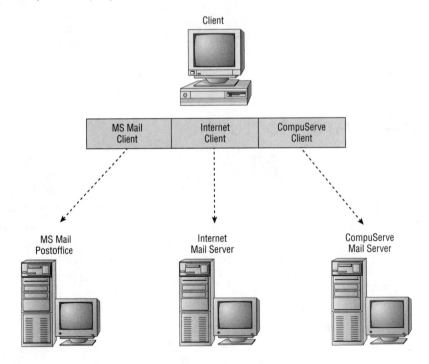

Microsoft decided to remedy this situation by creating a standard messaging architecture known as MAPI. MAPI provides a way for client messaging applications to communicate with multiple messaging systems (see Figure 6.4). Although MAPI is an abbreviation for Messaging Application Programming Interface, it is much more than an API. It is an architecture that specifies components, how they should act, and how they should interface with each other.

FIGURE 6.4   A single MAPI application accessing multiple message systems

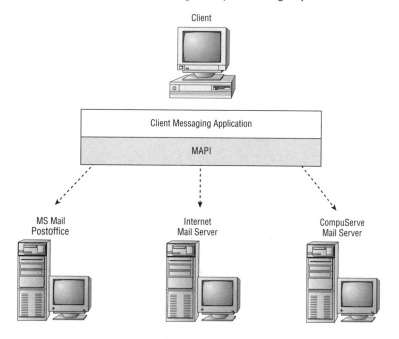

Figure 6.5 illustrates the basic architecture of MAPI. The top layer, the client application layer, includes client applications that enable users to perform messaging activities. These client applications are the front-end programs that request services from the back-end server programs. Client applications can include different messaging services (such as e-mail, fax, voicemail, and paging), as long as they are written to the MAPI specification. The concept of having messages from multiple sources delivered to one place is referred to as the *universal inbox*.

FIGURE 6.5   The basic MAPI architecture

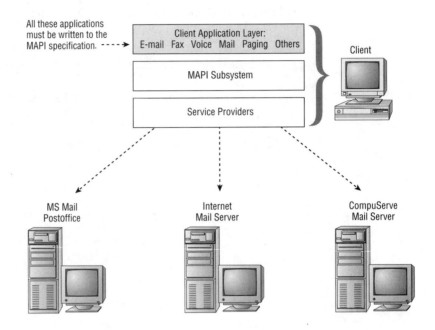

Previously, a single client program could not communicate with more than one server program, because the server programs all used different APIs. The MAPI architecture eliminates this limitation by providing a single layer through which the client programs and the server programs can communicate. This is the second layer and is called the MAPI subsystem (see Figure 6.6). The MAPI subsystem is referred to as *middleware* because it acts as a broker between two other layers.

Server programs can still use their own APIs on the back end. But the vendors of these programs must write a type of client component, called a *service provider*, that will interface their back-end system with the MAPI subsystem. Service providers comprise the third layer in the MAPI architecture (see Figure 6.7). Client software communicates with the MAPI subsystem, which communicates with a service provider, which communicates with the back-end message server. This is how a single client application, using multiple service providers, communicates with multiple back-end message servers.

FIGURE 6.6 The MAPI subsystem

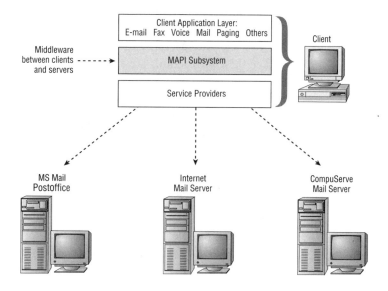

FIGURE 6.7 MAPI service providers

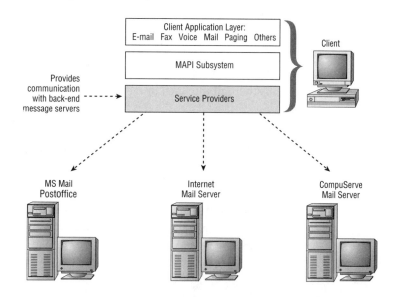

The next sections provide additional details on the MAPI architecture.

Client Application Layer

Client applications that need to perform messaging functions can have those functions implemented through the usage of MAPI function calls. Examples of these calls are MAPIReadMail, MAPISaveMail, and MAPISendMail. When these instructions are executed in a client application, they initiate an action in the MAPI subsystem, which then interfaces with service providers, which interface with a server messaging system, such as Microsoft Exchange Server or CompuServe Mail.

MAPI encompasses three major API sets:

Simple MAPI   This is a set of 12 straightforward messaging functions, like reading (MAPIReadMail) and sending (MAPISendMail) messages. It is included in *messaging-aware* applications like Microsoft Word.

Common Mail Call (CMC)   This is a set of 10 messaging functions similar to Simple MAPI. CMC is geared for cross-platform, operating system–independent development. CMC was developed by the X.400 Applications Programming Interface Association (XAPIA).

MAPI 1.*x* (also called Extended MAPI)   This is the newer, more powerful MAPI standard. It includes the abilities of Simple MAPI, but adds many other instructions for complex messaging functions, such as custom forms.

See Figure 6.8 for a depiction of these three APIs in the MAPI architecture.

These three API sets allow developers to create client messaging applications that fall into two broad categories:

Messaging-aware applications   These are applications like Microsoft Word that have some messaging functions included, like a Send option on the File menu. Messaging is not essential to these applications. Simple MAPI or CMC is most conveniently used as the messaging API.

Messaging-based or messaging-enabled applications   These are applications like Microsoft Outlook that require messaging functionality. The comprehensive function call set of Extended MAPI is normally required to implement these applications.

FIGURE 6.8   The three MAPI API sets

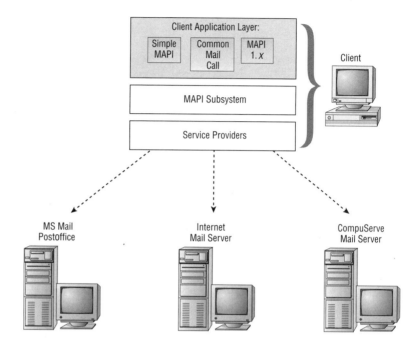

MAPI Subsystem

The second layer of the MAPI architecture is the *MAPI subsystem* (see Figure 6.9). This component is shared by all applications that require its services and is therefore considered a subsystem of the operating system. Microsoft includes the MAPI subsystem with the 32-bit Windows 98, Me, NT, and 2000 operating systems, and the file MAPI32.DLL is the primary function library for these operating systems. The MAPI subsystem for 16-bit Windows 3.*x* is loaded with the installation of the Exchange client, and the file MAPI.DLL is the primary function library.

FIGURE 6.9 MAPI subsystem

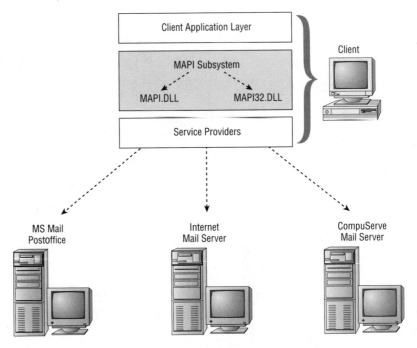

 The MAPI subsystem is also referred to as the MAPI runtime.

The MAPI subsystem provides a single interface for client applications. Communication with all MAPI-compliant server messaging systems is facilitated by interfacing with the MAPI subsystem. It is the middleware or broker in the messaging environment. The subsystem manages memory, administers profiles, routes client requests to the relevant service provider, and returns results from servers via service providers.

The MAPI subsystem also presents a single, virtual address book and a single, virtual storage area to the user. As you will learn in the next section, multiple service providers can create multiple address books and multiple message stores. The MAPI subsystem presents all of these through a unified interface. Consequently, even though an e-mail program and a fax program are being used, the user can view all addresses in one virtual address book. Because all data can be kept in the same virtual storage area, users can organize information based upon logical categories (e.g., all communication from Jane) rather than by application (e.g., e-mail directory, fax directory, etc.).

MAPI Service Providers

The MAPI architecture's third layer contains components called service providers. These replaceable components (manifested as DLL files) communicate with the messaging system back end. There are three main types of service providers:

- Address book providers
- Message store providers
- Message transport providers

The following three sections discuss these service providers.

A provider is sometimes called a driver.

Address Book Providers

An address book provider is a component that interacts with a database of message recipients. Some of these providers create their own address databases, called *personal address books (PABs)*; others can access address books on a server. Address book providers can be written for many kinds of back-end systems, and because they all interface with the MAPI subsystem, a user can still have a single, virtual address book.

The following are three examples of address book providers:

Global Address List (GAL)   This provider enables a client application to view an Exchange server's Global Address List (GAL). The GAL is a database of all the recipients in an Exchange organization, such as mailboxes, distribution lists, custom recipients, and public folders. The file extension of this address book is usually .GAL.

Personal Address Book   This provider, also called the Local Address Book, enables the creation of a customized address book. Users can include frequently used e-mail addresses, as well as custom recipients and distribution lists that the user creates. Message recipients are not the only type of information that can be stored. Phone and fax numbers, postal addresses, and other information can be stored here. This address book can be stored on the user's machine or on a server. The file extension of this address book is usually .PAB.

Offline Address Book (OAB) This address book provider permits an Exchange server's GAL to be downloaded to a user's machine. This can be useful when working offline. The file extension of this local database is usually .OAB.

See Figure 6.10 for a depiction of the address book providers in the MAPI architecture.

FIGURE 6.10 Address book providers

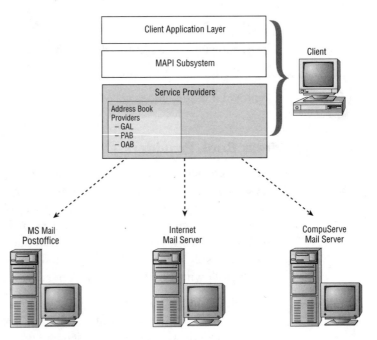

Message Store Providers

Message store providers are components that manage a database of messages. This entails client message storage, organization, and submission for sending and retrieving of messages and attachments. Storage is organized in a hierarchical tree of folders. Views can be created to allow the user to see messages based on certain criteria, like subject or date. Searches can also be conducted to retrieve specific information.

Message store providers can use server-based storage or client-based storage. Following are four examples of message store providers (see Figure 6.11):

Private folders   This provider enables client access to an assigned mailbox on an Exchange server (i.e., the home server of the mailbox). The term *private folders* is another name for what are more commonly referred to as mailboxes. They are called "private" because, more often than not, they are associated with a single user (even though several users can be given permission to use a single mailbox). All private folders are stored on an Exchange server in the Private Information Store, which is managed by the Information Store service. The advantages of this type of storage are compression, security, and centralized backup.

Public folders   Public folders are the groupware component of Exchange Server. This provider allows a client to access the hierarchical tree of public folder storage to which everyone in the Exchange organization has access. Public folders are stored on Exchange servers in the Public Information Store, which is managed by the Information Store service.

Personal folders (PST, Personal STore)   A personal folder store is a file-based storage container independent of the Exchange Server back end. The file that is composed of a set of personal folders has the .PST extension. A PST file can be stored on the user's local machine or on a shared directory on a network server. As with private folders, a user can create a hierarchical tree of folders within a personal folder store. Up to 16,000 entries and 2GB of data can be placed in a personal folder store.

Personal folder stores can be assigned a password for protection. Personal folders can also be designated as the location to where incoming mail messages are moved. Although all mail is always first sent to private folders on an Exchange server, users can configure their private folders to route messages to their personal folders. Because of storage technologies used in the Private Information Store, information moved from that location to a personal folder will take up more space in the personal folder. Note also that moving information to personal folders may make backing up more complicated than if everything is stored on a server. Of course, personal folders can also be stored on a server that is included in regular backups.

Passwords assigned to a personal folder cannot be viewed by the Exchange administrator. Therefore, if a user forgets this password, the information in that folder is inaccessible using tools provided in System Manager or Outlook. However, there are a number of third-party utilities that are usually able to crack personal folder and other application passwords.

Offline folders (OST, Offline STore)   If mailbox storage is left in the default location (the Private Information Store) and offline access to that data is also needed, the user can utilize *offline folders*. An offline folder is a local copy of the user's private folders in the Private Information Store. The mailbox on the server remains the master copy. Offline folders have the .OST file extension.

FIGURE 6.11   Message store providers

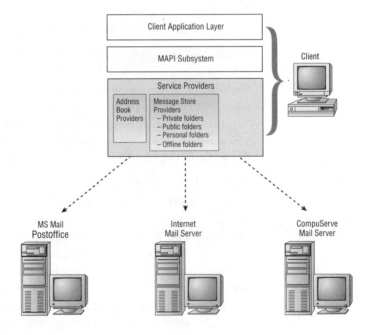

Message Transport Providers

Message transport providers manage the physical transportation of messages between a MAPI client and a back-end system (see Figure 6.12).

Like gateway components, they take a MAPI message, translate it to the format of the back-end system, and send it. They do the reverse for incoming messages. Message transport providers work with any of the Microsoft supported network protocols, such as TCP/IP, IPX/SPX, and NetBEUI.

The following are examples of back-end systems that have message transport providers:

- Microsoft Exchange Server

- Microsoft Network online service (MSN)

- Microsoft Fax

- Microsoft Mail

- Internet Mail

- CompuServe Mail

FIGURE 6.12   Message transport providers

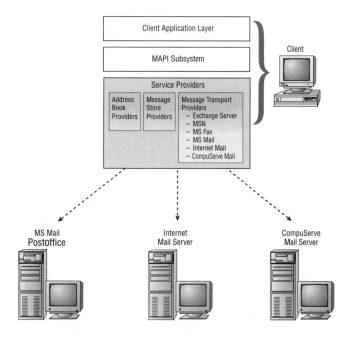

Message Spooler

The message spooler (also referred to as the MAPI spooler) is an independent process that manages the flow of messages between the message store and the transport providers. It is like a queue where incoming and outgoing messages are sent and from there are routed to the necessary providers. When a message is marked for sending, a message store provider will send it to the message spooler. The message spooler then selects, based on the destination address, a message transport provider that can send the message to the relevant messaging system.

Messaging Profiles

A messaging profile is a collection of configuration parameters for MAPI operations. The first time a user starts a MAPI-based application, the Profile Wizard runs and prompts for various operational parameters related to messaging. For example, the user is prompted to choose the information services to be used, such as Microsoft Exchange Server, Microsoft Fax, Internet Mail, and others. Information services are collections of the various providers described earlier. The user is also prompted to configure his personal address book information service. Other information in the profile relates to message handling, such as saving sent mail or generating a delivery receipt. When the MAPI subsystem starts, it reads this profile to see what services to load and how to operate (see Figure 6.13).

FIGURE 6.13 Messaging profile

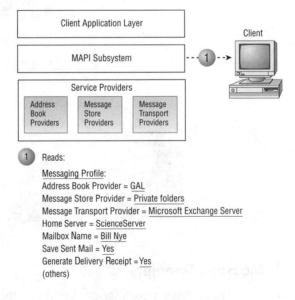

A user can have several profiles for one particular machine. For example, a user's computer might be a laptop that is used both at the office and on the road. When at the office, the user profile connects the user to an Exchange server at the office. When traveling, a different profile connects the laptop to the Internet. Multiple profiles for a particular machine are also useful when several people use the same machine.

Common Features of MAPI-Based Applications

Many common features are found in MAPI-based applications, including the following:

Universal inbox   Information from multiple sources (e.g., Exchange Server, Internet, etc.) and of varying types (e.g., e-mail, faxes, documents, and voicemail) is delivered to a single Inbox folder.

Single address book   A standard user interface to the address book is provided. Information from all the address books configured in the current profile is consolidated into one place.

Hierarchical storage   Messages and other items can be organized into a user-customizable hierarchical tree of folders. Four special folders are always present in the default store. They are the Inbox, Deleted Items, Sent Items, and Outbox folders.

Custom views   Information stored in folders can be sorted and viewed using many types of criteria, such as author, date, keyword, or type of content.

Rich-text formatting   Users can create message content that uses the rich-text format, which includes underlining, italic, bolding, bullet points, colors, fonts, different character sizes, and letter strikethrough.

Microsoft Outlook

Microsoft Outlook fits into several application categories. It is a personal information manager (PIM) because it functions as a personal calendar, scheduler, contact manager, and task manager. It is also a messaging application because it includes a powerful e-mail program and forms program. And finally, it is a groupware application because it can access Exchange Server public folders and enables calendars, schedules, contact information, and task information all to be used in a group context. All of this functionality exists through a single, integrated, desktop environment.

Microsoft Outlook 2000 for Windows and *Outlook 98 for Macintosh* are included with Microsoft Exchange 2000 Server as the premier client applications for use with Exchange. Outlook is also part of the Microsoft Office suite and as such is tightly integrated with the other Office applications, though it can also be purchased as a stand-alone product. Outlook is fully MAPI compliant.

Though no longer shipped with Exchange Server or supported by Microsoft, versions of Microsoft Outlook are available for Microsoft Windows 3.*x*.

Even though Microsoft Outlook is shipped with Microsoft Exchange Server, it requires a Microsoft Exchange Client Access License (CAL) to legally access Exchange Server. This is the same requirement for *all* client applications that access Exchange Server.

Architectural Design

Microsoft Outlook is designed to be a desktop information manager. This means it integrates personal and groupware tools, as well as their information, in a unified manner. This goal was achieved by including the following design features:

Single application, multiple functionality   From a single interface, users can execute numerous programs like e-mail, calendar, contact list, and task list.

Integrated user interface   All the tools in Outlook are seamlessly integrated. For example, Outlook includes a feature called the Outlook Bar. This is a navigation tool that creates shortcuts to a user's e-mail inbox, calendar, contacts, tasks, and folders. Outlook, as a MAPI program, provides a single address book that can be used for e-mail, phone dialing, faxing, and other functions. The Outlook interface permits users to access both local file folders and Exchange public folders.

Custom forms using Office 2000   One example of Outlook's tight integration with Office 2000 is its ability to create and send forms that include objects created in any of the Office 2000 applications. For instance, an expense report form that includes an Excel spreadsheet can be created.

Because of Microsoft object technology (see note below), the spreadsheet contained in the form will not be merely rows and columns, but will include the Excel code to execute the functions of the spreadsheet. The form's users can enter their numbers, have the spreadsheet calculate them, and then have the form automatically sent to a designated person. Outlook, along with Microsoft Office 2000, enables the creation of instant groupware applications.

ActiveX is an object technology developed by Microsoft. It is an extension of the earlier OLE technology. ActiveX allows programs to exchange objects that include both presentation data (i.e., what you see on the screen) and native data (i.e., the executable code to manipulate the presentation data).

Features of Microsoft Outlook

Microsoft Outlook includes some very powerful messaging, groupware, and personal productivity features. Tables 6.1, 6.2, and 6.3 describe many of those features.

TABLE 6.1   Messaging Features of Microsoft Outlook

Main Function	Features	Description
E-mail	Auto NameCheck	Outlook checks the name typed in message headers against the address book as soon as the user tabs out of the entry fields.
	Message recall	A user may recall a sent message, assuming the recipient has not already opened it.
	Voting	Users can create messages that include voting buttons in the message when received. Recipients can click one of the button choices and submit their choice back to the sender. The sender can automatically track responses to a question or issue.

TABLE 6.1 Messaging Features of Microsoft Outlook *(continued)*

Main Function	Features	Description
	Delegate access	Users can grant other users the right to send and receive messages using their mailbox.
	Message tracking	All the information about delivery, receipt, recall, and voting notifications is tabulated on the original message in the sender's mailbox.
	AutoPreview	The first few lines of each message can be displayed without requiring the user to open the message in a separate window. This allows users to quickly view the contents of messages.
	MessageFlags	Users can place flags (i.e., notices) on messages to aid in sorting and prioritizing messages. Flags include reply, read, "for your information," or any custom text.
	Hyperlinks to URLs	If a message includes a Web URL (Uniform Resource Locator) address, Outlook will recognize that address. If the user clicks the address, Outlook will start the user's Web browser and connect to that location.
	Retrieve deleted items	Users can retrieve deleted items from their mailboxes through the Recover Deleted Items command. Recovered mailbox items are placed in the Deleted Items folder. This functionality is made possible by the Exchange Information Store and is configured through the Private Folder Store and individual mailboxes.

TABLE 6.2 Groupware Features of Microsoft Outlook

Main Function	Features	Description
Group scheduling	Browsing free/busy information	Users can browse other users' free/busy schedule information.
	Meeting request processing	If a user sends another user a meeting request, that request is automatically copied from the inbox to the calendar as a tentative meeting.
	Delegate access	Users can grant other users the right to read and modify their schedules.
Group calendars, contact lists, and task lists	Public folder use	Calendars, contact lists, and task lists can all be published to public folders to allow group access to that information.
Group task management	Task tracking	Users can send tasks to other users, and the status of those tasks can be automatically tracked.
	Status reports	An automatic status report on a task (containing details such as whether the task has been started, the percentage completed, the hours spent working on the task, and the task owner's name) can be sent as a mail message.

TABLE 6.2 Groupware Features of Microsoft Outlook *(continued)*

Main Function	Features	Description
Forms and Office 2000 objects	Inclusion of Office 2000 objects	Microsoft Office 2000 applications can be used to create both presentation material and executable material for Outlook forms. For instance, Microsoft Word can compose the text of a form, and Microsoft Excel can add a spreadsheet to a form.

TABLE 6.3 PIM (Personal Information Manager) Features of Microsoft Outlook

Main Function	Features	Description
Functional integration within Outlook	Outlook Bar	This navigation tool permits the creation of shortcuts to a user's e-mail Inbox, calendar, contacts, tasks, and folders.
	AutoCreate	Outlook can automatically convert one Outlook item into another. For example, if an e-mail message represents a task a user needs to complete, the user can drag and drop the e-mail message into the Task folder, and Outlook will automatically convert it to a task.
Document browsing and retrieval	Outlook Journal	This feature maintains a log of users' actions, what they did, and when they did it. Users can then search for items based on when they were created, not just on what they are named or where they were saved.
	Outlook Views	Outlook comes with dozens of standard views of information, and users can create their own customized views.

TABLE 6.3 PIM (Personal Information Manager) Features of Microsoft

Main Function	Features	Description
Calendar/ Schedule features	AutoDate	Outlook understands natural language input for dates and can convert loosely worded dates into discrete calendar dates. For example, if a user types "the third Wednesday of November at 5:00 p.m.", Outlook will automatically convert that to "Wednesday 11/15/00 5:00 PM".
Contact Manager features	Single address book	The lists of contacts in Contact Manager can be used to address e-mail or a fax and even jump to a Web site or dial a phone.
Functions for portable computer users	Local replication	Information that users enter into Outlook while on the road with the portable computer can later be replicated back to their Exchange server.
	Time switching	Outlook can change the system time and time zone as mobile users move from one location to another.
Microsoft Office 2000 integration	Office 2000 interface	Outlook shares many user interface elements with the other Office 2000 applications, such as command bars, menus, shortcut menus, tabbed dialog boxes, and toolbars.
	Single address book	The other Office 2000 applications can use the Outlook Contact Manager address book.
	Attachments	Users can attach any Office 2000 document to any Outlook item, such as an e-mail, contact, or task.

TABLE 6.3 PIM (Personal Information Manager) Features of Microsoft

Main Function	Features	Description
	Mail merge	Users can perform a mail merge between the Outlook Contact Manager and Microsoft Word.
	Word 2000 and e-mail	Word can be used as the text editor for creating e-mail content.
	Drag-and-drop	Users can drag and drop information between Office 2000 applications and Outlook modules.
	Outlook Journal	Office files can be located using Outlook Journal.
	Office 2000 objects and forms	As stated earlier, objects created in Office 2000 applications can be included in Outlook forms.
Importing and exporting data	Import and export of data	Microsoft Outlook can import and export data from and to all Microsoft calendar and mail products, as well as many third-party PIM and messaging products.
Visual Basic for Applications (VBA)	VBA integration	Outlook includes Microsoft object technology and therefore can be used with Microsoft's Visual Basic for Applications to create compound applications.

Installing Outlook from the User's Perspective

As with most other Windows programs, Outlook 2000 is installed using a fairly intuitive Wizard that lets you choose the specific components of the program that you want installed (see Figure 6.14).

FIGURE 6.14 Choosing components in an Outlook 2000 installation

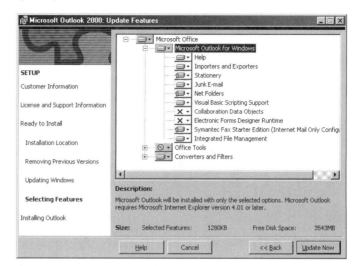

Once Outlook 2000 is installed, there is still some configuration left to do. The first time you start Outlook, you are asked to choose one of the following three modes in which to configure the program:

- Internet Mail Only

- Corporate or Workgroup Settings

- No E-Mail

The Internet Mail Only mode makes Outlook act as an Internet mail client that supports the POP3 or IMAP4 message retrieval protocols and uses SMTP as the message delivery protocol. Basically, you can think of this mode as an Internet e-mail program (like Outlook Express) that also offers PIM functions. Some of the functionality of Outlook, such as the use of voting buttons, is unavailable in this mode. A client machine must have a personal folder, or PST file, in order to store messages.

The Corporate or Workgroup Settings option is designed for use over a local area network (LAN) with Exchange Server or another LAN-based mail system. In this mode, Outlook 2000 provides all the features that are available in the other modes and also allows you to connect to Exchange. Depending on the mail server you are using, the client machine does not need to have a personal folder, or PST file, in order to operate with this option because the messages are stored on the server. However, if users want to maintain a PST file, they are free to do so. Users must be aware that the PST file exists only on their hard drives; it is their responsibility to ensure it is backed up properly to avoid losing mail if the PST file becomes unusable. Another important item about PST files is that they are not, by default, protected from prying eyes. However, there is an option for users to password-protect files if they so desire.

In the No E-Mail mode, Outlook acts as a stand-alone PIM, but you cannot send or receive e-mail. Even though the client machine is not utilized for mail, it must have a personal folder, or PST file, in order to store information used by the other features.

Once an operating mode is selected, Outlook starts up and prompts the user to configure an e-mail account. In an Exchange organization, this consists of the name of the Exchange server and the user's username. As you can see, Outlook 2000 is really a breeze to set up from the user's perspective. However, what the user sees during setup, is largely up to you.

The Office Custom Installation Wizard

As an administrator, you can customize the setup of Outlook in a few ways, including running the setup program with command-line options or using a settings file to answer various setup questions automatically instead of making the user answer them. However, the easiest and most powerful way to customize an installation of Outlook is with the *Office Custom Installation Wizard*, shown in Figure 6.15. This Wizard is available as part of the Office 2000 Resource Kit, by Microsoft Press.

FIGURE 6.15 Using the Office Custom Installation Wizard

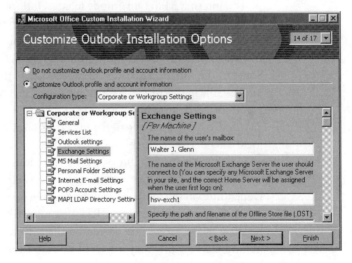

The Custom Installation Wizard works with Windows Installer to let you tweak almost every detail of the installation process. You can do the following:

- Define the path where Outlook is installed on client computers.

- Set the installation options (Run From Hard Drive, Install On First Use, Don't Install) for individual features of Outlook 2000.

- Define a list of network servers for Windows Installer to use if the primary installation server is unavailable.

- Specify other products to install or other programs to run on the user's computer when the Outlook installation is done.

- Hide selected options from users during setup.

- Add custom files and Windows Registry settings to the installation.

- Customize Desktop shortcuts for Outlook 2000.

- Set user default options.

- Use Office Profile settings created with the Profile Wizard for Office 2000 to preset user options.

To accomplish all of this, the Windows Installer uses two types of files to install Outlook: an *installer package (MSI file)* and an *installer transform (MST file)*. The package contains a database that describes the configuration information. The transform file contains modifications that are to be made as Windows Installer installs Outlook. The package file never changes; it is essentially a database that helps Windows Installer relate various features to actual installation files. The transform file is what the Custom Installation Wizard helps you create. This means that you can create unique setup scenarios that all use the same installation files. In other words, you could create different installation routines for different departments, but only use one network installation point for everyone to share.

Virtual Servers in Exchange 2000

As you learned in Chapter 2, Exchange 2000 relies heavily on Internet Information Server (IIS) to support access via Internet protocols. This integration with IIS also provides Exchange with the ability to configure virtual servers for Internet protocols. A *virtual server* enables you to host different protocols on the same physical server. The use of virtual servers provides added functionality and scalability. From the client perspective, there is no difference in connecting to a physical server or a virtual server. From the administrative perspective, virtual servers allow much greater flexibility and control than do individual physical servers that have to be created to support Internet protocols.

When Exchange 2000 Server is installed, a virtual server is created by default for each Internet protocol, including SMTP, NNTP, HTTP, LDAP, IMAP4, and POP3. Virtual servers are managed using the System Manager snap-in, as shown in Figure 6.16.

For the most part, the management of each type of virtual server is the same. You can right-click a virtual server and use the Pause, Stop, and Start commands to control the state of the service. Pausing a virtual server simply prevents new connections from being made to that server while the server itself remains running. Current connections are not disconnected. This is a graceful way of shutting down a virtual server that may be in use. When all users are finished, you can stop the server. Stopping the server will forcibly disconnect all connected users. If you want to disable certain protocols on a server-wide basis, stopping the virtual server for that protocol is usually the best way to go.

Aside from these basic commands, you can also open property pages for each kind of virtual server. These pages are covered in the sections later in this chapter that deal with the individual protocols themselves.

FIGURE 6.16 Viewing virtual protocol servers in System Manager

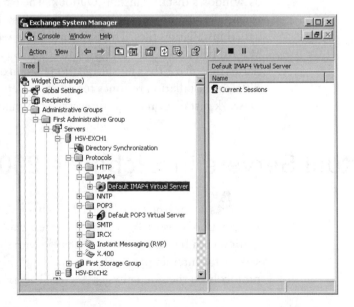

It is possible to configure virtual servers directly using IIS, but this is not recommended. When virtual servers are managed using System Manager, the Exchange System Attendant writes the configuration information to Active Directory. From there, the information is written to the IIS metabase. If you configure virtual servers directly in IIS, it is possible that the information you configure will be overwritten by older information configured in System Manager or Active Directory. The one exception to this rule is that the HTTP virtual server *must* be managed using the IIS Manager and cannot be accessed using System Manager.

Microsoft Outlook Web Access

*O*utlook Web Access (OWA) was first introduced to Exchange Server in version 5 and provides a way to access Exchange-based folders using a Web browser like Internet Explorer. OWA can be used to access e-mail, public folders, contact information, and calendar information. Since its introduction, OWA has become very popular, and its architecture has been completely overhauled with the introduction of Exchange 2000 Server. It has been redesigned to provide improved performance and a streamlined user interface.

Microsoft
✓ ***Exam***
Objective

Perform client deployments. Clients include Microsoft Outlook 2000, Outlook Web Access, POP3, IMAP4, and IRC.

- Configure Outlook Web Access.
- Configure client access protocols.

The "Configuring client access protocols" subobjective is covered later in this chapter.

OWA also provides a better way to support roaming users on a network than traditional messaging clients such as Microsoft Outlook. Supporting roaming users with Outlook requires the use of system policies and server-based profiles to ensure that a user's settings are available on multiple computers. With OWA, the only thing required on the client computers is Internet Explorer. This is also what makes OWA a good tool for cross-platform support, as versions of most Web browsers exist for Windows, Macintosh, and Unix. In fact, OWA is the primary Exchange Server access method for users of Unix.

Outlook Web Access is designed to work with any browser that supports HTML version 3.2 and JavaScript. This includes the latest versions of Internet Explorer and Netscape Navigator, as well as many other browsers. However, OWA is also designed to take advantage of a number of features provided in Internet Explorer 5 that are not supported by other browsers at this time, such as Dynamic HTML (DHTML) and eXtensible Markup Language (XML). Such features help provide many advanced collaborative functions.

OWA Features and Restraints

OWA is installed by default when you install Exchange 2000 Server. When the *Active Server Pages (ASP)* that are used to provide OWA access are installed, a user can access many of the functions available through Outlook, including functionality for basic e-mail, calendar and group scheduling, public folders, and collaborative applications (when the forms have been developed with Microsoft Visual InterDev). Following are some of the items that are *not* available when using OWA:

- Personal address books (because they are stored on your workstation)
- Personal folders (PST files)
- Spell-checking
- Message flags and Inbox rules
- Dragging and dropping to a folder
- Searching for messages
- WordMail and Microsoft Office integration
- Task lists and task management
- Electronic forms creation
- Synchronizing local offline folders with server folders

Outlook Web Access simulates the look and feel of Outlook 2000, as shown in Figure 6.17. The ubiquity of the browser client makes OWA an attractive choice in environments that have a widespread mix of client platforms (such as Windows, Macintosh, and Unix) and that require shared client computers. Outlook Web Access is extremely useful for users who frequently move around among different workstations during the day and users who must access the Exchange server remotely via the Internet.

FIGURE 6.17 Accessing Exchange via OWA

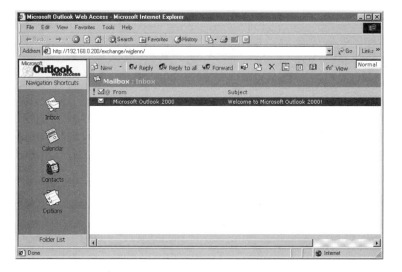

The OWA Process

The OWA process in Exchange 2000 is quite different from previous versions. OWA 5.*x* used Active Server Pages (ASP) to communicate with Exchange Server 5.5, which in turn used Collaboration Data Objects (CDO) 1.2 and MAPI. The effective number of users per server was limited by the overhead needed to support ASP and to run MAPI sessions within ASP. OWA was actually a part of IIS.

The new version of OWA does not use MAPI to communicate with the mailbox store and no longer uses ASP for client access. Instead, OWA is built into Exchange 2000 Server's new Web store and uses IIS only to receive requests and pass them to the Web store. Thus, IIS acts as an intermediary between the browser and OWA. IIS receives a client request, looks at the URL, and passes the appropriate information for the URL back to the Web browser. If the server houses the Exchange 2000 database, OWA uses a high-speed channel to access the mailbox store. If the server is a front-end server, OWA redirects the request to a back-end server using HTTP.

OWA is actually not a client itself, but rather a set of Active Server Pages that run in the context of Microsoft's IIS. Client Web browsers access IIS using HTTP over TCP port 80, and in turn IIS accesses the OWA component on behalf of the clients using an extended version of HTTP known as HTTP-DAV. HTTP-DAV adds several features to HTTP such as file locking, namespace management, and document property access.

Many components play an important role in the OWA process, including the following:

- Active Directory

- Information Store

- The *Exchange DSAccess* component, which enables Exchange 2000 components to communicate with Active Directory (DSAccess uses the LDAP protocol to perform this communication)

- OLE DB Provider for Exchange (ExOLEDB), which acts as the interface between DAVEx and EXIPC (both discussed a bit later)

- Directory Service to the IIS metabase (DS2MB), which provides a one-way synchronization of configuration information from Active Directory to the IIS metabase

- EXIPC, a queuing engine that is used to pass information between the IIS and Information Store components

- *IIS metabase*, which is a Registry database for IIS configuration

- *W3svc*, the World Wide Web publishing service of IIS

- *DAVEx*, a component that passes client requests between W3svc and the Information Store

- ExProx, which acts as a protocol proxy on a front-end server if a front-end/back-end server configuration is being used

- *Forms Registry*, which stores the OWA forms rendered by IIS and passed to the client

As you can see, the OWA process is fairly complicated and involves a number of components. The complexity of the process is basically designed to ensure that each major tool in use does what it is good at and that the client needs no special configuration. Since the client needs to be able to access Exchange using a standard Web browser, its only responsibility must be to request a simple URL, such as `http://owa.microsoft.com/exchange`, from a Web server (in this case IIS) and display the results in its window. Everything else must happen on the server end. For example, to open a user's contacts, type the path to the user's mailbox followed by /contacts, as in `http://owa.microsoft.com/exchange/user/contacts`, share user is the user's mailbox name.

Here is the actual process that occurs when a client's browser requests information from an Exchange server:

1. W3svc in IIS receives the request and authenticates the user by querying Active Directory.

2. Once authentication is complete, W3svc relays the request to the DAVEx component.

3. DAVEx transfers the request through the EXIPC queue to the Information Store.

4. The Information Store retrieves the appropriate data and returns it to DAVEx.

5. DAVEx retrieves an appropriate form from the Forms Registry and merges it with the information from the Information Store, creating an HTML or XML document.

6. DAVEx sends the formatted document back to W3svc.

7. W3svc sends the information back the client, which displays it in the browser window.

Installing and Configuring OWA

OWA is installed as part of the default setup of Exchange 2000 Server, and it is configured by default to allow access to users' mailboxes and the default public folder tree. However, you can configure the server to provide customized access for clients by specifying which users can access the server, which authentication method(s) to allow, and which public folders are exposed to users.

Since Outlook Web Access begins running when Exchange Server is installed, no special setup options are required other than a standard Exchange installation. The OWA client can offer your users much of the functionality offered by using Outlook 2000 from remote locations. Using a dedicated server for OWA can also increase network security by exposing only this dedicated server to the Internet.

When you install Exchange 2000 Server, Web access is installed and configured by default, and an Exchange virtual root and a Public virtual root are added to the IIS directory tree. These virtual roots point to their corresponding directories in Exchange 2000 Server—the directories that hold the public store and the mailbox store.

To access mail folders from within the corporate intranet, users will need to enter the following address in their Web browser: `http://servername/exchange/userid/`, where `servername` is the name of the Exchange server, `exchange` is the default private Web folder, and `userid` is the alias of the user. For connecting via the Internet, the above URL must be appended by the Fully Qualified Domain Name of the domain on which Exchange is running, for example, `http://servername.domain.com/exchange/userid/`.

Web access to Exchange 2000 is enabled for all users by default. To change this configuration, use Active Directory Users and Computers. First, make sure that View Advanced Features is enabled on the View menu. This allows you to see the Exchange Advanced tab in the user's properties. Use the Protocols Settings button to modify the HTTP, POP3, and IMAP4 access settings for the user, as shown in Figure 6.18.

FIGURE 6.18 Modifying protocol settings for a user

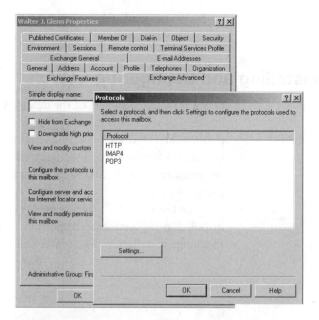

User Authentication in OWA

Users of OWA must be authenticated in some form before anything but Anonymous access is granted. A number of options are available for OWA authentication. Choosing the appropriate mechanism is usually a matter of the capabilities of the client operating system and specific security policies. In a single-server environment, the default authentication method for OWA is Anonymous authentication and Integrated Windows authentication (similar to NTLM). In a multi-server environment, the default authentication is Basic (Clear-Text) and NTLM. Authentication is set via the HTTP virtual servers configured for OWA. This configuration is actually set in Internet Information Server. Microsoft recommends configuring authentication on the back-end Exchange server only. The default authentication settings are the same on the front-end Exchange server, but securing the back-end server is much more important. In addition, authentication conflicts between the front end and back end could jeopardize user access. Exercise 6.1 outlines the steps for configuring OWA authentication, the available types of authentication are defined first.

Basic authentication *Basic authentication,* also referred to as plain-text or clear-text, is commonly used on intranets. Unlike the NTLM protocol, which accepts established users' identification through the access token, Basic authentication relies on users to enter their username, domain, and password. Basic authentication is independent of the browser, which also makes it independent of the platform being used. Basic authentication results in the transmission of unencrypted passwords over the network, which makes it a relatively insecure method of authentication. Users must enter their username, domain, and password each time they log on.

Integrated Windows authentication *Integrated Windows authentication* works differently depending upon the situation. The optimal authentication takes place when the client is running Windows 2000 and Internet Explorer 5, in which case Kerberos provides the best security available. With other non–Windows 2000 clients, Integrated Windows authentication uses the NTLM protocol instead of Kerberos. Integrated Windows authentication always encrypts the client's password, which provides excellent security. It also allows browser access without prompting the user for their user ID and password. Integrated Windows authentication does not work with browsers other than Internet Explorer 4 and 5, and it is not available in a front-end and back-end Exchange Server configuration.

Anonymous authentication *Anonymous authentication*, which IIS also allows, provides limited access to specific public folders and directory information. All browsers support Anonymous authentication, making it an easy way to provide insecure access to public folder data. A single point of configuration makes administration simple. Anonymous authentication does not identify users uniquely. Consequently, you cannot track usage by user.

Secure Sockets Layer authentication *Secure Sockets Layer (SSL)* provides the best level of security because the entire communications session is encrypted. SSL is not an authentication mechanism itself. Rather, SSL provides a secure channel for other authentication mechanisms. Although any authentication mechanism can be used with SSL, the most common implementation with SSL is Basic (Clear-Text). Most browsers support SSL communication. SSL creates a substantial amount of overhead in providing this security, so SSL communications tend to reduce the overall performance of an authenticating server and generate increased network traffic.

EXERCISE 6.1

Configuring Authentication for Outlook Web Access

1. Click Start ➤ Programs ➤ Administrative Tools ➤ Internet Services Manager.

2. Expand the container for the server running OWA.

3. Expand the default Web site container.

4. Right-click the Exchweb object and select Properties from the shortcut menu.

5. Click the Directory Security tab.

6. Click the Edit button in the Anonymous Access And Authentication Control section at the top of the page.

7. Select the forms of access that you want to allow.

8. Click OK twice to return to Internet Services Manager.

All in all, Outlook Web Access is a powerful means of providing cross-platform and remote access to your Exchange server. Authenticated users can log on to their personal accounts to access e-mail, public folders, and collaborative tools. Using Web-based public folder access, an organization could even build private and public discussion forums on the Internet or on private intranets.

Post Office Protocol (POP3) Clients

*P*ost Office Protocol version 3 (POP3) enables a client to retrieve mail from a remote server mailbox. A user who is not always attached to their network can have their mailbox on a server that is permanently attached to the network. Mail sent to that user would be delivered to the server-based mailbox, and the server acts as a sort of mail drop. Clients can remotely connect to the server and download their mail to their computer. The protocol used both to store the mail on the server and to download the mail to the client is POP3. In this capacity, the server is referred to as a POP server, and the client as a POP client. POP3 cannot be used to send mail; it is only a retrieval protocol. *Simple Mail Transfer Protocol (SMTP)* is still used to transfer mail between mailboxes.

Microsoft
✓ Exam
Objective

Perform client deployments. Clients include Microsoft Outlook 2000, Outlook Web Access, POP3, IMAP4, and IRC.

- Configure Outlook Web Access.
- Configure client access protocols.

Configure and monitor client connectivity. Clients include Outlook 2000, Outlook Web Access, POP3, IMAP4, and IRC.

Diagnose and resolve client connectivity problems. Problems include DNS structure, server publishing structure, DS Proxy/ DS Access, address resolution, Instant Messaging clients, various connection protocols, and non-Windows 2000 environments.

The "Configuring Outlook Web Access" subobjective is covered earlier in the chapter.

The remainder of this section covers these POP-related topics:

- POP3 architecture
- An overview of Exchange Server POP3 (including server and mailbox configuration)
- POP3 client configuration

POP3 Architecture

POP works through a simple request-response mechanism. A POP client sends request commands, and a POP server sends responses back to the POP client. These client-server interactions can be divided into three main states:

- Authorization
- Transaction
- Update

Authorization, also called greeting, is the client logon to the POP server. The POP username and password are sent to the POP server. After a successful authorization, transactions can take place between the POP client and server. The POP client can request the number and size of messages in its mailbox, and messages can be downloaded and deleted. After the POP server has responded and the POP client is finished, the POP client issues a QUIT command. This ends the POP session and causes the POP server to enter the update state for the user's mailbox. Messages may be deleted during the update state.

POP uses TCP/IP as its transport protocol. The session, or *conversation*, between the POP client and server takes place on TCP port 110. If Secure Sockets Layer (SSL) is being used to create an encrypted channel, port 993 is used instead. A *port* is a numeric identifier assigned to an application or protocol and is used to route incoming packets to the correct application. Although a packet has arrived at the correct computer, it still has to be delivered to the correct application on that computer. POP clients address the requests to port 110 on the POP server. The POP server listens to port 110 for those requests (this same principle is applicable to LDAP, HTTP, and other Internet protocols). The third revision of the POP standard, POP3, is documented in RFC 1939.

You may be familiar with Ethernet or Token Ring addresses, which are used to deliver a frame to a specific computer. You may even be familiar with network addresses, such as IP addresses, which are used to route packets to the correct networks and computers. Ports are yet another type of address that are used to route packets to the correct applications on a machine.

Exchange Server POP3 Overview

POP3 is integrated into the Internet Information Server (IIS) component of Windows 2000. Although it is not a separate service, the POP3 functionality is sometimes referred to as the POP3 Service. It permits any POP3-enabled e-mail program to connect to an Exchange server via IIS and retrieve mail (see Figure 6.19). Only messages in the Inbox folder of a mailbox can be accessed. The POP3 Service does not permit access to encrypted messages.

FIGURE 6.19   Exchange and POP3

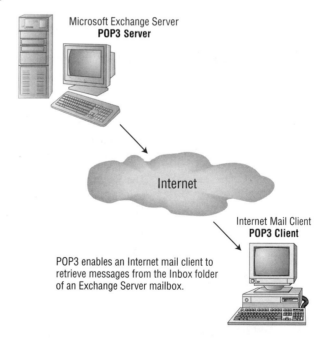

As mentioned previously, POP3 retrieves mail, but does not send it. The Simple Mail Transfer Protocol (SMTP) is used to send mail. SMTP functionality is also provided by IIS and uses TCP port 25.

POP3 Server Configuration

The site- and server-level POP3 objects have three property pages in common (four if the Permissions page is displayed). Table 6.4 lists and describes these property pages.

TABLE 6.4 Property Pages for the Site and Server POP3 Objects

Property Page	Description
General	This page is used to assign an IP address to the virtual server. The default is for the server to have access to all IP interfaces configured on the server. You can select a specific IP address or use the Advanced button to configure IP address and TCP port information. This page is used to configure how long an idle POP3 connection will be held open before automatically closing and to limit the number of connections that the virtual server will allow.
Access	The Authentication section of this page is used to select the authentication protocols that POP3 clients must use to log on to the Exchange server with the POP protocol. The options are Basic, which works using an unencrypted username and password, and Windows Integrated Authentication, which works using Windows 2000 network security and an encrypted password.
	The Secure Communication section of the Access page is used to configure a certificate server to provide POP3 security. This type of security is discussed in Chapter 14.
	The Connection Control section of the Access page is used to grant or deny access to the POP3 virtual server based on computer names or IP addresses.

TABLE 6.4 Property Pages for the Site and Server POP3 Objects

Property Page	Description
Message Format	This page sets the encoding method and character set used when converting Exchange messages for retrieval by POP3 clients. The encoding options include MIME and UUENCODE. Selecting UUENCODE makes available the option to use Binhex with Macintosh clients. The default character set used is US-ASCII, but you can choose from many international sets. You can also specify whether Microsoft Exchange rich-text format can be used in POP3 messages.

POP3 Mailbox Configuration

An administrator can override server-level settings at the mailbox level using the Protocols button on the Exchange Advanced page of a mailbox object. A mailbox can independently have POP3 enabled or disabled or have unique POP3 settings. As mentioned earlier, if a protocol is disabled at the server level, the settings at the mailbox level have no effect.

Configuring a POP3 Client

The following information must be configured on a POP3 client in order for it to connect to a POP3 server (in this case, the POP3 server is an Exchange server with the Exchange POP3 Service enabled):

POP3 server name   The computer name of the home server of the Exchange mailbox.

SMTP server name   The computer name of the Exchange server that is supporting SMTP.

Unless the client is connection to a server on the same network, you may need to indicate a Fully Qualified Domain Name for the POP3 and SMTP server names.

POP3 account name   The name the POP3 client must use when being authorized by a POP3 server. The Exchange POP3 Service requires a Windows 2000 domain and user account that has read permissions on the Exchange mailbox, followed by the alias name of the mailbox in the format *domain\account\alias*. If the account name and alias are the same, the alias name can be left off.

POP3 account password   The Exchange POP3 Service requires the password of the Windows 2000 user account that is specified in the POP3 account name field.

POP3 client e-mail address   The SMTP address of the POP3 client. For an Exchange mailbox, this is the SMTP address found on the E-Mail Addresses property page of the mailbox.

Table 6.5 provides sample information and shows how that information can be used to configure a POP3 client. Exercise 6.2 outlines the steps for configuring Outlook Express as a POP3 client. This exercise assumes that Outlook Express is already installed on your system.

TABLE 6.5   An Example of a POP3 Client Configuration

Sample Information	POP3 Client Configuration
Computer name running the POP3 Service=Education	POP3 server name=Education
Computer name running SMTP=Education	SMTP server name=Education
Window 2000 account with read permission on the mailbox=Domain\GeorgeW Alias name of mailbox=GeorgeW	POP3 account name=Domain\GeorgeW\GeorgeW or simply Domain\GeorgeW
Password of GeorgeW=woodenteeth	POP3 accountpassword=woodenteeth
Domain name=Chicago.com Alias name of mailbox=GeorgeW	POP3 client e-mail address=GeorgeW@Chicago.com

EXERCISE 6.2

Configuring Outlook Express as a POP3 Client

1. Click Start>Programs>Outlook Express.

2. Under the Tools menu, select the Accounts command.

EXERCISE 6.2 *(continued)*

3. Click the Add button and then click the menu's Mail command.

4. Enter a display name to appear in the From field of messages you send, and then click Next to continue.

5. Enter an e-mail address in the E-Mail Address field.

6. Click Next to go on.

7. Select the POP3 protocol from the drop-down menu.

8. In the Incoming Mail field, enter the name of the Exchange server that will service POP3 requests.

9. In the Outgoing Mail field, enter the name of the Exchange server that will service SMTP requests.

10. Click Next to go on.

11. In the Account Name field, enter the username of the mailbox to which you will connect.

12. Enter a password for the User, and then click Next.

13. Click Finish.

Internet Message Access Protocol version 4 (IMAP4) Clients

As with POP3, IIS provides *Internet Message Access Protocol version 4 (IMAP4)* support to Exchange. This enables Internet e-mail applications using IMAP4 to retrieve data from an Exchange server. As with POP3, IMAP4 can only retrieve data and must use the SMTP functions of the Exchange Internet Mail Service (IMS) to send data.

Perform client deployments. Clients include Microsoft Outlook 2000, Outlook Web Access, POP3, IMAP4, and IRC.

- Configure Outlook Web Access.
- Configure client access protocols.

Configure and monitor client connectivity. Clients include Outlook 2000, Outlook Web Access, POP3, IMAP4, and IRC.

Diagnose and resolve client connectivity problems. Problems include DNS structure, server publishing structure, DS Proxy/ DS Access, address resolution, Instant Messaging clients, various connection protocols, and non-Windows 2000 environments.

The "Configuring Outlook Web Access" subobjective is covered earlier in the chapter.

One of the main differences between IMAP4 and POP3 is the Exchange folders they can access. As mentioned earlier, POP3 can only access the Inbox folder of a mailbox. IMAP4, however, can also access personal and public folders. IMAP4 also includes other advanced features (and non-POP3 features) such as search capabilities and selective download of messages or even only the attachment of a message.

The IMAP4 virtual server has many of the same properties as the POP3 virtual server, such as authentication, message format, and idle time-out. Some of the pages for these properties have additional attributes not present with POP3. IMAP4, for instance, also allows anonymous user access, meaning that an IMAP4 user without a Windows 2000 user account could access the server. Table 6.6 lists and describes the property pages and attributes of the IMAP4 object. Exercise 6.3 outlines the steps for configuring Outlook Express as an IMAP4 client.

TABLE 6.6   Property Pages of the IMAP4 Object

Property Page	Description
General	This page is used to assign an IP address to the virtual server. The default is for the server to have access to all IP interfaces configured on the server. You can select a specific IP address or use the Advanced button to configure IP address and TCP port information. This page is used to configure how long an idle POP3 connection will be held open before automatically closing and to limit the number of connections that the virtual server will allow. The Include All Public Folders When A Folder List Is Requested option, which is enabled by default, permits a complete listing of public folders to be sent to an IMAP4 client in response to the IMAP List command. Some IMAP4 client applications, however, encounter poor performance when downloading a large list of public folders. If that is the case, this field can be cleared (i.e., unchecked). The Enable Fast Message Retrieval option, which is enabled by default, permits an Exchange server to approximate the size of messages when reporting to an IMAP4 client application. Approximating message sizes increases the speed of message retrieval. Some IMAP4 client applications, however, require a server to report the exact message size. If that is the case, this field can be cleared (i.e., unchecked).
Access	An Exchange server can allow IMAP4 clients to be authenticated with the same protocols that are available with POP3. While the options are the same for both IMAP4 and POP3, each can be configured with a different set of authentication protocols. This is also true for any of the other attributes IMAP4 and POP3 have in common.
Message Format	This page is used to set the encoding method and character set used when converting Exchange messages for retrieval by IMAP4 clients. The encoding options are as follows:

TABLE 6.6 Property Pages of the IMAP4 Object *(continued)*

Property Page	Description
	MIME Both the message body and attachments will be encoded with MIME.
	Provide Message Body As Plain Text The message body will be placed in plain text and any attachments in MIME.
	Provide Message Body As HTML The message body will be placed in HTML format and any attachments in MIME. If both this option and the Provide Message Body As Plain Text option are selected, Exchange will generate both plain-text and HTML versions of the message body.

EXERCISE 6.3

Configuring Outlook Express as an IMAP4 Client

1. Click Start≻Programs≻Outlook Express.

2. Click the Tools menu, and then choose the Accounts command.

3. Click the Add button, and then choose the Mail command.

4. Enter a display name to appear in the From field of messages you send, and click Next to continue.

5. Enter an e-mail address in the E-Mail Address field, and click Next.

6. Select the IMAP4 protocol from the drop-down menu.

7. In the Incoming Mail field, enter the name of the Exchange server that will service IMAP4 requests.

8. In the Outgoing Mail field, enter the name of the Exchange server that will service SMTP requests, and click Next.

EXERCISE 6.3 *(continued)*

9. In the Account Name field, enter the username of the mailbox to which you will connect.

10. Enter a password for the user, and click Next to go on.

11. Click Finish.

12. Outlook Express displays a dialog asking you whether you would like to download folders from the mail server you just configured. Click Yes to retrieve information on private folders other than your Inbox and any available public folders.

 Because of Exchange Server's support of IMAP4 and POP3, many Internet mail programs can be used as clients to Exchange Server.

Network News Transfer Protocol (NNTP)

As with the other Internet protocols, IIS provides support for the *Network News Transport Protocol (NNTP)*. Since the NNTP virtual server is installed and enabled by default when you install Exchange 2000 Server, any NNTP-based newsreader application can be used to connect to and use public folders right away. Like the other protocols, the NNTP virtual server is configured using a number of property pages. Table 6.7 provides an overview of the property pages for this object

<table>
<tr><td>

Microsoft
✓ ***Exam***
Objective

</td><td>

Perform client deployments. Clients include Microsoft Outlook 2000, Outlook Web Access, POP3, IMAP4, and IRC.

- Configure Outlook Web Access.
- Configure client access protocols.

Configure and monitor client connectivity. Clients include Outlook 2000, Outlook Web Access, POP3, IMAP4, and IRC.

Diagnose and resolve client connectivity problems. Problems include DNS structure, server publishing structure, DS Proxy/ DS Access, address resolution, Instant Messaging clients, various connection protocols, and non-Windows 2000 environments.

</td></tr>
</table>

The "Configuring Outlook Web Access" subobjective is covered earlier in the chapter.

TABLE 6.7   NNTP Property Pages

Property Page	Description
General	This page is used to assign an IP address to the virtual server. The default is for the server to have access to all IP interfaces configured on the server. You can select a specific IP address or use the Advanced button to configure IP address and TCP port information. This page is used to configure how long an idle POP3 connection will be held open before automatically closing and to limit the number of connections that the virtual server will allow. In addition, this page can be used to configure a path header, which is used by other Usenet servers to prevent a situation called "looping" that can happen when a Usenet server is connected to multiple providers. Finally, this page can be used to enable logging for the NNTP service for troubleshooting purposes.

TABLE 6.7 NNTP Property Pages *(continued)*

Property Page	Description
Access	An Exchange server can allow NNTP clients to be authenticated with the same protocols that were options with POP3. But while the options are the same for both NNTP and POP3, each can be configured with a different set of authentication protocols.
Settings	The Settings page provides a number of options for configuring the NNTP protocol:
	The Allow Client Posting option controls whether users with NNTP-based newsreaders can post messages using the NNTP protocol. If enabled, you can also control how large of a message, in kilobytes, may be posted and how much data, in megabytes, may be posted during a single user session.
	The Allow Feed Posting option works the same way as the Allow Client Posting option, but it controls whether or not messages may be automatically posted by newsfeeds, which are discussed later in the chapter.
	The Allow Server To Pull News Articles From This Server option controls whether other Usenet servers can use the NNTP protocol to pull messages in a public folder to their own server.
	The Control Messages option is used to allow Usenet servers to govern the traffic between servers.
	The final three options control the domain and address of moderators for moderated newsgroups. In a moderated newsgroup, a designated moderator must approve messages before they are posted to a folder.

Creating Newsgroups

When NNTP is installed, two virtual directories are created by default (see Figure 6.20):

- The default directory creates new newsgroups and stores them in the Newsgroups public folder.

- The control directory contains three folders for the three primary control commands: Remove Articles, Create Newsgroup, and Remove Newsgroup.

FIGURE 6.20 Viewing newsgroups in System Manager

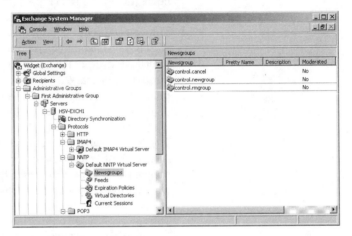

You can create new newsgroups using either a MAPI client or System Manager. The procedure for creating a newsgroup within a MAPI client varies, but it usually follows a pretty simple procedure of selecting a parent folder and creating a new folder inside of it. In System Manager, you can create a new newsgroup by expanding an NNTP virtual server, right-clicking the Newsgroups container inside of it, and selecting the New Newsgroup command from the shortcut menu.

In addition to creating your own newsgroups, you can also configure Exchange to pull newsgroups and their contents from a Usenet server on the Internet. Before you learn to do that, however, a brief overview of Usenet itself is in order.

A Usenet Overview

Usenet is a network within the Internet that is composed of numerous servers containing information on a variety of topics. Each organized topic is called a newsgroup, which can be thought of as a discussion group or a bulletin board. The Usenet servers are also referred to as newsgroup servers. Users access these newsgroups to post information or to read other people's postings. Users interact with newsgroups through client applications referred to as newsgroup readers.

Clients and servers use the Network News Transfer Protocol (NNTP) to transfer information across Usenet. When a client reads or posts information to a newsgroup server, NNTP is used for this exchange.

NNTP is also used to transfer newsgroup content between servers. This function is referred to as a *newsfeed*. A newsgroup server can be configured to send all or some of its newsgroups to other servers. When one server actively sends information to another server, it is referred to as a *push feed* (it is also referred to as publishing). A server also can be configured to request that information be sent to it from another server. This is referred to as a *pull feed*. Push feeds are usually used with large newsfeeds. A pull feed allows a local administrator to specify which and when newsgroups are received.

Exchange 2000 Server can function as a full Usenet server and exchange newsgroup information with other Usenet servers on the Internet. This is done through the Newsfeed Configuration Wizard. The Wizard prompts the installer for such information as the name of the Usenet host; the host's IP address; and the type of newsfeed, such as inbound (i.e., receiving data), outbound (i.e., publishing data), or inbound and outbound. Newsfeeds basically enable an Exchange server to function as a newsgroup server. It can publish public folder content as newsfeeds to other Usenet servers. It also can receive newsfeeds from the Usenet and place newsgroups in public folders. To receive newsfeeds, it can either pull a newsfeed or receive a push. See Figure 6.21 for an illustration of this process.

FIGURE 6.21 Newsfeeds and the Usenet

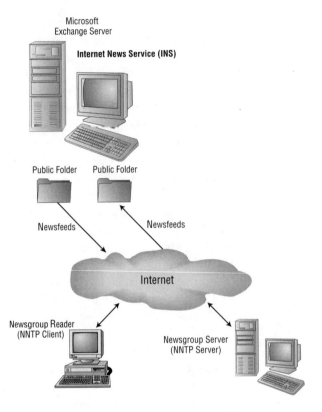

Once a newsfeed is configured, it is represented in the Feeds container of an NNTP virtual server as an object. The property pages of a newsfeed object can be used to configure the newsfeed after its creation. Much of the information that was entered in the Wizard can be later viewed and modified through the newsfeed object. For example, if the IP address of the Usenet host changes, the new address can be entered in the properties of that newsfeed rather than creating a new newsfeed with the Wizard.

Summary

A messaging profile is the collection of configuration information used by a MAPI application, such as Microsoft Outlook. Some of the information contained in a profile indicates the information services to be used, such as Microsoft Exchange Server, Microsoft Fax, or Internet Mail. Other information in the profile relates to information storage, delegate access, and remote mail. Profiles can be created at the time of the client software installation. They can also be created and edited after the installation.

Outlook 2000 for Windows and Outlook 98 for Macintosh both ship with Exchange 2000 Server and are considered the premier clients for use in an Exchange system.

Exchange Server also extends support for the IMAP4, POP3, HTTP, and NNTP Internet protocols, thus expanding the number of client applications that can access Exchange.

IMAP4 and POP3 enable an e-mail program to retrieve messages from a remote server mailbox. Internet users who have Exchange mailboxes can use these protocols to retrieve mail.

HTTP is the primary protocol used for client-server interactions on the World Wide Web. Exchange Server supports HTTP using Outlook Web Access and IIS, and thereby allows Web users to access Exchange resources such as mailboxes, public folders, and calendars using a standard Web browser.

Exchange Server supports NNTP and, therefore, can operate as part of the Usenet. Exchange can both publish public folders to the Usenet and receive newsfeeds from the Usenet. Newsgroups received from newsfeeds are published in public folders.

Key Terms

Before you take the exam, be certain you are familiar with the following terms:

Active Server Pages (ASP)	newsfeed
Anonymous authentication	Office Custom Installation Wizard
Basic authentication	offline folders
DAVEx	Outlook 98 for Macintosh
Exchange DSAccess	Outlook Web Access (OWA)
Forms Registry	personal address books
IIS metabase	Post Office Protocol version 3 (POP3)
installer package (MSI file)	private folders
installer transform (MST file)	Secure Sockets Layer (SSL)
Integrated Windows authentication	service provider
Internet Message Access Protocol version 4 (IMAP)	Simple Mail Transfer Protocol (SMTP)
MAPI	universal inbox
MAPI subsystem	Usenet
Microsoft Outlook 2000	virtual server
Network News Transport Protocol (NNTP)	W3svc

Review Questions

1. Jane uses Microsoft Outlook on both her office computer and her home computer. One night at home, Jane connects to her office server in order to read her mail. The next day at the office when Jane attempts to re-read the previous day's mail, there are no messages in her Inbox. What is the most likely cause of this situation?

   A. Jane's mail was delivered to an OST file on her home computer.

   B. Jane's home computer is still logged on to the server.

   C. Jane did not synchronize her mailbox with the server.

   D. Jane's mail was delivered to a PST file on her home computer.

2. Lou has a laptop computer for doing work away from the office and a desktop computer at the office. Microsoft Outlook is installed on both computers. Lou would like to see all of his messages while using either computer. The laptop computer does not have a continuous connection to the office server, but Lou would like to be able to read and compose messages while using the laptop offline. How should Lou configure his two computers?

   A. Configure the laptop computer with an OST file and the desktop computer to access his private folders in the Information Store.

   B. Configure both computers with PST files.

   C. Configure both computers to access his private folders in the Information Store.

   D. Configure the laptop computer with a PST file and the desktop computer to access his private folders in the Information Store.

3. Which of the following MAPI components manages memory, administers profiles, routes client requests to the relevant service provider, and returns results from servers via service providers?

   A. Client Application Layer

   B. MAPI subsystem

   C. Common Mail Call

   D. MAPI service provider

4. An IMAP4 client connects to your Exchange server and receives an error message stating that the message size is unknown. Which of the following should you do to fix this problem?

   A. Enable MCIS.

   B. Increase the Idle-Timeout setting.

   C. Use Plain-Text authentication.

   D. Clear the Enable Fast Message Retrieval checkbox.

5. A user has come to you after forgetting the password she assigned to her personal folders. What can you do to retrieve the messages in those folders?

   A. Use the Inbox Repair Tool to assign a new password.

   B. Use System Manager to assign a new password.

   C. Use System Manager to create a new set of personal folders and then import messages from the old personal folders.

   D. Use Outlook to create a new set of personal folders and then import messages from the old personal folders.

   E. Nothing—you cannot retrieve the information.

6. You are creating a custom electronic form for a public folder using Outlook 2000. Which of the following components could you include on the form?

 A. A functioning Excel spreadsheet

 B. Voting buttons that let users vote on the usefulness of that spreadsheet

 C. A button that automatically routes the form to the next person on a routing list

 D. All of the above

7. Your company receives newsfeeds from your Internet Service Provider. You notice a folder within the newsgroup hierarchy that you do not want to receive. What must you do to permanently remove this folder from the hierarchy?

 A. Rename the folder.

 B. Exclude the folder from the newsfeed.

 C. Clear the folder's Folder Visible attribute.

 D. Delete the folder through Microsoft Outlook.

8. Management has decided to allow company access to various newsgroups. Your ISP can provide full newsgroup access, but they do not configure newsfeeds on a customer-by-customer basis. How would you configure the transfer of the newsfeeds?

 A. No transfer type is necessary.

 B. Configure it for both push and pull.

 C. Configure it for a push transfer only.

 D. Configure it for a pull transfer only.

9. You have just configured your Exchange server for POP3 client access. POP3 clients can be authenticated with Basic, Basic with SSL, or Integrated Windows authentication. The administrator of your firewall informs you that the firewall will allow traffic from SMTP (port 25), POP3 (port 110), and HTTP (port 80). What additional traffic must the firewall be configured to allow for your Exchange server POP3 configuration to be used?

   A. 993

   B. 443

   C. 137

   D. 135

10. An Outlook 2000 user has just sent a message to a recipient who is also using Outlook 2000, and he realizes that he has forgotten to attach an important document to the message. He can recall the message so long as what has not happened?

   A. The recipient has not received the message.

   B. The recipient has not opened the message.

   C. The recipient has not replied to or forwarded the message.

   D. The recipient has not moved the message from the Inbox.

   E. The recipient has not deleted the message.

11. Your Exchange server is using TCP/IP and is configured with HTTP and POP3. A firewall sits between your network and the Internet. Your Exchange server has its name and IP address entered into a public DNS server on the Internet. Your network's firewall prohibits traffic on all ports that are not explicitly allowed. The ports that are open are port 25 (SMTP), port 53 (DNS), port 80 (HTTP), and all ports greater than port 1023.

   Required result:

   Users must be able to connect over the Internet to your Exchange server using Microsoft Outlook. Policy dictates that passwords be transmitted in a secure manner.

17. You have made certain configuration changes to the POP3 protocol using Internet Information Server. However, soon after you make the changes, you find that the configuration has reverted to its previous state. You try again, but the same thing happens. What is the problem?

    A. You can only make changes using System Manager.

    B. You must make the configuration changes in both System Manager and IIS.

    C. You must make the configuration changes in both Active Directory Users and Computers and IIS.

    D. You must configure IIS to replicate changes to System Manger.

18. Which of the following features are not available when accessing an Exchange server with a Web browser via Outlook Web Access? (Choose all that apply.)

    A. Personal folders

    B. Public folders

    C. Searching for messages

    D. Group scheduling

19. Which of the following components is responsible for merging a form with information from the Information Store to create an HTML or XML page that is delivered to a Web client?

    A. W3svc

    B. Information Store

    C. DAVEx

    D. Forms Registry

20. Which of the following components manages the flow of messages between a MAPI message store and MAPI transport providers?

A. MAPI client

B. Offline folder

C. Message spooler

D. Transport service

Answers to Review Questions

1 D. A personal folder store is a file-based storage container independent of the Exchange Server backend. The file that is composed of a set of personal folders has the PST extension. A PST file can be stored on the user's local machine or on a shared directory on a network server.

2. A. If mailbox storage is left in the default location (the Private Information Store) and offline access to that data is also needed, the user can utilize an offline folder. An offline folder is a local copy of the user's private folders in the Private Information Store. The mailbox on the server remains the master copy.

3. B. The MAPI subsystem provides a single interface for client applications. Communication with all MAPI-compliant server messaging systems is facilitated by interfacing with the MAPI subsystem. It is the middleware or broker in the messaging environment.

4. D. The Enable Fast Message Retrieval option, which is enabled by default, permits an Exchange server to approximate the size of messages when reporting to an IMAP4 client application. Approximating message sizes increases the speed of message retrieval. Some IMAP4 client applications, however, require a server to report the exact message size. If that is the case, this field can be cleared (i.e., unchecked).

5. E. Passwords assigned to a personal folder can be neither viewed by the Exchange administrator nor retrieved without the password. Therefore, if a user forgets this password, the information in that folder is inaccessible.

6. D. Because of Microsoft object technology, a spreadsheet contained in a form would not be merely rows and columns, but could include the Excel code to execute the functions of the spreadsheet. Voting buttons are a built-in function of Outlook 2000, and a routing function is an example of a simple custom code that could be placed into a form.

7. B. Exclude the folder from the newsfeed using the Subscription page of the newsfeed's property pages.

8. D. When one server actively sends information to another server, it is referred to as a push feed (it is also referred to as publishing). A server can also be configured to request that information be sent to it from another server. This is referred to as a pull feed.

9. A. POP uses TCP/IP as its transport protocol. The session, or conversation, between the POP client and server takes place on TCP port 110. If Secure Sockets Layer (SSL) is being used to create an encrypted channel, port 993 is used instead.

10. B. An Outlook 2000 user may recall a sent message, assuming the recipient has not already opened it.

11. A. Using the outlined procedure, each port in use is specifically allowed through the firewall. Allowing SSL and RPC traffic to pass ensures that Outlook can log on to the Exchange server securely. Allowing POP3 to pass through the firewall ensures that POP3 clients can access their mailboxes.

12. A, B. Both the Internet Mail Only and Corporate or Workgroup modes would allow Outlook to work as a POP3 or IMAP4 client. The Corporate or Workgroup mode would offer the additional advantage of allowing Outlook 2000 to connect to a local messaging system such as Exchange Server.

13. C. Internet Information Server (IIS) is used to provide management of the HTTP protocol.

14. A. POP3 clients can only be used to retrieve messages from the Inbox.

15. D. POP3 is a protocol used for message retrieval only. In order to send messages, POP3 clients use the SMTP protocol.

16. A, B. Windows Installer uses two types of files to install Outlook: an installer package (MSI file) and an installer transform (MST file). The package file contains a database that describes the configuration information. The transform file contains modifications that are to be made as Windows Installer installs Outlook. The package file never changes; it is essentially a database that helps Windows Installer relate various features to actual installation files. The transform file is what is modified using the Custom Installation Wizard.

17. A. When virtual servers are managed using System Manager, the Exchange System Attendant writes the configuration information to the Active Directory. From there, the information is written to the IIS metabase. If you configure virtual servers directly in IIS, it is possible that the information you configure will be overwritten by older information configured in System Manager or Active Directory.

18. A, C. While OWA provides many advanced Exchange features, not all of the features available in a MAPI client like Outlook are available through OWA.

19. C. DAVEx retrieves an appropriate form from the Forms Registry and merges it with the information from the Information Store, creating an HTML or XML document. DAVEx then sends the formatted document to the W3svc service for delivery to the client.

20. C. The message spooler is an independent process that manages the flow of messages between the message store and the transport providers. It is like a queue where incoming and outgoing messages are sent and from there are routed to the necessary provider. When a message is marked for sending, a message store provider will send it to the message spooler.

Building Administrative and Routing Groups

MICROSOFT EXAM OBJECTIVES COVERED IN THIS CHAPTER:

✓ **Create and manage administrative groups.**

✓ **Manage and troubleshoot messaging connectivity.**

- Manage Exchange 2000 Server messaging connectivity.

- Manage connectivity to foreign mail systems. Connectivity types include X.400, SMTP, and Internet messaging connectivity.

- Diagnose and resolve routing problems.

- Diagnose and resolve problems reported by non-delivery report messages.

n Exchange 2000, there are two ways to organize servers: according to the physical routing needs of your organization and according to administrative needs. *Routing groups* are physical groupings of Exchange servers that have full-time, full-mesh, reliable connections between each server and every other server in the group. *Administrative groups* are Exchange servers and other Active Directory objects that are logically grouped together for the purposes of administration and permissions management.

This chapter covers the configuration and management of both administrative and routing groups. It begins by examining the different models for using multiple administrative groups and how using multiple groups is affected if you are running a mixed-mode organization—one in which previous versions of Exchange Server coexist with Exchange 2000 Server. Next, this chapter looks at the process of creating and maintaining administrative groups. From there, the chapter turns to routing groups, examining the reasons an organization might benefit from using multiple routing groups and showing the actual process of creating new groups and linking them to one another using various types of connectors.

Creating and Configuring Administrative Groups

An *administrative group* is a collection of Active Directory objects that are grouped together for the purpose of permissions management. Administrative groups are logical, which means that you can design them to fit your needs—geographical boundaries, departmental divisions, different groups of Exchange administrators, or different Exchange functions. For example, one group of Exchange administrators might be responsible for managing the messaging and routing backbone of the organization, another might be responsible for managing public folders, and still another might be responsible for managing connectivity with a legacy messaging system. You could create an administrative group for each that contains only the objects the administrator needs.

The basic idea behind administrative groups is that they make it easier to assign permissions to groups of objects. Once you set permissions on an administrative group, any object moved to that group automatically inherits those permissions. You will learn more about assigning permissions in Chapter 9.

An administrative group can hold the following types of objects:

- Servers
- Routing groups
- Public folder trees
- System policies
- Conferencing services
- Chat communities

Mixed Mode versus Native Mode

Before you get started dividing up everything into administrative groups, it is important to understand that there are some differences in how they are handled, depending on whether Exchange 2000 is running in mixed mode or native mode. *Mixed mode* allows Exchange 2000 servers and servers running earlier versions of Exchange to coexist in the same organization. It allows this interoperability between versions by limiting functionality to features that both products share.

Some of the limitations of mixed mode include the following:

- Each Exchange 5.5 site in the organization is mapped directly to a single administrative group and a single routing group, and vice versa. This limits your ability to use administrative and routing groups in the way that best fits the needs of your organization.

- You can only move mailboxes between servers that are in the same administrative group.

- Routing groups can only contain servers that are part of the administrative group that is defined with the routing group.

When you first install Exchange 2000 Server, it defaults to running in mixed mode. If the entire organization will only be running Exchange 2000 servers and you do not plan to use any previous versions, you can switch to *native mode*. Native mode means you have a pure Exchange 2000 Server organization, which allows you to take full advantage of Exchange 2000 Server functionality. Be careful, though: If you change the operation mode of an Exchange 2000 Server organization from mixed mode to native mode, you cannot reverse this change, and the organization will no longer be interoperable with earlier versions of Exchange.

Native mode offers the following benefits:

- A server can belong to an administrative group, but it does not have to belong to one of the routing groups within that administrative group.

- Administrative groups do not have to contain any routing groups.

- A single administrative group can contain all routing groups within the organization.

- You can move mailboxes between any servers in the organization.

You can learn more about mixed-mode operations and managing the coexistence of Exchange 2000 and Exchange 5.5 in Chapter 11. From this point on, this chapter assumes that you are running Exchange 2000 in native mode and that all of the functionality of running in native mode is available.

Exercise 7.1 outlines the steps for switching an Exchange organization from mixed mode to native mode.

EXERCISE 7.1

Switching an Exchange Organization to Native Mode

1. Click Start menu➤Programs➤Microsoft Exchange, and then select System Manager.

2. In the left-hand pane, find the object for the organization that you want to switch to native mode. If you are only running one organization, this object is at the top of the pane.

3. Right-click the organization object, and choose Properties from the shortcut menu.

4. The Organization Mode field displays whether your organization is currently in mixed or native mode. Click the Change Mode button.

5. A warning appears stating that once you change to native mode, you cannot change back. Click OK to make the change.

6. You are returned to the organization object property pages. Notice that the Organization Mode field now identifies the organization as being in native mode and that the Change Mode button is no longer available. Click OK to return to System Manager.

Using Multiple Administrative Groups

For most small to medium companies, where there is a single Exchange manager or a single management team, there is usually no reason to use more than one administrative group. In larger companies, it often makes sense to divide up the administration of the Exchange organization by location, department, or administrative duties.

Microsoft defines three basic administrative models: centralized, decentralized, and mixed. It is important, both in the real world and for the exam, to know how these three models work.

Centralized Administrative Model

In the *centralized model*, one administrator or group of administrators maintains complete control over an entire Exchange organization. However, this does not necessarily mean that only one administrative group is defined. You might choose to create a few groups just to make it easier to assign permissions. Your routing topology does not need to match the administrative topology, of course. You may create many routing groups within a single administrative group.

Decentralized Administrative Model

The *decentralized model* is typically used to define administrative boundaries along real geographical or departmental boundaries. Each location would have its own administrators and its own administrative group. For example, a company with branch locations in three different cities would likely have administrators in each city. According to the decentralized model, an administrative group would be created for each location. Again, routing topology does not need to match administrative topology. You could create multiple routing groups within each administrative group. You could also have a routing group that spanned multiple administrative groups or an administrative group that spanned multiple routing groups.

Mixed Administrative Model

The *mixed model* is really a catchall model for any other ways you can think of to use administrative groups. It is useful for when you do not necessarily want the tight control of the centralized model and the strict geographic division of the decentralized model is not appropriate. Here are two examples of when the mixed administrative model is useful:

- You might want to keep most administration under the control of a single administrative group but restrict certain types of administration to certain administrators. For example, you might leave the default First Administrative Group intact for general Exchange management, but create a special administrative group that holds all system policies. This way, only specific administrators could create and manage policies.

- You might want to combine geographic boundaries and functional boundaries. For example, assume that your company has its main location in one city and a branch location in another. You might want to leave the First Administrative Group intact for general management of the main location. You might then want to create an administrative group specifically for the branch location, another group for policy management, and another for public folder management.

Creating Administrative Groups

By default, Exchange 2000 is configured with a single administrative group named First Administrative Group. Also by default, this administrative group is hidden from view in System Manager, as shown in Figure 7.1. After all, why add a layer of complexity to the administration program by displaying administrative grouping when there is only one group?

Microsoft Exam Objective	**Create and manage administrative groups.**

FIGURE 7.1   By default, administrative groups are not shown in System Manager.

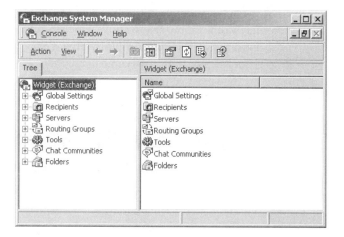

To enable the view of administrative groups, open the property pages for the organization object. Select the Display Routing Groups and Display Administrative Groups options on the General property page, and click OK to apply the new settings. You are informed that you must shut down and restart System Manager to see the changes. After you bring System Manager back up, it looks something like the view shown in Figure 7.2.

FIGURE 7.2 System Manager showing administrative and routing groups

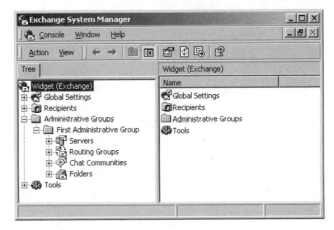

If you compare this view to the one shown in Figure 7.1, you'll notice that the Servers, Routing Groups, Chat Communities, and Folders containers have all been moved to show which administrative group they belong to—in this case, the First Administrative Group. All functionality remains the same, except that now you can create new administrative groups and arrange most resources among them however you like. Exercise 7.2 outlines the steps for creating a new administrative group.

EXERCISE 7.2

Creating a New Administrative Group

1. Click Start Menu➤Programs➤Microsoft Exchange, and then select System Manager.

2. Expand the organization object in which you want to create a new administrative group.

3. Right-click the Administrative Groups container and select the New Administrative Group command from the shortcut menu. This opens the property pages for the new group.

4. On the General page, enter a name for the new administrative group that identifies its purpose.

5. Optionally, you can switch to the Details page and enter some text that describes the purpose of the new group.

6. Click OK to return to System Manager. The new administrative group is displayed in the Administrative Groups container.

Once you have created a new administrative group, the first thing you'll want to do is assign the appropriate permissions to the group. By doing this first, you ensure that new objects created inside the group inherit those permissions. Permissions are covered in Chapter 9.

Once permissions have been assigned, it is time to structure the new administrative group. The first thing you must do is create one or more containers inside the group. Do this by right-clicking the group and selecting a new container type from the shortcut menu. The types of containers you can create include the following:

- Routing Groups containers
- Public Folders containers
- Chat Communities containers
- Policy containers

Figure 7.3 shows the new administrative group we created previously, now populated with a Routing Groups container and a System Policies container.

FIGURE 7.3 Creating containers inside a new administrative group

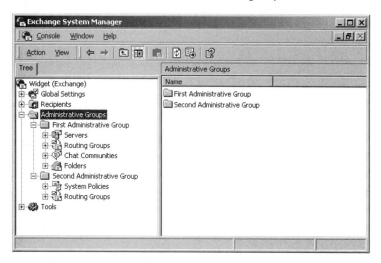

Once you have created the subcontainers for the administrative group and defined the new group's structure, you then have two options for filling up that structure with objects:

- You can create new objects within those subcontainers using the methods discussed throughout this book. For example, you can create a new public folder tree in a Folders container; the method for this is covered in Chapter 5. Creating new objects works in exactly the same way that creating objects in the default administrative group works. (Routing groups are discussed later in this chapter, policies in Chapter 9, and Chat communities in Chapter 10.)

- You can drag objects from other administrative groups and drop them into the corresponding folders inside the new administrative group. For example, once you create a Routing Groups subcontainer in the new administrative group, you could drag routing groups from other administrative groups to the new administrative group. You can also drag servers themselves to routing groups in the new administrative group. However, you cannot move servers between administrative groups.

There is one other item to be aware of regarding administrative groups. When you install Exchange servers into an organization after creating additional routing groups, the setup program lets you choose in which administrative group and routing group the server should be placed. This option never appears during setup if there is only one administrative group.

Creating and Configuring Routing Groups

A *routing group* is a collection of Exchange servers that have full-time, full-mesh, reliable connections between each and every server. Messages sent between any two servers within a routing group are delivered directly from the source server to the destination server. The message transport mechanism for this delivery is SMTP. Using SMTP as the native protocol provides several advantages. SMTP allows for a more flexible routing and administrative scheme because SMTP is more tolerant of low-bandwidth and high-latency topologies.

Microsoft Exam Objective

Manage and troubleshoot messaging connectivity.

- Manage Exchange 2000 Server messaging connectivity.

The "Manage connectivity to foreign mail systems. Connectivity types include X.400, SMTP, and Internet messaging connectivity" subobjective is covered in Chapter 12. The "Diagnose and resolve routing problems" and "Diagnose and resolve problems reported by non-delivery report messages" subobjectives are covered in Chapter 9.

Ideally, you would be in a networking environment in which all servers were well connected. Of course, this is not always the case. For this reason, Exchange 2000 lets you define routing groups that collect well-connected servers into different groups and then connect those groups using several different kinds of connectors.

This chapter deals mainly with the actual process of creating and linking routing groups. Before you get started, it is important that you are familiar with the concepts discussed in the "Routing Architecture" and "Message Transport" sections of Chapter 2. In particular, you should know the architectural concepts behind the use of routing groups and how messages flow when they are sent to recipients on the same server, within the same routing group, to a different routing group, or outside the Exchange organization.

Routing groups in Exchange 2000 should be planned similarly to sites in Exchange 5.5—according to available bandwidth and reliability of the connection. However, because Exchange 2000 uses SMTP, it is more tolerant of lower bandwidths and higher latency. This means you'll be able to group servers into the same routing group that may not have been possible with an Exchange 5.5 site.

The most important factor to consider when defining routing group boundaries is the stability of the network connection rather than the actual bandwidth of the connection. If the connection is prone to failure or is often too saturated with network traffic to be useful, then you should divide your servers into separate routing groups.

Be sure to have a Global Catalog server in each routing group and in each Windows 2000 site, if possible. This decreases traffic across slower WAN links when clients and servers need to look up information in the Global Access List (GAL).

In order for servers to exist in the same routing group, they must meet the following criteria:

- All servers running Exchange 2000 must have reliable, permanent, and direct network connectivity between them that supports SMTP.

- All servers must belong to the same Active Directory forest.

- All servers must be able to connect to the routing group master. The routing group master maintains data about all of the servers running Exchange 2000 in the routing group.

If your servers do not meet these criteria, or if you have a need to maintain greater control over the way messaging information flows on your network, you will need to create multiple routing groups.

Creating Routing Groups

You will need to create separate routing groups if you have any servers that are separated by slow or unreliable links. Creating a routing group is a very similar process to the one for creating an administrative group. Exercise 7.3 outlines the steps for creating a new routing group.

EXERCISE 7.3

Creating a New Routing Group

1. Click Start ➤ Programs ➤ Microsoft Exchange, and then select System Manager.

2. Expand the organization object in which you want to create a new administrative group.

3. Expand the Administrative Groups folder.

4. Expand the administrative group in which you want to create a new routing group. If this administrative group does not already have a Routing Groups container in which to create a routing group, you will have to create one using the procedure discussed previously in this chapter.

5. Right-click the Routing Groups container and select the New Routing Group command from the shortcut menu. This opens the property pages for the new routing group.

6. On the General page, enter a name for the new routing group that describes it.

7. Optionally, you can switch to the Details page and enter some text that describes the purpose of the new group.

8. Click OK to return to System Manager. The new routing group is displayed in the Routing Groups container.

The new routing group will hold two subcontainers, as shown in Figure 7.4. The Connectors container holds any connectors that you create to connect this routing group to other routing groups or to foreign messaging systems. These connectors are covered later in this chapter. The second object is a Members container, which holds the servers that are part of the routing group. Both of these containers are empty right after you create the new routing group.

FIGURE 7.4   Viewing a new routing group

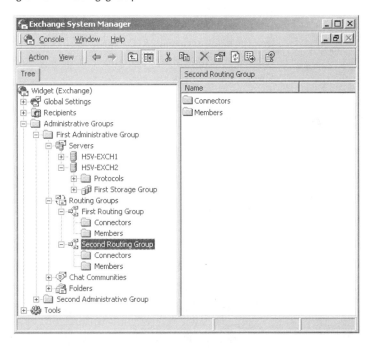

Adding Servers to a Routing Group

Once a routing group is connected, there are two primary tasks you will need to take on to configure the new group. The first is moving or installing servers into the new group. The second, which is discussed a bit later in the chapter, is connecting the routing group to other routing groups.

There are two ways to make a server a member of a routing group. The first way is to drag a server from the Members container of an existing routing group and drop it into the Members container of the new routing group. It really is just that simple.

When you move a server from one routing group to another, you are actually removing the SMTP virtual server or the X.400 service through which the server communicates and re-creating the virtual server or service in the new routing group.

The second way to get a server into a routing group is to put it there during Exchange installation. If your organization contains more than one routing group, the Exchange setup program will ask you into which routing group (and which administrative group, if applicable) you want to install the new server. After setup is finished, the new server is added to the chosen routing group. For more information on installing Exchange Server, see Chapter 3.

Connecting Routing Groups

Once you have created multiple routing groups, you will need to connect them together so that they can exchange messaging information. There are three types of connectors that you can create:

- The *Routing Group Connector (RGC)* is the main connector used to connect routing groups and is the simplest to configure. It used SMTP as its default transport mechanism, but it may also use a Remote Procedure Call (RPC) if the situation requires it.

- The *SMTP Connector* takes a bit more work to set up than the RGC and sports some different features. It is used mainly to connect routing groups where you want to force SMTP to be used for the transport mechanism. The SMTP Connector can also be used to connect an Exchange organization to a foreign messaging system using SMTP.

- The *X.400 Connector* can be used to connect routing groups and to connect to a foreign system. When used for connecting routing groups, its primary advantage is that it can be used over extremely low bandwidth and fairly unreliable connections.

The creation and configuration of each of these connectors is covered in the following sections.

In most cases, your best choice will be the Routing Group connector because it is the simplest to configure and manage. However, your choice will depend on the purpose the connector will serve. In addition, multiple connectors may be created between the same two routing groups to provide a level of fault tolerance and load balancing.

Routing Group Connector

The RGC is the preferred method of connecting two routing groups in the same organization because it is fast, reliable, and the simplest to configure (has the fewest settings). SMTP is the native protocol used by the RGC, and the connector consults Exchange 2000 Server's new link state table for routing information.

The RGC is a one-way connection from one server to another. Therefore, when you configure a connector in one routing group, you'll also need to create a connector in the other routing group to form a two-way. Fortunately, System Manager will automatically configure the other end of the link for you if you want it to.

A *bridgehead server* is one that is designated for passing messages from one routing group to another. The RGC offers a level of fault-tolerance by allowing multiple source and destination bridgehead servers. Bridgehead servers can be used in one of three ways:

- No bridgehead server is designated, and all of the servers in the routing group function as bridgehead servers for message transmission.

- One bridgehead server is designated, and all mail destined for other routing groups flows through that one server. This gives the administrator great control over messaging configuration.

- Multiple bridgehead servers are used, and all mail flows over one of these designated servers. This configuration offers the advantages of load balancing and fault-tolerance. Should one bridgehead server be unavailable for message transport, another will be available.

RGCs offer administrators the ability to control connection schedules, message priority, and message size limits.

Creating a Routing Group Connector

Creating a new RGC is a simple procedure. Exercise 7.4 outlines the steps involved.

EXERCISE 7.4

Creating a New Routing Group Connector

1. Click Start➤Programs➤Microsoft Exchange, and then select System Manager.

2. Expand the organization object, the Administrative Groups folder, the specific administrative group, and the routing groups folder in which you want to configure the connector.

3. Right-click the Connectors container and select the New Routing Group Connector command from the shortcut menu.

4. This opens the property pages that you must configure for the new connector. After you have configured these pages, which are described in the next section, System Manager offers to automatically create a connector for the other end of the link using the same properties you have just configured.

Configuring Routing Group Connector Properties

The RGC holds a number of property pages that can be configured. You have the option of configuring these pages when you first create the connector and later by opening the pages for the connector object, which is placed in the Connectors container for the particular routing group. Each of these, and the parameters they hold, are covered in the next several sections.

GENERAL PROPERTIES

The General page, shown in Figure 7.5, lets you enter several settings regarding the connector. These include the following:

- The name of the connector can be entered only when you are creating the connector. This field is unavailable after the connector is created.

- The Connects This Routing Group With drop-down box lists the routing group with which you want to connect. All routing groups in the organization should be listed here.

- The Cost field indicates the *cost value* of using the connector relative to any other connectors that may connect the two routing groups.

This value can range from 1 to 100, and lower cost links are always pre-ferred over higher cost links. This provides you with a way of assigning preference when there are multiple connectors configured between routing groups. For example, you might want to configure two connec-tors to share the main messaging load between two sites and assign both of them a cost of 1. Then you might configure a backup connector with a cost of 5 that is used when the two main connectors are unavailable. As a general rule, the cost value of a connector should be inversely pro-portional to the bandwidth the connector enjoys.

- While the option labeled Any Local Server Can Send Mail Over This Connector is enabled (which it is by default), all servers in the local routing group function as bridgehead servers and can route messages over the connector. You can specify that only particular servers be used as bridgehead servers by selecting the These Servers Can Send Mail Over This Connector option and then using the Add button to add servers to the list.

- The Do Not Allow Public Folder Referrals option specifies that clients may not access public folder content using this connector. When a cli-ent tries to access public folder content that does not exist on a server in that client's own routing group, it must try to find the content in other routing groups. This option gives you a way to govern the con-nections that can be used for this.

FIGURE 7.5   General properties of a RGC

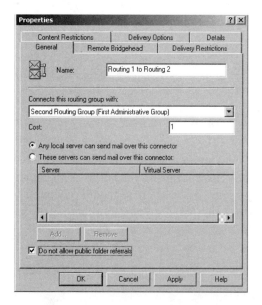

REMOTE BRIDGEHEAD PROPERTIES

The Remote Bridgehead page, shown in Figure 7.6, allows you to specify one or more servers in the remote routing group as the bridgehead server(s) with which this connector will attempt to establish connections before sending messages. The servers are contacted in order starting at the top of the list. Also, if the destination server has more than one *SMTP virtual server* configured, you'll need to select the appropriate virtual server that will allow messages to be sent across the connector you are setting up.

FIGURE 7.6   Remote Bridgehead properties of a RGC

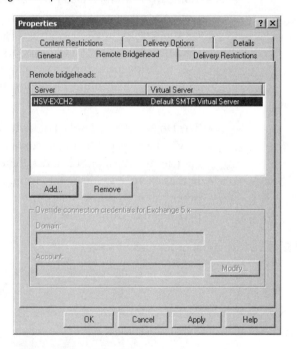

DELIVERY RESTRICTIONS PROPERTIES

The Delivery Restrictions page, shown in Figure 7.7, lets you specify who can use this connector, either by specifying that all messages are rejected except for specified users or that all messages are accepted save for specified users. You can add mailbox-enabled or mail-enabled users and contacts to this list, but you cannot add groups.

FIGURE 7.7 Delivery Restrictions properties of a RGC

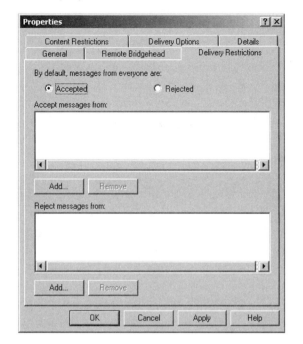

CONTENT RESTRICTIONS PROPERTIES

The Content Restrictions page, shown in Figure 7.8, lets you configure several parameters:

- The Allowed Priorities section lets you select what priority messages are allowed over the connection. This is a great way to establish connectors dedicated, for example, to passing high priority messages.

- The Allowed Types section lets you specify whether system messages and non-system messages are allowed over the connector. System messages would include any non–user-generated message, including directory replication, public folder replication, network monitoring, and delivery and non-delivery report messages.

- The Allowed Sizes section lets you restrict the size of messages that may be sent over the connector.

FIGURE 7.8 Content Restrictions properties of a RGC

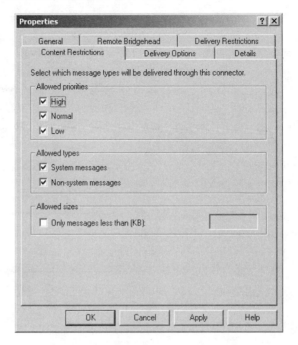

DELIVERY OPTIONS PROPERTIES

The Delivery Options page, shown in Figure 7.9, lets you specify when messages can flow through the connector. This is especially helpful if the connector uses a slow or unreliable WAN link. Click the Customize button to set up a schedule using a simple calendar interface. By selecting the Use Different Delivery Times For Oversize Messages option, you can channel larger messages to transfer at the times you configure, presumably when the connector would be experiencing little traffic.

FIGURE 7.9 Delivery Options properties of a RGC

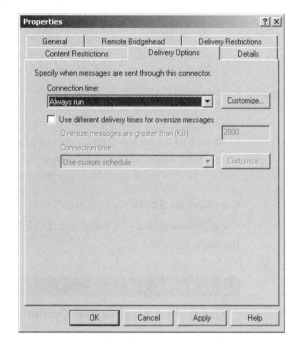

SMTP Connector

Although the RGC uses SMTP as its native transport mechanism, Exchange 2000 Server also provides an SMTP Connector that can be used to link routing groups. There are three reasons why you might want to use an SMTP Connector instead of a RGC:

- The SMTP Connector is more configurable than the RGC and offers a greater ability to fine-tune the connection. The SMTP Connector also offers the ability to issue authentication before sending mail, specifying *TLS encryption*, and removing mail from queues on remote servers.

- The SMTP Connector always has to use SMTP. When you are connecting an Exchange 2000 server with an Exchange 5.5 server, the RGC uses Remote Procedure Calls (RPCs) to communicate because it has no way of knowing whether the Exchange 5.5 server is configured to use SMTP, which was provided through the Internet Mail Service in previous versions of Exchange. There is no way to force the RGC to use SMTP, so an SMTP Connector may be used instead.

- The SMTP Connector is also capable of connecting independent Exchange forests within an organization so that messages can be transferred.

Another advantage of the SMTP Connector is that is can be used to connect an Exchange organization to the Internet or to a foreign (non-Exchange) messaging system that uses SMTP.

When connected to the Internet, the SMTP Connector uses a smart host or mail exchange (MX) records in DNS for next-hop routing. When configured internally between two routing groups, this connector will relay link-state information between routing groups but will still depend on the MX records in DNS for next-hop information.

Creating an SMTP Connector

Creating a new SMTP Connector is a simple procedure. Exercise 7.5 outlines the steps involved.

EXERCISE 7.5

Creating a New SMTP Connector

1. Click Start➤Programs➤Microsoft Exchange, and then select System Manager.

2. Expand the organization object, the Administrative Groups folder, the specific administrative group, and the routing groups folder in which you want to configure the connector.

3. Right-click the Connectors container and select the New SMTP Connector command from the shortcut menu.

4. This opens the property pages that you must configure for the new connector. After you have configured these pages, which are described in the next section, System Manager does not offer to automatically create a connector for the other end of the link. You must do this manually.

Configuring SMTP Connector Properties

The SMTP Connector holds a number of property pages that can be configured. You have the option of configuring these pages when you first create the connector and later by opening the pages for the connector object, which is placed in the Connectors container for the particular routing group. Two of these property pages, Content Restrictions and Delivery Restrictions, are identical to the RGC property pages of the same name. The rest are discussed in the following sections.

GENERAL PROPERTIES

The General page, shown in Figure 7.10, lets you configure the following options:

- The name of the connector can be entered only when you are creating the connector. This field is unavailable after the connector is created.

- The Use DNS To Route To Each Address Space On This Connector option makes the connector work with DNS to make direct connections to the destination SMTP server based on MX records. To forward mail upstream to another SMTP server instead, select the Forward All Mail Through This Connector To The Following Smart Hosts option. For this option, enter either the Fully Qualified Domain Name (FQDN) or IP address of the server.

- The Do Not Allow Public Folder Referrals option works the same way as the option for the RGC, and it is covered in that section.

FIGURE 7.10   General properties of the SMTP Connector

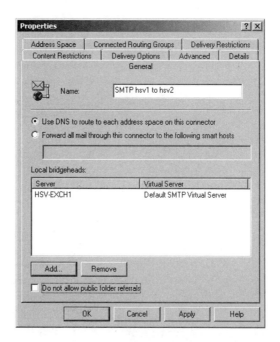

DELIVERY OPTIONS PROPERTIES

The Delivery Options page, shown in Figure 7.11, lets you specify when messages can flow through the connector. For the most part, this page works the same as the Delivery Options page for the RGC, except that one feature has been added. The Queue Mail For Remote Triggered Delivery option allows clients to periodically connect to the Exchange 2000 Server and download messages using a special command. You can select which Windows 2000 accounts can download mail.

FIGURE 7.11 Delivery Options properties of the SMTP Connector

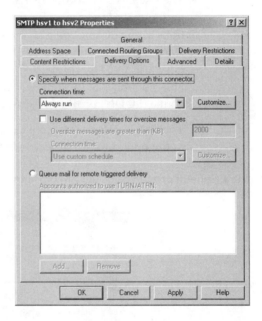

ADVANCED PROPERTIES

The Advanced page, shown in Figure 7.12, has a number of important configuration points. These include the following:

- Normally, an SMTP client connects to an SMTP server using a command named *HELO*, which signals the start of a session between two SMTP servers and identifies the sender of the coming message. By default, Exchange 2000 Server sends the *EHLO* command, another start command that indicates the Exchange 2000 server can use the Extended SMTP (ESMTP) commands. Not all SMTP servers are capable of dialogue using the extended commands, but you really only have to worry about this when connecting to non-Exchange servers.

- The Outbound Security button can be used to provide authentication credentials to the remote domain.

- The Do Not Send ETRN/TURN option prevents this connector from processing requests for remote servers to process mail sitting in their queues. This is selected by default.

- The Request ETRN/TURN When Sending Messages option is used to request that the server deliver queued mail to the client via a new ESMTP connection at certain times. Do this by selecting the Additionally Request Mail At Specified Times option and then scheduling the dequeuing time using the Connection Time drop-down list.

- Use the Request ETRN/TURN From Different Server option and type the server's name to request dequeuing from a server other than the one to which the message was sent.

- To specify either the ETRN or the TURN command for dequeuing, select either the Issue ETRN or Issue TURN options. The ETRN command can be issued on a per-domain basis by adding the domain names under the Domains button.

FIGURE 7.12   Advanced properties of the SMTP Connector

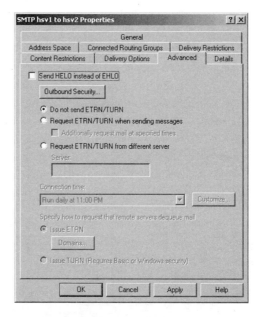

ADDRESS SPACE PROPERTIES

Whenever a message is sent that is not addressed to a recipient on the same server, that message is handed off for delivery to a remote server. To decide how to route that message to its destination, the routing engine used an *address space*. An address space is the addressing information associated with a connector. Typically, an address space is a subset of a complete address. The Address Space property page lets you configure the default address spaces used for different types of messages, including SMTP, X.400, and many others. For the most part, this page is used when you are configuring the SMTP Connector to be used with a foreign system. This aspect is covered in Chapter 12. The Connected Routing Groups page is used instead when you are connecting two routing groups together.

CONNECTED ROUTING GROUPS PROPERTIES

If you do not configure an address space on the Address Space tab, you must configure which routing groups are connected to the local routing group using the Connected Routing Groups page (shown in Figure 7.13). This is a much better (and easier) way of handling routing between routing groups than using the Address Space page is. The purpose of specifying connected routing groups is to inform the connector which routing groups are adjacent to it to enable internal routing of messages.

FIGURE 7.13 Connected Routing Groups properties of the SMTP Connector

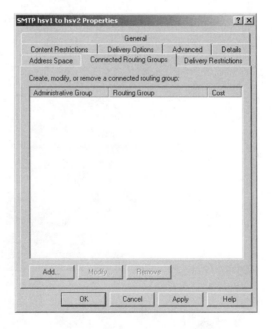

X.400 Connector

The X.400 Connector can be used to link Exchange routing groups and also to link an Exchange organization to a foreign, X.400-based messaging system. X.400 Connectors are useful for linking routing groups when there is very little bandwidth (less than 16K) available between servers or when X.400 is the only connectivity available. When linking routing groups with the X.400 Connector, a single server in each group must be designated as the bridgehead server. You must set up multiple X.400 Connectors between multiple servers in each routing group to gain a load-balancing feature.

Each end of an X.400 connection must be configured with the name of one remote Message Transfer Agent (MTA) to which it will connect. The local MTA name is assigned when an MTA Transport Stack is installed.

For details on the architecture of X.400, see Chapter 1.

Creating a Service Transport Stack

Creating an X.400 Connector to link routing groups is not too difficult. The one thing you must remember is that each end of an X.400 Connector must be configured separately and, unlike the RGC, System Manager does not offer to do this for you automatically. To configure the X.400 Connector in Exchange 2000 Server, you first must create an MTA *Service Transport Stack*. This transport stack is configured on a particular Exchange server and is basically a set of information about the software and hardware making up the underlying network. The use of the transport stack allows for a layer of abstraction between the X.400 Connector and the network itself.

Transport stacks exist at the server level and are associated with a particular Exchange server. This setup differs from the connector or connectors that will use the transport stack. Connectors exist at the routing group level. What this means to you is that multiple MTA Transport Stacks and X.400 Connectors can be configured within a routing group, giving you the ability to balance the load placed on servers by messaging connectors.

Exchange supports two different types of MTA Transport Stacks, each defined by the type of network hardware or software you have configured. The two types are as follows:

TCP/IP This type defines specifications for running OSI software, such as X.400 messaging systems, over a TCP/IP-based network. Microsoft Exchange 2000 Server uses Windows 2000 TCP/IP services.

TP0/X.25 This type uses an Eicon port adapter to provide both dial-up and direct communication in compliance with the OSI X.25 recommendation.

No matter which type of MTA Transport Stack you use, the configuration is nearly identical. Because it is easily the most-commonly installed, we cover the creation of a TCP/IP MTA Transport Stack in this chapter. Exercise 7.6 outlines the steps for creating a TCP/IP MTA Transport Stack.

EXERCISE 7.6

Creating a TCP/IP MTA Transport Stack

1. Click Start≻Programs≻Microsoft Exchange, and then select System Manager.

2. Expand the organization object in which you want to create a new administrative group.

3. Expand the Administrative Groups folder, the administrative group, and then the server on which you want to create the stack.

4. Expand the Protocols container, right-click the X.400 Container, and choose New TCP/IP X.400 Service Transport Stack from the shortcut menu.

5. Use the property pages to configure the new connector.

Once the stack is created, you will manage it using two property pages: General and Connectors.

GENERAL PROPERTIES

The General page is used to change the display name for the MTA Transport Stack and to configure OSI addressing information. Unless you plan to allow other applications besides Exchange 2000 Server to use the MTA Transport Stack, you do not need to worry about the OSI addressing values.

CONNECTORS PROPERTIES

The Connectors property page, shown in Figure 7.14, lists all of the messaging connectors in the routing group that are configured to use the current MTA Transport Stack. When you first create a stack, this list is blank. As new connectors are created that use the MTA Transport Stack, the connectors will be added to the list.

FIGURE 7.14 Viewing connectors for an MTA Transport Stack

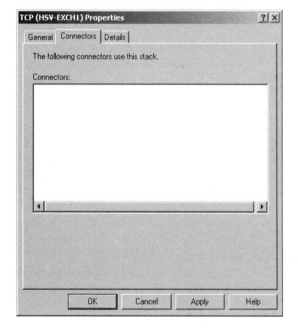

Creating an X.400 Connector

After you create an MTA Transport Stack, you must create the X.400 Connector itself. Exercise 7.7 outlines the steps involved.

Creating a TCP/IP X.400 Connector

1. Click Start ≻ Programs ≻ Microsoft Exchange, and then select System Manager.

2. Expand the organization object, the Administrative Groups Folder, the specific administrative group, and the routing group for which you want to create the connector.

3. Right-click the Connectors container and choose the New TCP X.400 Connector command from the shortcut menu.

4. Expand the Protocols container, right-click the X.400 Container, and choose New TCP/IP X.400 Service Transport Stack from the shortcut menu.

5. This opens the property pages that you must configure for the new connector. After you have configured these pages, which are described in the next section, System Manager does not offer to automatically create a connector for the other end of the link. You must do this manually.

Configuring X.400 Connector Properties

Many of the property pages that you see for the X.400 Connector are only used when you are connecting your Exchange organization to a foreign X.400 messaging system, and they do not pertain to connecting two routing groups to one another. This section only examines the property pages and parameters that are relevant to connecting routing groups. Also, the Delivery Restrictions and Content Restrictions pages are identical to the pages of the same names for the Routing Group Connector.

GENERAL PROPERTIES

For the most part, the General page does not hold any parameters that are useful when connecting routing groups. The exceptions are the following:

- The name of the connector can be entered only when you are creating the connector. This field is unavailable after the connector is created.

- The X.400 Transport Stack setting lets you change the MTA Transport Stack that the X.400 Connector is currently configured to use. You can change the MTA Transport Stack at any time.

- The Do Not Allow Public Folder Referrals option works the same way as for the Routing Group Connector and the SMTP Connector.

SCHEDULE PROPERTIES

The Schedule property page lets you restrict the times at which the X.400 Connector may be used. By default, the X.400 Connector can be used always and, for the most part, you will want to leave this value alone. There are times, however, when you may wish to limit connectivity, such as on a very busy network, or when you need to bring a network down for maintenance.

You can set an X.400 Connector schedule to one of four values:

- The Never option disables the connector altogether. It is useful for bringing down the connector while performing maintenance.

- The Always option allows connections to be made to and from the server at any time.

- The Selected Times option defines specific times at which the X.400 Connector is available. This can be useful on a busy network. If immediate messaging is not a concern, you can schedule messages only to be sent at specific periods during the day, when network traffic is otherwise low.

- The Remote Initiated setting allows remote servers to connect to the current server but does not allow the local server to initiate a connection.

STACK PROPERTIES

The Stack property page, shown in Figure 7.15, is used to specify transport address information about the server in the other routing group. If you input an IP address instead of a host name, be sure to enclose it in brackets, such as [192.168.2.200].

FIGURE 7.15 Stack properties for an X.400 Connector

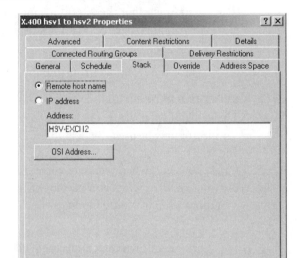

CONNECTED ROUTING GROUPS PROPERTIES

Just like with the SMTP Connector, the purpose of specifying connected routing groups is to inform the connector which routing groups are adjacent to it to enable internal routing of messages. If you were not connecting routing groups, you would use the Address Space page to configure actual address spaces.

Summary

In previous versions of Exchange Server, the concept of a site was used to define both the physical routing boundaries of a group of well-connected servers and the administrative boundaries within an organization. In Exchange 2000, sites have been replaced by administrative groups, which are objects logically grouped together for permissions management, and routing groups, which are physical groupings of Exchange servers used to define routing boundaries.

The use of both types of groups depends on whether your organization is running in mixed mode or native mode. Mixed mode allows Exchange 2000 servers and servers running earlier versions of Exchange to coexist in the same organization. It allows this interoperability between versions by limiting functionality to features that both products share.

Microsoft defines three basic administrative models: centralized, decentralized, and mixed.

- In the centralized model, one administrator or group of administrators maintains complete control over an entire Exchange organization. This can be done with one administrative group or a few administrative groups created to make certain functions earlier.

- The decentralized model is typically used to define administrative boundaries along real geographical or departmental boundaries. Each location would have its own administrators and its own administrative group.

- The mixed model is really a catchall model for any other ways you can think of to use administrative groups. It is useful for when you do not necessarily want the tight control of the centralized model and the strict geographic division of the decentralized model is not appropriate.

By default, Exchange 2000 is configured with a single administrative group that is named First Administrative Group. You can add new administrative groups, name them what you want, and then create Public Folder, Routing Group, Chat Community, and Policy containers inside the new group. Once these are created, you can move resources from other groups into the new group.

A routing group is a collection of Exchange servers that have full-time, full-mesh, reliable connections between each and every server. Exchange servers in the same routing group must also belong to the same Active Directory forest.

You create routing groups in System Manager in much the same way you create administrative groups. When created, they are simple containers waiting for you to fill them with servers.

Once your routing groups are defined, you must connect them together using one or more of three types of connectors. The Routing Group Connector (RGC) is the main connector used to connect routing groups and is the simplest to configure. It used SMTP as its default transport mechanism, but may also use a Remote Procedure Call (RPC) if the situation requires it. The

SMTP Connector is a bit more involved to set up than the RGC and sports some different features. It is mainly used to connect routing groups where you want to force SMTP to be used for the transport mechanism. The X.400 Connector can be used to connect routing groups and to connect to a foreign system.

Key Terms

Before you take the exam, be certain you are familiar with the following terms:

address space	mixed model
administrative group	native mode
bridgehead server	Routing Group Connector (RGC)
centralized model	routing group
cost value	Service Transport Stack
decentralized model	SMTP Connector
EHLO	SMTP virtual server
HELO	TLS encryption
mixed mode	X.400 Connector

Review Questions

1. You are configuring a connector between two routing groups that are in different buildings on your corporate campus. You have a dedicated, high-speed link between the buildings, but you have decided to create a routing group for each building anyway. You would like to use a connector that is fairly easy to set up and configure. What type of connector would you choose?

   A. Routing Group Connector

   B. Site Connector

   C. X.400 Connector

   D. SMTP Connector

2. Lou is managing mailboxes in an Exchange organization and needs to move several mailboxes to a server in a different administrative group. When he tries to move the mailboxes, System Manager returns an error. What is the cause of the problem?

   A. You can only move mailboxes between servers that are in the same administrative group.

   B. The organization is running in mixed mode.

   C. You cannot move mailboxes between servers, only between storage groups.

   D. You can only move mailboxes between servers that are in the same routing group.

3. Which of the following protocols can you use to create an MTA Transport Stack for an X.400 Connector? (Choose all that apply.)

   A. TCP/IP

   B. IPX

   C. X.25

   D. SMTP

4. Which of the following objects can an administrative group hold? (Choose all that apply.)

   A. Server container

   B. Recipients container

   C. System policy container

   D. Organization container

5. Which of the following connectors can be used to connect an Exchange organization to a foreign messaging system? (Choose all that apply.)

   A. Routing Group Connector

   B. SMTP Connector

   C. Active Directory Connector

   D. X.400 Connector

6. You are planning a large Exchange 2000 deployment. Your company has networks in four locations: New York, Toronto, London, and Madrid. Each of the locations has been configured as a Windows 2000 domain in the same Active Directory forest. Each of the networks in the four locations is maintained within a central building and all computers within the buildings enjoy a high-bandwidth, full-time connection. There is a high-speed T1 line connecting New York with Toronto. There is a switched 256K connection between New York and London. The connection between Toronto and Madrid uses a low-bandwidth X.25 connection.

   Required result:

   Group the servers in the various locations into routing groups using the fewest number of routing groups possible.

   Optional result:

   For each connection between groups, choose whichever routing group connector will work and is the simplest to configure and maintain.

Proposed solution:

Create a single routing group for each location: New York, Toronto, London, and Madrid. Connect the New York and Toronto routing groups with a Routing Group Connector. Connect the New York and London groups with an SMTP Connector. Connect the Toronto and Madrid groups with an X.25-based X.400 Connector.

Which of the results does the proposed solution produce?

A. The proposed solution produces the required result and the optional result.

B. The proposed solution produces the required result, but not the optional result.

C. The proposed solution produces the optional result, but not the required result.

D. The proposed solution produces neither the required result nor the optional result.

7. You are planning a large Exchange 2000 deployment. Your company has networks in four locations: New York, Toronto, London, and Madrid. Each of the locations has been configured as a Windows 2000 domain in the same Active Directory forest. Each of the networks in the four locations is maintained within a central building and all computers within the buildings enjoy a high-bandwidth, full-time connection. There is a high-speed T1 line connecting New York with Toronto. There is a switched 256K connection between New York and London. The connection between Toronto and Madrid uses a low-bandwidth X.25 connection.

Required result:

Group the servers in the various locations into routing groups using the fewest number of routing groups possible.

Optional result:

For each connection between groups, choose whichever routing group connector will work and is the simplest to configure and maintain.

Proposed solution:

Create a single routing group for the New York and Toronto locations. Create one routing group for the London location and one for the Madrid location. Connect the New York/Toronto routing group to the London routing group with a Routing Group Connector. Connect the New York/Toronto routing group to the Madrid routing group with an X.25-based X.400 Connector.

Which of the results does the proposed solution produce?

A. The proposed solution produces the required result and the optional result.

B. The proposed solution produces the required result, but not the optional result.

C. The proposed solution produces the optional result, but not the required result.

D. The proposed solution produces neither the required result nor the optional result.

8. You are planning a large Exchange 2000 deployment. Your company has networks in four locations: New York, Toronto, London, and Madrid. Each of the locations has been configured as a Windows 2000 domain in the same Active Directory forest. Each of the networks in the four locations is maintained within a central building and all computers within the buildings enjoy a high-bandwidth, full-time connection. There is a high-speed T1 line connecting New York with Toronto. There is a switched 256K connection between New York and London. The connection between Toronto and Madrid uses a low-bandwidth X.25 connection.

Required result:

Group the servers in the various locations into routing groups using the fewest number of routing groups possible.

Optional result:

For each connection between groups, choose whichever routing group connector will work and is the simplest to configure and maintain.

Proposed solution:

Create a single routing group for the New York and Toronto locations. Create one routing group for the London location and one for the Madrid location. Connect the New York/Toronto routing group to the London routing group with an SMTP Connector. Connect the New York/Toronto routing group to the Madrid routing group with an X.25-based X.400 Connector.

Which of the results does the proposed solution produce?

A. The proposed solution produces the required result and the optional result.

B. The proposed solution produces the required result, but not the optional result.

C. The proposed solution produces the optional result, but not the required result.

D. The proposed solution produces neither the required result nor the optional result.

9. You have an organization that consists of three routing groups: RG1, RG2, and RG3. Two Routing Group Connectors are configured between RG1 and RG2. RGConnector1 is configured with a cost of 5. RGConnector2 is configured with a cost of 10. One Routing Group Connector, RGConnector3, is configured between RG2 and RG3. Its cost is 5. One SMTP Connector, SMTPConnector1, is also configured between RG2 and RG3. Its cost is 9. Which of the following preferred routes will a message take from RG1 to RG3?

A. RGConnector1, SMTPConnector1

B. RGConnector1, RGConnector3

C. RGConnector2, RGConnector3

D. RGConnector2, SMTPConnector1

10. You have a large network that is located in a single building in downtown Dallas. You also have a smaller network in a branch office in Houston. You have created two routing groups in the Dallas location to help direct the flow of messaging traffic and a single routing group in Houston. Four Exchange administrators work in Dallas, and one works in Houston. You want to create one administrative group for Houston and let that administrator handle all Exchange administration for that network. You would like one administrative group in Dallas, as well. However, you find that you must create another administrative group in Dallas to handle system policies since you only want the lead Exchange administrator to create system policies. Which of the following administrative models does this plan fall under?

    A. Centralized

    B. Decentralized

    C. Mixed

11. Servers must meet which of the following criteria to be in the same routing group? (Choose all that apply.)

    A. They must belong to the same Active Directory forest.

    B. They must belong to the same Active Directory domain.

    C. They must be capable of supporting SMTP connectivity.

    D. They must all be in the same administrative group.

12. You are configuring a routing group to connect to a server in an Exchange 5.5 site. You want to ensure that the connector you use will definitely uses SMTP and no other protocol to pass messages. Which of the following options is valid?

    A. Configure a Routing Group Connector and specify that SMTP be used on the Protocols property page.

    B. Configure a Routing Group Connector and specify that SMTP be used on the General property page.

    C. Configure a Routing Group Connector and specify that SMTP be used on the Address Spaces property page.

    D. Configure an SMTP Connector.

    E. Configure an X.400 Connector.

13. You are currently running Windows 2000 in mixed mode and are considering making the switch to native mode. Which of the following would be valid concerns to take into account before making the switch?

    A. The switch to native mode is irreversible.

    B. If you later decide to switch back to native-mode, all object configuration is lost.

    C. Exchange 5.5 Server may not be run in a native-mode environment.

14. You are configuring a connector between two routing groups and want to have servers issue authentication before sending any mail. Which connector allows this?

    A. Routing Group Connector

    B. SMTP Connector

    C. X.400 Connector

    D. Active Directory Connector

15. You are configuring an SMTP Connector. You do not want to allow the connector to use a DNS server to make direct connections to other SMTP servers. Instead, you want the connector to route mail to a specific SMTP server that will handle the messages. How would you do this?

    A. Configure a smart host on the connector's General property page.

    B. Configure a smart host on the connector's Hosts property page.

    C. Configure an MX Record on the connector's Delivery Options page.

    D. Use the connector's Delivery Restrictions page to reject messages from all except a specified server.

16. You are creating a series of connectors between two routing groups that have a fairly low bandwidth connection. You want the connection to be available all the time, but you would like for messages over 5MB only to be sent at specific times during the day. For which of the following connectors can you schedule the delivery of messages based on the size of the message?

   A. Routing Group Connector

   B. X.400 Connector

   C. SMTP Connector

17. You are running an Exchange organization in mixed mode. Previously, the organization consisted of four sites running Exchange Server 5.5. Now that you have installed Exchange 2000 Server into the organization, how many administrative groups can you configure?

   A. None

   B. One

   C. Four

   D. As many as you want

18. Which of the following connector types may use multiple bridgehead servers? (Choose all that apply.)

   A. Routing Group Connector

   B. SMTP Connector

   C. X.400 Connector

   D. TCP Connector

19. Which of the following is an extended SMTP command that is used to initiate an SMTP connection?

   A. HELLO

   B. HELO

   C. EHLO

   D. ELHO

20. What primary advantage does SMTP offer over RPCs for connectivity between servers within a routing group?

   A. SMTP is faster.

   B. SMTP does not require full-time connectivity.

   C. SMTP does not require high-speed connectivity.

   D. SMTP does not require reliable connectivity.

Answers to Review Questions

1. A. The Routing Group Connector is the fastest and simplest to set up. It also offers the ability to automatically configure the other end of a link once one end is set up.

2. B. When running in mixed mode, you can only move mailboxes between servers that are in the same administrative group.

3. A, C. Before creating an X.400 Connector, you must create an MTA Transport Stack. Both TCP/IP and X.25 Transport Stacks are available.

4. A, C. Administrative groups can contain servers, routing groups, public folder trees, system policies, conferencing services, and chat communities.

5. B, D. Both the SMTP and X.400 Connectors can be used to connect routing groups together and to connect to foreign messaging systems. The Routing Group Connector can only be used to connect routing groups. The Active Directory Connector is used to connect an Exchange 5.5 site to the Windows 2000 Active Directory.

6. D. Since New York and Toronto enjoy a permanent, high-speed T1 connection between them, it is possible to configure them to be part of the same routing group, thus the required result of using the fewest groups possible is not met. The connector used between the New York/Toronto routing group and the London routing group should be a Routing Group Connector because it meets the optional result of using a connector that is the simplest to configure and maintain. The connector between the New York/Toronto routing group and the Madrid routing group should be an X.25-based X.400 Connector that supports both X.25 networks and the low-bandwidth connection.

7. A. Since New York and Toronto enjoy a permanent, high-speed T1 connection between them, it is possible to configure them to be part of the same routing group, thus the required result of using the fewest groups possible is met. The connector used between the New York/Toronto routing group and the London routing group should be a Routing Group Connector because it meets the optional result of using a connector that is the simplest to configure and maintain. The connector between the New York/Toronto routing group and the Madrid routing group should be an X.25-based X.400 Connector that supports both X.25 networks and the low-bandwidth connection.

8. B. Since New York and Toronto enjoy a permanent, high-speed T1 connection between them, it is possible to configure them to be part of the same routing group, so the required result of using the fewest possible number of groups is met. London and Madrid should be configured as individual routing groups. The connector used between the New York/Toronto routing group and the London routing group should be a Routing Group Connector because it meets the optional result of using a connector that is the simplest to configure and maintain.

9. B. Messages are sent over the preferred connectors when possible, and the preferred connectors are those with the lowest costs, regardless of what type of connector they are.

10. C. A centralized model is one where there is one administrative group or a tightly controlled set of groups used for functional purposes. A decentralized model is one where an administrative group is created for each of a set of geographical or departmental entities. A mixed model is one where both techniques are used. Since a group is being created for Houston and a main group is being created for Dallas, that makes the example at least partially decentralized. However, since another group is being created in Dallas for purely functional reasons, that makes it a mixed model.

11. A, C. In order to be in the same routing group, all servers must have reliable, permanent, and direct network connectivity that supports SMTP. They must also belong to the same Active Directory forest and be able to connect to a routing group master.

12. D. The only connector that you can force to use SMTP is the SMTP Connector. Actually, you don't force it; it's the only protocol it supports. This makes it ideal when you need to configure a connector to use SMTP between a routing group and an Exchange 5.5 site because the Routing Group Connector will default to RPC in this situation when an SMTP connection cannot be established.

13. A. The switch to native mode is a one-time, one-way switch and is irreversible. Native mode allows your Windows 2000 domain controllers to scale into the millions of objects per domain instead of the 40,000 accounts that Windows NT 4.0 can support.

14. B. The SMTP Connector is more configurable than the Routing Group Connector, offering the ability for more fine-tuning of the connection. The SMTP Connector offers the ability to issue authentication before sending mail, specifying TLS encryption, and removing mail from queues on remote servers.

15. A. To forward mail upstream to another SMTP server instead, select the Forward All Mail Through This Connector To The Following Smart Host option on the General property page for the connector. Also, you might want to specify the IP address instead of the name for the smart host so that no DNS query is required to resolve the name.

16. A. Although you can schedule delivery times on each of the connectors, only the Routing Group Connector also allows you to create a special schedule based on message size.

17. C. Each Exchange 5.5 site in the organization is mapped directly to a single administrative group and a single routing group, and vice versa.

18. A, B. Both the Routing Group Connector and the SMTP Connector can be configured to use multiple source and destination bridgehead servers. The X.400 Connector can only support one bridgehead server. There is no such thing as a TCP Connector.

19. C. Normally, an SMTP client connects to an SMTP server using a command named HELO, which signals the start of a session between two SMTP servers and identifies the sender of the coming message. By default, Exchange 2000 Server sends the EHLO command, another start command that indicates the Exchange 2000 Server can use the Extended SMTP (ESMTP) commands.

20. C. The primary advantage of SMTP over RPCs to transfer messages between servers in a routing group is its ability to transfer messages over slower connections than RPCs allow.

Chapter

8

Configuring the Information Store

MICROSOFT EXAM OBJECTIVES COVERED IN THIS CHAPTER:

✓ **Configure server objects for messaging and collaboration to support the assigned server role.**

- Configure information store objects.
- Configure multiple storage groups for data partitioning.
- Configure multiple databases within a single storage group.
- Configure virtual servers to support Internet protocols.
- Configure Exchange 2000 Server information in the Windows 2000 Active Directory.
- Configure Instant Messaging objects.
- Configure Chat objects.

✓ **Manage user and information store association.**

- Configure user information stores.

✓ **Manage growth of public and private message store databases.**

✓ **Optimize public folder and mailbox searching.**

- Configure the public folder store or mailbox store for full-text indexing.
- Perform full-text indexing.

In Exchange 2000, the Information Store is the service responsible for storing data in the proper places and maintaining the integrity of that data once stored. Unlike previous versions of Exchange Server, which only supported one private storage database and one public storage database per server, Exchange 2000 allows for the creation of multiple stores of each type on a server and the grouping of those stores into storage groups. It is these changes to the storage architecture that provide Exchange 2000 with much greater scalability and flexibility than previous versions. Also, these changes make new methods of accessing data—such as from standard Windows applications—possible.

This chapter provides a brief overview of how storage groups and stores interact and what you can do with them. It then looks at the creation, configuration, and management of both storage groups and stores. Finally, it examines a form of content indexing known as full-text indexing, which Exchange uses to provide greater search capabilities within the Information Store.

Overview of Storage Groups and Stores

Exchange 2000 Enterprise Server supports up to four storage groups on a server and up to five stores in each storage group, providing great flexibility in the storage design and planning. Before we get started with the actual process of creating and managing storage groups and stores, though, it is important to be familiar with the major components in the Exchange storage system and the method Exchange uses to store data.

This chapter deals mainly with the procedures for creating and managing storage groups and stores. Although this overview provides a brief look at how Exchange storage works, it is also important that you are familiar with the architectural concepts discussed in the "Information Storage" section of Chapter 2.

Main Storage Components

The *Information Store* is a Windows 2000 Service that provides storage management on an Exchange 2000 server. It is an actual process, named *Store.exe*, that runs on the server. The Information Store is responsible for making sure that data is placed into transaction logs, that transaction log entries are committed to actual Exchange database files, and that routing maintenance is performed on those files.

A *store* is a logical database that is actually made up of two database files: a *rich-text file* (*.edb) and a *streaming media file* (*.stm). You learned about these files in Chapter 2, so we won't go into too much detail about them here; in short, the rich-text file is used for holding standard Exchange content (such as messages), and the streaming media file is used for holding other types of content in its native format so that Exchange does not have to spend time converting it.

There are two types of stores that you can create on an Exchange server: public and private. *Public stores* are used to hold public folders that are generally accessible by multiple users. *Private stores* are used to hold mailboxes that are normally only accessible by a specified user. Unlike previous versions of Exchange, Exchange 2000 allows you to create multiple stores of each type on a single server.

This ability to create multiple stores leads to several benefits:

- User downtime in the event of a failure is decreased because a failure in one store does not affect users of another store.

- Backup and restore routines are typically faster and more flexible because you can back up or restore a single store at a time without affecting other stores. For example, backing up one out of four 10GB stores at different times of the day is often better than backing up a single 40GB store.

- You can assign different general settings to different stores. For example, you might configure one private store for general use and another for use only by executives. The general store might have certain limitations placed on it that the executive store would not.

Exchange 2000 Enterprise Server supports multiple mailbox stores and multiple private stores on a single server. Exchange 2000 Standard Server supports only one mailbox store on a server, but still supports multiple public stores. In addition, the single mailbox store allowed in the Standard edition is limited to 16GB in size, while the Enterprise edition allows mailbox stores of any size.

A *storage group* is a logical grouping of stores that share the same set of transaction log files, as shown in Figure 8.1. You can create up to four storage groups on a single server, and each storage group can hold up to five stores. The primary reason behind the use of storage groups is to reduce the amount of server overhead that would be caused if every store had its own set of transaction logs, resulting in greater scalability. There are some additional advantages to using multiple storage groups:

- You can manage the stores in a storage group as a group or individually.

- You can configure different properties for the transaction logs of different groups. For example, suppose you have one storage group that contains only public folders that would not be impacted too much by the use of circular logging. You could then configure another storage group to hold more critical mailbox stores for which circular logging would be disabled.

FIGURE 8.1 Storage groups hold stores that share a single set of transaction logs.

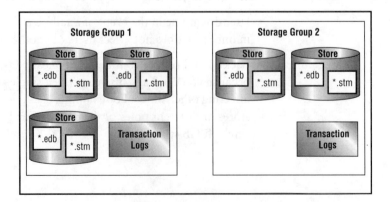

Exchange Storage Methods

When data is to be written to one of the Exchange databases, the database engine does not write the data to the database file immediately. The data is first committed (or written) to a *transaction log file*, and then later committed to the database through a background process. This method has two advantages, one of which is performance. When data is written to a transaction log file, it is entered sequentially, always at the end of the file. This can be done very fast. When data is committed to a database file, however, the database engine must search for the appropriate location to place the data. This is much slower than the simple sequential method. The second advantage is fault tolerance. If a database file becomes corrupt, a transaction log file can be used to re-create the database file.

As transactions in transaction log files are committed to the database files, a *checkpoint file* (EDB.CHK) is updated. The checkpoint file keeps track of which transactions in the sequential list still need to be committed to a database by maintaining a pointer to the last information that was committed. This tells the engine that everything after that point still needs to be committed to a database. If a server shuts down abnormally, Exchange can read the checkpoint file to learn where in the transaction logs it needs to start recovering data. Thus the checkpoint file assists in the fault tolerance of Exchange.

Transaction log files can contain up to 5MB of transactions, and they are always 5MB in size no matter how many transactions they contain. This is because the engine creates them as 5MB files and then proceeds to fill them with transactions. The current log file being written to is named EDB.LOG. When it is filled with 5MB of transactions, it is renamed to EDB*nnnnn*.LOG (where *nnnnn* is a hexadecimal number), and a new, empty EDB.LOG file is created. Therefore, the log files will accumulate on the hard disk. A way to minimize this is to perform regular full or incremental backups of the databases. During a full or incremental backup, fully committed log files are automatically flushed (deleted) because the data in them is backed up. This prevents the number of log files from growing until they take up the entire disk.

Circular Logging

Transaction log files can also be configured to recycle themselves to prevent constant accumulation on the hard disk. This process is called *circular logging*. Instead of continually creating new log files and storing the old ones, the database engine "circles back" to the oldest log file that has been fully committed and overwrites that file. Circular logging minimizes the number of transaction log files on the disk at any given time. The downside is that these logs cannot be used to re-create a database, because the logs do not have a complete set of data. They only have the data not yet committed. Another disadvantage of circular logging is that it does not permit a differential or incremental backup of the databases.

Circular logging is the default setting and can be enabled or disabled on a store's General property page (discussed later in the chapter). Table 8.1 presents a summary and comparison of when circular logging is enabled and disabled.

TABLE 8.1 Circular Logging Enabled vs. Disabled

Circular Logging Enabled (default)	Circular Logging Disabled
Transaction log files are recycled.	Old transaction log files are stored.
The re-creation of a database is not permitted.	The re-creation of a database is permitted.
Differential or incremental backups are not permitted.	Differential and incremental backups are permitted.
	A full or incremental backup automatically deletes old transaction log files.

Reserve Log Files

One other feature of the transaction-based databases is the use of *reserve log files*. Exchange creates two reserve log files (RES1.LOG and RES2.LOG) for each database. They are used if the system runs out of disk space. If that happens, Exchange shuts down the database service, logs an event to the Event Log, and writes any outstanding transaction information into these reserve log files. These two files reserve an area of disk space that can be used after the rest of the disk space is used.

Using Storage Groups

Since storage groups are basically containers that hold stores, they are fairly simple to create, and there is not much to manage about them other than a few simple details. This section describes the creation, configuration, and management of storage groups.

Microsoft
✓ ***Exam***
Objective

Configure server objects for messaging and collaboration to support the assigned server role.

- Configure multiple storage groups for data partitioning.

Creating a Storage Group

By default, a single storage group is created on each server and is named First Storage Group. Since every storage group is created on and associated with a single server, you will always find storage group containers inside a server container in the System Manager snap-in, as shown in Figure 8.2.

FIGURE 8.2 Storage groups always belong to a specific server.

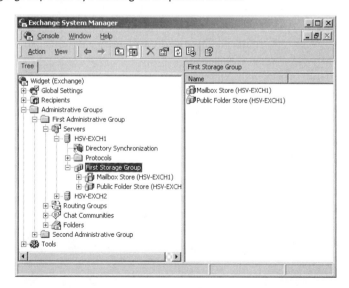

Exercise 8.1 outlines the steps for creating a new storage group.

EXERCISE 8.1

Creating a New Storage Group

1. Go to Start>Programs>Microsoft Exchange, and then select System Manager.

2. Expand the organization object, the Administrative Groups folder, the specific administrative group, and the server on which you want to add a storage group.

3. Right-click the server object and select the New Storage Group command from the shortcut menu. This opens the property pages for the new storage group.

4. Type a name for the new storage group in the Name field and click OK. This creates the storage group using the default properties suggested by System Manager.

Configuring Storage Group Properties

There is only one property page for a storage group—the General page, shown in Figure 8.3. You are given the chance to configure it when you first create the storage group, and you can change the properties later by right-clicking the storage group object and choosing Properties from the shortcut menu.

On the General page for a storage group, you can configure the following parameters:

- You can name the storage group during its creation. If the organization is running in native mode, you can change the name of the storage group at any time. If the organization is running in mixed mode, you cannot change the name after creation.

- The transaction log location is the directory in which the transaction log file for the storage group resides. By default, a location is created for the log file based on the name you give the storage group. You can change this location during creation of the storage group or anytime after creation.

- The system path location is where any temporary database files (named TMP.EDB) and checkpoint files (named EDB.CHK) are stored. You can change this location during or after creation.

- The log file prefix is chosen by the system and cannot be altered. It designates the prefix attached to the log file for the group.

- The Zero Out Deleted Database Pages option is used to remove all 4k pages of data for items when they are deleted from a database. This option automatically writes zeros to these pages within all stores of the storage group. This process occurs after an online backup is performed. This means that the database pages on the backup are not zeroed until the next backup. Be careful using this option, though, as it can significantly reduce your server performance.

- As mentioned earlier, circular logging enables Exchange to conserve disk space by maintaining a fixed number of transaction logs and overwriting those logs as needed. Without circular logging, Exchange creates new log files when old ones fill up. Circular logging is disabled by default, and it is generally recommended that you leave it disabled except possibly for storage groups that contain only public stores with non-critical data.

FIGURE 8.3 Configuring properties for a storage group

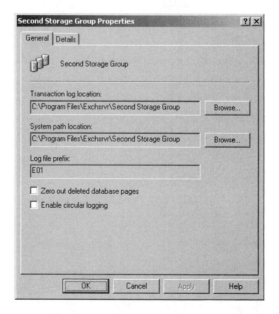

Using Stores

The default storage group, named First Storage Group, is created during Exchange installation. Two stores are also created within that storage group:

- A public store named Public Folder Store *(servername)*. This store is made up of two databases, pub1.edb and pub1.stm, which are stored in the \\Program Files\Exchsrvr\Mdbdata folder.

- A mailbox store named Mailbox Store *(servername)*. This store is made up of two databases, priv1.edb and priv1.stm, which are also stored in the \\Program Files\Exchsrvr\Mdbdata folder.

Microsoft ✓ *Exam Objective*

Configure server objects for messaging and collaboration to support the assigned server role.

- Configure information store objects.
- Configure multiple databases within a single storage group.

Manage growth of public and private message store databases.

You can create up to three new stores in the First Storage Group (unless you first delete the default stores), and you can create new stores in other storage groups, as well. The process for creating a private store and a mailbox store is identical and, for the most part, so is the configuration of the two different types of stores. In the sections that follow, we cover the creation, configuration, and management of a new mailbox store. When configuring a public store, many of the properties you will configure and much of the management are identical. Some differences in the configuration, like the replication of public folders, are discussed in detail in Chapter 5.

Creating a Store

Creating a new store is a straightforward process. You need only make sure that you are creating the store in a storage group with room for another store. Exercise 8.2 outlines the steps for creating a new mailbox store.

EXERCISE 8.2

Creating a New Mailbox Store

1. Go to Start➤Programs➤Microsoft Exchange, and then select System Manager.

2. Expand the organization object, the Administrative Groups folder, the specific administrative group, and the server on which you want to add a store.

3. Right-click the storage group object in which you want to create the store and select the New Mailbox Store command from the short-cut menu. This opens the property pages for the new store.

4. Type a name for the new mailbox store in the Name field of the General page and click OK. This creates the store using the default properties suggested by System Manager.

Configuring Store Properties

There are a number of property pages used to configure a mailbox store. You are given the chance to configure these pages when you first create the store and can change the properties later by right-clicking the store object and choosing Properties from the shortcut menu. The following sections detail the parameters found on many of these property pages. For information on configuring the Policies and Security pages, see Chapter 9.

Microsoft
✓ *Exam*
Objective

Manage user and information store association.

- Configure user information stores.

General Properties

A mailbox store's General page, shown in Figure 8.4, is used to configure the following properties:

- You can name the store during its creation. As with storage groups, you can change the name of a store after creation only if the organization is running in native mode.

- Every Exchange user must have a default public store that is used for public folder access. This does not limit access only to the chosen public store, but rather provides an entry point—the first place the client will look for public folder content. Click the Browse button to open a list of available public stores from which to choose.

- The Offline Address List field specifies the default offline address list that users of this mailbox store will download when synchronizing the Offline Address List on their client. Like the public folder setting, this is simply a default value and does not prevent other available offline address lists from being used.

- You have the option to Archive All Messages Sent Or Received By Users On This Store to a public folder. While this does increase the use of server resources and possibly increase network traffic, it also provides a way of logging e-mail sent in your organization—something your lawyers will love, and your users will hate.

- *Secure/Multipurpose Internet Mail Extensions (S/MIME)* is a secure version of the MIME protocol that supports encryption of messages. It is expected that S/MIME will be widely implemented, which will make it possible for people to send secure e-mail messages to one another, even if they are using different e-mail clients.

- The final option, Display Plain-Text Messages In A Fixed-Size Font, displays all messages sent using plain text in the 10-pt. Courier font, which makes reading many e-mail clients a bit easier.

FIGURE 8.4   General properties of a mailbox store

Database Properties

The mailbox store's Database page, shown in Figure 8.5, has controls that govern how Exchange handles the databases for the store. You can change the location and name of both the rich-text database and the streaming file database. One caveat, though: In order to move a database, you must be running System Manager on the server that holds the database you want to move.

FIGURE 8.5 Database properties of a mailbox store

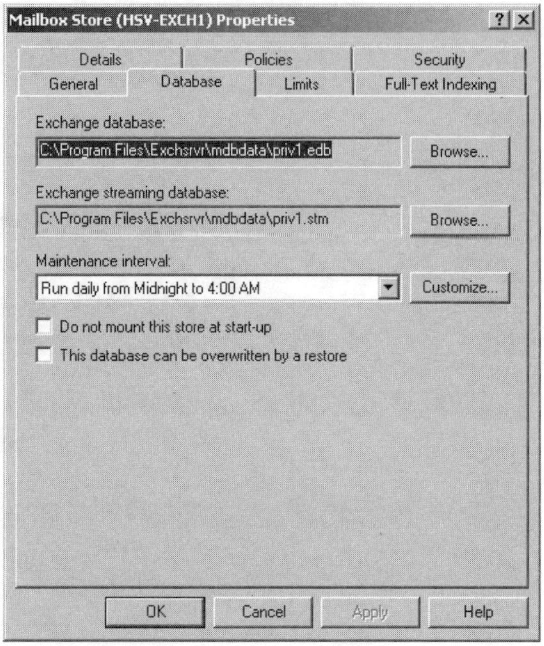

You can also use the Database page to specify the times at which you want the automatic store maintenance routines to run. Select from several preset values using the drop-down list, or click Customize to bring up a calendar-style interface. Finally, you can set options for whether to mount the store when the Exchange server starts up (if it doesn't, you'll have to do it manually) and whether the store can be overwritten during a restore from backup. Check out Chapter 13 for more on backup and recovery.

Limits Properties

The Limits page, shown in Figure 8.6, should look familiar to you. It is used to configure the same types of limits that you can set on individual mailboxes, as discussed in Chapter 4. At the mailbox level, you can set values that override any values you configure on this page, or you can elect to use the store defaults.

FIGURE 8.6   Limits properties of a mailbox store

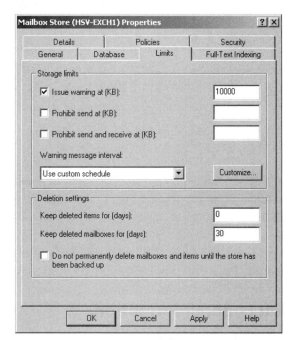

This page lets you set two parameters: storage limits and deletion settings. Storage limits refer to the limits (in kilobytes) placed on the size that mailboxes in the store can grow to and what happens when that limit is crossed. By default, no limits are set. You can set limits for when a warning is issued, when sending is prohibited, and when sending and receiving are prohibited. You can also configure the interval at which the Information Store checks these values and issues warnings.

Deletion settings refer to how long (in days) deleted items in a mailbox and deleted mailboxes are retained on a server after a user or administrator deletes them. You can also configure the store to keep deleted items and mailboxes until the store has been backed up, regardless of the actual values entered.

Full-Text Indexing Properties

Unlike other property pages, the Full-Text Indexing page is not available during the creation of a store. It only becomes available after creation. Full-text indexing is discussed in its own section later in the chapter.

Managing Stores and Storage Groups

Once created and properly configured, both storage groups and stores require proper management to keep everything running smoothly. Much of this management is covered elsewhere in this book:

- Backing up and restoring (Chapter 13)
- Managing public folders and replication (Chapter 5)
- Managing individual users and their mailboxes (Chapter 4)
- Tracking messages and monitoring the status of message flow (Chapter 9)
- Configuring client access to the store data (Chapter 6)

Aside from these major administrative functions, other administrative tidbits regarding stores and storage groups are covered in the next few sections.

Viewing Logon Information

In the store container itself, a number of objects provide some management and monitoring ability over the store. The Logons container, shown in Figure 8.7, shows information regarding who has logged on to the mailbox store. Among other things, this information includes the username, the logon time, the logoff time, and the type of client used to connect.

FIGURE 8.7 Viewing logon information for a store

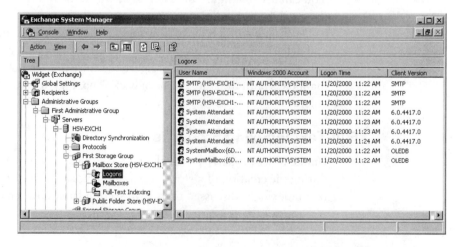

Viewing and Managing Mailbox Information

The mailbox container for a store, shown in Figure 8.8, shows all of the mailboxes configured in the store. Along with the actual mailbox name, you can see who last logged on to the mailbox, how much space the mailbox takes up on the server, how many actual items are in the mailbox, and the last logon/logoff times for the mailbox.

FIGURE 8.8   Viewing mailbox information for a store

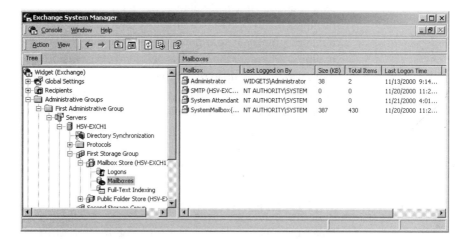

You cannot manage these mailboxes the same way you could in previous versions of Exchange. In fact, there are not even property pages to open. Almost all mailbox administration is performed using the Active Directory Users and Computers tool and the techniques described in Chapter 4.

However, there are two things that you can do to a mailbox from within System Manager. The first is to delete it, though this is called *purging* within the context of System Manager. To do this, right-click the mailbox and select Purge from the shortcut menu.

Once a mailbox is purged, it cannot be recovered.

Mailboxes can also be deleted from within Active Directory Users and Computers, although mailboxes deleted in this manner are not really deleted; they are simply disconnected from the user. This leads us to the second function that you can perform on mailboxes in System Manager, which is to reconnect a disconnected mailbox. Do this by right-clicking the mailbox and selecting Reconnect from the shortcut menu.

This business with purging, deleting, disconnecting, and reconnecting brings up an interesting point regarding not only an interesting interface design point, but something to be careful with on the exam. Why didn't Microsoft simply choose to call it deleting a mailbox in System Manager and disconnecting a mailbox in Active Directory Users and Computers? After all, purging a mailbox makes it sound like you are removing all the messages inside the mailbox. Whatever the reasons, this kind of confusing language and inconsistency can trip you up in real life and on the exam. On the exam, pay particular attention to the context of questions. For example, if an exam questions asks whether you can recover a deleted mailbox, paying close attention may clue you in to whether they really mean a deleted (purged) mailbox or a disconnected (deleted) mailbox.

Mounting and Dismounting Stores

One of the great advantages of having multiple stores is that individual stores can be taken down for maintenance without affecting other stores on the server. Taking a store offline is referred to as *dismounting*, and bringing it back online is referred to as *mounting*. To mount or dismount a store, simply right-click the store and choose the appropriate command from the shortcut menu.

Deleting Mailbox Stores

To delete a mailbox store, just right-click it and choose Delete from the shortcut menu. Before you can do this, however, you must either delete or move all mailboxes within that store. System Manager will not let you delete a store that contains mailboxes. In addition, if the store being deleted has any messages currently queued for outbound delivery, you will be informed that these messages will be lost if you proceed. If you choose to delete the store anyway, you will be asked to select a new store to be used for any messages in the inbound queue.

Deleting Public Folder Stores

Deleting public stores is a little more complicated than deleting mailbox stores. To begin with, the actual command is the same; right-click the store and choose the Delete command. However, there are several restrictions governing the process:

- The store cannot be the only store that contains a public folder tree.

- The store must not be the default public store for any mailbox stores or users.

- Before you can remove a public store that contains system folders, you must select a new public store for those folders.

- If the public store holds the only available replica of a public folder, you will be warned that all data in that folder will be lost.

Deleting a Storage Group

You can delete any storage group by right-clicking it and choosing Delete from the shortcut menu. However, the storage group must not have any stores associated with it. This means you must first remove all stores in the storage group before you can delete the group itself.

Full-Text Indexing

Any client can search the Exchange databases for information by default. However, Exchange 2000 also provides a feature called *full-text indexing*, in which every word in a store (including those in attachments) is indexed for much faster search results.

Microsoft
Exam
Objective

Optimize public folder and mailbox searching.

- Configure the public folder store or mailbox store for full-text indexing.

- Perform full-text indexing.

While full-text indexing does provide significant advantages, there are a few considerations you must make before you decide to use it:

- Building and updating the index consumes server resources. For large stores, the CPU usage and time involved in creating the index can be considerable.

- An indexed store requires about 20% more disk space than a non-indexed store.

- During the time that a store is being indexed or updated, clients may receive incomplete search results. Also, in general, search results are only accurate up to the time the store was last indexed.

Creating a Full-Text Index

Exercise 8.3 outlines the steps for creating a full-text index for a mailbox store.

EXERCISE 8.3

Creating a Full-Text Index for a Mailbox Store

1. Go to Start➤Programs➤Microsoft Exchange, and then select System Manager.

2. Expand the organization object, the Administrative Groups folder, the specific administrative group, the server, and the storage group that contains the store you want to index.

3. Right-click the store and select the Create Full-Text Index command from the shortcut menu.

4. In the dialog that opens, either type a path for the location of the index catalog or accept the default location, and then click OK.

Configuring Properties for a Full-Text Index

Once the full-text index is created (and this can take some time, depending on the size of the store being indexed), you can configure indexing properties by opening the property pages for the store and switching to the Full-Text

Indexing page, shown in Figure 8.9. This page holds three parameters you can configure:

- The Update Interval option is used to schedule the interval at which changes in the store are added to the index.

- The Rebuild Interval option is used to schedule the interval at which the entire index is rebuilt.

- The This Index Is Currently Available For Searching By Clients option opens the index for searching. It is recommended that you disable this during the initial creation of the index and also during complete rebuilds of the index. This helps prevent incomplete searches returned to clients who perform searches while the index is being built.

FIGURE 8.9 Viewing full-text indexing information for a store

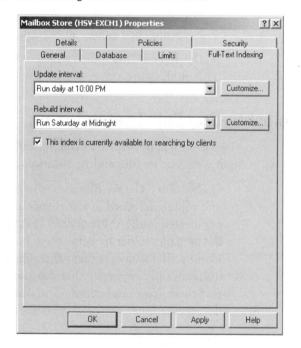

Managing a Full-Text Index

When you right-click a store for which full-text indexing has been enabled, several management tasks are available to you on the shortcut menu that opens. These tasks include the following:

- Start Incremental Population, which finds any changed information in the store and adds it to the index.

- Start Full Population, which rebuilds the entire index. During this process, Exchange purges the index one document at a time instead of purging the entire index and then rebuilding it. This helps speed up the rebuilding process.

- Pause Population, which stops any population process that is currently happening without causing any loss of indexing.

- Stop Population, which halts any population process that is currently happening and causes any updates to be lost.

- Delete Full-Text Index, which deletes the index catalog associated with the store.

Troubleshooting Full-Text Indexing

Two tools will be helpful to you in troubleshooting problems with full-text indexing: Gather files and Application Logs.

Gather files   Gather files are created whenever a full-text index is built and contain a record of errors encountered during indexing. These files are located in the `\\ProgramFiles\Exchsrvr\ExchangeServer\GatherLogs` folder by default and have the extension `.gthr`. These files identify all documents that were not successfully indexed. For the exam, it's really only important that you know what these files are and where to find them. You can learn more about using them from the Exchange documentation.

Application Log   If indexing cannot be performed on an item or is stopped altogether for some reason, a search error is logged in the Windows 2000 Application Log. If the service is experiencing problems, you can also find errors relating to the Microsoft Search Service itself.

Summary

Each Exchange server contains from one to four storage groups. Each of those storage groups contains from one to five stores and a set of transaction logs associated with those stores. Transaction logs are used as the intermediary storage area for transactions that are committed to the actual Exchange databases later. A store is a logical database represented by two files, a rich-text file and a streaming media file. There are two types of stores found on an Exchange server: Public stores hold public folders meant for multiple users, and mailbox stores hold the mailboxes that store messages for individual users.

This assembly of databases, stores, and storage groups provides a great deal of scalability to Exchange 2000 and flexibility in the way that you configure storage in your organization.

The default storage group created when you first install Exchange 2000 Server is named First Storage Group. It contains one public store and one private store when created, though if you wish, you can delete these and/or create more stores. You can create more storage groups on the server, also. Once created, stores and storage groups are configured just like any other object in System Manager—using a series of property pages. The store objects also contain subcontainers, such as the Logons and Mailboxes containers, that let you monitor the status of the store. You can also mount, dismount, and delete individual stores using the object's shortcut menu.

Full-text indexing is a form of content indexing available to all stores on an Exchange server. As an administrator, you can enable or disable full-text indexing on a store-by-store basis. Once a store is indexed, a client can search for items in the store much faster and more accurately than without indexing. Every word of every item in the store, including attachments, is made part of the index. Updating indexes happens automatically, and you can configure the scheduling of this using the Full-Text Indexing property page of the store object. You can also use the shortcut menu for a store to manually control indexing at any time. Two tools are used in troubleshooting problems with full-text indexing. Gather files are created whenever a full-text index is built and contain a record of errors encountered during indexing. The Windows 2000 Application Log records any errors logged by the Microsoft Search Service.

Key Terms

Before you take the exam, be certain you are familiar with the following terms:

checkpoint file	purging
circular logging	reserve log file
committed	rich-text file
dismounting	Secure/Multipurpose Internet Mail Extensions (S/MIME)
full-text indexing	storage group
Information Store	store
mounting	Store.exe
private store	streaming media file
public store	transaction log file

Review Questions

1. You have configured three storage groups on your Exchange server. One group holds five mailbox stores and no public stores. The other two groups are configured with two public stores each and no mailbox stores. How many transaction logs are maintained on the system?

   A. One

   B. Three

   C. Five

   D. Nine

2. You have just installed a new drive on your Exchange server and would like to move the transaction logs for one of your storage groups to that drive. Where would you go to do this?

   A. The Logging property page of the server object that holds the storage group.

   B. The Database property page for the storage group object.

   C. The General property page for the storage group object.

   D. You cannot do this. Once a transaction log is created, it cannot be moved.

3. Which of the following does the Standard edition of Exchange 2000 Server support? (Choose all that apply.)

   A. Multiple public stores

   B. Multiple mailbox stores

   C. Multiple storage groups

   D. Databases up to 16GB

   E. Databases of any size

4. You are an assistant Exchange administrator for a large network. Your supervisor asks you to check a set of mailboxes to determine the last time the user logged on. How would you do this?

   A. Use the Advanced General page of the user's profile in Active Directory Users and Computers.

   B. View the Tools container in System Manager.

   C. View the Mailboxes container in System Manager.

   D. View the Logons container in System Manager.

5. For security reasons, you have decided to configure your mailbox storage group to zero out deleted databases. You realize that this process does not occur until after an online backup is performed, but you have decided that is secure enough for your purposes. What other concern does using this feature raise?

   A. The performance of the server will suffer.

   B. Online backups will take considerably longer.

   C. Users will no longer be able to recover deleted items from their client application.

   D. Multiple log files will be created that must be included in a backup routine.

6. You are planning storage on an Exchange server. You need to create two mailbox stores, one for general use and one for executive use. You also need to create one public store.

   Required result:

   You must be able to re-create the database from uncommitted log files for the executive mailbox store, but this is not so important for the general mailbox store or the public store.

   Optional results:

   You would like to be able to perform both full and incremental backups on all stores on the server.

   You would like to minimize the amount of disk space that the general mailbox and public stores use by limiting the creation of new log files.

Proposed solution:

Create a single storage group. Configure the Executive mailbox store to use circular logging and to zero out deleted database pages.

Which of the results does the proposed solution produce?

A. The proposed solution produces the required result and both optional results.

B. The proposed solution produces the required result, but only one of the optional results.

C. The proposed solution produces the required result, but none of the optional results.

D. The proposed solution does not produce the required result.

7. You are planning storage on an Exchange server. You need to create two mailbox stores, one for general use and one for executive use. You also need to create one public store.

Required result:

You must be able to re-create the database from uncommitted log files for the executive mailbox store, but this is not necessary for the general mailbox store or the public store.

Optional results:

You would like to be able to perform both full and incremental backups on all stores on the server.

You would like to minimize the amount of disk space that the general mailbox and public stores use by limiting the creation of new log files.

Proposed solution:

Create three storage groups. Put the storage mailbox store in one group, and disable circular logging on that group. Put the general mailbox store in another group, and configure that group to zero out deleted pages. Put the public store in the remaining group, and configure that group to zero out deleted pages.

Which of the results does the proposed solution produce?

A. The proposed solution produces the required result and both optional results.

B. The proposed solution produces the required result, but only one of the optional results.

C. The proposed solution produces the required result, but none of the optional results.

D. The proposed solution does not produce the required result.

8. You are planning storage on an Exchange server. You need to create two mailbox stores, one for general use and one for executive use. You also need to create one public store.

Required result:

You must be able to re-create the database from uncommitted log files for the executive mailbox store, but this is not so important for the general mailbox store or the public store.

Optional results:

You would like to be able to perform both full and incremental backups on all stores on the server.

You would like to minimize the amount of disk space that the general mailbox and public stores use by limiting the creation of new log files.

Proposed solution:

Create two storage groups. Put the Executive mailbox store in one group, and configure that group not to use circular logging. Put the general mailbox store and the public folder store in the other group, and configure that group to use circular logging.

Which of the results does the proposed solution produce?

A. The proposed solution produces the required result and both optional results.

B. The proposed solution produces the required result, but only one of the optional results.

C. The proposed solution produces the required result, but none of the optional results.

D. The proposed solution does not produce the required result.

9. You have an organization that consists of three servers: Server1, Server2, and Server3. Server1 and Server2 contain only the default storage groups named First Storage Group, and each of those storage groups contain the default public store and mailbox store. The same is true of Server3, yet here you have also configured another storage group named Executive that holds a single mailbox store for executive mail and a storage group named Jupiter that contains a public store for a new public folder tree. Server1 and Server2 are in one routing group, and Server3 is in another. Server1 is a member of one Windows 2000 domain, and Server2 and Server3 belong to a second Windows 2000 domain. Your organization is running in native mode. Which of the following statements is true? (Choose all that apply.)

A. You could move a mailbox from the mailbox store on Server1 to the mailbox store on Server2.

B. You could move a mailbox from the mailbox store on Server1 to the mailbox store on Server3.

C. You could move a mailbox from the mailbox store on Server1 to the Executive store on Server3.

D. You could move a mailbox from the mailbox store on Server2 to the mailbox store on Server3.

E. You could move a mailbox from the mailbox store on Server2 to the Executive store on Server3

10. You are planning to index a large public store. You are concerned that during the time it takes to index the store, users will submit reports of incomplete or inaccurate searches. How can you solve this problem?

   A. Dismount the store while the indexing takes place.

   B. Use the Full-Text Indexing property page of the store object to disallow searching while the indexing takes place.

   C. Use the General property page of the index to disallow searching while the indexing takes place.

   D. E-mail your users and let them know that search functions will be unavailable for a certain amount of time.

11. Which of the following files is used to keep track of the information in a transaction log that has already been committed to the database?

   A. EDB.LOG

   B. CHECK.LOG

   C. EDB.CHK

   D. RES1.LOG

12. In which of the following directories would you find the database files for the default public and mailbox stores created during Exchange 2000 installation?

   A. \\Program Files\Exchsrvr\Mdbdata

   B. \\Program Files\Exchange\Mdbdata

   C. \\WINNT\Exchsrvr\Mdbdata

   D. \\WINNT\Exchange\Mdbdata

13. You have an Exchange server that contains three storage groups. The first storage group contains a single mailbox store that consumes 10GB of disk space. The second storage group contains two mailbox stores, each consuming 4GB of disk space. The third storage group holds a single public store that consumes 5GB of disk space. You want to enable full-text indexing on all of these stores. How much total disk space should the stores consume after indexing is complete?

A. 23GB

B. 25.3GB

C. 27.6GB

D. 34.5GB

E. 46GB

14. One of your Exchange servers has unexpectedly shut down its Information Store service. You check the Event Log and discover that the disk containing the log files for the Information Store has run out of space. What has happened to any transactions that were outstanding when the problem occurred?

A. The transactions are stored in memory and must be committed before shutting down the computer.

B. The transactions are stored in a reserve log and will be committed when the IS comes back online.

C. Circular logging is turned on, and the oldest committed transaction log is overwritten.

D. The transactions are lost.

15. Which of the following statements is true of working in a mixed-mode organization?

A. You cannot rename a storage group after its creation.

B. You can rename a storage group at any time.

C. You can rename a storage group, but you must dismount all stores in the group first.

D. You can rename a storage group, but only if all transaction logs are fully committed.

16. You recently created a mailbox store for use by executives in your company. You would like to create a public folder and have copies of all messages sent to users in that mailbox store sent to the folder as well. How could you do this?

    A. Configure the store to archive messages using the store's General property page.

    B. Configure the store to archive messages using the store's Advanced property page.

    C. Make regular backups of the mailbox store, and then restore those messages to the public store where the folder is kept.

    D. You cannot do this except by creating a custom program.

17. One of your assistant administrators has mistakenly purged a user's mailbox, thinking that the command was used to empty all messages from the mailbox. Instead, the mailbox has been deleted. How can you recover the mailbox?

    A. Purged mailboxes are only disabled for a specified period of time before being deleted. During this time, you can recover them from System Manager.

    B. Purged mailboxes are only disabled for a specified period of time before being deleted. During this time, you can recover them from Active Directory Users and Computers.

    C. You cannot recover the mailbox. You must create a new one for the user.

18. You are helping a small-business owner install Exchange Server on his network. He plans to use only one Exchange server and does not plan to use public folders. To save some system resources, you decide to remove the public folder store from the server. When you try to delete the store, however, System Manager will not let you. What could be the problem?

    A. You must remove all public folders from the store before deleting the store.

    B. You can only delete a store after dismounting it.

    C. You cannot delete the only store in an organization that contains a public folder tree.

    D. You cannot delete a public store from an Exchange server at all.

19. Which of the following statements is correct?

    A. You can create a full-text index for an individual store.

    B. You can create full-text indexes only for entire storage groups.

    C. You can create full-text indexes only for entire servers.

    D. Full-text indexing is either on or off for a whole organization.

20. Your users are complaining that the search results they get when looking for messages in certain public folders are always outdated by several days. You recognize that all of the folders are part of the same public store and that full-text indexing is turned on for the store. What is the best way to make the searches better for the users?

    A. Decrease the Update interval option on the Full-Text Indexing property page of the public store.

    B. Decrease the Update interval option on the Interval property page of the full-text index.

    C. Adjust the schedule at which updating occurs using the Schedule property page of the public store.

    D. Adjust the schedule at which updating occurs using the Schedule property page of the full-text index.

Answers to Review Questions

1. B. Only one transaction log is maintained for each storage group. Note that there may be multiple transaction log files that represent old transactions not yet committed to the database, but only one current log is used for each storage group.

2. C. The transaction log location is the directory in which the transaction log file for the storage group resides. By default, a location is created for the log file based on the name you give the storage group. You can change this location during creation of the storage group or anytime after creation using the General property page for the storage group object.

3. A, C, D. Exchange 2000 Enterprise Server supports multiple mailbox stores and multiple private stores on a single server. Exchange 2000 Standard Server supports only one mailbox store on a server, but still supports multiple public stores. In addition, the single mailbox store allowed in the Standard edition is limited to 16GB in size, while the Enterprise edition allows mailbox stores of any size.

4. C. The Mailboxes container displays a list of mailboxes and some related information, such as the size of the mailbox, how many items it contains, and the time of the last logon and logoff. The Logons container shows logons to the mailbox store itself.

5. A. The Zero Out Deleted Database Pages option is used to remove all 4k pages of data for items when they are deleted from a database by writing zeros to these pages within all stores of the storage group. This process occurs after an online backup is performed. This option can significantly reduce server performance, though, because of the additional overhead of writing to all the pages.

6. D. When circular logging is enabled, the database engine "circles back" to the oldest log file that has been fully committed and over-writes that file instead of creating a new one. This means that the log files cannot be used to re-create the database in the event of failure. In addition, incremental and differential backups may not be used when circular logging is turned on. Finally, circular logging can only be enabled at the storage group level, since all the stores in a group share a common set of logs. The best thing to do in this scenario is to create two storage groups. Place the executive mail store into one group, and make sure that circular logging is turned off. Place the general mailbox and public store into the other storage group. You will only be able to achieve one of the optional results. If you turn off circular logging, you can use incremental backups on those stores, but you cannot limit the disk space used by the creation of new logs.

7. B. When circular logging is enabled, the database engine "circles back" to the oldest log file that has been fully committed and overwrites that file instead of creating a new one. This means that the log files cannot be used to re-create the database in the event of failure. In addition, incremental and differential backups may not be used when circular logging is turned on. Finally, circular logging can only be enabled at the storage group level, since all the stores in a group share a common set of logs. The best thing to do in this scenario is to create two storage groups. Place the executive mail store into one group, and make sure that circular logging is turned off. Place the general mailbox and public store into the other storage group. You will only be able to achieve one of the optional results. If you turn off circular logging, you can use incremental backups on those stores, but you cannot limit the disk space used by the creation of new logs.

8. B. When circular logging is enabled, the database engine "circles back" to the oldest log file that has been fully committed and over-writes that file instead of creating a new one. This means that the log files cannot be used to re-create the database in the event of failure. In addition, incremental and differential backups may not be used when circular logging is turned on. Finally, circular logging can only be enabled at the storage group level, since all the stores in a group share a common set of logs. The best thing to do in this scenario is to create two storage groups. Place the executive mail store into one group, and make sure that circular logging is turned off. Place the general mailbox and public store into the other storage group. You will only be able to achieve one of the optional results. If you turn off circular logging, you can use incremental backups on those stores, but you cannot limit the disk space used by the creation of new logs.

9. A, B, C, D, E. Assuming you are running in native mode, you can move a mailbox to any other store in the same organization.

10. B. The This Index Is Currently Available For Searching By Clients option on the Full-Text Indexing page for a store opens the index for searching. It is recommended that you disable this during the initial creation of the index and also during complete rebuilds of the index. Not only should you not dismount the store during indexing, but you cannot index a dismounted store. Also, there are no property pages for an index.

11. C. As transactions in transaction log files are committed to the data-base files, a checkpoint file (EDB.CHK) is updated. The checkpoint file keeps track of which transactions in the sequential list still need to be committed to a database by maintaining a pointer to the last informa-tion that was committed. This tells the engine that everything after that point still needs to be committed to a database.

12. A. By default, the databases making up the mailbox and public stores are created in \\Program Files\Exchsrvr\Mdbdata.

13. C. An indexed store requires about 20% more disk space than a non-indexed store. Before indexing, the combined space consumed by the stores was 23GB. Following indexing, this would increase by 20%, making the combined space consumed 27.6GB.

14. B. Exchange creates two reserve log files (RES1.LOG and RES2.LOG) for each database. They are used if the system runs out of disk space. If that happens, Exchange shuts down the database service, logs an event to the Event Log, and writes any outstanding transaction information into these reserve log files. These two files reserve an area of disk space that can be used after the rest of the disk space is used.

15. A. In a mixed-mode organization, you can only name the storage group during its creation. Once created, you cannot change the name later.

16. A. You have the option of archiving all messages sent or received by users in the mailbox store to a public folder. While this does increase the use of server resources and possibly increase network traffic, it also provides a way of logging e-mail sent in your organization.

17. C. Mailboxes may be purged from the Mailbox container in System Manager. Once a mailbox is purged, it cannot be recovered.

18. C. You can delete public stores from System Manager. However, the store cannot be the only store in an organization with a public folder tree. Also, the store must not be the default public store for any users. If the store contains any system folders, you must select a new store to hold those folders. Finally, if the store holds the only available replica of a public folder, you can still delete the store, but System Manager will warn you that the folder will be deleted as well.

19. A. Full-text indexing is enabled at the store level.

20. A. To begin with, there are no property pages for an index. The Update interval is the interval at which changes in the store are committed to the index. Decreasing this option would provide more current search results for your users. The option can be found on the Full-Text Indexing property page of the store object.

Chapter 9

Administration and Maintenance

MICROSOFT EXAM OBJECTIVES COVERED IN THIS CHAPTER:

- ✓ **Configure server objects for messaging and collaboration to support the assigned role.**
  - Configure information store objects.
  - Configure multiple storage groups for data partitioning.
  - Configure multiple databases within a single storage group.
  - Configure virtual servers to support Internet protocols.
  - Configure Exchange 2000 Server information in the Windows 2000 Active Directory.
  - Configure Instant Messaging objects.
  - Configure Chat objects.
- ✓ **Manage messaging queues for multiple protocols.**
- ✓ **Monitor link status.**
  - Monitor messages between Exchange 2000 Server computers.
  - Monitor messages between Exchange 2000 systems and foreign systems.
- ✓ **Monitor services use. Services include messaging, Chat, public folder access, Instant Messaging, and calendaring.**
  - Monitor the Information Store service.
  - Monitor server use by configuring server monitors.
  - Manage Instant Messaging by using System Monitor.
- ✓ **Manage growth of user population and message traffic.**

✓ **Monitor the growth of client use. Clients include Outlook 2000, Outlook Web Access, POP3, IMAP4, and IRC.**

✓ **Manage recipient and server policies.**

✓ **Diagnose and resolve problems that involve recipient and server policies.**

✓ **Diagnose and resolve Exchange 2000 Server availability and performance problems.**

- Diagnose and resolve server resource constraints. Resources include processor, memory, and hard disk.

- Diagnose and resolve server-specific performance problems.

✓ **Manage and troubleshoot messaging connectivity.**

- Manage Exchange 2000 Server messaging connectivity.

- Manage connectivity to foreign mail systems. Connectivity types include X.400, SMTP, and Internet messaging connectivity.

- Diagnose and resolve routing problems.

- Diagnose and resolve problems reported by non-delivery report messages.

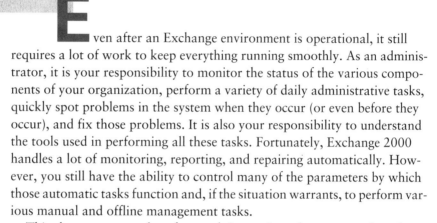

Even after an Exchange environment is operational, it still requires a lot of work to keep everything running smoothly. As an administrator, it is your responsibility to monitor the status of the various components of your organization, perform a variety of daily administrative tasks, quickly spot problems in the system when they occur (or even before they occur), and fix those problems. It is also your responsibility to understand the tools used in performing all these tasks. Fortunately, Exchange 2000 handles a lot of monitoring, reporting, and repairing automatically. However, you still have the ability to control many of the parameters by which those automatic tasks function and, if the situation warrants, to perform various manual and offline management tasks.

This chapter covers a lot of ground. In previous chapters, you have been using System Manager to perform many of the tasks in Exchange. In this chapter, you'll take a closer look at this powerful utility. You will also learn about the following topics:

- Running snap-ins in the Microsoft Management Console

- Using various Windows and Exchange tools to monitor an Exchange server

- Managing message queues and tracking messages

- Using system and recipient policies

- Troubleshooting clients and servers

Administering a Server with System Manager

Most of the chapters in this book discuss some element of administering an Exchange server, group, or organization. Much of this management happens inside the *System Manager* snap-in and, if you've been following along with the exercises in this book so far, you're probably already pretty comfortable with the tool. This section offers a closer look at using System Manager.

Microsoft Management Console

Microsoft Management Console (MMC) provides a common environment for management of system and network resources. MMC is a framework application in which modules called *snap-ins* are run. (System Manager is the snap-in used for managing Exchange 2000 Server.) Snap-ins provide all the real functionality of MMC, and you can run multiple snap-ins inside a single instance of MMC, often called a *console*. This allows administrators to create custom management consoles that are geared toward a specific administrative function or administrator. For example, you might have an administrator who manages an Exchange server and is also responsible for various other aspects of management on that server. You could create a custom console that contained the System Manager snap-in and any other snap-ins that this administrator might need.

Figure 9.1 shows MMC with the System Manager snap-in loaded.

MMC menu bar   The primary MMC menu bar always holds three menu items, regardless of any snap-ins that are loaded: Console, Window, and Help. The Window and Help menus are pretty much what you'd expect. The Console menu holds commands for opening and saving consoles and for adding new snap-ins.

MMC toolbar   The MMC toolbar appears to the right of the MMC menu bar and provides quick access to commands found in the Console menu.

FIGURE 9.1   The main MMC window

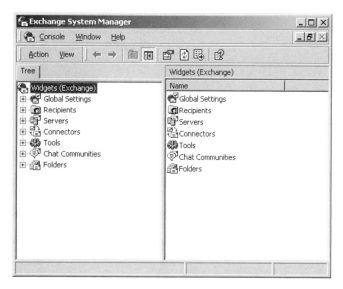

Snap-in action bar   The snap-in action bar appears directly below the MMC menu bar and holds menus that pertain to the snap-in loaded in the console. If a console window contains multiple snap-ins, the action bar changes according to whatever snap-in you are viewing. Most action bars sport three menus: Action, View, and Favorites. The Action menu contains commands that apply to whatever object you have selected in the console. This means that many of the commands found on that menu will change as you select different objects. The View menu is used to control how information is displayed in the console. The Favorites menu lets you add items to a list of favorites and organize that list into categories. The Favorites list can include shortcuts to tools, items in the console, or tasks. The Favorites tab in the Scope pane lets you view items on your Favorites list.

Scope pane   The Scope pane is on the left-hand side of the main MMC window. It shows a hierarchy of containers referred to as a console tree. Some containers are displayed as unique icons that graphically represent the type of items that they contain. Others are displayed as folders, simply indicating that other objects are held inside.

Results pane The Results pane is on the right-hand side of the console. This pane changes to show the contents of whatever container is selected in the Scope pane. In other words, the Results pane shows the results of the currently selected scope. The Results pane can display information in a number of different views. The standard views—large or small icon, list, and detail—are accessed through the View menu. In addition to the standard views, you can also create a taskpad view, which is a dynamic HTML (DHTML) page that presents shortcuts to commands available for a selected item in the Scope pane. As you can see on the bottom of the sample screen in Figure 9.2, each command is represented as a task that consists of an icon, a label, and a description that appears when you run the mouse over the icon.

FIGURE 9.2 Creating a custom taskpad view

Containers and objects All of the items you see in both panes of the console window are called objects. These objects are the primary management tools of a snap-in, and you will use them by opening their property pages, selecting them to view data in the Results pane, or right-clicking them to access pertinent commands. Objects come in two types. *Container objects* hold other objects, even other container objects. They are used to arrange objects into an administrative hierarchy. All container objects form the expandable tree that you see in the Scope pane of a console. *Leaf objects* differ from container objects only in that they cannot hold other objects.

Using the System Manager Snap-In

In previous chapters, you have seen how the System Manager snap-in is used to create and manage recipients; build routing, administrative, and storage groups; and configure protocol usage. This section discusses how it can be used to manage other Exchange activities relating to organization and server management.

Microsoft Exam Objective

Configure server objects for messaging and collaboration to support the assigned role.

- Configure Exchange 2000 Server information in the Windows 2000 Active Directory.

The "Configure information store objects," "Configure multiple storage groups for data partitioning," and "Configure multiple databases within a single storage group" subobjectives are covered in Chapter 8. The "Configure virtual servers to support Internet protocols" subobjective is covered in Chapter 12. The "Configure Instant Messaging objects" and "Configure Chat objects" subobjectives are covered in Chapter 10.

When System Manager is started, its default action is to try to connect to a domain controller that exists on the same subnet as the computer running System Manager. If no domain controller exists on the same subnet, System Manager tries to find one in the same Windows 2000 site. Once System Manager finds a domain controller, it queries Active Directory to fill the console with the current Exchange 2000 objects.

You can direct System Manager to connect to a specific computer by adding the snap-in to a blank MMC console rather than starting System Manager from the Start menu. To do this, select the Run command from the Start menu and type **MMC** into the Run box. When the blank console opens, use the File menu to add a snap-in, and choose the Exchange System Manager snap-in from the list of available snap-ins. When you add the snap-in, you will be prompted to supply the name of a specific domain controller when you add the snap-in. You can save the console at this point so that you don't lose any selections.

Figure 9.3 shows the System Manager snap-in for the Widgets server. No administrative groups or routing groups are displayed so that we may examine the primary hierarchy of containers (shown in the left-hand pane) that make up the System Manager administrative model.

FIGURE 9.3 The hierarchy of an Exchange container

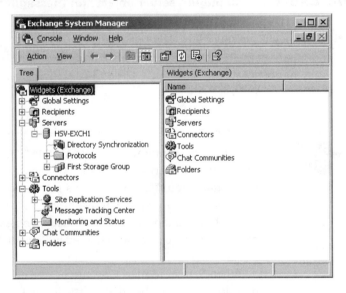

Organization The Organization container appears at the top of the hierarchy and is named for the organization itself (Widgets in Figure 9.3). The property pages for this object hold options for displaying administrative and routing groups and for changing your organization from mixed mode to native mode. These properties are discussed in detail in Chapter 7.

Global Settings   The Global Settings container holds objects governing settings that apply to your entire organization. The container itself has no property pages associated with it, but inside the container, you will find three objects. The first, Internet Message Formats, defines the formatting for SMTP messages sent over the Internet. The second object in the Global Settings container, Message Delivery, is used to configure message defaults for your organization. Open the property pages for this object (shown in Figure 9.4) to set message limit defaults that filter down to the information stores on your servers and to configure filters for handling messages from particular SMTP addresses. The final object in the Global Settings container, Instant Messaging Settings, is used to control default settings for the Instant Messaging Service, which is covered in Chapter 10.

FIGURE 9.4   Configuring Message Delivery settings for an organization

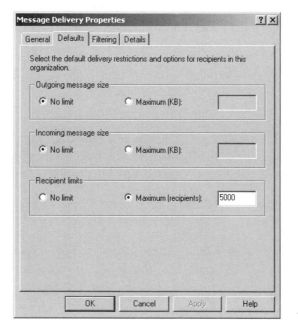

Recipients   The Recipients container is used to manage server settings that apply to recipients in your organization. You can define recipient policies, manage address lists, and even modify address templates. Recipient policies are covered later in this chapter. You can find information on managing address lists in Chapter 4.

Servers   Server containers hold configuration objects for managing the Protocols, Connectors, and Storage Groups configured on a server. You can find information on configuring these specific objects throughout this book.

Connectors   The Connectors container holds configuration items for each of the connectors available within your organization. The objects within the Connectors container represent both connectors between routing groups in your organization and to foreign messaging systems. Connectors between routing groups are covered in Chapter 7, and connectors to foreign messaging systems are covered in Chapter 12.

Tools   The Tools container holds objects that help you manage your Exchange organization. You'll find three containers within the Tools container. The Site Replication Services container lets you configure replication with existing Exchange 5.5 sites using the Active Directory Connector. This is covered in Chapter 11. The Message Tracking Center object is actually a shortcut for opening the *Message Tracking Center (MTC)*, which lets you track specific messages in your organization. The MTC is discussed in detail later in this chapter. The Monitors container holds objects that let you monitor the status of servers and connections in your organization. Both of these are covered later in this chapter.

Chat Communities   The Chat Communities container appears only if the Chat Service is installed and is used to configure Chat support. Chat services are covered in detail in Chapter 10.

Folders   The Folders container holds the public folders hierarchy and properties, but not their contents. It also contains the system folders, a list of folders that Exchange users do not see. The system folders hold the Offline Address Book and other system configuration objects. You can learn more about the Folders container in Chapter 5.

Customizing a Console

System Manager is actually a saved console file that connects to a Windows 2000 domain controller in order to get configuration information regarding your Exchange organization. While all Exchange administrative functionality can be controlled from the System Manager, there are reasons you might want to create a custom console.

For example, you could create a custom System Manager console that provides specialized taskpad views for helping new Exchange administrators get used to the system or that always connects to a specific server in another organization.

In addition to the full System Manger snap-in, there are a few other Exchange-related snap-ins you can use to create a custom console:

- The *Exchange Advanced Security snap-in* creates a console with only the tools for managing the Key Management (KM) Server. You can find details on using the KM Server in Chapter 14.

- The *Exchange Conferencing Services snap-in* creates a console displaying only the tools for managing Exchange Server's online collaboration features, including Chat and Instant Messaging. You can find details on using these features in Chapter 10.

- The *Exchange Folders snap-in* creates a console with only the tools for managing public folders.

- The *Exchange Message Tracking Center snap-in* creates a console displaying only the message tracking features.

Managing Administrative Security

Administrative access to Exchange objects can be configured. An administrator can assign permissions to specific users or groups at different levels of the Exchange hierarchy in order to determine who has what type of access to what information. To understand how permissions are assigned, you must understand the types of permissions available and the way that permissions are inherited by objects from their parent objects.

Types of Permissions

Exchange 2000 Server uses the Windows 2000 security model to manage access to objects. All Exchange objects are secured with a *discretionary access control list (DACL)* and individual *Access Control Entries (ACEs)* that give users and groups specific permissions on an object. In System Manager, you will configure permissions for an object using the Security property page for that object (see Figure 9.5).

FIGURE 9.5 Assigning permissions to an object

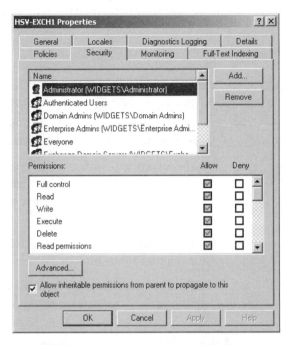

For the most part, the Security page is common across all objects. You select a user or group from the list (you can add more by clicking the Add button) and then either grant or deny each permission for that user or group.

WARNING If you do not specifically grant or deny a permission, the state of the permission is inherited from the parent container. Read on for more on permissions inheritance.

There are two types of permissions available to you. *Standard permissions* are part of the default permissions that come with Windows 2000. *Extended permissions* are added when Exchange 2000 is installed. Extended permissions change depending on the object you are viewing. For example, many recipient objects have the extended permissions Send As and Receive As. Server objects have an Administer Information Store permission that is used to specify the users and groups that can administer stores on the server.

Table 9.1 lists the standard permissions available to you. These are the permissions you should really be familiar with on the job—and on the exam.

TABLE 9.1   Standard Permissions for Administrative Objects

Permission	Description
Full Control	Gives full permissions on the object.
Read	View the object in System Manager.
Write	Make changes to the object.
Delete	Delete the object.
Read Permissions	View the Security page for the object.
Change Permissions	Modify the permissions for the object.
Take Ownership	Take ownership of the object.
Create Children	Create child objects inside the object.
Delete Children	Delete child objects from the object.
List Contents	View the contents of a container object.
Read Properties	View the properties of the object.
Write Properties	Modify the properties of the object.
List Object	View the objects in a container object.

Permissions Inheritance

By default, child objects in System Manager always *inherit* permissions from their parent objects. For the most part, this is a good thing, as it eliminates the need to manually assign permissions to every object, letting System Manager do much of the work for you. However, there will be times when you want to override this functionality. You can do so in two ways via the child object's Security property page (shown in Figure 9.5):

- Modify the permissions by specifically granting or denying the permission to the appropriate user or group.

- Disable the Allow Inheritable Permissions From Parent To Propagate To This Object option.

You can also prevent permissions from being inherited in the first place by visiting the parent object's Security page and clicking the Advanced button. In the Advanced dialog that opens, you can specify whether the permissions for each access control setting should or should not propagate to child objects.

Exercise 9.1 outlines the steps for assigning permissions to an object and preventing that object from propagating permissions to any of its child objects.

EXERCISE 9.1

Modifying Permissions on an Object in System Manager

1. Click Start ≻ Programs ≻ Exchange ≻ System Manager.

2. Double-click the Servers container to expand it.

3. Right-click a server object and select the Properties command.

4. Click the Security tab.

5. Select the Domain Admins group from the list.

6. Click the Deny option for the Full Control permission.

7. Click the Advanced button.

8. Select the Deny Domain Admins Full Control entry from the list.

9. Click the View/Edit button.

10. From the drop-down list, select This Object Only.

11. Click OK three times to return to System Manager.

The Exchange Administration Delegation Wizard

All users who will function as Exchange administrators must be granted the appropriate permissions on objects they will need to administer. Fortunately, System Manager provides a tool that makes the task of delegating administrative permissions in Exchange a good bit easier than having to assign them manually.

The *Exchange Administration Delegation Wizard* lets you select a user or group and assign them a specific administrative role. You can start the Wizard either from the organization object (right-click and choose the Delegate Control command) or from a specific administrative group.

Where you start the Wizard defines the scope of permissions that are assigned to the user or group. For example, if you start the Wizard from the organization object, the permissions assigned propagate all the way down through the hierarchy of objects. If you start the Wizard from a specific administrative group, permissions propagate down through that group only. However, read-only permissions also propagate upward along the hierarchy so that the administrators can view, at least, the objects in the full hierarchy.

The Exchange Administration Delegation Wizard is a separate utility from the Delegation of Control Wizard available in Active Directory Users and Computers.

In addition, to start the Wizard, you must have full administrative control yourself. Full administrative control is granted to the user who installed the first Exchange server in an organization.

There are three roles that you can assign using the Exchange Administration Delegation Wizard:

- The *Exchange Full Administrator role* gives full administrative capability. Administrators can add, delete, and rename objects, as well as modify permissions on objects.

- The *Exchange Administrator role* gives the same full administrative capability as the Exchange Full Administrator role, but does not give administrators permission to modify permissions for objects.

- The *Exchange View-Only Administrator role* lets administrators view Exchange configuration information, but not modify it in any way. This role is often useful to assign to administrators who might need to see the way an organization is structured, but do not perform any actual administration.

Monitoring a Server

By keeping close watch over your organization and its components, you can spot potential problems before they occur and quickly respond to the problems that do occur. Monitoring also allows you to identify trends in network use that signal opportunities for optimization and future planning.

This section covers many of the Windows 2000 and Exchange 2000 tools that you will use to monitor your servers.

<table>
<tr><td>

Microsoft
✓ *Exam*
Objectives

</td><td>

Manage growth of user population and message traffic.

Monitor the growth of client use. Clients include Outlook 2000, Outlook Web Access, POP3, IMAP4, and IRC.

Monitor services use. Services include messaging, Chat, public folder access, Instant Messaging, and calendaring.

- Monitor the Information Store service.

</td></tr>
</table>

Windows 2000 Tools

Exchange 2000 Server is tightly integrated into Windows 2000 Server and leverages the management tools built into the operating system. In this section, we discuss these tools:

- Control Panel ➢ Administrative Services ➢ Services
- Event Viewer
- Performance Monitor
- Registry Editor
- Computer Management
- Task Manager

Monitoring Services

Selecting Control Panel ➢ Administrative Tools ➢ Services (shown in Figure 9.6) can be used to check the status of the Exchange Server services. You can start, stop, and pause a service by selecting it and using the appropriate buttons on the toolbar. You can also configure the startup parameters of a service by double-clicking it to open the service's property pages.

FIGURE 9.6 Monitoring services in Windows 2000

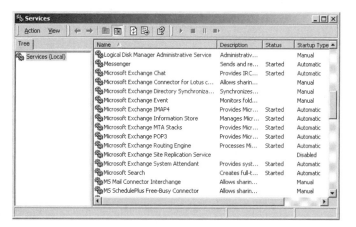

There are a number of Exchange-related services that you should be aware of, including the following:

- The Microsoft Exchange Information Store service manages the store databases.

- The Microsoft Exchange Routing Engine service processes the routing information for a server.

- The Microsoft Exchange System Attendant provides system-related services such as server maintenance.

There will be a number of other services listed depending on the components you have installed on the server.

Using Event Viewer

All Exchange services write event information to the *Windows 2000 Event Log*. Administrators should regularly (daily is recommended) view the Event Log for management and troubleshooting purposes using the Event Viewer application. Exchange services can be configured to log different amounts and types of events for diagnostics logging. Windows 2000 Server maintains three distinct logs:

- The Application log is a record of events generated by applications. All Exchange 2000 Server services write their status information to this log. If you enable diagnostics logging for any Exchange 2000 Server component, that information is also recorded in the Application log. This log is the most valuable log for monitoring the general health of an Exchange server.

- The Security log is a record of events based on the auditing settings specified in the Active Directory Users and Computers utility.

- The System log is a record of events that concern components of the system itself, including such events as device driver and network failures.

The vast majority of Exchange information is written to the Application Event Log. The administrator may want to increase the maximum size of this log (the default is 512KB) if logging levels are turned up for troubleshooting or just to maintain the events that have occurred over a longer period. Event Viewer can also be used to view the Event Logs of a remote server.

Microsoft ✓ ***Exam*** ***Objectives***

Diagnose and resolve Exchange 2000 availability and performance problems.

- Diagnose and resolve server resource constraints. Resources include processor, memory, and hard disk.

- Diagnose and resolve server-specific performance problems.

Monitor services use. Services include messaging, Chat, public folder access, Instant Messaging, and calendaring.

- Monitor Instant Messaging by using System Monitor.

Using the Performance Snap-In

The Exchange Server setup program adds Exchange-related counters to Windows 2000's *Performance snap-in*, also called Performance Monitor, making it possible to view the performance of various Exchange activities. Performance Monitor graphically charts the performance of hundreds of individual system parameters on a Microsoft Windows 2000 computer and can also be used to log those parameters over time. When Exchange 2000 Server is installed on a Windows 2000 Server, several Exchange-specific counters can be charted as well.

This book uses the terms System Monitor and Performance Monitor interchangeably.

Table 9.2 shows the major new performance objects added by Exchange and the counters for those objects.

TABLE 9.2 Exchange-Related Performance Objects and Counters

Object	Counter	Description
MSExchangeIS	User Count	Displays the number of users that are currently using the Information Store.
MSExchangeIS Mailbox and MSExchangeIS Public	Send Queue Size	Displays the queue of messages outbound from the Information Store.
	Receive Queue Size	Displays the queue of messages inbound to the Information Store.
	Message Sent/min	Shows the rate (per minute) at which messages are sent to the routing engine.
	Messages Delivered/min	Shows the rate (per minute) at which messages are delivered to all recipients.
SMTP Server	Local Queue Length	Indicates the number of messages in the local queue. A normal reading is 0. If the reading exceeds 0, the server is receiving messages faster than it can process them.
	Categorizer Queue Length	Displays the number of messages waiting for advanced address resolution to occur.

TABLE 9.2 Exchange-Related Performance Objects and Counters *(continued)*

Object	Counter	Description
	Inbound Connections Current	Measures the number of connections that are currently inbound.
	Message Bytes Received/sec	Measures the rate (per second) at which inbound messages are being received.
	Message Bytes Sent/sec	Measures the rate (per second) at which inbound messages are being sent.
MSExchangeMTA	Messages/sec	The number of messages the MTA sends and receives per second.
	Work Queue Length	The number of messages queued in the MTA.
MSExchangeMTA Connections	Queue Length	Displays MTA counters on a connection-by-connection basis
MSExchangeSRS	Replication Updates/sec	Measures the rate (per second) at which replication updates are applied to local site replication services. This object is used to monitor integration of Exchange 5.5 with Exchange 2000 Server.
	Remaining Replication Updates	Measures how many messages in the current replication update message have yet to be processed.

TABLE 9.2   Exchange-Related Performance Objects and Counters *(continued)*

Object	Counter	Description
MSExchangeIM Virtual Servers	Current Online Users	The number of Instant Messaging users currently logged on to the system.
	Current Subscriptions	The number of current subscription notifications sent by users to a server.
	Inbound SUBSCRIBEs/sec	The average number of SUBSCRIBE requests per second.

Don't underestimate the benefit of using the Performance snap-in in your Exchange environment. The Performance snap-in can be used to collect and analyze data, perform a baseline of your Exchange servers, and detect problems and provide the proper notification, as well as analyze the problems when they occur.

In addition to the Exchange-specific counters represented in the preceding table, there are several critical areas in which you should use the Performance snap-in to monitor an Exchange server's performance. These areas include the following:

Central Processing Unit (CPU)   The Processor object has several counters you can use to monitor the CPU for potential bottleneck issues.

Network   The Network Segment, Redirector, Server, and Server Work Queue objects hold counters that can help identify network subsystem bottlenecks.

Disk Input/Output (I/O)   You should monitor both the logical and physical disk counters to help identify disk subsystem bottlenecks.

Memory   The Memory object has several counters useful in determining the scope of memory-related bottlenecks.

Using Performance Monitor to Check Exchange

Here is a case study of using the Performance snap-in to monitor Exchange Server. An administrator is receiving reports from users that the Exchange server response time is slow. A quick examination shows that the server's disk is almost constantly active. The administrator decides to take a deeper look and, using Performance Monitor, collects the following information about that particular Exchange server:

%Processor time = 70

%Disk free space = 60

Pages/sec = 40

Avg. Disk sec/Transfer = 0.02

The administrator then compares these statistics to the "rule of thumb" thresholds that their organization has determined. The following are those thresholds, which when exceeded, have been associated with performance problems:

%Processor time > 80%

%Disk free space < 10%

Pages/sec > 5

Avg. Disk sec/Transfer > .3

Comparing the current statistics with the thresholds, the administrator sees that the Pages/sec number is over the threshold. This suggests that there is not enough memory to cache information, therefore leading the system to page data to the disk. The administrator decides to add memory to this server and continue to monitor the situation.

Performance Monitor can also be used to warn you of a situation and therefore help you prevent a particular problem. For example, if all available disk space is used, your IS will stop. You could configure Performance Monitor to send you an e-mail message when the available disk space reaches a specified low level. You could then take steps to prevent all disk space from being used and therefore prevent the IS from being stopped.

Using Registry Editor

Like all Windows applications, Exchange Server stores some configuration information in the Registry. This information can be read and modified using the Registry Editor application (`regedit.exe`). All the Registry settings for Exchange Server are stored under the keys `HKEY_LOCAL_MACHINE\SOFTWARE` and `HKEY_LOCAL_MACHINE\SYSTEM`. Normally, you will not need to edit the Registry directly (which can be dangerous, as there are no safeguards to prevent mistakes). Most configurations are made through the Exchange Administrator program and are written to the Registry automatically.

Computer Management

The *Computer Management snap-in* (available in Control Panel ➤ Administrative Tools) holds a variety of management utilities, including:

- Event Viewer
- Disk Management Tools, which allows you to partition and format hard disks
- Various pieces of information about services and applications running on the server

Using Task Manager

Task Manager displays the programs and processes running on a computer. It also displays various performance information, such as CPU and memory usage. An Exchange administrator can use this tool to view the overall health of a server. You access Task Manager by right-clicking the Taskbar and choosing Task Manager from the drop-down menu.

Exchange Tools

In addition to the Windows 2000 tools used for monitoring and managing a server, Exchange 2000 Server provides a number of its own tools, as well.

Microsoft
✓ *Exam*
Objective

Manage and troubleshoot messaging connectivity.

- Diagnose and resolve routing problems.

The subobjectives "Manage Exchange 2000 Server messaging connectivity" and "Manage connectivity to foreign mail systems. Connectivity types include X.400, SMTP, and Internet messaging connectivity" are discussed in Chapters 7 and 12, respectively. The "Diagnose and resolve problems reported by non-delivery report messages" subobjective is discussed later in this chapter.

Configuring Diagnostics Logging

All Exchange services log certain critical events to the Windows 2000 Server Application Log. For certain services, however, you can configure additional levels of logging. *Diagnostics logging* is one of the most useful tools for troubleshooting problems in Exchange 2000 Server.

You can modify the levels of diagnostics logging for all services on a particular Exchange server by using the Diagnostics Logging property page for the server object in System Manager (see Figure 9.7).

FIGURE 9.7 Configuring diagnostics logging

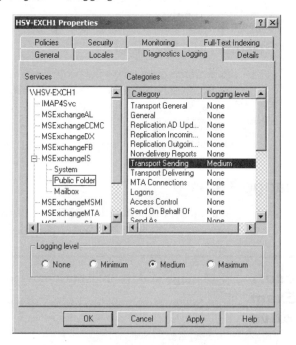

On the left side of this page, you'll find a hierarchical view of all the major services on the server for which you can enable advanced diagnostics logging. These services include the following:

MSExchangeCCMC (Microsoft Exchange cc:Mail Connector)   Use diagnostics logging on this service to troubleshoot problems with message delivery between Exchange 2000 Server and a cc:Mail post office.

MSExchangeDX (Microsoft Exchange Directory Synchronization Agent)   Use diagnostics logging on this service to troubleshoot problems with Directory Synchronization with foreign mail systems.

MSExchangeIS (Microsoft Exchange Information Store Service)   You do not actually enable logging for the Information Store service as a whole. The MSExchangeIS item expands, allowing you to enable diagnostics logging individually for the Public and Private Information Stores and for the various Internet protocols.

MSExchangeMSMI (Microsoft Exchange Microsoft Mail Connector)   The acronym MSMI stands for Microsoft Mail Interchange. Use diagnostics logging on this service to troubleshoot problems with message delivery between Exchange 2000 Server and Microsoft Mail post offices.

MSExchangeMTA (Microsoft Exchange Message Transfer Agent)   Use diagnostics logging on this service to troubleshoot problems with message delivery and gateway connectivity.

On the right side of the Diagnostics Logging page, you'll find a list of categories that can be logged for the selected service. You can enable four distinct levels of logging by using the radio buttons on the bottom of the page. All events that occur in Exchange 2000 Server are given an event level of 0, 1, 3, or 5. The logging level you set will determine which levels of events are logged:

- When the None option is selected, only events with a logging level of 0 are logged. These events include application and system failures.

- When the Minimum option is selected, all events with a logging level of 1 or lower are logged.

- When the Medium option is selected, all events with a logging level of 3 or lower are logged.

- When the Maximum option is selected, all events with a logging level of 5 or lower are logged. All events concerning a particular service are logged. This level can fill an Event Log quickly and is used mainly when working on an issue with Microsoft Product Support.

Monitoring Messages

Ensuring the efficient delivery of messages is paramount to an administrator's job. To accomplish this job, you need to first understand how messaging works within the Exchange system. Messaging architecture is covered in detail in Chapter 2. Chapter 7 also showed you how to construct and link routing groups and the role they play in the flow of messages in an Exchange organization. In this section, you will learn about managing message queues and tracking messages in the organization.

Microsoft ✓ **Exam Objectives**

Manage messaging queues for multiple protocols.

Monitor link status.

- Monitor messages between Exchange 2000 Server computers.
- Monitor messages between Exchange 2000 systems and foreign systems.

Managing Message Queues

Should you suspect a problem with a particular queue, System Manager provides a tool called the *Queue Viewer* that can help you troubleshoot it. In the Protocols container of each server in System Manager, you will find containers for each of the protocols configured on a server. Many of these protocol containers have a container inside them named Queues. Selecting a Queues container displays a list of queues on the server in the content pane of System Manager, along with useful information such as whether the queue is running and how many messages are in it. The Queues container for the Microsoft MTA is shown in Figure 9.8.

Selecting any particular queue within the Queues container shows you a list of messages within the queue and the attributes of those messages. You can freeze messages so that the MTA does not attempt to send them while you troubleshoot the queue and then unfreeze them to let the MTA go ahead with the send. You can also delete messages from the queue altogether.

FIGURE 9.8   Viewing the Queues container

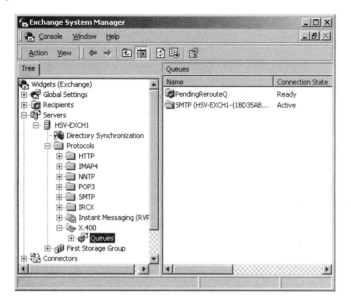

Tracking Messages

Message tracking is enabled at the server level using the General property page for the server container. You can also enable it using system policies, which are covered later in the chapter. Once message tracking is enabled, Exchange Server keeps a log of all messages transferred to and from the server. Log files are maintained by the System Attendant service on each server.

Microsoft Exam Objective

Manage and troubleshoot messaging connectivity.

- Diagnose and resolve problems reported by non-delivery report messages.

The subobjectives "Manage Exchange 2000 Server messaging connectivity" and "Manage connectivity to foreign mail systems. Connectivity types include X.400, SMTP, and Internet messaging connectivity" are discussed in Chapters 7 and 12, respectively. The "Diagnose and resolve routing problems" subobjective is discussed earlier in this chapter.

When message tracking has been enabled, you can track individual messages by using the Message Tracking Center, a component of System Manager. You can use the MTC to trace the route of test messages you send through the system or to help diagnose the cause of undelivered messages for which users have received non-delivery reports.

To use the MTC, open it by first navigating to and selecting the Message Tracking Center container in System Manager, as shown in Figure 9.9.

FIGURE 9.9 Using the Message Tracking Center

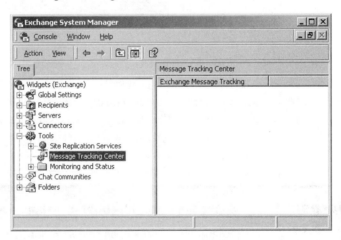

Next, choose the Track Message command from the Action menu. This opens the Message Tracking Center window, shown in Figure 9.10. Click the Browse buttons next to the From or Sent To boxes to open a standard address book, from which you can choose the originator or recipient of the message that you want to track in the MTC. You can also browse for the server(s) on which you would like to search for the messages. After you enter your criteria, click Find Now to perform the search.

FIGURE 9.10 Searching for a message to track

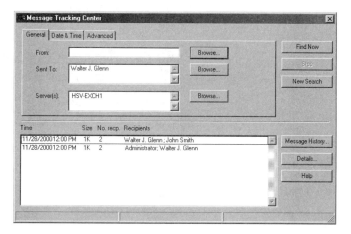

When the messages that meet your criteria are displayed in the bottom of the MTC window, you can open the property sheet of any message by selecting it and then clicking the Details button. Use this method to find the actual message that you want to track. When you find that message, select it and then click the Message History button to start the MTC tracking the history of the message. The results are displayed in the Message History window, shown in Figure 9.11. As you can see, the Message History window displays basic information about the message and a history of the message that shows each service the message has been through.

FIGURE 9.11 Viewing the tracking history for a message

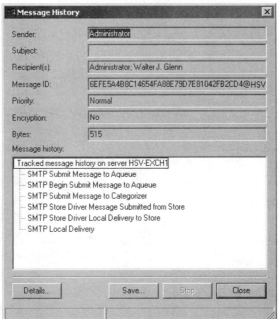

Using Exchange Monitors

By default, Exchange 2000 monitors the status of all connectors and a group of default services on every Exchange server. You can change the default services monitored, configure Exchange to monitor other services, and set up notification events to occur when problems arise. You do all of this using the *Monitoring and Status tool* (shown in Figure 9.12), which is actually a container in System Manager.

Microsoft
✓ *Exam*
Objectives

Monitor link status.

- Monitor messages between Exchange 2000 Server computers.

- Monitor messages between Exchange 2000 systems and foreign systems.

Monitor services use. Services include messaging, Chat, public folder access, Instant Messaging, and calendaring.

- Monitor server use by configuring server monitors.

FIGURE 9.12 Accessing the Monitoring and Status tool

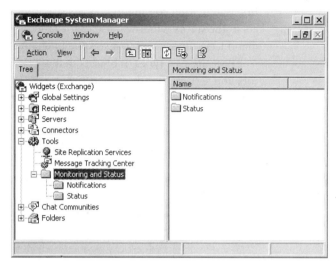

Monitoring Status

Status monitoring is configured using the Status container. Selecting the container in the System Manager snap-in, as shown in Figure 9.13, displays the basic status of all connectors and servers in the right-hand pane. This display gives you a quick overview of the names of the connectors and servers, the administrative group they belong to, and whether they are available or not.

FIGURE 9.13 Using the Status container

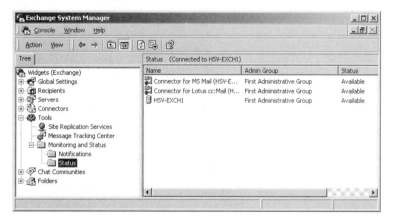

Right-clicking the Status container provides access to two commands. The first is a filtering command that lets you filter the view of connectors and servers in the status window—useful for large organizations. The second command lets you connect to a specific Exchange server in the organization.

There are two types of objects that appear in the Status container: connectors and servers. For the connector objects, you really can't do much more than see whether the connector is available or not. Connector objects don't have property pages, so they are not configurable at this location. Server objects, on the other hand, are quite configurable. Right-click any server and choose Properties to open the property page shown in Figure 9.14.

FIGURE 9.14 Configuring properties for a server monitor

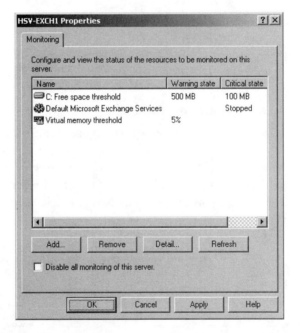

By default, Exchange 2000 monitors the following services on every Exchange server and logs a critical or warning state whenever any of the services stops:

- Microsoft Exchange Information Store service
- Microsoft Exchange MTA Stacks

- Microsoft Exchange Routing Engine

- Microsoft Exchange System Attendant

- Simple Mail Transfer Protocol (SMTP)

- World Wide Web Publishing service

You can add a new default service to be monitored by selecting the Default Microsoft Exchange Services entry and clicking the Detail button. This brings up a dialog box that lists the services currently being monitored. Use the controls on this dialog to add and remove service from the list. Note that you are not restricted to only monitoring Exchange-related services. You can add any service on the computer to be one of the default monitored services.

In addition to monitoring services, a server monitor can be configured to monitor other resources, as well. In Figure 9.14, the monitor is also configured to keep track of free disk space and a virtual memory threshold. By clicking the Add button on the Monitoring tab, you can add any of the following resources to the list to be monitored:

- Available virtual memory

- CPU utilization

- Free disk space

- SMTP queue growth

- Any Windows 2000 service

- X.400 queue growth

For each of these resources, you will need to configure what threshold must be crossed to send the monitor into a warning state or a critical state. For example, you might want the monitor to enter a warning state when the amount of free disk space on a server reaches 500MB and to enter a critical state when it reaches 100MB.

Exercise 9.2 outlines the process for configuring a server to monitor the free disk space and enter a critical state when space falls below 250MB

EXERCISE 9.2

Setting Up a Monitor

1. Click Start ➤ Programs ➤ Microsoft Exchange ➤ System Manager.

2. Expand the Tools container and the Monitoring and Status container inside it, and then select the Status container.

3. Right-click the server you want to monitor and select Properties from the shortcut menu.

4. Click Add.

5. In the dialog box that opens, select the Free Disk Space entry, and then click OK.

6. In the Disk Space Thresholds dialog, select the Critical State (MB) option and type **250**.

7. Click OK twice to return to System Manager.

SETTING UP NOTIFICATIONS

As the previous section just described, the Status container is used to configure whether stopped services or certain resource thresholds trigger a warning state or a critical state. A *notification* defines what happens when those states are entered. By default, the Notifications container is empty. This means that the only way you really have of noticing that a server or connector has entered a warning or critical state is by checking out the Status container yourself. The Notifications container lets you set up a notification that can either send you an e-mail or run an executable script when something goes amiss.

Figure 9.15 shows the property page for an e-mail notification. A script notification is quite similar, but has parameters for running a script instead of sending an e-mail.

FIGURE 9.15 Setting up an e-mail notification

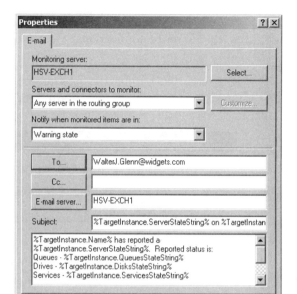

For each notification, you must set up the following in its property page:

- The monitoring server is the server that actually performs the monitoring and triggers the notification.

It is often good to put one server in charge of monitoring another, as a server often can't send out a notification when one of its own services goes down.

- Select an individual server, all servers or connectors, a routing group, or a customized list of servers and connectors to which the notification will apply.

- Choose whether the notification should occur when the monitored resource enters a warning or critical state. For example, you could set an e-mail notification to inform you when a warning state is entered and a script notification to run a script that pages you when a critical state is entered.

- For e-mail notifications, you must configure the e-mail address and server to which the notification is to be sent.

- For script notifications, you must enter the path to the executable file and any command-line parameters.

Exercise 9.3 outlines the steps for setting up an e-mail notification to warn you when a server enters a critical state.

EXERCISE 9.3

Setting Up an E-Mail Notification

1. Click Start ➤ Programs ➤ Microsoft Exchange ➤ System Manager.

2. Expand the Tools container and the Monitoring and Status container inside it.

3. Right-click the Notifications container and select New E-Mail Notification from the shortcut menu.

4. Click the Select button.

5. In the Select Exchange Server dialog box, select the Exchange server that you want to perform the monitoring and to send the notification, and click OK.

6. Click the To button.

7. In the Select Recipient dialog box, select the user to whom the notification should be sent, and click OK.

8. Click OK to create the notification and return to System Manager.

Using SNMP and the MADMAN MIB

Simple Network Management Protocol (SNMP) is used to collect information from devices on a TCP/IP network. SNMP was developed in the Internet community to monitor activity on network devices such as routers and bridges. Since then, SNMP acceptance and support have grown. Many devices, including computers running Windows 2000, can now be monitored with SNMP.

SNMP has a small command set and maintains a centralized database of management information. An SNMP system has three parts:

- The SNMP Agent is the device on a network that is being monitored. This device is typically a computer that has the SNMP Agent software installed. Windows 2000 includes SNMP Agent software in the form of the Microsoft SNMP Service, which you install by using the Add/Remove Windows 2000 Components utility in the Add/Remove Programs Control Panel.

- The SNMP Management System is the component that does the actual monitoring in an SNMP environment. Windows 2000 does not provide an SNMP Management System; third-party SNMP Management Systems include Hewlett-Packard's OpenView and IBM's NetView.

- The *Management Information Base (MIB)* is a centralized database of all the values that can be monitored for all the devices in an SNMP system. Different MIBs are provided for monitoring different types of devices and systems. Windows 2000 comes with four MIBs: Internet MIB II, LAN Manager MIB II, DHCP MIB, and WINS MIB. These four MIBs allow the remote monitoring and management of most components of Windows 2000.

Exchange 2000 Server includes a special MIB that you can use to enable an SNMP Management System that manages many Exchange 2000 Server functions. This MIB is based on a standardized MIB named the *Mail and Directory Management (MADMAN) MIB*, which is detailed in Internet Request for Comments (RFC) 1566.

Using Policies

Policies are a new feature of Exchange 2000 that allow an administrator to create collections of configuration settings that can be easily applied to large numbers of objects at once. For example, you might configure a policy that configures a group of server-related settings. You could then apply those settings across a group of servers without having to manually configure each server.

Manage recipient and server policies.

Diagnose and resolve problems that involve recipient and server policies.

There are two types of policies in Exchange 2000:

- *System policies* affect servers, mailbox stores, and public stores. These policies appear in the System Policies container in System Manager.

- *Recipient policies* are applied to mail-enabled Exchange objects to generate e-mail addresses. These appear in the Recipient Policies container inside the Recipients container in System Manager.

If you do not see a System Policies container in System Manager, you will need to create one. In order to do this, System Manager must be configured to display administrative groups, even if you only have one administrative group. To display administrative groups, open the property pages for the organization object and enable the administrative groups display. To create a System Policies container, right-click a specific administrative group and choose the New Server Policy Container command. Once the container is created, you can disable the viewing of multiple administrative groups if you want to.

System Policies

As mentioned, system policies can be created for and applied to servers, mailbox stores, or public stores. Once you define a policy, you can apply it to a set of objects throughout the organization. In addition, once a policy is associated with a group of objects, changing a setting in the policy changes that setting in all associated objects.

Creating a Policy

To create a new policy, right-click the policy container, point to New, and select the type of policy you want to create: Server, Mailbox Store, or Public Store. A set of property pages opens immediately for you to configure the policy. Each policy has a General page that lets you name the policy and a number of other pages that correspond to pages of the object for the type of policy you are creating. For example, the Server policy has only one extra page that represents the General property page of a server object.

Table 9.3 lists the pages available for each type of policy.

TABLE 9.3   Property Pages Available for System Policies

Type of Policy	Page	Description of Parameters
Server	General	Configuration of message tracking and log file maintenance
Public Store (see Chapter 5 for more information on specific settings)	General	General settings, such as support for S/MIME signatures and formatting of plain text messages
	Database	Maintenance interval for public store
	Replication	Replication interval and limits
	Limits	Storage and age limits, and deletion settings
	Full-Text Indexing	Update and rebuild intervals
Mailbox Store (see Chapter 8 for more information on specific settings)	General	General settings, such as default public folder and offline folder settings
	Database	Maintenance interval for mailbox store
	Limits	Storage and age limits, and deletion settings
	Full-Text Indexing	Update and rebuild intervals

Managing Policies

You can adjust the settings for a policy by opening its property pages. Selecting the policy in the left-hand pane displays all the objects attached to the policy in the right-hand pane. You can right-click an object to remove it from the policy.

You can also right-click a policy to find three useful commands:

- Delete A Policy From The Server: This command also dissociates the policy from any objects to which it is currently applied. However, the settings made by the policy remain in effect on objects unless otherwise modified.

- Copy A Policy To Use A Policy As A Template: Once a copy is made, you can make only the necessary adjustments to create a similar policy.

- Rename A Policy

Applying Policies

After creating and configuring a policy, you can apply it to objects throughout the organization. Exercise 9.4 outlines the steps for applying a server policy. The procedures for adding objects to the other types of system policies are almost identical.

EXERCISE 9.4

Applying a Server Policy

1. Start System Manager.

2. Expand the System Policies container.

3. Right-click the policy to which you want to add objects and select the Add Server command from the shortcut menu.

4. Select a server from the list in the dialog that appears, and click the Add button to add it to the list of servers to add.

5. If a dialog box opens asking you to verify that you want to add the server to the policy, click Yes to proceed.

6. If the server is under the control of another policy, another dialog will appear asking you whether you want to change to the new policy. Click Yes to proceed.

7. Repeat steps 4–6 to add as many servers to the policy as you want.

8. Once you are done, click OK to return to System Manager.

Recipient Policies

Recipient policies work somewhat like system policies, but are applied to groups of mail-enabled recipients instead of server objects. Recipient policies are used to generate e-mail addresses for recipients. By default, Exchange includes a single recipient policy that is used to generate SMTP and X.400 e-mail addresses for various mail-enabled recipients. You can create additional policies for other types of e-mail addresses.

Recipient policies use what is known as a background apply method, in which policies are defined and associated with recipients, but are not immediately applied to recipients upon association (system policies are immediately applied). Instead, recipient policies are actually applied during regular maintenance intervals when the System Attendant service updates the address list.

Client Troubleshooting Tools

Two tools are used to troubleshoot an Exchange client. The Inbox Repair Tool repairs personal folder storage, and the RPC Ping utility tests connections to a server.

Microsoft   ✓ ***Exam***   ***Objective***

Diagnose and resolve Exchange 2000 Server availability and performance problems.

- Diagnose and resolve server-specific performance problems.

The "Diagnose and resolve server resource constraints. Resources include processor, memory, and hard disk" subobjective is discussed earlier in this chapter.

Inbox Repair Tool   The *Inbox Repair Tool* (SCANPST.EXE) tests and repairs a personal folder store (*.PST). It scans for bad blocks and attempts to rebuild them. If a PST file is corrupted beyond repair, this program will try to evacuate the good blocks of data and remove the corrupted blocks. This program does not need to be run unless there are operational problems with personal folders. On rare occasions, if an Exchange client application is abnormally terminated, a personal folder can become corrupted. You will be notified of the corruption on the next startup of the client application. The Inbox Repair Tool is found in the Exchange client program group. You can also use this utility on OST files. For example, you could receive a message stating that your OST file is damaged. Running SCANPST on the OST file will allow you to access those messages without losing the unsynchronized changes in that file.

RPC Ping   The *RPC Ping* utility is used to test RPC connections between two computers. It can be used to test the RPC connection between a client and a server. The RPC Ping Server component (e.g., RPINGS.EXE for the Intel platform) is run first on the Exchange server. The RPC Ping Client component (e.g., RPINGC32.EXE for 32-bit clients) is then run on the client computer and sends a request to the server. This procedure tests the existence and quality of that connection. There are RPC Ping client versions for Windows 3.*x*, Windows 9*x*, Windows NT, and MS-DOS. Both the client- and server-side programs are on the Exchange Server CD, in the SUPPORT\RPCPING directory.

Summary

Many tools are included with Exchange Server to help manage an Exchange organization. An Exchange administrator can use various Windows NT Server tools, like Event Viewer. The main tool in an administrator's arsenal is the System Manager snap-in, which manages objects throughout the Exchange hierarchy.

System Manager is actually a saved console file that connects to a Windows 2000 domain controller in order to get configuration information regarding your Exchange organization. You can customize the console to your use or create custom consoles for other administrators.

Administrative access to Exchange objects can be configured. An administrator can assign permissions to specific users or groups at different levels of the Exchange hierarchy in order to determine who has what type of access to what information. The Exchange Administration Delegation Wizard lets you select a user or group and assign them a specific administrative role. Roles include the Exchange Full Administrator, Exchange Administrator, and Exchange View Only Administrator.

Many Windows tools are useful in monitoring an Exchange server. These include:

- Control Panel ➤ Administrative Services ➤ Services
- Event Viewer
- Performance Monitor
- Registry Editor
- Computer Management
- Task Manager

In addition, Exchange provides a number of tools useful for monitoring system performance and troubleshooting. These include the Monitoring and Status utility, the Queue Viewer, and the Message Tracking Center.

System and recipient policies allow an administrator to create collections of configuration settings that can be easily applied to large numbers of objects at once. For example, you might create a policy that configures storage limits and deletion times for mailbox stores. You could then apply those settings across a group of stores without having to manually configure each store.

Key Terms

Before you take the exam, be certain you are familiar with the following terms:

Access Control Entries (ACEs)	leaf object
Computer Management snap-in	Mail and Directory Management (MADMAN) MIB
console	Management Information Base (MIB)
container object	Message Tracking Center (MTC)
diagnostics logging	Microsoft Management Console (MMC)
discretionary access control list (DACL)	Monitoring and Status tool
Exchange Administration Delegation Wizard	notification
Exchange Administrator role	Performance snap-in
Exchange Advanced Security snap-in	Queue Viewer
Exchange Conferencing Services snap-in	recipient policies
Exchange Folders snap-in	RPC Ping
Exchange Full Administrator role	Simple Network Management Protocol (SNMP)
Exchange Message Tracking Center snap-in	standard permissions
Exchange View-Only Administrator role	System Manager
extended permissions	system policies
Inbox Repair Tool	Task Manager
inherit	Windows 2000 Event Log

Review Questions

1. You have installed Microsoft Exchange Server on a server that is heavily utilized. After installation, you notice that response times are slow and that the hard disk is constantly active. You use Windows NT Performance Monitor to collect the following statistics:

   %Processor time = 70

   %Disk free space = 60

   Pages/sec = 40

   Avg. Disk sec/Transfer = 0.02

   What should you do to reduce disk activity and improve server response time?

   A. Install more RAM.

   B. Install a faster CPU.

   C. Create additional swap files.

   D. Install an additional hard disk.

   E. Replace the hard disk with a faster hard disk.

2. A user receives a message stating that their OST file is damaged. What should you tell them so they can access their messages without losing the unsynchronized changes in that file?

   A. Move the OST file to the server and run ISINTEG.

   B. Use the Migration tool to import the OST into a new mailbox.

   C. Rename the OST file with a .PST extension and run SCANPST on the PST file.

   D. Run SCANPST on the OST file.

3. Your company has had problems with Exchange disk drives becoming full and stopping the IS service. What could you do to receive a warning before the IS reaches its limit again?

   A. Configure the Performance snap-in to send you an e-mail message when the Push Notification Cache Size has reached 100 percent.

   B. Configure an Exchange notification to send you a Microsoft Windows NT alert before the IS service stops.

   C. Configure an Exchange notification to send you an e-mail message when the IS service stops.

   D. Configure an Exchange notification to send you an e-mail message when disk space runs low.

4. You are an assistant Exchange administrator for a large network. Your supervisor asks you to send a test message to a recipient configured on a foreign messaging system and then determine the exact path that message took to get through the Exchange system. How would you do this?

   A. Use the Queue Viewer to monitor the message as it makes its way through the Exchange messaging queues.

   B. Use the Message Tracking Center to search for the message and see its history.

   C. Use the Monitoring and Status tool to send a test message that will automatically reply with a message that includes a trace.

   D. Use the Windows Event Viewer to trace the message's route.

5. Which of the following permissions would you assign on an object if you wanted a user to be able to view the object in System Manager, but not access the object's properties?

   A. Read

   B. Read Permissions

   C. Execute

   D. Visible

6. Recently, users have been complaining that it seems to be taking longer and longer to connect to their Exchange server to get their e-mail. You have determined that all of the users have mailboxes on the same server. You want to find out what is slowing down the server by creating a performance log using the Performance snap-in. Which of the following would be important objects to monitor to determine the bottleneck in the system? (Choose all that apply.)

A. The Pages/sec counter of the Memory object

B. The Messages/sec counter of the MSExchangeMTA object

C. The Local Queue length counter of the SMTP Server object

D. The % Disk free space counter of the Physical Disk object

7. You have 15 servers in your Exchange organization. Ten of those servers contain at least one mailbox store. Due to recent misuse of server-based storage, you have decided to limit the storage capacity of individual mailboxes.

Required result:

You need to create a storage limit of 30MB for all mailboxes.

Optional results:

You would like to be able to implement this storage limit without configuring each store manually.

You would like to be able to assign the Change Permissions permission on all of the mailbox stores to the Domain Admins security group.

Proposed solution:

Create a new server policy. On the Limits page of the policy, assign the limits you want for all stores on the server. On the Security page of the policy, assign the Change Permissions permission to the Domain Admins group. Add all the servers that contain mailbox stores to the new policy.

Which of the results does the proposed solution produce?

A. The proposed solution produces the required result and both optional results.

B. The proposed solution produces the required result, but only one of the optional results.

C. The proposed solution produces the required result, but neither of the optional results.

D. The proposed solution produces neither the required nor the optional results.

8. You have 15 servers in your Exchange organization. Ten of those servers contain at least one mailbox store. Due to recent misuse of server-based storage, you have decided to limit the storage capacity of individual mailboxes.

Required result:

You need to create a storage limit of 30MB for all mailboxes.

Optional results:

You would like to be able to implement this storage limit without configuring each store manually.

You would like to be able to assign the Change Permissions permission on all of the mailbox stores to the Domain Admins security group.

Proposed solution:

Create a new mailbox store policy. On the Limits page of the policy, assign the limits you want for all stores on the server. On the Security page of the policy, assign the Change Permissions permission to the Domain Admins group. Add all the mailbox stores to the new policy.

Which of the results does the proposed solution produce?

A. The proposed solution produces the required result and both optional results.

B. The proposed solution meets the required result, but only one of the optional results.

C. The proposed solution produces the required result, but none of the optional results.

D. The proposed solution produces neither the required result nor the optional results.

9. Your organization is configured to communicate with a legacy cc:Mail messaging system using the Exchange cc:Mail Connector. Recently, you have noticed that the address books have not been matching up between the two systems, even though everything had been working fine previously. E-mail messages are flowing correctly between the two systems. You want to use diagnostics logging to troubleshoot the problem. For what service would you need to enable logging?

A. MSExchangeCCMC

B. MSExchangeDX

C. MSExchangeIS

D. MSExchangeMTA

10. Which of the following permissions would you assign to a user if you wanted the user to be able to modify the properties of an object in System Manager?

A. Read Properties

B. Write Properties

C. Change Properties

D. Modify Properties

11. Which of the following tools represents the easiest way to get real-time information on items such as CPU and memory usage?

    A. Performance snap-in

    B. Computer Management

    C. Monitoring and Status

    D. Task Manager

12. Which of the following services does the Monitoring and Status tool monitor by default? (Choose all that apply.)

    A. Microsoft Exchange Information Store service

    B. Microsoft Exchange Event

    C. Microsoft Exchange Routing Engine

    D. Microsoft Exchange MTA Stacks

    E. Microsoft Exchange POP3

13. You have configured one of the servers in your organization with an X.400 connector so that users in the organization can exchange messages with users of a foreign X.400 system. Once configured, though, you have noticed that the X.400 traffic tends to stack up in the queue once in a while, and you would like an easy way to know when this happens without having to constantly monitor the server yourself. What would be the best way to do this?

    A. Configure the Queue Viewer to log messages to the Windows Event Log when messages stack up in the queue.

    B. Set up the Performance snap-in to monitor the queue and send an alert when messages stack up.

    C. Configure a server monitor to monitor the X.400 queue and configure a notification to e-mail you when the threshold is reached.

    D. You must monitor the queue manually using the Queue Viewer.

14. Which of the following is not a component of an SNMP system?

    A. SNMP Agent

    B. SNMP Management System

    C. SNMP Alerter

    D. Management Information Base

15. Which of the following properties can be configured with a public store system policy? (Choose all that apply.)

    A. The public folder tree associated with the store

    B. Support for S/MIME signatures

    C. The database associated with a store

    D. Storage limits

    E. Replication intervals

16. By default, what types of addresses are generated automatically for all recipients by the default recipient policy? (Choose all that apply.)

    A. X.400

    B. Microsoft Mail

    C. SMTP

    D. cc:Mail

17. You just hired two assistant administrators and want to provide them with the permissions necessary to administer the Exchange organization. However, you do not want them to be able to modify the permissions on any object. What should you do?

    A. Assign them the Full Control permission at the organization level, but explicitly deny them the Write Permissions permission, and then propagate those permissions down throughout the hierarchy.

    B. Assign them the Full Control permission for each administrative group, and then propagate those permissions down throughout the hierarchy.

    C. Use the Exchange Administration Delegation Wizard to assign them the Exchange Administrator role at the organization level.

    D. Use the Exchange Administration Delegation Wizard to assign them the Exchange Administrator role at each administrative group.

18. Your organization has three Exchange servers. All servers belong to a single administrative group and a single routing group. One server has an SMTP connector configured so that your organization can exchange mail with users on the Internet. You would like to be able to log the number of messages sent and received by your users to help establish a baseline of messaging activity to help with future troubleshooting efforts. Which tool would be best suited for this use?

    A. Performance Monitor

    B. Window 2000 Event Log

    C. Diagnostics logging

    D. Computer Management

    E. Monitoring and Status

19. A user has been granted the permission to modify permissions on objects at the organization level. That same user has been denied the permission to modify permissions on objects at the server level, but has been granted the permission on a specific server. The organization is set up to use the default inheritance settings. What effective permissions does the user have on the specific server?

   A. The user can modify permissions.

   B. The user cannot modify permissions.

   C. Permissions cannot be set for individual servers.

   D. Permissions cannot be set at the organization level.

20. Which of the following pieces of data regarding the Information Store service can you track with Performance Monitor? (Choose all that apply.)

   A. The number of users currently using the service

   B. The number of queries the service receives

   C. The amount of processor time the service consumes

   D. The numbered of messages queued in the service

Answers to Review Questions

1 A. Pages/sec is the key item here. This value indicates a high level of pages being written from memory to disk and means that RAM is the likely bottleneck. Even though the disk and CPU usage is also high, these values are likely a secondary effect of the memory bottleneck.

2. D. An OST file is a set of folders used for offline storage and uses the same format as the PST files used for personal folders. The Inbox Repair Tool (SCANPST.EXE) should be able to fix the problem.

3. D. The Exchange Monitoring and Status tool can be set up to monitor for certain resource thresholds, like low disk space, and to send e-mail notifications when thresholds are crossed.

4. B. The Message Tracking Center lets you search for specific messages sent within your organization and track those messages' progress through any server that has message tracking enabled.

5. A. The Read permission makes an object visible, but it does not allow a user to modify the object or even to view its property pages.

6. A, D. It would be best to start by logging the physical aspects of your computer, such as memory, networking, disk space, and CPU performance. The trouble with monitoring Exchange-specific counters and objects in relation to a noticeable slowdown in server performance is that most Exchange-related performance is going to be slowed down by a physical component bottleneck. Of course, if you determine that a physical bottleneck is not the likely culprit, you should move on to explore other areas.

7. D. Server policies can only be used to set message tracking and logging parameters for a server. They cannot be used to set security or limits for the stores on the servers. Mailbox store policies can be used to assign both age and storage limits to mailbox stores. However, no policies can be used to assign permissions to an object.

8. B. Server policies can only be used to set message tracking and logging parameters for a server. They cannot be used to set security or limits for the stores on the servers. Mailbox store policies can be used to assign both age and storage limits to mailbox stores. However, no policies can be used to assign permissions to an object.

9. B. You would use diagnostics logging on the MSExchangeDX service to troubleshoot problems with Directory Synchronization with foreign mail systems. The MSExchangeCCMC service would be used to troubleshoot problems with actual message delivery between the Exchange organization and the cc:Mail system.

10. B. The Write Properties permission allows a user to change the properties of an object.

11. D. Task Manager displays the programs and processes running on a computer. It also displays various performance information, such as CPU and memory usage. An Exchange administrator can use this tool to view the overall health of a server. Access Task Manager by right-clicking the Taskbar and choosing the Task Manager menu option.

12. A, C, D. By default, the Monitoring and Status tool monitors the Information Store service, MTA Stacks, Routing Engine, System Attendant, Simple Mail Transfer Protocol (SMTP), and World Wide Web Publishing services on every server. You can change these defaults or add services to any server.

13. C. Among other resources, a server monitor can be configured to monitor X.400 queue growth, and a notification can be set up to e-mail you when a threshold is reached. This is the best way to receive notification without having to monitor the system manually.

14. C. The SNMP Agent is the device on a network that is being monitored. The SNMP Management System is the component that does the actual monitoring in an SNMP environment. The Management Information Base (MIB) is a centralized database of all the values that can be monitored for all the devices in an SNMP system. There is no such thing as an SNMP Alerter component.

15. B, D, E. The General, Database, Replication, Limits, and Full-Text Indexing pages of a public store are available for configuration, but not all of the properties on those pages are available. You cannot configure a public folder tree or the database associated with a store because these are parameters that apply only to a specific store and cannot be applied to multiple stores using a policy.

16. A, C. Recipient policies are used to generate e-mail addresses for recipients. Exchange includes a single recipient policy by default that is used to generate SMTP and X.400 e-mail addresses for various mail-enabled recipients. In previous versions of Exchange Server, Microsoft Mail and cc:Mail addresses were also generated by default, but not in Exchange 2000 Server.

17. C. The Exchange Administrator role gives users the same full administrative capability as the Exchange Full Administrator role, but does not give them permission to modify permissions for objects. Running the Wizard at the organization level would provide these permissions throughout the organization.

18. A. Performance Monitor graphically charts the performance of hundreds of individual system parameters on a Microsoft Windows 2000 computer and can also be used to log those para-meters over time. Specifically, you would want to log the Messages Sent/min and Messages Delivered/min counters of the MSExchangeIS Mailbox object.

19. A. A specific permission granted or denied always takes precedence over any inherited permissions, no matter from where those permissions are inherited.

20. A. The MSExchangeIS Performance Monitor object includes only the User Count counter, which displays the number of users who are currently using the Information Store.

Chapter

10

Configuring Auxiliary Services

MICROSOFT EXAM OBJECTIVES COVERED IN THIS CHAPTER:

✓ **Configure server objects for messaging and collaboration to support the assigned server role.**

- Configure information store objects.
- Configure multiple storage groups for data partitioning.
- Configure multiple databases within a single storage group.
- Configure virtual servers to support Internet protocols.
- Configure Exchange 2000 Server information in the Windows 2000 Active Directory.
- Configure Instant Messaging objects.
- Configure Chat objects.

✓ **Configure Exchange 2000 Server for high security.**

- Configure Exchange 2000 Server to issue v.3 certificates.
- Enable Digest authentication for Instant Messaging.
- Configure Certificate Trust Lists.
- Configure virtual servers to limit access though firewalls.
- Configure Key Management Service (KMS) to issue digital signatures.

✓ **Configure a user object for messaging.**

- Configure a user object for e-mail.
- Configure a user object for Instant Messaging.
- Configure a user object for Chat.

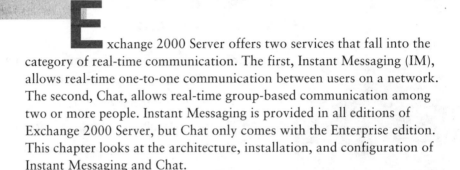

Exchange 2000 Server offers two services that fall into the category of real-time communication. The first, Instant Messaging (IM), allows real-time one-to-one communication between users on a network. The second, Chat, allows real-time group-based communication among two or more people. Instant Messaging is provided in all editions of Exchange 2000 Server, but Chat only comes with the Enterprise edition. This chapter looks at the architecture, installation, and configuration of Instant Messaging and Chat.

Instant Messaging

Traditional e-mail services work well for most communication, but are not well suited to more immediate needs. For these needs, most people still rely on the telephone. Instant Messaging provides another way to fill the need for immediate one-to-one communication that, like e-mail, lets people work with text and transfer files, and, like the telephone, lets people work in real time. In addition, Instant Messaging offers an extra benefit—the ability to determine whether the person on the other end of the line is available, busy, or away from the desk before making the call.

Configuring Instant Messaging servers and clients are straightforward procedures. Most of the intricacy comes in planning the right way to implement the service on your network. Our look at Instant Messaging begins with a brief overview of the technology that should help in planning your implementation and then turns to the actual installation and configuration of the service.

Instant Messaging Overview

It is likely that you have already used, or are at least familiar with, some form of Instant Messaging. ICQ, AOL Instant Messenger, Yahoo Pager, and the MSN Messenger are all forms of IM clients, and most are geared toward letting users determine whether people on their contact list are online and, if so, communicate with them. All of these clients offer a way for a user to send an instant message (one that is much like an e-mail message) that will immediately pop up on the other user's screen. Many of these clients also offer other forms of one-to-one communication such as the ability to use voice and video, open a chat window, collaborate on a virtual whiteboard, share documents, and transfer files.

Exchange 2000 Server now provides server mechanisms for supporting IM. Though Exchange 2000 Server ships with (and Microsoft only provides support for) the MSN Messenger client, Exchange does implement IM using standard Internet protocols. In this section, we look at some of the features and architectural components of Instant Messaging in an Exchange 2000 environment.

Presence Information

When a user runs an IM client, periodic notifications of that user's status are sent to the IM server. This status is referred to as *presence information*. There are seven presence settings that a user can choose from within the client:

- Invisible
- Busy
- Be Right Back
- Away From Computer
- On The Phone
- Out To Lunch
- Online

In addition to these seven settings that a user may choose, there are also two automatic settings:

- Idle, which is set automatically by the client whenever the user's system has been idle for a specified period of time. Idle status is set by the system's screen saver trigger.

- Offline, which is set by the client when the user is not logged on to the IM server. This usually means either that the IM client is not running or that the connection to the server is not working.

When using an IM client (such as MSN Messenger, shown in Figure 10.1), presence information allows you to quickly determine the status of other people on the network. For example, a quick check might reveal that your supervisor is out to lunch. You could then decide either to send an instant message that would be received when the supervisor returned or to check the supervisor's presence information again later.

FIGURE 10.1 Viewing presence information in MSN Messenger

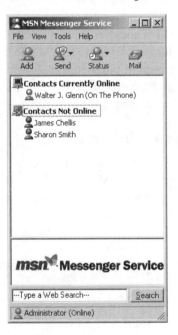

Instant Messaging Topology

When planning Instant Messaging topology for your network, it is important that you understand the roles played by the various IM components. An Instant Messaging topology consists of four basic elements:

- Domains, which are DNS names that identify groups of Instant Messaging user accounts

- Home servers, which communicate directly with clients and maintain presence information

- Routers, which forward messages between home servers and allow communication with external networks, like the Internet

- Clients, which send and receive instant messages

You will use these four elements to construct your Instant Messaging topology based on needs such as the number of servers you need to support your users, whether you need Internet connectivity, and the type of security you require. Figure 10.2 shows two different examples of Instant Messaging topology. The illustration on the top shows a simple network on which one home server and a number of clients are configured. The illustration on the bottom shows a more complex topology that has two home servers and uses an Instant Messaging router to provide inter-domain and Internet connectivity.

FIGURE 10.2   Comparing simple (top) and complex (bottom) Instant Messaging topologies

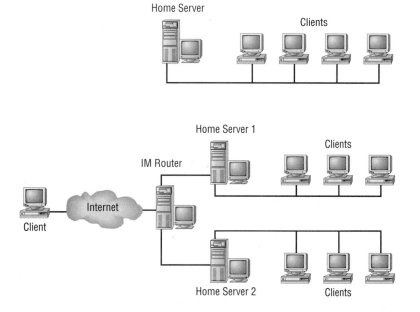

Domains

An *Instant Messaging domain* is a DNS name that identifies user accounts. Instant Messaging routers answer queries for an Instant Messaging domain and make Instant Messaging available to internal and Internet users. You must associate each Instant Messaging domain with at least one router, which routes messages for the domain.

The number of Instant Messaging domains you need to create corresponds to the number of e-mail domains in your organization. Many organizations have one e-mail domain and thus require only one Instant Messaging domain. If your organization does use multiple e-mail domains, the standard recommendation is that you consistently base the names of the IM domains on the e-mail domain names so that users can easily derive the IM domain names. For example, given the e-mail domains atlanta.widgets.com and huntsville.widgets.com, you might use the IM domain names im.atlanta.widgets.com and im.huntsville.widgets.com. The naming of domains and configuring DNS to support domain names is discussed later in this chapter.

Routers

An *Instant Messaging router* is a virtual server that receives messages, looks up the recipient of that message in Active Directory, determines the recipient's destination home server, and then forwards the messages to that home server. In a single-server IM environment, an IM router is not necessary. In fact, home servers can route messages just as routers do.

A single IM router can handle around 50,000 concurrent users. If your user load exceeds this number, you will need to configure multiple routers. However, it is also generally recommended that you use an IM router for every two home servers in a domain. In addition, you will have to configure at least one router for each IM domain that you configure, because routers are required to transfer messages between domains.

Also, you must use an IM router if you want to enable Internet connectivity for your IM users. This provides a high degree of security in that IM clients outside a network firewall will only be able to connect to the IM router. The router proxies the client operations to the home server on behalf of the client outside the firewall.

Home Servers

An *Instant Messaging home server* is a virtual server that actually hosts Instant Messaging user accounts. Home servers also communicate directly with clients to send and deliver instant messages and presence information. Home servers also cache information from the Instant Messaging routers, so clients do not have to communicate with the router often.

The number of Instant Messaging home servers you need depends on two factors:

- A single home server will support around 10,000 concurrent user accounts. If you anticipate more than 10,000 concurrent users, you need two or more home servers and at least one Instant Messaging router.

- If you have groups of users separated by low-bandwidth connections, you should deploy home servers in each area.

Clients

Instant Messaging users must have computers running Windows 95/98/Me, Windows NT 4 Server or Workstation, or Windows 2000. Also, the following software needs to be installed on the user's client computer:

- Internet Explorer version 5 or later

- The Microsoft proxy client, Winsock 2, if users will use Instant Messaging outside the Exchange organization

- Exchange Instant Messaging client, which is available from the `\InstMsg\I386\Client` directory on the Exchange 2000 Server CD-ROM

Configuring DNS

When users enter their IM address into the client logon screen, the address is translated into a URL that is used to access the IM server. For example, `walter@im.widgets.com` would be translated to `http://im.widgets.com/aliases/walter`. In order for clients to be able to reach your IM server using such a URL, you must create DNS "A" records for any Instant Messaging servers. An "A" record is a DNS resource record that matches a server's host name to its IP address.

If you maintain separate DNS servers for internal and external addresses and do not use HTTP reverse proxy servers, both internal and external DNS "A" records must refer to the Instant Messaging routers.

If you use HTTP reverse proxy servers, external queries must pass through the reverse proxy servers. This means that external DNS "A" records must refer to the reverse proxy server, and internal DNS "A" records for the same Fully Qualified Domain Names must refer directly to the Instant Messaging routers.

If you use DNS SRV records to allow users to use SMTP Instant Messaging addresses, each DNS zone containing an e-mail domain must have a DNS SRV record that refers to the Fully Qualified Host Name for that zone's Instant Messaging domain.

Authentication

IM supports two forms of user authentication: Integrated Windows (NTLM) authentication and HTTP Digest authentication. Both forms of authentication rely on Windows 2000 passwords already in effect so that users are not required to learn additional passwords.

Integrated Windows authentication is simpler to use for both administrators and users, so it is enabled by default. In this form of authentication, user credentials are prevented from being passed over a network as clear text. When a user logs on to Windows with a username and password, these same credentials are then used to log the user on to the IM server. Users do not have to enter their credentials again when starting up the IM client.

HTTP Digest authentication is an Internet standard that allows authentication of clients to occur using a series of challenges and responses over HTTP. It is intended primarily as a means of allowing users to log on to IM servers when they must connect to those home servers through an HTTP proxy server. Unlike with Integrated Windows authentication, users configured to use Digest authentication must always supply a username and password within the IM client application to log on to the IM server.

Configuring Instant Messaging Servers

A typical installation of Exchange 2000 Server (Standard or Enterprise edition) does not include Instant Messaging. Unless you performed a custom installation and specifically chose the Instant Messaging component, the first thing you'll have to do is run Exchange setup again and install the component. You can find detailed information on using the Setup Wizard in Chapter 3, but all you really have to do is run setup again and, on the component selection page, add the component.

Once IM is installed, there are five actions to take in configuring Instant Messaging on the server side:

- You must create at least one home server.
- If your network demands it, you may need to create a routing server.
- If you will use HTTP Digest authentication, you must set up the appropriate password policy on the domain controller.

- You must grant users access to IM.

- You must distribute the IM client.

Creating a Home Server

As with most objects, System Manager provides a helpful Wizard that steps you through the process for setting up a home server. Exercise 10.1 outlines the steps involved in using this Wizard.

EXERCISE 10.1

Creating an Instant Messaging Home Server

1. Click Start ➣ Programs ➣ Microsoft Exchange ➣ System Manager.

2. Expand the administrative group and server on which you want to create the IM home server.

3. Expand the Protocols container on the server.

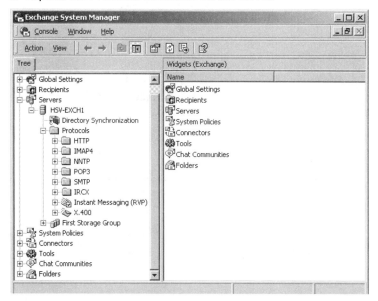

4. Right-click the Instant Messaging (RVP) object and select the Instant Messaging Virtual Server command from the New sub-menu on the shortcut menu.

5. On the welcome page of the New Instant Messaging Virtual Server Wizard, click Next to go on.

6. In the Display Name field, type a name for the server that will appear in System Manager, and then click Next.

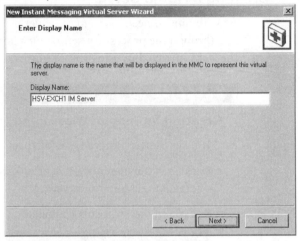

7. On the Choose IIS Web Site page, verify that the Default Web Site option is selected, and then click Next. A virtual directory is created under this Web site and named InstMsg.

8. In the DNS domain name field, type a Fully Qualified Domain Name for the IM server, and then click Next.

9. Select the Allow This Server To Host User Accounts option, and then click Next.

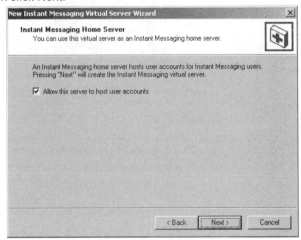

10. Click Finish to return to System Manager.

If you plan to install multiple IM servers on a single computer (something we generally do not recommend), there is an extra step you must take before using the Creation Wizard. One IIS virtual server must exist for each IM home server you create on a single computer. The first IM home server you create will use the default IIS virtual server, but you must configure an additional IIS virtual server for each IM home server you want to create.

Creating an IM Router

The procedure for creating a new IM router is nearly identical to the one for creating a new IM home server. In fact, you use the same Wizard, and the only difference is that in the final step of the Wizard (refer to the final graphic in the previous procedure), you simply do not select the Allow This Server To Host User Accounts option. Since the server is not capable of hosting user accounts, it will only be used as a router.

Configuring HTTP Digest Authentication

By default, Instant Messaging uses Integrated Windows authentication and, as discussed earlier in the chapter, this is a good way to leave things set up unless you need to support authentication through a proxy server. If this is the case, you will need to set up HTTP Digest authentication instead. When using this method, IM must be able to retrieve unencrypted user passwords from Active Directory. To enable this, you must first change the password policy on the domain controller to store the passwords in a reversible encrypted format. Exercise 10.2 outlines the steps for setting this password policy. Exercise 10.3 outlines the steps for enabling HTTP Digest authentication once the password policy has been changed.

Microsoft
✓ *Exam*
Objective

Configure Exchange 2000 Server for high security.

▪ Enable Digest authentication for Instant Messaging.

The "Configure Exchange 2000 Server to issue v.3 certificates," "Configure Certificate Trust Lists," "Configure virtual servers to limit access though firewalls," and "Configure Key Management Service (KMS) to issue digital signatures" subobjectives are discussed in Chapter 14.

EXERCISE 10.2

Configuring Password Policy for HTTP Digest Authentication

1. Click Start ➤ Programs ➤ Administrative Tools ➤ Active Directory Users and Computers.

2. Right-click the organizational unit for the domain and select Properties from the shortcut menu.

3. Switch to the Group Policy page.

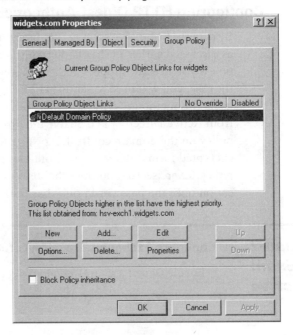

4. Select the Default Domain Policy entry and click Edit.

EXERCISE 10.2 *(continued)*

5. In the Group Policy window that opens, navigate to the Password Policy container.

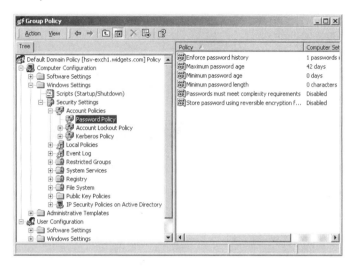

6. In the right-hand pane, double-click the Store Password Using Reversible Encryption For All Users In The Domain entry.

7. In the dialog that opens, select the Enable option, and click OK.

8. Close the Group Policy window and then click OK on the property page for the domain organizational unit.

9. Close Active Directory Users and Computers. It will take several minutes for the changes to take effect.

EXERCISE 10.3

Enabling HTTP Digest Authentication

1. Click Start ➤ Programs ➤ Administrative Tools ➤ Internet Services Manager.

2. In the left-hand pane, expand the server that you want to manage, and then expand the Default Web Site container on that server.

3. Right-click the InstMsg object, and select Properties from the short-cut menu.

4. Switch to the Directory Security page.

5. Click the Edit button in the Anonymous Access And Authentication Control section.

6. Select the Digest Authentication For Windows Domain Servers option.

7. A warning appears informing you that passwords will be stored in clear text. Click Yes to proceed.

8. Click OK twice, and then close the Internet Information Services window.

Granting Users IM Access

Once you have configured at least one home server in your IM domain, you can grant users access to that server. This is done using the user's profile in Active Directory Users and Computers. Exercise 10.4 outlines the steps involved.

Granting a User Instant Messaging Access

1. Click Start ➤ Programs ➤ Administrative Tools ➤ Active Directory Users and Computers.

2. In the left-hand pane, select the Users container.

3. In the right-hand pane, right-click the user for whom you want to grant IM access, and select the Exchange Tasks command from the shortcut menu. If you want to grant IM access to a number of users at once, select all of the users and then issue the Exchange Tasks command.

4. On the Available Tasks window that opens, select the Enable Instant Messaging entry, and then click Next.

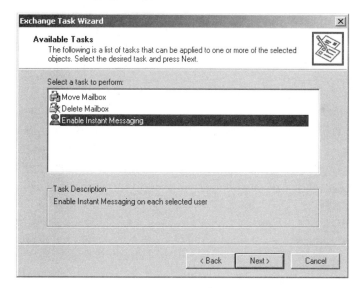

5. On the next page, click the Browse button to select a home server for that user, and then click Next.

6. Click Finish to exit the Wizard.

Distributing the IM Client

Probably the simplest way for you to distribute MSN Messenger (the IM client that comes with Exchange 2000) to your users is to create a shared folder with the setup files and then provide your users with directions on how to access and run setup themselves. You can find the setup files on the Exchange 2000 Server CD-ROM in the `\InstMsg\I386\Client\Usa` folder. There you'll find a single file named `Mmssetup.exe`, which you should make available to your users.

Managing Instant Messaging Users

Once you have configured Instant Messaging and granted access to users, management of those users is fairly simple. You will use both the Exchange Tasks command for a user and the user's property pages.

Microsoft ✓ *Exam* *Objective*	**Configure a user object for messaging.** • Configure a user object for Instant Messaging.

The "Configure a user object for e-mail" subobjective is covered in Chapter 4. The "Configure a user object for Chat" subobjective is covered later in this chapter.

Selecting the Exchange Tasks command for a user after Instant Messaging access has already been granted opens the window shown in Figure 10.3. Two new commands are added to the window for users who have IM access. Use the Disable Instant Messaging command to remove access that you have previously granted to a user. Use the Change Instant Messaging Home Server command to rehome the user to a different IM home server.

FIGURE 10.3   Managing an IM user

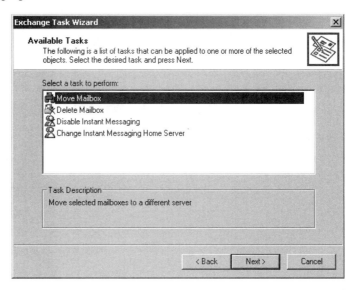

Certain IM features are also managed using the Exchange Features property page for a user. Among the services listed on this page, you'll find an entry for Instant Messaging. Select the entry and click the Properties button to open the property pages for Instant Messaging. The General page, shown in Figure 10.4, simply displays information about the user's IM configuration.

FIGURE 10.4   Configuring user properties for IM

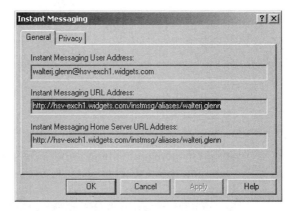

The Privacy page, shown in Figure 10.5, lets you set limitations on the IM service for the user. You can allow access to the user's information by all other users and servers except for those you specify, or you can deny access to everyone except those you specify. The former option is selected by default.

FIGURE 10.5 Configuring privacy for a user

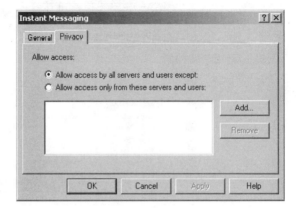

Managing Instant Messaging Servers

Managing Instant Messaging servers is not much more involved than managing IM users.

Microsoft ✓ Exam Objective

Configure server objects for messaging and collaboration to support the assigned server role.

- Configure Instant Messaging objects.

The "Configure information store objects," "Configure multiple storage groups for data partitioning," and "Configure multiple databases within a single storage group" subobjectives are discussed in Chapter 8. The "Configure virtual servers to support Internet protocols" and "Configure Exchange 2000 Server information in the Windows 2000 Active Directory" subobjectives are discussed in Chapters 12 and 9, respectively. The "Configure Chat objects" subobjective is discussed later in this chapter.

The following list shows the management tasks you can perform:

- You can delete an IM server by right-clicking it in System Manager and choosing Delete. A dialog opens that gives you the opportunity to move users on the server to another server prior to deletion.

- You can use the property pages of a particular IM server to change its display name and to view details about its DNS name and IIS virtual server.

- You can use the property pages of the service itself, named Instant Messaging (RVP), to change the database and log file locations for all the IM servers on the computer.

Since IM is run mostly by IIS using a Web site, there are a few properties you might want to configure using the Internet Service Manager tool. For example, by setting parameters on the property pages for the Default Web Site object, you can control such things as the number of incoming connections allowed and authentication methods used. You can also pause or stop the IIS virtual server for your IM server to take the service offline temporarily.

Chat

Microsoft Exchange 2000 *Chat Service* is provided only with the Enterprise edition of Exchange 2000 Server and provides a way for multiple users to communicate with one another in a text-based discussion.

Chat Service is based on *Internet Relay Chat (IRC)*, a client-server protocol that supports real-time conversation between two or more users over a TCP/IP network. Chat Service also supports *extended IRC (IRCX)*, which is a set of extensions developed by Microsoft that enhance the functionality of the IRC protocol and add several new commands you can use to manage users and channels on a chat server.

When users connect to a chat server, they can join real-time text-based conversations on any number of different *channels* (sometimes referred to as chat rooms). When a user joins a channel, that user can see and respond to anything that any user types to other members of the channel.

There are two types of channels used in Chat:

- Registered channels are permanent channels configured by an administrator that are always present in a community.

- Dynamic channels are created by users from their client applications. The first person to join a dynamic channel, usually the person who creates it, becomes the channel host and has special control over the channel that other users do not.

A group of channels and users make up a *chat community*, a virtual server on an Exchange server that is run by a single instance of the Chat Service. You can configure multiple chat communities on a single Exchange server to group together major topics or even separate businesses.

Installing Chat Service

As with Instant Messaging, a typical installation of Exchange 2000 Enterprise Server does not include Chat Service. Unless you performed a custom installation and specifically chose the Chat Service component, you'll have to run Exchange setup again and install the component.

Configuring Chat Communities

When Chat Service is installed, a default chat community is created named Default-Chat-Community. If you will only need one community, then all you need to do is connect it to a server (discussed later in this section) and possibly give it a better name by right-clicking it and choosing the Rename command.

Microsoft ✓ *Exam* *Objective*	**Configure server objects for messaging and collaboration to support the assigned server role.**
	- Configure Chat objects.

The "Configure information store objects," "Configure multiple storage groups for data partitioning," and "Configure multiple databases within a single storage group" subobjectives are discussed in Chapter 8. The "Configure virtual servers to support Internet protocols" and "Configure Exchange 2000 Server information in the Windows 2000 Active Directory" subobjectives are discussed in Chapters 12 and 9, respectively. The "Configure Instant Messaging objects" subobjective is discussed earlier in this chapter.

There are two reasons why you might want to create multiple chat communities. The first is that a single chat server can only host around 20,000 concurrent users. If you need to support more than that, you'll need to set up additional servers and possibly additional communities. The other reason for setting up multiple chat communities is to provide completely separate environments for different functions (or even for different businesses if you are a service provider).

You can set up multiple chat communities either on a single server or on different servers. Exchange 2000 Server does not support spanning a single chat community over multiple servers. To run more than one chat community on a single server, the IP address or port number settings must be different for each community; for example, you can have one community on port 6667 (the default port number) and another on port 6668, but both communities can use the same IP address. Conversely, both communities can be hosted on port 6667 if they use different IP addresses.

Creating a Chat Community

Creating a chat community is a simple procedure, and the steps are outlined in Exercise 10.5.

EXERCISE 10.5

Creating a Chat Community

1. Click Start ➢ Programs ➢ Microsoft Exchange ➢ System Manager.

2. If System Manager is set to display administrative groups, expand the group containing the Chat Service you want to configure. Otherwise, just right-click the Chat Communities container and select the New Chat Community command. This opens the property pages for the new community.

3. On the General page, type a name and title for the community into the appropriate fields. The name appears in System Manager. Both the name and title appear in the Chat client. Since clients must be able to connect to the community using standard IRC commands, no spaces are allowed in the name of the community.

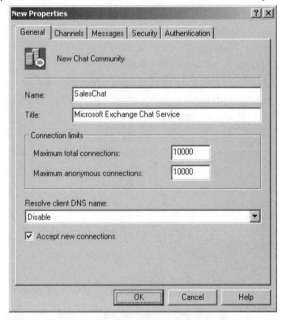

4. If you want, you can also modify the default number of concurrent total and anonymous connections allowed to the community. By default, each of these is set to 10,000.

5. You can also specify how the community handles client DNS names. By default, the Disable option is set, which means that client DNS names are not resolved. If you want the name resolved before a client connection is allowed, choose either the Attempt or the Require setting. Require is the most secure option.

6. The final option on the General page, Accept New Connections, can be used to temporarily disable a community for maintenance. Once you disable this option, new users are prevented from connecting to the community. When all of the current users have disconnected, you can perform your maintenance. This is much more graceful than simply stopping a service and disconnecting all the users immediately.

7. Switch to the Channels page to set the default number of users allowed in a single channel at once, to specify whether a user who creates a channel can become its owner or host, and to configure how dynamic channels are handled if they are allowed at all.

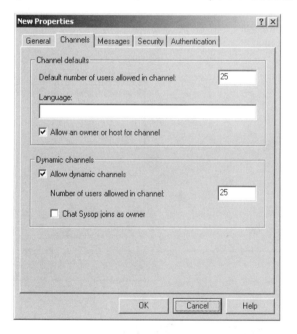

8. Switch to the Messages page to set up two different messages. The first is a message of the day (MOTD) that is displayed each time a user logs on to the community. The second is an ADMIN (administrative) message that displays information about the server when the ADMIN command is typed into a client.

Connecting a Chat Community to a Server

Once a community is created, it needs to be connected to a specific server. To do this, use System Manager to find and expand the container for the server that will host the community. Under that server container, right-click the IRCX object and choose Properties from the shortcut menu. This opens the property page shown in Figure 10.6. Click Add; in the window that opens, select the community you want to connect to the server, and select the Enable Server To Host This Chat Community option. The dialog also gives the option of designating a specific IP address for the community.

FIGURE 10.6   Connecting a chat community to a server

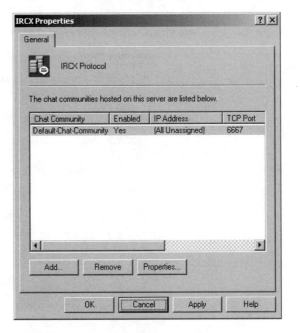

Removing a Community

There are two ways to remove a chat community from service. The first is the simple, but irreversible, way: Select the community in System Manager and delete it. The second way is to remove the community's association with the server. You can do this either by removing the chat community from the list of communities associated with the server (refer to Figure 10.6) or by opening the properties for the community entry on that list and disabling the Enable Server To Host This Chat Community option. Either option will do the job, but the latter is easier to reverse later.

Configuring Chat Channels

As an administrator, you will be responsible for creating and managing registered channels in your chat communities and for controlling the creation of dynamic channels.

Creating a Registered Channel

Exercise 10.6 outlines the steps for creating a registered channel.

EXERCISE 10.6

Creating a Registered Channel

1. Click Start ➤ Programs ➤ Microsoft Exchange ➤ System Manager.

2. Find and expand the chat community for which you want to create a channel.

3. Right-click the Channels folder and select the New Channel command. This opens the property pages for the new channel.

4. On the channel's General page, type a name for the channel in the Name field. A channel name can contain between 1 and 200 characters, must start with a valid IRC channel prefix (#, &, %#, or %&), and can contain no spaces. If you like, you can enter a topic, subject, content rating, and language on this page, as well.

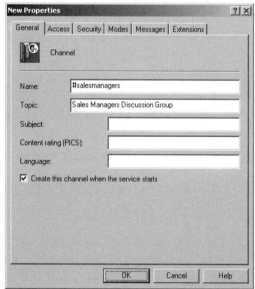

5. Make sure the Create This Channel When The Service Starts option is enabled to make the channel permanent.

6. Click OK to create the new channel. Once created, you can configure the channel later by modifying additional parameters on its other property pages.

Restricting Access to a Channel

You can configure parameters restricting access to a channel using two of a channel's property pages: Access and Modes.

The Access page, shown in Figure 10.7, lets you control a few parameters. The first is the visibility of the channel to users. There are four options:

- Public visibility means that nonmembers of the channel can obtain all information about the channel from their client.

- Private visibility means that nonmembers can only obtain the name, number of members, and PICS (Platform for Internet Content Selection) property of the channel from their client.

- Hidden visibility works the same as public visibility except that the channel cannot be found using the List or Listx commands in a chat client. In order to find the channel and see its properties, you must know its exact name.

- Secret visibility means that nonmembers cannot use queries to locate the channel.

You can also use this page to set passwords for different levels of users, to limit the number of users allowed in the channel (this setting overrides that configured for the community), and to limit the types of users allowed.

FIGURE 10.7 Configuring visibility of a channel

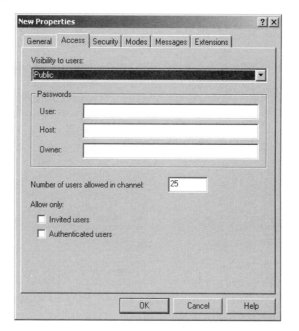

The Modes page, shown in Figure 10.8, is used to set additional parameters governing how the channel can be used and who can use it. The following parameters are available on this page:

- The Messages section contains options for how messages are treated within the channel. You can configure the channel so that only channel members may send messages.

- The Speaking Restrictions section is used to place restrictions on the types of messages that can be sent.

- Several miscellaneous options appear at the bottom of the page for further configuration. The one option of real interest here is the Allow This Channel To Be Cloned option. Cloning is useful for creating duplicates of channels either as an easy way to create a new channel with similar configurations or to create a duplicate channel to accommodate an overflow of users on a channel.

FIGURE 10.8 Configuring channel modes

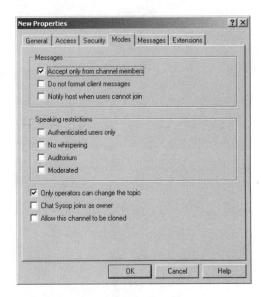

Managing Chat Users

There are several actions you can take to manage chat users, including the following:

- Banning users from a chat community due to inappropriate behavior
- Configuring user classes to impose restrictions on certain users or groups of users
- Disconnecting users from a chat service

Microsoft ✓ **Exam Objective**

Configure a user object for messaging.

- Configure a user object for Chat.

The "Configure a user object for e-mail" subobjective is covered in Chapter 4. The "Configure a user object for Instant Messaging" subobjective is covered earlier in this chapter.

Banning Users

User bans allow you to restrict access to a chat community for a specific user or group of users. Exercise 10.7 outlines the steps for setting up a user ban.

EXERCISE 10.7

Setting Up a User Ban

1. Click Start ➤ Programs ➤ Microsoft Exchange ➤ System Manager.

2. Find and expand the chat community for which you want to configure a ban.

3. Right-click the Bans folder and select the New Ban command from the shortcut menu.

4. On the property page that opens, you can ban a user or group of users by their chat nickname, their actual username, their domain name or IP address, or any combination of these. All of these fields accept the asterisk (*) and question mark (?) as wildcard characters for selecting groups of users.

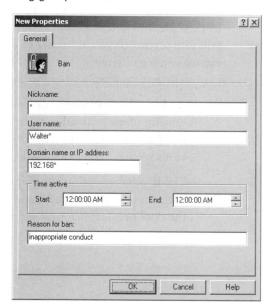

EXERCISE 10.7 *(continued)*

5. Optionally, you can set a schedule for the ban so that the user or users are only banned at certain times.

6. Also optionally, you can enter a reason for the ban.

7. Click OK to close the property page and institute the user ban.

Configuring User Classes

Instead of outright banning users or configuring system-wide limits on the Chat Service, you also have the option of grouping users into *user classes* and then configuring restrictions for those classes. To set up a new user class, simply right-click the Classes container in a chat community and choose the New Class command. This opens a set of property pages for the class object. Each of the property pages is covered in the next three sections.

General Properties

The General page, shown in Figure 10.9, is used to name and determine membership for the class. Be careful when you name the class. Restrictions by class are imposed in alphabetical order of class names. Thus, if one user falls into several classes, the order in which the class restrictions are applied can make a big difference. The Member Scope section of the General page is used to determine membership for the class. There are two options:

- An Identify mask identifies members by a nickname, username, a domain name or IP address, or any combination of these attributes. Configure this mask the same way you configured user bans in the previous section. You can include groups of users by using wildcards.

- The IP address option lets you select a group of users that all belong to the same range of IP addresses. Simply enter a starting IP address for the pool of addresses, and enter a subnet mask to define the range.

FIGURE 10.9   Determining membership for a class

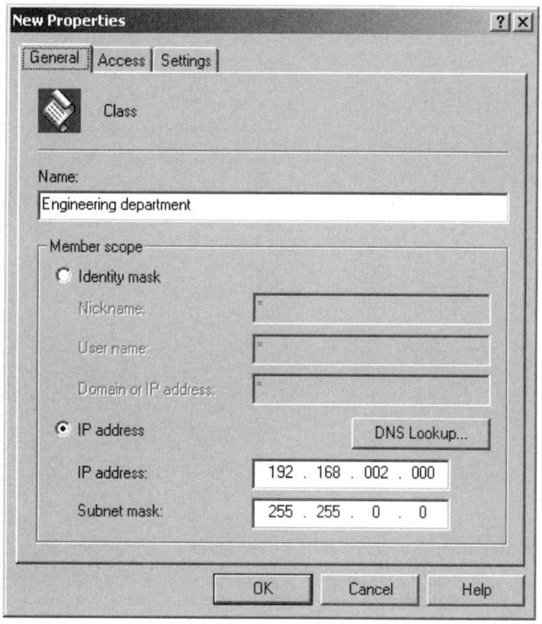

Access Properties

The Access page, shown in Figure 10.10, lets you further define the class membership based on how a user is logged on (authenticated or anonymous, or both) and lets you impose certain restrictions on members of the class, such as not being able to log on to the community at all, or not being able to create dynamic channels. This page also lets you configure a time schedule for the class restrictions to be in effect. The final option on the page, Hide Class Members' IP Addresses And DNS Names, provides a way to prevent one chat user from launching an attack on another chat user by flooding the user's IP address with large amounts of data.

FIGURE 10.10 Determining membership for a class

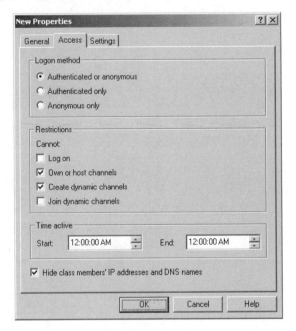

Settings Properties

The Settings page, shown in Figure 10.11, sets protection levels to prevent attacks from bringing down the chat server. There are four choices for levels: None, Low, Medium, and High. Depending on the level of protection you set, users are disconnected from the chat server after specific numbers of certain types of messages (such as bad passwords, standard messages, or even join messages) are reached.

The Limits section of the Settings page is used to set certain other restrictions (such as the maximum number of channels a user can join) for members of the class. The Delays section is used to configure how long certain delays are allowed before a user is assumed not to be present at the client side of the connection and the connection is terminated.

FIGURE 10.11 Setting protection levels for a community

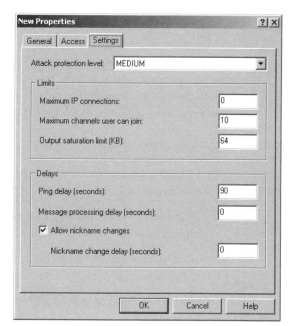

Disconnecting Users from a Chat Channel

In order to disconnect a user from a chat channel, you must first log on to that channel as a chat administrator. You can do this by opening your chat client directly and logging on to the channel. Once you have logged on, you can use either the Kick or the Kill command followed by a username to temporarily disconnect a user from the channel. This method will allow the user to log back on to the channel; to impose a permanent restriction on the user, set up a user ban or user class.

In order to use the Kick or the Kill command, first you must open the properties for a community in System Manager and, on the community's Channels property page, set the Chat Sysop Joins As Owner option.

Summary

Exchange 2000 Server offers real-time collaboration in the form of two services: Instant Messaging and Chat. Instant Messaging allows real-time one-to-one communication between users on a network. It is available in both the Standard and Enterprise editions of Exchange 2000 Server. Chat allows real-time group-based communication among two or more people. Chat is available only in the Enterprise edition.

An Instant Messaging topology consists of four elements:

- Domains are DNS names that identify groups of Instant Messaging user accounts.

- Home servers communicate directly with clients and maintain presence information on users.

- Routers forward messages between home servers and allow external communication with the Internet.

- Clients send and receive information and query servers for presence information.

Instant Messaging supports two forms of user authentication. Integrated Windows authentication is used by default and is highly secure. When a user logs on to Windows with a username and password, these same credentials are then used to log the user on to the IM server. Users do not have to enter their credentials again when starting up the IM client. HTTP Digest authentication is an Internet standard that allows authentication of clients to occur using a series of challenges and responses over HTTP. It is intended primarily as a means of allowing users to log on to IM servers when they must connect to those home servers through an HTTP proxy server.

Configuring Instant Messaging in an organization consists of several steps. First, you must ensure that the Instant Messaging service is installed. Next, you must create at least one home server. If necessary, you will need to create routing servers as well. If you will use HTTP Digest authentication, you must set up the appropriate password policy on the domain controller. Finally, you must grant users Instant Messaging access and distribute the client software.

Chat Service is based on Internet Relay Chat (IRC), a client-server protocol that supports real-time conversation between two or more users over a

TCP/IP network. When users connect to a chat server, they can join real-time text-based conversations on any number of different channels. Registered channels are persistent channels created by an administrator. Dynamic channels are temporary channels created by a user. A group of channels and users make up a chat community, which is a virtual server on an Exchange server that is run by a single instance of the Chat Service. You can configure multiple chat communities on a single Exchange server.

Once you make sure that the Chat Service is installed, setting up a chat environment is not too difficult. You can either use the default chat community or create additional communities. Either way, each community must be connected with a specific server; communities cannot span multiple servers. Once a community is connected with a server, you can begin creating and configuring channels in the community for users to join. You can configure the properties for a channel to limit the use of that channel, or you can manage users using bans and classes. User bans allow you to ban access to a chat community for a specific user or group of users. User classes allow you to create a set of membership criteria by which membership in the class is established. You can then apply different restrictions on Chat use to those classes.

Key Terms

Before you take the exam, be certain you are familiar with the following terms:

channels	Instant Messaging router
chat community	Integrated Windows authentication
Chat Service	Internet Relay Chat (IRC)
extended IRC (IRCX)	presence information
HTTP Digest authentication	user bans
Instant Messaging domain	user classes
Instant Messaging home server	

Review Questions

1. You are planning a deployment of Instant Messaging for your company network. You estimate that 18,000 users will use Instant Messaging. These users are divided into two e-mail domains, atlanta.widgets.com and huntsville.widgets.com. 12,000 users are in the atlanta.widgets.com domain, and 6,000 users are in the huntsville.widgets.com domain. You do not want to provide Internet access to Instant Messaging users. How many home servers and routing servers will you need?

   A. Two home servers and no routers

   B. Two home servers and one router

   C. Three home servers and no routers

   D. Three home servers and one router

   E. Three home servers and two routers

2. How would you enable HTTP Digest authentication?

   A. Using the property pages of the HTTP protocol container in System Manager

   B. Using the property pages of the Instant Messaging (RVP) container in System Manager

   C. Using the property pages of the Default Web container in Internet Services Manager

   D. Using the property pages of the InstMsg container in Internet Services Manager

3. Which of the following are valid presence settings that an Instant Messaging user may select? (Choose all that apply.)

   A. Busy

   B. Idle

   C. Online

   D. Offline

4. When setting up Instant Messaging, you configured two IM home servers and three IM routers on your network. However, you now realize that you only need two routers. Instead of deleting the third router, you would like to turn it into a home server. How can you do this?

    A. Use the General property page of the IM router to configure the router to host user accounts.

    B. Use the Hosting property page of the IM router to configure the router to host user accounts.

    C. Use the General property page of the InstMsg object in Internet Services Manager to configure the router to host user accounts.

    D. You cannot do this.

5. What must you do in order to configure multiple IM servers on a single computer?

    A. Create a virtual SMTP server for each IM server.

    B. Configure a separate IP address for each IM server.

    C. Create a virtual IIS server for each IM server.

    D. Configure a separate TCP port for each IM server.

6. Which of the following would be a valid name for a chat channel? (Choose all that apply.)

    A. #chatchannel1

    B. &chat channel 1

    C. %chatchannel1

    D. %&chatchannel1

7. You are the Exchange administrator for a large network. One of your primary duties is managing the chat communities on your network. In one community that is designated for general use, a small number of users have been creating dynamic channels used to host what your company considers inappropriate content.

    Required results:

    Temporarily prevent those users from accessing the community.

    Prevent all users of the community from creating dynamic channels.

    Restrict the use of the community to certain times of the day.

    Proposed solution:

    Create a separate user ban for each of the users you want to prevent from accessing the community. Create an additional ban that prevents all users from creating dynamic channels. Use the Schedule property sheet of the community to set up the times that the community is available.

    Which of the results does the proposed solution produce?

    A. Those users are temporarily prevented from accessing the community.

    B. All users of the community are prevented from creating dynamic channels.

    C. The use of the community is restricted to certain times of the day.

8. You are the Exchange administrator for a large network. One of your primary duties is managing the chat communities on your network. In one community that is designated for general use, a small number of users have been creating dynamic channels used to host what your company considers inappropriate content.

    Required results:

    Temporarily prevent those users from accessing the community.

    Prevent all users of the community from creating dynamic channels.

    Restrict the use of the community to certain times of the day.

Proposed solution:

Create a separate user ban for each of the users you want to prevent from accessing the community. Create an additional ban that prevents all users from creating dynamic channels. Create a user class that includes all users, and set scheduling restrictions for that class.

Which of the results does the proposed solution meet?
(Choose all that apply.)

A. Those users are temporarily prevented from accessing the community.

B. All users of the community are prevented from creating dynamic channels.

C. The use of the community is restricted to certain times of the day.

9. Your network consists of a single e-mail domain with one IM home server. An IM router is located outside the company firewall so that it may proxy IM requests between internal and external users. Your network is also configured to use reverse proxy servers. How should you configure your DNS records for the IM home server?

A. Set up an external "A" record to refer to the reverse proxy server and an internal "A" record to refer to the IM home server.

B. Set up an external "A" record to refer to the reverse proxy server and an internal "A" record to refer to the IM router.

C. Set up an external "A" record to refer to the IM router and an internal "A" record to refer to the reverse proxy server.

D. Set up an external "A" record to refer to the IM home server and an internal "A" record to refer to the reverse proxy server.

10. In order for clients to reach an IM server using an SMTP address such as user@im.widgets.com, what would you need to configure?

A. An MX record in DNS

B. An "A" record in DNS

C. An IM record in DNS

D. An SRV record in DNS

11. Which of the following types of visibility allow nonmembers to obtain all information about the channel using their client? (Choose all that apply.)

   A. Public

   B. Private

   C. Hidden

   D. Secret

12. How many concurrent users can a single IM router handle?

   A. 10,000

   B. 20,000

   C. 50,000

   D. 100,000

13. What must you do in order to configure multiple chat communities on a single computer?

   A. Create a virtual SMTP server for each community.

   B. Configure a separate IP address for each community.

   C. Create a virtual IIS server for each community.

   D. Configure a separate TCP port for each community.

   E. None of the above.

14. Which of the following statements about Instant Messaging routers is true?

   A. You must associate each IM domain with at least one router.

   B. You must associate each IM domain with at least one router only if the number of users in the domain exceeds 10,000.

   C. You must associate each IM domain with at least one router only if the number of users in the domain exceeds 50,000.

   D. You must associate each IM domain with at least one router only if your IM users need Internet connectivity.

15. You are planning a deployment of Instant Messaging on your network. You have 700 users. 500 users are located in the main corporate headquarters in downtown Dallas. 200 users are located in a branch office in Houston. Each location has its own Windows 2000 domain, and both domains are part of one domain tree. The two locations are connected via a low-bandwidth demand-dial connection. All users in both domains receive e-mail using the same e-mail domain. How many Instant Messaging domains and home servers will you need?

   A. One Instant Messaging domain and one home server

   B. One Instant Messaging domain and two home servers

   C. Two Instant Messaging domains and one home server

   D. Two Instant Messaging domains and two home servers

16. What two forms of user authentication are supported by Instant Messaging?

   A. Integrated Windows authentication (NTLM)

   B. Basic authentication

   C. HTTP Digest authentication

   D. Secure Sockets Layer

17. You have configured Instant Messaging on your network and now want to grant users access to use the service. What tool would you use to do this?

   A. System Manager

   B. Internet Services Manager

   C. Instant Messaging Manager

   D. Active Directory Users and Computers

18. Which of the following statements is true about chat communities?

    A. You can span a single chat community over multiple Exchange 2000 servers.

    B. You can span a single chat community over multiple Exchange 2000 servers only if you are running Exchange 2000 Server Enterprise edition.

    C. You can span a single chat community over multiple Exchange 2000 servers only if those servers are running in a cluster.

    D. You cannot span a single chat community over multiple Exchange 2000 servers.

19. Once a chat community is created, what other step must you take in order to set up the community before users can access it?

    A. Connect the community to a specific server.

    B. Connect the community to a specific administrative group.

    C. Configure chat channels in the community.

    D. Grant users access to the chat community.

20. You are the administrator of a chat community. The community is configured so that only a certain number of users can connect at a time. However, you have noticed that many users are not being allowed to connect even when the active number of connections to the community seems to be relatively low. You suspect that idle chat clients are not being disconnected, and those connections are preventing new users from joining. You would like to reduce the amount of time after which idle users are disconnected. What would you use to do this?

    A. The properties for the chat community

    B. The properties for the server associated with the chat community

    C. The properties for each individual chat channel in the community

    D. A user ban

    E. A user class

Answers to Review Questions

1. E. Since the atlanta.widgets.com domain has 12,000 users and a single home server can support only 10,000 users, you know that you will need two home servers for that domain. You will also need a home server in the huntsville.widgets.com domain. Even though no Internet access is needed, you still need to have one router for every two home servers. Since there will be three home servers, two routers should handle the job well.

2. D. You will control much of Instant Messaging through the Internet Services Manager, as it is implemented in large part as a set of Web folders. Use the InstMsg object of the appropriate Web site to set up HTTP Digest authentication.

3. A, C. Users can select seven presence settings: Invisible, Busy, Be Right Back, Away From Computer, On The Phone, Out To Lunch, and Online. Idle and Offline are presence settings that are applied automatically based on the user's situation. Idle is applied when the screen saver is activated, and Offline is applied when the client application is not connected to the IM server.

4. A. On the General property page of an IM server or IM router, you will find an option named Allow This Server To Host User Accounts. Home servers and routers are basically identical, except that the home server is allowed to host user accounts. You can change a router into a server by selecting this option. Note, however, that you cannot change a home server into a router. The option is unavailable.

5. C. Each IM server installed on a single computer must have its own virtual IIS server.

6. A, D. A channel name can contain between 1 and 200 characters, must start with a valid IRC channel prefix (#, &, %#, or %&), and can contain no spaces.

7. A. User bans are the most effective way to prevent a user from accessing the community. When you want the user to return, simply lift the ban. Unfortunately, you will have to create separate bans for each user unless the users share common naming or addressing characteristics

that let you select them as a group using wildcards. With a small number of users, however, separate bans are not much of a problem. Bans cannot be used to prevent users from creating dynamic channels; they are only used to prevent access. Also, the community property pages have no scheduling page. To prevent users from creating dynamic channels and to restrict the use of the community to certain times of the day, you will need to create a user class that includes all users, and set the appropriate restrictions on that class.

8. A, C. User bans are the most effective way to prevent a user from accessing the community. When you want the user to return, simply lift the ban. Unfortunately, you will have to create separate bans for each user unless the users share common naming or addressing characteristics that let you select them as a group using wildcards. With a small number of users, however, separate bans are not much of a problem. Bans cannot be used to prevent users from creating dynamic channels; they are only used to prevent access. Also, the community property pages have no scheduling page. To prevent users from creating dynamic channels and to restrict the use of the community to certain times of the day, you will need to create a user class that includes all users, and set the appropriate restrictions on that class.

9. B. If you use HTTP reverse proxy servers, external queries must pass through the reverse proxy servers. This means that external DNS "A" records must refer to the reverse proxy server, and internal DNS "A" records for the same Fully Qualified Domain Names must refer directly to the Instant Messaging routers.

10. B. When users enter their IM address into the client logon screen, the address is translated into a URL that is used to access the IM server. For example, walter@im.widgets.com would be translated to http://im.widgets.com/aliases/walter. In order for clients to be able to reach your IM server using a URL, you must create DNS "A" records for any Instant Messaging servers. An "A" record is a DNS resource record that matches a server's host name to its IP address.

11. A, C. Hidden visibility works the same as public visibility, except the channel cannot be found using the List or Listx command in a chat client. In order to find the channel and see its properties, you must know its exact name.

12. C. A single IM router can handle around 50,000 concurrent users. If your user load exceeds this number, you will need to configure multiple routers. However, it is also generally recommended that you use an IM router for every two home servers in a domain.

13. E. Chat communities do not require virtual SMTP or IIS servers. In addition, while each chat community must have its own combination of IP address and TCP port, they do not necessarily need separate instances of each. For sample, you can have one community on port 6667 (the default port number) and another on port 6668, but both communities can use the same IP address. Conversely, both communities can be hosted on port 6667 if they use different IP addresses.

14. A. An Instant Messaging domain is a DNS name that identifies user accounts. Instant Messaging routers answer queries for an Instant Messaging domain and make Instant Messaging available to internal and Internet users. You must associate each Instant Messaging domain with at least one router, which routes messages for the domain.

15. B. You only need one IM domain for each e-mail domain. An IM domain can span multiple Windows 2000 domains. You will need two home servers. While a single home server can support up to 10,000 IM users, it is best to deploy multiple home servers when you have groups of users separated by low-bandwidth connections.

16. A, C. IM supports two forms of user authentication: Integrated Windows (NTLM) authentication and HTTP Digest authentication. Both forms of authentication rely on Windows 2000 passwords already in effect so that users are not required to learn additional passwords.

17. D. Users are granted access to IM by right-clicking the user objects in Active Directory Users and Computers and using the Exchange Tasks command.

18. D. You can set up multiple chat communities on a single server or on different servers. Exchange 2000 Server does not support spanning a single chat community over multiple servers.

19. A. Once a community is created, it must be connected to a specific server. You do not need to connect the community to an administrative group, nor do you need to configure any channels or grant specific access before users can connect.

20. E. User classes are used to set up restrictions for classes of users that connect to a community. The Settings property page of a user class allows you to configure how long certain delays are allowed before a user is assumed not to be present at the client side of the connection and the connection is terminated.

Chapter

11

Connecting to Exchange 5.5

MICROSOFT EXAM OBJECTIVES COVERED IN THIS CHAPTER:

✓ **Manage coexistence with Exchange 5.5.**

  ▪ Maintain common user lists.

  ▪ Maintain existing connectors.

  ▪ Move users from Exchange 5.5 to Exchange 2000 Server.

  ▪ Configure the Exchange 2000 Active Directory Connector to replicate directory information.

✓ **Diagnose and resolve Exchange 2000 Active Directory Connector problems.**

Most companies that are installing Exchange 2000 Server will already have some messaging system in place. Many of those will be using a previous version of Exchange Server. Unless you are planning a full upgrade of all previous Exchange servers to Exchange 2000 and do not plan for users to access the system during the upgrade, there will be a time when Exchange 2000 servers and Exchange servers of previous versions need to coexist on the same network. You might choose to install an Exchange 2000 server into an existing Exchange 4.*x* or 5.*x* organization, or you might choose to create a new organization for the Exchange 2000 Server that runs alongside the previous organization. Either way, you will have to manage the communications and the synchronization of directory information between Exchange 2000 and previous versions. That is what this chapter is all about.

Mixed-Mode Operations

An Exchange 2000 organization can operate in two modes: native and mixed. In *native mode*, only Exchange 2000 Server is running, and the full Exchange 2000 functionality is present. No previous version of Exchange server can communicate with the native-mode organization, except possibly via a connector or gateway as if it were a foreign system.

In *mixed mode*, Exchange 2000 Server can coexist and communicate with previous versions of Exchange Server in the same organization. When you first install Exchange 2000 Server, it operates in mixed mode by default—even if you have no previous versions running on your network. Once you switch to native mode (described later in the chapter), you cannot go back, and direct interoperability with previous Exchange versions is lost.

There are two big changes between all previous versions of Exchange Server and Exchange 2000 Server:

- In previous versions, Exchange Server managed its own directory of configuration and user objects. For example, mailboxes were objects in the Exchange directory that were associated with Windows NT 4.0 user accounts. In Exchange 2000, all directory functions have passed to Active Directory.

- In previous versions, Exchange sites were used to provide routing, administrative, and namespace boundaries. In Exchange 2000, routing groups provide routing boundaries, administrative groups provide administrative boundaries, and Active Directory provides namespace boundaries.

In this section, we discuss the benefits and limitations of running an organization in mixed mode, provide an overview of how Exchange 5.*x* directories and Active Directory can coexist, and examine the interaction of Exchange 5.*x* sites with Exchange 2000 routing groups and administrative groups.

Benefits and Limitations of Mixed Mode

Before we get too deep into the mechanics of mixed-mode operations, it is helpful to examine some of the benefits and limitations of working in mixed mode. Working in mixed mode provides the following benefits:

- Interoperability between Exchange 2000 servers and servers running previous versions.

- Exchange 5.*x* directory objects are replicated to Active Directory and may be managed using System Manager and Active Directory Users and Computers.

- Exchange 2000 imports information from Exchange 5.*x* Gateway Address Routing Tables into its own link state tables and thus provides access to Exchange 5.*x* connectors and gateways.

- You can continue to install Exchange 5.x servers, should you want to do so.

- Public folders can be replicated between Exchange 2000 and Exchange 5.x servers.

There are also a number of limitations imposed by working in mixed mode. These limitations include the following:

- Exchange 5.x sites are mapped directly to Exchange 2000 administrative groups and vice versa. This gives you less flexibility in setting up administrative groups than when working in native mode.

- You can move mailboxes only between servers that are in the same administrative group. In native mode, you can move mailboxes between servers in different administrative groups.

- You can divide servers in an administrative group into different routing groups. However, these servers must all belong to the administrative group. In native mode, routing group boundaries and administrative group boundaries can cross.

Directory Interactions

Although many components and features are upgraded in Exchange 2000 Server, one of the most important aspects of coexistence is the synchronization between the Exchange 5.x directory service and Active Directory. In order to successfully manage directory interactions, it is important that you understand the following:

- How the Exchange 5.x Directory Service works. This includes how it is structured, how it is replicated among Exchange 5.x servers, and how it is managed. We provide a brief overview below, but for more information check out your Exchange 5.x documentation or, better yet, pick up a copy of the previous edition of this book.

- How Active Directory works in relation to Exchange 2000. This includes how Exchange configuration objects are stored in Active Directory and how Active Directory is replicated among domain controllers. For more information on this, see Chapter 2 of this book and refer to your Windows 2000 documentation.

- The components that are used to allow Exchange 5.x servers to synchronize directory information with Exchange 2000 servers that use

Active Directory. These components include the Site Replication Service (SRS) and the Active Directory Connector (ADC).

A Brief Review of the Exchange 5.*x* Directory Service

In Exchange 5.*x*, the *Directory Service (DS)* creates and manages the storage of all information about Exchange objects, such as the organization, site, servers, mailboxes, distribution lists, and public folders. The characteristics of these objects are called properties or attributes. The DS organizes all this information into a hierarchical database called the Directory, which is contained in a database file named DIR.EDB. The Directory hierarchy is patterned after the X.500 standard.

All Exchange servers in a site contain a complete copy of the Directory information. This is accomplished by automatic directory replication between servers of a site via *Remote Procedure Call (RPC)*. When an Exchange object, such as a mailbox, is created on a particular Exchange server, that object's information is automatically copied to all the other servers in that site.

There can also be directory replication between sites. This is not an automatic process, and must be configured by an administrator. Directory replication between sites occurs using e-mail messages over whatever connectors are used to connect the sites. This ability allows administrators to decide what resources to share with other sites. Directory replication between sites can be used to create an enterprise messaging environment.

The DS component supports directory access through the MAPI interface and through the LDAP interface. This enables both MAPI client software (like Outlook) and Internet LDAP-enabled applications (like Outlook Express) to access the Exchange Directory. Administrators access the Directory through Microsoft Exchange Administrator, which is a MAPI program.

Supporting Directory Coexistence

Two main components facilitate coexistence between the Exchange 5.*x* Directory and the Active Directory in mixed-mode organizations: the *Site Replication Service (SRS)* and the *Active Directory Connector (ADC)*.

Site Replication Service

The SRS runs on an Exchange 2000 server and actually simulates an Exchange 5.*x* system from the viewpoint of the Exchange 5.*x* servers in a site. In fact, the SRS is really the same service as the Directory Service from Exchange 5.*x*; it has just been disabled in a few critical areas so that clients cannot connect to it and so that it does not interfere with operations on the

Exchange 2000 server. Within a site, Exchange 5.*x* servers treat SRS as if it were just another Exchange 5.*x* server running Directory Service and replicate information with it freely. The information collected by SRS is then synchronized with Active Directory via the Active Directory Connector. SRS actually provides two functions:

- SRS provides a pathway for replicating configuration information between Active Directory and Exchange 5.*x* servers. As you'll learn in the next section, the ADC synchronizes directory information with Exchange 5.*x* servers directly, but must go through SRS for configuration information.

- SRS provides Exchange 5.*x* servers in the site with a means of accessing directory information concerning the Exchange 2000 server on which SRS is running.

Active Directory Connector

The ADC runs on an Exchange 2000 server and synchronizes directory information between Active Directory and Exchange 5.*x* servers in the site. ADC also synchronizes configuration information with those servers using the SRS as an intermediary (see Figure 11.1).

FIGURE 11.1 Active Directory Connector and Site Replication Service

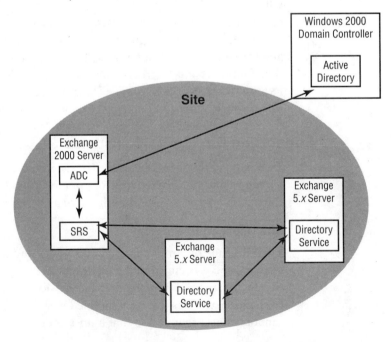

There is a good reason why the SRS is used as the synchronization endpoint for configuration information instead of allowing direct connection between Active Directory and the Directory Services. Different parts of the Exchange 5.*x* Directory are replicated to different areas within the Active Directory:

- Configuration information, such as the configuration of servers and connectors, is replicated to the configuration-naming partition of Active Directory.

- Recipient information is replicated to the domain-naming partition of Active Directory.

- Namespace information is replicated to the schema-naming partition of Active Directory.

Only one instance of the ADC can run on a single Exchange server, but you can configure multiple connection agreements for an ADC. A *connection agreement (CA)* is something like a virtual connector that runs over the ADC. Each connection agreement is defined to replicate certain directory objects to certain parts of the Active Directory, and can even be configured to replicate at certain times. Having the SRS perform as the endpoint of communication for the ADC means that you don't have to reconfigure the connection agreements each time the status of an Exchange 5.*x* server in your site changes (for example, you upgrade it to Exchange 2000). You can configure connections agreements between Active Directory and multiple sites, and you can configure multiple agreements to a single site.

There are two basic types of connection agreements:

- User connection agreements replicate recipient objects and their data between the SRS and Active Directory.

- Configuration connection agreements replicate Exchange-specific configuration information, such as connectors and site information.

You'll learn how to configure the SRS, ADC, and connection agreements later in this chapter.

There are actually two versions of the Active Directory Connector: one that ships with Windows 2000 Server and one that ships with Exchange 2000 Server. The ADC for Windows does replicate directory information between Exchange 5.x Directories and Active Directory. It is intended for people who want to prepare Active Directory for Exchange 2000 during Windows deployment but before installing Exchange 2000. The ADC for Exchange has all the features of the ADC for Windows, but it is enhanced so that it can replicate not only the actual Exchange objects, but also the configuration information about those objects. Because it includes all the features of the ADC for Windows and more, we always recommend upgrading to the ADC for Exchange.

Site and Administrative Group Interactions

In order to make Exchange 5.x and Exchange 2000 coexist, certain restrictions are placed on how you can configure Exchange 2000. When an organization is running in mixed mode, Exchange 2000 must follow the rules laid out by previous versions of Exchange. This means that administrative groups and routing groups must be mapped directly to Exchange 5.x sites so that, in essence, Exchange 2000 simulates the functionality of an Exchange 5.x site.

In an Exchange 5.x site, messages flow between Exchange 5.x Message Transfer Agents (MTAs) using RPC. When you add an Exchange 2000 Server to the site, messages flow between the Exchange 5.x MTAs and the Exchange 2000 MTA using RPC. When multiple Exchange 2000 servers exist in the site, messages flow between Exchange 5.x and Exchange 2000 using RPC, but using SMTP, they flow between Exchange 2000 servers.

Between Exchange 5.x sites, messages move across connectors in much the same way that connectors are used in Exchange 2000. The primary connector used between Exchange 5.x sites is the *Site Connector*, which makes use of RPC to transmit messages. In Exchange 2000 the *Routing Group Connector (RGC)* replaces the Site Connector used in previous versions. The RGC uses SMTP rather than RPC to transport messages between Exchange 2000 servers. For coexistence, however, the RGC uses RPC to transport messages to Exchange 5.x sites that use the Site Connector. This means you can target Exchange 2000 servers as bridgehead servers for Exchange 5.x sites that use the Site Connector. For all other connectors (such as X.400), Exchange 2000 uses its equivalent connector to communicate with Exchange 5.x sites.

Going Native

Once you switch an Exchange organization to native mode (see Chapter 7 for details on the process), the organization is no longer directly interoperable with Exchange 5.*x* servers. Native-mode organizations may only contain Exchange 2000 servers.

You must also be aware that the switch is one-way. Once you switch an organization to native mode, you cannot switch back to mixed mode. Therefore, it is important that your organization be ready for the switch. Here are a few guidelines to help you decide if switching to native mode is the right action to take:

- You no longer have any Exchange 5.*x* servers in your organization.

- You do not plan to add any Exchange 5.*x* servers at a later date.

- If you do have Exchange 5.*x* servers still running on your network, you do not require interoperability between them and the Exchange 2000 organization (i.e., you are maintaining separate organizations).

Site Replication Service

As you learned earlier in the chapter, SRS is used to make Exchange 2000 servers appear as Exchange 5.*x* servers to other Exchange 5.*x* servers in a site. It is also used by ADC to synchronize configuration information. SRS is installed automatically when the first Exchange 2000 server is introduced to an Exchange 5.*x* site. When it is installed, a connection agreement is also created so that the ADC can manage synchronization of configuration information.

There is really not much for you to manage about the SRS; Exchange 2000 Server handles the configuration and maintenance of SRS pretty much automatically. However, there are a few points about SRS that you should be aware of.

SRS and LDAP   SRS runs the *Lightweight Directory Access Protocol (LDAP)* in order to communicate with Active Directory. Because Windows 2000 also uses LDAP and locks the well-known port 389 for its own use, SRS defaults to using port 379 for its LDAP communications. No special configuration is needed for SRS to communicate with Active Directory, but on occasion, you may need to configure special firewall access for the port. You can learn more about configuring ports for LDAP in Chapter 14.

Super Knowledge Consistency Checker   The *Super Knowledge Consistency Checker (SKCC)* is an updated version of the Knowledge Consistency Checker from Exchange 5.*x*. The SKCC ensures that knowledge consistency is maintained for sites and administrative groups when operating in mixed mode. It does this by dynamically configuring multiple connection agreements to establish the most efficient replication.

SRS database   SRS uses the same ESE database technology that the Information Store uses and that the Exchange 5.*x* Directory Services uses. When SRS is installed, a set of databases and transactions logs much like those for a storage group are installed in the `\Program Files\Exchsrvr\srsdata` folder. Unlike the stores in a storage group, the SRS database cannot be mounted or dismounted. However, you can stop and start SRS manually using the Services tool provided with Windows.

Creating an additional SRS for a site   Only one instance of SRS can run on a single Exchange 2000 server, and normally, only the first Exchange 2000 server installed into an Exchange 5.*x* site is configured with SRS. Additional Exchange 2000 servers installed into the site do not really need the service because they can simply rely on Active Directory for their directory information. However, it is sometimes useful to have another instance of SRS running in a site; for example, it may help to balance the replication load in a busy site. You can install an additional instance of the service in System Manager by expanding the Tools container, right-clicking the Site Replication Service object, and selecting the New Site Replication Service command from the shortcut menu. Each additional instance of SRS requires an additional Exchange 2000 server in the site.

Active Directory Connector

The Active Directory Connector is installed automatically when you install Exchange 2000 Server into an existing Exchange 5.*x* site. You can also install the ADC before installing Exchange 2000 Server if you want to set up a replication model first. In this section, we discuss the installation of ADC and the creation and configuration of connection agreements.

Installing ADC

You will install the ADC from the Active Directory Connector folder on the Exchange 2000 CD-ROM or from the splash screen that appears when you

insert the disc. During the installation, the Setup Wizard prompts you to
install two components, as shown in Figure 11.2:

- The Active Directory Connector Service component is the actual connector itself. If you are installing the first ADC in a forest, you will
  need to have the appropriate permissions to modify the Active Directory Schema. If an ADC or an instance of Exchange 2000 is already
  installed in the forest, you will not need these permissions, as the
  Schema will already have been modified. You can find more information on how the installation routine modifies the Schema in Chapter 3.

- The Active Directory Connector Management components is a snap-in
  that lets you manage the ADC outside of the System Manager
  snap-in, useful if you want to install the ADC before installing
  the first Exchange 2000 server into an organization. You can
  install the snap-in on any computer from which you would want
  to manage the ADC.

FIGURE 11.2 Installing the ADC

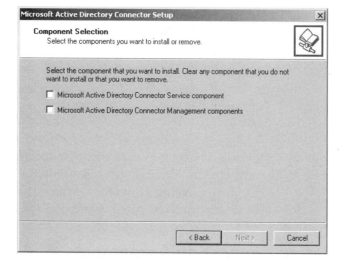

If ADC is already installed on the computer on which you run SETUP, you are
given the option of removing the ADC from the computer—useful when you
have decommissioned all of your Exchange 5.x servers. Before you can unin-
stall the ADC, however, you must first use System Manager to remove all of
the connection agreements.

Exercise 11.1 outlines the steps for installing the ADC.

EXERCISE 11.1

Installing the Active Directory Connector

1. Insert the Exchange 2000 Server CD-ROM into the drive.

2. On the CD-ROM, open the ADC folder, then open the I386 folder.

3. Double-click setup.exe.

4. On the Welcome page, click Next to go on.

5. On the Components Selection page, select the Active Directory Connector Service and Active Directory Connector Management components, and click Next to go on.

6. Leave the installation location at its default directory, and click Next to go on.

7. Exchange 5.*x* uses a special user account named the Site Service Account that lets other Exchange 5.*x* computers log on to the local computer to perform their functions. The SRS service on your Exchange 2000 Server needs one, too. Enter the name of the account you would like to use as well as the password, and click Next to go on.

8. On the summary page, click Finish.

Once you have installed the ADC, you can open its property pages to reveal general details and to enable diagnostic logging for the connector, but not much else. Most of the management of the ADC actually happens by creating and managing connection agreements.

Creating Connection Agreements

When you install Exchange 2000 Server into an existing Exchange 5.*x* site, SRS and ADC are installed automatically. A configuration connection agreement named configCA is also created that replicates configuration information between the SRS and Active Directory. Before directory replication can be performed, however, you must configure a recipient or public folder connection agreement manually.

Microsoft
✓ **Exam**
Objective

Manage coexistence with Exchange 5.5.

- Maintain common user lists.

- Maintain existing connectors.

- Configure the Exchange 2000 Active Directory Connector to replicate directory information.

Whether you are creating a recipient or public folder connection agreement, the creation process is basically the same. Exercise 11.2 outlines the steps for creating a recipient connection agreement.

EXERCISE 11.2

Creating a Recipient Connection Agreement

1. Click Start ➤ Programs ➤ Microsoft Exchange ➤ Active Directory Connector.

2. Right-click the Active Directory Connector *(computername)* object and select New ➤ Recipient Connection Agreement. This opens the property pages for the new connection agreement, which are discussed in detail in the next section.

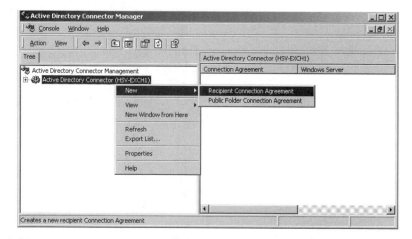

3. Enter a name for the connection agreement on the General page. Try to make the name one that suggests the use of the CA.

4. Enter the name of the Exchange 5.*x* server to which you want to connect on the Connections page.

5. All of the other properties throughout the property pages are optional. When you are finished configuring the connection agreement, click OK to finish.

Configuring Connection Agreement Properties

Whether you are creating a recipient or public folder connection agreement, the property pages you use to configure the agreements are identical. The property pages for a configuration connection agreement are also identical, except that two of the property pages, Deletion and Advanced, are not present. The following sections detail all of the available property pages for a CA.

General Properties

The General page, shown in Figure 11.3, is used to name the CA, to specify whether the CA is two-way or one-way, and to designate a server to run the CA.

FIGURE 11.3   General properties of a CA

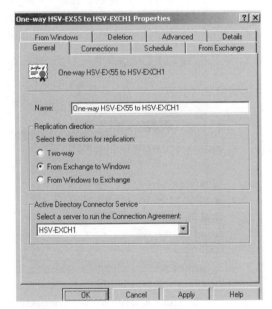

Connections Properties

The Connections page, shown in Figure 11.4, is used to enter connection information for the bridgehead servers of the connection: the Windows server (the Active Directory server) and the Exchange server (the server running Exchange 5.x). The Windows server must be a server running Active Directory. The Exchange server must be running Exchange Server 5.5 with at least Service Pack 1 applied, even though the rest of the servers in the site do not need to run this recent a version of Exchange.

FIGURE   11.4   Connections properties of a CA

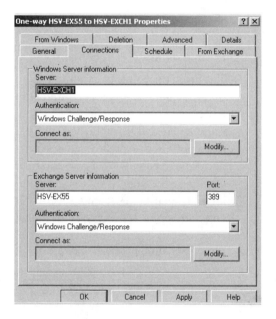

You use the Connections page to specify the authentication method to use for each end of the connection agreement. For more information on authentication methods, see Chapter 14. Also, you use the Connections page to enter the authentication credentials for each server. The account you enter allows each server to connect to the directories on the other end of the connection. The permissions account defined for each server requires only write permissions for its directory.

Finally, you use the Connections page to specify the LDAP port number used by the Exchange 5.x server. Unless Exchange 5.x is running on a Windows 2000 domain controller, this option is not important. However, Windows 2000 locks port 389 for its own use and renders the Exchange 5.x server unable to accept LDAP connections. Common alternative port numbers are 379 and 390.

Schedule Properties

The Schedule page is like all the other Schedule property pages you've seen in this book and throughout Windows 2000. It allows you to specify the times during which replication can take place.

You can also start an unscheduled replication at any time by right-clicking a connection agreement and choosing the Replicate Now command from the All Tasks submenu.

From Exchange Properties

The From Exchange page, shown in Figure 11.5, lets you specify the location of the Exchange Directory container or containers that will be replicated, the location in Active Directory to which they will be replicated, and the specific objects that will be replicated. For public folder connection agreements, these options are already set, and you can't change them. For recipient connection agreements, you can fine-tune the options to meet your needs. For example, you might want to configure one connection agreement to replicate all of the mailboxes from a specific recipients container throughout the day and another agreement to replicate all other types of objects only at night.

FIGURE 11.5 From Exchange properties of a CA

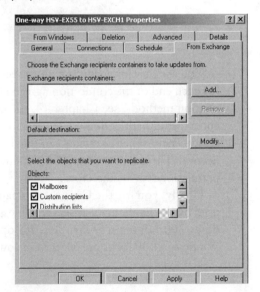

From Windows Properties

The From Windows page is basically the opposite of the From Exchange page. It lets you configure the organizational units in Active Directory that should be replicated, the destination container they should be replicated to on the Exchange 5.*x* end, and the types of objects to replicate.

Deletion Properties

By default, objects deleted in one directory are not deleted in the other directory. Instead, a record of the deletion is stored in a file on the server running ADC in the MSADC\MSADC\<*connection agreement name*> folder. The Deletion page, shown in Figure 11.6, lets you change this behavior. For each direction of replication, you can choose whether objects deleted in the source directory are deleted in the target directory or not. Note that in a one-way connection agreement, one section of this page will be unavailable, as in Figure 11.6.

FIGURE 11.6   Deletion properties of a CA

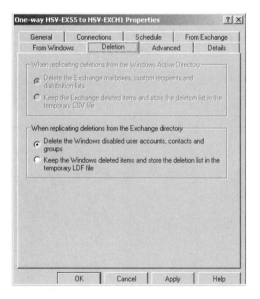

Advanced Properties

The Advanced page, shown in Figure 11.7, lets you configure a number of properties. These include the following:

- The Paged Results section lets you specify the number of entries that are paged together to be replicated as a single action. Paging helps improve replication performance, as a separate replication message does not have to be generated for each entry.

- A primary connection agreement is able to create new entries in the target directory. A CA that is not a primary agreement can only replicate properties to existing objects in the target directory. There are two primary agreement options on this page, one for each direction of the agreement.

- Use the This Is An Inter-Organizational Connection Agreement option if you are replicating information between two different Exchange organizations. Note that this option is not available for public folder connection agreements.

- The When Replicating A Mailbox Whose Primary Windows Account Does Not Exist In The Domain menu lets you specify what should happen when a mailbox being replicated does not have a primary Windows account in the domain. This setting applies only to primary CAs, because many of the options call for creating new accounts in the target directory.

- Use the final setting on the page to specify the direction in which replication should occur first if you are configuring a two-way connection agreement.

FIGURE 11.7 Advanced properties of a CA

Managing a Mixed-Mode Organization

For the most part, managing a mixed-mode organization is not too difficult. You will just have to keep in mind the distinction between your Exchange 2000 servers and Exchange 5.x servers.

Managing Servers

Once an Exchange 2000 server is added to an Exchange 5.x site, the Exchange 5.x servers become visible in System Manager as semi-transparent icons. This is really just to let you know that those servers exist. Even though all configuration information for Exchange 5.x servers is replicated to Active Directory with the ADC, you cannot manage Exchange 5.x servers from System Manager. To manage the queues, connectors, address book views, and other configuration details for Exchange 5.x servers, you will have to use the *System Administrator* tool. System Administrator comes with previous versions of Exchange Server, and you can also install it as a custom option during the installation of Exchange 2000 Server.

Managing Users

Assuming that the ADC is in place and that replication has occurred between Exchange 5.x and Active Directory, you can manage all users from both Exchange 2000 servers and Exchange 5.x servers with Active Directory Users and Computers. The property pages of a user object in Active Directory Users and Computers contain all of the same properties that you can find on the property pages of an Exchange 5.x mailbox in System Administrator. This offers the advantage of performing user management from a single location.

Moving Users

Moving users from an Exchange 5.x server to an Exchange 2000 server can be an important step in migrating to Exchange 2000. Chapter 3 discussed several high-level strategies for upgrading an organization by moving mailboxes in different ways. At the time of this writing, a bug in the software prevents you from moving mailboxes from the Exchange 5.x side using Exchange Administrator. Even though you can begin the process, an error occurs. We expect this problem will be fixed in a future update.

Microsoft
Exam
Objective

Manage coexistence with Exchange 5.5.

- Move users from Exchange 5.5 to Exchange 2000 Server.

In order to move mailboxes from Exchange 5.*x* to Exchange 2000, you must use Active Directory Users and Computers. Exercise 11.3 outlines the steps for performing this operation. This exercise assumes that an ADC is in place and that the user objects in the Exchange 5.*x* directory have already been replicated to Active Directory.

EXERCISE 11.3

Moving Mailboxes from an Exchange 5.*x* Server to an Exchange 2000 Server

1. Click Start ➤ Programs ➤ Administrative Tools ➤ Active Directory Users and Computers.

2. Expand the container for the appropriate domain.

3. Expand the user container that contains the Exchange 5.*x* user you want to move to Exchange 2000.

4. Right-click the user and select the Exchange Tasks command from the shortcut menu.

5. On the welcome page of the Wizard that opens, click Next.

6. Select the Move Mailbox option, and then click Next.

7. Select the server and mailbox store to which you want to move the user, and then click Next.

8. On the summary page, click Finish.

Active Directory Account Cleanup Wizard

The *Active Directory Account Cleanup Wizard* is designed to merge duplicate accounts that may be created when multiple directories are migrated to Active Directory. This tool can be used to clean up after upgrading from

Windows NT, migrating user accounts from another operating system, synchronizing with a foreign messaging system, or, as we are most concerned with here, synchronizing with Exchange 5.*x* directories.

Microsoft ✓ ***Exam Objective***	**Manage coexistence with Exchange 5.5.** ▪ Maintain common user lists.

The Wizard searches for two types of criteria when performing its cleanup routines:

- It attempts to match active user accounts and disabled user accounts that represent the same object.

- It attempts to match active user accounts with contact accounts representing the same object.

Exercise 11.4 outlines the steps for using Active Directory Account Cleanup Wizard to automatically search for duplicated accounts.

EXERCISE 11.4

Using the Active Directory Account Cleanup Wizard

1. Click Start ➣ Programs ➣ Microsoft Exchange ➣ Active Directory Cleanup Wizard.

2. On the welcome page of the Wizard, click Next to go on.

3. On the Identify Merging Accounts page, select the containers and subcontainers that you want to search by clicking Add and browsing for directories. By default, the Wizard searches the entire Active Directory forest.

4. Make sure that the Search Based On Exchange Mailboxes Only option is enabled so that only objects created by the ADC are included in the search results.

5. Begin the search by clicking Next.

EXERCISE 11.4 *(continued)*

6. When the search is complete, you can review the list of suggested merge operations on the Review Merging Accounts page. We strongly recommend reviewing the operations. Just double-click any merge operation to review the details of the source and target accounts. If you see that a merge is missing, you can add a merge operation to the list using the Add button. You can also remove operations using the Remove button. Once you're done with the review, click Next to go on.

7. On the Begin Merging Accounts screen, click Begin The Merge Process Now.

8. The Wizard will warn you that merge operations cannot be undone once they are performed. Click Yes to go on.

9. To begin the merge process, click Next.

10. You can cancel the merge process at any time, but any operations that have already been completed are irreversible. Once the process is done, an Account Merge Results screen is displayed where you can review the results of the merge operations.

Troubleshooting

Because you are relying on the Exchange 5.*x* Directory Service, the Active Directory, and the components that tie the two together, ADC and SRS, troubleshooting coexistence problems can be tricky. This section provides some troubleshooting tips and places to start looking when things go wrong.

Microsoft Exam Objective	**Diagnose and resolve Exchange 2000 Active Directory Connector problems.**

The first action to take when troubleshooting is to check the more obvious sources of potential error. These include the following:

- Are all your servers running?

- Are the ADC and SRS services actually running on the Exchange 2000 server? Are the Directory Services running on any Exchange 5.*x* servers? Use the Services tool or Task Manager to make sure.

- Is a connection agreement configured between the Active Directory and the appropriate Exchange 5.*x* server? If so, is it properly configured?

- Is the container to which you want an entry replicated displayed in the Export Containers list? If not, you'll need to add it.

- Do you have sufficient permissions on the target directory to which you are trying to replicate?

- Have you checked the Windows Application Log for any error messages?

- Can you connect to the SRS port (379 by default) on the Exchange 2000 server?

Once you have exhausted these possibilities, there are a few situations you should be aware of in which an object would not replicate between an Exchange 5.*x* Directory and Active Directory. These are outlined in Table 11.1.

TABLE 11.1 Causes for an Object Not to Replicate When Using ADC

Active Directory to Exchange 5.*x*	Exchange 5.*x* to Active Directory
The Active Directory and Exchange objects being replicated match, but the Exchange object was deleted.	The Exchange and Active Directory objects being replicated match, but the Active Directory object was deleted.
The Active Directory and Exchange objects being replicated match, but the Exchange object is not in the same site as the Exchange 5.*x* server specified in the connection agreement.	The Exchange and Active Directory objects being replicated match, but the Active Directory object is not in a domain to which the ADC can write.
The connection agreement is not the primary connection agreement for the organization.	ADC is attempting to match an Exchange 5.*x* mailbox to a mail-enabled user instead of a mailbox-enabled user.

TABLE 11.1 Causes for an Object Not to Replicate When Using ADC *(continued)*

Active Directory to Exchange 5.*x*	Exchange 5.*x* to Active Directory
The object in Active Directory does not contain e-mail information.	ADC is attempting to match an Exchange 5.*x* custom recipient or distribution list to a mailbox-enabled user.
	The object could not be matched.

Summary

In this chapter, you learned how to use the tools that enable Exchange 2000 Server and previous versions of Exchange Server to coexist in the same organization. An organization running multiple versions of Exchange Server is referred to as mixed mode. An organization running only Exchange 2000 Server is referred to as native mode. Exchange 2000 Server operates in mixed mode by default, even if you have no previous versions running on your network. Once you switch to native mode, you cannot go back, and direct interoperability with previous Exchange versions is lost.

The primary advantage of running in mixed mode is that you can continue to use previous versions of Exchange (and any connectors and software specific to those versions) while upgrading your organization to Exchange 2000 Server. There are also some limitations imposed by running in mixed mode. Exchange 5.*x* sites are mapped directly to Exchange 2000 administrative groups, meaning that administrative groups lose some of their flexibility. You can also not move mailboxes between administrative groups when running a mixed-mode organization.

The primary components used in supporting mixed-mode operations are the Site Replication Service (SRS) and the Active Directory Connector (ADC). The SRS runs on an Exchange 2000 server and actually simulates an Exchange 5.*x* system from the viewpoint of the Exchange 5.*x* servers in a site. The ADC runs on an Exchange 2000 server and synchronizes directory information between Active Directory and Exchange 5.*x* servers in the site.

ADC also synchronizes configuration information with those servers using the SRS as an intermediary. Only one instance of the ADC can run on a single Exchange server, but you can configure multiple connection agreements for an ADC. Each connection agreement is defined to replicate certain directory objects to certain parts of the Active Directory.

Once replication of directories is established, management of a mixed-mode organization is fairly straightforward. You can use Active Directory Users and Computers to manage all users from both Exchange 2000 and Exchange 5.*x*, although you can continue to manage users from System Administrator should you choose. Exchange 2000 servers and other Exchange 2000–specific configuration is managed through System Manager. Exchange 5.*x*–specific configuration must be managed using System Administrator.

Key Terms

Before you take the exam, be certain you are familiar with the following terms:

Active Directory Account
Cleanup Wizard

Active Directory Connector (ADC)

connection agreement

Directory Service (DS)

Lightweight Directory Access
Protocol (LDAP)

mixed mode

native mode

Remote Procedure Call (RPC)

Routing Group Connector (RGC)

Site Connector

Site Replication Service (SRS)

Super Knowledge Consistency
Checker (SKCC)

Review Questions

1. You have an Exchange organization that consists of a single site with four servers running Exchange Server 5.5 with Service Pack 3. You have upgraded all of these servers to run Windows 2000 Advanced Server with Service Pack 1 and have designated two of them as domain controllers. You have just installed an Exchange 2000 server into the site. That server also runs Windows 2000 Server with Service Pack 1. Users that have mailboxes on the two domain controllers complain that they are having problems accessing their address book. You check the Application Log on your Exchange servers and notice that a lot of errors have been generated by servers attempting to contact the domain controllers. What steps should you take to remedy the situation? (Choose all that apply.)

   A. Reapply Windows Service Pack 1 to the domain controllers.

   B. Apply Exchange Server 5.5 Service Pack 4 to all Exchange 5.5 servers.

   C. Change the LDAP port for the Exchange service on the domain controllers.

   D. Change the LDAP port used by the ADC connection agreements to connect to the domain controllers.

   E. Relocate the Exchange 5.5 servers so that they are not on domain controllers.

2. To which of the following Active Directory partitions is recipient information replicated?

   A. Configuration-naming partition

   B. Domain-naming partition

   C. Schema-naming partition

   D. Organization-naming partition

3. Which of the following is a limitation of working in a mixed-mode organization?

    A. You can only move mailboxes within the same storage group.

    B. You can only move mailboxes within the same administrative group.

    C. You cannot move mailboxes from an Exchange 5.*x* server to an Exchange 2000 server.

    D. You cannot move mailboxes from an Exchange 2000 server to an Exchange 5.*x* server.

4. You are the administrator of a mixed-mode organization and are responsible for monitoring the queues on all servers. You receive an alert that one of the connectors on a server running Exchange Server 5.5 is down. What program could you use to check the status of the queue?

    A. System Manager

    B. Exchange Administrator

    C. Active Directory Users and Computers

    D. Task Manager

5. When an Exchange 2000 server is installed into an existing Exchange 5.*x* site, with what services on the Exchange 2000 server do the Exchange 5.*x* servers directly interact? (Choose all that apply.)

    A. SRS

    B. ADC

    C. MTA

    D. Active Directory

6. You are the Exchange administrator for a large mixed-mode organization. You are about to decommission one of your Exchange 5.5 servers and need to move all of the mailboxes on that server to a single mailbox store on one of your Exchange 2000 server. Which of the following tools could you use?

   A. Active Directory Users and Computers

   B. System Manager

   C. Exchange Administrator

   D. Active Directory Account Cleanup Wizard

7. You are the Exchange administrator for an organization that consists of two Exchange sites. Each of these sites contains two servers running Exchange Server 5.5 with Service Pack 3 and Windows 2000 Advanced Server with Service Pack 1. None of these servers is a domain controller. You have created a separate organization on your network that consists of a single administrative group with two servers running Exchange 2000 Server. Neither of these servers is a domain controller. You plan to gradually move users over to the Exchange 2000 organization and then remove the Exchange 5.5 organization altogether.

   Required results:

   Prevent replication of configuration information to the Exchange 2000 organization.

   Allow replication of all recipient information to the Exchange 2000 organization.

   Allow replication of all public folder information to the Exchange 2000 organization.

   Allow users in the Exchange 2000 organization to exchange messages with users in the Exchange 5.5 organization.

Proposed solution:

Switch the Exchange 2000 organization to native mode. Install the Active Directory Connector on a server in the Exchange 2000 organization. Create a recipient and a public folder connector agreement. Configure both agreements so that they connect the Exchange 2000 server to a server in the Exchange 5.5 organization. Set both agreements to be primary connection agreements.

Which of the results does the proposed solution produce?

A. Prevent replication of configuration information to the Exchange 2000 organization.

B. Allow replication of all recipient information to the Exchange 2000 organization.

C. Allow replication of all public folder information to the Exchange 2000 organization.

D. Allow users in the Exchange 2000 organization to exchange messages with users in the Exchange 5.5 organization.

8. You are the Exchange administrator for an organization that consists of two Exchange sites. Each of these sites contains two servers running Exchange Server 5.5 with Service Pack 3 and Windows 2000 Advanced Server with Service Pack 1. None of these servers is a domain controller. You have created a separate organization on your network that consists of a single administrative group with two servers running Exchange 2000 Server. Neither of these servers is a domain controller. You plan to gradually move users over to the Exchange 2000 organization and then remove the Exchange 5.5 organization altogether.

Required results:

Prevent replication of configuration information to the Exchange 2000 organization.

Allow replication of all recipient information to the Exchange 2000 organization.

Allow replication of all public folder information to the Exchange 2000 organization.

Allow users in the Exchange 2000 organization to exchange messages with users in the Exchange 5.5 organization.

Proposed solution:

Install the Active Directory Connector on a server in the Exchange 2000 organization. Create a recipient and a public folder connector agreement. Configure both agreements so that they connect the Exchange 2000 server to a server in the Exchange 5.5 organization. Set both agreements to be primary connection agreements. Establish a messaging connector between the two organizations.

Which of the results does the proposed solution produce? (Choose all that apply.)

A. Prevent replication of configuration information to the Exchange 2000 organization.

B. Allow replication of all recipient information to the Exchange 2000 organization.

C. Allow replication of all public folder information to the Exchange 2000 organization.

D. Allow users in the Exchange 2000 organization to exchange messages with users in the Exchange 5.5 organization.

9. You are the Exchange administrator for an organization that consists of two Exchange sites. Each of these sites contains two servers running Exchange Server 5.5 with Service Pack 3 and Windows 2000 Advanced Server with Service Pack 1. None of these servers is a domain controller. You have created a separate organization on your network that consists of a single administrative group with two servers running Exchange 2000 Server. Neither of these servers is a domain controller. You plan to gradually move users over to the Exchange 2000 organization and then remove the Exchange 5.5 organization altogether.

Required results:

Prevent replication of configuration information to the Exchange 2000 organization.

Allow replication of all recipient information to the Exchange 2000 organization.

Allow replication of all public folder information to the Exchange 2000 organization.

Allow users in the Exchange 2000 organization to exchange messages with users in the Exchange 5.5 organization.

Proposed solution:

Install the Active Directory Connector on a server in the Exchange 2000 organization. Create a recipient and a public folder connector agreement. Configure both agreements so that they connect the Exchange 2000 server to a server in the Exchange 5.5 organization. Set both agreements to be inter-organizational connection agreements. Establish a messaging connector between the two organizations.

Which of the results does the proposed solution produce? (Choose all that apply.)

A. Prevent replication of configuration information to the Exchange 2000 organization.

B. Allow replication of all recipient information to the Exchange 2000 organization.

C. Allow replication of all public folder information to the Exchange 2000 organization.

D. Allow users in the Exchange 2000 organization to exchange messages with users in the Exchange 5.5 organization.

10. To which of the following Active Directory partitions is namespace information replicated?

    A. Configuration-naming partition

    B. Domain-naming partition

    C. Schema-naming partition

    D. Organization-naming partition

11. Which of the following actions are taken by the Active Directory Account Cleanup Wizard? (Choose all that apply.)

    A. It attempts to match active user accounts and disabled user accounts that represent the same object.

    B. It attempts to match active user accounts and contact accounts that represent the same object.

    C. It attempts to match active groups and contact accounts that represent the same object.

    D. It attempts to match active user accounts and mail-enabled accounts that represent the same object.

12. Which of the following statements is true?

    A. Exchange 2000 servers in a mixed-mode organization can use connectors installed on Exchange 5.x servers in the same organization.

    B. Exchange 2000 servers in a mixed-mode organization can use connectors installed on Exchange 5.x servers in other organizations.

    C. Exchange 2000 servers in a mixed-mode organization cannot use connectors installed on Exchange 5.x servers.

    D. Exchange 5.x servers can use connectors installed on Exchange 2000 servers in a mixed-mode organization.

13. You are running a mixed-mode organization that contains a number of Exchange 2000 and Exchange 5.5 servers in a single site. How do Exchange 5.x servers in that site exchange directory information?

    A. Using SMTP

    B. Using MAPI

    C. Using RPCs

    D. Using LDAP

14. Which of the following statements is true about public folders in mixed-mode organizations?

    A. Public folders may not be replicated.

    B. Public folders may be replicated from Exchange 5.x servers to Exchange 2000 servers only.

    C. Public folders may be replicated from Exchange 2000 servers to Exchange 5.x servers only.

    D. Public folders may be replicated in both directions.

15. You are the administrator of an Exchange 5.x organization consisting of a single site. You create a new site containing a single Exchange 5.x server and then install an Exchange 2000 server into that new site. Which of the following statements is true about directory replication in the organization?

    A. Directory replication happens automatically between all servers in the organization.

    B. Directory replication happens automatically between all Exchange 5.x servers in the organization, but must be manually configured to the Exchange 2000 server.

    C. Directory replication happens automatically between all servers in the same site, but must be configured to happen between sites.

    D. Directory replication cannot happen between the Exchange 2000 server and the Exchange 5.x servers in the other site.

16. Which of the following types of connection agreements would be used to replicate the information about a legacy Microsoft Mail connector configured on an Exchange 5.x server?

    A. Recipient connection agreement

    B. Configuration connection agreement

    C. Connector connection agreement

    D. Link state connection agreement

17. What protocol does the Routing Group Connector use to transport messages to Exchange 5.x sites that are connected using Exchange 5.x Site Connectors?

    A. SMTP

    B. X.400

    C. RPC

    D. LDAP

18. What is the default port number used by SRS for LDAP communications?

    A. 369

    B. 379

    C. 389

    D. 399

19. Which of the following statements about the Active Directory Connector is true? (Choose all that apply.)

    A. The ADC must run on the same computer as Active Directory.

    B. The ADC must run on an Exchange 5.x server.

    C. Only one ADC can run in any given site.

    D. Multiple ADCs can run in a given site.

    E. Only one ADC can run on a single server.

    F. Multiple ADCs can run on a single server.

20. You are configuring a recipient connection agreement in a mixed-mode site. What two requirements exist for the bridgehead servers on either end of the agreement?

A. One end of the connection must be a computer running Exchange 2000 Server.

B. One end of the connection must be a computer running Active Directory.

C. One end of the connection must be a computer running Exchange 5.5 with Service Pack 1.

D. One end of the connection must be a computer running Exchange 5.5 with Service Pack 1 on a Windows 2000 Server.

Answers to Review Questions

1 C, D. Windows 2000 domain controllers lock LDAP port 389 for their own use. This renders Exchange Server 5.5 unable to accept LDAP connections when running on a domain controller, since the default LDAP port is 389. You must change the LDAP port that the Exchange servers use and then change the LDAP port that the ADC uses to connect to the servers.

2. B. Configuration information, such as the configuration of servers and connectors, is replicated to the configuration-naming partition of Active Directory. Recipient information is replicated to the domain-naming partition. Namespace information is replicated to the schema-naming partition of Active Directory. There is no such thing as an organization-naming partition.

3. B. When operating in mixed mode, you can only move mailboxes between servers in the same administrative group. You can always move mailboxes between servers of different versions.

4. B. Even though all configuration information for Exchange 5.*x* servers is replicated to Active Directory with the ADC, you cannot manage Exchange 5.*x* servers from System Manager. To manage the queues, connectors, address book views, and other configuration details for Exchange 5.*x* servers, you will have to use the Exchange Administrator. Active Directory Users and Computers can be used for managing users on both Exchange 2000 and Exchange 5.*x* servers.

5. A, B. The SRS behaves like an Exchange 5.*x* Directory Service running on the Exchange 2000 server. SRS provides Exchange 5.*x* servers in the site with a means of accessing configuration information concerning the Exchange 2000 server on which SRS is running. The ADC is used to replicate directory information between the Active Directory and the Exchange 5.*x* servers. Exchange 5.*x* servers communicate with the Exchange 2000 server in the same site using RPCs. If the servers were in different sites, the MTA would be used.

6. A. In order to move mailboxes from Exchange 5.*x* to Exchange 2000, you must use Active Directory Users and Computers.

7. A. Configuration information may not be replicated between organizations using a connection agreement, so this option is prevented by default. In order to accomplish the results, you must leave the Exchange 2000 organization in native mode, install ADC on one of the servers, establish recipient and public folder connection agreements that connect that server with a server in the Exchange 5.5 organization, and then enable the This Is An Inter-Organizational Connection Agreement option on the Advanced property page of the CAs to allow for replication between organizations. Once these steps are taken, recipient directory information is exchanged between the two organizations. However, you must also create a messaging connector between the two organizations for users to be able to transfer messages.

8. A, D. Configuration information may not be replicated between organizations using a connection agreement, so this option is prevented by default. In order to accomplish the results, you must leave the Exchange 2000 organization in native mode, install ADC on one of the servers, establish recipient and public folder connection agreements that connect that server with a server in the Exchange 5.5 organization, and then enable the This Is An Inter-Organizational Connection Agreement option on the Advanced property page of the CAs to allow for replication between organizations. Once these steps are taken, recipient directory information is exchanged between the two organizations. However, you must also create a messaging connector between the two organizations for users to be able to transfer messages.

9. A, B, C, D. Configuration information may not be replicated between organizations using a connection agreement, so this option is prevented by default. In order to accomplish the results, you must leave the Exchange 2000 organization in native mode, install ADC on one of the servers, establish recipient and public folder connection agreements that connect that server with a server in the Exchange 5.5 organization, and then enable the This Is An Inter-Organizational Connection Agreement option on the Advanced property page of the CAs to allow for replication between organizations. Once these steps are taken, recipient directory information is exchanged between the two organizations. However, you must also create a messaging connector between the two organizations for users to be able to transfer messages.

10. C. Configuration information, such as the configuration of servers and connectors, is replicated to the configuration-naming partition of Active Directory. Recipient information is replicated to the domain-naming partition. Namespace information is replicated to the schema-naming partition of Active Directory. There is no such thing as an organization-naming partition.

11. A, B. The Active Directory Account Cleanup Wizard is designed to merge duplicate accounts that may be created when multiple directories are migrated to Active Directory. It works by searching for user accounts that match either disabled accounts or contacts and then allowing you to merge those accounts.

12. A. The configuration connection agreement of the ADC imports information from Exchange 5.*x* Gateway Address Routing Tables into Exchange 2000 server link state tables and thus provides access to Exchange 5.*x* connectors and gateways.

13. C. All Exchange 5.*x* servers in the same site automatically replicate directory information using RPCs. Replication of directory information between Exchange 5.*x* servers in different sites must be configured manually and occurs by sending e-mail messages over whatever connector is used to connect the sites.

14. D. Public folders can be replicated freely between Exchange 2000 and Exchange 5.*x* servers.

15. C. The SRS on the Exchange 2000 server makes the server appear as an Exchange 5.*x* server to other 5.*x* servers. Directory replication between Exchange 5.*x* sites is not an automatic process and must be configured by an administrator. Directory replication between sites occurs using e-mail messages over whatever connectors are used to connect the sites. This ability allows administrators to decide what resources to share with other sites.

16. B. There are two basic types of connection agreements: user agreements (which come in the form of recipient and public folder agreements) and configuration agreements. Configuration agreements replicate Exchange-specific configuration information, such as connectors and site information.

17. C. The primary connector used between Exchange 5.x sites is the Site Connector, which makes use of RPC to transmit messages. In Exchange 2000, the Routing Group Connector (RGC) replaces the Site Connector used in previous versions. The RGC uses SMTP rather than RPC to transport messages between Exchange 2000 servers. For coexistence, however, the RGC uses RPC to transport messages to Exchange 5.x sites that use the Site Connector.

18. B. Because Windows 2000 also uses LDAP and locks the well-known port 389 for its own use, SRS defaults to using port 379 for its LDAP communications.

19. D, E. The ADC runs on an Exchange 2000 server. Only one instance of the ADC can run on a single Exchange server, but you can configure multiple connection agreements for an ADC. An instance of ADC can run on each server in a site that is running Exchange 2000.

20. B, C. The computer running the ADC service will have Exchange 2000 installed. The Windows server at one end of the connection agreement must be a computer running Active Directory. The Exchange server must be running Exchange Server 5.5 with at least Service Pack 1 applied, even though the rest of the servers in the site do not need to run this recent a version of Exchange.

Connecting with Other Messaging Systems

MICROSOFT EXAM OBJECTIVES COVERED IN THIS CHAPTER:

✓ **Configure server objects for messaging and collaboration to support the assigned server role.**

- Configure information store objects.
- Configure multiple storage groups for data partitioning.
- Configure multiple databases within a single storage group.
- Configure virtual servers to support Internet protocols.
- Configure Exchange 2000 Server information in the Windows 2000 Active Directory.
- Configure Instant Messaging objects.
- Configure Chat objects.

✓ **Manage and troubleshoot messaging connectivity.**

- Manage Exchange 2000 Server messaging connectivity.
- Manage connectivity to foreign mail systems. Connectivity types include X.400, SMTP, and Internet messaging connectivity.
- Diagnose and resolve routing problems.
- Diagnose and resolve problems reported by non-delivery report messages.

As you learned in Chapter 7, Exchange 2000 Server relies on various connectors to provide messaging links between routing groups in an organization. Connectors are also used to provide messaging links between Exchange organizations and external messaging systems. The external messaging system could be a legacy system you have in place on your own network, a messaging system (even another Excha\nge organization) on someone else's network, or the Internet itself. Exchange 2000 comes with a few general-use connectors, such as the X.400 and SMTP Connectors, that are used to establish communications with other systems capable of using these same protocols. In addition, Exchange 2000 comes with several specialized connectors used to establish communications with proprietary messaging systems. Examples include the Microsoft Mail and Lotus cc:Mail Connectors.

This chapter begins with a look at two of the general-purpose connectors: the X.400 Connector and the SMTP Connector. Since the basic configuration of these was covered when we discussed linking routing groups together in Chapter 7, we will look at the differences in configuring the connectors to be used with external systems. We will also look at the details of using the SMTP Connector to enable communications with the Internet. From there, we will turn our attention to the Microsoft Mail and Lotus cc:Mail Connectors.

Connecting to an X.400 System

If you recall from Chapter 7, the *X.400 Connector* can be used to link Exchange routing groups in the same organization and also to link an Exchange organization to a foreign, X.400-based messaging system.

When you create an X.400 Connector, the computer on which the connector is configured becomes the bridgehead server to the foreign system.

Microsoft **Manage and troubleshoot messaging connectivity.**
Exam
Objective - Manage connectivity to foreign mail systems. Connectivity types include X.400, SMTP, and Internet messaging connectivity.

The "Manage Exchange 2000 Server messaging connectivity" subobjective is covered in Chapter 7. The "Diagnose and resolve routing problems" and "Diagnose and resolve problems reported by non-delivery report messages" subobjectives are covered in Chapter 9. This section provides a brief overview of setting up an X.400 Connector. For more detail, see Chapter 7. Also, for more detail on the X.400 protocol itself, please refer to Chapter 1.

To configure the X.400 Connector in Exchange 2000 Server, you first must create a *Message Transfer Agent (MTA) Service Transport Stack*. This Transport Stack is configured on a particular Exchange server and is basically a set of information about the software and hardware making up the underlying network. The use of the Transport Stack allows for a layer of abstraction between the X.400 Connector and the network itself. You can configure Transport Stacks that support either the TCP/IP or X.25 protocols.

After creating the Transport Stack, you must create the connector. Exercise 12.1 outlines the basic steps for creating a new TCP/IP Transport Stack and an X.400 Connector to use that stack.

EXERCISE 12.1

Creating a TCP/IP Transport Stack and X.400 Connector

1. Start➤Programs➤Microsoft Exchange➤System Manager.

2. Expand the organization object in which you want to create a new administrative group.

3. Expand the Administrative Groups folder, the administrative group, and then the server on which you want to create the stack.

EXERCISE 12.1 *(continued)*

4. Expand the Protocols container, right-click the X.400 container, and choose New TCP/IP X.400 Service Transport Stack from the shortcut menu.

5. Use the property pages that open to configure the new stack, and click OK when you are done.

6. Expand the organization object, the Administrative Groups folder, the specific administrative group, and the routing group for which you want to create the connector.

7. Right-click the Connectors container and choose the New TCP X.400 Connector command from the shortcut menu.

8. Expand the Protocols container, right-click the X.400 container, and choose New TCP/IP X.400 Connector from the shortcut menu.

9. This opens the property pages that you must configure for the new connector. After you have configured these pages, you must get the administrator of the external X.400 system to create the corresponding connector to your system.

Many of the property pages used to configure an X.400 Connector were covered in detail in Chapter 7. However, three of the pages are only relevant to configuring external X.400 connections. Those pages are covered in the next few sections.

Override Properties

The Override page, shown in Figure 12.1, lets you configure settings that override the local MTA settings when messages are sent over the X.400 Connector. For the most part, you can leave these advanced settings alone. When connecting to a foreign X.400 system, that system's administrator will be able to tell you the settings that need to be adjusted.

You can also override the name and password of your local MTA. This is used mainly when the name and password of the local MTA are too long or use characters or spaces that MTAs on foreign systems cannot accept. The overriding values are used only for the X.400 connection.

Address Space Properties

Foreign systems do not necessarily use the same addressing scheme as
Exchange 2000 Server. For this reason, the Exchange MTA relies on address
spaces to choose foreign gateways over which messages should be sent. An
address space is the part of an address that designates the system that should
receive the message. For example, look at a typical Internet address:
user@company.com. Everything after the @ sign is the address space. The
format of the address space is enough to tell the MTA that the message
should be sent via SMTP.

The Address Space property sheet, shown in Figure 12.2, lets you configure an address space for the foreign X.400 system to which you are connecting. The Exchange MTA compares the destination address of outgoing
messages with this address space to determine whether the outgoing messages should be sent over the X.400 Connector.

FIGURE 12.2 Configuring address spaces for an X.400 Connector

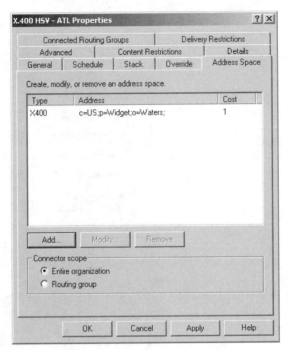

Clicking the Add button opens an Add Address Space dialog box, shown in Figure 12.3, which allows you to specify the type of address space that you want to add. Because you are connecting to a foreign X.400 system, you want to configure an X.400 address space.

FIGURE 12.3 Choosing an address space type

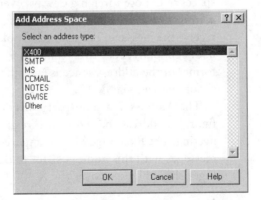

After you choose the X.400 address space type and click OK, the X.400 Address Space Properties dialog box appears, as shown in Figure 12.4. The particular addressing information that needs to be configured for the foreign system should be provided by the administrator of the foreign system. X.400 addresses are case-sensitive and need to be typed in exactly the same format as provided.

FIGURE 12.4   Configuring the address space

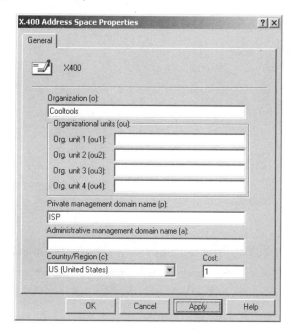

Advanced Properties

The Advanced page, shown in Figure 12.5, is used to specify options for MTA conformance, links, and message attributes. The settings depend mostly on the specifications of the foreign system to which you are connecting.

FIGURE 12.5 Configuring Advanced properties for an X.400 Connector

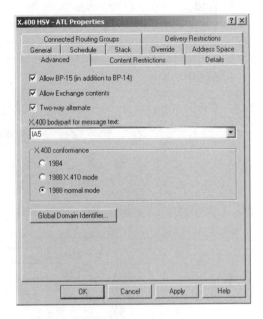

Table 12.1 lists the properties available on the Advanced page.

TABLE 12.1 Advanced Properties for an X.400 Connector

Property	Description
Allow BP-15 (in addition to BP-14)	The Body Part 15 (BP-15) standard is part of the 1988 X.400 recommendation and supports several advanced messaging features, such as the encoding of binary attachments. The Body Part 14 (BP-14) standard is part of the older 1984 X.400 recommendation, which supports fewer features. If you do not select the Allow BP-15 option, only the BP-14 standard is used.
Allow Exchange contents	Microsoft Exchange supports the use of Extended MAPI-compliant clients, which in turn support such features as rich-text format. Make sure that any foreign X.400 system to which you are connecting supports such features before you allow them to be transferred.

TABLE 12.1   Advanced Properties for an X.400 Connector *(continued)*

Property	Description
Two-way alternate	The two-way alternate specification is an X.400 standard in which two connected X.400 systems take turns transmitting and receiving information. If the foreign system to which you are connecting supports this option, enabling it can greatly improve transmission speed.
X.400 bodypart for message text	This option specifies how message text should be formatted. Unless you are communicating with foreign systems that use foreign-language applications, leave this value at its default setting, International Alphabet 5 (IA5).
X.400 conformance	X.400 standards are periodically published as recommendations. Exchange 2000 Server supports the two primary recommendations: those issued in 1984 and those from 1988. New updates have been made to the standard since 1988, but they don't really form a new recommendation. The 1988 recommendation itself has two versions: normal mode and X.410 mode. The default setting is 1988 normal mode, and you can expect it to work with most foreign X.400 systems.
Global Domain Identifier	The global domain identifier (GDI) is a section of the X.400 address space of the target system. The GDI is used to prevent message loops that can occur with outgoing messages. The administrator of the foreign X.400 system will let you know if you need to modify these values.

SMTP and Internet Connectivity

In Chapter 7, you saw how the SMTP Connector could be used to connect routing groups in the same organization and to connect an Exchange 2000 routing group to an Exchange 5.5 server. You can also use SMTP Connectors to connect an Exchange organization to the Internet or to a foreign messaging system that uses SMTP.

Microsoft.
Exam
Objective

Manage and troubleshoot messaging connectivity.

- Manage connectivity to foreign mail systems. Connectivity types include X.400, SMTP, and Internet messaging connectivity.

SMTP Overview

The *Simple Mail Transfer Protocol (SMTP)* defines the methods for exchanging mail messages between applications. The protocol addresses mail transfer between an SMTP client and an SMTP server (the client may itself be another SMTP server). This section discusses SMTP and outlines how it works.

SMTP Process

The SMTP process involves a TCP connection, a series of client-server commands and replies, and the use of spooling. We will discuss each of these in the following sections.

TCP Connection

When an SMTP client application sends mail to an SMTP server, it uses TCP to establish a connection with port 25 on the SMTP server. Port 25 is the application doorway on the SMTP server for mail activity. Once that connection is established, a series of commands and replies are exchanged between the client and the server. The connection is similar to a telephone connection, and the commands and responses are similar to verbal communication over a telephone connection.

SMTP Commands and Replies

Now we will examine the steps in the SMTP process (including the TCP connection). In this example, we will send a message. You do not need to remember the reply code numbers. They are included here merely to provide a complete picture.

1. A client establishes a connection with the server at port 25.

2. The server confirms the connection by replying with a 220 reply code, which means "ready for mail."

3. The client computer identifies itself to the server by sending the HELO command with the computer's identity (for example, HELO server1.acme.com).

4. The server confirms the HELO by responding with the 250 reply code (which means "all is well") and its identity. The server may also require a password or some other form of authentication.

5. The client sends the MAIL FROM command that contains the identification of the sender.

6. The server responds with the 250 reply code ("all is well").

7. The sender then sends the RCPT TO (Recipient To) command with the identity of a recipient of the mail message.

8. The server responds with either a 250 reply code or a 550 reply code (which means "no such user here").

9. After all the RCPT TO commands are sent (one command is sent per recipient), the client sends the DATA command indicating that it is ready to send the actual mail message.

10. The server responds with a 354 reply code (which means "start mail input").

11. Upon receiving the 354 reply, the client sends its outgoing mail messages line by line. The data must be in 7-bit ASCII format. If the data is in 8-bit format, it must be translated into 7-bit format using either Multipurpose Internet Mail Extensions (MIME) or UUEN-CODE(UNIX-to-UNIX encode).

12. After the data has been sent, the sender sends a special sequence of control characters (e.g., CRLF.CRLF) to signal the end of the transfer.

13. The client sends a QUIT command to end the session.

14. The server responds with the 221 reply code (which means that it "agrees with the termination"). Both sides of the communication close the TCP connection.

SMTP and Spooling

The word "spooling" in this context means "queuing." SMTP uses *spooling* to delay message delivery. For example, when a client sends a message addressed to another user, that message is spooled on the sender's SMTP server. The SMTP server will periodically check its spooled messages and try to deliver them to the relevant users. If it cannot deliver a message, the SMTP server will keep the message spooled and try to deliver it at a later time. When the recipient's server comes online, the SMTP server can deliver the message. If a message cannot be delivered within a time period set by the administrator, the spooled message is returned to the sender with a non-delivery message.

The advantage of the spool mechanism is that the message sender does not have to establish a connection with a recipient's computer in order to send a message. After sending a message, the sender can proceed with other computing activities because he or she does not need to wait online for the message to reach the recipient. The recipient also does not have to be online in order for mail to be sent to him or her.

DNS and SMTP

Transferring messages between SMTP hosts is dependent on the Domain Name Service (DNS). When an SMTP host sends an e-mail message to another SMTP host, DNS must resolve the domain name of the receiving host to an IP address. DNS does this by storing special records named *Mail Exchanger (MX) records* in the DNS database. Each MX record in a DNS database represents an SMTP host to which mail can be forwarded. You can also assign each MX record a preference relative to the other MX records in the database.

A sending SMTP host retrieves all MX records for the receiving domain from DNS, resolves the IP address for the SMTP host with the lowest preference number, and attempts to send its message to that host. If that host is unavailable, the sender tries the host with the next higher preference number.

SMTP Folders in Exchange 2000 Server

SMTP uses three file system folders to manage messages on an Exchange 2000 Server. By default, all of these folders are created in the C:\Program Files\Exchsrvr\Mailroot folder. The three folders are:

- The *Pickup folder* is used for outbound messages on some SMTP hosts. Exchange 2000 creates, but does not normally use, this folder.

- The *Queue folder* is where SMTP stores inbound messages as they are received. Once received, Internet Information Server (IIS) processes them for delivery.

- The *Bad Mail folder* is where undeliverable messages that cannot be returned to the sender are stored.

Configuring Multiple SMTP Domain Names

SMTP can be configured in a number of different ways. For example, you might provide your users with one or multiple SMTP addresses. You might also segregate users into virtual organizations, each with their own SMTP address spaces. For example, you might configure some of your users to receive mail using the @widgets.com address space, while others receive mail using the @cooltools.com address space. To do this, you must configure separate SMTP virtual servers for these users and configure MX records to resolve the IP address associated with those virtual servers.

The SMTP Virtual Server

With Exchange 2000, you can create multiple virtual servers for every supported Internet protocol, including SMTP. Creating multiple *SMTP virtual servers* allows you to segment SMTP traffic to use different IP addresses or TCP ports, each with their own configuration. This allows you a good bit of leeway in your SMTP configuration. For example, you might configure one SMTP virtual server with stricter authentication policies than another. Or, you might configure one virtual server to send and receive SMTP messages between all Exchange 2000 servers inside an organization, and configure another virtual server to send and receive SMTP messages from the Internet.

Microsoft ✓ *Exam* *Objective*

Configure server objects for messaging and collaboration to support the assigned role.

- Configure virtual servers to support Internet protocols.

The "Configure information store objects," "Configure multiple storage groups for data partitioning," and "Configure multiple databases within a single storage group" subobjectives are covered in Chapter 8. The "Configure Exchange 2000 Server information in the Windows 2000 Active Directory" subobjective is covered in Chapter 9. The "Configure Instant Messaging objects" and "Configure Chat objects" subobjectives are covered in Chapter 10.

As with most other objects, you'll configure the SMTP virtual server using its property pages. Just expand the protocols container under the Exchange server on which the virtual server is configured, and then expand the SMTP container, as shown in Figure 12.6.

FIGURE 12.6   Viewing SMTP virtual servers

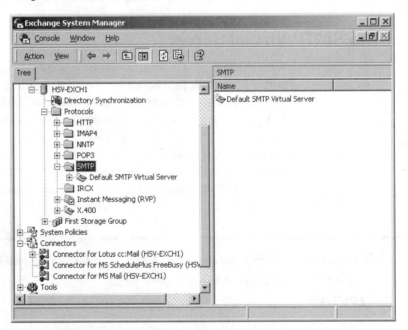

To start with, only the Default SMTP Virtual Server exists. You can add new virtual servers by right-clicking the SMTP container and selecting the New SMTP Virtual Server command. This command opens the property pages for configuring the new server. Each of the available pages is discussed in the upcoming sections.

General Properties

The General page, shown in Figure 12.7, is used to set several general parameters, including the following:

- The IP address assigned to the virtual server (this is unassigned by default)

- The number of concurrent connections the server is allowed to support (no limit is set by default)

- The maximum amount of time a connection may be idle before being timed out (again, no default is set)

- Whether logging is enabled

FIGURE 12.7   General properties of an SMTP virtual server

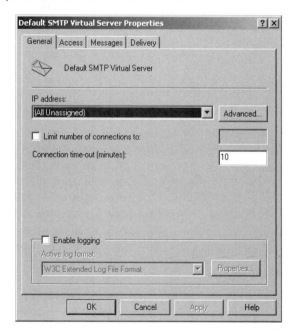

Access Properties

The Access properties page provides access to a number of separate dialog boxes used to control access to the virtual server. Table 12.2 describes the parameters you can configure using the buttons on this page.

TABLE 12.2 Setting Access Properties for an SMTP Virtual Server

Button	Settings
Authentication	It is often useful to require an SMTP host or client to authenticate before allowing message transfer. You can use this button to choose from Anonymous, Basic, or Integrated Windows authentication methods. This dialog also lets you configure TLS encryption. Authentication and encryption are covered in Chapter 14.
Certificate	This button launches a Wizard for creating and configuring Web server certificates (also discussed in Chapter 14).
Communication	This button lets you configure whether a secure channel is required to transfer messages using the SMTP virtual server and whether that secure channel should use 128-bit encryption.
Connection	This button opens a dialog that lets you configure a specific list of hosts to grant or deny access to.
Relay	By default, an SMTP virtual server will accept messages from any host, but will only relay messages sent from authorized clients. This allows clients in your domain using POP3 or IMAP4 clients to send SMTP messages using the SMTP virtual host. If you want to configure your SMTP virtual server to act as a smart host for relay messages coming in from other domains, you can configure the specific clients to relay messages for using this button. Note that this is used to configure only inbound relay restrictions. Outbound restrictions are configured using the SMTP Connector.

Messages Properties

The Messages page, shown in Figure 12.8, lets you configure how messages are handled by the SMTP virtual server. You can place several limits on messages, including the message size, the cumulative size of messages that can be transferred during a single session, the number of messages that may be sent per connection, and the number of recipients a single message can name.

You can also use this page to designate a recipient to receive Non-Delivery Reports (NDRs) and change the directory in which bad mail is stored.

FIGURE 12.8   Configuring message properties

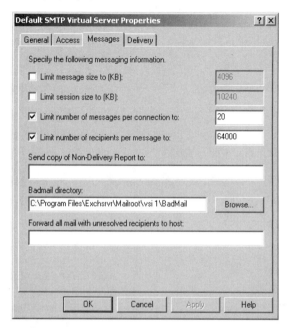

The final field on this page, Forward All Mail With Unresolved Recipients To Host, is probably not featured prominently enough in the list of options. This field lets you name a *smart host* to which messages are forwarded when they cannot be resolved within your domain. This offers the powerful ability to configure a single host to which all external mail (such as to the Internet) should go. For example, you could configure your SMTP virtual server to forward all unresolved messages (those not to recipients in your own organization) to an SMTP host at your ISP or to a smart host of your own that you have placed outside the company firewall.

Delivery Properties

The Delivery page lets you set several options governing how the SMTP virtual server tries to deliver mail and some parameters governing the security and configuration of outbound connections. The parameters you can configure on this page include are shown in Table 12.3.

TABLE 12.3   Setting Delivery Properties for an SMTP Virtual Server

Property	Description
Retry intervals	By default, each virtual server tries to deliver messages as they arrive. When delivery fails for some reason, the virtual server queues the message for retries. The first through third and subsequent retry interval settings let you configure how long it takes the server to attempt to send a message after a failure.
Delay notification	If a message has been queued for 12 hours (the default setting), the sender is notified that the message has not been delivered yet.
Expiration timeout	After two days (again, the default setting), the message is returned to the sender with an NDR.
Local	The Delay Notification and Expiration Timeout settings in the Local section work the same as those in the Outbound section, but apply only to recipients within the organization.
Outbound security	As you saw in the previous section, inbound security is set using the Authentication button on the Access page. Outbound security is configured using this button. Usually, you should configure outbound security to use the same authentication protocols that you require for inbound security.
Outbound connections	Use this button to assign limits on the allowable number of outbound connections.
Advanced	One common security problem with Internet mail occurs when the person sending the message misrepresents their identity. This is referred to as spoofing. To help prevent spoofing, you can configure an SMTP virtual server to perform a reverse DNS lookup on people who send messages. This confirms that the IP address of the sender is from the same network as is registered in DNS. Use the Advanced button to enable Reverse DNS lookup. One caution, however: Using reverse DNS lookup can significantly decrease performance.

Managing SMTP Virtual Server Queues

SMTP maintains four queues in which messages are held for various stages of processing. These queues are:

- local_domain_name (Local Delivery), which contains messages waiting for delivery to a local mailbox. If this queue backs up, look for problems within IIS or the Information Store.

- Messages awaiting directory lookup, which contains messages waiting for recipient addresses to be resolved. If this queue backs up, look for problems between Exchange 2000 and Active Directory.

- Messages waiting to be routed, which contains messages waiting for Exchange 2000 Server to determine the best route along which to send them. Once the route is determined, messages are moved to various temporary link queues for delivery. If this queue backs up, look for problems with connectors.

- Final destination unreachable, which contains messages the SMTP virtual server was unable to deliver. If this queue backs up, look for problems with the SMTP virtual server, the destination SMTP server, or improper addressing.

For more information on managing queues, see Chapter 9.

EXERCISE 12.2

Creating an SMTP Virtual Server

1. Click Start>Programs > Microsoft Exchange > System Manager.

2. Expand the organization object in which you want to create a new administrative group.

3. Expand the Administrative Groups folder, the administrative group, and the server on which you want to create the new virtual server, and then expand the Protocols container.

4. Right-click the SMTP container and select New SMTP Virtual Server from the shortcut menu.

5. On the first page of the Wizard that appears, enter the name for the new SMTP virtual server.

6. Select the specific IP address configured on your server to the new SMTP virtual server. Note that the IP address and port number combination you configure must be separate from any that are already in use on your server.

7. Click Finish to create the new connector and return to System Manager.

8. In System Manager, expand the SMTP container.

9. Right-click the new SMTP virtual server, and select Properties from the shortcut menu.

10. Click the Access tab.

11. Click the Authentication button.

12. Remove the checkmarks next to the Anonymous and Basic authentication options.

13. Click the Messages tab.

14. Select the Limit Message Size To (KB) option, and enter a maximum message size into the corresponding field.

15. Click OK to set the new properties and return to System Manager.

The SMTP Connector

While an SMTP virtual server is used to define basic SMTP transport properties, an SMTP Connector is used to define properties for a specific address space. In Chapter 7, we covered the creation and configuration of SMTP Connectors in detail. Even though that discussion was aimed primarily at using the SMTP Connector to connect routing groups, the process of setting up the SMTP Connector for other uses is almost identical, so we refer you to Chapter 7 for specifics.

Connecting to Microsoft Mail

Exchange 2000 Server offers connectivity to the Microsoft Mail for PC Networks messaging system (referred to as MS Mail from here on) via the *MS Mail Connector*. This section provides an overview of MS Mail and how MS Mail and Exchange 2000 Server communicate.

Microsoft ✓ *Exam* *Objective*

Manage and troubleshoot messaging connectivity.

- Manage connectivity to foreign mail systems. Connectivity types include X.400, SMTP, and Internet messaging connectivity.

MS Mail Overview

To understand the MS Mail Connector, you need to have a basic understanding of MS Mail. We will examine four elements of the MS Mail architecture:

- Postoffices
- MS Mail MTA
- Directory synchronization across postoffices
- Gateways from MS Mail to non–MS Mail systems

Postoffices

MS Mail is a shared-file mail system. The mail messages are stored as files in a shared directory on a designated computer, called a *postoffice*. An MS Mail system can have more than one postoffice.

MS Mail MTA

If an organization has several postoffices, the MS Mail MTA component routes messages between them. The MTA is implemented by either the External MTA or the Multitasking MTA.

Directory Synchronization across Postoffices

MS Mail postoffices exchange directory information through the MS Mail Directory Synchronization Protocol. A single postoffice is designated as a *dirsync server (directory synchronization server)*. DISPATCH.EXE is the MS Mail program that executes the functions of a dirsync server. The dirsync server stores the master copy of a network's directory information (the Global Address List) and sends that list to the other postoffices. These other postoffices are designated as *dirsync requestors (directory synchronization requestors)*.

They send new, locally created directory information to the dirsync server, and they receive the Global Address List from the dirsync server.

Three primary events occur during synchronization: A requestor sends directory information to the server, the server compiles the Global Address List and sends it to requestors, and a requestor rebuilds its Global Address List. Each of these events is initiated at a certain timed interval configured through the following parameters:

T1   The *T1 event* defines the interval used by dirsync requestors to send their postoffice address lists to the dirsync server.

T2   The *T2 event* defines the interval used by the dirsync server to compile a new Global Address List and to send that list to the dirsync requestors.

T3   The *T3 event* defines the interval used by the dirsync requestors to rebuild their postoffice address lists.

The default setting for each of these events is once every 24 hours. Each event can also be manually initiated.

Gateways from MS Mail to Non–MS Mail Systems

MS Mail includes optional software that allows it to exchange messages with non–MS Mail systems. Gateways exist to the following foreign mail systems:

- AT&T EasyLink
- IBM PROFS, OfficeVision, and SNADS
- Novell Message Handling System (MHS)
- MCI Mail
- SMTP mail systems

In a typical MS Mail gateway configuration (see Figure 12.9), a dedicated computer runs the gateway software and connects to the foreign mail system. Another postoffice (the *Gateway Postoffice*) is configured to receive all the messages destined for the foreign mail system. The rest of the postoffices send their foreign addressed messages to the Gateway Postoffice, which then sends them to the gateway computer. To send foreign addressed messages to the

Gateway Postoffice, a postoffice must have a special software program (the MS Mail 3.*x* Gateway Access Component) installed.

FIGURE 12.9   MS Mail gateway configuration

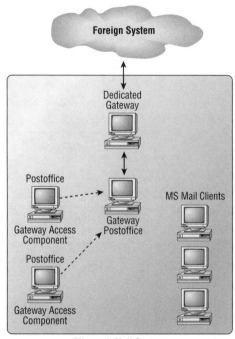

Figure 12.10 illustrates the four architectural elements of MS Mail:

- Postoffice
- MTA
- Directory synchronization
- Gateways

FIGURE 12.10 A typical MS Mail system

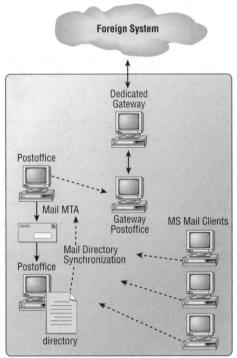

Microsoft Mail System

Exchange and MS Mail Interoperability

For Exchange and MS Mail systems to interoperate, they must be able to exchange messages, directory information, and client schedule information. Three Exchange components enable these operations: the MS Mail Connector, the Directory Synchronization Agent (DXA), and the Schedule+ Free/Busy Connector. This section provides an overview of these components and their processes.

MS Mail Connector Architecture

The MS Mail Connector enables an Exchange server to function like an MS Mail postoffice. The MS Mail Connector translates Exchange messages addressed to MS Mail users into an MS Mail message format and sends those messages to MS Mail postoffices. It can also receive MS Mail messages addressed to Exchange recipients and translate them into the Exchange message format.

To understand how the MS Mail Connector functions, you need to understand its architecture. This section provides information on the following topics:

- MS Mail Connector Postoffice
- MS Mail Connector components
- Message flow
- Physical connections
- Using multiple MS Mail Connectors

MS Mail Connector Postoffice

The *MS Mail Connector Postoffice* is an area on an Exchange server used to store MS Mail messages. This postoffice serves a slightly different purpose than an actual MS Mail postoffice. Rather than sending, receiving, and permanently storing MS Mail messages, this postoffice is used only to send and receive MS Mail messages. When an MS Mail message is received by the MS Mail Connector, it is temporarily stored before it is translated to the Exchange format and sent to the relevant Exchange recipients. When an Exchange message is to be sent to an MS Mail user, it is translated into the MS Mail format and temporarily stored before being transferred to the relevant postoffice. Because it is dedicated to message delivery and has no local mailboxes, this storage is sometimes referred to as a *shadow postoffice*. Figure 12.11 illustrates the role of the MS Mail Connector Postoffice.

FIGURE 12.11   MS Mail Connector Postoffice

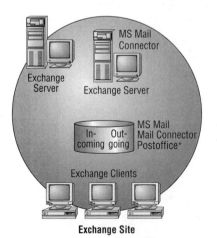

Exchange Site   **MS Mail**

*Temporary storage of incoming and outgoing messages

The component that submits and retrieves messages from the MS Mail Connector Postoffice and the component that sends and receives MS Mail messages are discussed next.

MS Mail Connector Components

The MS Mail Connector is made up of two components:

- MS Mail Connector Interchange

- MS Mail Connector (PC) MTA

Both of these run as Windows 2000 services, and both use the MS Mail Connector Postoffice to temporarily store MS Mail messages.

MS MAIL CONNECTOR INTERCHANGE

The *MS Mail Connector Interchange* translates messages from the Exchange format to the MS Mail format, and vice versa. When an Exchange user sends a message to an MS Mail user, the Interchange receives the outgoing message, translates it to the MS Mail format, and submits it to the MS Mail Connector Postoffice. From there it will be sent to the MS Mail system.

If an MS Mail message that is addressed to an Exchange recipient is in the MS Mail Connector Postoffice, the Interchange reads the message, translates it to the Exchange format, and passes it to the other Exchange components for delivery to the Exchange recipients. Figure 12.12 illustrates both of these processes.

FIGURE 12.12 MS Mail Connector Interchange

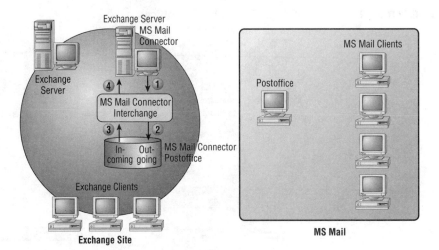

1) Exchange message
2) MS Mail message
3) MS Mail message
4) Exchange message

MS MAIL CONNECTOR (PC) MTA

The *MS Mail Connector (PC) MTA* transfers MS Mail messages between an Exchange server and MS Mail postoffices. The MS Mail Connector (PC) MTA is similar to the Exchange MTA in that it routes and transfers messages.

While an Exchange server can have only one instance of the MS Mail Connector installed, the MS Mail Connector (PC) MTA can be configured with up to 10 instances, allowing a single MS Mail Connector to connect to more than one postoffice. Figure 12.13 illustrates the role of this component.

FIGURE 12.13   MS Mail Connector (PC) MTA

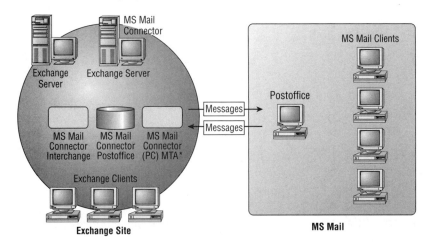

*Sends and receives MS Mail messages.

The MS Mail Connector (PC) MTA can be configured to make direct or indirect connections to MS Mail postoffices. Both of these options are explained here:

Direct connection to a postoffice   When an MS Mail Connector (PC) MTA is configured to send messages directly to a postoffice, the connection is referred to as a direct connection to an external postoffice. Mail sent over a direct connection does not go through any other postoffices, and it is sent directly to the destination postoffice. Figure 12.14 illustrates a direct connection to an external postoffice.

FIGURE 12.14 Direct connection to a postoffice

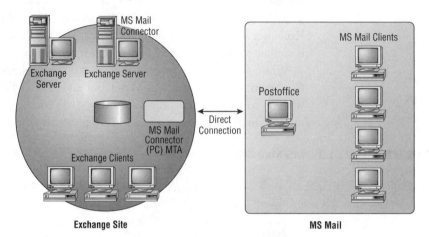

Indirect connection to a postoffice When an MS Mail Connector (PC) MTA has a direct connection to a postoffice that has connections to other postoffices, the MS Mail Connector can use its directly connected postoffice to forward messages to other postoffices. The connection to these "downstream" postoffices is referred to as an indirect connection. Figure 12.15 illustrates indirect connections.

FIGURE 12.15 Indirect connections to external postoffices

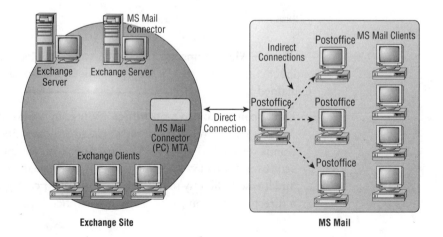

Message Flow

This section describes the flow of a message through an Exchange server when the MS Mail Connector is used.

RECEIVING AN MS MAIL MESSAGE

After an MS Mail user has created and sent a message addressed to an Exchange recipient, and after that user's postoffice has transferred the message to the Exchange server, the following processes (illustrated in Figure 12.16) occur:

1. The MS Mail Connector (PC) MTA receives the message and places it in the MS Mail Connector Postoffice.

2. The MS Mail Connector Postoffice temporarily stores the message until the MS Mail Connector Interchange processes it.

3. The Interchange reads the queued message, translates it to the Exchange format, passes it to the Exchange MTA for delivery, and then deletes the message that was temporarily stored in the MS Mail Connector Postoffice.

4. The Exchange MTA compares the message destination with the Exchange Directory. If the message recipient is on that server, the message is passed to the Information Store (IS) for local delivery. If the recipient is on a remote Exchange server, the MTA transfers the message to that remote server.

FIGURE 12.16 An exchange server receiving an MS Mail message

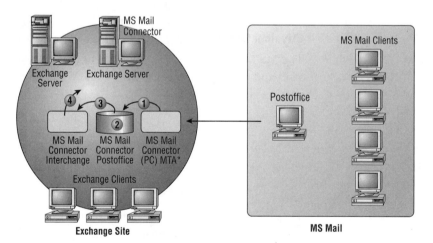

1) Mail message
2) Temporary storage, MS Mail message
3) Translates, Exchange message
4) Exchange MTA, Exchange message

SENDING A MESSAGE TO AN MS MAIL POSTOFFICE

After an Exchange user has created and sent a message addressed to an MS Mail recipient, the following processes occur on the Exchange server with the MS Mail Connector:

1. The IS compares the destination address to the Exchange Directory and determines that this message is for remote delivery. Therefore, the IS passes the message to the Exchange MTA.

2. The Exchange MTA temporarily queues the message and then compares the destination address with the Exchange Directory. (This is to determine how the message is to be delivered.) In this case, the Exchange MTA determines that it must use an MS Mail Connector. It then passes the message to the MS Mail Connector Interchange.

3. The Interchange translates the message content from the Exchange format to the MS Mail format. It then passes the message to the MS Mail Connector Postoffice.

4. The MS Mail Connector (PC) MTA scans the MS Mail Connector Postoffice for outgoing messages. When it detects one, it sends the message to the MS Mail postoffice to which it is connected. After sending the message, the MS Mail Connector (PC) MTA deletes the message from the MS Mail Connector Postoffice.

Physical Connections

The MS Mail Connector can use any of three physical connection types to send and receive messages from an MS Mail postoffice. These three connection types are:

- LAN
- Asynchronous modem
- X.25

LAN

The default and preferred connection option between an MS Mail Connector and an MS Mail postoffice is a LAN (local area network) connection. This connection is the easiest to configure and performs the best. You must configure the network path to the shared directory that serves as the postoffice on the MS Mail server. After you enter that primary piece of information, the MS Mail Connector automatically configures almost everything else.

An advantage of using a LAN connection is that it enables automatic uploading of information about downstream postoffices. You will need to manually enter downstream postoffices when using asynchronous modem and X.25 connections.

ASYNCHRONOUS MODEM

Asynchronous modems can be used to connect an MS Mail Connector and its external postoffice when they are not connected by a LAN. This connection option will normally be slower than a LAN connection, and it will require more configuration and administration on both sides of the connection. The remote network name, postoffice name, telephone number, and other information must be manually entered when configuring the MS Mail Connector.

The remote network containing the MS Mail postoffice must have a computer running either the MS Mail 3.*x* External MTA or Multitasking MTA. Use the External MTA on a computer running MS-DOS. Use the Multitasking MTA if the computer is running Windows NT. The MS Mail Connector will connect to the MS Mail MTA computer in order to deliver messages to the remote postoffice.

X.25

An X.25 connection is another WAN connection that can be used between an MS Mail Connector and an MS Mail environment. This connection can be slower than the LAN option and will require more configuration and administration.

Using Multiple MS Mail Connectors

If your organization has a large number of MS Mail postoffices and a large number of messages passed between them and your Exchange system, you might need to configure multiple MS Mail Connectors to handle the load. Although an individual Exchange server can have only one instance of the MS Mail Connector, more than one Exchange server can be configured with an MS Mail Connector. Because all of the MS Mail Connectors in an Exchange site use the same address space, the site appears to the MS Mail environment as one big postoffice.

Directory Synchronization Agent (DXA)

The MS Mail Directory Synchronization protocol has been incorporated in other messaging products such as Exchange, permitting them to exchange directory information with MS Mail. The Exchange component that supports this protocol is the *Directory Synchronization Agent (DXA)*. When this component is used, Exchange can automatically swap directory information with an MS Mail system. Information about Exchange recipients is sent to the MS Mail system, and information about MS Mail recipients is sent to the Active Directory via Exchange. MS Mail recipients are entered into the Exchange Directory as contacts. Although the MS Mail Connector provides for message transfer between the two systems, the DXA allows the users on each system to see the directory information (e.g., e-mail addresses) of the other system.

The DXA enables an Exchange server to function as either a dirsync server or dirsync requestor. Although it can assume either role, it can only perform one of these roles at a time (i.e., the Exchange server cannot be a dirsync server and a dirsync requestor concurrently). Also, there can be only one dirsync server in an MS Mail network. An Exchange site can have only one Exchange server designated as a dirsync server, but a site is not required to have a dirsync server. All Exchange servers in a site can be dirsync requestors using an MS Mail postoffice as the dirsync server.

When configured as a dirsync server, an Exchange server receives the new directory information sent by the postoffices configured as dirsync requestors and compiles the Global Address List. This master list of directory information is then sent to all requestor postoffices. Figure 12.17 illustrates this configuration.

FIGURE 12.17   An Exchange server as a dirsync server

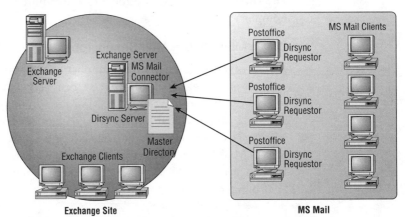

If configured as a dirsync requestor, an Exchange server will send its new directory information to the postoffice designated as the dirsync server and receive the Global Address List from that postoffice. Figure 12.18 illustrates this configuration.

FIGURE 12.18   An Exchange server as a dirsync requestor

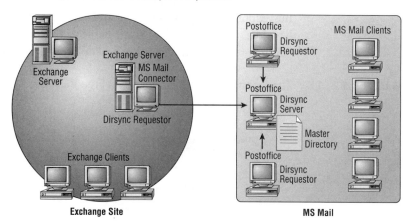

Schedule+ Free/Busy Connector

Schedule+ is a personal and group scheduling program. One of its many features allows users to view the free/busy schedule information of other users. MS Mail ships with Schedule+ version 1.0, and Exchange ships with Schedule+ version 7.5 (Schedule+ 7.5 is now called Outlook Calendar). Exchange includes the Schedule+ Free/Busy Connector to allow users with one version to view information from users of the other version. In the following two sections, we discuss the elements and processes for sending scheduling information in both directions (from Exchange to MS Mail and from MS Mail to Exchange).

Sending Information from Exchange to MS Mail

All Schedule+ 7.5 free/busy information is stored in the Exchange *Schedule+ Free Busy public folder* (it's one of the system folders in System Manager). The Schedule+ Free/Busy Connector uses a special mailbox agent (ADMINSCH) to translate and address that information for delivery to a designated distribution list (DL) on the MS Mail network. (When Exchange Server is installed, ADMINSCH is automatically created.) The MS Mail DL contains the administrative user accounts that are used to distribute free/busy information to the users of that network.

Sending Information from MS Mail to Exchange

On an MS Mail network, a program called Schdist.exe can be used to collect free/busy information and send it in the form of a message to the ADMINSCH mailbox agent on the designated Exchange server. The Free/Busy Connector then translates it and places it in the Schedule+ Free Busy public folder. This information is available to Exchange clients using Schedule+ 7.5. Figure 12.19 illustrates the Schedule+ Free/Busy Connector architecture.

FIGURE 12.19 The architecture of the Schedule+ Free/Busy Connector

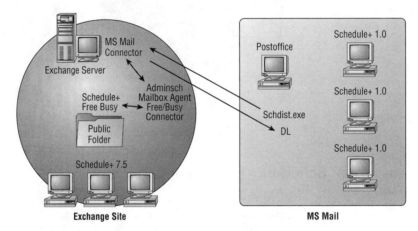

Now that you have a firm understanding of the components that enable communication between Exchange 2000 and MS Mail, it's time to look at the actual implementation of these components.

Configuring Exchange for MS Mail

This section discusses implementing the components necessary for the following types of interoperability between Exchange and MS Mail:

- Message exchange
- Directory synchronization
- Schedule+ information access
- Troubleshooting interoperability with Microsoft Mail

Message Exchange

The MS Mail Connector must be installed, configured, and started before messages can be exchanged between Exchange and MS Mail. MS Mail post-offices must be configured to route messages to the MS Mail Connector.

MS Mail Connector Installation

When you install Exchange Server, one of your options is to install the MS Mail Connector. If you choose this option, the MS Mail Connector will be installed and will appear in the Exchange hierarchy as an object in the site Connectors container.

If the MS Mail Connector is not installed during the initial Exchange Server setup, it can be installed later by executing the Exchange setup program (SETUP.EXE) and adding the component.

MS Mail Connector Configuration

The MS Mail Connector configuration process can be organized into four main procedures:

1. Define and configure a physical connection to an external postoffice.

2. Define and configure message transfer.

3. Configure destination addresses.

4. Configure other settings.

These steps and procedures are explained in the following sections. All of these procedures are executed through System Manager and configured on the Connector for MS Mail object, found in the Connectors container.

DEFINE AND CONFIGURE A PHYSICAL CONNECTION TO AN EXTERNAL POSTOFFICE

To send and receive messages from an MS Mail postoffice, you must configure a physical connection on the Connections property page. As you learned earlier, three connection types can be used: LAN, asynchronous, and X.25.

Some of the important attributes of each of these connections are listed here:

LAN connection   Only two pieces of information must be entered for this connection type:

Postoffice path   The network path to the shared directory on an MS Mail postoffice in which mail messages are stored. The path must be entered using the Universal Naming Convention (UNC). In a Microsoft networking environment, the path format would be *computer_name**share_name**directory_path*. If the postoffice is located on a NetWare server, the path format would be *server_ name**volume_name**directory_path*.

Connection attempts   The number of times the MS Mail Connector will attempt to send a message before it returns the message to the sender with a Non-Delivery Report (NDR). The default is 3.

Asynchronous connection (Async)   Asynchronous connections require more settings than LAN connections. The primary settings are as follows:

Network name   The name of the MS Mail network to which the MS Mail Connector is attaching.

Postoffice name   The name of a specific postoffice to which the MS Mail Connector will connect.

Sign-on ID   The serial number of the external postoffice to which a connection is being made.

Password   The password used at the external postoffice. This is an optional attribute at the external postoffice.

Connection attempts   The number of times the MS Mail Connector will attempt to send a message before it returns the message to the sender with a Non-Delivery Report (NDR). The default is 3.

Phone number   The phone number to the external postoffice.

Optional settings   Accessed by clicking the Options button.

X.25 connection   For this connection option to be used, the X.25 protocol must already be installed and configured on the Exchange server. The X.25 option has many of the same properties as the async option, including network and postoffice name, sign-on ID, password, and connection attempts. The primary difference is that this connection type requires the X.121 address of the external postoffice. A 16-digit number identifies the computer on the X.25 network that contains the external postoffice.

DEFINE AND CONFIGURE MESSAGE TRANSFER

Once a physical connection has been configured, you can configure message transfer. You must create one or more instances of the MS Mail Connector (PC) MTA. As you learned earlier, only one instance of the MS Mail Connector can exist on an Exchange server. However, that single instance of the MS Mail Connector can use multiple instances of the MS Mail Connector (PC) MTA to transfer messages. The Connector MTA's property page is used to create and configure an MTA.

To create a new Connector MTA instance, click the New button on the Connector MTA's property page. The main attributes to configure are as follows:

Service name The name that represents a particular instance of this MTA. This name is registered with the Windows operating system as a service that can be started and stopped with the Services applet in the Control Panel.

Polling frequency Can be set to indicate how long this instance of the MTA waits before checking the external postoffice for new mail to be picked up. The default is 5 minutes.

Connection parameters The MTA must use a physical connection to send and receive messages. That connection is chosen under Connection Parameters. The default is LAN.

After an MTA instance is created, you can determine the external postoffices with which it will exchange messages. This information can be entered after clicking the List button on the Connector MTA's property page.

If a particular MS Mail Connector (PC) MTA will use an asynchronous or an X.25 connection, additional properties need to be set for the MTA (such as the communication port and the modem timeout value).

CONFIGURE DESTINATION ADDRESSES

Like other connectors, the MS Mail Connector is configured with the destination addresses to which it will route messages. These addresses are configured on the Address Space property page.

Four address templates can be used to enter addresses:

- X.400

- MS Mail

- Internet

- General (can be used to create any type of address)

Addresses can be to specific recipients on a foreign system, or they can be to an entire network of recipients. An example of an MS Mail address space is

```
MS:Sprockets/Manufacturing/*
```

where MS refers to the address space type (MS Mail in this example), Sprockets is the network name, Manufacturing is the postoffice name, and the asterisk (*) is a wildcard, meaning all recipients.

CONFIGURE OTHER SETTINGS

The General, Interchange, and Local Postoffice property pages contain the following configurable MS Mail Connector properties:

General   Use this page to set a maximum message size and indicate an administrative note for this connector.

Interchange   Use this page to select an administrator's mailbox to receive information messages and alert notifications from this connector. Other properties on this page include the primary language used by clients accessing this connector and message tracking. If message tracking is enabled, information about messages sent through this connector will be written to the tracking logs.

Local Postoffice   The MS Mail Connector allows an Exchange server to function as an MS Mail postoffice. As such, it must have a network and postoffice name. By default, the Exchange organization name is used as the network name, and the Exchange site name is used for the postoffice name. This page allows you to change these values. The MS Mail Connector can also require a password to be used by external postoffices that are connecting to and sending messages to this connector. This page is where you enter this password.

MS Mail Postoffice Configuration

The previous procedures configured the MS Mail Connector to transfer messages to the external postoffices. Those postoffices also need to be configured to send messages to the MS Mail Connector. The primary information that must be entered at these postoffices is the network and postoffice name used by the MS Mail Connector. If the MS Mail Connector uses a password, it must also be configured on the MS Mail postoffices.

Directory Synchronization

The primary steps to implement directory synchronization between Exchange and MS Mail are as follows:

1. Configuring and starting the DXA.

2. Use an Exchange server as a dirsync server,

   or

3. Use an Exchange server as a dirsync requestor.

Each of these primary steps is covered in the following sections.

Configuring and Starting the DXA

The Exchange DXA component is installed when the MS Mail Connector is installed. As a Windows 2000 service, it can be stopped and started through the Services applet. It is represented by the Directory Synchronization object in the Exchange hierarchy. As with other Exchange objects, it has properties that can be configured, such as delivery restrictions and the use of addressing templates.

Exchange Server as a Dirsync Server

To use an Exchange server as a dirsync server, the following procedures must be performed:

A dirsync server object must be created and configured. In System Manager, right-click the Connectors container and choose the New Dirsync Server command. This creates the dirsync server object and opens its property pages. Some of this object's properties are as follows:

Name The directory name of this object.

Dirsync administrator The Exchange recipient that receives administration notifications pertaining to this object.

Server The name of the Exchange server that will function as the dirsync server.

Schedule A schedule can be defined to execute the T2 event, namely the compilation of the Global Address List and submission of it to the dirsync requestors.

Remote dirsync requestors must be created and configured. The Exchange server acting as a dirsync server must maintain the list of the dirsync requestors with which it will be communicating. This information is configured by the Exchange administrator by creating a remote dirsync requestor object for each MS Mail postoffice. These objects are created in System Manager by right-clicking the Connectors container and choosing the New Remote Dirsync Requestor command. One of the most important properties of this type of object is the list of recipient containers that are to be exported to the remote requestor. This information is entered on the Export Containers property page. Attributes on this page include the following:

Recipient containers The Exchange recipient containers to export to this particular remote requestor. These containers can be located in any site.

Trust level   The trust level used to select objects for synchronization with this remote requestor. All Exchange objects in the designated containers with a trust level less than or equal to this value will be synchronized.

Configure the MS Mail postoffices that are dirsync requestors.   The MS Mail administrator must configure the dirsync requestors with information about the dirsync server.

Exchange Server as a Dirsync Requestor

If an Exchange server will be a dirsync requestor, the following procedures must be performed:

A dirsync requestor object must be created and configured.   In System Manager, right-click the Connectors container and choose the New Dirsync Requestor command to configure the dirsync requestor. The Dirsync Requestor object includes many of the same attributes as the dirsync server, such as name, server, and schedule. On the Export Containers property page, you can designate which recipient containers to send to the dirsync server and which trust levels to use. On the Import Container property page, you can designate the recipients container in which to create directory entries received from the dirsync server.

Configure the Mail dirsync server.   The postoffice serving as the dirsync server must be configured with information about the Exchange server functioning as a dirsync requestor.

Schedule+ Information Access

Procedures must be performed in both the Exchange site and the MS Mail network for free/busy information to be accessible from one system to the other system. On the Exchange site, the following must be operational in order for the Schedule+ Free/Busy Connector to work:

- MS Mail Connector

- Directory synchronization between the Exchange site and MS Mail network

The Schedule+ Free/Busy Connector is installed when the MS Mail Connector is installed. If the MS Mail Connector was not installed at the initial Exchange Server setup, run the Exchange Server Setup program in maintenance mode and choose the Add/Remove option to install the MS Mail Connector.

Troubleshooting Interoperability with Microsoft Mail

Many troubleshooting situations related to interoperability with Microsoft Mail involve directory synchronization. For example, your Microsoft Exchange server could be configured as a dirsync server with remote dirsync requestors defined. You configure the synchronization time on the Exchange server to Always. Three hours later, you notice that Microsoft Mail recipients have not yet replicated to your Exchange Global Address List. The solution to this problem is to run a utility named REQMAIN (request maintenance) on the Microsoft Mail postoffice. Running that utility with the Transmit option (i.e., `reqmain -t`) will force the postoffice to transmit its updates.

Connecting to Lotus cc:Mail

The *Connector for Lotus cc:Mail* provides both message exchange and directory synchronization between Exchange and cc:Mail systems. This connector is installed using the Exchange Server setup program. The Connector for Lotus cc:Mail uses two Lotus cc:Mail utilities, `IMPORT.EXE` and `EXPORT.EXE`. The connector and these two utilities are described here:

Lotus cc:Mail Connector   Transfers messages and synchronizes directories between Exchange and cc:Mail.

IMPORT.EXE   Imports information, both mail messages and directory information, into the cc:Mail environment.

EXPORT.EXE   Exports information, both mail messages and directory information, from the cc:Mail environment.

Figure 12.20 illustrates an organization using the Connector for Lotus cc:Mail.

FIGURE 12.20 The Connector for Lotus cc:Mail

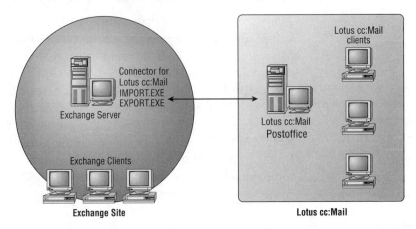

Summary

Exchange 2000 Server relies on connectors to communicate with external messaging systems. Two protocol-based connectors, the X.400 Connector and the SMTP Connector, can be used either to connect two Exchange routing groups together or to connect an Exchange organization to an external messaging system that uses the same protocol.

SMTP is also used to provide messaging connectivity with the Internet. Creating multiple SMTP virtual servers allows you to segment SMTP traffic to use different IP addresses or TCP ports, each with their own configuration. Virtual servers are used to define basic SMTP transport properties. SMTP Connectors are configured on virtual servers to define properties for a specific address space.

Exchange Server also comes with the proprietary connectors used to exchange messages and perform directory synchronization with Microsoft Mail (MS Mail) and Lotus cc:Mail systems.

The MS Mail Connector enables message exchange between an Exchange system and an MS Mail system. This connector creates a temporary storage area (the MS Mail Connector Postoffice) for messages transmitted between Exchange and MS Mail. The MS Mail Connector is implemented as two Windows 2000 services (components), the MS Mail

Connector Interchange and the MS Mail Connector (PC) MTA. The Interchange translates messages from the Exchange format to the MS Mail format, and vice versa. The MS Mail Connector (PC) MTA transfers messages between Exchange and MS Mail systems.

Environments that contain both Exchange and Lotus cc:Mail can use the Connector for Lotus cc:Mail to enable both message exchange and directory synchronization between the two systems.

Key Terms

Before you take the exam, be certain you are familiar with the following terms:

address space	postoffice
Bad Mail folder	Queue folder
Connector for Lotus cc:Mail	Schedule+ Free Busy public folder
Directory Synchronization Agent (DXA)	shadow postoffice
dirsync requestors (directory requestors)	Simple Mail Transfer Protocol (SMTP)
dirsync server (directory synchronization server)	smart host
Gateway Postoffice	SMTP Connector
Mail Exchanger (MX) record	SMTP virtual server
Message Transfer Agent (MTA) Service Transport Stack	spooling
MS Mail Connector	T1 event
MS Mail Connector (PC) MTA	T2 event
MS Mail Connector Interchange	T3 event
MS Mail Connector Postoffice	X.400 Connector
Pickup folder	

Review Questions

1. You have configured SMTP on your network to allow users to exchange messages with the Internet. Exchange recipients can send mail to Internet users, but Internet users cannot send mail to the Exchange recipients. You verify that your SMTP virtual server is accessible from the Internet. What is the most likely cause of the problem?

   A. Your firewall is not open to port 110 (POP3).

   B. Your firewall is not open to port 25 (SMTP).

   C. Your client computers are not configured with TCP/IP.

   D. Your client computers are not directly connected to the Internet.

   E. Your domain has no MX record in DNS.

2. Which of the following SMTP folders is not normally used by Exchange 2000?

   A. Pickup folder

   B. Queue folder

   C. Bad Mail folder

   D. DNS folder

3. How would you set the maximum size of messages allowed over an X.400 Connector?

   A. Using the General property page of the connector.

   B. Using the Limits property page of the connector.

   C. Using the Content Restrictions property page of the connector.

   D. You cannot set this limit on an X.400 Connector.

4. Your Exchange environment uses SMTP to exchange mail with a company named Sockets & Wrenches, which uses a host-based SMTP mail system. When users on your system send mail to the name of the host at Sockets & Wrenches, it is not delivered. But if those users use an IP address for addressing, the mail is delivered. You are informed that other systems can send mail to Sockets & Wrenches using a host name in the addressing. What should you do to enable your users to be able to send mail to Sockets & Wrenches using a host name in the addressing? (Select the best answer.)

   A. Configure a mapping on the DNS server on your network.

   B. Configure a HOSTS file on each client.

   C. Configure an LMHOSTS file on each client.

   D. Configure SMTP to forward all mail to Sockets & Wrenches.

5. As administrator of an Exchange organization, you have been asked to have all outgoing SMTP mail sent to a single SMTP server. How should you configure this?

   A. Enter the SMTP server as an MX record in the DNS.

   B. Enter the SMTP server as a CN record in the DNS.

   C. Enter the SMTP server in the SMTP virtual server properties.

   D. Enter the SMTP server in the SMTP Connector properties.

   E. Make the SMTP server the default gateway in the TCP/IP settings of your IMS computer.

6. SMTP relies on which of the following components to resolve addresses of Exchange recipients on inbound messages?

   A. DNS

   B. SMTP

   C. Resolver program

   D. Active Directory

7. Your company has both Exchange Server and MS Mail. Eventually, there will be a migration from MS Mail to Exchange, but right now you need to come up with a coexistence strategy. Part of that strategy is to make a distribution group available that contains recipients from both systems. How could you do that?

   A. Create both an MS Mail distribution list that includes all Microsoft Mail users and an Exchange distribution group that includes all Exchange users. Create an Exchange distribution group that includes the MS Mail distribution list and the Exchange distribution group.

   B. Create Internet mail connectivity between the two systems. Create SMTP contacts for each MS Mail user. Create a distribution group that includes all Exchange users and all SMTP contacts.

   C. Configure directory synchronization between the two systems. After synchronization has taken place, create a master distribution list on the MS Mail postoffice.

   D. Configure directory synchronization between the two systems. After synchronization has taken place, create a master distribution group on the Exchange server.

8. A company uses an MS Mail gateway for SMTP to exchange mail between its three MS Mail postoffices and the Internet. This company has also just installed Exchange 2000 Server. They have hired you as a consultant to outline the steps necessary to replace their current Mail gateway for SMTP with the SMTP on Exchange. What are those steps? (Choose all that apply.)

   A. Make sure SMTP is correctly configured on Exchange the server.

   B. Install the MS Mail Connector on an Exchange server.

   C. Add the MS Mail Connector to the external postoffice list on each MS Mail postoffice.

   D. Reinstall the SMTP Gateway Access Component on the existing MS Mail postoffices. Specify the Microsoft Exchange Mail Connector postoffice as the gateway postoffice.

   E. Install the Gateway Access Component on the Exchange server to allow the Mail users to access SMTP on Exchange.

9. Your company currently uses MS Mail. You have just added an Exchange server to the network. Management would like both systems to coexist and be able to exchange both messages and directory information. Management would also like to keep the current dirsync strategy. Consequently, you install the MS Mail Connector on the Exchange server. What other step must you take on the Exchange server?

   A. Create a dirsync server on the Exchange server.

   B. Configure the Exchange server as a dirsync requestor.

   C. Create a directory replication bridgehead server.

   D. Reinstall MTA.

10. Your network has three Microsoft Mail postoffices, named PO-1, PO-2, and PO-3. You replace PO-2 with an Exchange server and establish directory synchronization between the two mail systems. Management has asked if you could hide certain Exchange recipients from the two Microsoft Mail postoffices. They also want Exchange recipients to see all recipients from both systems. You decide to create two groups, called Visible Recipients and Hidden Recipients. You place all Exchange users who are to be hidden into the Hidden Recipients group. How should you configure the trust levels of these two groups?

    A. Configure the trust level of the Visible Recipients group to be higher than that of the dirsync requestor. Configure the trust level of Hidden Recipients group to be lower than that of the dirsync requestor.

    B. Configure the trust level of the users in the Visible Recipients group to be lower than that of the dirsync requestor. Configure the trust level of the recipients in the Hidden Recipients group to be higher than that of the dirsync requestor.

    C. Configure the trust level of both groups to be higher than that of the dirsync requestor. Configure the trust level of the Hidden Recipients group to be lower than that of the Visible Recipients group.

    D. Configure the trust level of both groups to be lower than that of the dirsync requestor. Configure the trust level of the Visible Recipients group to be lower than that of the Hidden Recipients group.

11. Directory synchronization is configured between Exchange organization and a foreign mail system (i.e., a non-Exchange system). What is the best way to prevent certain Exchange recipients from being replicated to the foreign system?

    A. Mark as hidden the recipients you do not want replicated.

    B. Create a new recipients container. Move the recipients that you do not want to be replicated to this container.

    C. Create a dirsync distribution list. Add all the recipients that are to be hidden to this list.

    D. Configure the trust levels for the recipients that you do not want replicated to be higher than that of the connector.

12. Your Exchange server is configured as a dirsync server and has remote dirsync requestors defined. You configure the synchronization time on the Exchange server to Always. Three hours later, you notice that MS Mail recipients have not yet replicated to Exchange. What is the solution to this problem?

    A. In MS Mail, set the T1, T2, and T3 times to be the same.

    B. Set the T2 time on the Exchange server to be one hour later than the T2 time in MS Mail.

    C. Run the REQMAIN utility with the Transmit option on the MS Mail postoffice.

    D. Run the REQMAIN utility with the Receive option on the Exchange server.

13. Your company uses an MS Mail gateway for SMTP to transfer messages between its five postoffices and the Internet. Your network is connected to the Internet through a filtered router. Management has had you install an Exchange server and configure the MS Mail Connector.

    Required result:

    Replace the MS Mail gateway for SMTP with the Exchange server.

    Optional results:

    POP3 clients should be able to send and receive messages.

Anonymous users on the Internet should be prevented from using the Exchange SMTP server as a relay host for other destinations.

Proposed solution:

Configure SMTP in Exchange. Reconfigure the Gateway Access Components on each MS Mail postoffice to point to the MS Mail Connector postoffice as the downstream postoffice. Disable relaying of SMTP messages. Make no other changes to the SMTP server.

What results does the above proposal produce?

A. The proposed solution produces the required result and both of the optional results.

B. The proposed solution produces the required result and only one of the optional results.

C. The proposed solution produces the required result but does not produce either of the optional results.

D. The proposed solution does not produce the required result.

14. Which of the following does not relate to restricting Exchange objects from being synchronized with an MS Mail system?

A. Trust level of the object

B. Trust level of the Exchange dirsync server or requestor

C. The recipients container

D. EXPORT.EXE

15. Which of the following are required when using the Schedule+ Free/ Busy Connector?

A. Directory synchronization with MS Mail

B. A Windows 2000 user account named FreeBusy

C. IMPORT.EXE running on the designated MS Mail postoffice

D. Both A and C

16. Where is Schedule+ 7.5 free/busy information exchanged between Exchange and MS Mail users stored?

    A. A specially designated system folder

    B. A specially designated mailbox

    C. A specially designated distribution group

    D. Active Directory

17. Which of the following MS Mail directory synchronization events is used by an MS Mail dirsync server to recompile the Global Address List?

    A. T1

    B. T2

    C. Newsfeed push

    D. T3

18. The administrator of an X.400 messaging system with which your Exchange organization is connected tells you that the speed of the connection could be enhanced if you were to turn on the two-way alternate option. Where would you go to do this?

    A. The Connection property page of the MTA Transport Stack used by the X.400 Connector

    B. The Connection property page of the X.400 Connector

    C. The Override property page of the X.400 Connector

    D. The Advanced property page of the X.400 Connector

19. In the basic SMTP process, what command does the client computer use to identify itself to the SMTP server?

    A. EHLO

    B. HELO

    C. MAIL FROM

    D. REQ

20. You would like to require SMTP hosts and clients to authenticate themselves before allowing messages to be transferred using your Exchange server. What forms of user authentication does the SMTP virtual server support? (Choose all that apply.)

A. Anonymous

B. Basic

C. Digest authentication

D. Secure Sockets Layer

E. Integrated Windows

Answers to Review Questions

1. E. Transferring messages between SMTP hosts is dependent on the Domain Name Service (DNS). When an SMTP host sends an e-mail message to another SMTP host, DNS must resolve the domain name of the receiving host to an IP address. DNS does this by storing special records named Mail Exchanger (MX) records in the DNS database. Each MX record in a DNS database represents an SMTP host to which mail can be forwarded.

2. A. SMTP creates three file system folders to manage messages on an Exchange 2000 Server: Pickup, Queue, and Bad Mail. However, the pickup folder is not used. By default, all of these folders are created in the `C:\Program Files\Exchsrvr\Mailroot` folder.

3. C. As with most connectors, the X.400 Connector allows you to set limits on messages sizes. You do this using the Content Restrictions property page of the connector.

4. A. Since your users cannot connect to the remote host by name, but can connect by IP address, it is apparent that there is a problem resolving the server name through DNS. Since other hosts can resolve the name, it is also apparent that the problem is local.

5. C. You would need to configure the name of the SMTP server on the Message property page of the SMTP virtual server. This page lets you name a smart host to which messages are forwarded when they cannot be resolved within your domain. This offers the powerful ability to configure a single host to which all external mail should go (such as to the Internet).

6. D. All information about users, including their addresses, are stored in the Active Directory.

7. A. The idea here is that you cannot create an MS Mail distribution list that contains Exchange recipients. Instead, you must create a distribution list in MS Mail and a distribution group in Exchange that each contain all recipients of their respective systems. Then, you can create a second group in Exchange that contains these two groups. Once directory synchronization occurs, both Exchange and MS Mail users will be able to send messages to this group and thus to all recipients in both messaging systems.

8. A, B, C, D. Basically, this process redefines the SMTP Gateway Access Component already used on the MS Mail systems to use the connector to the Exchange system for all SMTP messages.

9. B. In order for directory synchronization (dirsync) with MS Mail to work, you must first install the MS Mail Connector. As a dirsync requester, your Exchange server will exchange directory messages with the MS Mail system using the connector.

10. B. The trust level is used to select objects for synchronization with a remote requestor. All Exchange objects with a trust level less than or equal to this value will be synchronized.

11. D. The trust level is used to select objects for synchronization with a remote requestor. All Exchange objects with a trust level less than or equal to this value will be synchronized.

12. C. Running the REQMAIN utility with the Transmit option (i.e., reqmain -t) will force the postoffice to transmit its updates.

13. B. This solution meets the required result of replacing the MS Mail gateway for SMTP with the Exchange server. By disabling relaying for the SMTP server, it also meets the optional result of preventing anonymous users from using the Exchange SMTP server as a relay host for other destinations. However, by disabling relaying altogether, you also prevent POP3 users from being able to send messages using the server. A better solution would be to permit authorized users to relay messages, but prevent all others.

14. D. EXPORT.EXE is a Lotus cc:Mail utility that exports both mail messages and directory information from the cc:Mail environment.

15. A. In order to use the Schedule+ Free/Busy Connector, the MS Mail Connector must be installed, and directory synchronization with MS Mail must be configured correctly.

16. A. All Schedule+ 7.5 free/busy information is stored in an Exchange system folder called Schedule+ Free Busy.

17. B. Three primary events occur during synchronization: a requestor sends directory information to the server (T1), the server compiles the Global Address List and sends it to requestors (T2), and a requestor rebuilds its Global Address List (T3).

18. D. The two-way alternate specification is an X.400 standard in which two connected X.400 systems take turns transmitting and receiving information. If the foreign system to which you are connecting supports this option, enabling it can greatly improve transmission speed.

19. B. The client computer identifies itself to the server by sending the HELO command with the computer's identity (for example, HELO server1.widgets.com).

20. A, B, E. It is often useful to require an SMTP host or client to authenticate before allowing messages transfer. You can choose from Anonymous, Basic, or Integrated Windows authentication methods. You can also configure TLS encryption for the virtual server.

Chapter

13

Backup and Recovery

MICROSOFT EXAM OBJECTIVES COVERED IN THIS CHAPTER:

- ✓ Configure separate Exchange 2000 Server resources for high-volume access. Resources include stores, logs, and separate RAID arrays.

- ✓ Diagnose and resolve problems that involve user and information store placement. Problems include security, performance, and disaster recovery.

- ✓ Apply a backup and restore plan.

- ✓ Diagnose and resolve backup and restore problems.

- ✓ Restore user data and System State data.
  - ▪ Recover deleted mailboxes.
  - ▪ Recover deleted items.

- ✓ Restore information stores.

- ✓ Configure a server for disaster recovery. Configurations include circular logging, backup, and restore.

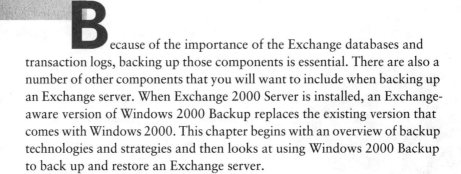

Because of the importance of the Exchange databases and transaction logs, backing up those components is essential. There are also a number of other components that you will want to include when backing up an Exchange server. When Exchange 2000 Server is installed, an Exchange-aware version of Windows 2000 Backup replaces the existing version that comes with Windows 2000. This chapter begins with an overview of backup technologies and strategies and then looks at using Windows 2000 Backup to back up and restore an Exchange server.

Understanding Backups

Before you fire up your backup program and start backing things up, it's important to have a clear understanding of the technologies involved and to create a good backup plan. This section looks at the various components of Exchange and Windows that you should back up, the types of backups available to you, and several backup strategies.

What to Back Up

An Exchange server is composed of a great deal of information, including the Exchange databases of user messages and public messages and the transaction logs associated with those databases. Configuration information is stored in the Microsoft Windows 2000 Registry, in various places in the Exchange Server installation path, in Active Directory, and even on some users' computers. This section covers the information that you should include when backing up an Exchange server.

Microsoft
✓ Exam
Objective

**Configure a server for disaster recovery. Configurations
include circular logging, backup, and restore.**

Much of the information in this section is a recap of how the Information
Stores in Exchange 2000 Server work. You can learn more about the
Exchange storage architecture in Chapter 2.

Databases

Much of the information in Exchange 2000 Server, including private and
public user messages, is stored in two databases: PRIV*x*.EDB and PUB*x*.EDB.

PRIV*x*.EDB Each mailbox store database on an Exchange server is
named using the format PRIV*x*.EDB, where *x* ranges from 1 to the number
of databases on the server. The private store databases hold user mailboxes and messages. By default, these databases are located in `Program`
`Files\Exchsrvr\Mdbdata\`.

PUB*x*.EDB Each public store database on an Exchange Server is named
using the format PUB*x*.EDB, where *x* ranges from 1 to the number of databases on the server. The public store databases hold messages and documents stored in public folders. By default, these databases are also located
in `Program Files\Exchsrvr\Mdbdata\`.

In addition to these core databases, a streaming database with the extension .STM is associated with each mailbox and public database. Several
optional databases might also be available on any given Exchange server.
These optional databases represent various services that may be installed on
a server, such as a *Key Management Server (KMS) database* or *Site Replication Services (SRS) database*.

Transaction Logs

Whenever a transaction occurs on an Exchange server, that transaction is
first recorded in a *transaction log*. Transactions are written to the database
later during idle time. Transaction logs are the primary storage areas for new
transactions. One set of transaction logs exists for each storage group on a

server. A set is composed of a current log, any number of previous logs, reserve logs, and a checkpoint file. The current transaction log file, named EDB.LOG, resides in the \Exchsrvr\Mdbdata directory by default.

Data is written to log files sequentially as transactions occur. Regular database maintenance routines commit changes in the logs to the actual databases later. The most current state of an Exchange service, therefore, is the .EDB database and .STM database, *plus* the current log file. Thus, transaction logs are an essential part of the backup routine.

Checkpoint files are used to keep track of transactions that are committed to the database from a transaction log. Using checkpoint files ensures that transactions cannot be committed to a database more than once. Checkpoint files are named EDB.CHK and reside in the same directories as their log files and databases.

Log files are always given 5MB of reserved disk space. When a log file fills, it is renamed, and a new log file is created. Old, renamed log files are called *previous logs*. Previous logs are named sequentially, using the format EDB*xxxxx*.LOG, in which each *x* represents a hexadecimal number. Previous logs are stored in the same directories as their current-log-file counterparts.

During an online backup of an Exchange server, previous log files that are fully committed are purged. Previous log files can still consume a good deal of disk space. Exchange 2000 Server provides a feature called *circular logging* that can help prevent that waste of disk space. When circular logging is enabled, only previous log files with uncommitted changes are maintained for each storage group. This can significantly reduce the amount of hard disk space that is required for your Exchange server, compared with keeping all transaction logs until a backup is completed. Circular logging is disabled by default, but you can enable it on the General property sheet of a storage group container in System Manager.

You can find more information on using circular logging in Chapter 8.

In addition to all of the current and previous transaction logs, the online backup process also creates *patch files* that serve as temporary logs to store transactions while the backup is taken place. Transactions in these logs are committed when the backup is finished.

Other Items to Back Up

In addition to Exchange databases and transaction log files (all of which are included automatically in a regular online backup of Exchange), you will want to consider several other items:

EXCHSRVR subdirectories   Many valuable pieces of information, including message-tracking data, are located in various subfolders of `Program Files\Exchsrvr`.

Site Replication Service (SRS) database   The SRS database is used in mixed Exchange Server 5.5 and Exchange 2000 Server environments. You can learn more about the SRS database itself in Chapter 11.

Key Management Server (KMS) database   KMS provides advanced security to an Exchange organization in the form of encryption and digital signatures. If you are running KMS, you will need to back up the KMS database, the CA certificates for each Certification Authority server, and the KMS database startup password. You can learn more about KMS in Chapter 14.

User information   Many administrators allow the storage of users' personal folders (.PST files) and address books on the Exchange server or another network server. Always make sure that information of this sort is included in your backup strategy. When users store personal folders on their local workstations, you will need to involve the users in the backup procedure.

Backing Up System State Information

A *System State backup* is new to the Windows 2000 Backup utility and is used to back up configuration information critical to a Windows 2000 server. You'll learn how to create a System State backup later in the chapter. System State information includes the following:

Windows 2000 Registry   The Windows 2000 Registry contains a great deal of configuration information relating to Exchange 2000 Server, especially information relating to the coexistence of Exchange 2000 Server with previous versions. You should perform regular System State backups on Exchange servers to include the Windows 2000 Registry.

Internet Information Server metabase   Since Exchange 2000 relies so heavily on IIS for protocol support, it is only natural that IIS be a part of any good backup plan. The IIS metabase, a database of configuration information, is included in a System State backup. Running regular System State backups on the Exchange server also backs up the IIS metabase.

Active Directory   While Active Directory is not really a part of Exchange, most of the configuration information for Exchange 2000 is stored in Active Directory. Recipient objects are also kept in Active Directory. You should run regular System State backups of domain controllers to capture Active Directory information. You should back up Active Directory and Exchange 2000 databases at the same time to avoid losing configuration of user objects on the domain controllers or in global catalogs.

Preparing a System for Backup and Disaster Recovery

When your Exchange server has only one hard disk, system information, databases, and log files are all stored on that disk. More often, however, an Exchange server is configured with more than one local hard disk. This is because Exchange offers flexibility in partitioning data across multiple locations to help with performance and for purposes of restoration.

Microsoft ✓ *Exam* *Objective*

Diagnose and resolve problems that involve user and information store placement. Problems include security, performance, and disaster recovery.

Configure separate Exchange 2000 Server resources for high-volume access. Resources include stores, logs, and separate RAID arrays.

In general, we recommend the following practices to optimize performance and disaster recovery:

Keep log files on separate hard disks.   The speed of an Exchange 2000 database depends a good deal on how quickly transactions are copied from memory to the transaction log. For this reason, we recommend that you place the log files for each storage group on a dedicated hard disk so that the transaction logs do not compete with any other read/write operations. The best performance is usually obtained from a mirrored disk device. Also, it is a good idea to keep transaction logs on a separate disk from the Information Store to ensure recoverability.

Keep storage groups on separate disks.   We also like to keep storage groups on separate disks from other storage groups. This decreases the damage that a single drive failure can do. However, it is more important to have transaction logs on a separate disk than to separate the storage groups themselves. Storing log files on separate disks dramatically increases your odds of successful recovery in the event of failure. For example, if you had three free hard disks (aside from the hard disk holding system information) and two storage groups, it would be better to put the two storage groups on one disk and then to put the transaction logs for each storage group onto their own disks than to try to separate the storage groups. In Figure 13.1, storage groups 1 and 2 are placed on a single disk array (F:). The logs for each storage group are placed on their own volumes (D: and E:).

FIGURE 13.1   Separating log files is more important than separating storage groups.

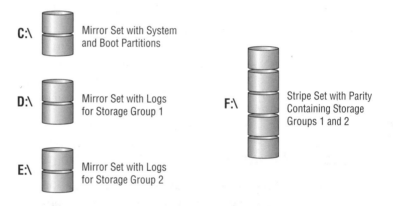

Keep databases small.   Within a storage group, data can be partitioned into multiple databases. We recommend that you keep these databases smaller rather than larger. If you have a particularly large database, dividing it into multiple databases improves recovery for two reasons:

- Users can begin accessing a database as soon as it is restored.

- If you use multiple backup media, you can actually restore the multiple databases in parallel. Restoring a smaller database takes less time than restoring a larger database.

Turn off circular logging for all storage groups.   The disadvantage of using circular logging is that it prevents you from using differential or incremental backups (discussed later in this chapter). Also, because some log files are discarded before backup, you may not be able to fully restore a server by replaying the log files, a potentially serious situation. For this reason, we generally recommend that you leave circular logging disabled for all your Exchange servers.

You may want to turn on circular logging when importing a large amount of data. However, you must remember to disable it afterward and do a full backup. You may also want to turn on circular logging for servers where recovery is not so important, such as for front-end servers that do not contain mailboxes or public folders.

Back up whole storage groups at once.   We recommended that you back up an entire storage group at the same time. This makes the backup process easier to manage because the databases within the storage group share the same set of log files. The log files can be truncated only after all databases have been backed up.

Back up storage groups to different media.   To prepare for a failure of all storage related to a server, you could partition data into separate storage groups and back up these storage groups to different media. As long as you initiate separate restore sessions for each storage group, Exchange can restore multiple storage groups at the same time. The storage groups should also be hosted on separate physical disks and RAID disk arrays so the physical disk media does not become a bottleneck for the restore. This is known as a *parallel restore*.

Types of Backups

You can perform five basic types of backups using the Windows 2000 Backup utility (and most other backup programs). The key difference between these backup types is how each one handles the archive bit in every Windows 2000 file. When a file is created or modified, the archive bit is set to on. When some types of backups run, the archive bit is set to off, which indicates that the file has been backed up.

The five backup types are as follows:

Normal   During a *normal backup*, all selected files are backed up, regardless of how their archive bit is set. After the backup, the archive bit is set to off for all files, indicating that those files have been backed up.

Copy   During a *copy backup*, all selected files are backed up, regardless of how their archive bit is set. After the backup, the archive bit is not changed in any file.

Incremental   During an *incremental backup*, all files for which the archive bit is on are backed up. After the backup, the archive bit is set to off for all files that were backed up.

Differential   During a *differential backup*, all files for which the archive bit is on are backed up. After the backup, the archive bit is not changed in any file.

Daily   During a *daily backup*, all files that changed on the day of the backup are backed up, and the archive bit is not changed in any file.

Backup Strategies

Although there are many backup strategies, three basic strategies serve most purposes. Table 13.1 describes these three basic strategies, along with some of their advantages and disadvantages. A five-day work week is assumed.

TABLE 13.1   Three Basic Backup Strategies

Backup Strategy	Description	Advantages	Disadvantages
Full daily (also called normal)	A full (i.e., complete) backup is performed every day. Given the storage capacity and speed of modern backup devices and that the Windows 2000 Backup utility allows you to back up to any available drive, daily full backups are the choice of most Exchange administrators, and we recommend them.	Only one tape is needed to perform a restoration. This strategy requires the least amount of time to restore (assuming an entire backup fits onto one media).	This strategy requires the longest amount of time to perform the backup.

T A B L E 1 3 . 1 Three Basic Backup Strategies *(continued)*

Backup Strategy	Description	Advantages	Disadvantages
A full backup once per week and an incremental backup every other day	A full backup is done on day one. An incremental backup (using a new tape every day) is performed every day for the next four days. This procedure only backs up the new and changed data since the last full or incremental backup (whichever is more recent).	This strategy takes the least amount of time to back up.	This strategy could require up to five tapes to perform a restoration. This strategy takes the most time to restore.
A full backup once per week and a differential backup every other day	A full backup is done on day one. A differential backup (using a single new tape) is performed every day for the next four days. This procedure only backs up the new and changed data since the last full backup.	No more than two tapes (the full and the last differential) are required to perform a restoration, making restoration faster than with the incremental method.	This strategy takes progressively longer to back up each day.

Using Windows 2000 Backup

When you install Exchange 2000 Server, an enhanced version of Windows 2000 Backup is installed that supports online Exchange server backups. This section briefly explains how to use Windows 2000 Backup to perform an online backup of an Exchange server.

Microsoft
Exam
Objective

Apply a backup and restore plan.

Performing a Backup

You can find Windows 2000 Backup in the System Tools program group, assuming that it was included in the Windows 2000 installation. When the program starts, you can run a Backup Wizard or to go right to the Backup tab and configure everything yourself. In this section, we look at how to use the Backup tab. If you choose to use the Backup Wizard, you make all of the same selections that are shown in this section, but in a different fashion. The Backup tab is shown in Figure 13.2 with the System State option selected and the Microsoft Exchange Server container expanded.

FIGURE 13.2   Configuring a backup

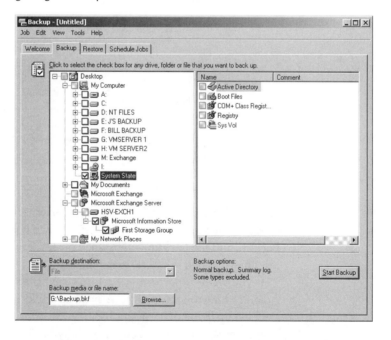

The Backup tab shows a hierarchical directory of the entire system. You can back up anything on your server that you like, including Microsoft Exchange Server. You can choose as much or as little of your Exchange organization to back up as you like—a single database on one server or even multiple servers from different routing groups. You can even back up one database on one server and one on another, should you wish.

If you choose to back up System State information, you must back up all of it. You cannot select individual components within the System State container.

Once you have selected all of the components you wish to back up, you must specify where to back them up. Use the Backup Destination drop-down list to specify whether you want to back up to tape or to file. Then, use the Backup Media Or Filename field to specify the tape drive or the drive and filename to which you want to back up. When you're satisfied with your choices, click Start Backup. This opens the Backup Job Information dialog box, shown in Figure 13.3.

FIGURE 13.3 Setting backup information

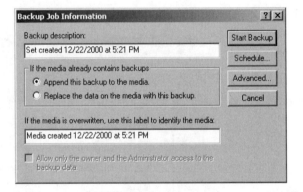

The basic information you need to supply is the name of the backup set and whether or not media should be overwritten or appended if there is already a backup present on the media. When you are ready to go, click Start Backup, and the backup will begin. You are shown the backup progress and a summary when the backup is finished.

If you wish to perform a backup type other than normal, click the Advanced button to open the Advanced Backup Options dialog box. From the Backup Type drop-down list, you can choose to perform a normal, incremental, differential, copy, or daily backup. You can also use the Advanced Backup Options dialog to set additional options, such as verifying and compressing data. The steps for performing a backup are outlined in Exercise 13.1.

EXERCISE 13.1

Backing Up an Exchange Server

1. Click Start ➤ Programs ➤ Accessories ➤ System Tools ➤ Backup.

2. Click the Backup tab.

3. Select the check box next to the System State container.

4. Expand the Microsoft Exchange Server container.

5. Expand the server that contains the databases you want to back up.

6. Expand the Microsoft Information Store container.

7. Select the check boxes next to the stores you want to back up. If you want to back up individual databases, expand the store containers and select the check boxes next to the databases.

8. Click the Browse button and select a location to hold the backup.

9. Click the Start Backup button.

10. Enter a backup description and choose whether to append the backup to any backups already on the media or to overwrite information on the backup media.

11. Click the Advanced button.

12. On the Advanced Backup Options dialog box, make sure that the normal backup type is selected.

13. Click OK.

14. Click Start Backup.

15. When the backup is finished and the summary dialog box is displayed, click OK.

Performing a Restore

Restoring from an online backup is basically the reverse process of performing the backup. First, you have to specify which backup set you want to restore. In Windows 2000 Backup, click the Restore tab (see Figure 13.4). All available backup jobs are displayed, and you simply have to drill down and select what backup job and what components of that job you want to restore.

FIGURE 13.4 Selecting a backup set to restore

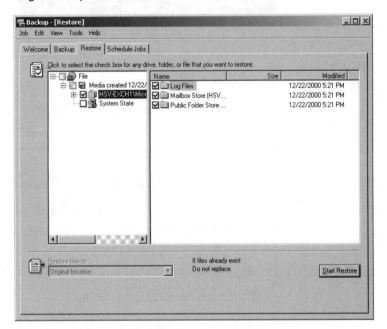

Microsoft Exam Objective

Restore user data and System State data.

- Recover deleted mailboxes.
- Recover deleted items.

Restore information stores.

In the bottom-left corner of the Restore tab, you need to specify whether to restore files to their original location, to an alternate location, or to an individual folder. If you are restoring an Exchange server, you will use the first option. If you are using a backup to move items to another server or to a newly installed server, you will usually use the second option. Restoring to an individual folder is useful if you want to try to find some particular piece of data within the backup job.

The Start Restore button opens the Restoring Database Store dialog box shown in Figure 13.5. Here, you can redirect the restore to another Exchange server, if you want. Also, you need to enter a temporary folder to hold the backed up log and patch files during the restore. First, Exchange 2000 will apply the older transaction logs from the temporary location to the database, and then it will apply the more recent logs from the original location.

FIGURE 13.5 Setting restore options

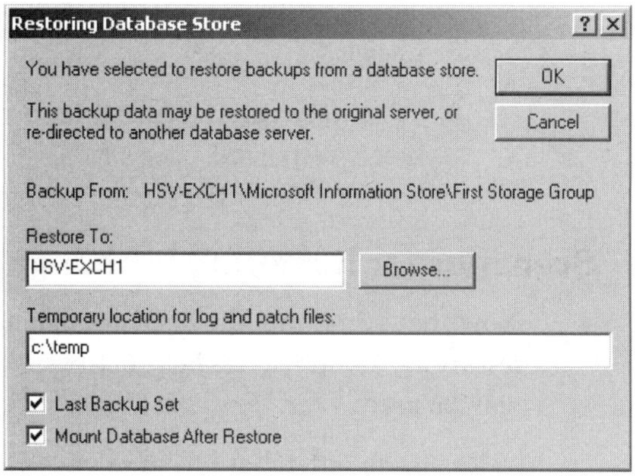

If the Last Backup Set option is specified, Exchange 2000 will begin replaying the log files to rebuild the database as soon as the backup set is restored. If you will be restoring multiple databases in the same storage group, you should not set this option until the final backup set is being restored. Click OK when you are done, and the restore will start. When it is done, you are shown a summary of the job. If you selected the Mount Database After Restore option, the database is now mounted. Exercise 3.2 details the process of restoring backup set.

EXERCISE 13.2

Restoring a Backup Set

1. Click Start ➢ Programs ➢ Accessories ➢ System Tools ➢ Backup.

2. Click the Restore tab.

3. Expand the media hierarchy, and select the check boxes next to items you want to restore.

4. Choose whether to restore files to their original location or to an alternate location.

5. Click the Start Restore button.

EXERCISE 13.2 *(continued)*

6. Enter a temporary location for the log files.

7. Select the Last Backup Set and Mount Database After Restore options.

8. Click OK.

9. When the restore process is completed and the summary dialog box is displayed, click OK.

Scenarios for Restoring Exchange Server

Now that you know the basics of using the Windows 2000 Backup tool to restore a backup set, it is helpful to examine a few scenarios in which restores may be used.

Restoring a database to the same server   Restoring a mailbox or public folder store to the same server on which you perform the backup is useful if one of your databases becomes damaged. You must dismount the damaged database, replace it from the last successful backup, and then mount the database again.

Restoring multiple databases to the same server   If you want to restore two databases from the same storage group during one operation, you must choose different directories in which to save the temporary logs. If you choose to use only one temporary location, you must ensure that the first restore is complete before starting a second restore of another database in the same storage group. To complete the first restore, you must choose the Last Backup Set option and then allow the log file replay to complete.

Restoring a database to a different server   Restoring a database to an Exchange server that is different from the one on which you performed the backup provides one way to move a database to a different storage group. It also provides a way to recover individual items from a backup without restoring over a server that is in use.

Restoring after a complete server failure   Performing a complete server restore involves several important steps.

Reinstalling Windows 2000 Server   First, you must reinstall the same version of Windows 2000 Server that was on the failed computer. You must also install Windows on the same hard disk and using the same paths as the previous installation. Be sure that you use the same computer name and that you select all of the same components that were installed on the original computer. Do not rejoin the domain during installation.

Restoring the system drive   Next, you should run Windows 2000 Backup to restore full backups of the system drive and any other drive on which application data was installed.

Restoring the System State information   Next, run Windows 2000 Backup to restore the System State information for the computer. This returns the computer to its original domain and restores the IIS metabase and Windows 2000 Registry information. After restoring the System State information, you'll have to restart the computer. When it restarts, you may see a number of error messages relating to failed services. These are usually Exchange services that Windows expects to find but does not, because Exchange has not yet been restored.

Running Exchange Setup in Disaster Recovery Mode   Next, run Exchange setup in *Disaster Recovery Mode* using the command line `setup /DisasterRecovery`. For the most part, the setup program works the same as when performing a normal installation. However, at the component selection screen, you must ensure that Exchange is installed to the same drive and path as the original installation and that the Disaster Recovery option is set for all components that were previously installed.

Restoring the Exchange databases   Finally, you must run Windows 2000 Backup using the procedures you've learned in this chapter to restore the Exchange databases to the server.

Recovering deleted mailboxes   If you set a deleted-item retention period on a mailbox or public store, users can restore messages after they have been deleted from their mailbox. By default, the deleted-item retention period is 0 days. If you do not set a deleted-item retention period, or if the retention period has expired for an item, you must restore deleted messages from backup. You do this by restoring the appropriate mailbox store to an alternate server, moving the messages to a .PST file, and then making the .PST file available to the user.

Being Prepared for Disaster

Performing regular backups is only part of a good disaster recovery plan. You must also test your plans and be prepared for when disaster does strike. We generally recommend the following practices:

Using recovery servers   A computer that you have prepared to take the place of a failed Exchange server is called a *recovery server* (sometimes referred to as a standby server or cold server). A recovery server would have Windows 2000 Server and Exchange Server already installed. It should also have the Exchange database files loaded. At the least, the database files should be loaded on media that would facilitate loading on that server. Some organizations create a batch file that stops the Exchange services on the primary server and copies the relevant files to the standby server. These files could also be copied to removable media and then uploaded to the standby server when needed. Recovery servers are also useful for restoring single mailboxes.

Validating your backups   It is important to validate that each backup occurs without errors. Check the Windows 2000 Backup Log and the Windows 2000 Event Log to ensure your backup has completed as scheduled.

Documenting backups   It is important to document your backup strategy and provide step-by-step instructions describing how to use backups to restore data. You should also keep track of old backup logs in case you need to refer to them.

Running fire drills   You should schedule regular fire drills in which administrators are required to restore a failed server from backup under different scenarios. This process accomplishes two things. First, it helps train administrators on how to perform restore procedures. Second, it helps verify that your backup media and plans really work.

Troubleshooting

Problems can occur when you back up or restore servers. Table 13.2 lists some problems (and possible causes and solutions) that you may encounter when you perform two common procedures.

Microsoft
Exam
Objective

Diagnose and resolve backup and restore problems.

TABLE 13.2 Backup and Restore Problems, Causes, and Solutions

Situation	Problem	Cause/Solution
Information Store will not start after restoring from backup.	The Information Store may need to be patched before it can be operational.	The Information Store may be corrupted. Execute the following command line: `ISINTEG -PATCH`.
The Information Store was restored to a different server.	After the restore, users cannot access the Information Store.	The restore was performed on a server in a different Windows 2000 domain than the original server. Restore to a server in the same domain.

You can also use the backup log file, `BACKUP.LOG`, which resides in your Windows 2000 directory (e.g., `\WINNT`), as a diagnostic tool when you troubleshoot.

Summary

This chapter demonstrated how to back up and restore an Exchange server. The first step in backing up a server is deciding what you need to back up. This can include the main Exchange databases (`PRIVx.EDB`, `PUBx.EDB`, and their corresponding .STM files), as well as transaction logs. You might also elect to back up items in the Exchange Server subdirectories, any server-stored user information, and System State information.

Once you have decided what to back up, you must decide how to perform the backup. There are five basic types of backups: normal, copy, incremental, differential, and daily. Exchange 2000 Server supports the use of the normal, incremental, and differential backup types. When you install Exchange 2000 Server, you also install an enhanced version of Windows 2000 Backup that provides support for online backups.

Restoring a database from an online backup using Windows 2000 Backup is essentially the reverse process of performing the backup in the first place. If you are restoring multiple databases to the same server, you must choose different directories in which to save the temporary logs or you must restore one database at a time. When restoring after a complete system failure, you must first reinstall Windows 2000 Server, restore the system drive and the system state backup information, reinstall Exchange 2000 Server using Disaster Recovery Mode, and then restore the Exchange databases.

Performing regular backups is one part of a good disaster recovery plan. You should also verify and document your backups, perform practice restores, and have recovery servers standing by in case of emergency.

Key Terms

Before you take the exam, be certain you are familiar with the following terms:

checkpoint files	normal backup
copy backup	patch files
daily backup	previous logs
differential backup	recovery server
Disaster Recovery Mode	Site Replication Services (SRS) database
incremental backup	System State backup
Key Management Server (KMS) database	transaction log

Review Questions

1. You are configuring the backup of a single Exchange server that holds two mailbox stores and no public folder store. Both of the mailbox stores are in a single storage group. You are not using Key Management Server. How many database files and transaction log sets will need to be backed up?

   A. Two database files and one transaction log set

   B. Four database files and one transaction log set

   C. Two database files and two transaction log sets

   D. Four database files and two transaction log sets

2. You are an Exchange administrator for a large company. One of your Exchange servers recently suffered a complete failure. You have repaired the computer and now must rebuild the server before you can restore your Exchange backups. Which of the following actions should you take? (Choose all that apply.)

   A. Install the same version of Windows 2000 Server that was running before.

   B. Join the same domain of which the computer was originally a member.

   C. Use Windows 2000 Backup to restore the System State information.

   D. Run Exchange setup in Disaster Recovery Mode.

3. You are the backup administrator for a set of Exchange servers in your company's organization. Recently, you had to restore the mailbox stores on one of your servers. After the restore, the Information Store service would not restart. What should you do?

   A. Restore the databases to a different server and then move the stores to the proper server.

   B. Perform the restore again and choose the Last Backup Set option.

   C. Run the command-line utility ISINTEG -PATCH.

   D. Perform the restore again, and restore the System State information.

4. You are the backup administrator for a large Exchange organization. Recently, one of your users discovered that he had deleted an important file by mistake. Unfortunately, the deleted-item retention time on your server was set to zero, so the file is not recoverable from the user's client. What should you do?

   A. Use the mailbox object for the user in System Manager to recover the file.

   B. Restore the latest backup of the mailbox store to the production server.

   C. Restore the latest backup of the mailbox store to an alternate server and then move the user's mailbox to the production server.

   D. Restore the latest backup of the mailbox store to an alternate server and then copy the files in the user's mailbox to a .PST file.

   E. Tell the user that you cannot recover the file.

5. Which of the following information is contained in a System State backup? (Choose all that apply.)

   A. The IIS metabase

   B. The Windows 2000 Registry

   C. Active Directory

   D. System Manager configuration information

6. An Exchange server is configured with two storage groups, as shown below. The first storage group (SG1) contains four mailbox stores and one public store. The second storage group (SG2) contains one mailbox store. Which of the following actions would have the most beneficial effect on server performance?

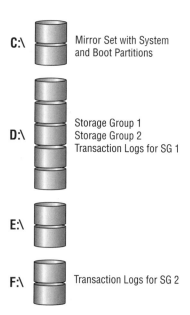

C:\ — Mirror Set with System and Boot Partitions

D:\ — Storage Group 1
Storage Group 2
Transaction Logs for SG 1

E:\

F:\ — Transaction Logs for SG 2

A. Move SG2 to the E: drive.

B. Move the transaction logs for SG1 to the E: drive.

C. Move the transaction logs for SG1 to the F: drive.

D. Move the transaction logs for SG2 to the D: drive.

7. Which of the following would be the best backup scheduling strategy?

   A. Back up Active Directory for a domain at the same time you back up Exchange databases in the domain.

   B. Separate the backup of Active Directory and the Exchange databases by at least an hour.

   C. Separate the backup of Active Directory and the Exchange databases by at least a day.

   D. Separate the backup of Active Directory and the Exchange databases by at least the amount of time it takes the Active Directory to replicate throughout the domain.

   E. Separate the backup of Active Directory and the Exchange databases by no more than the amount of time it takes the Active Directory to replicate throughout the domain.

8. Which of the following backup types causes the archive bit for a file that is backed up to be set to the off position? (Choose all that apply.)

   A. Normal

   B. Copy

   C. Incremental

   D. Differential

   E. Daily

9. You are the backup administrator for a large Exchange organization and are currently designing a backup plan. You have decided that the time it takes to restore after a failure is more critical than the time it takes to back up. Which of the following backup methods would be the best choice?

   A. A full normal backup every day

   B. A full normal backup once per week and an incremental backup every other day

   C. A full normal backup once per week and a differential backup every other day

   D. A daily backup every day

10. You have just finished repairing and rebuilding a server after a complete failure and are ready to restore the databases. You have three different backup sets—one for three mailbox stores in one storage group, one for two mailbox stores in another storage group, and one for a public store in yet another storage group. You plan to restore the backup sets in that order and to use only one temporary location during the restores. Which of the following should you do?

   A. Enable the Last Backup Set option only when restoring the public store in the final storage group.

   B. Enable the Last Backup Set option for each of the three backup sets.

   C. Enable the Last Backup Set option only when restoring the public store in the final storage group, but enable the Mount Database After Restore option for all three backup sets.

   D. Enable the Last Backup Set option and the Mount Database After Restore option for all three backup sets.

   E. Restore each database individually, and enable the Last Backup Set option for each database.

11. Which of the following files would be useful in troubleshooting a failed backup?

   A. BACKUP.LOG

   B. BACKLOG.TXT

   C. NTBACK.TXT

   D. SYSTEM.BAK

12. You are the administrator of a small organization with a single Exchange server. You are preparing to restore a mailbox store on that server. Which of the following should you do first?

   A. Dismount the database you intend to restore.

   B. Dismount all databases in the same storage group as the database you intend to restore.

   C. Stop the Information Store service on the Exchange server.

   D. Nothing—Windows 2000 Backup will take care of dismounting the appropriate databases and stopping any services.

13. You are the backup administrator for a large Exchange organization. One of your Exchange servers currently has a single storage group with four mailbox stores. Each store hosts around 2,000 users. While the performance of your server has been fine, you are concerned that the amount of time it will take to restore the server in the event of failure will be too long.

    Required result:

    You must be able to restore each store of 2,000 users simultaneously.

    Optional result:

    All of the stores will use a common transaction log.

    Proposed solution:

    Keep all of the stores in the same storage group. Back up each store to separate backup media.

    What results would the proposed solution produce?

    A. The proposed solution produces the required result and the optional result.

    B. The proposed solution produces the required result but does not produce the optional result.

    C. The proposed solution produces the optional result but does not produce the required result.

    D. The proposed solution does not produce the required or the optional result.

14. You are the backup administrator for a large Exchange organization. One of your Exchange servers currently has a single storage group with four mailbox stores. Each store hosts around 2,000 users. While the performance of your server has been fine, you are concerned that the amount of time it will take to restore the server in the event of failure will be too long.

Required result:

You must be able to restore each store of 2,000 users simultaneously.

Optional result:

All of the stores will use a common transaction log.

Proposed solution:

Create a separate storage group for each store, and move the stores into those groups. Place each storage group onto a separate physical disk. Back up each storage group to separate backup media.

What results would the proposed solution produce?

A. The proposed solution produces the required result and the optional result.

B. The proposed solution produces the required result but does not produce the optional result.

C. The proposed solution produces the optional result but does not produce the required result.

D. The proposed solution does not produce the required or the optional result.

15. You are the backup administrator for a large Exchange organization. One of your Exchange servers currently has a single storage group with four mailbox stores. Each store hosts around 2,000 users. While the performance of your server has been fine, you are concerned that the amount of time it will take to restore the server in the event of failure will be too long.

Required result:

You must be able to restore each store of 2,000 users simultaneously.

Optional result:

All of the stores will use a common transaction log.

Proposed solution:

Create a separate storage group for each store, and move the stores into those groups. Place each storage group onto a separate physical disk.

What results would the proposed solution produce?

A. The proposed solution produces the required result and the optional result.

B. The proposed solution produces the required result but does not produce the optional result.

C. The proposed solution produces the optional result but does not produce the required result.

D. The proposed solution does not produce the required or the optional result.

16. One of your users has come to you complaining that she has forgotten the password she used for her personal folders (.PST file). She needs to get something out of those folders. What can you do with the tools provided by Exchange 2000 Server and Outlook 2000?

A. Use `scanpst.exe` to recover the personal folders.

B. Use System Manager to import the messages in the personal folders to the user's mailbox.

C. Use your administrative password to open the personal folders and assign a new password to the user.

D. Nothing—you cannot access the personal folders without the password.

17. Which of the following actions would generally offer the greatest performance enhancement on an Exchange server?

A. Turning off circular logging

B. Breaking large stores into smaller ones

C. Putting storage groups on separate disks from one another

D. Putting transaction logs on disks separate from their storage groups

18. Which of the following statements is true?

   A. You must dismount a store before performing a backup.

   B. You must dismount a store before performing a backup only if you are backing up multiple stores in the same backup set.

   C. You must dismount a store before performing a restore.

   D. You must dismount a store before performing a restore only if you are restoring multiple stores in the same backup set.

19. You are restoring two stores from the same storage group during the same restore operation. Which of the following should you do?

   A. Enable circular logging while the restore is being performed, and turn it off again afterward.

   B. Choose different directories for each store in which to store the temporary logs during the restore process.

   C. Restore both stores at once, and enable the Last Backup Set option.

   D. Restore both stores at once, and enable the System State option.

20. Which of the following statements is true of backing up Exchange 2000 Server?

   A. A single backup set can only include stores within a single storage group.

   B. A single backup set can only include stores on a single server.

   C. A single backup set can only include stores within a single routing group.

   D. A single backup set can only include stores within a single administrative group.

   E. A single backup set can include stores throughout the organization.

Answers to Review Questions

1. B. Each store is composed of two database files: a rich-text file and a streaming file. Since there are two mailbox stores, four files will be backed up. Each storage group maintains a single set of transaction logs. Since all stores are in a single group, only one set of logs is used.

2. A, C, D. You should not rejoin the domain during or after installation of Windows 2000 Server. When you restore the System State information, the computer will be made a member of the domain again.

3. C. The Information Store may need to be patched before it can be operational. The ISINTEG utility can be used to perform checks on the integrity of a database, and the -PATCH switch is used to patch the databases.

4. D. If you set a deleted-item retention period on a mailbox or public store, users can restore messages after they have been deleted from their mailbox. By default, the deleted-item retention period is 0 days. If you do not set a deleted-item retention period or if the retention period has expired for an item, you must restore deleted messages from backup. You do this by restoring the appropriate mailbox store to an alternate server, moving the messages to a .PST file, and then making the .PST file available to the user.

5. A, B, C. A System State backup includes the Windows 2000 Registry, the IIS metabase, and the Active Directory if the computer is a domain controller.

6. B. Storing log files on separate disks dramatically increases performance and your odds of successful recovery in the event of failure. Putting multiple storage groups on one disk and then putting the transaction logs for each storage group onto their own disks would be better than trying to separate the storage groups.

7. A. You should back up Active Directory and Exchange 2000 databases at the same time to avoid losing configuration of user objects on the domain controllers or in global catalogs.

8. A, C. When a file is created or modified, the archive bit is set to on. When some types of backups run, the archive bit is set to off, which indicates that the file has been backed up. The normal and incremental backup types set the archive bit to off so that the same files will not be backed up in subsequent backups unless the files change.

9. A. Given the speed of modern backup devices, there is really no reason to do anything other than a full normal backup every day. The actual backup does take the longest time of any backup method to perform, but it provides the easiest and fastest restore.

10. A. If the Last Backup Set option is specified, Exchange 2000 will begin replaying the log files to rebuild the database as soon as the backup set is restored. If you want to restore two databases from the same storage group during one operation, you must choose different directories in which to save the temporary logs. If you choose to use only one temporary location, you must ensure that the first restore is complete before starting a second restore of another database in the same storage group. To complete the first restore, you must choose the Last Backup Set option and then allow the log file replay to complete.

11. A. BACKUP.LOG resides in your Windows 2000 directory (e.g., \WINNT) and serves as a good diagnostic tool when you troubleshoot.

12. A. Restoring a mailbox or public folder store to the same server on which you perform the backup is useful if one of your databases becomes damaged. You must dismount the damaged database, replace it from the last successful backup, and then mount the database again.

13. C. To prepare for a failure of all storage related to a server, you could partition data into separate storage groups and back up these storage groups to different media. As long as you initiate separate restore sessions for each storage group, Exchange can restore multiple storage groups at the same time. The storage groups should also be hosted on separate physical disks or disk arrays so the physical disk media does not become a bottleneck for the restore. This is known as a parallel restore.

14. B. To prepare for a failure of all storage related to a server, you could partition data into separate storage groups and back up these storage groups to different media. As long as you initiate separate restore sessions for each storage group, Exchange can restore multiple storage groups at the same time. The storage groups should also be hosted on separate physical disks or disk arrays so the physical disk media does not become a bottleneck for the restore. This is known as a parallel restore.

15. D. To prepare for a failure of all storage related to a server, you could partition data into separate storage groups and back up these storage groups to different media. As long as you initiate separate restore sessions for each storage group, Exchange can restore multiple storage groups at the same time. The storage groups should also be hosted on separate physical disks or disk arrays so the physical disk media does not become a bottleneck for the restore. This is known as a parallel restore.

16. D. Once the password to personal folders is forgotten, it cannot be recovered, nor can the folders be accessed. For this reason, it is important that you include personal folders in your backup plan.

17. D. Although each of these actions can increase the performance of an Exchange server, putting transaction logs on separate disks from their storage groups typically offers the greatest increase if you have to make a choice.

18. C. You do not need to dismount a store before performing a backup, even if you are backing up multiple stores. You do need to dismount a store before restoring it, however.

19. B. If you want to restore two databases from the same storage group during one operation, you must choose different directories in which to save the temporary logs. If you choose to use only one temporary location, you must ensure that the first store is restored completely by choosing the Last Backup Set option before restoring another store in the same storage group.

20. E. You can back up as much or as little of your Exchange organization as you like—a single store on one server or multiple stores throughout the organization.

Chapter 14

Securing Exchange 2000 Server

MICROSOFT EXAM OBJECTIVES COVERED IN THIS CHAPTER:

✓ **Configure Exchange 2000 Server for high security.**

- Configure Exchange 2000 Server to issue v.3 certificates.
- Enable Digest authentication for Instant Messaging.
- Configure Certificate Trust Lists.
- Configure virtual servers to limit access through firewalls.
- Configure Key Management Server (KMS) to issue digital signatures.

✓ **Diagnose and resolve security problems that involve user keys.**

As computer networking has become more pervasive, the information transported over networks has become more valuable. As a result, some unscrupulous people try to steal information and disrupt business affairs. E-mail messages are susceptible to eavesdropping, tampering, and forgery. Implementing the proper security measures can prevent these and other security threats.

This chapter covers three aspects of security that you must concern yourself with as an Exchange administrator. The first feature is the collection of basic security services built into Windows 2000, including permissions, policies, and auditing. The second is network security, which includes authentication, the configuration of firewalls and proxy servers, and the prevention of virus attacks. The final aspect (and primary focus of the chapter) is messaging security, which includes the digital signature and encryption of messages using the Key Management Server (KMS) that comes with Exchange 2000 Server in conjunction with Windows 2000 Certificate Services.

Windows 2000 System Security

As you know, Exchange 2000 is heavily integrated with Windows 2000. Since much of the Exchange configuration lies in Active Directory, good Windows 2000 security practices are essential for good Exchange security. This section is intended to provide a brief overview of the security features in Windows 2000 that Exchange is designed to take advantage of. The integration of Windows 2000 and Exchange 2000 is covered in detail in Chapter 2, and Exchange-specific permissions and groups are covered in Chapter 9. You can also learn more about Windows 2000 security from your system documentation.

User Accounts and Authentication

Before users or services can access Exchange, they must log on to Windows 2000 by supplying a valid username and password. Windows 2000 must then authenticate the logon information, which it does using *Kerberos version 5 authentication*. Once a user is validated, that user is assigned a token that identifies the user whenever the user attempts to access resources during that logon session.

Each resource on a Windows 2000 network maintains an *Access Control List (ACL)*, a list of users and groups that are allowed access to the resource and the specific permissions they are assigned. A *permission* provides specific authorization to perform an action, such as deleting an object.

All objects in Exchange also maintain an ACL that defines the level of access users have to that object. You will grant users permissions on the various Exchange-related objects in Active Directory and in System Manager to create security for your organization. Check out Chapter 9 for details on the permissions available on most Exchange objects and the various administrative roles you can assign.

Administrative Groups

An *administrative group* is a collection of Active Directory objects that are grouped together for the purpose of permissions management. Administrative groups are logical, which means that you can design them to fit your needs—geographical boundaries, departmental divisions, different groups of Exchange administrators, or different Exchange functions. For example, one group of Exchange administrators might be responsible for managing the messaging and routing backbone of the organization, another might be responsible for managing public folders, and still another might be responsible for managing connectivity with a legacy messaging system. You could create an administrative group for each that contained only the objects the administrator needs. You can find details on using administrative groups in Chapter 7.

Policies

A *policy* is a collection of configuration settings that you can apply across any number of objects in the Active Directory at once. Making a change in a policy affects every object that is attached to that policy. *System policies* affect server objects such as servers, mailbox stores, and public stores, while *recipient policies* affect objects such as users and groups. Since you can use policies to make changes to such large numbers of objects, they are an important part of Exchange security. You can find detailed coverage of both types of policies in Chapter 9.

Auditing

Auditing is a feature in Windows 2000 that logs the actions of users and groups based on certain criteria. For example, a Windows 2000 server can audit successful and failed logon attempts or access to certain files. Because Exchange 2000 essentially works as a collection of Windows 2000 services, you can use auditing to track significant Exchange events, such as mailbox or server access.

Networking Security

These days, Internet access for a company network is a vital asset. However, along with the benefits that Internet access can provide come the risks of having your network permanently connected to the outside world. Thus it is essential that a network be secured from unauthorized access. This affects you as an Exchange administrator because the methods put in place to keep unwanted outsiders from connecting to your network must often allow connection by any Exchange users outside the network. For example, you may want traveling employees to be able to connect to their mailboxes over the Internet. This section describes several methods used for securing network access.

Authentication

If users are authenticated with a Windows 2000 domain controller using Kerberos V5, then those users are automatically granted the appropriate access to Exchange objects without having to be authenticated again. If users are not authenticated by a domain controller, they must be authenticated by another means. For example, a user connecting to an Exchange server over the Internet with a POP3 client would not necessarily be authenticated by a domain controller.

If authentication is not already granted to a user, a virtual server (such as the POP3 server) may authenticate the user instead. Each virtual server on an Exchange server can be configured to use different forms of authentication. With the exception of HTTP, you can configure the authentication method for all protocols by opening the property pages for the appropriate virtual server in System Manager and switching to the Authentication page.

Virtual servers support the following forms of authentication:

Anonymous   *Anonymous authentication* allows any user to access the virtual server without providing a username or password.

Basic (Clear-Text)   *Basic (Clear-Text) authentication* requires the user to submit a valid Windows username and password. The username and password are sent across the network as unencrypted clear text.

Basic over Secure Sockets Layer (SSL)   *Basic over Secure Sockets Layer (SSL) authentication* extends the Basic authentication method by allowing an SSL server to encrypt the username and password before they are sent across the network.

Integrated Windows authentication   *Integrated Windows authentication* also requires the user to provide a valid Windows username and password. However, the user's credentials are never sent across the network. If you are running a mixed-mode Windows 2000 network, this method uses the NTLM authentication protocol used by Windows NT 4.0. If your network is running in native mode, this method uses Kerberos V5.

In addition to the methods on the previous list, the IIS can also use a form of authentication called *Digest authentication* when validating HTTP clients. See Chapter 10 for details on enabling Digest authentication.

Firewalls

A *firewall* is a set of mechanisms that separates and protects your internal network from unauthorized external users and networks. Firewalls can restrict inbound and outbound traffic, as well as analyze all traffic between your network and the outside. Different criteria can be used by a firewall to analyze traffic, such as IP addresses and TCP/IP port numbers. The remainder of this section covers port numbers and example security scenarios that use a firewall.

Port Numbers

A *port number* is a numeric identifier used to route packets to the correct application on a computer. Just as Media Access Control (MAC) addresses are used to deliver frames to the correct physical computer (actually to the network adapter) and IP addresses are used to route packets to the correct logical computer (e.g., 147.4.56.76), port numbers are used to route a packet to the correct application after the packet has arrived at its destination computer. Multiple applications often run on a single server. When a packet arrives at that server, it cannot be delivered to just any application. POP3 client requests are not going to be understood by an LDAP server application.

Port numbers range from one to over 65,000. Most established Internet protocols have assigned port numbers, referred to as *well-known port numbers*, somewhere below port 1024. Table 14.1 lists some of the protocols discussed in this book and their well-known port numbers.

TABLE 14.1 Protocols and Their Well-Known Port Numbers

Protocol	Port Numbers
SMTP	25
DNS	53
HTTP	80
Kerberos V5	88, 750–754
MTA - X.400 over TCP/IP	102
POP3	110
NNTP	119
RPC	135
NetBIOS name service	137
IMAP4	143
IRC	194
LDAP	389
HTTP (over SSL)	443
SMTP (over SSL)	465
NNTP (over SSL)	563

TABLE 14.1   Protocols and Their Well-Known Port Numbers *(continued)*

Protocol	Port Numbers
LDAP (over SSL)	636
IMAP (over SSL)	993
POP3 (over SSL)	995
Instant Messaging	2890
Global Catalog lookup	3268

Microsoft
✓ *Exam*
Objective

Configure Exchange 2000 Server for high security.

- Configure virtual servers to limit access through firewalls.

One way a firewall can work is by prohibiting certain port numbers or allowing only designated port numbers to pass through the firewall. This functionality can be used to restrict the applications that can be used to access your network. For example, if a firewall were configured to prohibit port 80, HTTP clients would not be able to pass through the firewall and communicate with any internal virtual servers. Many firewalls are configured to prevent all but the most well-known port numbers (such as POP3, HTTP, and SMTP) from passing through. Often, you will have to open specific ports in order to let the proper traffic pass.

For an extra measure of security, you can usually change the port numbers that an application uses. For example, you might change your POP3 virtual server and all POP3 clients to use port 28,345 instead of the default 110. The downside of doing this is that you will have to manually change any application that will need to communicate with the server. Exercise 14.1 outlines the steps for changing the regular and SSL port numbers for the POP3 virtual server.

EXERCISE 14.1

Changing Port Numbers for a POP3 Virtual Server

1. Click Start ➤ Programs ➤ Microsoft Exchange ➤ System Manager.

EXERCISE 14.1 *(continued)*

2. Expand the administrative group and server that contain the virtual server you want to alter.

3. Expand the Protocols container and then the POP3 container.

4. Right-click the Default POP3 Virtual Server object and select Properties from the shortcut menu.

5. On the General page, click the Advanced button.

6. Select the IP address for which you want to change the port number, or leave the default All Unassigned option selected.

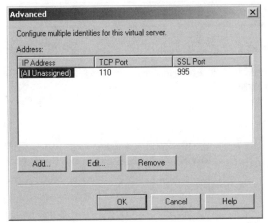

7. Click the Edit button.

8. In the TCP Port and SSL Port fields, type the new port numbers you want to use. Make sure that the new port numbers do not conflict with the port numbers in use by any other application.

9. Click OK three times to return to System Manager.

Security Scenarios Using a Basic Firewall

Firewalls are useful in a number of ways, some of which are illustrated in the following scenarios.

Scenario 1

You have just configured your Exchange server for IMAP4 client access. IMAP4 clients can be authenticated with either the Basic (Clear-Text) or Basic over SSL authentication methods. The administrator of your firewall tells you that the firewall will allow traffic from SMTP (port 25), IMAP4 (port 143), and HTTP (port 80). What additional traffic must the firewall be configured to allow for your Exchange server IMAP4 configuration to be used? Because the Exchange server is using SSL as one of its authentication methods, IMAP over SSL (port 993) would also need to be opened on the firewall.

Scenario 2

A new Exchange server has been installed and configured for LDAP, HTTP, and POP3. The network project plan calls for allowing the following clients to access this server: LDAP, Web software using Integrated Windows NT, POP3, and Microsoft Outlook using secure passwords. You refer to the current firewall configuration and see that it is open to DNS, HTTP, SMTP, and ports higher than 1023. What, if anything, must you do to enable the desired Exchange clients to pass through the firewall? The answer is: Open LDAP (port 389), POP3 (port 110), and the RPC Endpoint Mapper Service (port 135). Without these changes, the firewall would not allow traffic from LDAP, POP3, or Exchange MAPI clients (which Outlook is).

Scenario 3

In each of the next three scenarios (including this one), you will see the same starting situation. But each scenario requires different mandatory and optional results, and presents different possible courses of action.

CURRENT SITUATION

Your Exchange server is using TCP/IP and is configured with LDAP, HTTP, and POP3. A firewall sits between your network and the Internet. Your Exchange server has its name and IP address entered into a public DNS server on the Internet.

Your network's firewall prohibits traffic on all ports that are not explicitly allowed. The open ports are port 25 (SMTP), port 53 (DNS), port 80 (HTTP), and all ports greater than port 1023.

REQUIRED RESULTS

Management requires that users are able to connect over the Internet to your Exchange server using Microsoft Outlook and LDAP applications. Policy dictates that passwords be transmitted in a secure manner.

OPTIONAL RESULTS

While not required, management would like Web clients that do not support Integrated Windows authentication to be able to connect to your Exchange server. Another preference is for POP3 clients to connect to the Exchange server and download their messages.

PROPOSED COURSE OF ACTION

One proposed course of action is to do the following:

- Assign port numbers to the Exchange Directory Service and Information Store. Then allow those ports through the firewall.

- Configure LDAP on the Exchange server to allow Anonymous access.

- Configure the Exchange protocols to use SSL as an authentication method.

- Allow SSL traffic through the firewall.

- Allow LDAP traffic (port 389) through the firewall.

- Allow RPC traffic (port 135) through the firewall.

- Allow POP3 traffic (port 110) through the firewall.

See Figure 14.1 for a depiction of this scenario.

FIGURE 14.1 Scenario 3 illustrated

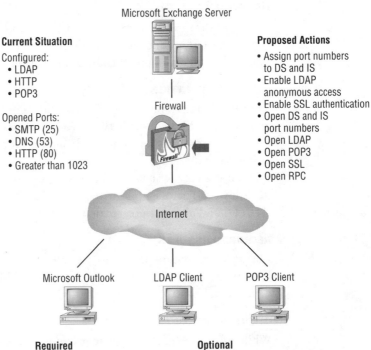

Microsoft Exchange Server

Current Situation

Configured:
- LDAP
- HTTP
- POP3

Opened Ports:
- SMTP (25)
- DNS (53)
- HTTP (80)
- Greater than 1023

Firewall

Proposed Actions

- Assign port numbers to DS and IS
- Enable LDAP anonymous access
- Enable SSL authentication
- Open DS and IS port numbers
- Open LDAP
- Open POP3
- Open SSL
- Open RPC

Internet

Microsoft Outlook   LDAP Client   POP3 Client

Required
- Microsoft Outlook and LDAP clients to access server
- Secure password transmission

Optional
- Web clients without Integrated Windows to access server
- POP3 clients to access server

RESULTS OF THE PROPOSED ACTIONS

This course of action would meet both required results and both optional results. The key actions were forcing Exchange to use fixed port numbers for the DS and IS, configuring of SSL on the Exchange server, and enabling the firewall to allow LDAP, POP3, SSL ports, RPC, and the fixed port numbers for the DS and IS.

Scenario 4

As mentioned, the following current situation, required results, and optional results are the same as above. The difference in this scenario is the proposed actions and, possibly, the results of those actions.

CURRENT SITUATION

Your Exchange server is using TCP/IP and is configured with LDAP, HTTP, and POP3. A firewall sits between your network and the Internet. Your Exchange server has its name and IP address entered into a public DNS server on the Internet.

Your network's firewall prohibits traffic on all ports that are not explicitly allowed. The open ports are port 25 (SMTP), port 53 (DNS), port 80 (HTTP), and all ports greater than port 1023.

REQUIRED RESULTS

Management requires that users are able to connect over the Internet to your Exchange server using Microsoft Outlook and LDAP applications. Policy dictates that passwords be transmitted in a secure manner.

OPTIONAL RESULTS

While not required, management would like Web clients that do not support Integrated Windows authentication to be able to connect to your Exchange server. Another preference is for POP3 clients to connect to the Exchange server and download their messages.

PROPOSED COURSE OF ACTION

One proposed course of action is to do the following:

- Assign port numbers to the Exchange Directory Service and Information Store. Then allow those ports through the firewall.

- Configure LDAP on the Exchange server to allow Anonymous access.

- Allow LDAP traffic (port 389) through the firewall.

RESULTS OF THE PROPOSED ACTIONS

This course of action would not meet the required results because port 135, used by the Mapper service, is not open on the firewall, and there is no capability to use secure passwords. Only one of the optional results is met, namely Web access to your server (that ability was already inherent in the current situation). The POP3 optional result is not met because POP3 is not allowed through the firewall.

Scenario 5

The final scenario presents the same situation as the previous scenario, but proposes a different course of action.

CURRENT SITUATION

Your Exchange server is using TCP/IP and is configured with LDAP, HTTP, and POP3. A firewall sits between your network and the Internet. Your Exchange server has its name and IP address entered into a public DNS server on the Internet.

Your network's firewall prohibits traffic on all ports that are not explicitly allowed. The open ports are port 25 (SMTP), port 53 (DNS), port 80 (HTTP), and all ports greater than port 1023.

REQUIRED RESULTS

Management requires that users are able to connect over the Internet to your Exchange server using Microsoft Outlook and LDAP applications. Policy dictates that passwords be transmitted in a secure manner.

OPTIONAL RESULTS

While not required, management would like Web clients that do not support Integrated Windows NT authentication to be able to connect to your Exchange server. Another preference is for POP3 clients to connect to the Exchange server and download their messages.

PROPOSED COURSE OF ACTION

One course of action would be to do the following:

- Assign port numbers to the Exchange Directory Service and Information Store. Then allow those ports through the firewall.

- Configure LDAP on the Exchange server to allow Anonymous access.

- Allow LDAP traffic (port 389) through the firewall.

- Allow RPC traffic (port 135) through the firewall.

RESULTS OF THE PROPOSED ACTIONS

This course of action would meet one of the required results, namely, allowing Microsoft Outlook and LDAP clients to access the Exchange server. The second required result, secure passwords, is not met, because an authentication method using SSL is not used. Only one of the optional results is met, namely, Web access to the server. The other optional result, POP3 client access, is not met because the firewall does not allow POP3.

Firewalls and Front-End/Back-End Servers

In addition to the basic use of firewalls outlined previously, the introduction of *front-end servers* and *back-end servers* in Exchange 2000 presents other possible configurations for the use of firewalls. There are three basic configurations that you can use, each offering a different level of security.

Using a Firewall Between a Front-End Server and a Back-End Server

In this configuration, a front-end server sits outside the firewall for your network, as shown in Figure 14.2. This type of configuration can be useful for authenticating and then redirecting clients using different protocols to various back-end servers behind the firewall. Keep in mind, though, that no firewall protects the front-end server.

FIGURE 14.2   Firewall between a front-end and a back-end server

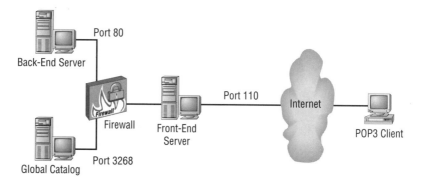

Figure 14.2 illustrates the following process:

1. A POP3 client connects to the front-end server using port 110.

2. The front-end server connects to the Global Catalog through the firewall over port 3268 and identifies the correct back-end server to receive the POP3 request.

3. The front-end and back-end servers communicate using HTTP over port 80.

4. The front-end server returns the information to the client using port 110.

Using a Firewall between a Client and a Front-End Server

In this configuration, the front-end server sits inside the network firewall, as shown in Figure 14.3. This method offers a higher level of security for the front-end server than placing it outside the firewall, but also requires more configuration of the firewall. Instead of having to open just two ports (3268 for the Global Catalog and 80 for the HTTP communications between front and back-end servers), you must open a port for each type of communication that you want to allow. For example, to allow POP3, IMAP, and HTTP clients to connect, you would have to open ports 110, 143, and 80.

FIGURE 14.3 Firewall between clients and a front-end server

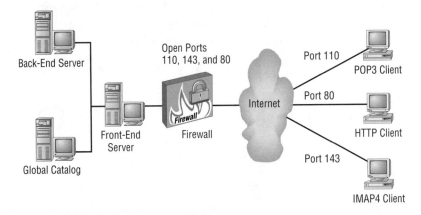

Placing the Front-End Server in a Perimeter Network

One highly secure firewall configuration calls for placing two firewalls between the outside world and your private network. A front-end server is then placed between the two firewalls, as shown in Figure 14.4. The area between the two firewalls is commonly referred to as a *perimeter network* or a *demilitarized zone (DMZ)*. When using this configuration, you must open all ports on the outside firewall for the clients that should be able to connect to the front-end server (i.e. POP3, IMAP, or HTTP) and then open ports 3268 and 80 on the interior firewall so that the front-end server can query the Global Catalog and pass information to the back-end server. Also, if you are using Kerberos V5 authentication, you must open port 88 on both firewalls.

FIGURE 14.4 A perimeter network

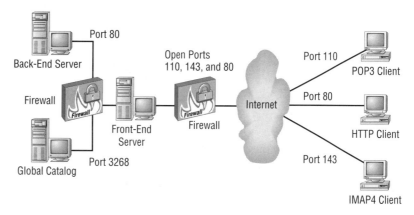

Viruses

Viruses can enter a system in a number of ways—through an infected file on a floppy disk that someone brings in, by downloading a file from the Internet, through e-mail, and even through shared documents. Most networks implement a number of virus protection schemes that work together to help prevent the problems viruses can cause. Some of these schemes are as follows:

- Virus protection built in to the network firewall that tries to prevent viruses from entering the network in the first place.

- Virus software that works with Exchange Server to scan all messages transferred through Exchange.

- Virus scanning software on servers and clients that examines files as they are transferred or used and examines messages as they are received by a client application. One great advantage this scheme has over the others is that messages that are encrypted for security cannot be effectively scanned for viruses, allowing those messages to slip through the firewall and Exchange Server virus scanners. Once decrypted on the client computer, however, any virus protection on that computer can scan the contents of the message and any attachments.

Messaging Security

Even if you have the best system and network security in place, it is often important to secure the actual messages being transferred within your organization and to users outside the organization. To accomplish this, Exchange 2000 Server provides the Key Management Server (KMS) component that works in conjunction with Windows 2000 Certificate Services.

Overview of Certificate Services

Certificates and public key encryption were originally designed for use on the Internet. Encryption keys are handed out between Web servers and from Web servers to clients using certificates or cookies. These keys are used primarily to give the client some assurance that the server is a trusted source for data. However, the trend toward requiring increasing levels of security while at the same time requiring greater scalability and exposure to the Internet has led to the incorporation of certificate services on many private networks.

To answer these needs, Windows 2000 implements security using a technology called *public key infrastructure (PKI)*, which is a system of components working together to verify the identity of users who transfer data on a system and to encrypt that data if needed. PKI is still an emerging standard, so you'll likely find that many systems incorporate a rather loose version of it.

Encryption Methods

Theft, tampering, and forgery can be countered through cryptology, which is the study and implementation of hiding and revealing information. Cryptology provides for confidentiality by preventing stolen data from being read or altered, making it useless to the thief.

The word cryptology comes from two Greek words, *kryptos*, which means "hidden," and *logos*, which means "word." A cryptological method can take information in standard format, called plaintext or clear text, and hide it by scrambling it to make it unintelligible. This is called *encryption*. Encrypted information is sometimes called cipher text. Most methods of hiding information do so by rearranging patterns or substituting characters with other characters (see the following sidebar, "The Caesar Code"). The procedure used to unscramble the information back to plaintext, so that it can be read, is called *decryption*.

The terms *encryption* and *authentication* are often substituted with the terms *sealing* and *signing* in Exchange Server and its documentation.

Modern encryption methods scramble information by running a mathematical algorithm involving a number called a *key* on the data to be encrypted. The key is added to the algorithm by a user or by software.

The Caesar Code

One early form of cryptology was the Caesar code:

```
a b c d e f g h i j k l m n o p q r s t u v w x y z
D E F G H I J K L M N O P Q R S T U V W X Y Z A B C
```

To encrypt a message, its letters are taken one by one and substituted with the letters appearing below them. The message "Send spears" would be encrypted as "VHQG VSHDUV". The substitution method used today is much more complicated.

Because the algorithm can remain constant, and may even be published, the keys are what add the variations and secrecy to the encryption. For example, a sender encrypts data using an agreed-upon algorithm and a secret key. The recipient, using the same algorithm, must supply the same secret key for the algorithm to decrypt the data.

The length of a key determines the difficulty of breaking the encryption. Each bit in a key can be in one of two states, a one or a zero. A key of 4 bits would have only 16 (2^4) unique combinations. If the algorithm were known, it would be simple to try every possible key with the algorithm and decrypt any message. But a key of 56 bits would have 2^{56} unique combinations, which is 72 quadrillion possible keys. Keys do not make encryption unbreakable, but they make it costly, time-consuming, and impractical to break. With the computer hardware available in the 1970s, it would take over 2,000 years to decrypt a message encrypted with a 56-bit key. Recently, a network of computers working together was able to decrypt a message with 56-bit encryption in fewer than six months. Therefore, as computers get more powerful, more bits are needed to keep encryption strong. In the following sections, we discuss the two basic types of key mechanisms: public/private key pairs and secret keys.

Public/Private Key Pairs

Some encryption methods assign each user a key that is divided into two mathematically related halves, called a *key pair*. One half of the key is made public and is called the *public key*. The other half is known only by one user and is called the *private key*. Some encryption protocols have the sender encrypt a message using the recipient's public key. The only key that can be used to decrypt the message is the other half of the key, the private key, which is known only to the recipient. Because there are two different keys, this method is referred to as being *asymmetrical*.

Figure 14.5 illustrates the use of public/private key pairs. This technique is often called simply *public key encryption*.

FIGURE 14.5 Public key encryption

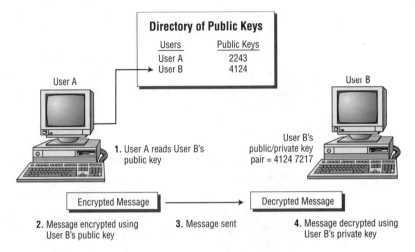

One of the most frequently used public key algorithms is called *RSA*. The RSA algorithm was developed in the late 1970s by Ron Rivest, Adi Shamir, and Leonard Adleman. They used the first letters of their last names, RSA, to name the algorithm. The RSA algorithm is computationally intense and slower than other methods, so it is not usually used to encrypt large amounts of data. However, it is used for secure user authentication.

Just as a fingerprint or retinal pattern can be used to uniquely identify a person, a key pair can be used to identify a message sender. When keys are used in this manner, they help to create *digital signatures*. A sender adds a digital signature to a message. When the recipient receives the message, they use the digital signature to authenticate (or prove) the sender's identity. Digital signatures help protect against message forgeries.

Thus, the public-key system provides two capabilities:

- Users can digitally sign data so that the recipient of the data can verify the authenticity of both the sender and the data. During this process, the sender of the data uses her own private signing key to sign the data. The data is not encrypted in any way during the signing process. The recipient of the data uses the sender's public signing key to verify the digital signature. The message is valid if the public and private signing keys correspond to one another.

- Users can encrypt data to be transferred securely. During this process, the sender uses the recipient's public key to encrypt the data, and the recipient uses her own private key to decrypt the data.

Secret Keys

A *secret key* mechanism uses the same key to both encrypt and decrypt information. When a message is encrypted, the key used by the algorithm is sent along with the message. The recipient uses the single secret key to decrypt the information. Because there is only one key, the secret-key scheme is a symmetrical method, and sometimes referred to as the *shared-secret method*. The *Data Encryption Standard (DES)* and *CAST* algorithms both use the secret-key method.

DATA ENCRYPTION STANDARD (DES)

DES was developed by IBM and in 1977 was accepted by the United States government as an official standard. DES is extremely secure and is used by many financial institutions for electronic fund transfers. DES uses a 64-bit key. The only method of cracking a DES-encrypted message is the brute-force approach of attempting every possible key.

Software-based DES encryption can be performed about 100 times faster than RSA encryption. Because of its speed, DES is suited for encrypting and decrypting large amounts of data.

When a message is encrypted in Exchange using DES, the secret key is encrypted with RSA and sent in a *lockbox* with the message. This type of hybrid system leverages the speed advantages of DES and the strength of 512-bit public-key RSA. When the message is received, the recipient's private key is used to decrypt the secret-key lockbox, and the secret key is used to decrypt the message. Figure 14.6 illustrates this type of hybrid system.

FIGURE 14.6 A hybrid encryption system using both RSA and DES

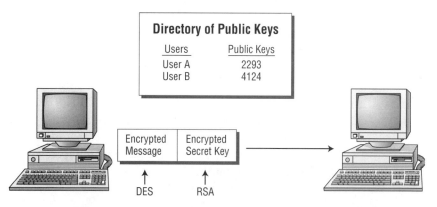

CAST

Another algorithm that uses a secret-key mechanism is the CAST algorithm. CAST derives its name from the initials of its developers, Carlisle Adams and Stafford Tavares, who worked at Northern Telecom Research. CAST uses a variable-length key between 40 and 128 bits. Exchange can use CAST 40, which uses a 40-bit key, and CAST 64, which uses a 64-bit key. A 64-bit key is 16 million times more secure than a 40-bit key.

Table 14.2 provides a summary of the encryption algorithms Exchange supports, and the locales where they can be used.

TABLE 14.2 Summary of Encryption Algorithms

Protocol	Use	Key Length	Locations
RSA	Authentication (digital signatures)	512-bit	All
DES	Data encryption	64-bit	U.S. and Canada
CAST 64	Data encryption	64-bit	U.S. and Canada
CAST 40	Data encryption	40-bit	International, except France

Certificates

While the public-key encryption method is a highly secure one, there is still a piece missing. How do you know that the public key being used is valid? The answer to this question comes in the form of a *certificate*, which you can think of as a message of authenticity associated with a public key and coming from a trusted source. Certificates allow verification of the claim that a given public key actually belongs to a given individual. This helps prevent someone from using a phony key to impersonate someone else.

The most widely used format for certificates is defined by the International Telecommunications Union (ITU) in Recommendation X.509. An *X.509 certificate* contains not only the public key, but also information that identifies the user and the organization that issued the certificate. This information includes the certificate's serial number, validity period, issuer name, and issuer signature.

Certificate Authorities

The issuer of a certificate is called a *Certificate Authority (CA)*. The CA is any trusted source that is willing to verify the identities of the people to whom it issues certificates and to associate those people with certain public and private keys. Because anyone can become a CA, certificates are only as trustworthy as the CA that issues them.

A CA issues certificates in response to a request to do so and based on the CA's policy for issuance. CAs can issue certificates to end users, computers, and other CAs. A CA accepts a certificate request, verifies the requester's information according to the policy for the CA, and then uses its own private key to digitally sign the certificate. The CA then issues the certificate to the subject (end user, computer, or other CA) of the certificate.

A CA can be provided by a third party, like VeriSign, or you can set up your own CA for use in your organization. Windows 2000 provides the Certificate Services component for setting up a CA.

CA Classes

There are two different classes of CAs:

Enterprise CA   The *Enterprise CA* acts as a CA for an enterprise, so it should come as no surprise that this type of CA requires access to the Active Directory. However, the Active Directory does not have to be installed on the same server functioning as the CA. Enterprise CAs have a number of special features:

- All users and computers in the same domain always trust the Enterprise CA.

- Certificates issued by an Enterprise CA can be used to log on to Windows 2000 domains using smart cards.

- Enterprise CAs publish certificates and Certificate Revocation List (CRL) information to the Active Directory so that the information is available throughout the enterprise.

- Enterprise CAs use certificate types and templates stored in the Active Directory (discussed a bit later in the chapter) to construct the content of new certificates.

- Enterprise CAs will always approve or reject a certificate request immediately and never mark a request as pending. The CA makes the decision based on the security permissions on the security template and on permissions and group memberships in the Active Directory.

Stand-Alone CA   The *stand-alone CA* is used to issue certificates to users outside the enterprise and does not require access to the Active Directory. For example, a stand-alone CA might be used to issue certificates to Internet users who access your company's Web site. Unlike Enterprise CAs, stand-alone CAs typically mark incoming certificate requests as pending, because the CA is not presumed to have access to the Active Directory to validate the request. Also, certificates generated by stand-alone CAs are not published if no Active Directory access is present—they must be manually distributed. Finally, certificates generated by stand-alone CAs cannot be used for smart card logons.

CA ROLES

Within each class, a CA can operate in one of two roles:

Root CA   A *root CA* is at the top of a CA hierarchy and is trusted unconditionally by a client. All certificate chains terminate at a root CA. The root CA must sign its own certificate because there is no higher authority in the certification hierarchy. Enterprise root CAs can issue certificates to end users, but are more often used to issue certificates to subordinate CAs, which in turn issue certificates to end users.

Subordinate CA   A *subordinate CA* is found underneath the root CA in the CA hierarchy and maybe even under other subordinate CAs. Subordinate CAs are typically used to issue certificates to users and computers in the organization; an organization does not have to have its own root CA. For example, you may establish a subordinate CA that receives certificates from another CA that belongs to a third-party company like VeriSign. That way, you can let a trusted third party take care of the security policy and use a subordinate CA mainly for convenience within your own network.

Certificate Trust List

The *Certificate Trust List (CTL)* for a domain holds the set of root CAs whose certificates can be trusted. You can designate CTLs for groups, users, or an entire domain. If a CA's certificate is not on the CTL, a client responds to the untrusted certificate depending on the client's configuration.

Microsoft ✓ *Exam Objective*

Configure Exchange 2000 Server for high security.

- Configure Certificate Trust Lists.

Trust in root CAs can be set by policy or by managing the CTL directly. In addition to establishing a root CA as trusted, you can also set usage properties associated with the CA. If specified, these restrict the purposes for which the CA-issued certificates are valid.

In previous versions of Exchange, the KM server managed the CTL. In Exchange 2000, that duty has passed to Windows 2000 and, for the most part, Windows manages the CTL with little or no user intervention required. One time when you may need to interact directly with the CTL is when you want to add the root certificates of outside parties (such as a company with which you are partnered) to your internal CTL. You do this by installing the external organization's root certificate on your domain controller and letting that domain controller's Group Policy Object (GPO) publish the certificate automatically. Exercise 14.2 outlines the steps for doing this. To perform this exercise, you will need to have a copy of the external certificate saved to a floppy or hard disk.

EXERCISE 14.2

Publishing an External Certificate to a Domain Controller's GPO

1. Go to Start ➢ Run.

2. In the Run field, type **MMC**, and then click OK.

3. From the Console menu of the Microsoft Management Console window, select the Add/Remove Snap-In command.

4. In the Add/Remove Snap-In window, click Add.

5. In the Add Standalone Snap-In window, select the Certificates entry, and then click Add.

6. In the Certificates Snap-In window, select the Computer Account option, and then click Finish.

7. In the Select Computer window, select the Local Computer option, and then click Finish.

8. Close the Add Standalone Snap-In window, and then click OK in the Add/Remove Snap-In window.

9. In the main console window, double-click the Certificates (Local Computer) object and then double-click Trusted Root Certification Authorities.

EXERCISE 14.2 *(continued)*

10. Click Certificates to view all of your organization's trusted root certificates. To add the external certificate, right-click Certificates, and go to All Tasks ➤ Import.

11. During the Import Wizard, you are given the chance to designate the location of the external certificate. Once the Wizard is done, click Finish to return to the Certificates snap-in.

Certificate Templates

You can configure Enterprise CAs to issue specific types of certificates to authorized users and computers. *Certificate templates* are stored in Active Directory and define the attributes for certificate types. Table 14.3 lists the standard certificate templates.

TABLE 14.3 Standard Certificate Templates

Certificate Template	Description	Note
Administrator	Used for authenticating clients and for Encrypting File System (EFS), secure mail, certificate trust list (CTL) signing, and code signing	Installed by default with Certificate Services
Authenticated Session	Used for authenticating clients	
Basic EFS	Used for Encrypting File System (EFS) operations	Installed by default with Certificate Services
CEP Encryption	Used to enroll Cisco routers for IPSec authentication certificates	
Code Signing	Used for code signing operations	

TABLE 14.3 Standard Certificate Templates *(continued)*

Certificate Template	Description	Note
Computer	Used for authenticating clients and servers	Installed by default with Certificate Services
Domain Controller	Used for authenticating domain controllers	Installed by default with Certificate Services
EFS Recovery Agent	Used for EFS data recovery operations	Installed by default with Certificate Services
Enrollment Agent	Used for authenticating administrators that request certificates on behalf of smart-card users	
Enrollment Agent (Computer)	Used for authenticating services that request certificates on behalf of other computers	Required before installing Key Management Server
Exchange Enrollment Agent (offline request)	Used for authenticating Exchange administrators who request certificates on behalf of secure mail users	
Exchange Signature Only (offline request)	Used by Exchange Server for client authentication and secure mail (used for signing only)	Required before installing Key Management Server

TABLE 14.3 Standard Certificate Templates *(continued)*

Certificate Template	Description	Note
Exchange User (offline request)	Used by Exchange Server for client authentication and secure mail (used for both signing and encryption)	Required before installing Key Management Server
IPSec	Used for IPSec authentication	
IPSec (offline request)	Used for IPSec authentication	
Root Certification Authority	Used for root CA installation operations	
Router (offline request)	Used for authentication of routers	
Smart Card Logon	Used for client authentication and logging on with a smart card	
Smart Card User	Used for client authentication, secure mail, and logging on with a smart card	
Subordinate Certification Authority (offline request)	Used to issue certificates to subordinate CAs	Installed by default with Certificate Services
Trust List Signing	Used to sign CTLs	
User	Used for client authentication and secure mail (used for signing and encryption)	Installed by default with Certificate Services

TABLE 14.3 Standard Certificate Templates *(continued)*

Certificate Template	Description	Note
User Signature Only	Used for client authentication and secure mail (used for signing only)	
Web Server (offline request)	Used to authenticate Web servers	Installed by default with Certificate Services

Certificate Store

The *Certificate Store* is a database created during the installation of a CA. If certificate services are installed on an Enterprise root CA, the store is created in the Active Directory. If services are installed on a stand-alone root CA, the store is created on the local server. The store is a repository of certificates issued by the CA, and each store can support up to 250,000 certificates.

Installing Advanced Security

There are a couple of steps you must take before you can install the Key Management Server (KMS) component of Exchange and start using advanced security. These include installing Certificate Services if they are not already installed, and installing the necessary certificate templates. Once these steps are taken, you can install and start the KMS component.

Microsoft ✓ *Exam Objective*

Configure Exchange 2000 Server for high security.

- Configure Exchange 2000 Server to issue v.3 certificates.
- Configure Key Management Server (KMS) to issue digital signatures.

Installing Microsoft Certificate Server

If *Windows 2000 Certificate Services* was not included in the installation of Windows 2000 Server (and it is not by default), you will have to install it. Exercise 14.3 outlines the steps involved in the installation. Before you get started, make sure you have access to the Windows 2000 installation files and whatever Windows Service Pack is currently installed.

EXERCISE 14.3

Installing Certificate Services

1. Click Start ➤ Settings ➤ Control Panel.

2. Double-click the Add/Remove Programs icon.

3. Click the Add/Remove Windows Components button.

4. From the list of components, select Certificate Services.

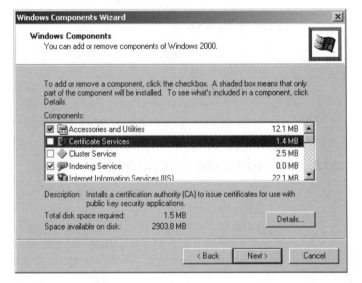

5. A dialog box opens, warning you that once you install Certificate Services, you will not be able to change the name of the computer or change your domain status. Click Yes to go on.

6. Click Next to go on.

7. Select the appropriate type for your new CA. If this is the first CA you are installing in an organization, you will probably want to choose the Enterprise Root CA option.

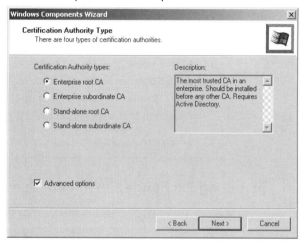

8. Click Next to go on.

9. Enter the identifying information for your CA. The CA name is required, and each CA in an organization must have a unique name. The country and expiration information is also required. All of the other information is optional and is used solely to help you identify the CA. Click Next to go on.

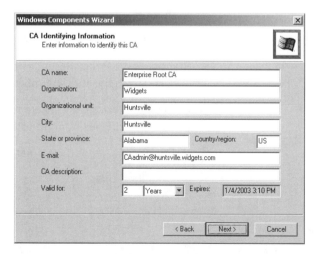

10. Confirm the location where the certificate database and certificate log should be stored. By default, these are both stored in the C:\WINNT\System32\CertLog folder. Click Next to go on.

11. A dialog box appears, letting you know that the IIS services must be stopped for installation to continue. Click OK to go on.

12. At this point, the Wizard prompts you for the location of the Windows 2000 Server installation files and the files for the latest Windows Service Pack you have applied. Once you have directed the Wizard to these locations, the Wizard begins copying files.

13. When the summary screen is displayed, click Finish.

Installing Exchange Certificate Templates

When Certificate Services is installed, a default collection of certificate templates is installed along with it (refer to Table 14.3 for a list). Before you can install KMS, you will need to install three more. Exercise 14.4 outlines the steps for doing this.

Installing Exchange Certificate Templates

1. Click Start ➤ Programs ➤ Administrative Tools ➤ Certification Authority.

2. Expand the Enterprise Root CA object in the left-hand pane.

3. Right-click the Policy Settings object and choose New Certificate To Issue from the shortcut menu.

4. Select the following certificate templates from the list (hold down the Ctrl key while clicking to select all three):

   - Enrollment Agent (Computer)

   - Exchange User

EXERCISE 14.4 *(continued)*

- Exchange Signature Only

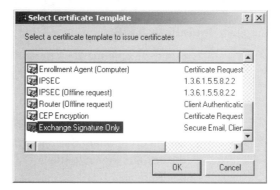

5. When all three templates are selected, click OK.

Installing KMS

Once Certificate Services and the three certificate templates are installed, it is time to install the *Key Management Server (KMS)* component. Exercise 14.5 outlines the steps involved in the installation. You will need access to the installation files for Exchange 2000 Server to install KMS.

You will also need to make a decision about how to handle the *KMS password*. Every time the KMS service starts, the KMS password is required. Setup can create the password in one of two ways:

- It can display the password so that you can write it down. If you choose this option, make sure you write it down correctly, because the password is long, and this is your *only* chance to see it. Also make sure you keep it in a very safe place. This option requires that you either be at the physical computer running the KMS service to enter the password whenever the service needs to start or that you include the key in the command-line parameter/or starting the service.

- It can copy the password to a floppy disk. You will actually need two disks for this operation—a master copy and a backup. Whenever the KMS service starts, the floppy disk must be in the A: drive of the computer running KMS for the service to start. This option allows you to start the KMS service while you are not physically at the computer (by leaving the disk in the drive), but we suggest you make sure that the server is in a secure location. We generally recommend using this option.

EXERCISE 14.5

Installing KMS

1. Run the Exchange 2000 Server setup program. You can do this from the CD-ROM or from a shared installation point. For details on running setup, see Chapter 3.

2. On the Welcome page of the Setup Wizard, click Next to go on.

3. On the Component Selection page, select the Change action from the drop-down list to the left of the Microsoft Exchange 2000 component.

4. Select the Change action from the drop-down list to the left of the Microsoft Exchange Messaging And Collaboration Services component.

5. Select the Install action from the drop-down list to left of the Microsoft Exchange Key Management Service component.

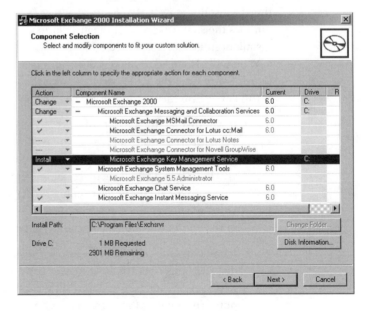

6. Click Next to go on.

7. Choose the Read Password From Disk option, and then click Next. If you choose the Manual Password Entry option, the password is displayed for you to write down; in this case, skip to step 12.

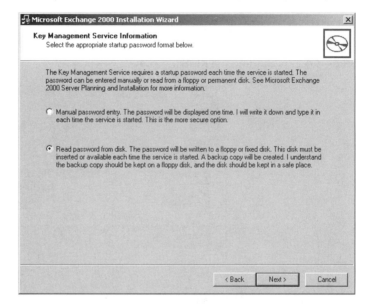

8. Leave the master and backup locations at their default and click Next. If you leave the locations at their default (A:), setup will prompt you for each disk.

9. When setup prompts you for the master disk, insert a blank floppy disk and click OK.

10. When setup prompts you for the backup disk, insert another blank floppy disk and click OK.

11. When the Component Summary page appears, click Next. Setup will begin copying files.

12. When the summary page is displayed, click Finish.

Starting the KMS Service

The KMS service does not start automatically when installation is finished or when Windows starts. To start the KMS service manually, open System Manager. If you installed KMS correctly, you'll notice that there is a new container named Advanced Security. Selecting that container reveals two components inside: Encryption Configuration and Key Manager. Right-click the Key Manager object and choose All Tasks ➢ Start Service, as shown in Figure 14.7.

FIGURE 14.7 Starting the KMS service

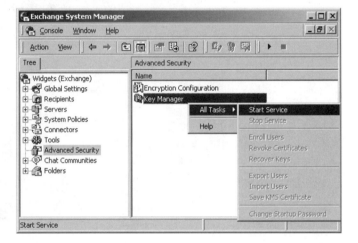

In order to start the service, you will need to enter the password in a dialog box or put the password disk in the floppy drive, depending on the option you selected during setup.

If you want the service to start automatically with Windows, you can set up the service to do so using the Service utility. If you do this, you must make sure that the password floppy is left in the A: drive and that the server is not configured to boot from the A: drive if there is a disk present.

Managing Advanced Security

The Encryption Configuration object that you saw in Figure 14.7 is used to set the encryption algorithm (DES or CAST) used by KMS; these algorithms were discussed earlier in the chapter.

The Key Manager object is used for the bulk of KMS management. Until you start the KMS service, as described previously, the only command available from the Key Manager object's shortcut menu is the Start Service command. When the service is started, a number of other commands become available. These are described in the following sections.

Microsoft ✓ ***Exam*** ***Objective***

Configure Exchange 2000 Server for high security.

- Configure Key Management Server (KMS) to issue digital signatures.

Enrolling Users

KMS uses Active Directory to enroll users in advanced security. You can enroll individual users, groups, Exchange administrative groups, or servers. When users are enrolled, KMS requests certificates for those users from Certificate Services. KMS then uses those certificates to generate and distribute two key pairs for the users. One key pair is used for signing messages and is stored on each user's client computer; the other pair is used for encryption and is stored on the KMS server.

Most of the commands for the Key Manager object require that you enter a password to access the command. By default, this password is the word "password", but you can change it using the Key Manager property pages as described later in this chapter.

To enroll users, right-click the Key Manager object and choose
All Tasks ➤ Enroll Users. This opens the dialog box shown in Figure 14.8.

FIGURE 14.8   Enrolling users in advanced security

Choosing the first option on this dialog lets you select from a simple list of users from the Global Catalog. You can enroll any number of users at a time. The second option lets you enroll groups of users by administrative group, server, or mailbox store, as shown in Figure 14.9. Simply select the objects containing users you want to enroll, and all users will be enrolled.

FIGURE 14.9   Enrolling groups of users

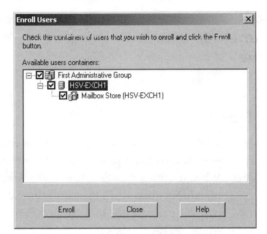

Once enrolled, a user should be able to configure advanced security within Outlook using a security token that is distributed either by e-mail or by hand, depending on the distribution method you select using the Enrollment property page of the Key Manager object, as described later in this chapter.

Revoking Certificates

Revoking a certificate disables advanced security for a user. All revoked certificates are placed on a *Certificate Revocation List (CRL)* that may be viewed at any time using the Certification Authority utility. To revoke a certificate, right-click the Key Manager object and choose the Revoke Certificates command from the All Tasks submenu. You will be presented with a list of users that have certificates. You can only revoke one user's certificate at a time. A revoked user will still be able to enroll in advanced security again with a new certificate.

Users for whom advanced security has been revoked are kept in the CRL until they are marked for deletion, which by default is about 18 months from when Exchange advanced security was first enabled. Within that time, you can recover advanced security for a user using the method described in the next section.

In order to revoke certificates from KMS, the KM server must be given the Manager permission on the Certificate Services server that issued the certificate. For this reason, it is often a good practice to give the KM server this permission on all Certificate Services servers that issued certificates to Exchange users.

Recovering Keys

There will be times when you will need to recover a user's private key. This might occur when a user forgets their password or suffers hardware failure, when users are imported from another location, or when you change the encryption used by KMS. Recovery prevents users from losing encrypted e-mail when they lose their existing keys.

Recovering a key is quite similar to enrolling a user. A new security token is generated and distributed using the same method configured for enrolling new users. After the user enters this recovery token in their client, KMS creates a new key pair for the user and returns all the user's old keys as well.

To recover a user's keys, right-click the Key Manager object and choose the All Tasks ➤ Recover Keys. You are presented with the same choices as when enrolling a new user; you can recover keys for individual users or for groups of users.

You can also enroll users, revoke certificates, and recover keys on a per user basis in Active Directory Users and Computers. Just open the properties for a user, switch to the Exchange Features page, select the E-Mail Security entry, and click Properties to access these features.

Changing the Startup Password

Unlike previous versions of Exchange, it is possible to change the startup password for the KMS service. Right-click the Key Manager object and choose the All Tasks ➤ Change Startup Password. This command presents the same dialog box you saw during KMS setup (refer to Exercise 14.5), which lets you create a new password and specify whether the password is displayed or written to floppy disk. Once you create a new password, you will need to stop and restart the KMS service for the change to take effect.

Configuring Key Manager Properties

You can access many properties for KMS by right-clicking the Key Manager object and choosing Properties from the shortcut menu. Each of the property pages is covered in the next few sections.

General Properties

The General page, shown in Figure 14.10, is used to view the certificate servers available to issue certificates to KM servers in the organization. Use the View Details button to see advanced information about a selected certificate server, including the certificate issued to the certificate server itself.

FIGURE 14.10   Configuring general properties for the Key Manager

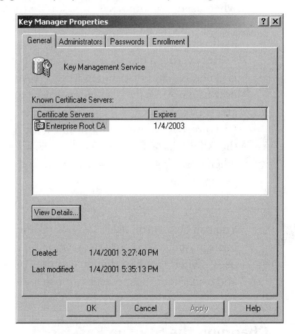

Administrators Properties

The Administrators page, shown in Figure 14.11, is used to grant administrative permissions for KMS. When KMS is installed, only the user account with which you were logged on during installation has any administrative permissions. You can add administrators to and remove administrators from the list, and each administrator can change his or her own password. As you see in the discussion of the Passwords property sheet later in this chapter, it is important that individual KM administrators are able to set their own passwords.

FIGURE 14.11   Configuring administrator properties for the Key Manager

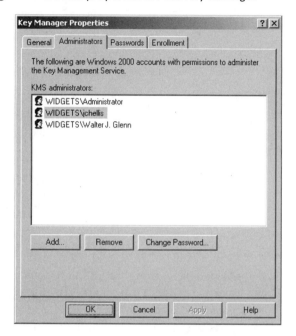

Passwords Properties

The Passwords page, shown in Figure 14.12, is used to set certain policies for administering KMS. You can require that certain administrative functions require the authorization of more than one KM administrator. The settings in Figure 14.12, for example, require that the passwords of three KM administrators be provided before a user's security keys are revoked. You cannot specify a required number of passwords that is greater than the number of administrators configured on the Administrators property sheet.

FIGURE 14.12 Configuring password properties for the Key Manager

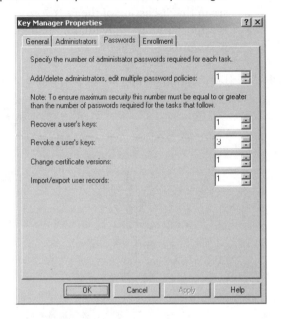

 As you have seen throughout this section, you must enter a startup password in order to use almost any of the KMS commands. By default, this password is actually "password", so you'll want to change it as soon as possible using the Passwords property page.

Enrollment Properties

When a user is enrolled in advanced security, a temporary key is generated, and this key must be given to the user. The temporary key is used by that user's mail client to establish an initial connection to KMS. During the initial connection, KMS generates the user's permanent key pair.

Microsoft
✓ *Exam*
Objective

Configure Exchange 2000 Server for high security.

- Configure Exchange 2000 Server to issue v.3 certificates.

The temporary key can be distributed by e-mail or in person. Personal distribution is much more secure and is usually done by having users pick up their tokens in person. Sending the key out by e-mail does not guarantee that the intended recipient is the one who receives it. Anyone who reads the e-mail has the key. If you want to allow distribution by e-mail, you must choose the Send Token In An E-Mail option on the Enrollment property page, shown in Figure 14.13. Click the Customize Message button to change the message that is sent to users along with the temporary keys.

FIGURE 14.13 Configuring enrollment properties for the Key Manager

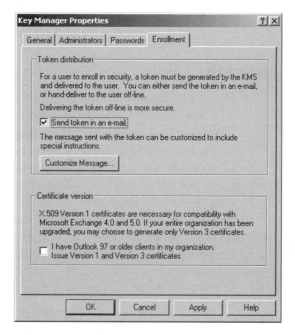

You can also use the Enrollment page to configure the version of X.509 certificate issued by KMS. Users running Outlook 98 or later can use X.509v3, the default selection. Users running Outlook 97 or earlier require X.509v1 certificates, the distribution of which you can enable at the bottom of the Enrollment page. Enabling this option causes KMS to issue both v1 and v3 certificates. Exercise 14.6 outlines the steps for enabling v1 certificates and v3 certificates.

EXERCISE 14.6

Enabling v1 and v3 X.509 Certificates

1. Click Start ➤ Programs ➤ Exchange ➤ System Manager.

2. Select the Advanced Security container.

3. Right-click the Key Manager object, and choose Properties from the shortcut menu.

4. Switch to the Enrollment page.

5. Select the I Have Outlook 97 Or Older Clients In My Organization option.

6. Click OK.

Configuring the Client

The user configures the client security components through Outlook by choosing Tools ➢ Options and selecting the Security property page (see Figure 14.14). The user can choose to encrypt messages and attachments, and to add digital signatures to messages. Before a user can configure advanced security, they must request and receive their keys and certificates from the KM server. To do this, the user must click Get A Digital ID and enter the security token they received from the KM administrator. They are prompted to enter a password to protect the digital ID they receive. Following this, an enrollment message is sent to KMS, and the user will usually get a reply within a few moments letting them know the enrollment succeeded.

FIGURE 14.14 The Security property page in the client software

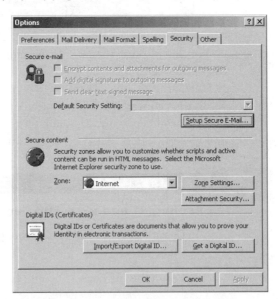

Securing Client Communications

Earlier versions of Exchange used Remote Procedure Calls (RPCs) for communication between MAPI clients (like Outlook) and the Exchange server and for communication between Exchange servers. Although Exchange 2000 now uses SMTP for most communication between servers, client-server communication still uses RPC. Therefore, one easy way to secure client-server transactions is to encrypt RPC in a client.

Encrypting RPC communications is different from encrypting messages using the advanced security provided by Exchange Server. Encrypting data for RPCs provides protection of data only while it is traveling from client to server; a message encrypted using advanced security encryption is encrypted until a recipient decrypts it within the client. Exercise 14.7 outlines the steps for configuring encrypted RPC communication in Outlook 2000.

EXERCISE 14.7

Encrypting RPCs from Outlook 2000

1. In Outlook 2000, select Tools ➢ Services.

2. On the Services page, make sure that Microsoft Exchange Server is selected, and click the Properties button.

3. Click the Advanced tab.

4. In the Encrypt Information section, select both the When Using The Network and When Using Dial-Up Networking options.

5. Click OK twice to return to Outlook 2000.

Troubleshooting Security Problems

Common security problems involve the startup password for the KM Server service and issues relating to enabling clients for advanced security. These problems and their solutions are covered next.

Microsoft ✓ **Exam Objective**	**Diagnose and resolve security problems that involve user keys.**

Table 14.4 provides a list of common advanced security problems and their solutions.

TABLE 14.4 Common Security Problems and Their Solutions

Problem	Solution
KM Server service will not start.	Either the startup floppy disk is not inserted, or the password value is not entered (or is entered incorrectly) in the startup parameters for the KMS service. The latter situation can be checked through the Services utility. Also note that the password is case sensitive.
The KM server is not running immediately after its installation.	Manually start the KMS service from the Services tool.
A user cannot use advanced security.	Enable advanced security for the user. Inform the user of their security token. Instruct the user how to enable advanced security in Outlook.
A user forgets their password for access to their private security keys.	The KM administrator must perform a recovery of that user's security keys. That is done using the Key Manager object in System Manager or the user object in Active Directory Users and Computers.
A user's security keys expire, and she cannot use advanced security.	The KM administrator must perform a renewal of that user's security keys. That is done using the Key Manager object in System Manager or the user object in Active Directory Users and Computers.

Summary

Three aspects of security were covered in this chapter. The first aspect was Exchange Server's basic reliance on the Windows 2000 security services. These include user accounts and authentication, Exchange administrative groups, system and recipient policies, and auditing.

The second aspect concerns networking security. This includes the protection of virtual servers through authentication, as well as the use of firewalls to protect private network resources from unauthorized access. Firewalls provide protection by closing access to port numbers, except for those applications that are permitted to pass data through the firewall. Exchange 2000 Server extends the use of firewalls with application of front-end and back-end servers.

Advanced security facilitates the authentication of a message sender's identity and the privacy of message data. Authentication is accomplished using digital signatures, and message privacy is maintained using encryption. In Exchange terminology, *signing* refers to authentication, and *sealing* refers to encryption.

The RSA algorithm is used by Exchange to implement digital signatures. RSA uses a key pair that includes a public key that can be accessed by anyone, and a private key that is only known by one user. While these two keys are different, they are mathematically related, and information is unlocked with the other half of the key that was used to lock it.

The algorithms that Exchange uses for sealing data are DES and CAST. These algorithms utilize a single secret key that is used to both seal and unseal message content. This secret key is itself sealed using RSA and sent along with the message.

KM server management duties include key and certificate revocation and client security information recovery and renewal. The KM server can also be configured to support multiple administrators.

Most of the problems that occur when using KMS relate to starting the service and enabling clients. When starting the service, make sure that you are entering the correct password or that the password floppy is in the drive. When users experience trouble, make sure that they are enrolled and that they are using the correct token when they try to enable advanced security on their client.

Key Terms

Before you take the exam, be certain you are familiar with the following terms:

Access Control List (ACL)	Enterprise CA
administrative group	firewall
Anonymous authentication	front-end servers
auditing	Integrated Windows authentication
back-end servers	Kerberos version 5 authentication
Basic (Clear-Text) authentication	key
Basic over Secure Sockets Layer (SSL) authentication	Key Management Server (KMS)
CAST	key pair
certificate	KMS password
Certificate Authority (CA)	lockbox
Certificate Revocation List (CRL)	perimeter network
Certificate Store	permission
Certificate templates	policy
Certificate Trust List (CTL)	port number
Data Encryption Standard (DES)	private key
decryption	public key
demilitarized zone (DMZ)	public key encryption
digital signature	public key infrastructure (PKI)
encryption	recipient policies

root CA

secret key

stand-alone CA

subordinate CA

system policies

well-known port numbers

Windows 2000 Certificate Services

X.509 certificate

Review Questions

1. You have just installed the Exchange Key Management Server. During the setup, you chose to use the floppy disk option for the KMS services password. You are administering Exchange from your workstation and shut down the KMS service. When you are done, you are ready to restart the KMS service. You put the password disk into your drive, but the KMS service will not start. What is the problem?

   A. You can only start the service from the actual KMS server.

   B. The password disk must be in the A: drive of the actual KMS server.

   C. Your workstation does not have the Manage permission on the KMS server.

   D. Your workstation has not been issued a certificate.

2. As administrator of a KM server, you receive a request to enable advanced security from a user named Alex. What must you do to accomplish that? (Choose all that apply.)

   A. Instruct Alex how to use Windows 2000 domain logons.

   B. Enroll Alex's user object in advanced security.

   C. Instruct Alex how to perform person-to-person key exchange.

   D. Instruct Alex to configure his workstation as a Certificate Authority.

   E. Provide a security token to Alex and have him enter it in his Microsoft Outlook application.

3. Your KM server is configured to use CAST-40 encryption. You now want to change the encryption protocol to CAST-64. What must you do to change and enable clients to use the new algorithm? (Choose all that apply.)

   A. Reinstall KM server.

   B. Stop and restart the System Attendant.

   C. Configure each Exchange client application to use the new algorithm.

   D. Change the preferred encryption algorithm in the properties of the Encryption Configuration object.

   E. Recover the client encryption keys from all of the Exchange users.

4. Which of the following types of Windows authentication may be used in a mixed-mode Windows 2000 network? (Choose all that apply.)

   A. Kerberos V3

   B. Kerberos V5

   C. NTLM

   D. Basic

   E. Basic over SSL

5. You have just configured your Exchange server for IMAP4 client access. IMAP4 clients can be authenticated with either Basic (Clear-Text) or Basic over SSL. The administrator of your firewall informs you that the firewall will allow traffic from SMTP (port 25), IMAP4 (port 143), and HTTP (port 80). What additional port must be opened on the firewall to allow for your Exchange server IMAP4 configuration to be used?

   A. 993

   B. 443

   C. 137

   D. 135

6. Which of the following constructs is used to verify the identity of a person associated with a public key?

   A. Certificates

   B. Private key

   C. Trust

   D. Certificate Authority

7. Which of the following authentication protocols passes a person's username and password over the network? (Choose all that apply.)

   A. Basic

   B. Basic over SSL

   C. NTLM

   D. Kerberos V5

8. You are currently upgrading your client base from Outlook 97 to Outlook 2000. However, you still expect many people to be using Outlook 97 for some time and want them to be able to sign and seal messages. What types of certificates should you configure KMS to distribute? (Choose all that apply.)

   A. X.509 v1

   B. X.509 v2

   C. X.509 v3

   D. X.509 v5

9. A new Exchange server has been installed and configured for HTTP and POP3. The network project plan calls for allowing the following clients to access this server: HTTP using Windows Integrated authentication, and POP3 and Microsoft Outlook using secure passwords. You refer to the current firewall configuration and see that it is open to DNS, HTTP, SMTP, and ports higher than 1023. What ports, if any, must you open to enable the desired Exchange clients to pass through the firewall? (Choose all that apply.)

   A. 389

   B. 110

   C. 443

   D. 135

   E. All of the above

10. When a user digitally signs a message, what two keys are used in the process?

   A. The sender's public signing key

   B. The sender's private signing key

   C. The recipient's public signing key

   D. The recipient's private signing key

11. Your Exchange server is configured for anonymous HTTP clients, but those clients that are outside your firewall report that they cannot access the directory. What is the problem?

   A. The DS needs to be stopped and restarted.

   B. Windows Integrated authentication needs to be enabled.

   C. The HTTP port is not open on the firewall.

   D. Basic (Clear-Text) authentication is needed.

12. When a user encrypts a message, what keys are used in the process? (Choose all that apply.)

    A. The sender's public encryption key

    B. The sender's private encryption key

    C. The recipient's public encryption key

    D. The recipient's private encryption key

    E. A secret key

13. Your network is configured as shown below. Your company uses two firewalls to create a perimeter network. Your front-end server has its name and IP address entered into a public DNS server on the Internet. Both firewalls prohibit traffic on all ports that are not explicitly allowed. The ports that are currently open on both firewalls are port 25 (SMTP), port 53 (DNS), and port 80 (HTTP)

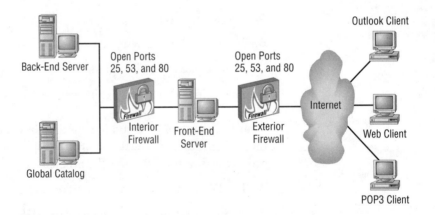

    Required result:

    Management requires that users are able to connect over the Internet to your Exchange server using Microsoft Outlook. Policy dictates that passwords be transmitted in a secure manner.

Optional results:

Management would like Web clients that do not support Windows Integrated authentication to be able to connect to your Exchange server, but not transmit user information in clear text.

Management would like POP3 clients to be able to connect to the Exchange server and download their messages.

Proposed solution:

Open port 135 on the exterior firewall.

Open port 110 on the exterior firewall.

Open port 443 on the exterior firewall.

What results does the proposed solution produce?

A. The proposed solution produces the required result and the optional results.

B. The proposed solution produces the required result and produces only one of the optional results.

C. The proposed solution produces the required result but does not produce either of the optional results.

D. The proposed solution does not produce the required result.

14. Your network is configured as shown below. Your company uses two firewalls to create a perimeter network. Your front-end server has its name and IP address entered into a public DNS server on the Internet. Both firewalls prohibit traffic on all ports that are not explicitly allowed. The ports that are currently open on both firewalls are port 25 (SMTP), port 53 (DNS), and port 80 (HTTP).

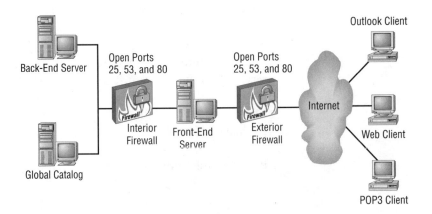

Required result:

Management requires that users are able to connect over the Internet to your Exchange server using Microsoft Outlook. Policy dictates that passwords be transmitted in a secure manner.

Optional results:

Management would like Web clients that do not support Windows Integrated authentication to be able to connect to your Exchange server, but not transmit user information in clear text.

Management would like POP3 clients to be able to connect to the Exchange server and download their messages.

Proposed solution:

Open port 135 on the exterior firewall.

Open port 110 on the exterior firewall.

Open port 443 on the exterior firewall.

Open port 3268 on the interior firewall.

What results does the proposed solution produce?

A. The proposed solution produces the required result and the optional results.

B. The proposed solution produces the required result and produces only one of the optional results.

C. The proposed solution produces the required result but does not produce either of the optional results.

D. The proposed solution does not produce the required result.

15. Your network is configured as shown below. Your company uses two firewalls to create a perimeter network. Your front-end server has its name and IP address entered into a public DNS server on the Internet. Both firewalls prohibit traffic on all ports that are not explicitly allowed. The ports that are currently open on both firewalls are port 25 (SMTP), port 53 (DNS), and port 80 (HTTP).

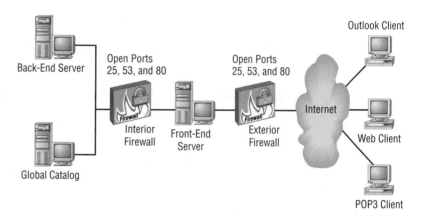

Required result:

Management requires that users are able to connect over the Internet to your Exchange server using Microsoft Outlook. Policy dictates that passwords be transmitted in a secure manner.

Optional results:

Management would like Web clients that do not support Windows Integrated authentication to be able to connect to your Exchange server, but not transmit user information in clear text.

Management would like POP3 clients to be able to connect to the Exchange server and download their messages.

Proposed solution:

Open port 135 on the exterior firewall.

Open port 110 on the exterior firewall.

Open port 3268 on the interior firewall.

What results does the proposed solution produce?

A. The proposed solution produces the required result and the optional results.

B. The proposed solution produces the required result and produces only one of the optional results.

C. The proposed solution produces the required result but does not produce either of the optional results.

D. The proposed solution does not produce the required results.

16. What security feature of Windows 2000 Server lets you log the actions of users and groups based on certain criteria?

   A. Auditing

   B. Diagnostics logging

   C. Accounting

   D. Tracking

17. You have configured an X.400 Connector between your mixed-mode organization and a foreign messaging system. The ports that are currently open on your company's firewall are port 25 (SMTP), port 53 (DNS), and port 80 (HTTP). What additional port would you need to open to allow the traffic for the X.400 Connector to pass?

   A. 98

   B. 102

   C. 110

   D. 119

8. A, C. You can use the Enrollment property page of the Key Manager object to configure the version of X.509 certificate issued by KMS. Users running Outlook 98 or later can use X.509v3, the default selection. Users running Outlook 97 or earlier require X.509v1 certificates, the distribution of which you can enable at the bottom of the Enrollment page. Enabling this option causes KMS to issue both v1 and v3 certificates. Exercise 14.6 outlines the steps for enabling v1 certificates and v3 certificates.

9. B, D. Opening port 110 allows POP3 traffic to pass. Opening port 135 allows RPC traffic to pass and thus enables Microsoft Outlook clients. Since the HTTP port 80 and all ports over 1023 are already open, HTTP is already allowed using Windows Integrated authentication.

10. A, B. The sender's own private signing key is used to sign the data. The data is not encrypted in any way during the signing process. The recipient of the data uses the sender's public signing key to verify the digital signature. The message is valid if the public and private signing keys correspond to one another.

11. C. If outside users report that they are having trouble making a connection, one of the first things you should check is whether the firewall is configured to allow the traffic to pass. One way to verify that the problem is with the firewall is to determine whether an internal user can connect to the same server with the same protocol.

12. C, D, E. First, the sender's client generates a secret key to encrypt the actual message and any attachments. Next, the recipient's public encryption key to encrypt the secret key in a lockbox is sent to the recipient. The receiving client then uses the recipient's private encryption key to decrypt the secret key, which is then used to decrypt the message.

13. D. In order to let the appropriate clients access the front-end server, you must open port 135 (RPC) for Outlook, port 110 (POP3) for POP3 clients, and port 443 (HTTP over SSL) for Web clients on the exterior firewall. The front-end and back-end server communicate using port 80 (HTTP), which is already open on the interior firewall. However, the front-end server must also be able to look up information in the Global Catalog so that it knows the appropriate back-end server to use. Therefore, you must also open port 3268 on the interior firewall.

14. A. In order to let the appropriate clients access the front-end server, you must open port 135 (RPC) for Outlook, port 110 (POP3) for POP3 clients, and port 443 (HTTP over SSL) for Web clients on the exterior firewall. The front-end and back-end server communicate using port 80 (HTTP), which is already open on the interior firewall. However, the front-end server must also be able to look up information in the Global Catalog so that it knows the appropriate back-end server to use. Therefore, you must also open port 3268 on the interior firewall.

15. B. In order to let the appropriate clients access the front-end server, you must open port 135 (RPC) for Outlook, port 110 (POP3) for POP3 clients, and port 443 (HTTP over SSL) for Web clients on the exterior firewall. The front-end and back-end server communicate using port 80 (HTTP), which is already open on the interior firewall. However, the front-end server must also be able to look up information in the Global Catalog so that it knows the appropriate back-end server to use. Therefore, you must also open port 3268 on the interior firewall.

16. A. Auditing is a Windows 2000 feature that logs the actions of users and groups based on certain criteria. For example, a Windows 2000 server can audit successful and failed logon attempts or access to certain files.

17. B. MTA traffic using X.400 over TCP/IP operates on port 102.

18. C. RSA is the only public-key encryption algorithm provided with Windows 2000. Kerberos is an authentication algorithm. DES and CAST are secret-key encryption algorithms.

19. C. Enterprise CAs are used as a CA for an enterprise and require Active Directory access. The stand-alone CA is used to issue certificates to users outside the enterprise and do not require access to the Active Directory. There is no such thing as an organization CA or a domain CA.

20. A, C. Trust in root CAs can be set by policy or by managing the Certificate Trust List (CTL) directly. You would add the root certificate of an outside party to your CTL by installing the root certificate on your domain controller and letting that domain controller's Group Policy Object (GPO) publish the certificate automatically.

Glossary

A

Access Control Entries (ACEs)   Entries on an Access Control List (ACL) that define a user's permission for an object.

Access Control List (ACL)   A list of users and groups allowed to access a resource and the particular permissions each user has been granted or denied.

Active Directory   Stores information about objects on a Windows 2000 network and makes this information easy for administrators and users to find and use.

Active Directory Account Cleanup Wizard   Designed to merge duplicate accounts that may be created when multiple directories are migrated to Active Directory.

Active Directory Connector (ADC)   Runs on an Exchange 2000 server and synchronizes directory information between Active Directory and Exchange 5.*x* servers in the site. ADC also synchronizes configuration information with those servers using the SRS as an intermediary.

Active Server Pages (ASP)   A specification for a dynamically generated Web page that uses ActiveX scripting. IIS uses ASP to generate many of the pages it displays.

ActiveX   The set of Microsoft protocols that specify how software components can communicate with each other through the use of objects.

address encapsulation   Placing a sender's native Exchange address in the form of a valid SMTP address. The encapsulated address is placed in the From field of the message.

address space   The set of remote addresses that can be reached through a particular connector. Each connector must have at least one entry in its address space.

administrative group   Used to define administrative boundaries within an Exchange environment.

age limit   A property that specifies the length of time a unit of data may remain in its container (e.g., public folder).

alias   An alternative name for an object. In Exchange 2000, an alias is normally generated for a user based on the user's name.

All Public Folders   The name for the default public folder tree in an Exchange 2000 organization. This tree is accessible by all clients that can access public folders.

Anonymous access   Accessing a server by logging in using a Windows 2000 account set up for general access.

Anonymous authentication   *See* Anonymous access.

Application Programming Interface (API)   A collection of programming commands (frequently called interfaces) that can invoke the functions of a program. Other programs can use a program's API to request services or communicate with that program. For example, Windows 98 contains an API referred to as the win32 API. For an application to request a service from Windows 98, it must issue that request using a win32 API.

architecture   The description of the components of a product or system, what they are, what they do, and how they relate to each other.

attribute   A characteristic of an object. For example, attributes of a mailbox-enabled user include display name and storage limits. The terms *attribute* and *property* are synonymous.

auditing   Windows 2000 can be configured to monitor and record certain events. This can help diagnose security events. The audit information is written to the Windows 2000 Event Log.

authentication   A process whereby the credentials of an object, such as a user, must be validated before the object is allowed to access or use another object, such as a server or a protocol. For instance, the Microsoft Exchange Server POP3 protocol can be configured to only allow access to POP3 clients that use the Integrated Windows authentication method.

B

back-end server   Exchange 2000 allows the use of front-end servers, which accept incoming client requests for information and then forward those requests to back-end servers that actually hold user information. This lets you balance the load between servers and provide a single namespace from your client's perspective.

backfill   The process used in public folder replication to fill in messaging data that is missing from a replica.

Bad Mail folder   The folder in which SMTP stores undeliverable messages that cannot be returned to the sender.

Basic (Clear-Text) authentication   Requires the user to submit a valid Windows username and password. The username and password are sent across the network as unencrypted clear text.

Basic over Secure Sockets Layer (SSL) authentication   Extends the Basic (Clear-Text) authentication method by allowing an SSL server to encrypt the username and password before they are sent across the network.

bridgehead server   A server within one bounded area, such as a routing group, that is designated to deliver data or messages to another area.

C

caching   Temporarily storing data in random access memory (RAM) where it can be accessed much faster than it could be from the disk.

CAST   A protocol that uses a secret-key mechanism, CAST uses a variable-length key between 40 and 128 bits. Exchange can use CAST 40, which uses a 40-bit key, and CAST 64, which uses a 64-bit key. *See also* Data Encryption Standard (DES).

Categorizer   A component of the Exchange 2000 routing engine used to resolve the sender and recipient for a message, expanding any distribution groups as needed. In previous versions of Exchange Server, this task was performed by the MTA.

centralized model   An administrative model in which one administrator or group of administrators maintains complete control over an entire Exchange organization.

certificate   Allows verification of the claim that a given public key actually belongs to a given individual. This helps prevent someone from using a phony key to impersonate someone else. A certificate is similar to a token.

Certificate Authority (CA)   The central authority that distributes, publishes, and validates security keys. The Windows 2000 Certificates Services component performs this role. *See also* public key, private key.

Certificate Revocation List (CRL)   A list containing all certificates in an organization that have been revoked.

Certificate Store   A database created during the installation of a Certificate Authority (CA) that is a repository of certificates issued by the CA.

certificate templates   Stored in Active Directory and define the attributes for certificates. The Enrollment Agent, Exchange Signature Only, and Exchange User certificate templates must be installed before installing Key Management Server (KMS).

Certificate Trust List (CTL)   Holds the set of root CAs whose certificates can be trusted. You can designate CTLs for groups, users, or an entire domain.

challenge/response   A general term for a class of security mechanisms, including Microsoft-authentication methods, that use Windows 2000 network security and an encrypted password.

change number   One of the constructs used to keep track of public folder replication throughout an organization and to determine whether a public folder is synchronized. The change number is made up of a globally unique identifier for the Information Store and a change counter that is specific to the server on which a public folder resides.

channel   A specific discussion forum within a chat community.

chat   A real-time, text-based, conversation performed over a computer network or networks. Exchange 2000 Server Enterprise edition features a Chat Service component. *See also* Internet Relay Chat (IRC), Chat Service.

chat channel   Often referred to as a chat room; a channel represents a topic of conversation in a chat community.

chat community   A virtual server on an Exchange server that is run by a single instance of the Chat Service.

Chat Service   The Exchange 2000 Server implementation of the IRC chat protocol. *See also* chat, Internet Relay Chat (IRC).

checkpoint file   The file (EDB.CHK) that contains the point in a transaction log which is the boundary between data that has been committed and data that has not yet been committed to an Exchange database.

child domain   Any domain configured underneath another domain in a domain tree.

circular logging   The process of writing new information in transaction log files over information that has already been committed. Instead of repeatedly creating new transaction logs, the Exchange database engine "circles back" and reuses log files that have been fully committed to the database. Circular logging keeps down the number of transaction logs on the disk. These logs cannot be used to re-create a database because the logs do not have a complete set of data. The logs contain only the most recent data not yet committed to a database. Circular logging is disabled by default.

Client Access License (CAL)   Gives a user the legal right to access an Exchange server. Any client software that has the ability to be a client to Microsoft Exchange Server is legally required to have a CAL purchased for it.

client/server messaging   A system in which tasks are divided between the client processes and server processes. Each side works to accomplish specific parts of the task.

cluster   A group of servers (also called nodes) that function together as a single unit.

Clustering   A Windows service that enables multiple physical servers to be logically grouped together for reasons of fault tolerance.

coexistence   When two different systems of any type are present on the same network. For example, Exchange 2000 Server can coexist with MS Mail or previous versions of Exchange.

committed   When a transaction is transferred from a transaction log to an Exchange database, it has been committed.

Computer Management snap-in   An administrative tool holding a variety of utilities, including Event Viewer and disk management tools.

connection agreement   Defined for an Active Directory Connector to replicate specified directory objects on an Exchange 5.x server to the Active Directory and can even be configured to replicate at certain times.

directory replication   The transferring of directory information from one server to another. In Active Directory, directory information is replicated between domain controllers. In previous versions of Exchange, directory information is replicated between Exchange servers.

directory replication bridgehead server   In previous versions of Exchange, the Exchange server designated as the server that will send site directory information to another site. Only one server in a site can be assigned to replicate information with each remote site. There can be more than one directory replication bridgehead server in a site, but each must connect with a unique remote site. However, one server can perform directory replication with multiple remote sites.

Directory Service (DS)   In Exchange 5.*x*, creates and manages the storage of all information about Exchange objects, such as the organization, site, servers, mailboxes, distribution lists, and public folders. This functionality is assumed by Active Directory in Exchange 2000.

Directory Synchronization Agent (DXA)   The Exchange 2000 component used to replicate information with MS Mail postoffices.

Directory Synchronization Protocol   The MS Mail protocol used to synchronize directory information between MS Mail postoffices. One server is designated as the dirsync server, and the other servers are designated as dirsync requestors. The dirsync server maintains the master copy of a network's directory. The dirsync requestors send any new directory information to the dirsync server, and request a copy of the master directory. *See also* dirsync requestor, dirsync server.

dirsync requestor   A type of MS Mail postoffice that sends its new directory information to the designated dirsync server, and requests a copy of the master directory. These actions are triggered by the T1, T2, and T3 events. *See also* Directory Synchronization Protocol, T1 event, T2 event, and T3 event.

dirsync server   A type of MS Mail postoffice that maintains the master copy of a network's MS Mail directory information. It also responds to requests by sending a copy of the master directory to dirsync requestors. These actions are triggered by the T1, T2, and T3 events. *See also* Directory Synchronization Protocol, T1 event, T2 event, and T3 event.

Disaster Recovery Mode   A mode in which you can run Exchange 2000 Server setup that lets you recover an Exchange installation after a failure.

discretionary access control list (DACL)   A list of Access Control Entries (ACEs) that give users and groups specific permissions on an object.

discussion thread   A collection of postings to a public folder related to a single subject.

dismounting   The process of taking a public or private store offline.

distribution group   An Active Directory group formed so that a single e-mail message may be sent to the group and then sent automatically to all members of the group. Unlike security groups, distribution groups don't provide any security function.

domain   A group of computers and other resources that are part of a Windows 2000 network and share a common directory database.

domain controller   A computer running Windows 2000 Server that validates user network access and manages Active Directory.

domain forest   A group of one or more domain trees that do not necessarily form a contiguous namespace, but may share a common schema and Global Catalog.

Domain Name Service (DNS)   The primary provider of name resolution within an organization.

DomainPrep   An Exchange 2000 Server setup switch that is used to prepare an Active Directory domain prior to Exchange installation.

domain tree   A hierarchical arrangement of one or more Windows 2000 domains that share a common namespace.

DNS   *See* Domain Name Service (DNS).

E

EHLO   The ESMTP command used by one host to initiate communications with another host.

e-mail   Electronic messages sent between users of different computers.

encryption   The process of scrambling data to make it unreadable. The intended recipient will decrypt the data into plaintext in order to read it.

Enterprise CA   Acts as a Certificate Authority for an enterprise and requires access to the Active Directory. *See also* Certificate Authority (CA).

Enterprise edition   Edition of Exchange 2000 Server that contains all the features of the Standard edition as well as Chat Service, Clustering, and distributed configurations. The Enterprise edition permits servers to contain more than one mailbox store and allows stores to be over 16GB.

ETRN   An SMTP command used by SMTP clients using dial-up connections to request their queued mail from their SMTP server.

Event Log   A set of three logs (Application, Security, and System) maintained by Windows 2000 Server. The operating system and many applications, such as Exchange 2000 Server, write software events to the Event Log.

Exchange 2000 Conferencing Server   Add-on product for Exchange 2000 Server that features advanced data, voice, and video conferencing tools.

Exchange Administration Delegation Wizard   Tool in System Manager that lets you select a user or group and assign them a specific administrative role in an Exchange organization. *See also* Exchange Administrator role, Exchange Full Administrator role, Exchange View-Only Administrator role.

Exchange Administrator role   Gives users the same full administrative capability as the Exchange Full Administrator role, but does not give them permission to modify permissions for objects. *See also* Exchange Administration Delegation Wizard, Exchange Full Administrator role.

Exchange Advanced Security snap-in   The Microsoft Management Console utility used to control Exchange 2000's KM server.

Exchange Conferencing Services snap-in   The Microsoft Management Console utility used to control Exchange 2000's Chat and Instant Messaging services.

Exchange DSAccess   A component that enables other Exchange 2000 components to communicate with Active Directory using the LDAP protocol.

Exchange Folders snap-in   The Microsoft Management Console utility used to control Exchange 2000's public folders.

Exchange Full Administrator role   Gives users full administrative capability within an organization. They can add, delete, and rename objects, as well as modify permissions on objects. *See also* Exchange Administration Delegation Wizard.

Exchange Interprocess Communication Layer (ExIPC)   The process that manages several queues used for communications between IIS and Exchange 2000 Server.

Exchange Message Tracking Center snap-in   The Microsoft Management Console utility used to control Exchange 2000's Message Tracking Center. *See also* Message Tracking Center (MTC).

Exchange System Manager   A snap-in for the Microsoft Management Console used to manage an Exchange 2000 organization.

Exchange View-Only Administrator role   Lets users view Exchange configuration information, but not modify it in any way. *See also* Exchange Administration Delegation Wizard.

expanding a distribution group   The process of determining the individual addresses contained within a distribution group. This process is performed by the home server of the user sending the message to the group unless an expansion server is specified for the group.

extended IRC (IRCX)   A set of extensions developed by Microsoft that enhance the functionality of the IRC protocol and add several new commands with which you can manage users and channels on a chat server.

extended permissions   Permissions added to the standard Windows 2000 permissions when Exchange 2000 Server is installed.

Extensible Storage Engine (ESE)   The database engine used by Exchange 2000 Server.

F

firewall   A set of mechanisms that separate and protect your internal network from unauthorized external users and networks. Firewalls can restrict inbound and outbound traffic, as well as analyze all traffic between your network and the outside.

folder-based application   An application built within a public folder by customizing properties of the folder, such as permissions, views, rules, and the folder forms library to store and present data to users.

foreign system   A non-Exchange message system.

ForestPrep   An Exchange 2000 Server setup switch that is used to prepare an Active Directory forest prior to Exchange installation.

forest root domain   The first domain installed in a domain forest and the basis for the naming of all domains in the forest.

Forms Registry   Stores the Outlook Web Access (OWA) forms rendered by Internet Information Server (IIS) and passed to the client.

frame   The unit of information sent by a Data Link protocol, such as Ethernet or Token Ring.

free/busy   Terminology used in the Microsoft Schedule+ application to denote an unscheduled period of time (free) or a scheduled period of time (busy).

front-end server   *See* back-end server.

full-text indexing   A feature that can be enabled for a store in which every word in the store (including those in attachments) is indexed for much faster search results.

Fully Qualified Domain Name (FQDN)   The full DNS path of an Internet host. An example is `sales.dept4.widget.com`.

function call   An instruction in a program that calls (invokes) a function. For example, MAPIReadMail is a MAPI function call.

G

GAL   *See* Global Address List (GAL).

gateway   Third-party software that permits Exchange to interoperate with a foreign message system. *See also* connector.

Gateway Address Routing Table (GWART)   Used by previous versions of Exchange; contains all the address space entries for all the connectors in a site. In Exchange 2000, this is replaced by the link state table.

gateway postoffice   The MS Mail postoffice configured to receive messages to be delivered through a gateway.

general-purpose trees   Public folder trees added to an Exchange organization beyond the default public folder tree. General-purpose trees are not accessible by MAPI clients like Microsoft Outlook.

Global Address List (GAL)   A database of all the recipients in an Exchange organization, such as mailboxes, distribution lists, custom recipients, and public folders.

Global Catalog   Used to hold information about all objects in a forest. The Global Catalog enables users and applications to find objects in an Active Directory domain tree if the user or application knows one or more attributes of the target object.

group   A collection of users and other groups that may be assigned permissions or made part of an e-mail distribution list.

groupware   Any application that allows groups of people to store and share information.

GWART   *See* Gateway Address Routing Table (GWART).

H

HELO   The SMTP command used by one host to initiate communications with another host.

hierarchy   Any structure or organization that uses class, grade, or rank to arrange objects.

home server   The Exchange server on which an object physically resides.

HTML   *See* HyperText Markup Language (HTML).

HTTP   *See* HyperText Transfer Protocol (HTTP).

HTTP Digest authentication   An Internet standard that allows authentication of clients to occur using a series of challenges and responses over HTTP.

HyperText Markup Language (HTML)   The script language used to create content for the World Wide Web (WWW). HTML can create hyperlinks between objects on the Web.

HyperText Transfer Protocol (HTTP)   The Internet protocol used to transfer information on the World Wide Web (WWW).

I

IIS metabase   The Registry-like database of configuration information maintained by Internet Information Server.

Inbox   The storage folder that receives new incoming messages.

Inbox Repair tool   A utility (Scanpst.exe) that is used to repair corrupt personal folder (.PST) files.

incremental backup   Method in which all files are backed up that have changed since the last normal or incremental backup.

Information Store   *See* Store.exe

inheritance   The process through which permissions are passed down from a parent container to objects inside that container (child objects).

in-place upgrade   Performing a direct upgrade to Exchange 2000 Server on a computer running Exchange Server 5.5 with Service Pack 3.

Installable File System (IFS)   Permits normal network client redirectors, such as Exchange, to share folders and items. This is a means of exposing the Exchange Information Store to users and applications on the network.

installer package (MSI file)   One of the files generated by Windows Installer; used to control configuration information during installation. The installer package contains a database that describes the configuration information. *See also* installer transform (MST file).

installer transform (MST file)   One of the files generated by Windows Installer; used to control configuration information during installation. The transform file contains modifications that are to be made as Windows Installer installs Outlook. *See also* installer package (MSI file).

Instant Messaging domain   A DNS name that identifies user accounts. Instant Messaging routers answer queries for an Instant Messaging domain and make Instant Messaging available to internal and Internet users.

Instant Messaging home server   A virtual server that actually hosts Instant Messaging user accounts. *See also* Instant Messaging router.

Instant Messaging router   A virtual server that receives messages, looks up the recipient of that message in Active Directory, determines the recipient's destination home server, and then forwards the messages to that home server. *See also* Instant Messaging home server.

Instant Messaging   A real-time communication service that also lets users determine presence information about other users.

Integrated Windows authentication   Requires the user to provide a valid Windows username and password. However, the user's credentials are never sent across the network. If you are running a mixed-mode Windows 2000 network, this method uses the NTLM authentication protocol used by Windows NT 4.0. If your network is running in native mode, this method uses Kerberos V5.

Internet Information Server (IIS)   A built-in component of Windows 2000 Server that allows access to resources on the server through various Internet protocols, such as POP3, IMAP4, and HTTP.

Internet Locator Server (ILS)   A Microsoft server that monitors which users are online and available for collaboration, such as participating in a chat, a whiteboarding session, or even a videoconference.

Internet Message Access Protocol version 4 (IMAP4)   An Internet retrieval protocol that enables clients to access and manipulate messages in their mailbox on a remote server. IMAP4 provides additional functions over POP3, such as access to subfolders (not merely the Inbox folder), and selective downloading of messages.

Internet Relay Chat (IRC)   An Internet protocol used to enable real-time, text-based conversations on a network or networks. Conversations are called chats or sessions, and the organization of a number of chats on a particular topic is called a channel.

interoperability   The ability of different systems to work together (for example, the ability of two different messaging systems to exchange messages).

K

Kerberos version 5 (V5)   The primary form of user authentication used by Windows 2000.

key   A randomly generated number used to implement advanced security, such as encryption or digital signatures. *See also* key pair, public key, private key.

Key Management Server (KMS)   A component of Exchange 2000 that distributes security keys to users based on certificates issued by Windows Certificate Services.

Key Management Server (KMS) database   The database used to hold information created by KMS.

key pair   A key that is divided into two mathematically related halves. One half (the public key) is made public; the other half (the private key) is known by only one user.

KMS password   The password used to start the KMS service. The password can be stored on a floppy or entered manually when the service starts.

L

leaf object   An object in a Microsoft Management Console window that does not contain any other objects.

Lightweight Directory Access Protocol (LDAP)   An Internet protocol used for client access to an X.500-based directory, such as Active Directory.

link   Generic term referring to the connection between two systems. In Exchange, a link is generally synonymous with a connector.

Link State Algorithm   The process used by Exchange 2000 Server to apply the information in the link state table when determining a route.

link state table   A table maintained by Exchange 2000 Server that specifies the routes a message can pass over and whether any given link on the route is up or down.

local delivery   The delivery of a message to a recipient object that resides on the same server as the sender.

Local Procedure Call (LPC)   When a program issues an instruction that is executed on the same computer as the program executing the instruction. *See also* Remote Procedure Call (RPC).

lockbox   The process of using a secret key to encrypt a message and its attachments and then using a public key pair to encrypt and decrypt the secret key.

M

Mail and Directory Management (MADMAN) MIB   *See* Management Information Base (MIB).

mailbox   The generic term referring to a container that holds messages, such as incoming and outgoing messages.

mailbox-enabled user   A user who has been assigned an Exchange Server mailbox.

mailbox store   A set of two databases (a rich-text file and a streaming media file) on an Exchange server that hold mailboxes. *See also* store.

mail-enabled user   A user who has been given an e-mail address, but no mailbox.

Mail Exchanger (MX) Record   A record in a DNS database that indicates the SMTP mail host for an organization.

mainframe computing   Consists of a powerful host computer, such as a mainframe computer or minicomputer, and numerous input-output devices attached to the host, such as terminals, printers, and personal computers running terminal emulation software.

Management Information Base (MIB)   A set of configurable objects defined for management by the SNMP protocol.

MAPI   *See* Messaging Application Programming Interface (MAPI).

MAPI client   A messaging client that used the Messaging Application Programming Interface (MAPI) to connect to a messaging server. *See also* Messaging Application Programming Interface (MAPI).

MAPI subsystem   The second layer of the MAPI architecture; this component is shared by all applications that require its services and is therefore considered a *subsystem* of the operating system.

message state information   Information that identifies the state of a message in a public folder. Message state information is made up of a change number, a time stamp, and a predecessor change list.

Message Tracking Center (MTC)   An interface within System Manager used to search for messages sent within an Exchange organization and then track the route taken by those messages.

Message Transfer Agent (MTA) X.400 component that is used to route messages in previous versions of Exchange Server and is still used with the X.400 Connector.

Message Transfer Agent (MTA) Service Transport Stack A set of information about the software and hardware making up the underlying network that is used by an X.400 Connector. The use of the transport stack allows for a layer of abstraction between the X.400 Connector and the network itself.

Messaging Application Programming Interface (MAPI) An object-oriented programming interface for messaging services, developed by Microsoft.

Microsoft Exchange 2000 Conferencing Server An add-on product to Exchange 2000 Server that supports advanced voice, video, and data conferencing.

Microsoft Exchange Event Service A service in previous versions of Exchange Server that watched for certain events to occur and then fired predetermined scripts using the Microsoft Exchange Scripting Agent.

Microsoft Exchange Scripting Agent *See* Microsoft Exchange Event Service.

Microsoft Management Console (MMC) A framework application in which snap-ins are loaded to provide the management of various network resources. System Manager is an example of a snap-in.

Microsoft Outlook 2000 The premier client application for use with Exchange 2000 Server. Outlook 2000 ships with Exchange 2000 Server and also is part of Microsoft Office 2000.

Microsoft Search Service The service that performs full-text indexing of mailbox and public stores.

migration Moving resources, such as mailboxes, messages, etc., from one messaging system to another.

minimum installation type This installation type installs only the Exchange 2000 Server software and the basic Messaging and Collaboration components.

mixed administrative model   An administrative model that is really a catchall model for any ways (other than the centralized or decentralized models) that you can think of to use administrative groups.

mixed mode   In mixed mode, Exchange 2000 Server can coexist and communicate with previous versions of Exchange Server in the same organization.

Monitoring and Status tool   A tool within System Manager used to set up the services monitored on a server and configure the notifications that are triggered when a monitored service fails.

mounting   The process of bringing a private or public store online. *See also* dismounting.

MS Mail Connector   Connects an Exchange organization with an MS Mail system.

MS Mail Connector (PC) MTA   Transfers MS Mail messages between an Exchange server and MS Mail postoffices. The MS Mail Connector (PC) MTA is similar to the Exchange MTA in that it routes and transfers messages.

MS Mail Connector Interchange   Translates messages from the Exchange format to the MS Mail format, and vice versa.

MS Mail Connector Postoffice   An area on an Exchange server used to store MS Mail messages.

MSN Messenger   The Instant Messaging client that comes with Exchange 2000 Server.

multimaster replication model   A model in which there is no master copy of the information being replicated; each system that holds a replica is considered equal.

Multipurpose Internet Mail Extensions (MIME)   An Internet protocol that enables the encoding of binary content within mail messages. For example, MIME could be used to encode a graphics file or word processing document as an attachment to a text-based mail message. The recipient of the message would have to be using MIME also to decode the attachment. MIME is newer than UUENCODE and in many systems has replaced it. *See also* Secure/Multipurpose Internet Mail Extensions (S/MIME), UUENCODE.

MX   *See* Mail Exchanger (MX).

N

name resolution   The DNS process of mapping a domain name to its IP address.

namespace   Any bounded area in which a given name can be resolved.

native mode   In a native-mode organization, only Exchange 2000 Server is running, and the full Exchange 2000 functionality is present.

Network News Transfer Protocol (NNTP)   An Internet protocol used to transfer newsgroup information between newsgroup servers and clients (newsreaders), and between newsgroup servers.

newsfeed   The newsgroup data that is sent from one newsgroup server to other newsgroup servers.

NNTP   *See* Network News Transfer Protocol (NNTP).

node   In a Microsoft Management Console window, a node is any object that can be configured. In clustering, a node is one of the computers that is part of a cluster.

normal backup   During this backup, all selected files are backed up, regardless of how their archive bit is set. After the backup, the archive bit is set to off for all files, indicating that those files have been backed up.

notification   Defines the event that is triggered when a service or resource being watched by a server or link monitor fails. Notifications can send e-mail and alerts, and even run custom scripts.

O

object   The representation, or abstraction, of an entity. As an object, it contains properties, also called attributes, that can be configured. For example, each Exchange server is represented as an object in System Manager. An Exchange server object can have properties that give certain administrators permission to configure that server.

Object Linking and Embedding version 2 (OLE 2)   The Microsoft protocol that specifies how programs can share objects and therefore create compound documents.

Office Custom Installation Wizard Part of the Office 2000 Resource Kit that lets you customize and automate installations of Microsoft Office 2000.

Offline Address Book (OAB) A copy stored on a client's computer of part or all of the server-based Global Address List (GAL). An OAB allows a client to address messages while not connected to their server.

offline folder *See* Offline Storage folder (OST).

Offline Storage folder (OST) Folders located on a client's computer that contain replicas of server-based folders. An OST allows a client to access and manipulate copies of server data while not connected to their server. When the client reconnects to their server, they can have their OST resynchronized with the master folders on the server.

OLE 2 *See* Object Linking and Embedding version 2 (OLE 2).

Open Shortest Path First (OSPF) A routing protocol developed for IP networks based on the Shortest Path First or Link State Algorithm.

Organization The highest-level object in the Microsoft Exchange hierarchy.

organizational unit An Active Directory container into which objects can be grouped for permissions management.

Originator/Recipient Address (O/R Address) An X.400 address scheme that uses a hierarchical method to denote where on an X.400 network a recipient resides. An example is: c=us;a= ;p=widgetnet;o= widget;s=wilson;g=jay;.

Outlook 98 for Macintosh The version of Microsoft Outlook shipped with Exchange 2000 Server for the Macintosh platform.

Outlook Web Access (OWA) A service that allows users to connect to Exchange Server and access mailboxes and public folders using a Web browser.

P

patch files Temporary logs that store transactions while a backup is taking place. Transactions in these logs are committed when the backup is finished.

Performance Monitor *See* Performance snap-in.

public-key encryption   An encryption method that employs a key pair consisting of a public and a private key.

public key infrastructure (PKI)   A system of components working together to verify the identify of users that transfer data on a system and to encrypt that data if needed.

public store   A set of two databases that hold public folders on an Exchange server. *See also* store.

pull   Procedure where a user finds and retrieves information, such as when browsing a public folder. Users accessing a public folder containing a company's employee handbook is a type of pull communication.

pull feed   Procedure where a newsgroup server requests newsfeed information from another newsgroup server. The opposite of a push feed.

public folder   A folder used to store data for a group of users. Some of the features of a public folder are permissions, views, and rules.

purging   The process of deleting a user's mailbox in System Manager.

push   Procedure where information is sent (pushed) to users. Users do not need to find and retrieve (pull) the information. Exchange Server pushes incoming messages to MAPI-based Exchange clients.

push feed   Procedure where a newsgroup server sends information to another newsgroup server without requiring the receiving server to request it. The opposite of a pull feed.

Q

Queue folder   A folder in which messages that have yet to be delivered are stored.

Queue Viewer   A part of System Manager that lets you view and manipulate the messages in a queue.

R

recipient   An object that can receive a message. Recipient objects include users, contacts, groups, and public folders.

recipient policies   *See* policy.

recovery server   A server separate from the organization that is used as a dummy server for recovering individual mailboxes or messages from a backup. *See also* standby server.

replica   A copy of a public folder located on an Exchange server.

replication   The transferring of a copy of data to another location, such as another server or site. *See also* directory replication, public folder replication.

remote delivery   The delivery of a message to a recipient that does not reside on the same server as the sender.

Remote Procedure Call (RPC)   A set of protocols for issuing instructions that can be sent over a network for execution. A client computer makes a request to a server computer, and the results are sent to the client computer. The computer issuing the request and the computer performing the request are separated remotely over a network. RPCs are a key ingredient in distributed processing and client/server computing. *See also* Local Procedure Call (LPC).

reserve log files   Two transaction log files created by Exchange Server that are reserved for use when the server runs out of disk space.

resolving an address   The process of determining where (on which physical server) an object with a particular address resides.

resource group   Functions in a cluster that are not bound to a specific computer and can fail over to another node.

rich-text (EBD) file   The database used by Exchange Server to store general messages and attachments.

Rich-Text Format (RTF)   A Microsoft format protocol that includes bolding, highlighting, italics, underlining, and many other format types.

role   A group of permissions that define what activities a user or group can perform with regards to an object.

root CA   At the top of a Certificate Authority hierarchy; is trusted unconditionally by a client. All certificate chains terminate at a root CA. *See also* Certificate Authority (CA).

root domain   The top domain in a domain tree.

routing group   A collection of Exchange servers that have full-time, full-mesh, reliable connections between each and every server. Messages sent between any two servers within a routing group are delivered directly from the source server to the destination server.

Routing Group Connector (RGC)   The primary connector used to connect routing groups in an organization. The RGC uses SMTP as its default transport mechanism.

Routing Group Master   A server that maintains data about all of the servers running Exchange 2000 in the routing group.

RPC Ping   A utility provided on the Exchange CD-ROM for testing the RPC connectivity between two systems. *See also* Remote Procedure Call (RPC).

rule   A set of instructions that define how a message is handled when it reaches a folder.

S

scalable   The ability of a system to grow to handle greater traffic, volume, usage, etc.

Schedule+ Free Busy public folder   A system folder that contains calendaring and synchronization information for Exchange users.

schema   The set of rules defining a directory's hierarchy, objects, attributes, etc.

Scripting Agent   The Microsoft Exchange component that reads and executes a script attached to a public folder. It can carry out instructions by accessing databases, spreadsheets, gateways, and many other programs and services.

sealing   The process of encrypting data.

secret key   A security key that can be used to encrypt data and that is only known by the sender and the recipients whom the sender informs.

Secure/Multipurpose Internet Mail Extensions (S/MIME) An Internet protocol that enables mail messages to be digitally signed, encrypted, and decrypted.

Secure Sockets Layer (SSL) An Internet protocol that provides secure and authenticated TCP/IP connections. A client and server establish a "handshake" whereby they agree on a level of security they will use, such as authentication requirements and encryption. SSL can be used to encrypt sensitive data for transmission.

security group A group defined in Active Directory that can be assigned permissions. All members of the group gain the permissions given to the group.

Server License Provides the legal right to install and operate Microsoft Exchange 2000 Server (or another server product) on a single-server machine.

service provider A MAPI program that provides messaging-oriented services to a client. There are three main types of service providers: address book, message store, and message transport.

Service Transport Stack *See* Message Transfer Agent (MTA) Service Transport Stack.

shadow postoffice A postoffice without mailboxes. The Exchange MS Mail Connector Postoffice is referred to as a shadow postoffice because it does not contain user mailboxes and only temporarily stores incoming and outgoing MS Mail messages.

shared-file messaging system A messaging system in which active clients deposit messages and poll for new messages in shared folders on a passive server.

signing The process of placing a digital signature on a message.

simple display name An alternate name for the mailbox that appears when, for some reason, the full display name cannot.

Simple Mail Transfer Protocol (SMTP) The Internet protocol used to transfer mail messages. It is now the default transport protocol for Exchange 2000 Server.

Simple Network Management Protocol (SNMP) Internet protocol used to manage heterogeneous computers, operating systems, and applications. Because of its wide acceptance and applicability, SNMP is well suited for enterprise-wide management.

single-instance storage   Storing only one copy. A message that is sent to multiple recipients homed in the same storage group has only one copy (i.e., instance) stored on that server. Each recipient is given a pointer to that copy of the message.

single-seat administration   The ability to manage a number of sites, servers, etc., from a single application on a single computer.

site   A logical grouping of servers in previous versions of Exchange that are connected by a full mesh (every server is directly connected to every other server) and communicate using high-bandwidth RPC. All servers in a site can authenticate one another either because they are homed in the same Windows domain or because of trust relationships configured between separate Windows domains. A site is also a group of Windows 2000 servers that are connected with full-time, reliable connections.

Site Connector   A connector used to connect Exchange 5.x sites. The Site Connector has been replaced by the Routing Group Connector (RGC) in Exchange 2000.

Site Replication Service (SRS)   Runs on an Exchange 2000 server and simulates an Exchange 5.x system from the viewpoint of the Exchange 5.x servers in a site. SRS also provides a pathway for replicating configuration information between Active Directory and Exchange 5.x servers.

Site Replication Service (SRS) database   Contains information maintained by the Site Replication Service (SRS).

Site Services Account   The Windows user account that Exchange Server 5.5 components within a site use to communicate with each other.

smart host   An SMTP host designated to receive all outgoing SMTP mail. The smart host then forwards the mail to the relevant destination.

S/MIME   *See* Secure/Multipurpose Internet Mail Extensions (S/MIME).

SMTP   *See* Simple Mail Transfer Protocol (SMTP).

SMTP Connector   Using SMTP as its transport mechanism, the SMTP Connector can be used to connect routing groups to one another and to connect Exchange to a foreign SMTP system.

SMTP virtual server   A logical representation of the SMTP protocol on a physical server.

SNMP   *See* Simple Network Management Protocol (SNMP).

spooling   The process used by SMTP to temporarily store messages that cannot be delivered immediately.

stand-alone CA   Used to issue certificates to users outside the enterprise and do not require access to the Active Directory. *See also* Certificate Authority (CA), Enterprise CA.

Standard edition   The basic edition of Exchange 2000 Server that includes support for most features except Chat. The Standard edition is limited to having one mailbox store per server, and all databases can grow to only 16GB.

standard permissions   Permissions that are defined in a standard installation of Windows 2000 Server. Extended permissions are created when Exchange 2000 Server is installed.

standby server   A server configured to be used in place of another server. If a server goes down because of a failure or is taken down for maintenance, a standby server can be brought online to provide continued service to users. *See also* recovery server.

storage group   A collection of stores (up to four) that all share a common set of transaction logs.

storage limit   A limit placed on the amount of data that may be stored in a mailbox or public folder. Limits may be assigned at the store level and at the folder or mailbox level.

store   There are two types of stores in Exchange 2000 Server: public stores that hold public folders meant to be accessed by groups of users, and private stores that hold user mailboxes. Each store is composed of two databases: a rich-text database and a streaming media database.

Store.exe   The actual process that governs the use of stores on an Exchange server. Often referred to as the Information Store service.

store-and-forward   A delivery method that does not require the sender and recipient to have simultaneous interaction. Instead, when a message is sent, it is transferred to the next appropriate location in the network, which temporarily stores it, makes a routing decision, and forwards the message to the next appropriate network location. This process occurs until the message is ultimately delivered to the intended recipient, or an error condition causes the message to be returned to the sender.

streaming media (STM) file   One of two files that comprise every Exchange store, the streaming media file is used to hold content that does not need to be translated by Exchange Server before it is presented to the client.

subordinate CA   A CA found underneath the root CA in the CA hierarchy and maybe even under other subordinate CAs. *See also* Certificate Authority (CA), root CA.

subsystem   A software component that, when loaded, extends the operating system by providing additional services. The MAPI program, MAPI32.DLL, is an example of a subsystem. MAPI32.DLL loads on top of the Windows 98 or Windows 2000 operating system and provides messaging services.

Super Knowledge Consistency Checker (SKCC)   An updated version of the Knowledge Consistency Checker from Exchange 5.*x*. The SKCC ensures that knowledge consistency is maintained for sites and administrative groups when operating in mixed mode.

swing server method   A method of upgrading organizations from previous versions of Exchange Server by installing a new Exchange 2000 server, migrating mailboxes from an Exchange 5.*x* server, upgrading that server to Exchange 2000, migrating mailboxes from another Exchange 5.*x* server, and so on.

system folders   Special public folders that are hidden by default and are only accessible through System Manager. System folders contain items that facilitate the capabilities of many Exchange clients, such as collaborative scheduling in Outlook.

System Manager   The Microsoft Management Console used to manage an Exchange 2000 Server organization.

System Monitor   *See* Performance snap-in.

system policies   *See* policy.

system state backup   A form of backup that includes the Windows 2000 Registry, the IIS metabase, and the Active Directory (if run on a domain controller).

T

Task Manager   Displays the programs and processes running on a computer. It also displays various performance information, such as CPU and memory usage.

template   An object, such as a user or group, that contains configuration information that is applicable to multiple users. Objects for each user can be easily created by copying the template and filling in individual information.

time stamp   The Information Store marks each message with the time and date the message was last modified.

TLS encryption   Transport Layer Security (TLS) encryption is a generic security protocol similar to Secure Sockets Layer encryption.

token   The packet of security information a Certificate Authority sends to a client during advanced security setup. Information in the packet includes the client's public key and its expiration. A token is similar to a certificate.

top-level folders   The folders found in the root level of a public folder tree.

transaction log   A file used to quickly write data. That data is later written to the relevant Exchange database file. It is quicker to write to a transaction log file because the writes are done sequentially (i.e., one right after the other). Transaction log files can also be used to replay transactions from the log when rebuilding an Exchange database. All stores in a single storage group share the same set of transaction logs.

trust level   A numeric value given an object that is used to determine if that object should be replicated to another location, such as a foreign directory.

typical installation type   This option installs the Exchange Server software, the basic Messaging and Collaboration components, and the System Manager snap-in program. It does not include the additional connectors, the Chat Service, or the Instant Messaging Service.

T1 event   The interval used by dirsync requestors to send their postoffice address list to the designated dirsync server.

T2 event   The interval used by the dirsync server to compile a new Global Address List (GAL) and to send that list to the dirsync requestors.

T3 event   The interval used by the dirsync requestors to rebuild their post-office address list.

U

Uniform Resource Locator (URL)   An addressing method used to identify Internet servers and documents.

universal Inbox   A single folder or service that receives incoming items from all outside sources and of all types, such as e-mail, voice mail, faxes, pages, etc.

upgrading by moving mailboxes   A method for upgrading to Exchange 2000 Server in which a new server is installed in the organization, mailboxes are moved to that server from an older server, and then the older server is decommissioned or upgraded.

URL   *See* Uniform Resource Locator (URL).

Usenet   A network within the Internet that is composed of numerous servers containing information on a variety of topics. Each organized topic is called a newsgroup.

user ban   Used to prevent defined groups of users from accessing a chat community.

user class   Used to apply restrictions for accessing a chat community to certain groups of users.

user object   An object in Active Directory that is associated with a person on the network. Users can be mailbox-enabled or mail-enabled in Exchange 2000.

UUENCODE   Stands for UNIX-to-UNIX Encode, and is a protocol used to encode binary information within mail messages. UUENCODE is older than MIME. *See also* Multipurpose Internet Mail Extensions (MIME.)

V

virtual server   A representation of a particular protocol (such as HTTP or SMTP) that is separately configurable from other virtual servers for the same protocol.

W

W3svc   The World Wide Web (WWW) publishing service of Internet Information Server (IIS).

Web   The World Wide Web (WWW).

Web Storage System   The name given to the Exchange 2000 storage system to emphasize the new Web-enabled features that Exchange 2000 Server supports.

Web store   A term used to refer to the Information Store in Exchange 2000 Server, particularly to its Web-enhanced capabilities.

well-known port numbers   Numbers that are commonly used as the TCP port numbers for popular applications.

Windows 2000 Event Log   *See* Event Log.

Windows 2000 site   A group of computers that exist on one or more IP subnets. Computers within a site must be connected by a fast, reliable network connection.

Windows Clustering Service   *See* Clustering.

Windows Internet Naming System (WINS)   A name resolution service for resolving NetBIOS names on a Windows network.

workflow application   An application that can route electronic forms to users based on various criteria.

World Wide Web (WWW)   The collection of computers on the Internet using protocols such as HTML and HTTP.

WWW   *See* World Wide Web (WWW).

X

X.400   An International Telecommunications Union (ITU) standard for message exchange.

X.400 Connector   Using X.400 as its transport mechanism, the X.400 Connector can connect routing groups or connect Exchange to a foreign X.400 messaging system. An X.400 Connector requires the use of a TCP/IP or X.25 MTA Service Transport Stack.

X.500   An International Telecommunications Union (ITU) standard for directory services.

X.509 certificate   The most widely used format for certificates, X.509 certificates contain not only the public key, but also information that identifies the user and the organization that issued the certificate.

Index

A

A records, 455
Accept New Connections command, 471
Access Control Entries (ACEs), 403, 682
Access Control Lists (ACLs), 623, 682
Access page
   in Chat, 474, *475*, **479**, *480*
   in IMAP4, 285
   in NNTP, 289
   in POP3, 280
   for SMTP virtual servers, **549–550**, *554*
account cleanup in mixed-mode operations, **514–516**
account names in POP3, 281
Accounts command, 282
ACEs (Access Control Entries), 403, 682
ACLs (Access Control Lists), 623, 682
Action menu in MMC, 397
Active/Active clustering, 65, 113
Active Directory, **51**, 682
   backing up, 594
   domains in, **101–102**
   and Exchange 2000, **57–59**
   forests in, **98–101**
   logical components in, **51–55**, *53–55*
   physical components in, **55–57**
   preparation for, **97–98**
   and public folders, **185–186**
   requirements for, 93
Active Directory Account Cleanup Wizard, **514–516**, 682
Active Directory Connector (ADC), **59**, **500–502**, 682

connection agreements for. *See* connection agreements (CAs)
   installing, **504–506**, *505*
   troubleshooting, **516–518**
Active Directory Connector Management component, 505
Active Directory Connector Service component, 505
Active Directory Users and Computers tool
   for contacts, 156
   for groups, 152
   for IM, **460–463**
   for key recovery, 657
   for mail-enabled users, 149
   for mailboxes, 137, 161, 371
   for OWA, 274
   for recipients, **158–159**
   for users, **138–140**, **513–514**
Active/Passive clustering, 65, 113
Active Server Pages (ASP), 62, 270, 682
ActiveX technology, 682
Adams, Carlisle, 640
ADC (Active Directory Connector), **59**, **500–502**, 682
connection agreements for. *See* connection agreements (CAs)
   installing, **504–506**, *505*
   troubleshooting, **516–518**
Add Address Space dialog box, 540, *540*
Add/Remove Snap-In window, 643
Add/Remove Windows Components option, 648
Add Server command, 432
Add Standalone Snap-In window, 643

B

C

F

H

hard disk space requirements, 92
hardware
    requirements for, **92–93**
    scalability of, 19
HELO command, 330, *545*, 694
help in MMC, 396
Hidden visibility option, 474
Hide Class Members' IP Addresses And DNS
    Names option, 479
Hide From Exchange Address Lists option,
    146, 200
Hide Group From Exchange Address Lists
    option, 155
hiding
    groups, 155
    mailboxes, 146, 200
    public folders, 194–195
hierarchies and hierarchical storage, 694
    in MAPI-based applications, 257
    in Outlook, 4–5
    in public folders, 184–185, *184*, **205–206**
home servers, **454–455**, **457–459**, 694
HTML (HyperText Markup Language), 694
HTML files, 62
HTML pages, 185
HTTP (HyperText Transfer Protocol), 242,
    694
HTTP Digest authentication, 456, **459–464**,
    694
HTTP reverse proxy servers, 455
hyperlinks in Outlook, 260
HyperText Markup Language (HTML), 694
HyperText Transfer Protocol (HTTP), 242,
    694

I

I Have Outlook 97 Or Older Clients In My
    Organization option, 662
Identify masks, 478
Identify Merging Accounts page, 515
Idle setting in instant messaging, 451
IFS (Installable File System), **64**, 201–202, 695
IIS (Internet Information Server), 6, **63**, *64*, 696
    POP3 in, 279
    requirements for, 93
IIS metabase, 272, 695
ILS (Internet Locator Service), 147, 696
ILS Settings page, **147**
IMAP4 (Internet Message Access Protocol
    version 4), **7**, **283–287**, 696
Import Containers page, *574*
IMPORT.EXE utility, *575*
importing data, 264
in-place upgrades, **111**, 695
Inbound Connections Current counter, 412
Inbound SUBSCRIBEs/sec counter, 413
Inbox folder, 695
    in Outlook, 4
    in POP3, 279
Inbox Repair Tool, 433–434, 695
inboxes, universal, 4, 245, 257, 713
Include All Public Folders When A Folder List
    Is Requested option, 285
incremental backups, 597–598, 695
indexing, full-text. *See* full-text indexes
indirect postoffice connections, 562, *562*
industry standards, **18–19**, 23
    CCITT X.400, 29–30, 715
        addressing in, **30–32**, *31*
        message format in, **32**
        message routing in, **32–33**
    CCITT X.500, 33–34, 715
        directory access in, **36**
        directory structure in, **34–36**, *34*

N

W

X